PRELUDE TO STALINGRAD

The Red Army's Attempt to Derail the German Drive to the Caucasus in World War II

Igor' Sdvizhkov

Translated and edited by Stuart Britton

STACKPOLE
BOOKS
Guilford, Connecticut

Published by Stackpole Books
An imprint of The Rowman & Littlefield Publishing Group, Inc.
4501 Forbes Blvd., Ste. 200
Lanham, MD 20706
www.rowman.com

Distributed by NATIONAL BOOK NETWORK
800-462-6420

2019 paperback edition published by The Rowman & Littlefield Publishing Group, Inc.

British Library Cataloguing in Publication Information available

Library of Congress Cataloging-in-Publication Data available

ISBN 978-0-8117-3866-8 (paperback)

™ The paper used in this publication meets the minimum requirements of American National Standard for Information Sciences—Permanence of Paper for Printed Library Materials, ANSI/NISO Z39.48-1992.

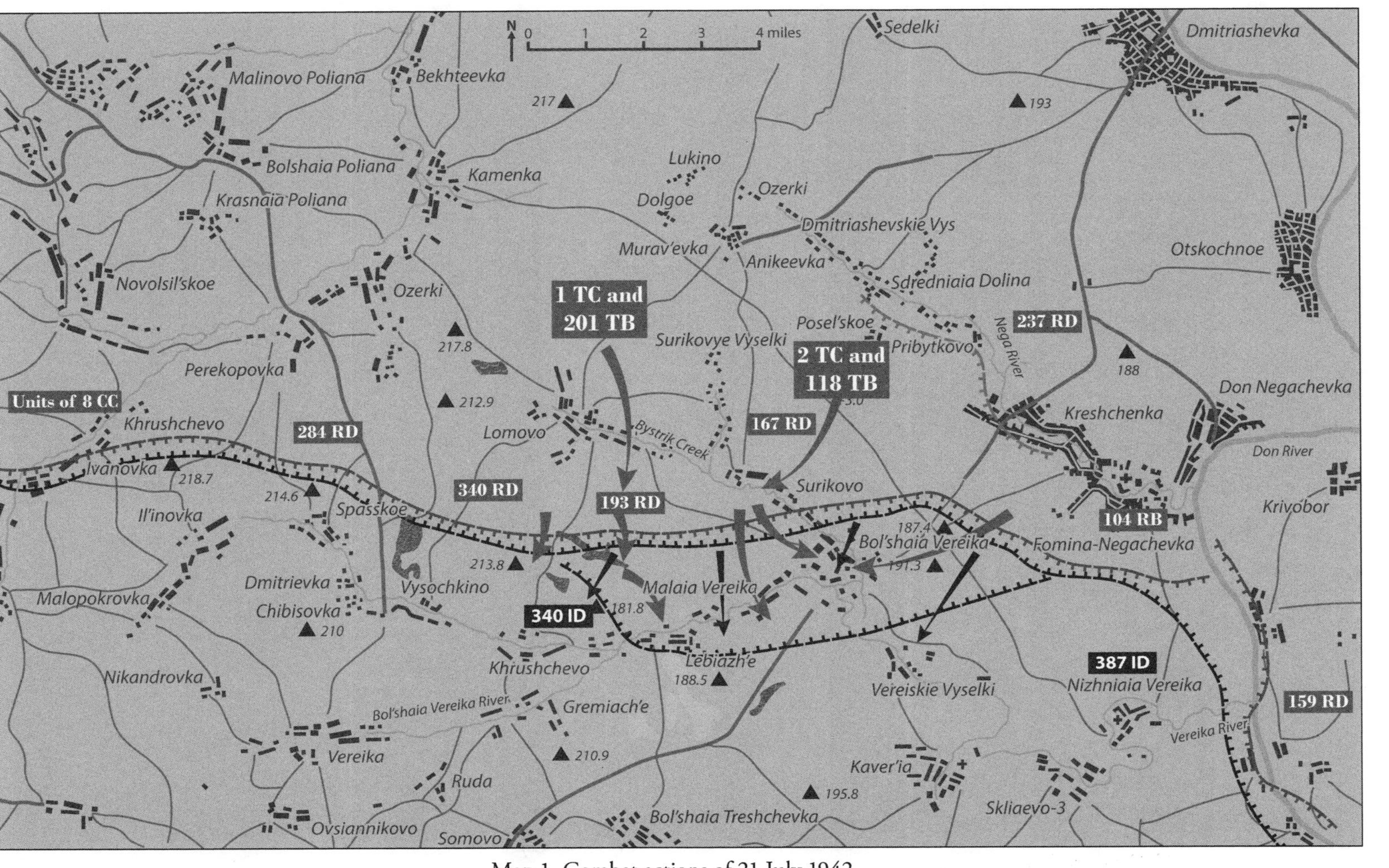

Map 1 Combat actions of 21 July 1942.

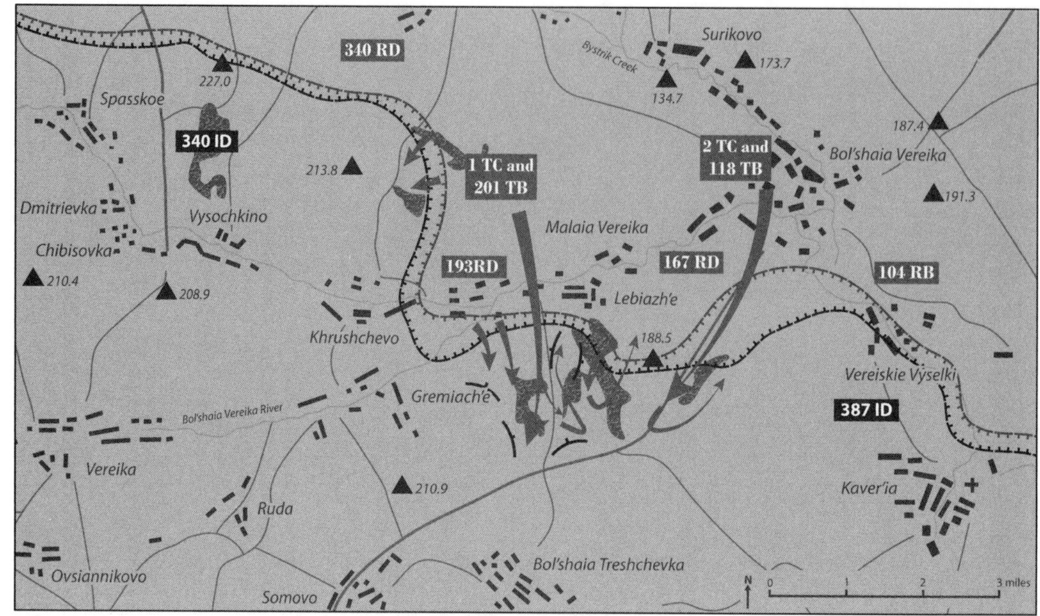

Map 2 Combat actions of 22 July 1942.

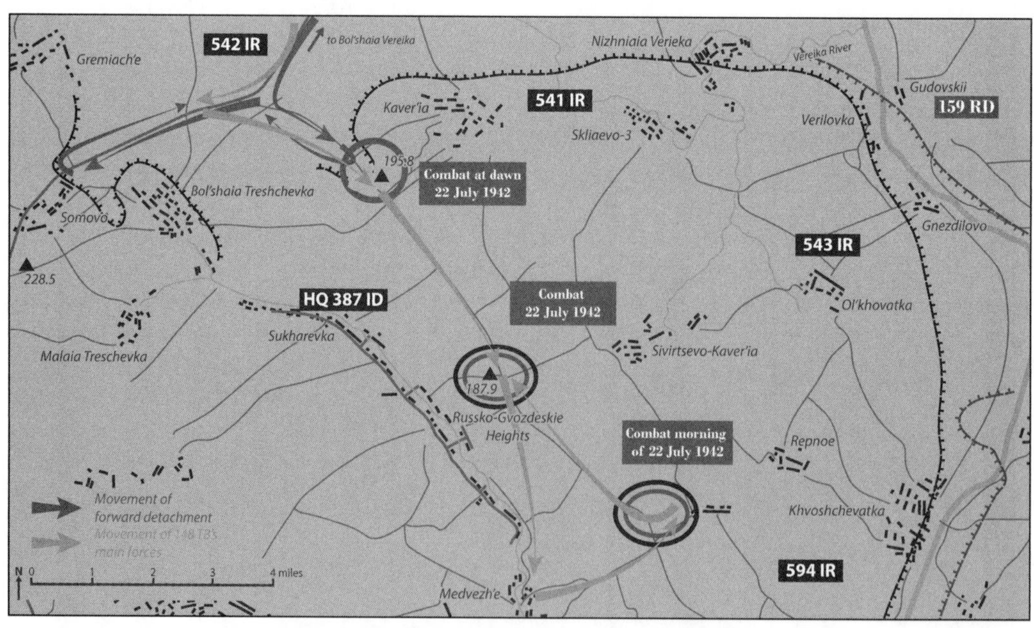

Map 3 148th Tank Brigade, 21-22 July 1942.

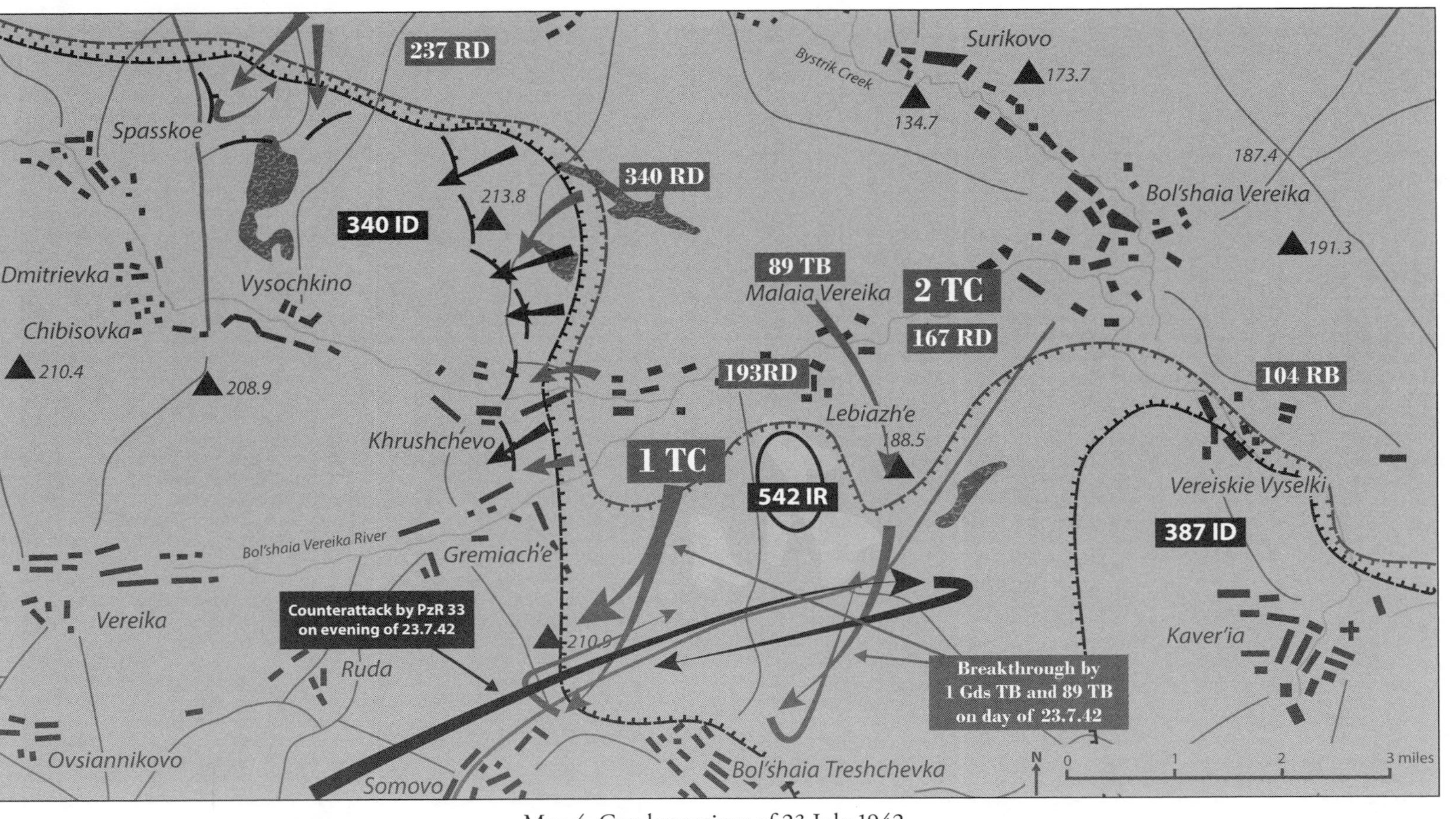

Map 4 Combat actions of 23 July 1942.

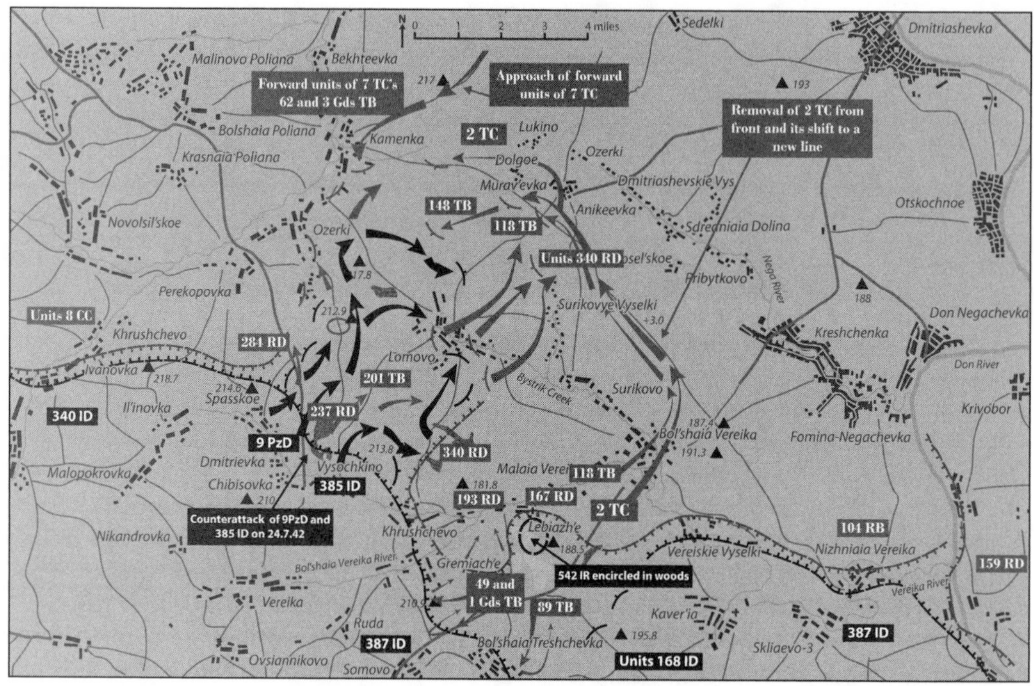
Map 5 Combat actions of 24 July 1942.

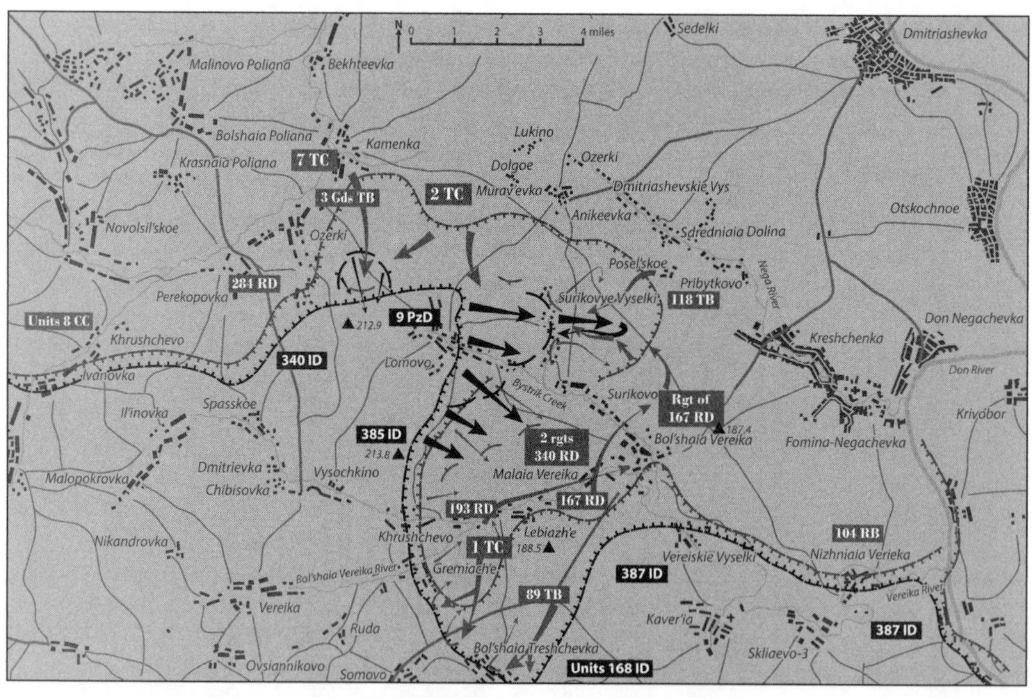
Map 6 Combat actions of 25 July 1942.

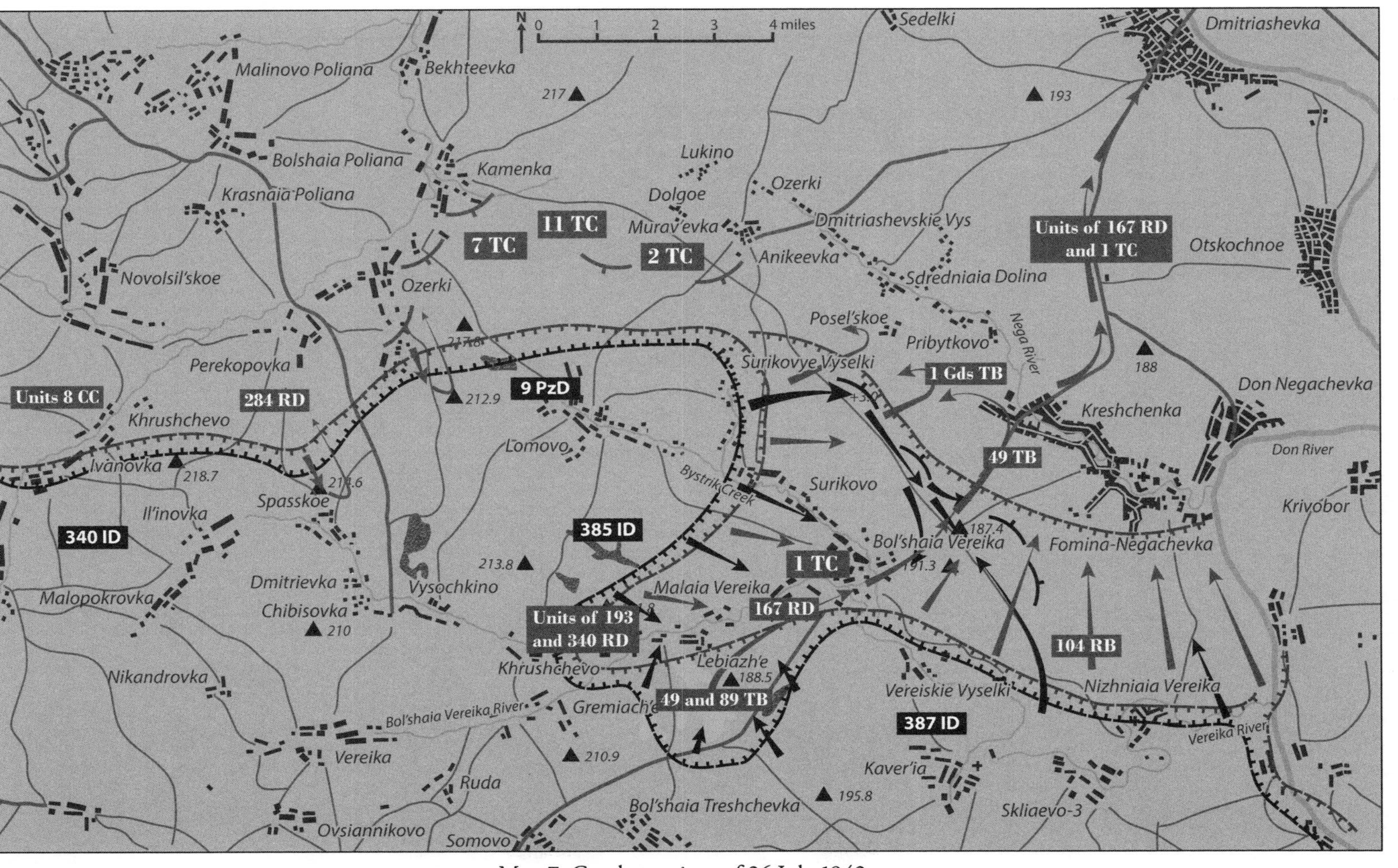

Map 7 Combat actions of 26 July 1942.

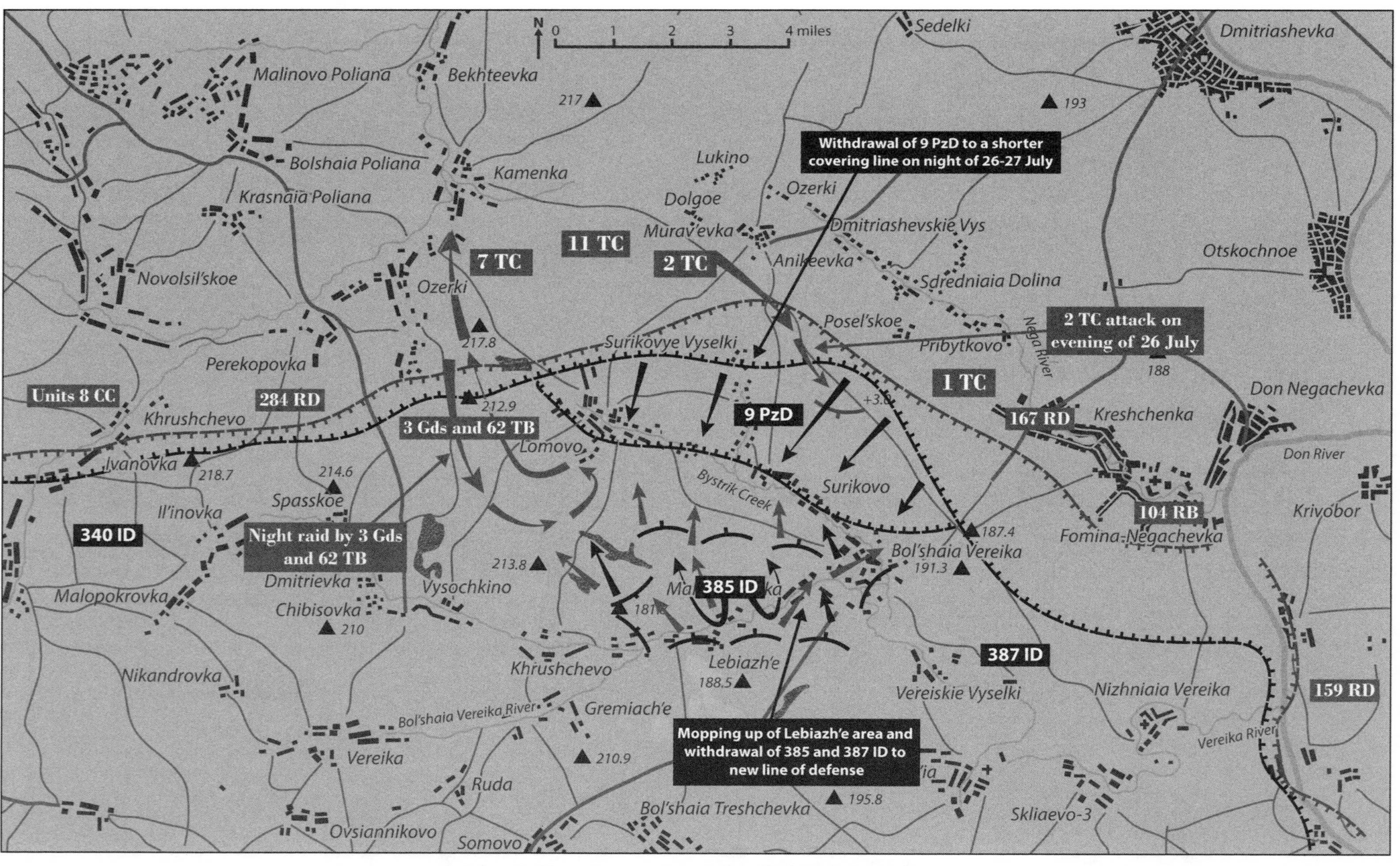

Map 8 Situation on the night of 26-27 July 1942.

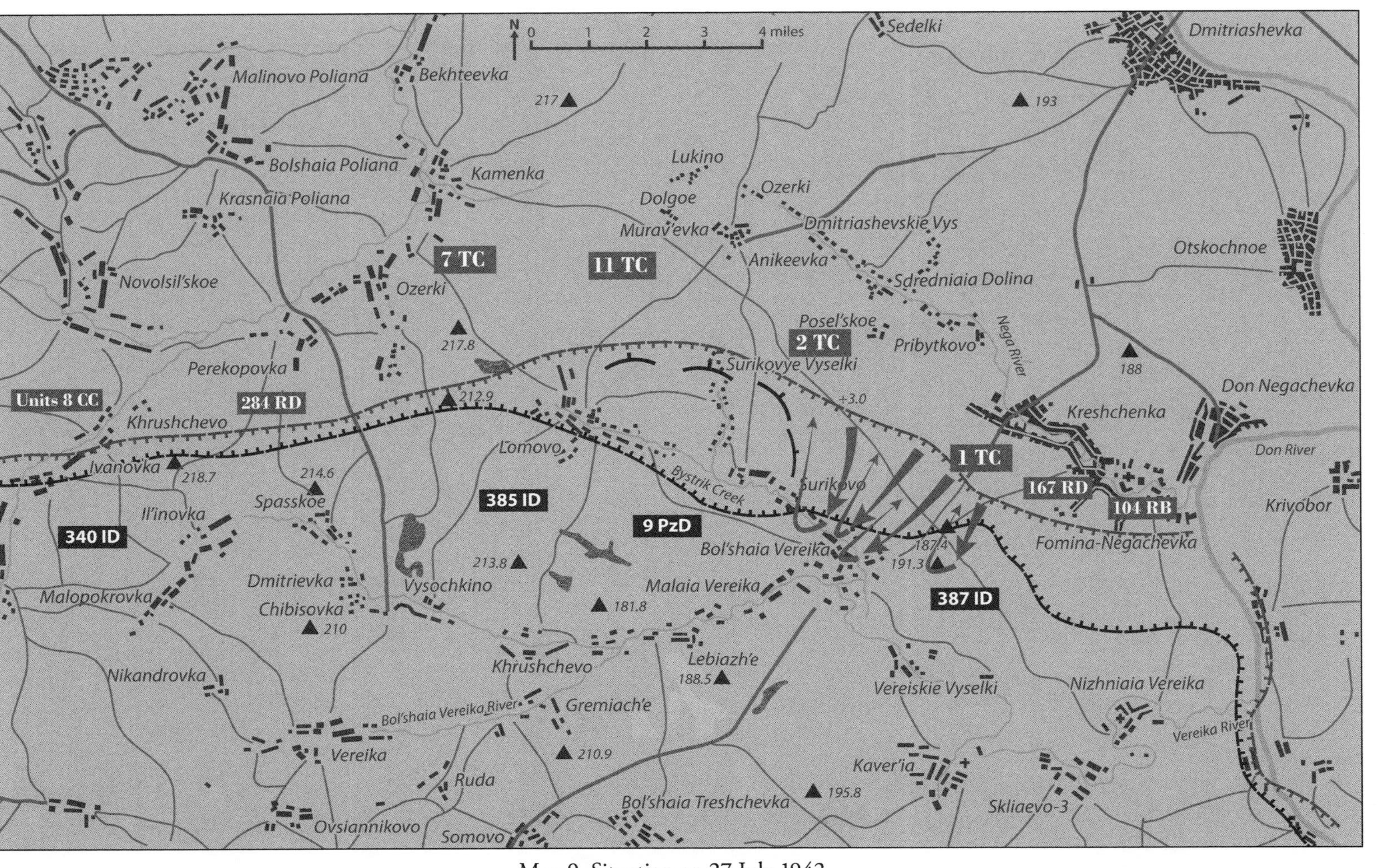

Map 9 Situation on 27 July 1942.

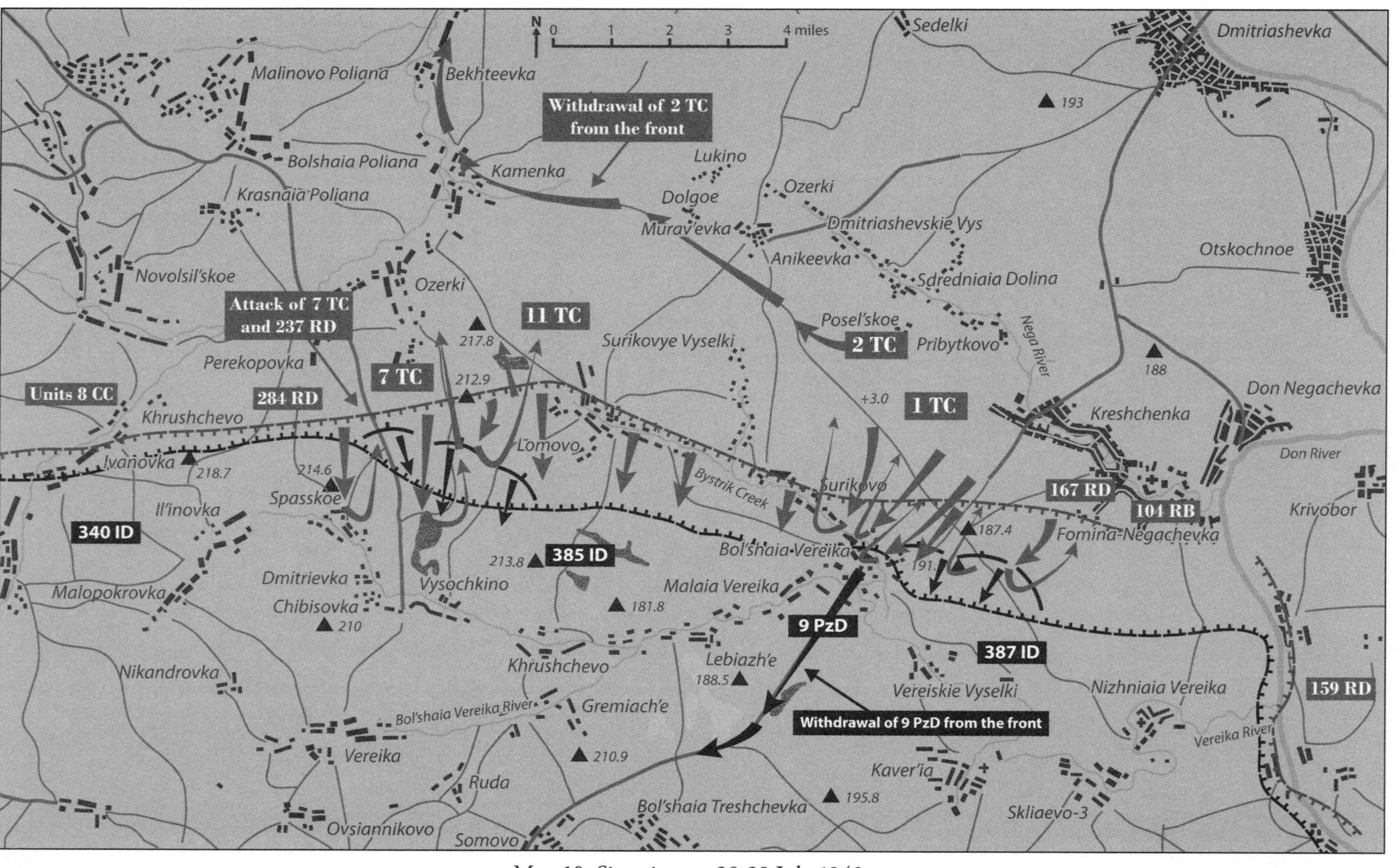

Map 10 Situation on 28-29 July 1942.

Contents

List of Photographs

Instead of a Prologue

Directive of the *Stavka* VGK [Supreme High Command] No.170516

To the Briansk Front Commander-in-Chief regarding the launching of an attack along the right bank of the Don River
CC: Commander-in-Chief of the Voronezh Front

17 July 1942, 1630hrs

In connection with the fact that Voronezh Front's 60th Army, which is attacking along the eastern bank of the Don River, has surged ahead and is tied up in prolonged fighting in the area of Podkletnoe and on the northern outskirts of Voronezh, while the left flank of Briansk Front is continuing to be held up on the western bank of the Don River on the line Fomina-Negachevka, Lomovo, Spasskoe, Khrushchevo and further to the west, the threat has arisen that the enemy might force a crossing of the Don River and emerge on the Voronezh River, thereby encircling and capturing the 60th Army.

The *Stavka* of the Supreme High Command is ordering Briansk Front, using the 340th, 284th and 193rd Rifle Divisions, the 104th Rifle Brigade, and the 1st Tank Corps, to initiate active offensive operations along the western bank of the Don River on the morning of 18 July, with the mission at whatever the cost to clear the enemy from the western bank of the Don River and to seize it in the Fomina-Negachevka, Malyshevo sector, for which: reach by the end of 18.07 – the line Lebiazh'e, Kaver'ia, Ol'khovatka; by the end of 19.07 – the line Bol'shaia Treshchevka, Treshchevka River, Russkaia Gvozdevka; by the end of 20.07 – Vereika, Perlevka, Semiluki and by the end of 21.07 – Golosnovka, Zemliansk, Veduga River, Ust'e, having secured a crossing at Malyshevo.

The *Stavka* compels you with all of your available strength and means to achieve the fulfillment of this assignment within the [given] timetable at whatever the cost.

The *Stavka* of the Supreme High Command
I. Stalin
A. Vasilevsky

1

And once again into battle ...

Combat Order No.9 of the 2nd [Tank] Corps headquarters

Sedelki, 14:00 20 July Map 100:000

1. Up to two enemy infantry divisions with tanks are defending on the front: Ozerki – Don River. Up to two infantry regiments are defending the Bol'shaia Vereika, Hills 187.4 and 191.3 nest of resistance. Tanks have been dug into the ground. Minefields are in front of the forward line.

2. Supporting the advance of the 104th Rifle Brigade with fire and maneuver, the corps has the task to enter the breakthrough behind the 167th Rifle Division in the direction of Surikovo, Malaia Vereika, destroy the enemy's infantry, artillery batteries and tanks in the area of Kaver'ia, Vereiskie Vyselki and Skliaevo-3 and to emerge in the Medvezh'e area. Subsequently push forward to the bridge across the Don River in Medvezh'e in order to destroy the reserves of the enemy's Voronezh grouping.

3. I have decided that the 26th and 148th Tank Brigades are to exploit the breakthrough by the 167th Rifle Division and the 2nd Motorized Rifle Brigade in the direction of Bol'shaia Vereika. The 27th Tank Brigade is my reserve. Prior to the introduction of the corps into the breakthrough, support the attack of the 104th Rifle Brigade with fire or maneuver.

4. I am ordering:
   A) The 26th Tank Brigade is to be ready to enter the breakthrough of the enemy's defenses in the direction of Surikovo and Malaia Vereika, to destroy the enemy's infantry, tanks and artillery in the area of Kaver'ia and Vereiskie Vyselki, and subsequently is to attack Medvezh'e. Intermediary assembly places are the northern outskirts of Kaver'ia, and then the northern patch of woods east of Medvezh'e.
   B) The 148th Tank Brigade is to stand ready to exploit the breakthrough in the Surikovo – Malaia Vereika – Kaver'ia direction, to destroy the enemy's infantry, tanks and artillery in the Rubtsovo, Skliaevo-3 area, and subsequently is to advance toward Medvezh'e on the 26th Tank Brigade's right. Intermediary assembly places are Rubtsovo, and then the woods on the southern outskirts of Medvezh'e.
   C) The 2nd Motorized Rifle Brigade with a company of T-60 tanks from the 27th Tank Brigade is to take up a jumping-off position by 2:00 21 July directly opposite the enemy defending Bol'shaia Vereika, and is to seize Bol'shaia Vereika in cooperation with the 104th Rifle Brigade and to secure the passage of the 27th Tank Brigade. Subsequently attack together with the 26th Tank Brigade.

D) The 27th Tank Brigade (minus the T-60 company) with the company of KV tanks is my reserve. As the corps enters the breakthrough, support the 104th Rifle Brigade's attack with fire from fixed positions and accompany it with the T-60 tanks. The main areas for concentrated fire from the fixed positions are: Bol'shaia Vereika, Hill 191.3 and the woods east of Surikovo. Expend half of a combat load of ammunition on 21 July for firing from fixed positions. With the introduction of the corps into the breakthrough, be ready to advance behind the 148th Tank Brigade. Clear the minefields in front of the forward edge of Bol'shaia Vereika. With the arrival of the 26th and 148th Tank Brigades in the Kaver'ia area, the 27th Tank Brigade is to shift to the woods south of Surikovo. Subsequently, advance in the wake of the 148th Tank Brigade. The artillery preparation is to start at 3:30. The infantry attacks at 4:00. The 2nd Motorized Rifle Brigade's chief of artillery is to organize centralized control of the 2nd Motorized Rifle Brigade's artillery with the addition of the 27th [Tank Brigade]'s anti-tank battalion, having coordinated their actions with the 104th Rifle Brigade's chief of artillery.

5. The signal for the start of the introduction of the tank brigades will be by radio: for the 148th Tank Brigade – "Storms", for the 26th Tank Brigade – "Thunderstorm", for the 27th Tank Brigade – "Lightning", and will be repeated by the signals officer. Recognition signs with the air force will be white flags of a large dimension made out of sheets, underclothing and so forth, and green flares between our tank units.

6. The axis of communications, of combat supply and repair will be along the axis of movement: Verkhniaia Kolybelka, Murav'evka, Bol'shaia Vereika, Medvezh'e, Privol'e, Endovishche.

7. My command post from 1700 20 July will be in the patch of woods north of Dmitriashevskie Vyselki. When the 27th Tank Brigade crosses the Bol'shaia Vereika River, [my command post will be] with the 27th Tank Brigade.

Commander of the 2nd Tank Corps Hero of the Soviet Union
Guards Major General LIZIUKOV
Military Commissar Regimental Commissar ASSOROV
2nd Tank Corps chief of staff Colonel Nagaibakov[1]

Three days separated General Liziukov from the end of his 5th Tank Army's failed operation and the start of a new operation – now as part of Briansk Front's newly-formed operational group as commander of the 2nd Tank Corps. Seventy-two hours of rest between two offensives, in order to re-invigorate himself physically and emotionally after all that had happened over the previous two weeks, to restore his spirits and again commit the troops to battle. But through all this time, only little was left for him when he might catch his breath.

The restoration of strength and catch-up on sleep after the extraordinary exertions of the recent days and sleepless nights was hindered by concerns arising in connection with his new appointment, which could not be dumped on the shoulders of the commissar and chief of staff, from whom he had remained aloof after all that was happening. The army was being disbanded, and it was necessary to transfer files and papers (the headquarters of Briansk Front's recently-formed

1 TsAMO, F. 202, op. 50, d. 1, l. 300

operational group was taking over the premises of the 5th Tank Army headquarters in Slepukha) and drive to his new command post, in order to take command of the tank corps on the spot, having relinquished his command of the tank army. There is hardly any point in speaking about any emotional respite after the arrival of the Front's order – Liziukov's direct superior was now the same man, who just a week before had already "awarded" him with a stinging psychological slap in the face, having publicly accused him of cowardice. Now the former army commander would have to serve under the command of this same man.

Moreover, he was no longer the fresh and well-rested commander after spending three months in the rear, with the opportunity to see his family during trips to Moscow; he was not the rising commander, emboldened by prior successes and the highest trust of The Boss, but a physically exhausted and emotionally wrecked man, and in the eyes of *other* commanders an unsuccessful general as well, who had failed to carry out the task that had been entrusted to him.

With the disbanding of his army, Liziukov had to part from his commissar and chief of staff. While he faced a return to the front to fight once again, they together with the army's headquarters were on their way to Vodop'ianovo in the rear. Whereas the 5th Tank Army's chief of staff Colonel Drugov could now fully concentrate on the past, analyzing and studying the recently concluded operation in the quiet of his office, Liziukov, essentially, had no time to ponder the lessons of the recent fighting; he had to think about looming battles.

On the very same day of the order to disband the 5th Tank Army, the Commander-in-Chief of Briansk Front K.K. Rokossovsky gave the commander of the Front's newly-formed operational group General Chibisov a directive to launch a new offensive. At the time, General Liziukov still wasn't aware that his army was being disbanded, or that the next battle was already looming in front of him. He didn't even have time to issue a farewell order to the 5th Tank Army, before he was to issue the order to the 2nd Tank Corps regarding the offensive. As far as working out the plan for the new offensive and pondering the received mission and the means for implementing it, he was hardly given any more time for all of this than he'd been granted prior to the 5th Tank Army's recent star-crossed offensive. In fact, the operational directive to conduct the new operation was issued by Lieutenant General Rokossovsky on 17 July, but the commander of the operational group General Chibisov (due to hitches in the Front headquarters and problems with communications) didn't receive it in Slepukha until 21:15 on 18 July, that is, on the evening of the following day![2] Briansk Front headquarters was requiring Chibisov to present the plan for the offensive on the morning of 19 July, while the offensive itself was to be launched between 20 and 24 July, but the operational group's small headquarters was simply unable to prepare for the offensive in the remaining available hours.

After processing the received directive, the just-formed headquarters of the operational group hastily set to work on planning the operation, while simultaneously working to resolve a multitude of tasks with respect to establishing communications with the units subordinate to the operational group, arranging logistical support, and organizing their march and assembly in the jumping-off areas. The combat order for the operation was ready only on 20 July and distributed to the subordinate units with the demand to start the offensive at dawn on 21 July.[3] Liziukov received this order in the tiny Don River hamlet of Sedelki, which was located almost 30 kilometers from the operational group's headquarters in Slepukha. Considering as a rule the lengthy time required by the liaison officers to deliver the papers along the farm roads and cross-country, this left him in the best case only several hours to put together his own attack orders to the tank corps that had recently been entrusted to his command.

2 TsAMO, F. 202, op. 5, d. 234, l. 13.
3 TsAMO, F. 1657, op. 1, d. 22, l. 145.

In these circumstances, taking into account as well the need to resolve the numerous questions regarding the organization of cooperation among the different types of troops, their resupply and communications, it is hardly possible to speak about any thorough elaboration of the operation's conception and the development of a detailed plan for the offensive. The commanders of the subordinate brigades had even less time for any of this.

True, in distinction from the preceding operation, Liziukov didn't face the thorny issue of moving his forces by rail – all of his brigades were already close to the area of forthcoming combat operations, which would finally allow him to launch a concentrated attack with all of his forces simultaneously, and not a piecemeal attack as he had made two weeks previously. There was also no *Stavka* insistence to keep part of his forces in deep reserve – now in command at a much lower rank, Liziukov's own responsibility was accordingly much lower.

However, now a different problem arose: after its recent fighting as part of 5th Tank Army, the 2nd Tank Corps' combat capabilities had diminished as a result of losses and the combat exhaustion of many units. Only the 26th Tank Brigade remained fresh and combat-ready; the remaining brigades needed replenishments and rest. However, instead of rest, they had to attack once again. (For the sake of justice it should be noted that the 7th and 11th Tank Corps, which had also fought as part of the 5th Tank Army, were so depleted and worn out that they were totally unable to take part in the new offensive; they remained in the rear for refitting. In comparison with them, the 2nd Tank Corps was in much better shape!)

Prior to the start of the 5th Tank Army's operation, the 2nd Tank Corps had 183 tanks. By the end of the fighting, there remained only 78 combat-ready tanks in the brigades, of which 38 were medium tanks; there was not a single heavy tank.[4] This was just 40% of the corps' initial strength in combat machines. The 2nd Motorized Rifle Brigade had lost more than half of its more than 3,000 men and was also in great need of replenishments.[5] General Liziukov, the former army commander took command of the 2nd Tank Corps in this condition. A portion of the corps' elements were still located back beyond the Snova and Don Rivers, to where they had retreated on 14 July; only several days later did they begin returning. All of these units had to be brought together in the assembly area, restored to order, and replenished.

Having decided to launch a new offensive, of the three tank corps of the former 5th Tank Army the Briansk Front command allotted replenishments primarily to the 2nd Tank Corps. The 26th Tank Brigade received only 7 tanks, while the 27th Tank Brigade received 15 T-34 and 10 KV tanks.[6] In contrast, the 2nd Tank Corps' 148th Tank Brigade received 20 KV and 20 T-60 tanks, which allowed it to bring the brigade's tank battalions up to full strength.[7] In addition, Liziukov was given a separate reconnaissance battalion (the 12th Separate Reconnaissance Battalion) which had only recently arrived at the Briansk Front. In the recently concluded failed offensive, neither any of the tank corps nor the 5th Tank Army itself had a reconnaissance battalion. The battalion had 20 armored personnel carriers and 12 armored cars, which despite the small amount of personnel (205 men) offered much greater prospects for reconnaissance and reconnoitering than previously to the commander of the tank formation.[8]

True, by the morning of 20 July the KV tank company (of 10 tanks) that had been directed to reinforce the 27th Tank Brigade hadn't yet arrived.[9] The replenishing of the motorized rifle elements with personnel was going slowly. Not having enough infantry to bring the 2nd Motorized

4 TsAMO, F. 331, op. 5041, d. 18, l. 37, appendix 40.
5 TsAMO, F. 5TA, op. 5041, d. 26, l. 113.
6 TsAMO, F. 202, op. 5, d. 238, l. 496.
7 TsAMO, F. 148, op. 1, d. 3, l.31.
8 TsAMO, F.2TK, op. 1, d. 224(b), l.159.
9 TsAMO, F. 27 tbr, op. 1, d. 5, l. 207.

Rifle Brigade back up to strength, Liziukov decided to strengthen the brigade with 10 light T-60 tanks, taken from the 27th Tank Brigade, after which this tank brigade was left with only 9 T-60 and 8 T-34 tanks.[10]

The KV tank company arrived in the 27th Tank Brigade only shortly before the attack order was put together, while 15 T-34 tanks with their crews in fact didn't show up on 20 July.[11] Obviously, anticipating the reinforcement of the 27th Tank Brigade with tanks, the crews of which (for the most part, totally green) still had to be received, checked and brought up to speed, and given their combat assignments and the time to work them out, Liziukov decided in the meantime to hold the tank brigade in his reserve.

In order to understand better the tasks that the 2nd Tank Corps was to carry out, it is necessary to pause here to analyze the situation and the plan conceived by the headquarters of Briansk Front to address it. With the arrival of the *Stavka* order regarding the disbanding of the 5th Tank Army, the Briansk Front command wound up facing the need to set up centralized command and control over those units that had been previously subordinate to the headquarters of the 5th Tank Army. Lacking an army headquarters for this, Lieutenant General Rokossovsky with his order on 17 July 1942 organized a Front operational group "in order to command the forces situated between the Olym and Don Rivers" and placed it under the command of General Chibisov.[12] On this same day of 17 July, in a personal meeting Rokossovsky gave Chibisov a directive to conduct a new offensive operation (even while formally the 5th Tank Army's operation was still continuing!), which was soon laid out and fleshed out in an operational directive. The overall objective of the operation was "to destroy the enemy units occupying the Voronezh node of resistance" and to seize the Nikol'skoe – Livenka – Zatsepino – Stadnitsa – Veduga River line.[13] In order to carry out this task, the seizure of the town of Zemliansk and an advance to the south of 5 kilometers (on the right flank) to 30 kilometers (on the left flank) was foreseen.

The depth of the planned attack was less than the one given in the 5th Tank Army's offensive, while the forces assigned to the new operation were significantly greater. Whereas Liziukov initially had only one rifle division for his 5th Tank Army's offensive, Chibisov received under his command five rifle divisions (the 340th, 284th, 193rd, 167th and 237th Rifle Divisions), not including the 1st Guards Rifle Division, the 106th Separate Rifle Brigade and the three cavalry divisions of the 8th Cavalry Corps, which prior to the formation of the operational group had been part of the 13th Army and was activated for the planned operation on a secondary axis. In addition, Chibisov's operational group received the 104th Separate Rifle Brigade. In place of the single light artillery regiment of 76-mm guns that had supported the 5th Tank Army's offensive with its fire, Chibisov would have seven separate artillery regiments (not including the authorized artillery regiments of the rifle divisions and the two brigades of the 2nd Destroyer Division that were equipped with 45-mm and 76-mm guns), of which two were heavy (122-mm and 152-mm) artillery regiments of the Supreme Command Reserve and two were anti-aircraft artillery regiments. In place of the single Guards mortar regiment (of Katiusha rocket launchers) in the 5th Tank Army, Group Chibisov would have three. Chibisov's operational group was slightly inferior to Liziukov's 5th Tank Army only in the number of tank formations – Chibisov had two tank corps and two separate tank brigades in place of the three tank corps and one separate tank brigade in the 5th Tank Army, which is to say, he had two fewer tank brigades. Regarding air support for the

10 Ibid.
11 Ibid., l. 208.
12 TsAMO, F.202, op. 5, d. 234, l. 5.
13 Ibid, l. 13.

upcoming operation, Rokossovsky confidently wrote that "the units' offensive will be supported by the entirety of the Front's aviation forces."[14]

In order to carry out the objective, the command of Briansk Front gave Group Chibisov four days to reach the designated line, but at the same time demanded that the tank corps seize the Zemliansk – Perlevka line by the end of the offensive's first day (the rifle divisions were to reach this line on the operation's third day). This meant that the 1st and 2nd Tank Corps would have to make an advance of 20-25 kilometers to the south on the first day and to create a threat to the rear areas and supply lines of the enemy's entire Voronezh grouping. It should be noted that the planned operation was not conducted separately by Operational Group Chibisov, but in cooperation with the rest of Voronezh Front, and was put together as part of the *Stavka*'s overall plan – finally through the combined actions of two *fronts* to cut off the Voronezh salient that had been seized by the foe and to smash the enemy grouping defending it. In addition to the offensive by Group Chibisov's main forces, the Briansk Front command was requiring a secondary offensive operation by the forces of the 1st Guards Rifle Division, the 106th Separate Rifle Brigade and the 8th Cavalry Corps on the operational group's right flank.

In his own order regarding the offensive Chibisov itemized the tasks of the forces subordinate to him, giving special attention to the actions of the tank corps. Moreover, the assignments he gave to them were even more ambitious than those that had been set for them in Briansk Front's directive (evidently, they were a consequence of Rokossovsky's thoughts that he had verbally expressed to Chibisov during their personal meeting). To wit, after carrying out the immediate tasks, the commander of the operational group was directing the 1st and 2nd Tank Corps to defeat the enemy at the Semiluki bridges on the Don River (35 kilometers from the attack's start line), with the subsequent possibility of pivoting to the west and attacking in the direction of Kastornoe (another 70 kilometers).[15] In the planned operation, the two tank corps were to enter the battle only after the rifle divisions had created a breach in the German defenses, and having emerged in operational space, they were to destroy the foe's rear echelons and lines of communication. Based upon this conception, Chibisov also arranged the combat formation of the operational group. In the first echelon, the rifle divisions and two separate tank brigades (the 201st and 118th Tank Brigades) were to attack, with the assignment of breaking through the enemy defense. The 1st and 2nd Tank Corps were assembled in the second echelon for introduction into a breakthrough.

The 1st Tank Corps was supposed "to enter the breakthrough in the Gremiach'e – patch of woods 2.5 kilometers east of Gremiach'e sector upon the seizure of Khrushchevo and Lebiazh'e by the 340th and 193rd Rifle Divisions', with the immediate task of destroying the enemy's reserves, headquarters and artillery in the Gremiach'e – Ovsiannikovo – Somovo area, and subsequently to advance in the direction of Kondrashovka, bypassing Zemliansk from the northeast."[16] (On 20 July, directly on the eve of the operation's start, the commander of the 1st Tank Corps Major General M.E. Katukov fell ill. The doctors recommended that he be hospitalized; however, he believed that it was totally impossible for him to leave the tank corps at such an important moment. This decision, unquestionably, deserves respect and characterizes Major General Katukov as a genuine commander, who put his duties before his own health. Other commanders in similar situations acted differently ….).[17]

The 2nd Tank Corps was specifically given the task "to enter the breakthrough in the sector: woods west of Hill 188.5 – Bol'shaia Vereika once the 167th Rifle Division takes Malaia Vereika,

14 Ibid.

15 TsAMO, F.1657, op. 1, d. 22, l. 145.

16 Ibid.

17 TsAMO F. 1 Tank Corps, op. 1, d. 4, l. 10.

with the immediate task to overwhelm and destroy the enemy's reserves, headquarters and artillery in the Churikovo – Kaver'ia – Sklaievo-3 area" and "in the future take the Medvezh'e area".[18] Chibisov's infantry were given 0430 as the H-hour for the offensive, but prior to this rifle units were to drive in the enemy's combat outposts by 0300 with a night attack and expose the enemy's forward edge. Before entering the breakthrough, units of the 2nd Tank Corps with one tank battalion were to support the actions of the 104th Separate Rifle Brigade to seize the German strongpoint atop Hill 187.4. Chibisov decided to set up his command post in Murav'evka and obliged his subordinate commanders to report every two hours starting at 0400 on 21 July 1942.

General Liziukov issued his order for the offensive at 1400 on 20 July, just 14 hours prior to the start of the infantry's attack, while the commanders of the subordinate brigades received it even later (for example, the headquarters of the 148th Tank Brigade received the order at 1600). The commander of the 148th Tank Brigade issued his combat order only at 2000, just 6 hours prior to the start of the attack.[19]

As was written in the documents of the 148th Tank Brigade "the entire night of 20-21.7.42 passed in preparation for the offensive." Having contacted the headquarters of the 167th Infantry Division that was attacking in the first echelon, the tank brigade headquarters sent forward a company of sappers to ensure the crossing of the tanks in Surikovo.[20] Similar preparations were going on in other tank brigades as well.

Meanwhile, that evening Liziukov shifted his command post to a patch of woods north of Dmitriashevskii Vyselok. The commissar of the 2nd Tank Corps, Regimental Commissar Assorov and staff members of the Intelligence and Operations Departments accompanied Liziukov. The chief of staff Colonel Nagaibakov remained in Sedelki, where in fact Combat Order No. 9 was written. This order became the first combat document of the corps headquarters in the forthcoming offensive.

However, neither Liziukov nor Assorov, and not even Nagaibakov was aware at the time that this order would not only be the tank corps' first, but also the final formal order of this operation. In addition, for two of them, it would be the last order in their lives.

18 Ibid.
19 TsAMO, F. 148 tp, op. 1, d. 3, l. 31.
20 Ibid.

2

The start of the operation: 21 July 1942

The terrain across which Operational Group Chibisov was to attack was a hilly steppe plain, cut by deep ravines. Here and there in the ravines were patches of woods, which in places extended far onto the plain. The Bystrik Creek and the Bol'shaia Vereika River flowed through the 2nd Tank Corps' path of advance. Villages were nestled in their valleys, some of which still had people living in them, but the rest (wherever the Germans had time to drive the citizens forcibly into their rear area) were unpopulated. The commanding hills offered splendid fields of vision stretching out for many kilometers, and were good sites for observation posts and defensive positions.

A considerable factor was also the fact that the Bystrik Creek and Bol'shaia Vereika River, although small and narrow, presented difficult obstacles to cross, not only for wheeled transport, but also tanks because of their muddy bottoms and marshy basins. Along most of their courses, they were impossible to cross in the absence of bridges or fords. The deep ravines overgrown with woods were also completely impenetrable for tanks, which to a great degree deprived the tank units of freedom to maneuver.

The terrain possibilities for organizing a defense were used by the troops in full measure, not only by the Germans, over ten July days, but also by the Soviets, long before the start of the fighting. The point is that a sector of the Voronezh defensive line of fortifications ran through this exact area, which at an order from the Soviet command had begun to be built back in the autumn of 1941, then abandoned, but was taken up to complete with fresh energy in the spring of 1942. An enormous amount of work was done by the hands of troops of the 6th Sapper Army and the local population: deep anti-tank ditches had been dug; the banks of brooks and streams were scarped; defensive strongpoints with concrete bunkers, firing positions and lines of trenches had been constructed.

Officially, a 14-hour work day was scheduled for the construction work.[1] With the time necessary to travel to and from the construction sites (a distance that quite often reached 5 or 6 kilometers) and breaks for meals, which naturally wasn't counted, the work day might extend even to 16 hours. There could also not be even any talk about days off – the country was at war! Attempts by the soldiers to "be clever" and to "harvest" more time for rest by showing up late for work or leaving early gave rise to the just indignation of political cadres who stopped by and issued harsh admonitions to cease idleness and slack work performance. They had the same attitude to manifestations of lice infestations among the sappers, prompted partially by the fact that despite all of the stern warnings, the soldiers were regularly visiting villages in order to exchange the soap they had been given for food items – plainly the rumbling of empty stomachs was more important for the men than cleanliness and lice.[2]

1 TsAMO, F.202, op. 36, d. 129, l. 161.
2 Ibid, l. 165.

In order to reinforce discipline, it goes without saying that regular political training sessions with *agitprop* specialists and public readings of newspapers and conversations with political instructors were scheduled of course not during hours on duty, but in free time for the men. The procurator's eye was also not slumbering in the struggle for labor discipline: a certain Sergeant Goncharov, unable to help himself, dozed off at work, and for his 3-hour nap he was sentenced to 5 years by a tribunal.[3] All of these measures enabled the command to impose high norms of work on the labor brigades and to achieve a lot ... and all of this with the aim of defending Voronezh from the enemy and to prevent him from approaching the city. By the beginning of July, a majority of the work to construct the Voronezh line of defensive fortifications had been finished.

However, due to the evil irony of fate, because of the foe's impetuous offensive that targeted a different location, this sector of defenses never delayed the fascist tanks and proved to be useless for the defense of Voronezh. However, the enemy, which had occupied them without fighting, immediately spotted the great advantage of the defensive positions to organize their own defense. So tens of thousands of man-hours, spent by our own compatriots to build the line, allowed the Germans not to start from scratch, but to continue the work already done, thereby economizing on others' work, effort, means and time.

Starting on 8-9 July, the enemy units began to improve the sectors of defense that had been achieved at no cost to them, and with German pedantic thoroughness corrected the mistakes made by the previous designers and builders (the tactically poor position of a number of defensive positions with respect to terrain; the shallow trenches dug well enough for government work, but not meeting their own standards, etc.) and built their own strongpoints, day after day digging more deeply into the earth. The German command explained to the infantry units that they had come here *seriously and for a long time ...*

The first test of the enemy's defenses took place in combat with the 5th Tank Army. Since then, units of the German 387th and 340th Infantry Divisions, taking full advantage of the week's respite in fighting at the front, strengthened their positions even more. Knowing that his infantry corps had limited possibilities, the commander of the German VII Corps *General der Artillerie* Ernst-Eberhard Hell strove to offset his lack of forces with a well planned system of defense and required his soldiers not to spare their strength when setting up their defensive positions, instructively reminding them that "whatever we cannot achieve with sweat, we'll be forced to pay for with a lot of blood."[4] So the soldiers under the direction of their officers constantly worked to improve their positions, knowing well that nothing less than their own lives depended on this. Thus, in the tense atmosphere of waiting before the battle, the German infantry divisions prepared to repulse a new Russian offensive, the looming imminence of which was completely obvious to the German command.

* * *

Pursuant to the order he had received from Chibisov, Liziukov in his turn ordered the 26th and 148th Tank Brigades to advance in the wake of the 167th Rifle Division and to enter the breakthrough in the sector between the villages of Malaia and Bol'shaia Vereika with the subsequent task to attack to the southeast toward the village of Medvezh'e. The 2nd Motorized Rifle Brigade, 104th Separate Rifle Brigade and the reserve 27th Tank Brigade were to support the tank corps' offensive from the left flank and take Bol'shaia Vereika.

3 Ibid., l. 162.
4 NARA, T-314, roll 364, fr. 000143-144.

The success of the operation greatly depended on the actions of the first echelon troops of the operational group, which were to break through the German defenses in order to give the tank corps the opportunity to enter a breach, without the need to lose tanks in combat with German anti-tank guns in the main line of defense. In the sector of the 2nd Tank Corps' offensive, the forces of the 167th Rifle Division, 118th Tank Brigade and 104th Separate Rifle Brigade were in the first echelon. All of these units had recently completed their process of forming up in the spring of 1942, after which they had been directed to Briansk Front.

The 104th Separate Rifle Brigade began forming up in December 1941 in Gor'ky Oblast and arrived at the front in May 1942. Almost no archival documents of the brigade remain for the summer of 1942. A certain impression of the 104th Separate Rifle Brigade can be gleaned from the recollections of veterans and memoirs. Veterans of the brigade recalled:

> The brigade was called a "cadet brigade", because the entire rank and file and noncommissioned officer staff came from cadets schools in the Far East. The brigade numbered 4,000 men. The senior and middle command echelon were convalescents from military hospitals; these men already had prior combat experience on the Western front and in the Finnish Winter War.
>
> The first brigade commander was Nikolai Vasil'evich Khriastov, a veteran of the Winter War with Finland. Back then there were intense days of training; everyone was preparing for departure to the front. But the poor nutrition and fat deficiency led to the fact that the healthy soldiers became afflicted with night blindness. After hard tactical exercises in snow-covered fields, the soldiers returned to their barracks in single file, clinging to the man in front of him.
>
> In March 1942 K.V. Voroshilov arrived from the *Stavka* to inspect the training. He saw that the brigade had been reduced to exhaustion and was not ready for the front. Brigade commander N.V. Khriastov was dismissed from his post. Colonel Zinovyi Nikolaevich Garanin became the new brigade commander.
>
> In the middle of April Voroshilov arrived again with a cluster of generals to inspect tactical exercises. After this, the brigade in April 1942 departed by rail for the front. The brigade took up a defense in Tula Oblast, not far from Belev.[5]

The men of the 104th Separate Rifle Brigade received their first impression of the front in May-June 1942, when as part of Briansk Front's 61st Army they took up a defensive position along the eastern bank of the Oka River. In truth, the situation on the Oka River provided only a taste of genuine combat experience – the exchange of fire with the enemy and a defense in a quiet sector of the front didn't give the brigade command the opportunity to check their rifle companies in offensive fighting. On 5 July 1942 the brigade was loaded aboard trains and sent to Elets. Starting on 7 July the 104th Separate Rifle Brigade spent 6 days preparing a line of defense south of that city, but then at an order from Operational Group Chibisov's headquarters, it began to move up to the front.

One of the last documents written by Regimental Commissar Assorov is an order to the commissar of the 104th Separate Rifle Brigade, dated 19 July 1942. This dispatch adds sharp lines to the portrait of the 2nd Tank Corps' commissar, just as it allows one a better view of the reality of life at the front, where anything could happen:

5 Materials of a school museum in the village of Sklaievo, Ramonskii District, Voronezh Oblast.

> To the military commissar of the 104th Rifle Brigade.
>
> It has been established that during the passage of the 1st Battalion of your brigade through the settlement of Pribytkovo, certain soldiers of this brigade took part in plundering the civilian population, stole things from the civilian population, scrounged meat and milk, uncovered [indecipherable in the text], and took money. One Red Army soldier took from a civilian woman her money and passport, and so forth. Neither the brigade commander nor the brigade commissar took any measures to curtail the marauding and thievery ... the command staff of this battalion also took part in the plundering and thievery.
>
> I am ordering an investigation into the facts of the plundering and thefts. Identify the parties guilty of thievery and shoot one or two of them. Report on the fulfillment of this order.[6]

The forthcoming operation, if not a combat baptism for the brigade, would unquestionably be its first test in offensive fighting.

The 167th Rifle Division began its second forming in December 1941 in the area of the hamlet of Sukhoi Log in Sverdlovsk Oblast (the original division perished in encirclement in September 1941) and was staffed with recruits from the Urals. There was a layer of commanders within the division who had been at the front, but the overwhelming majority of the personnel didn't have any combat experience.

One of the division's veterans recalled his training in its artillery regiment: "Initially we lacked a lot for giving the soldiers full-value training. We had to teach them using wooden mock-ups. However, this didn't reduce enthusiasm, and the exercises went with great zeal and diligence. The quality and content of training improved after the regiment received a 122-mm howitzer and one 107-mm cannon from the Odessa Artillery School that had been evacuated to Sukhoi Log." Guns in an artillery regiment (!) were such a rarity that the training of the artillerymen took place both day and night, under the light of lanterns, "since the positions of all the batteries had to be trained on these two guns."[7]

The former chief of the division's medical service recalled that "during the division's process of formation, the doctors of the medical-sanitation battalion mastered practical surgery, visiting a military hospital in Sukhoi Log, and twice a week performed operations on dogs, supplied for this purpose by local residents. The pinnacle of training was participation in field exercises ..."[8]

In April 1942 the division arrived in the town of Morshansk, where it finally received combat weapons, equipment and ammunition. Then the 167th Rifle Division conducted a march through Lipetsk to Zadonsk, where some of the soldiers and commanders became witnesses to fascist air raids. In general for the overwhelming majority of our units arriving at the front, bombing attacks by enemy aviation was their first encounter with the adversary even before entering combat.

On 7 July the chief of staff of the 3rd Reserve Army with great agitation wrote about the condition of the army's rifle divisions (one of which was the 167th Rifle Division):

> All of the divisions have gone through a very brief period of training according to a one- or two-month program of training, and still haven't mastered their weapons, since they received them quite late. There is one sapper battalion, unarmed and untrained. There is a large shortage of motorized transport in the divisions, which adversely affects their mobility. When

6 TsAMO F. 2 TK, op. 1, d. 224(b), l. 53.

7 *Poklonimsia velikim tem godam: Vospominaniia veteranov 167* sd [We *bow down before those great years: Recollections of veterans of the 167th Rifle Division*] (Lipetsk, 1995), l. 6.

8 Ibid., l. 7

> moving out, this causes a stretching of the column … In all of the divisions, chemical means of defense, other than gas masks, are lacking. In the divisions there is less than one standard combat load of ammunition, and nothing in the field army dump. […] There is an extremely limited quantity of horse-drawn carts and motorized transport in the divisions and in the field command of the army; this complicates the organization of communications, command and control of the army, as well as the delivery of ammunition and food to the units, which creates a difficult situation in places. The divisions cannot manage with the available transport means.[9]

On 19 July the 167th Rifle Division became subordinate to Operational Group Chibisov, and already on 20 July received an order to launch an offensive at sunrise on 21 July. The headquarters of a division that was going into battle for the first time had less than one day to prepare for the operation – for reconnaissance, intelligence-gathering, setting up communications, organizing cooperation among the different types of forces, working out a plan of attack, transmitting the tasks to the subordinate units and for many other matters.

The 118th Tank Brigade, which was supposed to support the rifle units' offensive, arrived at Briansk Front on 1 July 1942. The brigade was up to table strength in personnel and equipment, and had 8 heavy KV tanks, 16 T-34 and 20 light T-70 tanks (this new tank with a 45-mm main gun had only just begun to appear at the front, and of all the tank units in Operational Group Chibisov, only the 1st Guards Tank Brigade and 118th Tank Brigade had them).[10] At first the 118th Tank Brigade was made subordinate to the commander of the 284th Rifle Division, and then to the commander of the 1st Tank Corps, before becoming directly subordinate to the commander of the operational group, at whose decision the tank brigade was supposed to break through the forward edge of the German defenses together with the infantry.

On the night of 19-20 July the units of Operation Group Chibisov began to move out toward the jumping-off area for the attack. Thousands of men, and hundreds of tanks, vehicles and artillery guns began movement toward the front across poorly-scouted or else totally unfamiliar terrain.

The 2nd Motorized Rifle Brigade and the 104th Separate Rifle Brigade were moving up to the line of attack north and northeast of the village of Bol'shaia Vereika. The 118th Tank Brigade and 167th Rifle Division were moving out toward Surikovye Vyselki. The assembly of the forces was taking place in darkness, which complicated both movement and orientation. Alas, the units suffered their first casualties even before entering combat. Two T-34 tanks of the 118th Tank Brigade collided during the march, as a result of which the commander of one of the tanks broke the bridge of his nose and had to be sent off to a hospital. Then the driver of a different tank didn't notice men of the 167th Rifle Division who were sleeping on the side of a road and crushed two of them to death and crippled two others.[11] (The men had to have been so worn out in order to fall asleep by the road and not hear the rumbling of the tanks! On the other hand, in the darkness and road dust, it was simple for the driver-mechanic to lose sight of the road and swerve onto the scarcely-noticeable shoulder of the road.) A hasty questioning of the incident's participants who remained uninjured (the units had to move into their jumping-off positions within a set time, and now the entire column had stopped!) plainly reached a deadlock, and quickly ended because of the absence of clear guilt.

During the night march, the Party organizer of an anti-tank battery of the 118th Tank Brigade was severely wounded by an unexpected gunshot. As is written in the documents, "…the

9 TsAMO, F. 60 Army, op. 10564, d. 35, l. 1
10 TsAMO, F. 118 tbr, op. 1, d. 47, ll. 1 and l. 10.
11 Ibid., l. 10.

investigation of the incident revealed that the shot had been fired from the direction of the 104th Rifle Brigade's position. In general, random gunfire from the direction of that brigade at the forest fringe where our brigade's units are positioned is noticeable." Because of accidents, breakdowns and delays on the march to the jumping-off area for the offensive, 2 T-34, 1 KV and 1 T-70 of the 118th Tank Brigade failed to arrive.

The operation, which had been designated by the headquarters of the Briansk Front to begin on 20 July, was postponed to the following day by General Chibisov, but judging from the documents, this happened at the last moment. Some units of the operational group received the order to take up their jumping-off areas for the attack on the night of 19-20 July, and after the postponement of the offensive remained in their jumping-off positions for the entire day of 20 July, which didn't go unnoticed by German reconnaissance. Moreover, many Soviet rank-and-file soldiers knew not only of the pending offensive, but also the fact of when it was supposed to begin. Senior Battalion Commissar Kuznetsov, a Briansk Front Political Department instructor who visited the 193rd Rifle Division, reported:

> The fact that a military secret is poorly kept in the preparation of a combat operation leaps to the eye … On the night of 19-20 July I arrived at the observation post of this division, which was located 10 kilometers from the command post. I overheard conversations of Red Army soldiers that the division's offensive was set to begin at 0300 hours with an artillery preparation. However, when the operation was postponed to 21 July because of the lack of readiness and there had been no artillery preparation that morning, the Red Army soldiers became indignant – why had there been no artillery preparation, when the offensive was supposed to begin? This indicates that they knew of the division's offensive, designated for 20 July, long before the start of the operation.

Considering the woeful detail of that difficult period of the war, when prisoners and turncoats of many of our units fell into enemy hands almost daily (which is mentioned many times in German documents), it is fully possible that in addition to observation and aerial reconnaissance, the German command received evidence of the forthcoming operation from this "operational source" as well, and thus was fully aware of the pending operation and was ready to repel it. There can be no talk of any surprise offensive in these circumstances.

The offensive by Briansk Front's operational group began on 21 July at 0430. After a 30-minute artillery preparation, units of the first echelon went on the attack.[12] In the sector of the 1st Tank Corps, the 340th Rifle Division with a battalion of tanks from the 89th Tank Brigade, and the 193rd Rifle Division with the 201st Tank Brigade attacked on an 8-kilometer front south of Lomovo. In the sector of the 2nd Tank Corps, the 167th Rifle Division and the 118th Tank Brigade began to advance toward Bol'shaia Vereika from the northwest, while the 104th Separate Rifle Brigade and a portion of the 27th Tank Brigade's light T-60 tanks attacked from the northeast. Fighting on the northeastern approaches to Bol'shaia Vereika developed in the vicinity of Hills 191.3 and 187.4, and at the beginning was protracted. However, in the 2-kilometer sector of the 167th Rifle Division, the offensive began to develop more promisingly. Two regiments of the division escorted by approximately 40 tanks of the 118th Tank Brigade attacked here against an incomplete German battalion that was defending this sector. Yet no matter how much the German machine guns sputtered, their barrels red-hot from the hail of bullets they were sending out, and no matter how quickly the losses began to mount among the packed combat formations of the attackers, the wall of attacking infantry and tanks drew ever more closely to the enemy's positions.

12 TsAMO, F.202, op. 5, d. 337, l. 33.

Soon the forward battalions of the 167th Rifle Division, supported by tanks, overcame the serried rows of barbed wire and the minefield arranged in front of the German defenses and reached the German trenches. The enemy infantry wavered, abandoned their occupied positions, and began to retreat. The 2nd Motorized Rifle Brigade was also committed into the battle, attacking Bol'shaia Vereika from the north.

The attacks by the 340th Rifle Division, together with a mobile artillery group of the 4th Destroyer Brigade and the 203rd Tank Battalion (8 KV tanks and 3 T-60 tanks[13]), and by the 193rd Rifle Division together with a mobile artillery group of the 3rd Destroyer Brigade (the artillery groups each had 3 batteries of 76-mm guns)[14] and the 201st Tank Brigade (18 Lend-Lease British Mk-II Matilda tanks and 16 T-60 light tanks)[15] developed more slowly; the infantry of the rifle divisions were for the most part separated from the tanks and stopped by fire on the approaches to the forward German positions, which ran along the fringe of a lengthy patch of woods north of Hill 181.8, the slopes of Hill 213.8, and the hills north of Vysochkino.

Only after Hill 213.8 was worked over by a Katiusha rocket salvo (6 rocket launchers of the 66th Guards Mortar Regiment from their firing positions on the northern outskirts of Lomovo fired more than 100 rockets at the hill)[16] were soldiers of the 340th Rifle Division's 1144th Rifle Regiment able with the support of the 203rd Tank Battalion to break into the trenches of the German strongpoint on the crest of the hill.

Although all of the units of the first echelon went on the attack simultaneously, it seemed to certain commanders during the battle that their neighbors were being slow and acting without sufficient energy. For example, the commissar of the 118th Tank Brigade wrote, "I consider it necessary to report that the 193rd Rifle Division and 201st Tank Brigade on our right went on the attack two hours late, as a result of which all the [enemy] firepower from the right flank was concentrated against the attacking units of our brigade. The 167th Rifle Division, with which our brigade was cooperating, failed to carry out the order to build a bridge across the Vereika River for our brigade and the 2nd Tank Corps. The bridge was laid down by the 2nd Tank Battalion under the direction of the deputy brigade commander, which led to a delay in the advance."[17]

The command of the 1st Tank Corps also had complaints against its neighbors. In the account of the 1st Tank Corps' headquarters, we read:

> Having launched the offensive at 04:30 on 21 July, the 340th and 193rd Rifle Divisions throughout the entire first half of the day failed to carry out their tasks fully and created no breach in the enemy's defenses. The 340th Rifle Division, having taken the northeastern slopes of Hill 213.8, made no further advance … the 193rd Rifle Division, bypassing Point 181.8 from the east, broke into the northern outskirts of Lebiazh'e, but the enemy, which had fallen back to the southern outskirts of Lebiazh'e, was continuing to defend stubbornly along the southern bank of the Sukhaia Vereika River.[18]

Here it is necessary to clarify that the 193rd Rifle Division was able to bypass Point 181.8 from the east because at this time there was no longer any enemy defending there; the German elements had been driven from their positions northwest of Bol'shaia Vereika by the attack of the 167th

13 TsAMO, F. 89 tbr, op. 1, d. 3, l. 26.
14 TsAMO, F. 2 id, op. 1, d. 4, l. 13.
15 TsAMO, F. 201 tbr, op. 1, d. 5, l. 5.
16 TsAMO, F. 66 gmp, op. 1, d. 1, l. 83.
17 TsAMO, F. 118 tbr, op. 1, d. 47, l. 14.
18 TsAMO, F. 1 tk, op. 1, d. 4, l. 16.

Rifle Division, the 118th Tank Brigade and a portion of the 201st Tank Brigade[19] and compelled to initiate a retreat to the south. Soon the enemy units also abandoned the strongpoints northeast of this village. At 1030, according to documents of the 27th Tank Brigade, Bol'shaia Vereika was occupied by our troops.[20] According to a report from the commander of the 104th Rifle Brigade, the brigade's 4th Battalion "fought its way to the southern outskirts of Bol'shaia Vereika" already by 0810 that morning, and "fully mopped up" the village of enemy submachine gunners by midday.[21] (According to other information this happened later.)

Having learned of this success, Liziukov believed that the moment had arrived to set his tanks in motion. At 1045 he informed the commanders of his tank brigades that "the enemy forward edge has been breached and his units are retreating to the south and southeast."[22] Simultaneously he ordered the command of the 26th and 148th Tank Brigades to cross the Bol'shaia Vereika River, pursue the enemy and "to destroy the retreating enemy units, artillery and tanks, as well as the approaching reserves."[23]

The start of the operation was encouraging: already in the morning on the offensive's first day, the enemy's defenses had been breached and under the attacks by units of the first echelon, the enemy was beginning to roll back in retreat. This, undoubtedly, emboldened the former commander of the 5th Tank Army, who recalled well how agonizingly slowly and difficultly the offensive of his units had developed two weeks before. In addition to the rapid success during the breakthrough of the enemy's defenses, there was one more circumstance, which could not help but gladden the commander of the 2nd Tank Corps. In distinction from the preceding operation, when his tank corps had been forced to fight their way through the enemy's defenses by themselves and suffered heavy losses in the process, this time the tank corps wouldn't have to contend with the enemy anti-tank guns in the forward zone and could conserve their strength for operations in the depth. Much better also was the artillery support. Now it was necessary not to slow the pace of the offensive and as soon as possible introduce the tank corps into the breakthrough. Having issued the necessary orders to the brigade commanders, Liziukov began to wait with impatience for their reports to arrive at his command post in Kreshchenka.

The 26th and 148th Tank Brigades began to move up to the front from their assembly areas approximately three hours after the start of the first echelon's offensive. From the areas of Anikeevka and Sredniaia Dolina, they had to move out to Surikovo, cross a stream there, and continue the offensive toward Malaia Vereika. The brigades traveled the 9 kilometers separating them from Surikovo relatively quickly, but delays began at the bridge there. Enemy air raids were pinning down the tank units, hindering the sappers from repairing damage to the bridge, and forcing the commanders to disperse their combat formations. The tanks crossed the stream one by one and began assembling on the southern outskirts of Surikovo. In view of the fact that the 26th Tank

19 It is worth noting that in the headquarters of the 201st Tank Brigade, the brigade's contribution to the success of the overall offensive was undoubted and significant. We read in the brigade's account: "21.7.42 the brigade in cooperation with the 193rd Rifle Division, having broken through the enemy's defense and seized Malaia Vereika and Lebiazh'e, allowed the 2nd Tank Corps to pass through their combat formations. 28 enemy soldiers were taken prisoner … In the fighting for Lebiazh'e the 295th Tank Battalion distinguished itself, which with an impetuous attack put the enemy to flight. The crew of battalion commander Senior Lieutenant Kryzhanovsky, operating in the vanguard of the attack, destroyed two enemy earth and timber bunkers and killed up to 40 enemy infantry soldiers. Lieutenant Volkov's crew was the first to break into Lebiazh'e, crushing Nazis under the tank's tracks, and overcoming a water obstacle, captured a German headquarters vehicle that contained documents and mail. (TsAMO F. 201 tbr, op. 1, d. 5, l. 6).

20 TsAMO, F. 27 tbr, op. 1, d. 5, l. 208.

21 TsAMO, F. 38 Army, op. 9005, d. 19, l. 25.

22 TsAMO, F. 148 tp, op. 1, d. 3, l. 33.

23 Ibid.

Brigade had more than 60 combat machines, the crossing took a long time. The 26th Tank Brigade was still in the process of crossing the bridge when the 148th Tank Brigade arrived in Surikovo. Since the bridge was completely tied up, the 148th Tank Brigade halted on the banks of the stream and began to wait for the 26th Tank Brigade to complete its crossing. In agonizing waiting and under intensifying enemy shellfire and enemy air raids, the brigade stood motionless for several hours. From documents it follows that the 148th Tank Brigade didn't complete its crossing over the bridge in Surikovo until 1330.[24] But after climbing the hills that lay between the rivers, where there were the positions that had been abandoned by the enemy, both tank brigades had to descend into another river valley and overcome a new water obstacle – the Bol'shaia Vereika River. The bridge there for the tanks wasn't ready, and everything had to start all over again: the construction of a bridge under enemy artillery fire and aerial attacks; the indecisive, cautious advance across the river by the ranks of the infantry that had become thinned in battle; and the motionless standing of the tanks on the riverbank instead of an impetuous dash forward.

Having learned of the delays, Liziukov sent first one, then a second radio message to the commander of the 148th Tank Brigade, demanding "attack immediately in pursuit of the fleeing enemy." At 1410 he had received a short reply: "I am advancing slowly. The crossing is being held up because of Burdov's 26th Tank Brigade."

Plainly frustrated by the delays and the slowing of the offensive's pace, Liziukov at 1450 ordered the commander of the 148th Tank Brigade not to wait for the completion of the 26th Tank Brigade's crossing, but instead to cross the river at a nearby location in order to keep pace with the 26th Tank Brigade and carry out his assignment. At 1620 yet another order arrived at the 148th Tank Brigade, but this time from the commander of the operational group General Chibisov himself. Dissatisfied by the tanks' "dawdling" in place after the breakthrough of the German defenses, with a special radio message he demanded that the commander of the 148th Tank Brigade "advance immediately."[25]

Meanwhile, the day was beginning to decline toward evening, while the brigades of the 2nd Tank Corps still hadn't crossed the Bol'shaia Vereika River and begun a pursuit of the retreating foe. From the documents it is difficult to determine who was at fault for this. Many units, scrupulously noting their services and successes, blamed their failures on their neighbors. In the headquarters of the 148th Tank Brigade they blamed the forward 26th Tank Brigade, which "completely blocked the bridge"[26]; in the 26th Tank Brigade, they complained that the "delay with the river crossing took place because the bridge wasn't ready"[27], as a result of which the brigade wasn't able to begin crossing until 1800. From documents of the 118th Tank Brigade, as we've seen, it follows that the 167th Rifle Division "failed to carry out its order to construct a bridge for the brigade and the 2nd Tank Corps, which led to a slowing of the advance", and the bridge had been laid down by tankers of the 118th Tank Brigade "under the direction of the deputy brigade commander".[28] However, the 167th Rifle Division's own account indicates that its engineer battalion built the bridge.[29]

Another characteristic example of the finger-pointing at listless neighbors and the emphasizing of one's own merits can be seen in the comments of the 148th Tank Brigade's deputy chief of staff: "The cause for the delay at the bridge: the 167th Rifle Division didn't carry out the order to construct a bridge, and the corps' engineers also didn't do anything. A bridge had to be built through the efforts of the brigade's own engineer platoon and mine-laying company. No one from

24 Ibid.
25 Ibid.
26 TsAMO, F. 148 tp, op. 1, d. 3, l. 33.
27 TsAMO, F. 8 gv. TK, op. 1, d.224(b), l. 162.
28 TsAMO, F. 118 tbr, op. 1, d. 47, l. 14.
29 TsAMO, F. 202, op. 5, d. 334, l. 63.

among the staff of the corps headquarters was at the bridge, but there were representatives from the army. According to plan the brigade was to be the last to cross, but instead it was the first, since the 26th Tank Brigade was held up at the [original] crossing site."[30] At the same time the common denominator among the tankers was to berate the infantry, which, supposedly, hadn't prepared enough bridges and in general fought poorly.

Similar assessments were given as well by the command of the 1st Tank Corps, which was attacking a bit to the west of the 2nd Tank Corps. In its own post-action account, its commander General Katukov regularly complained about the 193rd and 340th Rifle Divisions, which in his opinion with their sluggish actions prevented him from carrying out his assignment. Characterizing the course of the fighting on 21 July, he wrote:

> The enemy's nests of resistance in the area of Point 181.8 and the grove 1 kilometer northwest of there weren't liquidated by the forces of the 193rd Rifle Division. Therefore, from 0430 to 1600 on 21 July, a breakthrough on the Khrushchevo – Lebiazh'e front never happened and the conditions for the introduction of the tank corps into a breakthrough hadn't been prepared. According to a supplementary decision by the Group's command, at 1600 on 21 July the 1st Guards Tank Brigade attacked the enemy in the area of Point 181.8 out of the Lomovo area with one tank company and liquidated this knot of resistance.[31] The rest of the tank brigade attacked toward Lebiazh'e and by the end of the day drove the enemy out of this settlement in cooperation with separate infantry groups of the 193rd Rifle Division, which the tankers had managed to gather on the field during the process of the attack, since the rifle division's offensive zeal as a whole had been weakened and the division headquarters subsequently failed to provide leadership over the units in the offensive to ensure the full execution of the order to create a breakthrough.[32]

However, what was the situation with the rifle units, the soldiers and commanders of which the tankers were so uniformly scolding? The 340th Rifle Division (curiously, it was being opposed by a German infantry division with the same numerical designation that had been transferred from France) throughout the day was engaged in heavy fighting for Hill 213.8 and an elongated patch of woods east of it [called the "Crocodile Woods" by the Germans], striving to overcome tough enemy resistance. In the process the division's command complained about its neighbor on the right – the 284th Rifle Division, which "didn't attack and all the [German] firepower from the patch of woods fell upon the flank and partially the rear of the division's attacking units."[33]

However, the documents of the 284th Rifle Division state that the division did attack, but the condition of its rifle regiments was such that they couldn't launch a strong attack. After the fighting at Kastornoe and its withdrawal from encirclement, the 284th Rifle Division lost the majority of its men and weapons, and even after re-assembling the units and being brought back into order, the division was still in a greatly weakened state. On the eve of its re-commitment into battle, the division's commissar Tkachenko reported:

30 TsAMO, F.202, op. 50, d. 1, l. 301.

31 From the account of the 1st Guards Tank Brigade it follows that the order for the brigade's first echelon to go over to the attack was personally given by the commander of Operational Group Chibisov, who was plainly irritated by the fact that the infantry of the 193rd Rifle Division had been totally unable to crush the enemy resistance in the German strong points that were hindering its advance. (Arkhiv IRI RAN, razdel 1, op. 36, d. 13, l. 40).

32 TsAMO, F. 1 TK, op. 1, d. 4, l. 12.

33 TsAMO, F. 340 sd, op. 1, d. 24, l. 211.

> I bring to your attention that the poor provisioning of the 284th Rifle Division with transport, horses, rifles and machine guns places it in an extremely difficult situation with respect to conducting combat operations, especially regarding the supply of rations. The following numbers testify to the poor provisioning of the division with transport and separate types of weapons:
>
> 1. In the division there are 3,172 military servicemen; a batch of replacements numbering 1,312 men has arrived and another 2,000 replacements are expected, but in the division there are only a total of 1,921 rifles, 98 automatic rifles and 202 PPSh submachine guns.
> 2. There are 21 motorized vehicles in the division, but according to the TO&E [Table of Organization and Equipment] there should be 114. There are just 7 heavy machine guns, but according to the table 108 are necessary.
> 3. 47 light machine guns, but according to the table there should be 350.
> 4. 36 anti-tank rifles, but 277 according to the table.
> 5. The division's separation from its supply base extends up to 100 kilometers and aggravates the supply with food. I persistently request, Comrade Division Commissar, with the aim of enhancing the division's strength and the future execution of combat tasks to take all necessary measures to give the division:
>   1. 75 vehicles, including 6-7 ambulances. Of the supposed number of ambulances, the medical-sanitation battalion has not a single one.
>   2. Issue 3,500-4,000 rifles, 30 heavy machine guns and 50 light machine guns, and 75-100 anti-tank rifles.
>   3. Issue 350-400 horses, especially artillery draught horses, since tow vehicles are lacking.
>   4. Bring the division's fuel, food and ammunition supply base closer to the division or move it either to Dolgorukovo Station or to the Ploty side track.[34]

Even though Tkachenko on the day of the offensive noted that "the soldiers received the information that we were going on the offensive with joy" and "many of them declared: 'The Germans must be given a blow such that they can't bear it … we'll thrash the Fritzes so that they drop their trousers!"[35], but in the regiments there was nothing in particular with which to "give the Germans a blow" or to "thrash the Fritzes" – **almost half the division's service personnel were unarmed!**

After the first day of the battle, Commissar Tkachenko wrote:

> It needs to be said that the lack of artillery fragmentation and shrapnel shells reflects on the course of the fighting; the artillerymen accordingly fired armor-piercing shells at the enemy's firing points and troops. There are no cartridges for the PPSh submachine guns; many of the soldiers have tattered uniforms and worn-out shoes. It is impossible to commit soldiers of the new batch of replacements into the fighting because of the lack of weapons. The absence of the necessary quantity of transport slows the bringing up of ammunition, food especially, and the evacuation of the wounded. We ask to give assistance with the division's provisioning with rifles, machine guns and transport, and to hasten the replacement of the worn-out uniforms and shoes …."[36]

34 TsAMO, F. 202, op. 36, d. 179, l. 21.
35 TsAMO F. 202, op. 36, d. 179, l. 29.
36 Ibid., l. 29.

It is not surprising that in these conditions, the 284th Rifle Division "advanced" to the very same lines from which it had started the attack, and its neighbor the 340th Rifle Division believed that the 284th Rifle Division hadn't attacked at all. On the first day of the offensive, the 284th Rifle Division lost 48 men killed and 93 wounded.[37]

In addition to the intense flanking fire, which didn't allow the right flank of the 340th Rifle Division to advance, the division's offensive in the center and on the left ran into organized enemy resistance, which employed heavy fire from automatic weapons and mortars to stop the attackers on the approaches to the German forward edge. The enemy artillery also became increasingly active. For a successful advance it was necessary to destroy or suppress numerous German firing points and artillery and mortar batteries, but this could not be done. It cannot be said that our artillery and air force didn't make an appearance at the battlefield: both Soviet and German documents note attacks by our aircraft and the fire of our artillery, but unfortunately their activity was ineffective.

From the post-action account of the Briansk Front's artillery units it follows that "direction over the operational group's artillery by the headquarters of the Front's artillery was implemented from the chief of artillery's command post. The 193rd Rifle Division was in the center of the assault grouping. On the night of 20-21 July the units had the task to drive in the combat outposts and close upon the forward edge of the enemy's defense. This task was not carried out by the infantry of the 340th Rifle Division."[38] (Again, it's the infantry's fault!)

The observation posts of many artillery units because of features of the terrain were positioned 4-6 kilometers away from the enemy's forward trenches, which greatly restricted the possibility of placing targeted, adjusted fire at most of his firing positions. The majority of the German defense was not even visible from such distant observation posts, but at the time the enemy's combat outposts, which remained in their positions right up to the start of the offensive, kept them from moving up closer to the front. Thus the artillery units that were supporting the infantry had to switch to unobserved fire at grid coordinates and "assembly areas of enemy reserves"; however, without the possibility of aerial spotting and the corresponding adjustment of the fire, the presence of these "reserves" in places where the barrages fell was more likely a supposition of the artillery chief's than a fact.

As an example, one can cite lines from the account of Briansk Front's artillery chief regarding the actions of General Chibisov's operational group, where it was written:

> On 21 July at 0430, all of the artillery worked over the forward edge of the enemy's defense for 30 minutes, ending with rocket salvoes from Guards Mortar regiments and an attack by bomber and ground attack aircraft. The infantry under the cover of the artillery fire closely followed the explosions. With the shifting of the artillery fire into the depth, it slowly advanced forward. ... The struggle with the enemy artillery was conducted against batteries that had been revealed by observation, but in view of the lack of artillery instrument reconnaissance (sound ranging devices), the fire was ineffective. The fire of the 152-mm howitzers was used primarily against aggregations of enemy reserves.[39]

The actions of the 89th Tank Brigade's 203rd Tank Battalion and the rocket launching units (on this day the 66th Guards Mortar Regiment and 8th Separate Guards Mortar Battalion fired approximately 600 rockets in 5 salvoes at areas of the enemy's defense) that were supporting the

37 Ibid.
38 TsAMO, F.202, op. 5, d. 337, l. 33.
39 Ibid.

340th Rifle Division went completely unnoticed by its headquarters.[40] It was as if they hadn't been there at all, even though the tankers and Guards mortar crews fought together with the infantry over the entire day. Moreover, the 340th Rifle Division's sole initial success – the penetration to Hill 213.8 and the capture of prisoners and booty there – was undoubtedly connected with the actions of the tank platoons that were supporting it (the command of the 66th Guards Mortar Regiment believed that our units took the hill as a result of salvo of the regiment's 6 rocket launchers at it at 0410 21 July).[41] We read in the 89th Tank Brigade's account:

> The tanks went on the attack at 0500 on 21.7.42. During the approach to the forward edge, the enemy met the tanks with heavy artillery and mortar fire. As a result of this the accompanying infantry became pinned down and could go no further; the artillery wasn't supporting the tanks' attack; and thus the tanks fought alone. The enemy infantry under the effects of the tank fire took cover in the trenches and was offering light resistance. In the battle, Lieutenant Krotov's crew and Lieutenant Borovyi's crews demonstrated resolve, courage and valor. During the battle they exited the tanks, leading our infantry [the 340th Rifle Division's 1144th Rifle Regiment – I.S.] behind them, and having spotted a group of enemy infantry pinned down on the battlefield, took 61 enemy soldiers prisoner. Our tanks, operating alone, upon reaching the southern slopes of Hill 213.8 were greeted with intense artillery and mortar fire; suffering losses, they made no further advance ...."

Likely the number "6" of the 61 prisoners mentioned in the 89th Tank Brigade's report was a typo, which was inserted there in place of the number "3". Data on the losses of the German 340th Infantry Division suggests this thought; from them it follows that all of the infantry division's units (and not only the battalions of its 695th Infantry Regiment, which was defending in the sector of offensive of the 203rd Tank Battalion and 340th Rifle Division's 1244th Rifle Regiment) lost irrecoverably over the entire day 46 men.

In the documents of the 340th Rifle Division it is given that the 29 prisoners captured on Hill 213.8 (according to some data, 31) were taken precisely by units of the 1144th Rifle Regiment; thus no merits whatsoever of the tankers in capturing the German soldiers (among whom were 3 *Unteroffizier* and 14 *Gefreitors*) were noted in the headquarters of the 340th Rifle Division.[42]

In a political report of the 340th Rifle Division it is written: "When the 1144th Rifle Regiment took 29 German soldiers and officers as prisoner on 21.7.42, submachine gunner Sergeant Major Fedorov and Political Instructor Matchenkov, Sergeant Grishokhin, Corporal Misiagin and Lieutenant Golubev particularly stood out; the latter was killed heroically while carrying out the combat task." Nevertheless, it is completely apparent that this success was achieved by the joint efforts of both the tankers and infantry.

It should be noted that "traces" of the fighting for Hill 213.8 were left in captured documents. For example, according to the report of the commander of the 340th Infantry Division's anti-tank battalion, in the fighting on 21 July the battalion, which was equipped on 22 July with seven 75-mm guns (3 German and 4 French), two Russian 76.2-mm guns and 1 50-mm German gun, knocked out 5 Russian tanks (including one KV) and lost 2 men dead, 9 wounded, and 17 missing-in-action.[43]

40 The data on the rocket artillery fire comes from TsAMO, F. 66 gmp, op. 1, d. 1, l. 83.
41 Ibid.
42 TsAMO, F. 340 sd, op. 1, d. 90, l. 425, 429; Ibid., d. 26, l. 211.
43 NARA, T-315, roll 21-20, fr. 000459.

In the course of the battle for Hill 213.8, the 203rd Tank Battalion lost 1 KV tank and 1 T-60 tank destroyed, and 3 KV tanks knocked out, plus 3 men killed and 3 badly wounded (one of whom soon died).[44] Over the day of fighting, 228 wounded (419 wounded according to a political report of the 340th Rifle Division's commissar[45]) arrived in the 340th Rifle Division's medical-sanitation battalion; losses in dead and missing-in-action still hadn't been determined.[46]

Regarding the results of the fighting, the 340th Rifle Division's commissar wrote, "The five vehicles attached to the medical-sanitation battalion are insufficient to transport the wounded, even though all of the lightly wounded are sent to the hospital on foot. I request assistance in providing the necessary amount of transport."[47]

There are practically no documents whatsoever for the 193rd Rifle Division in the archives for the summer of 1942, thus it seems impossible to determine precisely what prevented its regiments from carrying out their orders. However, judging from all the available evidence, the division was experiencing the same problems as the other rifle divisions. It must not be forgotten as well that the 193rd Rifle Division's single preceding frontline experience was a catastrophic defeat, which had occurred just a week before, when over two days of fighting as part of the 5th Tank Army the division had been rendered combat-ineffective and withdrawn from the front in order to gather personnel and bring the units back into order. The heavy losses and the defeat in the very first battle affected in a most negative way the mood of the remaining personnel, the motivation and training of a significant part of which even before the fighting hadn't been on a high level.

Battalion Commissar Prokof'ev, a member of Briansk Front's Political Department who had been assigned to the 193rd Rifle Division, reported:

> In the division, approximately 50% of the personnel are not Russian … and poorly understand the Russian language. The division didn't receive the People's Commissar of Defense's Order No. 130 [Stalin's 1 May 1942 address to the people regarding the nature of the war and the enemy, and calling upon the Red Army to make 1942 the year of the final rout of the German-fascist troops] in their languages and it is available only in Russian; there are also no newspapers, and thus education work and the passing of orders to these nationalities, as the chief of Political Department Comrade Ovcharenko declared, are very difficult to organize …
>
> In places where the 193rd Rifle Division fought, many rifles, light machine guns, gas masks, metal helmets and other items of supply and armament lay scattered about in the ravines and on the fields. The collection of weapons and gas masks is poorly organized, which I have brought to the attention of the chief of the 193rd Rifle Division's Political Department, and directives have been given to collect all the rifles, gas masks and metal helmets immediately.[48]

It isn't surprising that the spiritless actions of the 193rd Rifle Division and its weak combat capability prompted the disgust of the commander of the 1st Tank Corps that was cooperating with it. According to dispatches, over the day of fighting the 193rd Rifle Division lost 201 men wounded; the number of dead and missing-in-action in the division couldn't even be reported to higher command the following day.[49] The 201st Tank Brigade that was supporting the 193rd Rifle

44 TsAMO, F. 89 tbr, op. 1, d. 2, l. 27.
45 TsAMO, F. 340 sd, op. 1, d. 90, l. 429.
46 Ibid., l. 425.
47 Ibid., l. 429.
48 TsAMO, F.202, op. 36, d. 129, l. 452-453.
49 TsAMO, F. 202, op. 5, d. 251, l. 6.

Division lost 4 Matilda tanks and 6 T-60 light tanks over the course of the day, and suffered 75 casualties, including 18 dead and 57 wounded.[50]

The offensive on Operational Group Chibisov's right flank immediately ran into stubborn enemy resistance and despite all the efforts of the 1st Guards Rifle Division, 106th Rifle Brigade and 8th Cavalry Corps that were operating there, failed. Our units made no significant progress there whatsoever.

However, the 167th Rifle Division and 118th Tank Brigade that were attacking on the operational group's left flank achieved a definite success, having reached the Bol'shaia Vereika River and taken the village of the same name there. However, their achievement didn't come easily. As a result of the fighting the 118th Tank Brigade lost 5 tanks destroyed (2 T-70, 2 T-34 and 1 KV) and 4 tanks knocked out (2 T-34 and 2 T-70), plus 15 men killed and 23 wounded.[51]

The 167th Rifle Division suffered much heavier losses; its regiments had to attack across the completely exposed ground lying between the two rivers. In contrast with the tankers that were so unhappy with the infantry's actions, the foot soldiers couldn't take cover from bullets and shell fragments behind armor plating, and took heavy casualties from artillery barrages and airstrikes. A driver of the 535th Separate Chemical Company of the 167th Rifle Division M.I. Morozov recalled: "In the first battles near Bol'shaia Vereika, the German air force bombed us pitilessly. Messerschmitt fighters were literally hunting down every vehicle, wagon and soldier. When moving to the front, fascist aircraft dove on me twice. I was wounded by a machine-gun burst."[52]

The German air raids particularly intensified when our units reached the river at Malaia Vereika. Hostile aircraft bombed and strafed troops and equipment that were approaching this place; they were disrupting the infantry's advance and didn't give the engineers a possibility to lay down bridges across the river. With the appearance of our rifle units on the southern bank of the river, the resistance of the enemy infantry also noticeably increased; before this, they had quickly rolled back from positions they had occupied that morning. The losses of our troops were heavy.

Battalion Commissar Kifman, the chief of the 167th Rifle Division's Political Department, reported on the offensive's first day:

> According to preliminary information from our side more than 500 men have been killed or wounded. In the fighting with the German fascists, the 520th Rifle Regiment alone had 211 men killed and wounded. Of them, the regiment commander Major Sergei Nikiforovich Dubov was wounded … there is a large number of losses among the political staff, which is explained by their ignorance of their place in battle. The blocking detachment detained 2 Red Army men that were attempting to desert: Red Army man R. of a battalion of the 520th Rifle Regiment, 1919 year of birth, and Red Army Man S. of a battalion of the 465th Rifle Regiment. [Here and throughout the book, in order to protect identities I've given only the first letter of their surnames – I.S.] They were both shot in front of their assembled units. I am sending documents and letters found on the bodies of the dead and captured Germans. Appendix: About 22 letters, 10 photographs, 1 booklet, a personal military document and one newspaper.[53]

A doctor of the 167th Rifle Division's 615th Rifle Regiment I.Iu. Tsverdlina recalled:

50 TsAMO, F. 201 tbr (3256), op. 1, d. 5, l. 5.
51 TsAMO, F. 118 tbr, op. 1, d. 47, l. 13.
52 *Poklonimsia velikim tem godam*, p. 14.
53 TsAMO, F. 202, op. 36, d. 179, l. 41.

> In the first battle our medical-sanitation company was located in a field on a hillside south of Surikovye Vyselki. Wounded men were lying on stretchers or simply lying or sitting on the ground. Doctor Nina Aleksandrovna Kozhina, medical assistants Nikolai Dnepro and Dernov and I were rendering initial, most necessary medical aid. Sanitary stretcher bearers or comrades were bringing in some of the wounded; others were arriving under their own power, and there were those coming on foot that in peacetime wouldn't have been able to get out of bed: men with broken leg bones or serious traumas to the head and abdomen. The regiment's senior doctor Viacheslav Sergeevich Matveev was helping us. The commander of the medical-sanitation company Aleksandr Mikhailovich Rozenshtein was busy with the evacuation of the wounded from the battlefield. I remember they brought in a young soldier, almost a boy. One of his legs had been torn off and the bones in the other smashed. He had lost a lot of blood. I still hear his beseeches in my ears: "Save me, I want to live". We gave him all the necessary aid that we could, but he still died.[54]

According to the operation's plan, the rifle divisions upon reaching a river were supposed to construct bridges quickly for the tanks, but as it turned out in reality, this was much easier to put down on paper than it was to do. Of course, the divisional engineer elements possessed the numbers and means to lay down the necessary number of bridges on schedule, and theoretically might have secured the passage of the tanks on time, if their work had gone without hindrance!

However, the bold staff calculations were plainly based upon the supposition that the enemy would be driven from the line of the river by the attacks of our infantry and would not be able to interfere with the construction of bridges, while Briansk Front's air force would reliably cover the area of the bridges against attacks by enemy bombers. In reality, neither the first nor the second supposition was realized. Moreover, in the center sector of the offensive, where the 193rd and 340th Rifle Divisions had been totally unable to reach the river, the German troops received the possibility of placing targeted flanking fire on the area of the crossing site from the hills they occupied. As a result, units of the 167th Rifle Division, which did reach the Bol'shaia Vereika River, were deprived of a saving dead space, where they might have been able to take some cover during a barrage from the southern bank, and wound up instead under crossfire from both banks of the Bol'shaia Vereika.

The calculations to cover the area of the operation with fighters also failed; they appeared over the battlefield only sporadically, as a result of which enemy aircraft soon began to arrive in the sky above the battlefield more frequently. Under their attacks time and again the advance of our rifle units was disrupted, the attacks of tanks came to a halt, while the sappers were not so much building bridges as they were trying to save themselves from bombings and artillery barrages in crevices and shell craters next to the river, or else directly in the water beneath the precipitous bank of the river. In such conditions work on bridges across the Bol'shaia Vereika River went on throughout the day of 21 June 1942.

With the advance of our troops across the abandoned German positions and particularly with their arrival at the river, a different threat to the attackers became increasingly evident – mines. Before retreating the Germans had time to mine roads, bypasses, likely avenues leading to the river, but with particular density – at the places of possible crossings themselves. In liberated Bol'shaia Vereika, our soldiers frequently encountered booby traps or taut wires leading to some similar "surprise" left behind by the enemy, which indirectly speaks to a planned German withdrawal and its engineer support.

54 *Poklonimsia velikim tem godam*, p. 18.

The commissar of the 27th Tank Brigade reported:

> During our troops' occupation of the village of Bol'shaia Vereika, we found the entire village had been mined. The following booby traps were uncovered:
>
> 1. On a front porch by the door, there was a man lying without legs, but still alive. Soldiers approached to take him, but when they grabbed him a mine exploded; the man had been mined.
> 2. In one home there was a case with papers left behind by the Germans. As soon as one commander (not from our unit, but some unknown one) attempted to open the case, there was an explosion – the commander was killed.
> 3. There was a new flexible steel cable lying in the grass. A Red Army man, a Komsomol member of the 27th Tank Brigade's 436th Tank Battalion Comrade Nesterenko grabbed the cable, an explosion was heard, and the eyes of the Red Army man were seared.
>
> There was a whole bunch of other incidents. Explanatory work is going on among the soldiers and commanders, so that in such cases they approach things left behind by the Germans with greater caution. Roads and buildings are being swept of mines. The commander of a company of tankettes Senior Lieutenant Danilov himself has detected and exploded 25 mines.[55]

As a result of mine explosions, the 27th Tank Brigade lost a KV tank and a T-34; two T-60 tanks and one T-34 were disabled.[56]

German mines at crossing sites especially caused a lot of harm. During an attempt to cross the river by the 26th Tank Brigade, four tanks blew up on mines, after which the tankers had to stop and search for and disarm mines together with the engineers.[57] Soon it became clear that upon retreating, the Germans had mined not only the approaches to crossing sites, but also the riverbanks, emplacing mines right on the waterline. A similar situation was seen in the 1st Tank Corps' sector of actions as well. Its brigades, taking advantage of the penetration by the 167th Rifle Division and 118th Tank Brigade, reached the Bol'shaia Vereika River in Lebiazh'e. During a crossing attempt by the 1st Guards Tank Brigade, eight tanks blew up on mines, and the crossing was stopped until the area had been cleared of mines.[58]

The 1st Guards Tank Brigade wrote in its official account:

> At 1600 on 21.7.42, the brigade's 2nd Tank Battalion reached the northern bank of the Sukhaia Vereika River; the bank and river bottom had been mined, and in addition scarps and counterscarps had been created. The bridge was damaged by the constant aerial attacks and artillery fire [...]. The 1st Tank Battalion and the motorized rifle battalion reached the southwestern slopes of Hill 181.8. Despite the demands of the commanders of the tank battalions for the infantry to render assistance by clearing mines and laying down bridges, the riflemen didn't do this, and it was only through the efforts of a sapper company of the 535th Engineer Battalion that the mines were cleared by 18:00 and 9 tanks were able to cross the bridge, before it collapsed.[59]

55 TsAMO, F. 2 TK, op. 1, d.224(b), l. 100.
56 Ibid., l. 56, 167.
57 Ibid, l. 162.
58 TsAMO, F. 1 TK, op. 1, d. 4, l. 12.
59 Arkhiv IRI RAN, F. 2, razdel 1, op. 36, d. 13, l. 40.

Thus, the frequent lengthy aerial bombings, the constant artillery and mortar barrages and the enemy's mining of approaches to the river led to the fact that the crossing of the tanks to the southern bank of the Bol'shaia Vereika River went very slowly. The total lack of combat seasoning of a lot of the rifle units was also telling; for the first time they were facing intense enemy fire, and instead of a rapid dash forward (like the dissatisfied tank commanders wanted who were following the course of the battle from their distant observation posts, or else from a command post in a secure bunker), they hung back, hugging the earth, or at times even scattered across the fields to escape the ferocious bombing runs (as Katukov asserted[60]). They didn't get by without mistakes made by the command staff either; a significant portion of them didn't have adequate classroom training and combat experience, but had immediately wound up in such a difficult situation.

Knowing all the above, is it worth being surprised that the tank units on this day took so long to cross the river? More likely, it is worth emphasizing that despite the stubborn enemy resistance, they nevertheless managed to cross the Bol'shaia Vereika River, and that one must bow one's head in front of the sacrifices and courage of our soldiers, commanders and political workers who enabled this most difficult river crossing.

By the evening of 21 July, elements of two regiments of the 167th Rifle Division were able not only to cross the river in Malaia Vereika, but also to drive the Germans from the line of hills along the riverbank adjacent to Malaia Vereika, from where the enemy had been keeping the area of the crossing site under targeted rifle and machine-gun fire. Now, sheltered by a dead space from enemy artillery and rifle fire, the engineers and tankers were able to complete the construction of corduroy roads and the strengthening of fords, so that the tanks could cross to the southern bank without hindrance. Doubtlessly encouraged by their presence, the infantry of the 167th Rifle Division pushed forward to the northern approaches of Hill 188.5 and began to dig in. One rifle battalion of the 2nd Motorized Rifle Brigade also managed to concentrate here late in the evening.

The crossing of the 2nd Tank Corps' 26th and 148th Tank Brigades was completed only 6-plus hours after their appearance at the riverbank. The brigades assembled on the southern outskirts of Malaia Vereika around 1800 hours. Altogether in the two tank brigades of the 2nd Tank Corps on the southern bank of the river there were 16 KV, 35 T-34 and approximately 25 light T-60 tanks.[61] Combat-capable tanks of the 118th Tank Brigade were also here; by the end of the day, it had 7 KV, 9 T-34 and 12 T-70 still operational. The rest of the machines needed repairs.[62] Thus, the total number of tanks in the tank grouping of the 2nd Tank Corps and the 118th Tank Brigade that had reached Malaia Vereika amounted to more than 100 tanks (23 KV, 44 T-34, 12 T-70 and approximately 25 T-60).

The 27th Tank Brigade was assembled in Bol'shaia Vereika. The losses in personnel among the tank units, despite the bombings and shelling, were minimal. From political reports of the tank brigades it follows that the 26th Tank Brigade had lost 1 man killed and 3 wounded, while the 27th Tank Brigade had lost 1 killed and 5 wounded.[63]

At the same time, a brigade commissar observed that "there are victims only thanks to the heedless attitude of certain soldiers and commanders to the need to take cover with the appearance of hostile aircraft. A directive has gone out to the military commanders to explain to all the personnel that to take cover in crevices and slit trenches with the appearance of hostile aircraft is not a sign of cowardice, but protects the men from pointless sacrifices."[64]

60 TsAMO, F. 1 TK, op. 1, d. 4, l. 12.
61 TsAMO, F. 148 tp, op. 1, d. 3, l. 31; F. 2 TK, op. 1, d. 224(b), l. 162.
62 TsAMO, F. 118 tbr, op. 1, d. 47, l. 1, 13.
63 TsAMO, F. 8 gv. TK, op. 1, d. 224(b), l. 162, 167.
64 TsAMO, F. 2 TK, op. 1, d. 224(b), l. 170.

Judging from everything, the losses of the 148th Tank Brigade were just as light. The losses of the 2nd Motorized Rifle Brigade for 21 July amounted to 6 dead and 30 wounded.[65]

In the brigade commissar's political reports, certain episodes of the battle for Bol'shaia Vereika have been preserved:

> The soldiers and commanders fought courageously with the Hitlerites and pushed forward. In the evening, the village of Bol'shaia Vereika was completely in our hands. [...] Among the killed is the political instructor of the 3rd Company of the 448th Motorized Rifle Battalion Junior Political Instructor Grishaev; the company's commander went down with wounds. Political Instructor Comrade Skulkin took command of the company into his hands and confidently led the soldiers toward the foe and through his personal example showed how it is necessary to destroy the fascist beasts. The fascists had fully moved the civilian population out of Bol'shaia Vereika back into their rear. The enemy mined roads and the entire river. Our engineer platoon successfully cleared the road and river of mines and gave our tanks the opportunity to advance without delay. The brigade's sanitation-medical platoon took in and sent on to the hospital 80 wounded soldiers and commanders.[66]

Much greater were the losses in the 104th Separate Rifle Brigade and 167th Rifle Division, the infantry of which spent the entire day on completely exposed ground under artillery barrages and bombing raids. The losses of the 104th Separate Rifle Brigade for 21 July amounted to 394 men, of which 43 were killed.[67] According to the roster of the 167th Rifle Division, the irrecoverable losses of the division in dead alone on this day amounted to 177 men. I don't possess any information on the wounded and missing-in-action of this division. Nevertheless, based upon the characteristic statistical relationship between killed and wounded at this stage of the war, one can presume that the total losses of the 167th Rifle Division on this day amounted to no less than 700 men, and thus the total casualties for these two formations (the 104th Rifle Brigade and 167th Rifle Division) were approximately 1,100. The chief of the division's medical service A.E. Rapoport recalled that on the first day of the fighting, approximately 2,000 men passed through the division's medical-sanitation battalion (although most likely, not all of these men were from the 167th Rifle Division).[68] Nevertheless, these units remained combat-worthy and continued to take part in the offensive.

By the end of 21 July 1942, elements of the 167th Rifle Division, the 118th Tank Brigade and the 2nd Tank Corps, the only ones of Briansk Front's entire operational group, were able to force a crossing of the Bol'shaia Vereika River, create a small bridgehead on the river's southern bank, and cross tanks into it. In the center of Group Chibisov's offensive, the 1st Tank Corps and 193rd Rifle Division took Lebiazh'e, but the tank brigades were unable to cross the Bol'shaia Vereika River with their main forces. The construction of bridges and the clearance of mines from the passages to the river continued all night. As a result of the day's action, the 1st Tank Corps lost 3 KV, 12 T-34 and 2 T-60 tanks. During one bombing raid, the commander of the 49th Tank Brigade Colonel Chernienko received a severe wound.[69]

65 Ibid., l. 150.
66 Ibid.
67 TsAMO, F. 202, op. 5, d. 251, l. 6.
68 *Poklonimsia k velikim tem godam*, l. 18.
69 TsAMO, F. 1 TK, op. 1, d. 6, l. 26: Operational Summary No.20, 21.

To the right of the 1st Tank Corps, the 340th and 284th Rifle Divisions spent the entire day fighting near their jumping-off positions and with the exception of elements of the 340th Rifle Division essentially made no progress. On the extreme left flank of Operational Group Chibisov, the 104th Separate Rifle Brigade with part of its strength fought for Bol'shaia Vereika and reached the line of the river at Churikovo. The rest of the brigade remained in their previous positions and exchanged fire with the enemy's combat outposts. To the left of the 104th Separate Rifle Brigade on the opposite bank of the Don River was the right flank of Voronezh Front, where the 60th Army's 159th Rifle Division was defending.

(It is worth noting that scouts of the 159th Rifle Division regularly conducted reconnaissance patrols on the western bank of the Don River out to a depth of 15 kilometers, and observing the flank and rear of the enemy units opposing the 104th Separate Rifle Brigade from the eastern bank of the Don River, they might have provided their neighbor with a lot of useful information about the nature of the enemy's defense and the location of the enemy's firing positions in the area adjacent to the Don River. But alas, separated not so much by a river as by their subordination to different *fronts*, the divisions of the two *fronts* never cooperated in any way, and the information of the scouts of the 159th Rifle Division never reached the neighboring units of Briansk Front. Mutual assistance was also not evident in the actions of the 104th Separate Rifle Brigade, the command of which banned other units from scouting in its sector, and deprived Voronezh Front's 159th Rifle Division of the possibility of knowing the operational situation in the sector of the brigade's defense.)[70]

By the end of the first day of the operation, the commander of the operational group General Chibisov had a lot of grounds for dissatisfaction. The forces of his operational group were supposed to have breached the German defenses and have advanced far beyond the line of the Bol'shaia Vereika River, but had been able only to reach it, and at that, only on the left flank. Moreover, the offensive that had started so successfully that morning in the sector of the 2nd Tank Corps had quickly bogged down, and while the tank units were immobile at the crossing sites, they were losing the opportunity to pursue the fleeing foe! As a result the enemy gained a breathing space and over the course of the night was able to regroup his forces and to consolidate on a new line. In the eyes of General Chibisov, this delay by the 2nd Tank Corps was a consequence of the indecisiveness of its tank commanders, which didn't display the necessary willpower and authority in such cases, in order to force the subordinates to carry out the assigned task. The first among these commanders of the 2nd Tank Corps was none other than the commander of the 2nd Tank Corps himself, General Liziukov.

Obviously experiencing ever increasing exasperation and impatience, Chibisov (over the head of Liziukov and completely ignoring his headquarters) sent a direct radio message to the commander of the 148th Tank Brigade Lieutenant Colonel Mikhailin with a demand to hasten the brigade's advance.[71] Such open disdain could not help but prick Liziukov's sense of self-esteem. After all, Chibisov should have contacted him first as Mikhailin's direct superior. But what could Liziukov do? During a battle, draw up the line of command within the operational group and show it to Chibisov? Alas, there was nothing left for him to do but to swallow the insulting (moreover, one shown before subordinates!) disregard of the operational group commander and continue to carry out his duties.

The first day of the operation was coming to an end. Time was passing inexorably, the sun was setting and night was approaching. The encouraging beginning, when it seemed that the 2nd Tank Corps would soon break into operational space, was alas deceptive. A breakthrough never happened,

70 TsAMO, F. 1186, op. 1, d. 73, l. 44.
71 TsAMO, F. 148 tp, op. 1, d. 3, l. 33.

and the offensive didn't lead to the success, which was so necessary for Liziukov right now, in his tottering position after the failure of the 5th Tank Army. He, the former army commander, at which it seemed that other displeased chiefs had already dismissively waved their hand, had to show at whatever the cost that he was capable of commanding troops and achieving victories, and demonstrate that the recent failure was only a puzzling episode in his irreproachable frontline biography that had existed up to that point. He simply could not permit another failure …

Understanding that the day was already coming to an end, yet the day's objective remained unfulfilled, Liziukov agonizingly searched for a way out of the situation that had arisen. Of course, it was not just the 2nd Tank Corps that had failed to carry out the order. In essence, all of his neighbors had performed no better than Liziukov, but this didn't make things any easier for him. In his situation he couldn't rely on the fact that other units had also failed to reach their objectives: bridges hadn't been built, the enemy line wasn't breached and the phase lines set for them hadn't been attained. He had every basis to believe that in the eyes of his "new" old commander, all of this would hardly justify his, Liziukov's, failure to carry out his assigned task. The experience of their last meeting spoke eloquently to this.

There is little doubt that the evening of 21 July 1942 and the decisions taken back then to a great extent determined the fate of the commander of the 2nd Tank Corps. However, knowing how future events would develop, it is worth pondering the question, to which there is no answer in the documents and to which, alas, there is now no one to give an unambiguous answer.

In reality, what stood behind the decisions taken on that evening? Why did the commander of the 2nd Tank Corps believe that he had to act in one way, and not another? In order to understand this, we can't avoid a detailed analysis of the situation that had developed by the evening of 21 July 1942.

The day's objectives, which can be seen on the map of the headquarters of the 2nd Tank Corps, by the evening of 21 July, could seem to the brigade commanders as simply unattainable. There still remained almost 20 kilometers to Medvezh'e – the objective of the 2nd Tank Corps' offensive on the first day of the operation, a distance 4 times greater than the brigades had been able to cover over the entire day thus far! Yet to cover the remaining distance would not be a march through their own rear area, but through territory still held by the enemy! In addition, after the first day of fighting, the tanks had to be topped up with fuel and ammunition (none of which had yet been brought up), and the crews had to be given some rest. For this it was necessary to stop for the night, bring up the rear services, and prepare the brigades to resume the offensive in the morning.

However, on the other hand, the operational map plainly spoke to the fact that although the path to the objective was a long one, there was now not a single river, nor a single stream or even deep ravine that might force another search for a crossing or require the construction of another bridge for the tanks. The last water obstacle on the way to the objective had already been overcome: the muddy Bol'shaia Vereika River, the crossing of which had already forced the expenditure of much precious time, and which many of the tankers regarded with unkind words since the previous operation by the 5th Tank Army, was finally behind them. Facing them, all the way to Medvezh'e, there were only enormously expansive fields and unwooded hills.

That evening, having done enough work for the day, the Luftwaffe finally disappeared from the skies above the battlefield, and the onset of darkness also blinded the hostile artillery batteries. However, it was abundantly clear that the German infantry that had been thrown back from the Bol'shaia Vereika River wouldn't sit still with their hands folded, but would unquestionably use the night to dig in along a new line. Then instead of a headlong dash to the south, the tank corps would be forced in the morning to break through an enemy defense in heavy fighting against enemy anti-tank weapons that had been brought up to the place of the breakthrough …

The 2nd Tank Corps commander had to have considered all of these factors on that July evening, and most likely it was these considerations that lay at the basis of his risky decision, but one that still offered a chance for success. Having discussed his proposal with Commissar Assorov, Liziukov decided to act.[72] At this late hour, when with one final effort he could still attempt to achieve the fulfillment of his assigned task, the commander of the 2nd Tank Corps made the decision not to stop on the line that had been attained, but to continue the offensive.

Not setting it aside until morning – right away; that very night.

72 Ibid.

3

The enemy's situation: 21 July 1942

At the start of the operation by Briansk Front's operational group, two German infantry divisions were defending in the offensive's designated sector: the 340th and 387th. They both had formed up in the spring of 1942 and had been transferred to the Eastern Front to Army Group South. The 340th Infantry Division had formed in France, the 387th Infantry Division – in Germany, but in July 1942 they had wound together on the Don steppes, and after a short period of intense fighting, they took up a position side by side as part of the VII Army Corps. General Otto Butze commanded the 340th Infantry Division, while General Arno Jahr commanded the 387th Infantry Division.[1]

Despite the losses they had suffered in the previous fighting, the combat capability of both divisions was sufficiently high, and the corps command gave them significant sectors to defend: the 340th Infantry Division occupied approximately 20 kilometers of the front, and the 387th Infantry Division – approximately 24 kilometers.[2]

In the lull between the two Red Army offensives the divisions worked to improve their positions and literally burrowed themselves into the ground, since lacking the strength to occupy the sectors assigned to them in compact combat formations, they were counting upon holding the front with the assistance of a carefully-conceived system of defense. In each division all of the infantry regiments were extended along the front in a single echelon and had practically no reserves. The division's reserves were quite meager and in the best case, consisted of one infantry battalion and various small elements. Each division had an artillery regiment equipped with horse-drawn heavy artillery (105-mm and 150-mm howitzers). The divisions' anti-tank defenses were based upon authorized anti-tank battalions, which were equipped with 37-mm, 50-mm, and 75-mm German anti-tank guns, as well as captured French 75-mm and Soviet 76.2-mm guns.[3]

The several days of rest granted to the divisions after the end of the fighting with the 5th Tank Army allowed the divisional supply trains to replenish the fighting troops with ammunition and food. In addition, they were able to evacuate the collected wounded after the fighting to rear hospitals, having readied the regimental medical points for the soon-to-be-expected fresh stream of patients.

After the conclusion of the counterattacks by the German 9th and 11th Panzer Divisions against the 5th Tank Army, units of the 340th and 387th Infantry Divisions had taken up advantageous positions on commanding heights, and exploiting the withdrawal of the units of the 5th Tank Army to the north, pushed their combat outposts forward. Clashes between our reconnaissance groups and the German combat outposts prevented our scouts from advancing to the south in

1 NARA, T-314, roll 253, fr. 001266.
2 Ibid., fr. 000342.
3 NARA, T-314, roll 353, fr. 001326.

order to gather vital information about the enemy's main line of resistance. From information gleaned through observation of the enemy (including from the eastern bank of the Don River), it was known that the German infantry was digging in on the hills opposite Gorozhanka; along a lengthy ravine northwest of there; on Points 191.3 and 187.4; north of Bol'shaia Vereika; and extending further to the west along commanding heights while mining the approaches to their forward edge.[4]

General Liziukov estimated the enemy strength in the Bol'shaia Vereika area as two infantry regiments, strengthened with tanks that had been dug into the ground.[5] In actual fact two German infantry battalions were holding the defense in the Bol'shaia Vereika area, while the enemy had no tanks at all here.[6] (Possibly, the Soviet observers had taken knocked-out and burned-out machines left behind on the battlefield after the fighting with the 5th Tank Army as the "dug-in German tanks".)

By dawn on 21 July, the combat outposts of the German infantry divisions had been pulled back and had taken up positions closer to the German main line of defense. In the sector of the 2nd Tank Corps' offensive, the German command considered Hill 191.3 and Hill 187.4 to be the most important strongpoints; the possession of these two hills offered superb views of the surrounding terrain.

Soon after 0300 on 21 July (the chronology in German documents corresponded to Berlin time), reports came into the 541st Infantry Regiment from a forward battalion, and from there the information was passed to division headquarters, that to the northeast of Bol'shaia Vereika, Russians were attacking the forward positions of the battalion's companies in strength of 2-3 companies supported by tanks.[7] This was the first report on the start of the offensive by Briansk Front's operational group that was reflected in the German documents. Reports on the start of an offensive also came in from elements that were defending northwest of Bol'shaia Vereika, but soon the division headquarters wound up in the dark about what was happening there because of a break in the cable line.[8]

At the same time, reports on the start of the fighting also arrived from the 340th Infantry Division. The headquarters of the VII Army Corps noted the very high activity of Soviet aircraft over the entire sector of the corps' front, as well as the fact that "the enemy is conducting attacks with the support of artillery, the strength of which has substantially grown in comparison with the preceding days."[9]

By 0700 in the morning, the attacking 167th Rifle Division and 118th Tank Brigade had managed to break through the enemy's forward edge of defense. The VII Army Corps' journal of combat operations noted: "In the sector of the 387th Infantry Division after a 10-minute artillery preparation from all types of guns, the enemy attacked the sector of II/542nd Infantry Regiment northwest of Bol'shaia Vereika with up to 2 regiments supported by major tank forces. At 0700 they managed to break into the positions. The adjacent battalion of the 541st Infantry Regiment on the right after the breakthrough of the neighbor's position on the left began to withdraw from the battle in the direction of Bol'shaia Vereika."[10]

The breakthrough on the narrow front south of Surikovo led to the withdrawal of the two attacked battalions, but also the forced retreat of the entire 542nd Infantry Regiment, which

4 TsAMO, F. 1186, op. 1, d. 206, ll. 321-328.
5 TsAMO, F. 202, op. 50, d. 1, l. 300.
6 NARA, T-314, roll 353, fr. 000396.
7 NARA, T-314, roll 353, fr. 001334.
8 Ibid.
9 Ibid.
10 NARA, T-314, roll 353, fr. 000396.

ultimately forced the enemy to abandon the village of Bol'shaia Vereika. However, on the front of the 340th Infantry Division, all of our units morning attacks were repulsed, as a result of which the elements of the 167th Rifle Division that had surged ahead came under flanking fire from the right and suffered serious losses.

Explaining the causes of the failure of the offensive on 21 July in the center of the operational group, the headquarters of the 340th Rifle Division observed:

> The forward edge of his [the enemy's – I.S.] defense ran not along the Sukhaia Vereika River, as was supposed and was reported from the 193rd Rifle Division, but along the line of Hill 213.8 and a lengthy patch of woods, where according to the information from the 193rd Rifle Division and in an order from the VPU [that is, the headquarters of the operational group – I.S.], the enemy's combat outposts were assumed to be. As a result, attempts to drive in this supposed line of combat outposts had no success. The enemy strongpoints had strong anti-tank artillery, supported by artillery out of Khrushchevo and Vysochkino and a roaming rocket launching battery. Each strongpoint had 2-3 mortar batteries, 7-9 heavy machine guns and strong groups of submachine gunners.[11]

In its account the command of the 1st Tank Corps also noted that during the artillery preparation our artillery struck not the enemy's forward edge of defense, but its second line along the Sukhaia Vereika River, which wasn't occupied by German troops. Thus the artillery batteries that had been gathered at the breakthrough sector for the most part fired on empty terrain, and expended hundreds if not thousands of shells without weakening the enemy main line of resistance in any way, and failed to help the infantry that had gone on the attack.

In fact, the headquarters of Briansk Front's operational group had mistakenly determined where the enemy's main belt of defenses ran, and accordingly passed this incorrect information down to the divisions subordinate to it. (Although their headquarters were also capable: they in fact were the ones that were supposed to keep the higher command informed about the real location of the German front line with their own reconnaissance information.) Thus, to the anguish of the tank commanders, the attacks of the Soviet infantry against the enemy's "combat outposts" didn't at all bring about the desired results. The actions of the 201st Tank Brigade also brought no success.

True, the failure of the offensive in the center of Group Chibisov, obviously, was connected with the fact that in the sector of defense of the 340th Infantry Division, the enemy had the largest concentration of anti-tank artillery. It was also precisely here that the 654th Panzerjäger Battalion directly subordinate to VII Army Corps had been positioned since the period of fighting with the 5th Tank Army, and it had been strengthened with the 340th Infantry Division's own anti-tank battalion. Combined, they had 30 heavy 75-mm anti-tank guns, not counting the 37-mm and 50-mm anti-tank guns that were less effective in the struggle against Russian tanks.[12]

The 387th Infantry Division could only count upon its own anti-tank means under the division's TO&E. Given a front of defense of 24 kilometers, the division had only 14 heavy 75-mm anti-tank guns, of which only 5 were up among the combat formations of the infantry regiments.[13] In comparison with the 340th Infantry Division, the anti-tank defense of the 387th Infantry Division was substantially weaker, and probably this factor played a role in the breakthrough of our tanks and infantry toward the villages of Malaia and Bol'shaia Vereika and their emergence on the bank of the Bol'shaia Vereika River.

11 TsAMO, F. 340 sd, op. 1, d. 24, l. 211.

12 NARA, T-314, roll 353, fr. 001325-326

13 Ibid.

Having received a report from the 387th Infantry Division about the Russian breakthrough, the chief of staff of VII Army Corps Colonel Hilscher considered the situation to be sufficiently serious, and at 0930 reported on what had happened to the headquarters of the Second Army with a request for air support. For its part the command of VII Army Corps began to take measures to reinforce the 387th Infantry Division with whatever it had at hand. The division was given one company of the 559th Panzerjäger Battalion that had been withdrawn to the rear after the fighting in Voronezh, but time was needed before this company would arrive in the area of fighting.

By 1400 the breach in the front of the 387th Infantry Division had increased to 5 kilometers and had begun to threaten the stability of the entire front of defense not only of this division, but also that of its neighbor on the left. In order to cover the increasingly exposed flank, the command of the 340th Infantry Division was forced to refuse the flank to the southeast and to abandon a section of its previously-held forward positions here. The Russian pressure increased, and in order to cover the boundary with the adjacent 387th Infantry Division that had retreated to the Bol'shaia Vereika River, the commander of the 340th Infantry Division committed his reserve infantry battalion.[14]

Alarmed by the situation in the sector of the breakthrough, the VII Army Corps command searched for reserves in order to counter the threat that had arisen. Counting, obviously, on a future positive decision from the headquarters of the Second Army, which had the 9th Panzer Division directly subordinate to it, the VII Army Corps' chief of staff delivered a briefing on the unfolding situation to the commander of the 9th Panzer Division and a query about possible options for the employment of the panzer division in the VII Army Corps' sector of defense.[15]

Having taken the received appeal to account, the commander of the 9th Panzer Division announced that in the event that his division would be ordered to enter the battle, it would be necessary to return the two battalions of the artillery regiment that had been detached for fighting in the Voronezh bridgehead to him. For the VII Army Corps command, this meant a substantial weakening of the "Don" artillery grouping, which was supporting with its fire the "land" front (this is what the German command called the line of defense on the northern outskirts of Voronezh as opposed to the "water" front along the Voronezh and Don Rivers,) of the Germans' Voronezh bridgehead. As it turned out, in order to counter threats in one place, it was necessary to weaken the front in a different place!

At 1345 the Second Army's chief of staff arrived at the headquarters of VII Army Corps. Having visited the headquarters of the 387th Infantry Division in Dolgovskii prior to this, using the communications post of VII Army Corps he reported on the situation that had developed to the commander of Second Army General von Salmuth. After receiving the report and discussing the operational situation the Second Army command decided to take the following measures:

1. To make maximum use of the Luftwaffe over the breakthrough area.
2. To transfer a battalion of the 62nd Artillery Regiment (equipped with 100-mm guns) and the II Battalion of the 71st Artillery Regiment (equipped with 12 105-mm and 150-mm howitzers) to the VII Army Corps command.
3. To request Army Group South to subordinate the 385th Infantry Division to VII Army Corps.
4. To shift the 9th Panzer Division to the Zemliansk area.[16]

14 NARA, T-314, roll 353, fr. 001334.
15 NARA, T-314, roll 353, fr. 000336-397.
16 Ibid.

At 1845 at the request of the Second Army command, the commander of VII Army Corps reported on the situation. He informed them that the breakthrough was being "localized" by the committed reserves of the 387th Infantry Division, but that approximately 50 Russian tanks had broken through to the river valley in the Bol'shaia and Malaia Vereika sector. It could be possible to strike them with anti-tank guns, only if they would exit the dead space of the river valley and emerge on the steppe above it; therefore, according to the worked-out plan, the anti-tank artillery was being towed back and would be concentrated south of the breakthrough place (according to the terrain, the most favorable position for the anti-tank guns were the woods along both sides of the Bol'shaia Vereika – Somovo road that were inaccessible to tanks).

Having heard the report, the Second Army commander informed the corps commander that for the army it was undesirable to commit the 9th Panzer Division, which had just recently been removed from the front, although after seven days of rest, the panzer division was in fact at a state of combat readiness. However, if the breakthrough couldn't be contained and if it expanded, the Second Army command was planning to launch a counterattack with the 9th Panzer Division and 385th Infantry Division. In the process, it was clearly stated to the corps commander that "only 24 July might be regarded" as the nearest date for the counterattack.[17]

Thus, by the evening of 21 July, of the four points in the plan of assistance announced by the commander of Second Army von Salmuth, the command of VII Army Corps and its subordinate 340th and 387th Infantry Divisions could count upon only one, but a substantial one at that – air support. In reality, German air strikes became more intensive in the latter half of the day of 21 July, and by evening the German aerial activity reached its peak. Otherwise, VII Army Corps in the meantime had to count upon only its own forces.

Wasting no time, General Hell issued an order to the commander of the 168th Infantry Division to organize switch positions on the northern outskirts of Terny with the forces of the 417th Infantry Regiment that was positioned in Stadnitsy.[18] The regiment had only just been withdrawn from the Voronezh bridgehead after a week of extremely heavy fighting as part of 168th Infantry Division. It was completely worn out and had suffered such losses that it was in acute need of rest and replenishments. However, the commander of VII Army Corps had no other choice, since the corps didn't have any other available reserves to reinforce the dangerously sagging front!

The situation facing the 387th Infantry Division had indeed become increasingly serious. In the evening the division headquarters reported that its engaged units had expended almost all of their ammunition, while II and III Battalions of the 542nd Infantry Regiment (which had been right in the middle of the breakthrough sector) had been greatly weakened because of high casualties.[19] Indeed, if the losses of the neighboring 340th Infantry Division while holding its front amounted over the day to 156 men (46 killed and 110 wounded – chances are that initially, all of the prisoners taken by the 340th Infantry Division's 1144th Rifle Regiment and the 89th Tank Brigade's 203rd Tank Battalion on Hill 213.8 were added to the number of killed), then the retreating 387th Infantry Division had lost, primarily in the sector of its 542nd Infantry Regiment, 475 men (89 killed, 338 wounded and 48 missing-in-action).[20] This meant that less than half the personnel remained in the two battalions on the axis of the Russians' main attack. (To be sure, some of the wounded remained in formation, which follows from the information of VII Army Corps' medical chief, according to whom the share of such wounded men approached 15-20%).[21]

17 Ibid.
18 Ibid.
19 NARA, T-314, roll 353, fr. 001334-335.
20 NARA, T-314, roll 354, fr. 000726-737.
21 NARA, T-314, roll 355, fr. 000501-505; also data found in T-314, roll 354, fr. 726-730.

The concern of the German command over the breakthrough on the front of VII Army Corps was so deep that repercussions of it even reached the chief of the OKH (*Oberkommanda des Heeres*, or Supreme Command of the Army) General Staff Colonel General Halder. In his war diary he noted in the entry for 21 July 1942: "Northwest of Voronezh, sizeable enemy attacks breach our line on a 10-km front (3 km deep)."[22]

Excerpts from the account of VII Army Corps' chief of artillery also testify to the severity of the fighting and the alarm of the German command regarding the stability of the front of defense in the sector of the Russian breakthrough:

> 21.7.1942: The enemy with a large number of tanks and infantry went on the offensive to the south and took Lebiazh'e, and Bol'shaia and Malaia Vereika. The enemy also managed to capture Hill 191.3. Elements of the 387th Artillery Regiment are being given an order: "In case of necessity use the ammunition previously designated for conducting blocking fire with the aim of self-defense for firing over open sights at hostile infantry that have reached the firing positions! Given the need to switch firing positions, every effort must be made to avoid that such a change prompts the infantry's desire to retreat!"[23] (A sensible order; plainly on this day the infantry of the 542nd Infantry Regiment had demonstrated such a "desire to retreat" that in places it had fled, leaving the artillerymen without cover.)

From the contents of an order from the commander of one of the battalions of the 387th Infantry Division, one can assess the unenviable state of morale shown at times by the enemy units that were fighting to repel our attacks. Drawing conclusions from the recent fighting, which judging from the date of the order was mainly the fighting against troops of Briansk Front's operational group, he appealed to his company and platoon commanders:

> During the recent fighting such crude mistakes were made, which made any sort of leadership impossible, that I am compelled to familiarize [you] with the following basic tenets of a service character.
>
> During a battle, a platoon commander must not under any circumstances abandon his command post in order to give a report to the company commander. He can leave his command post only when he must hurry forward from a threatened location, but backward – never!
>
> Not a single commander should trust a verbal report from pickets. Given a complex situation it is important to light up a cigarette or cigar and say: "50% exaggerated, 30% made up, 90% fear, for a total of 170%. Just what is true?" That, which the subordinates report (I emphasize, in critical situations) must primarily be considered false.
>
> Recently I have also received information that was shocking. During an actual attack by two enemy companies (one of which struck the right flank, the other the left flank of one of our reinforced companies in an advanced position), after our company's retreat I met one soldier while he was standing in line for grub and asked him about the enemy's strength; he answered: "Several battalions". When I asked him how many he had actually seen with his own eyes, he had to confess that he hadn't seen a single Russian. Fantasy, momentary fear, a

22 Halder, F. *Voennyi dnevnik: Ezhednevnye zapisi nachal'nika General'nogo Shtaba Sukhoputnykh voisk, 1939-1942* (Sankt Peterburg: AST, 2003), p. 822. This is the Russian language edition of Halder's war diary. The English translation comes from Charles Burdick and Hans-Adolf Jacobsen (ed.), *The Halder War Diary, 1939-1942* (Novato: Presidio Press, 1988). The specific entry can be found on page 645.

23 NARA, T-314, roll 353, fr. 001081-1087.

> fleeting observation of swaying cornstalks or brownish sunflowers – and the enemy movement is underway!
>
> Then there is the cry "The enemy has turned our right!" The platoon commander at this moment can't be found and a panicked state surely results. The troops will abandon their positions in flight, leaving behind gear, weapons and ammunition. This might sound like an exaggeration, but it serves as a better illustration. If some also maintain that the enemy attack was that strong, then having later returned to the occupied position I should have at least found several dead. But it is possible that the company fled without having fired a single shot, or else the company had been trained for sharpshooting beyond any criticism.
>
> When the commander remains in his place, the soldiers don't retreat. Given calm, clear, firm command and control, routs don't happen.[24]

Having recoiled to the south, the remnants of two battalions of the 542nd Infantry Regiment were stopped by the regiment's command on Hill 188.5 and began to dig in. Because of the heavy losses and the significant reduction in combat capability (chances are, also for reasons of their state of morale), the regiment's defense began to coalesce around the positions of anti-tank batteries, where the rallied infantry soldiers were deployed to screen the guns. In the situation that had developed, the 387th Infantry Division command's main calculations were also based on the fortitude of the anti-tank gun batteries. Although the situation in the sector of the 542nd Infantry Regiment became even more precarious by nightfall, the organization of the anti-tank defense on the new line was eased by two significant factors. First, all of the division's main anti-tank means were now positioned close to the breakthrough area, and not to the side of it, as had been the case that morning. Second, the patches of woods with the deep ravines that were impenetrable by tanks didn't leave the Russians much choice about the direction of the attack, and thereby made the determination of the best positions for their anti-tank guns easier for the Germans.

After bringing the retreating troops back into order and after localizing the penetration on the Lebiazh'e – Bol'shaia Vereika line, the 387th Infantry Division command demanded of all the units to begin work immediately on fortifying their occupied line. By morning, the defense was supposed to be ready! With the onset of darkness, the artillery crews received an order to hold their positions at whatever the cost.

24 TsAMO, F. 331, op. 5041, d. 3, l. 87.

4

The night of 21-22 July 1942

At some point after 2100 that evening, General Liziukov and Regimental Commissar Assorov arrived in Malaia Vereika and ordered the commanders of the 26th and 148th Tank Brigades to gather. Soon, the corps commander and corps commissar were joined by the commander of the 26th Tank Brigade Colonel Burdov; the 26th Tank Brigade's commissar (plainly, Regimental Commissar Alekseev); the operations chief of the 2nd Tank Corps Lieutenant Colonel Pupko; the commander of the 148th Tank Brigade Lieutenant Colonel Mikhailin; the 148th Tank Brigade's chief of staff Major Mikhalev; the commissar of the 148th Tank Brigade Senior Battalion Commissar Lesnoi; and the deputy commander of the 148th Tank Brigade Hero of the Soviet Union Major Il'chenko.[1] (On that evening, three Heroes of the Soviet Union were in tiny Malaia Vereika. The third, in addition to Liziukov and Il'chenko, was a battalion commander in the 118th Tank Brigade Captain Plotnikov. They were all storied officers, and were undoubtedly thirsting for new victories. They didn't know, however, that one of them had less than 24 hours to live, the second – less than two days, and the third – less than four days.)

Judging from everything, Liziukov's and Assorov's conference with the assembled commanders took place in one of the homes left abandoned on the outskirts of Malaia Vereika (almost 2 weeks before, the Germans had forcibly driven its residents into the German rear). No sooner had he been briefed by the arriving officers, the commander of the 2nd Tank Corps got down to business: "Major General Liziukov announced that he and the commissar had discussed and decided upon a night raid into the enemy rear, for which they were revealing their decision."[2] General Liziukov also gave a short speech, and judging from everything, spoke with great emotional agitation. He revealed that the planned raid was a government mission, and that "such a task is the first for the Red Army's tank forces and has fired up the men." Subsequently the corps commander gave his subordinates the concrete objective (obviously, Liziukov had a staff map with him that showed the situation and contained his notes):

> The corps moves at night and by morning reaches the Medvezh'e area, where it assembles and takes Medvezh'e. The 148th Tank Brigade will take the lead, setting out at 2300, behind it, with no gap, is the 26th Tank Brigade, and the 27th Tank Brigade, together with which the corps commander marches, takes up the rear. The brigade rear services arrive in the Medvezh'e area after the 26th Tank Brigade, and replenish the tanks with fuel and ammunition. Everyone marches with their lights on and fires indiscriminately.[3]

The documents don't clarify whether or not there was any sort of discussion of the upcoming raid after Liziukov issued the tasks. Most likely, the subordinate commanders who had arrived, for which Liziukov's decision likely came as a big surprise, attempted to familiarize themselves with

1 TsAMO, F. 148 tp, op. 1, d. 3, l. 33.
2 Ibid.
3 Ibid.

their orders, but there was very little time for a detailed discussion of the planned operation – the column was to move out in less than an hour. The commanders who attended the meeting didn't receive any written orders; all of the orders and instructions were given verbally and only later were they put on paper from memory.

Why did Liziukov call the forthcoming raid "a government mission"? It is totally clear that Stalin's government hadn't given him any sort of "mission" for a raid toward Medvezh'e. Chances are that Liziukov said this, hoping to impart particular significance to the order he had given and to mobilize all of the tank brigades' efforts to carry it out. He also had no assurance that their planned nighttime offensive would be the first for a tank corps in the history of the Red Army. It was the first in his own frontline experience, but obviously not aware of any other similar instances, he was hoping to prompt not only a sense of responsibility in the subordinate commanders, but also a sense of pride over the task they'd been given.

Most likely, Regimental Commissar Assorov had a direct connection to all of this; it was at his recommendation that an important "government mission" arose on the Don steppes so distant from the government in Moscow, as well as the thesis regarding the "first employment of the Red Army's tank forces for such a task". Well, naturally it was the commissar's job to inspire people, and at that critical hour he was in fact attempting to do so, dramatizing the moment and concocting whatever of motivational idea to make the case. But from the heights of the modern day, can we now rebuke him for this? Hardly. He was carrying out the duties of a political officer as he understood them, and was assisting Liziukov by every means at his disposal.

There can be no doubt that the commander of the 2nd Tank Corps wanted the attack to be a concentrated one, employing all of his available strength. Taking into account the 27th Tank brigade by the end of 21 July the corps had 105-107 tanks, including 24 KV and 42 T-34, which follows from the compiled data for the corps' brigades. If he managed to include the 118th Tank Brigade that had also crossed the Bol'shaia Vereika River, then the number of tanks in his tank grouping would have increased to more than 130. A strike by such a mass of tanks, which had been gathered on a narrow front at Malaia Vereika, might not only quickly rupture the enemy's organized defense, but also lead to a remorseless rampage through the supply and support services in the immediate German rear. Moreover, in the event of a successful breakthrough by the 2nd Tank Corps, reinforced with the 118th Tank Brigade, into the depth of the enemy's defenses, its consequences might become a genuine catastrophe for the entire front of the German VII Army Corps.

By the end of 21 July, once the 2nd Tank Corps had caught up with the 167th Rifle Division and the 118th and 201st Tank Brigades at the bridges, the first and second echelons of Briansk Front's operational group became re-united and now had a common task. In these conditions, the subordination of the 118th and 201st Tank Brigades to the 2nd Tank Corps would have not only reinforced the 2nd Tank Corps, but would also have unified command and control over all the tank units. However, in order to do this, it was necessary to contact the commander of Group Chibisov, propose to him the plan of actions, and convince him of the sensibleness of such a decision.

It is well known that Liziukov was never a submissive executive; he could disagree with superiors and had the courage to propose his own alternative plan, if he considered it superior. One example of this was his telegram to Vasilevsky on 3 July 1942, in which Liziukov argumentatively contested a decision made by the General Staff, and his actions that night were also a clear confirmation! It would seem that in the operation of Briansk Front's Operational Group Chibisov, both the authorizing level of command was lower and the advantage of unifying the tank forces was plain!

But … Liziukov balked at contacting Chibisov and proposing anything to him. Was he recalling his previous difficult discussions with him, or did he now have neither the time nor the strength for arduous negotiations to persuade his overbearing and prickly boss?

Having crossed the Bol'shaia Vereika River, the 118th Tank Brigade and at least one battalion of the 201st Tank Brigade stopped for the night and remained totally separate from the forward grouping of the 2nd Tank Corps. Thus Liziukov could only count upon his own tank brigades. However, one of these, the 27th Tank Brigade, was still on the opposite bank of the river in Bol'shaia Vereika and was unable to join the two forward tank brigades in time. As it happened, of the five tank brigades that had assembled with their main forces by the evening of 21 July in Lebiazh'e, Malaia Vereika and Bol'shaia Vereika, for an immediate raid toward Medvezh'e Liziukov was able to use only two, and of the total 156 tanks, only 76.

Unfortunately, none of those present at the meeting with Liziukov and Assorov left behind recollections of it, and details of the discussion, the responses of the participants and the course of the conversation itself remained unrecorded. However, one of the archival documents preserved a genuinely invaluable piece of evidence, which allows us not only to picture the atmosphere of this brief meeting, but also "to see" Liziukov at one of the most dramatic moments of his life: "After issuing the order, Major General Liziukov kissed everyone, promising after the breakthrough to decorate all of the raid's participants. They coordinated their watches. The time was 2150."[4]

He kissed everyone ....

It wasn't often that generals promised to decorate all the participants of an upcoming battle. Still more rarely did they kiss them. Something extraordinary must have happened, if Liziukov threw aside the formalities of the chain of command and impulsively stepped forward to greet his subordinates, not simply to shake their hands, but *to embrace and kiss them*. This was a special, deeply personal, almost fatherly parting, which for any one of them might become (and alas, did become!) a farewell forever ....

I could not read the lines of this final piece of testimony about General Liziukov, which has been preserved in documents, without agitation. It is a piece of evidence, which in its power and clarity is worthy of an artistic production, but at the same time a completely reliable one. There are not many words in this laconically described scene, but how striking they are! At that hour nothing yet had happened, but literally as if sensing that something bad was looming, Liziukov made no attempt to restrain himself, and giving freedom to all the emotions surging inside him, hurried to express his gratitude and respect to his fellow servicemen – while still alive, and in the face of death.

He was sending them into a difficult battle and was placing all of his hopes on them. *They* would not let him down.

After receiving the order, the commander of the 148th Tank Brigade Lieutenant Colonel Mikhailin ordered his chief of staff Major Mikhalev to gather the battalion and company commanders and commissars in order to relay his combat instructions to them. The brigade command had literally only 20 minutes to work out a plan of action. At 2210 the subordinate commanders convened and the brigade commander gave them the following combat assignment:

1. The brigade continues to carry out its given assignment, by the morning of 22.7.42 reaches the Medvezh'e area, where it tops up the tanks with fuel and ammunition.
2. The route of advance: southern outskirts of Bol'shaia Vereika, route [connecting] Hills 195.8, 187.9, 181.5, Medvezh'e. The re-assembly area is the woods east of Medvezh'e. The order of march: the GPZ [*golovnaia pokhodnaia zastava*, forward mobile detachment] – a KV platoon of the 260th Tank Battalion and T-60 platoon from the 89th Tank Battalion. The chief of the GPZ – Major Mikhalev. Set out at 2300.

4 TsAMO, F. 148 tp, op. 1, d. 3, l. 34.

3. The main forces: the 89th Tank Battalion, the 260th Tank Battalion and the light tanks follow behind each KV tank.
4. I am at the head of the 89th Tank Battalion. The lead machines will march with all lights on. Inform each crew member of the task. Communications by radio. Major Il'chenko remains here in order to organize the headquarters and rear service.[5]

After the sun set (at 2156), it quickly became dark; night was approaching. No matter all the hustle and bustle in the brigades to prepare for the raid, the start of the march became increasingly delayed. Fuel had to be brought up, tanks had to be serviced, and ammunition had to be loaded aboard the tanks. Likely, the fuel and ammunition first went to the forward mobile detachment tanks, which were to set out less than 30 minutes after receiving the order. The other crews had to wait their turn.

The 148th Tank Brigade's chief of staff Major Mikhalev was given an important assignment: he, as the commander of the GPZ, was not only to precede the march of the main forces, but also had to make his way accurately to the Medvezh'e area at night. Preparing for departure, Mikhalev studied the map again and again. Almost the entire route to Medvezh'e ran across a steppe plain without any sort of noticeable landmarks. Only during the first part of the march could he keep to the road leading to Somovo, but once the GPZ turned to the east, it faced a march across a broad steppe that stretched for many kilometers. True, Mikhalev's task was eased by the fact that after turning off the road on the way to the village of Somovo, the GPZ's route of advance remained virtually straight, and only on the approach to the objective did it bend a little to the south.

The GPZ set off on the brigade's route with a 10-minute delay: at 2310.[6] The lead KV turned on its headlight, and heading the group of 3 KV and several T-60 tanks climbed the slope of the river valley. But barely had the tanks emerged from the dead space of the river valley, when fire was opened up at them (in the document, it is written "immediately, after 100 meters").[7] True, it wasn't anti-tank guns that were firing at the tanks, but only machine-gun and rifle fire, which couldn't harm the crews within the tanks. Nevertheless, the first bullets or machine-gun bursts shattered the headlight on the lead KV tank and the tank stopped.[8] Seeing this, Major Mikhalev bypassed the stopped tank and led the GPZ onward, having become its lead machine. The tanks began to take fire from every direction and bullets were hammering the armor; almost immediately after setting out, the GPZ had run into German positions. However, there was no anti-tank artillery fire ….

Major Mikhalev led the GPZ across a broad field on Hill 188.5, making no response to the small arms fire. Having no possibility to clamber out of the tank, he was compelled to use a periscope to direct the tank. (On that night, the moon was almost full, and judging from the documents, it wasn't obscured by clouds, so this somewhat eased observation. True, the only orienting landmarks in those conditions might be only the dark masses of woods close to the road on the left and more distant to the right, but whether the crews could see them from their tanks remains unclear.)

The continuous fire of German submachine gunners[9] continued for the extent of several kilometers and ended only once the GPZ pivoted to the southeast and moved away from the road to

5 Ibid.
6 TsAMO, F. 202, op. 50, d. 1, l. 307.
7 TsAMO, F. 148 tp, op. 1, d. 3, l. 34.
8 Ibid. The material on the rest of the events also come from TsAMO, F. 202, op. 50, d. 1, ll. 301-307.
9 The term "submachine gunners" in relation to the enemy soldiers is regularly encountered in the documents of Soviet units, but considering the TO&E of the German infantry divisions of that period of the war, this term rarely reflected the true state of matters. Most likely, ordinary soldiers, who as a rule were equipped with carbines, and not submachine guns (machine pistols), were mistakenly called "submachine gunners". How-

Somovo. Soon the tanks emerged from the zone of fire. Mikhalev opened his hatch, climbed out onto the tank's turret, and saw that only one KV tank was following him. There were no other tanks around. Midnight was approaching. According to calculations, the GPZ had reached Hill 195.8 (in investigative documents of the Briansk Front headquarters, it is given that the GPZ reached this hill at 0100 on 22 July).

Mikhalev ordered the driver-mechanic to stop the tank. What was he to do now? Keep moving forward, or wait for the brigade on the hilltop? There were no radio communications with the brigade commander and tank battalions, so he could only wait and keep peering back across the dark steppe. Time passed, but the brigade didn't show up, and he could not hear the distant rumble of any tank engines, by which he might have detected the approach of a tank column.

Pondering the situation for a certain amount of time, Mikhalev assumed that the brigade, possibly, had missed the turn-off toward Medvezh'e and had advanced further along the road toward Somovo. Having come to this conclusion, he turned around and began to head back. Having traveled approximately 3 kilometers, he arrived back at the Somovo road at the turn-off point. The road was empty. He could see no columns.

Next the chief of staff of the 148th Tank Brigade issued an order to head toward Somovo in the hope of finding the brigade there. After 4 kilometers, the GPZ (or what was left of it) reached Somovo and stopped. The dial on his watch showed that it was already 0200. The brigade was nowhere to be found.

So once again Mikhalev had to reach a decision in a situation that he hardly could have imagined before setting out. He was supposed to be leading the rest of the 148th Tank Brigade, and his main duty was not to diverge from the path and bring the column out near the objective. However, suddenly it had turned out that instead of this, he had to search for tank battalions that had gone missing somewhere!

Time was passing, he had to hurry, but Mikhalev had to rack his brains and think of where else he might search for the brigade! Assuming that it, most likely, was located somewhere behind him, he decided to return to the place where his adventure had begun. Thus, for the third time that night, the GPZ turned around and headed back ....

The column of the 148th Tank Brigade's main forces were late in starting out by almost an hour, and when the battalions finally began to clamber out of the river valley, the GPZ was now nowhere in sight. The 260th Tank Battalion (led by Senior Lieutenant Tiunin) headed the column, and the brigade's commander and commissar were moving with it in their tanks. Behind the 260th Tank Battalion was the 89th Tank Battalion. The tail of it was supposed to be the 26th Tank Brigade. Nine KV and 4 T-60 of the 260th Tank Battalion and 6 KV and 4 T-60 of the 89th Tank Battalion had been sent out on the raid.

Together with the brigade command, deputy brigade commander Major Il'chenko had set off with the 89th Tank Battalion; he had initially been left behind by Mikhailin in Malaia Vereika. Plainly Il'chenko had pleaded with the brigade commander to allow him to join the march together with everyone else, since he simply could not remain in the rear, when the brigade was leaving on such an important assignment. General Liziukov's adjutant Captain Pendak also set out on the raid in one of the tanks of the 89th Tank Battalion; he also, chances are, couldn't hide behind the backs of his combat comrades, protected by his special position, and received permission from the

ever, the high saturation of the German infantry elements with machine guns often created the impression that almost everywhere, numerous and ever-present hostile "submachine gunners" were doing the fighting. Nevertheless, the author believes it necessary to keep to the style and terms of the wartime documents, and thus in the text left behind references to "submachine gunners" without changes.

commander of the 2nd Tank Corps to join the march. (Likely, he also received the special, almost fatherly parting words and gestures of Liziukov, who appreciated his adjutant's wish not to sit out the raid in the rear, but to fight. In the book *Povest' o brat'iakh* [*Tale of brothers*] the Belorussian authors Rodinsky and Tsar'kov brilliantly describe a scene, when Captain Pendak asks Liziukov to send him to a tank battalion. However, it isn't clear what sources the authors used to reconstruct this conversation.[10]) The 89th Tank Battalion was commanded by Senior Lieutenant Zaporozhets, and Captain Pendak went on the raid as his deputy commander. The battalion commissar was Political Instructor Vystavnoi.

Having lost visual contact with the GPZ, the 148th Tank Brigade's column began to move on independently. From the documents, it isn't clear whether the brigade was moving "under continuous fire of submachine gunners", as was the case with the forward mobile detachment; however, these documents also make it clear that the German anti-tank artillery was still silent. The brigade slowly and cautiously advanced across an enormous field. An hour passed in this way, then another half-hour. This was followed by another 15 minutes. The field wasn't coming to an end. Neither the GPZ, nor Medvezh'e was anywhere in sight. Finally, the brigade commander and commissar decided to stop and get their bearings. The column halted. However, it was extremely difficult to figure out where they were. None of the commanders had ever been here before, and the brigade had wound up in a completely unknown place – without reconnaissance and at night.

A monotonous plain stretched all around without any noticeable landmarks, while the darkness covered everything that was in the distance. Having consulted, the brigade commander and commissar decided that the column had reached the vicinity of Russko-Gvozdevskie Vyselki and needed to continue onward. After a 10-minute halt, the march was resumed, but the 260th Tank Battalion hadn't even managed to cover several hundred meters when tanks appeared up ahead that were advancing toward them. There were plainly a lot more of them than the GPZ had. The column again stopped. (Oppressed by the unknown, the crews, obviously, experienced several nervous moments, preparing just in case for combat …).

However, it turned out that these tanks were the 89th Tank Battalion, which had originally been following the 260th Tank Battalion, but somehow wound up in front of it and was simultaneously moving toward it. Surprisingly, the GPZ was with the 89th Tank Battalion; Mikhalev announced to the 148th Tank Brigade's commander and commissar that the column had missed the turn toward Medvezh'e and that by mistake they were heading toward Somovo. (One has to believe that this came as a most unpleasant surprise for the brigade command. Believing that they had already covered half the distance to Medvezh'e, they in fact were heading in the totally wrong direction. Probably, Mikhalev was also very much surprised, when he found out where Mikhailin and Lesnoi thought the brigade was located.)

It turned out that having become stretched out in the darkness, the tank battalions lost contact with each other and that the 89th Tank Battalion had passed the forward 260th Tank Battalion, arriving at a patch of woods at Somovo. There, at approximately 0200, it encountered the GPZ as it was on its way back; together, they turned around and moved off in the direction from which the 89th Tank Battalion had come, where they soon came across the 260th Tank Battalion that was unknowingly advancing toward Somovo. Thus, deep into the night, the 148th Tank Brigade had finally reassembled. However, this happened just 6 kilometers from their jumping-off area and 16 kilometers from their objective. Meanwhile, just a couple of hours remained before dawn.

Having finally figured out where they were located, the brigade commander and commissar pivoted the entire brigade around and the battalions began to return to the turn-off point toward

10 Rodinsky, D., and Tsar'kov, N., *Povest' o brat'iakh* [*Tale of brothers*] (Moscow: Politizdat, 1976), pp. 92-93.

Medvezh'e that they had missed previously. The GPZ again took the lead, heading the entire column that was following it. However, the vexing oddities and incoherent actions didn't come to an end with this ....

The brigade commissar's tank, having lost sight of the brigade commander's tank, continued on its own way and ultimately veered from the column's path. Several other crews also became confused and drifted away from the main column. From documents it isn't simple to understand how, where and why this happened, and even more difficult to get a general picture of what occurred, since there are a lot of contradictions and confusion in the testimonies that were written later. Take, for example, what the 148th Tank Brigade's commissar Senior Battalion Commissar Lesnoi later wrote:

> At the time the brigade turned around, the driver-mechanic lost sight of the brigade commander's tank (for orientation, the brigade commander's tank had a rear lamp burning). I open the hatch – I see no machine out in front. Two KV tanks are trailing my tank. Moving on, I couldn't detect the rest of the brigade's column, and the two KV tanks, which had been behind me, also disappeared somewhere. Before even reaching the bend in the road on Hill 188.5, I met the 26th Tank Brigade [according to documents, the 26th Tank Brigade was in fact more to the north – I. S.]. The enemy opened up anti-tank artillery fire at us and we joined battle. With me were 3 KV tanks. About 30 minutes later (during the battle I wasn't paying attention to the machine) and wound up alone; two T-34 tanks were towing two smoking T-34 tanks; I reached some woods, where I met our infantry. Here, I stayed up until 1100-1200 hours and after that I arrived in Malaia Vereika.[11]

What of the 26th Tank Brigade, which was supposed to have been following the 148th Tank Brigade? The brigade column that night actually did move out behind the 148th Tank Brigade and soon came upon three KV tanks standing 1 kilometer south of Hill 188.5. One of them was disabled, and the two others were standing behind it. The column of the 26th Tank Brigade "stretched out behind these tanks" and also stopped. It seems that the 26th Tank Brigade's command was waiting for when the two serviceable KV tanks of the 148th Tank Brigade would "take the lead of the attack" and move out. However, they didn't budge from place. So the 60-plus (!) tanks of the 26th Tank Brigade also didn't move and remained standing behind them. *After all, according to the order the brigade was to trail behind the 148th Tank Brigade, and not move in front of it.* That's why it was waiting ...

Just what was happening with the 27th Tank Brigade at this time? There, the shift to the offensive was totally dragging out. It still had to get its tanks across the river. At night. There was also the need to reassemble them – and inform the crews of their task. Moreover, the order directed that the brigade follow the 26th Tank Brigade, and for some reason the latter wasn't moving. *The orders gave the 27th Tank Brigade no choice but to wait ... and so the tanks remained parked.*

It was somewhere after 0200 when Major Mikhalev, having at last located the 148th Tank Brigade, turned it around and finally led it in the correct direction. Shortly after 0300, the column followed the GPZ as it turned off the road and headed to the southeast along the hills. The battalions became jumbled, some of the tanks fell behind, while others (like, for example, Commissar Lesnoi's tank) in the darkness became confused and took the old road to Bol'shaia Vereika. In essence, only the forward portion of the brigade column was confidently following the GPZ; those crews in the tanks that were following behind were more likely guessing about the correct direction of movement and didn't know it exactly.

11 TsAMO, F. 202, op. 50, d. 1, ll. 302-303.

Meanwhile, it began to grow light, which did help the crews in the still intact portion of the column see the tanks in front of them. Around 0400, what remained of the brigade's column (most likely, 11 KV and 8 T-60) reached Hill 195.8.

The tank battalions were moving in an extended mobile formation toward the horizon, which to the northeast was beginning to be suffused with a luminous pink, when suddenly they came under fire from German anti-tank guns that had been silent up to that point. The first tank to be knocked out was the KV of Major Mikhalev, the only one still remaining in the mobile forward detachment by that time (the first KV with the headlight that had been shot up by bullets "*remained behind to repair the light*" back on Hill 188.5; the second KV tank lost the column in the darkness and by morning showed up back in Malaia Vereika. From the documents, it isn't fully clear where the T-60 tanks of the GPZ were or what had happened to them.) Soon Major Mikhalev's tank burst into flames. The other tanks of the 260th Tank Battalion joined combat with the German anti-tank guns, covering the crew of the brigade's chief of staff.[12]

Alas, the heavy KV tanks, because of the height of their silhouette, clearly stood out in the field, and were forced to accept battle in conditions very unfavorable for them, because it was very difficult for the crews to spot the enemy's low, well-camouflaged anti-tank guns among the tall plantings. The limited field of view from the tanks and the impossibility of stopping in the open field for thorough observation, which would also make them immobile targets, reduced the possibility of detecting the enemy's anti-tank guns. Meanwhile, the German anti-tank gunners could clearly pick out targets while remaining unspotted, and hastening to take advantage of this favorable opportunity, fired at the tanks from their camouflaged positions.

The 89th Tank Battalion with the start of the German anti-tank fire at the brigade on Hill 195.8, opened up a rapid fire toward the enemy guns, but "not becoming tied up in combat, in the highest gear slipped past the German area of defense" and continued on toward Medvezh'e. One KV tank of the 260th Tank Battalion moved off together with the 89th Tank Battalion, but at the same time one of the 89th Tank Battalion's KV tanks remained together with the 260th Tank Battalion. Practically all of the 89th Tank Battalion's T-60 tanks joined combat with the enemy on Hill 195.8 together with the 260th Tank Battalion, and only two of them continued on with their own 89th Tank Battalion. Soon the 89th Tank Battalion emerged from the zone of German fire and began to move increasingly away from the combat area to the southeast, toward Medvezh'e. The battalion commander had continuous radio contact with the brigade commander right up until reaching Hill 195.8, but after passing this point the contact was broken. When the 89th Tank Battalion reached the area of Hill 187.9 near Russko-Gvozdevskie Vyselki, the battalion commander lost contact with the 260th Tank Battalion as well. The battalion command kept trying to make contact with the brigade headquarters, but received no response. All the attempts to make contact with anyone else proved unsuccessful. In response to the calls, the radiomen heard only a crackling silence ....

The sun rose. What remained of the 89th Tank Battalion was moving across the steppe in the direction of Medvezh'e in almost complete silence, except for the roaring of the engines in their own tanks. There was no one around, the steppe was empty, and only a few kilometers remained to Medvezh'e. Unknowingly, the battalion's tankers in that hour passed by the headquarters of the 387th Infantry Division just a couple of kilometers away, which was located in the northwestern outskirts of Sukharevka.[13] Considering that the headquarters' security had no substantial anti-tank means, or more likely, none at all (there wasn't enough anti-tank artillery even at the front), one can only imagine what the Soviet tanks that had broken through might have done with the

12 Ibid.

13 NARA, T-314, roll 354, fr. 000344.

German division headquarters, had they happened to turn into this village. However, the tank battalion kept advancing along the hills toward Medvezh'e, didn't veer from this course, and having learned of the Soviet breakthrough, the German staff officers on that morning got away with just a scare. At the same time, behind the remaining tanks of the 89th Tank Battalion, there was no sign of any other Soviet tank striving to catch up with them.

If the reduced 89th Tank Battalion was moving toward Medvezh'e practically without firing a single shot, the 260th Tank Battalion and the T-60 tanks of the 89th Tank Battalion that had remained with it were still engaged in a hard battle with the German anti-tank artillery on Hill 195.8. Increasing numbers of KV and T-60 tanks were becoming immobilized with combat damage. The adversary continued to pour shells into them, until they burst into flames. As was written in one Soviet document: "Expecting the 26th Tank Brigade's arrival, up until 07:00 the [crews of the] immobilized tanks continued to struggle, and abandoned it only when the tank became enveloped in flames." The majority of the crew members here died in the flames, or was killed when trying to exit them. Altogether in the vicinity of Hill 195.8 on the morning of 22 July, 7 KV and 6 T-60 were knocked out or destroyed. The commander of the 148th Tank Brigade Lieutenant Colonel Mikhailin was killed in the fighting (his name doesn't appear on the list of the 148th Tank Brigade's irrecoverable losses. According to other documents he was counted as missing-in-action). The casualties of the 260th Tank Battalion amounted to 8 killed and 6 missing in action. The tank crew of the brigade's chief of staff Major Mikhalev managed to clamber out of their burning tank, after which they took cover in the tall plantings and together with the surviving members of other crews, began to wait for the 26th Tank Brigade to reach the hill. However, the brigade was still not showing up ….

Meanwhile, what was happening at this time with the 148th Tank Brigade's forward battalion? Around 0800 on the morning of 22 July, 8 hours after moving out on the raid, the 89th Tank Battalion (or what was left of it) was nevertheless able to reach the area of Medvezh'e. The village lay in the deep valley of a branch of the Treshchevka River, and from the hill to the north of it, the tankers finally caught sight of the 2nd Tank Corps' objective. The streets of Medvezh'e were empty; the residents were hiding or had been driven away by the Germans. In addition, no enemy could be seen in the village. The battalion halted. An unusual silence was all around. The front was far behind them and the 89th Tank Battalion was now deep behind enemy lines. However, there was no sign of an enemy presence in Medvezh'e. Of the entire tank brigade, only several crews had made it this far. Of the 34 tanks of the 148th Tank Brigade that had crossed into Malaia Vereika, only 4 KV and 2 T-60 had made it to Medvezh'e (approximately 5% of the number of tanks in the 2nd Tank Corps before the offensive!): 6 tanks and 24 tankers – lacking infantry, artillery, and supplies.

It would seem that the raid's objective had been reached and that the mission had been carried out. However, the situation in which the crews found themselves upon reaching Medvezh'e more likely prompted alarm in them, not celebration. In reality, what should they do now? The attack order didn't give the brigade the task of advancing any further than Medvezh'e. Indeed, where could they go without the delivery of fuel and ammunition? They had no contact with anyone, and the tankers found themselves almost 15 kilometers behind enemy lines. They could only wait for the arrival of the corps' main forces and hope that this would take place soon. However, the hills over which the 26th and 27th Tank Brigades were to attack toward Medvezh'e remained empty. Thus, approximately an hour passed in uncertainty and conjecturing.

Then, in the distance, trucks appeared, from which infantry began to unload. Next this infantry began to cordon off the area occupied by the Soviet tanks.

5

22 July 1942

The 26th Tank Brigade stood idle on Hill 188.5 until morning. With the morning light, the enemy opened anti-tank artillery fire at the brigade's tanks as they stood idle in the field. Having come under such fire and later aerial bombing as well, the 26th Tank Brigade began to suffer losses, so Colonel Burdov made the decision to turn the brigade around and escape the beaten zone. This was no sooner said than done. The 26th Tank Brigade fell back to the northern slopes of Hill 188.5, and then took cover in a small patch of woods lying east of the road. Even though the bombing continued, the fire of the German anti-tank guns couldn't reach them here. The brigade commander considered the cover in the woods fully amenable and *opted not to leave it ...* Where precisely the 27th Tank Brigade was on the morning of 22 July isn't fully clear from the documents. However, it is totally obvious that it was even further from Medvezh'e than the 26th Tank Brigade that was "attacking" in front of it.

The headquarters of the 148th Tank Brigade was located in Malaia Vereika. In the absence of the brigade commander, commissar, chief of staff and chief of the Political Department, the senior officer in the brigade was the assistant chief of staff Captain Putsienko. Out of the entire brigade, he had only its understrength motorized rifle battalion left – about 300 men. The 148th Tank Brigade headquarters spent all night trying to restore contact with the tank battalions that had departed on the raid, but all of the efforts of the radiomen went to naught: the battalions didn't answer.

Only at 0920 did a single solitary reply to all of the numerous calls come out of the heretofore silent radio waves. The brigade commissar unexpectedly made contact, but his brief radio message was more than strange: "I'm moving to yesterday's position," Senior Battalion Commissar Lesnoi transmitted.[1] These five words in the radio message raised more questions at the headquarters about what was going on than answers. (Subsequently, in the course of the investigation by Briansk Front's headquarters of the 2nd Tank Corps' actions, Putsienko substantially expanded Lesnoi's radio message, writing that "he reported that he had lost contact with the commanders and his bearings, and was moving toward Malaia Vereika."[2] However, it isn't clear where the 148th Tank Brigade's commissar was and what Lesnoi was doing during the 5-plus hours of daylight, when he might have fully gotten his bearings.) The headquarters wasn't able to obtain any further information from Lesnoi: he made no further attempt to make contact. That's how the morning of 22 July 1942 began in the 148th Tank Brigade. The 2nd Motorized Rifle Brigade that morning remained in the positions it had occupied the evening before in expectation of a general attack. However, the corps' tank brigades weren't moving and neither were the motorized riflemen, who in turn were waiting for the tanks to move out.

The 167th Rifle Division and 118th Tank Brigade on the morning of 22 July went on the attack in the 2nd Tank Corps' sector of operations. The infantry rose to the attack behind the tanks, but were soon cut off from them by intensive fire and became pinned down close to the jumping-off

1 TsAMO, F. 148 tp, op. 1, d. 3, l. 38.
2 Ibid.

positions. The tanks of the 118th Tank Brigade continued on briefly, but then returned for the infantry, but the rifle companies, pinned down by the artillery shelling and air strikes, were digging in on the exposed field and made no further advance. The attack by the 104th Separate Rifle Brigade also bogged down; after reaching the Bol'shaia Vereika River, it began to fortify the line it had attained. The German units that had reeled back to the line of the river the day before, had rallied over the night and were everywhere putting up dogged resistance.

West of Malaia Vereika, in the area of Lebiazh'e, the 1st Tank Corps and 193rd Rifle Division launched their attack on 22 July only in the afternoon. Prior to this the 1st Tank Corps had worked all night and through the morning clearing mines from the banks of the river and repairing the damaged bridges. The forward units of the 193rd Rifle Division reached the southern outskirts of Lebiazh'e and waited for the tanks to attack while under enemy artillery fire and aerial bombings. In its account, the 1st Tank Corps command wrote:

> Only at 1300 22 July, having cleared passages through the minefields and repaired the bridge, did a brigade [the 1st Guards Tank Brigade – I.S.] begin crossing its tanks to the southern bank of the river and attack the enemy, which was stubbornly defending Point 188.5, the northern fringe of the patch of woods south of Lebiazh'e and Khrushchevo with anti-tank artillery and infantry. The infantry of the 193rd Rifle Division, arriving in the southern outskirts behind the 1st Guards Tank Brigade, didn't follow the tanks into the attack and under aerial attacks and artillery barrages on the enemy's part, broke and fled from the battlefield. As a result the tanks were left unsupported and were forced to try to crack the enemy's resistance only with their own numerically-weak rifle battalions.[3]

As on the operation's first day, the Luftwaffe reigned above the battlefield, subjecting almost all of Operational Group Chibisov's units to intense bombings. Even though they weren't as massed as they'd been in the prior period of the 5th Tank Army's offensive, when up to 30-40 aircraft often took part in the missions, the prolonged "influence" of the bombers on the attacking troops inevitably led to a slowing of the pace of the offensive, pinned down the tank units, and forced the infantry to hug the earth. The fascist air strikes in the vicinities of the bridges, where a large number of troops and vehicles had accumulated, led to heavy losses in both men and equipment. At the same time, the aerial cover of the operational group's units by Soviet fighters was completely inadequate. Time and again enemy dive bombers struck clusters of our troops without meeting any opposition in the air, and only the anti-aircraft batteries were attempting to protect the units from air strikes. It cannot be said that our aircraft never appeared above the battlefield. German documents note the high activity of Soviet aircraft in the operational area "with bombings and strafing attacks with their on-board weapons."[4] In documents of the Soviet 2nd Air Army, there are mentions of combat sorties to cover the troops and to strike the enemy opposing them.[5] However, the sporadic appearance of our aircraft was unable to exert significant influence on the course of the combat operations. If the topic of discussion regards the support of the attacking units directly on the battlefield, where the aircraft might "work over" panzer units, suppress enemy anti-tank guns and clear a path forward for the tanks in response to direct requests, which means tight cooperation with the ground troops and contributes to their progress on the ground, then the

3 TsAMO, F. 1 TK, op. 1, d. 4, l. 16.
4 NARA, T-314, roll 353, fr. 001339.
5 Check, for instance, the operational summaries of the 2nd Air Army for the period between 21-26.7.42 in TsAMO, F. 2 VA, op. 4196, d. 14, l. 88-96.

situation was even worse. Numerous references to this in the documents of all types of units state that they frequently never observed the activity of our air force above the battlefield.

For example, the 1st Tank Corps command wrote regarding the combat actions on 22 July:

> The enemy, offering stubborn resistance with opposing anti-tank guns and artillery means from the line Khrushchevo – Gremiach'e, the northern fringe of the woods south of Lebiazh'e and Point 188.5, actively worked over our combat formations from the air with continuous air strikes by 20-30 aircraft. The enemy with bombing from the air disrupted the combat formations of the attacking units, holding up their forward advance. Our fighter aircraft didn't appear in the skies above the battlefield, and moreover, an entire number of cases were identified when our ground attack aircraft, appearing in the area of our units' operations, struck and shot up their own units with their cannons and rockets, sometimes in the rear up to 80 kilometers from the frontline.[6]

A document of the 26th Tank Brigade states:

> Over the period from 21 July, the delivery of food for the men in their forward positions was made difficult as a result of a massed enemy airstrike. In view of this, food for the men was brought up to the frontline only early in the morning or late in the evening. There was a case where the 2nd Rifle Company didn't receive a hot breakfast, but was given a dry ration.[7]

The commissar of the 2nd Motorized Rifle Brigade reported on 22 July:

> The enemy subjected our positions throughout the day to intense artillery and mortar fire, as well as bombings from the air. [...] Uninterrupted enemy attacks from the air continued throughout the day from 05:00. Our aircraft showed up three times. [...] The entire area of Bol'shaia Vereika throughout the day was located under constant enemy air activity".[8]

Just as in the previous operation of the 5th Tank Army, enemy bombers pounced on the units' anti-aircraft batteries with the aim of eliminating any resistance from the ground. In the 27th Tank Brigade, on this day a direct hit by a bomb destroyed 2 DShK anti-aircraft machine guns, left 3 vehicles burned out (including one truck that was carrying all of the ammunition for the anti-aircraft machine guns), and left 33 men killed and 12 wounded.[9] In the 148th Tank Brigade, a 37-mm anti-aircraft gun was knocked out by bombs; three commanders and several members of the anti-aircraft gun crews were wounded.[10]

In the 167th Rifle Division's account of the operation, there is the statement: "At 0600 on 22 July, enemy fighter and bomber aircraft appeared above the units' combat formations; they focused all of their fire on the forward edge, on bridges, and on the tanks and combat formations of the infantry positioned at the bridge and attacking to the south out of Malaia Vereika."[11]

---

6 TsAMO, F. 1 TK, op. 1, d. 4, l. 16.
7 TsAMO, F. 2 TK, op. 1, d.224(b), l. 52.
8 Ibid., l. 151.
9 TsAMO, F. 27 tbr, op. 1, d. 9, l. 150; F. 2 TK, op. 1, d. 224 (b), l. 56.
10 TsAMO, F. 2 TK, op. 1, d. 224 (b), l. 155.
11 TsAMO, F. 202, op. 5, d. 334, l. 63.

Battery commander of 167th Rifle Division's artillery regiment N.M. Epimakhov recalled:

> I received my combat baptism in the first battle at Bol'shaia Vereika. I was then a deputy commander of the 576th Artillery Regiment's 5th Battery. On the eve of the battle we shifted our concealed firing position 4 kilometers closer to the front. We concealed our horse trains in a ravine that was overgrown with dense shrubbery. Over the night we dug emplacements for the guns, slit trenches for the men, and pits for storing the shells. The drivers built shelters for the horses. Signalmen under the leadership of Lieutenant Smirnov unrolled a telephone line to the observation post. In the morning, squadrons of German aircraft appeared above the forward edge of our defense. Having assembled into a ring, they winged over into a dive, released their bombs and shot up the trenches from their machine guns. Driver Ponomarev, who refused to leap into a slit trench, was badly wounded, but continued to unload the shells. The next day the ravine in which our artillery trains were located was subjected to an accurate bombing and machine-gun fire. Several horses were killed or wounded. Those animals that in fright escaped their harnesses came galloping into the firing position with whinnying and snorting, searching for protection from the enemy gunners. We suffered losses in these attacks. Gun commander Tsibulko was badly wounded; Lieutenant Podkhineichenko was mortally wounded; battery commander Senior Lieutenant Andreev received a severe wound in the head; and the commander of the fire direction platoon Lieutenant Meitus' right arm was broken by a shell fragment.[12]

Due to the artillery barrages and air strikes, neither the 167th Rifle Division, nor the 118th Tank Brigade, nor even the 2nd Tank Corps were able to push forward. The afternoon of 22 July went by, and they still remained on the northern slopes of Hill 188.5.

General Liziukov spent the morning of 22 July at the 2nd Tank Corps command post in Kreshchenka. With impatience he was waiting for reports from the brigades that had left on the raid the night before, but was unable to make contact with any of them. In these conditions he could only conjecture how the battle was going, and guess at the lines that the tank brigades of his corps had reached.

Later it became known to him that the 26th and 27th Tank Brigades had been totally unable to make progress. From their messages it followed that they had become separated from the 148th Tank Brigade and were still located north of Hill 188.5! This meant that instead of an attack by a clenched fist of more than 100 tanks, only the 148th Tank Brigade had headed out on the raid, which meant ... one-third of all the corps' available combat machines! Future clarifications from the headquarters of the 148th Tank Brigade were even more disquieting: it turned out that not all of the tanks even in this brigade had gone on the attack.

Having no reliable information from the 148th Tank Brigade that had set out the night before, and receiving vague explanations from the other tank brigades about the reasons for the delay, the commander of the 2nd Tank Corps with growing impatience was hounding the other brigades and demanding that they get moving. The lack of any contact with the 148th Tank Brigade weighed upon him and he didn't know what to do with himself at the command post that was isolated from the brigades. In this respect it is worth citing excerpts from the recollections of the 2nd Tank Corps' former chief of intelligence, E. F. Ivanovsky, who in his words was a witness to these ever more alarming hours of the corps commander's stay in Kreshchenka:

12 *Podklonimsia velikim tem godam*, p. 14.

A tense atmosphere reigned at the observation post. Everyone was waiting for a decisive word from General A.I. Liziukov, who was intently staring at a map.

-- "Comrade General," a signaler reported, "The commander-in-chief is on the line."

Liziukov approached the device and picked up the phone – all of this calmly and deliberately.

The staff officers in the observation post immediately fell silent, some of them even holding their breath. We knew that Colonel General K.K. Rokossovsky, who by that time was already a prominent Soviet military commander, had recently taken command of Briansk Front.

From everything that A.I. Liziukov said, with alternating official precision and trustworthy warmth, it was possible to picture both the contents of the dialogue and to guess that both of its participants were long-time comrades and possibly close friends.

Liziukov initially said, "I am reporting on the situation of the brigades that have broken free, Comrade Commander."

After several questions and answers, the talk was now: "I will do everything that depends on me, Konstantin Konstantinovich. I fully understand. Thank you for the advice." Before setting down the phone, he repeated: "Comrade Front Commander, everything will be carried out!"

[In his memoirs, Rokossovsky doesn't mention any conversation with Liziukov. There is also no confirmation in the documents that this phone call took place – I.S.]

After the conversation, A.I. Liziukov took a seat at a small table and became lost in thought. He then stood up with a decisive expression on his face and ordered that he be connected by radio with the commander of the 26th Tank Brigade. As he heard the report, the corps commander became increasingly gloomy.

-- "What sort of tale are you spinning, Burdov!?" he thundered, irritated by something; "I have a hunch … I know what you have going on there. So I'm heading out now; I'll take a look myself and figure things out …"

Then he turned to me and directed, "Ivanovsky, stay here. Keep a watch on the situation and keep in touch. Soon the chief of staff will arrive at the observation post."

"Yes, sir, Comrade General!"

A.I. Liziukov climbed into a tank, and the machine took off at high speed.[13]

Archive documents indirectly confirm the conversation between Liziukov and Rokossovsky described by Ivanovsky. For example, the combat journal of the 148th Tank Brigade states:

The brigade headquarters throughout the day stayed in contact with the 2nd Tank Corps headquarters and with the 26th and 27th Tank Brigades and the 167th Rifle Division, reminding them of the need to carry out the order regarding the offensive and to link up with the tanks of the 148th Tank Brigade. The 2nd Tank Corps commander Major General Liziukov repeatedly radioed the brigades about this. For example, at 1345 the 2nd Corps commander radioed the 26th Tank Brigade the following: "This is Liziukov. Immediately report how things are going with the execution of the order. Why have you lagged behind Mikhailin? You sly old dog! Act decisively and carry out the task! Mikhailin's coordinates: 12847.[14]

13 E.F. Ivanovsky, *Ataku nachinali tankisty* [*Tankers launched the attack*] (Moscow: Voenizdat, 1984), p. 64.
14 TsAMO, F. 148 tp, op. 1, d. 3, l. 38.

Whether Liziukov had direct contact with the Commander-in-Chief of Briansk Front Rokossovsky through his direct superior Chibisov remains an open question. The 1st and 2nd Tank Corps were both subordinate to Briansk Front's operational group and were to maintain direct contact with its headquarters. Most likely, Rokossovsky called Liziukov through the operational group's communications center, so this dialogue did take place. However, it mustn't be forgotten that in accordance with the chain of command, Liziukov was obligated to report on the course of the offensive not to Rokossovsky, but to Chibisov, from whom he repeatedly and unsuccessfully requested air support.

The worst days of the 5th Tank Army's fighting, when the Luftwaffe worked over Liziukov's units from morning to nightfall with impunity, were being repeated, but the requests of the 2nd Tank Corps commander for air cover went unanswered. Moreover, now analogous requests weren't finding the understanding of the commander of the operational group, but provoking his increasing temper. Being unable to provide air cover to the troops, Chibisov, as had been the case before, "decided the problem" by imperiously demanding that Liziukov *stop complaining*!

At 1430 the operations chief of the 2nd Tank Corps Lieutenant Colonel Pupko, who was at the command post of the 167th Rifle Division, received and jotted down the following order from Chibisov to the commander of the 2nd Tank Corps:

> Take control of the corps into your hands; prepare with the support of the 167th Rifle Division's artillery and of your own tanks to break through in the sector between Hill 188.5 and the woods southeast of Churikovo and carry out the order for an attack toward the Medvezh'e area and destroy the enemy in the Kaver'ia, Skliaevo, Nizhniaia Vereika area. Personally oversee the fighting. I am demanding the strict fulfillment of the order. By the end of the day, the areas indicated in the order must be overwhelmed and captured. Cease referring to the enemy air force. Carry out the order.[15]

Fifty minutes after Chibisov's order, the 148th Tank Brigade's commissar made contact with his headquarters for the second time in 24 hours. At 1520 he reported over the radio: "I'm in Malaia Vereika. Send me a "Pigmy" [Ed. note: The Ford Pigmy was a prototype jeep submitted to the U.S. Army prior to World War II for testing, but only two were ever built. Likely, he was referring to a Willys jeep]; I'm going to report to Liziukov."[16]

As with his first radio message, there are strange aspects to Lesnoi's second transmission. From his message, it was apparent that Lesnoi was connecting with the headquarters of the 148th Tank Brigade from the very same tiny village in which this headquarters was in fact located. He didn't clarify where in the village the Willys had to be delivered. From Commissar Lesnoi's communication it turns out he had arrived in Malaia Vereika soon after noontime, and was there, where the headquarters of his brigade was located for 2-3 hours, but for some reason never went to the headquarters and only later contacted it by radio.[17]

From the documents it isn't clear, whether Lesnoi was ever sent the "Pigmy" that he requested (and to where??), but Lesnoi nevertheless later did arrive in Kreshchenka to report to Liziukov, although no one from the headquarters of the 148th Tank Brigade took him there, and no one from the headquarters in fact ever saw him on that day. Meeting with Lesnoi at the command post of the 2nd Tank Corps in Kreshchenka, for the first time Liziukov found out about what had happened the night before with the 148th Tank Brigade. In the process the brigade commissar

15 TsAMO, F. 202, op. 50, d. 1, ll. 304-307.
16 Ibid.
17 Ibid.

could more or less reliably report to the corps commander only what he had personally observed before he had wandered from the brigade's main column. From Lesnoi's words it turned out that after the confusions in the night, the 148th Tank Brigade by morning had nevertheless found its way and had headed toward Medvezh'e. But where it had later arrived and with what forces, the brigade commissar couldn't say.

Nevertheless, Liziukov believed that the 148th Tank Brigade had carried out its assignment and had broken through to Medvezh'e with its main forces. Now the entire fate of the operation depended on giving timely support to the tankers that had penetrated into the German rear. The 148th Tank Brigade needed urgent reinforcements; fuel, ammunition and food; but all this could not be quickly organized. Unable to render immediate assistance to the brigade, the commander of 2nd Tank Corps decided to boost its morale at least (which in the present situation was also very important!) and somehow give heart to Lieutenant Colonel Mikhailin. As before, there was no contact with the brigade, but in the hope that the silent brigade radios might at least receive a radio message, Liziukov sent his personal gratitude to the commander of the 148th Tank Brigade.[18] Liziukov's message was sent via a radio of the 27th Tank Brigade (plainly because the 27th Tank Brigade was closer to Medvezh'e and the radiomen were relying on the fact that is was more likely that the 148th Tank Brigade would receive this radio message, than if it was sent from the corps' command post in Kreshchenka), but in response to Liziukov's radio appeal, there was only oppressive silence – and the longer that there was no news from the brigade now deep behind German lines, the greater was the concern of the commander of the 2nd Tank Corps.

Liziukov still didn't know that the commander of the 148th Tank Brigade was no longer able to hear his expression of gratitude, even had it reached him through the radio waves. He was completely unaware that Lieutenant Colonel Mikhailin that morning had perished inside his burning tank and would now never be able to answer him.

I believe that the lack of any message at all from the 148th Tank Brigade over the course of many hours, together with the complete silence of the radios available in the tank brigade, made the rest of the commanders at the command post, and primarily Liziukov himself, increasingly agitated, but also prompted great apprehensions. One can say the same about the 148th Tank Brigade's commissar, who plainly didn't know what to do with himself on 22 July and was behaving most oddly and impulsively.

From the testimony of the 148th Tank Brigade's assistant chief of staff Captain Putsienko in the course of Colonel Sukhoruchkin's subsequent investigation, Battalion Commissar Lesnoi never appeared at the headquarters of his brigade, and from General Liziukov he headed to the 26th Tank Brigade, attached the remaining three KV tanks to it, and intended to go in support of his brigade."[19] However, Lesnoi's desire to set out immediately to the relief of his combat comrades made no sense to the commander of the 26th Tank Brigade, who was plainly waiting (or more exactly – enduring bombing and artillery barrages in the patch of woods) for more favorable conditions to start active operations, or simply didn't have the stomach to set out toward the hilltop from the woods while under heavy German fire.

Later, having analyzed in detail the course of the operation and having interrogated the executive officers and eyewitnesses, the Chief of Briansk Front's Armored Forces Colonel Sukhoruchkin considered the actions (or more properly – the inactivity) of the 26th Tank Brigade's command to be criminal and asked the Briansk Front Military Council to turn the guilty parties over to a military tribunal.[20]

18 Ibid.
19 Ibid.
20 Ibid.

The 27th Tank Brigade's command received General Liziukov's next verbal order about "entering the breakthrough" at 1530.[21] According to this order, the 27th Tank Brigade was to assemble on the southern outskirts of Bol'shaia Vereika by 1700 in readiness to attack in the wake of the 26th Tank Brigade. However, the 27th Tank Brigade was unable to assemble in the jumping-off area by the designated time and arrived there two hours later! It would seem that this is a criminal failure to carry out an order from a senior commander, but at higher command levels everything was more complicated than that and it wasn't possible to identify any plainly guilty parties in the matter. The point is that just that afternoon the brigade had finally received replenishments in the form of 15 new T-34 tanks with crews that were just as new. The tanks hadn't been inspected and fully serviced, but the totally unseasoned crews were expected to go into battle almost within an hour of their arrival. Yet it had been necessary at the very least to prepare the arriving tanks for battle, and at least briefly inform the crews of their assignment.

Note that there was no mention of the need to conduct reconnaissance and gather intelligence; to obtain and analyze information about the enemy and his anti-tank defense means; or to organize matters regarding cooperation and communications – just as long as the tanks were able to move out on time. One must again and again deplore the fact that "the introduction into combat" of newly-arrived young replacements often went just this way. Is it so surprising that the inexperienced crews, who hadn't had time to familiarize themselves with the terrain or the situation, or hadn't even yet had time to grasp their assignments, were often at a loss on the battlefield and lost their tanks without having inflicted serious damage to the enemy; at times fired at friendly tanks; or else were killed in their first battle?

At 1700 Liziukov arrived at the command post of the 167th Rifle Division in Surikovo, where he attempted to work out joint actions with the division command in the forthcoming attack.[22] For the 167th Rifle Division, this was the second day of combat operations in its entire brief history, and the extremely complicated situation on the battlefield greatly exacerbated the natural difficulties of the division's combat footing. On the first day of the operation, a significant number of the command staff had been killed or wounded, including the commander of the 520th Rifle Regiment Major Dubov, who had received a severe wound.[23]

Lacking any artillery of his own, the 2nd Tank Corps commander was counting upon the artillery of the 167th Rifle Division to work over the enemy's defense, by which assistance the corps' tanks might be able to overrun the enemy's anti-tank defense on Hill 188.5 and advance onward. The division's artillery regiment was equipped with large-caliber guns and together with the artillery of the rifle regiments had the possibility of silencing the German anti-tank guns in the breakthrough sector with their fire. However … the next blow was awaiting Liziukov: at the command post of the 167th Rifle Division, he was informed that the division's artillery had almost run out of shells, because a German airstrike had destroyed its ammunition depot in Fomina-Negachevka.[24] In the airstrike, the division's chief of artillery supply and ordnance inspector had been killed, and the commandant of the artillery depot wounded, among the other Red Army men killed and wounded in the attack.[25] According to the recollections of the 167th Rifle Division's artillery commander P.I. Botko, because of the acute shortage of ammunition, a strict limit on the expenditure of shells was enacted, amounting to just half a shell per gun per day. In other words, a battery of four guns could fire just two shells a day![26] The neighboring 193rd Rifle Division

21 Ibid.
22 Ibid.
23 *Poklonimsia velikim tem godam*, p. 18.
24 Materials of the Kon'-Kolodez' Museum, Khlevenskii District, Lipetsk Oblast.
25 *Poklonimsia velikim tem godam*, p. 19.
26 Materials of the Kon'-Kolodez' Museum, Khlevenskii District, Lipetsk Oblast.

was in a similar situation; because of a lack of shells, the division's artillery regiment had been directed to cease fire and was completely pulled back into the second echelon.[27] Thus, Liziukov was unable to count upon powerful artillery support from the 167th Rifle Division. Nevertheless, the commander of the 2nd Tank Corps agreed upon a joint attack by the tank corps and rifle division (the documents make no mention of any agreements with the 118th Tank Brigade, which was operating in the same area).

About 1800 that evening, Liziukov and his signals officer Senior Lieutenant Vafin arrived in Bol'shaia Vereika, where they visited the 27th Tank Brigade and 2nd Motorized Rifle Brigade; from there, they returned to the corps command post in Kreshchenka. Liziukov gave an order to Vafin to drive to the corps headquarters and to pass it his order: "the headquarters' leadership is to move out to the 26th Tank Brigade in Malaia Vereika and direct the preparation for battle."[28] Plainly, he wanted for the staff officers by their own personal presence to prompt the excessively cautious 26th Tank Brigade command to initiate active operations and on the spot ensure that it carried out the order he had issued.

Then, at approximately 1900 on 22 July, Liziukov and Assorov took a seat in a KV tank and headed out from the 2nd Tank Corps' command post to Bol'shaia Vereika, in order to direct the fighting from the forward observation post. The operational summary of the headquarters of the 2nd Tank Corps gives us solid grounds to assume that on the evening of 22 July Liziukov believed that the 148th Tank Brigade, which had departed on the nighttime raid, was in the Sivertsevo – Kaver'ia area, just 12-14 kilometers from present combat area.[29] To breakthrough to it with the rest of the 2nd Tank Corps' brigades had become for Liziukov the main task of the day.

27 TsAMO, F. 202, op. 36, d. 129, l. 460.
28 TsAMO, F. 202, op. 50, d. 1, ll. 304-305.
29 TsAMO, F. 202, op. 5, d. 238, l. 508.

6

The 148th Tank Brigade in the enemy rear

The chief of staff of the 148th Tank Brigade Major Mikhalev and his four surviving crew members had remained in the vicinity of Hill 195.8 all morning. Their tank, like all the brigade's other tanks that had joined combat on this hill, had been knocked out, and then set ablaze by the German anti-tank guns. The surviving tankers hid in the tall vegetation and waited for the arrival of the 26th and 27th Tank Brigades. Alas, those brigades didn't appear. An hour passed, then another … and another. The sounds of battle could be heard coming from the fields to the northwest, but came no closer. Noontime arrived, and still neither of the 2nd Tank Corps' two remaining tank brigades showed up. So Major Mikhalev decided to wait no longer and to try to get back to friendly lines. Sooner or later, the other tankers hiding in the field made the same decision. The remnants of the crews of the 260th Tank Battalion began a dangerous journey back, making their way across the fields to the north.[1] Their 13 burned-out tanks and the remains of the tankers that had burned to death inside them remained behind as sad monuments to the destroyed tank battalion.

Having reached the Medvezh'e area, the 89th Tank Battalion numbering just 4 KV tanks and 2 T-60 light tanks since 0800 that morning had been waiting for the approach of the corps' main forces. The tank crews remained in the small village, even when it became clear that the Germans were encircling the battalion's location. The tankers caught sight now and then of the approaching German infantry and fired at them, but gradually and inexorably they were coming ever closer. The tall stalks of rye greatly contributed to this, offering fine concealment to the enemy infantry, but unable to conceal the tanks. What could the tankers do? Chase the German infantry around the field? But they could easily hide among the tall stalks of grain, switch positions, and appear somewhere else. Moreover, the fuel in the tanks was running low, and the supply of ammunition wasn't unlimited. The tanks had no escorting motorized riflemen, and they had no way to drive away the German infantry that were creeping toward them from multiple directions.

Soon, there happened what could be expected in that situation: "Molotov cocktails" sailed through the air toward the tanks. However, as can be understood from the account of the 89th Tank Battalion, not a single one of them caused the tanks any harm: the German infantry were plainly afraid to approach any closer; they had thrown the bottles from a distance and none of them had reached their targets. However, the crews, encircled and literally besieged from every direction by the foe, were plainly unsettled. They recognized that by remaining in their position, it would inevitably sooner or later lead to the event where one or more of the flaming bottles would hit a target.

Major Il'chenko, who in the absence of Lieutenant Colonel Mikhailin was commanding the brigade (or more accurately, its remnants) decided to break out of the encirclement and head toward the hills. Scattering and killing enemy soldiers they met in their path, the tanks easily broke out of

1 TsAMO, F. 148 tp, op. 1, d. 3, l. 35.

the encirclement and headed to the northeast. After 4 kilometers, the battalion stopped in an area west of the village of Pankovo and again began to wait for the approach of the corps' other tank brigades. Time passed, and still there was no sign of the other tank brigades.

Instead, German soldiers once again began to close upon the area occupied by the 89th Tank Battalion. The situation was repeated. As stated in the account of the 89th Tank Battalion: "The battalion left the area of Medvezh'e at 10:00 22 July because up to a battalion of [enemy] submachine gunners [sic] had stolen up to the area of our tanks' location and had begun tossing "Molotov cocktails" at the machines."[2]

In reality, the enemy strength had been greatly exaggerated by the crews (which isn't a wonder, considering the confusion of battle in encirclement, the poor visibility, and the gunfire coming from every direction). The enemy had no "battalion of submachine gunners" in the Medvezh'e area. The command of the 387th Infantry Division would have been happy to have one at hand, but by this time an entire infantry battalion was an unimagined luxury for the division – all of its reserves had been thrown into the fighting. Thus, in order to cordon off the Russian tanks that had broken through, the enemy might have been able to detach no more than one company hastily assembled from whatever was available. After the receipt of reconnaissance reports, the elements that had been hastily formed up were trucked to Medvezh'e. These groups of German infantry (one must note the determination and pluck of the enemy infantry, brave enough to encircle tanks, steal up to them, and toss "Molotov cocktails" at them) became the first German detachments that "besieged" the Russian tank battalion that had broken through and were keeping watch on its movements while waiting for anti-tank guns to come up. Battalion Commissar Golovin subsequently wrote [the document's style has been preserved – I.S.]:

> We took up the forest fringe, but soon came under mortar fire and here enemy submachine gunners began to advance on us … and with their fire began to force matters. Having consulted with Hero of the Soviet Union Major Il'chenko, from the patch of woods we moved to a hillock. Here, artillery fire joined with the submachine gunners and mortar fire. We reached a decision: to leave the fringe of woods and head 4-5 kilometers in the direction of Kaver'ia.[3]

After waiting in vain in the area west of Pankovo for the other tank brigades, Major Il'chenko decided once again to change position and to set out to meet the anticipated 26th and 27th Tank Brigades. The battalion moved to the southern slopes of Hill 187.9 and stopped once again to wait. Again, an hour passed and then another – the tank brigades didn't appear. The radiomen never ceased their attempts to make contact with the command, but neither the brigade commander or the brigade's chief of staff, nor the headquarters of the 148th Tank Brigade that remained in Malaia Vereika or the corps headquarters ever respond.

The battalion was isolated behind enemy lines and was in complete ignorance of the surrounding situation and of the changes occurring at the front. The situation of the tankers that had broken through was worsened by the fact that there was still no delivery of fuel or ammunition as foreseen by the order, while the absence of the corps' other tank brigades spoke to the fact that there might not be any resupply at all.

At Major Il'chenko's order, the crews calculated the remaining amount of fuel and ammunition: enough fuel was left to cover 8-10 kilometers, and a half-load of ammunition, while the tank engines' radiators that had begun to boil in the heat needed water. There was no talk of water or

2 Ibid. ll. 36-37.
3 TsAMO, F. 202, op. 50, d. 1, ll. 304-305.

food for the men; they might endure, but the crews also might not be able to choke down their dry rations with water for very long. Moreover, after a full day of fighting, the night march without any rest, the lengthy roaming and searches, and then the perpetual stress of fresh combat in encirclement, the tankers were worn out both physically and psychologically, yet no rest was in sight.

The shortage of fuel was sharply restricting Il'chenko in the choice of alternative plans of action and threatening to convert his remaining tanks from a maneuvering shock unit into relatively immobile (or entirely immobile) firing points. However, even then, the shortage of ammunition would make them *firing* points only for a time. Once the crews had fired all of their shells and machine-gun ammunition, the menacing combat machines would turn into immobile targets – and then what?

Two days on his feet without sleep or rest, having no information where the 2nd Tank Corps was or where the Germans were (perhaps the Germans had already initiated a retreat?), what was Major Il'chenko to do? What sole, reliable decision could he take as senior commander? His ignorance of the surrounding situation because of the lack of communications didn't allow him to assess the situation properly, but the fact that the corps' main forces had suffered a setback was becoming increasingly apparent. Having exerted so much effort, and having lost so many casualties, the 148th Tank Brigade had carried out its task and with a final desperate lunge, losing tanks and men on the way, a portion of it had nevertheless broken through to Medvezh'e. But having reached there with only an incomplete tank battalion, the brigade was suddenly no longer the vanguard of a following tank corps, but a solitary and played-out combatant in the midst of the enemy. Back in the morning, the occupied area might have been considered a forward staging area. By noon it began strongly to suggest a trap.

Having wound up at Hill 187.9, Major Il'chenko decided to discuss the situation with the other commanders and summoned them for a brief conference. Of the battalion's senior command staff among the crews were Hero of the Soviet Union Major Il'chenko himself; Battalion Commissar Zuev, the chief of the 148th Tank Brigade's Political Department; the 260th Tank Brigade's commissar Battalion Commissar Golovin (who had wound up together with the 89th Tank Battalion after the nighttime confusions and the fight near Kaver'ia); the 89th Tank Battalion's commander Senior Lieutenant Zaporozhets; his deputy and General Liziukov's adjutant Captain Pendak; Senior Lieutenant Samartsev; and the battalion's commissar Political Instructor Vystavnoi. The question was one: What to do? Today we don't know how long the discussion went or what proposals were made by those present, nor will we ever know, but it is clear that as a result of this meeting, the decision was to remain in place and to wait for the arrival of the other tank brigades, and if they failed to do so – to make their way back to friendly lines.

Of course, from the vantage point of today it is clear that this decision doomed the 89th Tank Battalion to inactivity and the complete loss of initiative. The enemy received the opportunity to bring up forces to the area of the breakthrough, while the Soviet tank crews had nothing else to do but wait helplessly for events to unfold. However, it shouldn't be forgotten that the shortage of fuel (we'll remember that there was enough left to travel only 8-10 kilometers) in essence left Il'chenko only two options: to break out to friendly lines or to wait for them on the hill they occupied.

If we also recall that the officers who attended this conference were still following an order that no one had cancelled, then it must be recognized that Major Il'chenko didn't even have this choice. Had they decided upon an immediate breakout attempt back to friendly lines, this would have meant a voluntary failure to comply with this order and an undermining of the entire operation. He did not take such a responsibility on his shoulders. Moreover, Major Il'chenko didn't know the reason why the 26th and 27th Tank Brigades hadn't made it to Medvezh'e and could fully suppose that ultimately, they'd still show up.

The hope that the main forces of the 2nd Tank Corps would reach the hill, perhaps, was indeed that factor, which together with a sense of duty and fealty to their oaths (as well as to their commander, who when parting the night before had not so much ordered, as he did ask that they do everything possible and even impossible to carry out the order) lay at the basis of the decision they took back then. The officers of the 89th Tank Battalion were unable to abandon the position and head back without waiting for the approach of the rest of the 2nd Tank Corps.

At 1600 Major Il'chenko decided to camouflage the tanks and to send out a patrol on foot in the direction of Kaver'ia.[4] However, coming under heavy fire, the scouts couldn't get to Kaver'ia and soon had to return. They reported that German troops were assembling on the northern slopes of Hill 187.9. Then observers spotted two German self-propelled guns that were moving toward the hill. Before the eyes of the battalion's tank crews, the German self-propelled guns began to take up firing positions. German infantry also began to advance through the grain fields. Seeing all this, Major Il'chenko set out a second reconnaissance group. However, the patrol didn't get very far when the Germans suddenly opened fire at the tanks. One KV was set ablaze with the very first shot, and then almost immediately, a second. In the words of Battalion Commissar Golovin, who judging from the identification numbers of the tanks in the brigade was in the second KV tank (No. 209), this happened around 1900. Golovin wrote: "My tank took two hits. The tanks parked in front started to move out toward Kaver'ia. I wasn't able to grab a ride in any of the tanks."[5] Golovin remained on the hill with two other crew members, while the rest of the 89th Tank Battalion's tanks set off, and judging from everything, quickly left his field of view, because later Golovin could say nothing about their fate.

The quick destruction of the two heavy KV tanks most likely is explained by the fact that the enemy somehow was able to roll up an anti-tank gun without being spotted and to open fire from point-blank range. But why did this gun (or these guns) remain unnoticed by the tank crews until the very final moment? Apparently, the reason for this was the demonstrative maneuvering of two German self-propelled guns in the distance, which diverted the attention of the crews and preventing them from spotting a threat from the rear. As a result, the action began so unexpectedly and so unsuccessfully for the battalion: of the four KV tanks, two were lost immediately.

The remaining tanks sped away and escaped the zone of fire, but having moved a short distance, they wound up in the zone of fire of other guns. The further action for our tankers went confusingly and extremely unsuccessfully. Having been attacked unexpectedly and not having had time to look around as they should and spot the positions of the guns that were firing at them, the crews in their scramble to get away inadvertently went into a head-on attack against the previously detected targets – the two German self-propelled guns. However, before having had time to strike them, 2 KV and 2 T-60 were knocked out and set ablaze one after the other by German anti-tank guns, which obviously had previously taken position on the flanks. Only 8 surviving tankers managed to scramble out of the burning tanks; a terrible death within the burning tanks awaited the crew members who hadn't been able to get out. Altogether in the battalion's final battle, 24 men were killed. General Liziukov's adjutant, the 21-year-old Captain Pendak, was burned alive in his tank.

The fate of Hero of the Soviet Union Major Il'chenko, who after the death of Lieutenant Colonel Mikhailin took command of the 148th Tank Brigade, remained unknown. None of the surviving tankers could confirm that Il'chenko had been killed, but he also wasn't among the survivors.

The possibility that he'd been taken prisoner, unquestionably, is impossible to reject completely, but nevertheless the chance of it is small. According to statistics, a significant share of the Red Army's senior command staff who became German prisoners after the winter of 1941-1942 survived their captivity and returned to the Motherland. Il'chenko wasn't among them. However,

4 TsAMO, F. 148 tp, op. 1, d. 3, l. 35.
5 TsAMO, F. 202, op. 50, d. 1, ll. 304-305.

even if we assume that he died in captivity, there would have been mentions of this in the captured German documents (given German meticulousness in keeping records). Such notes haven't been found. Moreover, the capture of members of the Red Army's senior command staff, as a rule, was recorded in documents of the Wehrmacht's combat units, but there is no trace of the capturing of Major Il'chenko in them.

The fate of the 148th Tank Brigade's political chief Battalion Commissar Zuev is also not fully known; according to the brigade's political report, just like Mikhailin, Il'chenko and many other officers of the 148th Tank Brigade, he failed to return from the raid. True, this political report written on 26 July mentions several other men of the brigade's command staff as missing, who nevertheless later made their way back to friendly lines. However, in later documents there is also no mention that Zuev was among this group.

The 11 surviving men, including the commissar of the 260th Tank Battalion Golovin and the two members of his crew, split into two groups and began to head off toward the front. The group containing Battalion Commissar Golovin and the commander of the 89th Tank Battalion Senior Lieutenant Zaporozhets began to head to the north, while Senior Lieutenant Samartsev's group set out to the northeast. At that moment they were just 8-10 kilometers from the frontlines, but it took more than a week for these exhausted and weary men to make their way back through the German lines.

Only on 30 July did Golovin's group emerge from the pocket in the vicinity of Vereiskie Vyselki southeast of Bol'shaia Vereika. Samartsev's tankers made their way to the Don River north of Verilovka, headed to the north away from the German front, and having crossed the Don River at Gorozhanka, emerged in the sector of the Voronezh Front.[6] Unfortunately, there are no records or recollections of what they had to go through on this difficult and lengthy path, when for 8 days without food or water they stubbornly made their way back to friendly lines. In the documents there is only a brief statement: they came into our lines on 30 July. Apparently, this portion of the ill-fated "raid through the enemy rear" was of little interest to the staff officers.

Was the complete destruction of the 89th Tank Battalion justified by the losses inflicted on the foe? Alas, the documents say "No". The battalion's tankers, or even those of the brigade as a whole, didn't know what damage they did to the foe. However, it is telling that at a time when enemy losses were far and wide counted up "in the crew's own statements" and all too often reached gigantic dimensions, the surviving tankers of the 148th Tank Brigade made no attempt to conjure up anything and didn't boast of their "victories".

Only the commissar of the 260th Tank Battalion (possibly because his post obliged him to do so, and because it was necessary to justify somehow the battalion's destruction) reported that on the way to Medvezh'e "the brigade killed a lot of enemy personnel and destroyed a large quantity of artillery and wagons, as well as 10 aircraft at an airfield."[7] However, of all the other tankers who gave statements about the raid, he was the only one to mention "a large quantity of artillery", and no one else said anything about German supply wagons or "10 German aircraft", even though they were likely tempted to claim more damage to the accursed foe in their summary accounts.

The commander of the 89th Tank Battalion Senior Lieutenant Zaporozhets, who in distinction from Golovin wasn't burdened by political tasks, spoke much more cautiously in his account. He reported only that there was a German airfield in the area of Skliaevo-4, but didn't write a word about any German aircraft destroyed there.

One can hardly doubt that if enemy aircraft actually had been destroyed there, then all of the returning participants would have trumpeted this clearly victorious episode of the raid. Was it

6 Ibid., l. 6. Also see TsAMO, F. 148 tp, op. 1, d. 3, l. 35.
7 Ibid.

an ordinary matter – to burst onto a German airfield and at a stroke destroy 10 aircraft there?! Golovin all on his own couldn't have done this … but I repeat, he was the only one to claim this triumphant episode. Captured German documents also do not confirm Golovin's statement.

Of all the tankers of the 148th Tank Brigade who were killed or went missing on this raid, only Captain Pendak was honored decades later with a monument. However, this was the result of the efforts of the fallen man's relatives, and not that of government officials. According to the head of the administration in Bol'shaia Vereika A.M. Russky, in the 1960s Captain Pendak's brother, who at that time was occupying a high post in the army, came to visit the village. He persuaded the village government to erect a monument to his brother, and said that he would cover the cost of the monument and its transportation. With the Soviet Army's benevolence of that time, the important military chief promised the villagers that he would donate the truck that would deliver the monument to the local school, and a motorcycle to boot. After some time passed a letter actually did arrive in Bol'shaia Vereika informing them that the monument was ready. Village representatives travelled by train to the far western boundary of the Soviet Union and soon returned with a truck carrying the monument and motorcycle. The monument was then ceremoniously erected in the center of the village, while the truck and motorcycle served the village school for many years. Unfortunately, today no one knows the name, address or fate of this important village serviceman. However, they still tend the monument and care for it.

This monument stone with a portrait of General Liziukov's adjutant stands in Bol'shaia Vereika. But just as in the case with the monument to General Liziukov, which was recently erected in Voronezh, the monument to the general's adjutant is purely symbolic. Alas, the fate of the fallen general and his adjutant, who were one time linked by war, is today linked by another sorrowful circumstance: there remains are not buried beneath the established monuments, and the location of their graves is still unknown.

* * *

On the evening of 22 July 1942, the 148th Tank Brigade's 89th Tank Battalion, the only one of the 2nd Tank Corps' elements to break through to Medvezh'e, perished in its final battle on Hill 187.9. The night raid, which was supposed to crush the enemy's defenses and lead Briansk Front's operational group to the Don River, ended in failure and as a tragedy for the 148th Tank Brigade. However, neither the headquarters of the 148th Tank Brigade which remained in Malaia Vereika, nor the commander and commissar of the 2nd Tank Corps, who were impatiently waiting for messages, were even yet aware of this. To them, the 148th Tank Brigade was still pursuing its successful fulfillment of its combat task in a continuing raid through the enemy rear …

7

The fighting on the evening of 22 July 1942

It is extremely difficult to follow the course of combat operations on the evening of 22 July. Here, the matter is not so much that the available sources are insufficiently informative as it is that they contradict each other. Several of our units took part in the battle simultaneously, and in their documents the course and outcome of the combat actions are described differently. Nevertheless, comparing and analyzing the available sources, we'll try to clarify that which conforms to reality in the cited reports and summaries, and that which does not, and critically evaluating the subjective assessments and conclusions, we'll attempt to approach the truth.

We'll begin with the 1st Tank Corps' documents. In its official account of the conducted operation, the corps command wrote the following about the fighting on 22 July: "In savage fighting against the enemy's artillery, infantry and anti-tank means, the 1st Guards Tank Brigade and 49th Tank Brigade by the end of 22 July reached the southern fringe of woods labeled 'Mel' [on the map] and the southern slopes of Hill 188.5, having encircled a group of enemy submachine gunners [sic] in the woods southeast of Lebiazh'e. In hand-to-hand fighting, the enemy was completely destroyed by the motorized rifle battalion, supported by tank fire ...."[1]

Alas, the truth here is tightly intertwined with the false. Units of the 1st Guards Tank Brigade were in fact engaged in combat, and it is fully possible that they reached the line indicated in the account (although in the documents of the 49th Tank Brigade, the day of 22 July is reflected in a complete contradictory fashion: the operational summary mentions combat actions and losses on 22 July, but according to the 49th Tank Brigade's own account and combat diary, the brigade's units were not involved in combat on 22 July[2]), but the bold declaration regarding the complete destruction of the foe in the woods southeast of Lebiazh'e doesn't correspond with reality. Elements of the German 387th Infantry Division's 542nd Infantry Regiment were neither destroyed nor driven out of the woods, but continued to defend them stubbornly, which follows not only from German documents, but also numerous Soviet documents, where one comes across constant references to the heavy enemy fire coming from this patch of woods.

Thus, the command of the 1st Tank Corps here plainly exaggerated the accomplishments of its units. In addition, when describing the combat operations in the manner typical back then for many units, the headquarters of the 1st Tank Corps claimed all the honors and made no reference to what its neighbors fighting beside it did, recalling them only when it was necessary to find someone to blame. From the 1st Tank Corps' official account, it turns out that only the corps' tankers and motorized riflemen fought for the woods and destroyed the German "submachine gunners" in them. Meanwhile, units of the 167th Rifle Division were also taking part in this very same action, and its account, in turn, doesn't make the least mention of the 1st Tank Corps.

1 TsAMO, F. 1 TK, op. 1, d. 4, ll. 12-13.
2 TsAMO, F. 3163, op. 1, d. 9, l. 24; and d.11, l. 8.

But that isn't all: neither the 1st Tank Corps nor the 167th Rifle Division noted the 118th Tank Brigade, which fought side-by-side with them. We read in the 167th Rifle Division's account:

> By the end of the day the regiments of the first echelon reached the second phase line, having smashed the enemy's 542nd Infantry Regiment and its headquarters; the regiment commander [whose name isn't given – I.S.] was killed by a bayonet thrust. The regiments seized 19 guns, several bicycles, horses and saddles, and wiped out up to a battalion of infantry. Due to the lack of transport, the captured items could not be removed and in subsequent days the enemy regained possession of them.[3]

Here again, lies are tightly intertwined with the truth. In fact the 542nd Infantry Regiment was not smashed and was continuing to defend stubbornly, led by both its headquarters and its commander, who was not at all killed by a "bayonet thrust", but continued to direct the fighting.[4]

But let's continue with the 167th Rifle Division's account:

> The exploitation of the initial success began at 1600 22 July and by 2000 the 615th and 520th Rifle Regiments, operating in the first echelon, reached the southern fringe of the woods south of Lebiazh'e and crossed the ravine and small patch of woods southwest of Churikovo. In the course of the attack, in addition to enemy aviation the 615th and 520th Rifle Regiments were under heavy enemy machine-gun and mortar fire from the woods south of Lebiazh'e and the woods southwest of Churikovo, which pinned down the attacking units and inflicted heavy losses. Mopping up detachments from the 465th Infantry Regiment and units of the 193rd Rifle Division were assigned to destroy the enemy elements lurking in the woods.[5]

As we see, it wasn't the 1st Tank Corps' motorized riflemen alone who were engaged in combat with the enemy in the woods, but other units as well. As concerns the "enemy elements lurking in the woods", the authors of the division's account preferred not to note the fact that the assigned "mopping up detachments" in fact failed to destroy the enemy there, although this was known in the headquarters of the 167th Rifle Division. The engaged rifle units were even more aware of the enemy's presence there whenever they attempted to advance across the field, and each time were met by flanking fire from these woods.

How accurate are the assertions of the 167th Rifle Division headquarters about the concerted arrival of the two regiments and other elements at the southern fringe of the woods south of Lebiazh'e (which lay much farther to the south than Point 188.5) and their passage of the ravine and the small patch of woods? Let's turn to the documents of other of our units. In the sector of breakthrough between the patches of woods, brigades of the 2nd Tank Corps and the 118th Tank Brigade attacked in concert with the 167th Rifle Division. The headquarters of the 2nd Tank Corps reported on the evening of 22 July:

> The 26th Tank Brigade was checked by an intense crossfire of anti-tank artillery coming **from the woods west and southwest of Hill 188.5** [emphasis the author's] and by enemy bombers. The brigade is holding Hill 188.5 and taking losses. The 2nd Motorized Rifle Brigade is occupying the northern slopes of Hill 188.5 [which is to say that the corps' motorized riflemen were located behind and not in front of the tanks – I.S.]. The start of the attack [was] through

3 TsAMO, F. 202, op. 5, d. 334, l. 63.
4 NARA, T-314, roll 353, fr. 001263, 001266, 001268.
5 TsAMO, F. 202, op. 5, d. 334, l. 63.

> Bol'shaia Vereika with the task to destroy the enemy in the area of Vereiskie Vyselki and Kaver'ia. Subsequently, destroying the enemy, it was to make contact with the 148th Tank Brigade .... Comrade Liziukov, in order to secure the success of the 148th Tank Brigade and of the 2nd Tank Corps, [considers] the most rapid advance of the 1st Tank Corps to be necessary and progress [made by] the rifle divisions to be mandatory. In the opposite event the 2nd Tank Corps might come to a stop without the delivery of ammunition and fuel and lubricants in area of the brigades' actions.[6]

According to the combat report from the 2nd Tank Corps' headquarters, this means that the 167th Rifle Division's attack had made no forward progress by 18:00. We can find indirect proof of this in the combat journal of the 38th Army as well, where it is stated that the 2nd Tank Corps was operating **"in front of the 167th Rifle Division"** [emphasis the author's].

In general, in the documents of the various units it has been scrupulously noted how much effort they had exerted to achieve success, but from what has been cited above it is difficult to figure out just who then was guilty for the attack's failure. The commissar of the 118th Tank Brigade, which was attacking toward the very same Hill 188.5 together with the 167th Rifle Division, complained: "Incidents of the infantry's lagging behind the tanks are frequent. The tankers are required to countermarch in order to pull up the infantry. This is being reflected in many of the tankers' statements, which express indignation with the infantry and blame them for the failure."[7] In turn, the command of the 167th Rifle Division was dissatisfied with the tankers' actions: "The tanks were not supporting [us] energetically; a fear of being left without infantry was perceptible."[8]

Just try to determine who was right, and who was at fault! However, one thing is completely clear: The tankers and the infantry wanted to fight, but did so without any mutual cooperation and support.

In the operational summary of the 1st Tank Corps for 22 July, it was written that the 49th Tank Brigade "broke the enemy resistance in the area of Point 188.5" and by 2000 arrived with its main forces in the vicinity of a major road 1.5 kilometers south of Point 188.5, after which the tanks began to exploit in the western direction."[9] (According to the 49th Tank Brigade's own combat diary and account, the brigades reached the indicated area only by 0600 on 23 July.)[10] As we can see, the command of the 1st Tank Corps totally failed to note the presence of two tank brigades (the 26th and 118th Tank Brigades) and two regiments of the 167th Rifle Division on the very same battlefield, and presumptuously assigned the success only to one of its brigades (and to itself). Again it comes off that the infantry, which in the opinion of the 1st Tank Corps' command was unready for battle, made no advance, left the tanks without support, scattered at "the least fire opposition" and "lay low in the rye".[11]

The commander of the 1st Guards Tank Brigade Colonel Chukin, who saw first-hand the actions of the 193rd Rifle Division's infantry in Lebiazh'e, added that the command staff of the rifle units didn't lead their elements on the battlefield, as a result of which "upon taking Lebiazh'e, the men of the 193rd and partially of the 340th Rifle Divisions boiled potatoes in the residences."[12] (Well, most likely the soldiers were doing this not at all because they were living high off the hog. – I.S.)

6 TsAMO, F. 202, op. 5, d. 238, l. 508.
7 TsAMO, F. 118 tbr, op. 1, d. 47, l. 23.
8 TsAMO, F. 202, op. 5, d. 238, l. 508.
9 TsAMO, F. 1 TK, op. 1, d. 8, l. 15.
10 TsAMO, F. 3163, op. 1, d. 9, l. 24; d.11, l. 8.
11 TsAMO, F. 1 TK, op. 1, d. 4,ll. 12-13.
12 Arkhiv IRI RAN, F. 2, r. 1, op. 36, d. 13, l. 42.

In a different document Katukov is even more categorical about the infantry's actions: "The enemy is not so strong, while the infantry of the cited divisions [the 340th and 193rd Rifle Divisions – I.S.] behaves disgracefully and flees in panic."[13]

The commander of the 1st Guards Tank Brigade, Katukov's subordinate, also wrote about the shameful behavior of the infantry while enumerating the shortcomings in the shaping of the battle: "The command of the 193rd Rifle Division doesn't believe the reports from the brigade's command that the infantry isn't advancing south of Lebiazh'e and in places is retreating, while the rifle regiment commanders are lying to the division command that the advance is continuing."[14]

But how objective are the assessments of the 1st Tank Corps command regarding its own successes and the failures of others? How accurate are its conclusions regarding the effectiveness of its own forces' actions and the strength of their attacks against the enemy? Finally, how reliable is the information given in its operational summaries and reports? In its own account, the 1st Tank Corps command plainly sought to present its own actions in the best possible light and regularly accused its neighbors. Thus in order to obtain the possibility of looking at the discussed events from a different angle, it is worth reading a document written by an observer who was independent from the 1st Tank Corps headquarters.

The senior instructor of Briansk Front's Political Department Senior Battalion Commissar Nikishin reported to the chief of Briansk Front's Political Directorate about the results of his trips to the 1st Tank Corps:

> The headquarters of the 49th Tank Brigade and the 1st Motorized Rifle Brigade do not contemplate the shaping of a battle and do not organize genuine communications, for example: in the course of 22 July the 1st Motorized Rifle Brigade had no contact with its battalions; reports arrived late and as a rule, **did not reflect the units' true condition** [emphasis the author's], their losses or booty. The shoulder-to-shoulder contact with the neighbors was poor. Reconnaissance during the battle and after the battle is lacking, fails to ascertain the presence of enemy forces, and from this the fulfillment of an assignment bogs down …
>
> Information from the headquarters to the battalions isn't organized; the battalion headquarters failed to keep higher headquarters informed and do not carry out an order from the brigade command. Information from above proves unreliable … I personally had conversations with the commanders and military commissars of the 49th Tank Brigade and 1st Motorized Rifle Brigade regarding matters of dishonesty [here it is impossible not to recall the enemy that was "completely destroyed" in the woods and the German defense that was "broken" by the 49th Tank Brigade – I.S.]; the corps' chief of staff Major General Kravchenko has been given directives.
>
> **An incorrect opinion has formed in some of the leadership of the command staff that the tankers fight best of all … while the other units are no good at all, and everyone needs to be shot. Such an opinion was expressed by the chief of staff of the corps, Major General Kravchenko. This attitude is passed along to the subordinates, which affected the communications and cooperation with the rifle units. I pointed out these shortcomings to Kravchenko, who claimed that "a lot is being written in the newspapers about**

13 TsAMO, F. 202, op. 5, d. 238, l. 463.
14 Arkhiv IRI RAN, F. 2, r. 1, op. 36, d. 13, L. 42.

us" and that "we in fact fight better than all the others",[15] **and that the commander of the 340th Rifle Division "must absolutely be shot"** [emphasis the author's].[16]

Thus from the report cited above it is apparent that far from all that was written in the documents of the 1st Tank Corps should be trusted. At the very least, one must compare what was written in them to other sources. This particularly concerns information about the enemy, which the command of the above named Soviet units lacked almost entirely. Therefore, in order to obtain an objective picture of the events we are examining, it is important to "take a glance" at what was happening from the opposite side of the frontline, which can be done using German documents. We'll try to take a look at the general course of the battle on the evening of 22 July 1942 on the basis of an entire array of sources available in our possession.

Unfortunately, the precise time when our units launched their attack is unknown; most likely, it started at various times, because judging from the documents, there was no joint, simultaneous attack by the 167th Rifle Division and the all of the tank brigades operating in this area. The sole mention of the start of the attack by one of our units is in the operational summary of Briansk Front's Group Chibisov, where it is stated that the 26th Tank Brigade "… at 1800 together with the 27th Tank Brigade at the order of the army commander [Which army commander? Liziukov? He was no longer an army commander. Chibisov? He wasn't an army commander either… I.S.] broke through the enemy's defensive front and by 2000 reached the southern slopes of Hill 188.5, and is continuing to pursue the enemy."[17] However, according to the documents of the 27th Tank Brigade, on the evening of 22 July it was located in the reserve of the 2nd Tank Corps in Bol'shaia Vereika and took no part in the fighting.

In addition to the tank brigades, the 167th Rifle Division was also advancing in this sector. However, the division's attack was not so much an advance as a trial by bombings and artillery barrages. Just as the infantry rose to attack, the enemy concentrated artillery, mortar, machine-gun and rifle fire on them, striving to separate them from the tanks. The rifle companies suffered losses and their men became pinned down again. The tanks continued forward, before conducting a countermarch to rally the infantry and get them moving again, but had no real success in doing so. Meanwhile the attack in one area simultaneously by several units, having no knowledge of the situation or precise knowledge of the enemy's positions or those of friendly units, and no communications or cooperation, hindered the brigades' attack and played right into the enemy's hands.

The snafu led to hard consequences. Moving out of the jumping-off area (probably after returning in order to top up their tanks), the 26th Tank Brigade deployed into a combat formation on Hill 188.5 and began to advance to the south. As they approached the "enemy's positions", the tank crews opened up intensive fire from their cannons and machine guns at the infantry occupying them, unaware that this infantry belonged to the 167th Rifle Division. Seeing what was happening, the commander of the forward 615th Rifle Regiment attempted to stop the tankers, but was killed by them on the spot. It isn't difficult to guess what the infantrymen were experiencing and what sort of words they were uttering at the address of the tankers, as all this was happening in front of their eyes.

15 The assessment given by the Briansk Front command on 22 July of the 1st Tank Corps' actions, alas, was far from complimentary. On this day, the following radio message arrived from the Front commander at the headquarters of the 1st Tank Corps: "The actions of the corps are not worthy of the title "tankers". The corps is criminally spinning its wheels in place. I am ordering to break the resistance of the enemy infantry with a decisive blow by all the corps' forces and to contribute to a forward advance. Report on the execution. Rokossovsky" (TsAMO, F. 19 mbr, op.1 d. 6, l. 146).

16 TsAMO, F. 202, op. 36, d. 132, l. 51.

17 TsAMO, F. 202, op. 5, d. 251, l. 6.

Furious at what had happened, the command of the 167th Rifle Division wrote:

> Cooperation on the scale of the group wasn't organized. Units and formations were operating in one and the same sector, didn't know the orders of their neighbors (the tank corps) or the task of the units that were operating in front, which made a mess of things and caused confusion in the troops' combat actions, as a result of which the 26th Tank Brigade when approaching the combat formations of the 167th Rifle Division began to riddle them with fire. The commander of the 615th Rifle Regiment Major Simonov was killed by a shot from a KV tank. Information on the part of higher headquarters about the actions of their own units wasn't distributed[18]

How much the rank and file infantrymen suffered from the fire of the 26th Tank Brigade (and possibly of other of our tank brigades) can be only guessed; they weren't mentioned in the division's account.

The density of the enemy fire grew in step with the advance to the south and the constriction of the enormous field between the patches of woods. The Germans could support their elements defending atop Hill 188.5 with flanking fire from the fringes of the woods. From the east, the infantry of the 167th Rifle Division was also struck by fire coming from the woods south of Churikovo, which Group Chibisov had failed to take. Under such fire, the units of the 167th Rifle Division could make no further advance together with the tanks and became pinned down in the narrowing neck of open ground between the patches of woods. It is obvious that only its forward elements were able to reach the southern fringe of the woods (if they were able even to achieve this!). At the same time, the tanks managed to penetrate through the narrow neck of open ground between the woods and break out onto the plain to the south. According to the documents of the 118th Tank Brigade, the brigade's units by 2100 on 22 July reached Hill 195.8 and then "arrived at the assembly point south of the patch of woods on the right, which is 2 kilometers north of 195.8."[19] However, the brigade's tank battalions were unable to consolidate on the achieved lines without the support of infantry, and by nightfall the tanks began to turn back in order to top up their fuel tanks and replenish their ammunition. The 26th Tank Brigade together with a composite battalion of the 2nd Motorized Rifle Brigade made an attempt to attack toward Kaver'ia, but by nightfall also returned to its jumping-off positions in the area on the southern outskirts of Malaia Vereika.[20]

With the onset of darkness and the withdrawal of our tanks that had broken through, the elements of the 167th Rifle Division also began to pull out of the narrow neck of fields that was being swept by German fire toward Hill 188.5, where the flanking fire was less intense. Not knowing the situation on the battlefield, nor the position of its neighbors and especially the plans of the Germans that were lurking in the woods, our infantrymen, isolated and semi-encircled by the Germans, plainly felt uncomfortable in the narrow neck of open ground, especially because German troops were filtering through the rye into the rear of our thinned elements and opening up desultory fire there.[21] A position on a broad section of the fields, closer to the main bulk of friendly forces, where it was possible to count upon the support of their own tanks and artillery, seemed less dangerous. One way or another, the forward elements of the 167th Rifle Division by

18 TsAMO, F. 202, op. 5, d. 238, ll. 508-509.
19 TsAMO, F. 118 tbr, op. 1, d. 47, l. 1, ll. 22-23.
20 TsAMO, F. 8 gv TK, op. 1, d. 224(b), l. 151.
21 TsAMO, F. 202, op. 5, d. 334, l. 65.

the morning wound up north of the area of the prior evening's penetration and were digging in on the slopes of Hill 188.5.

German documents acknowledge that on 22 July, Russian tanks managed to break through the positions of the 387th Infantry Division. However, further they insist on a very important fact for our entire understanding of the course of the battle: the attacks of our rifle units were repulsed.[22] That is to say, the tanks broke through without the infantry, and correspondingly there was nothing with which to exploit the breakthrough and to dig in on the lines attained. The situation map of the VII Army Corps headquarters at the end of 22 July 1942 also confirms this. It is possible that the frontlines on the map as drawn by the staff officers shouldn't have been marked as continuous and thick, but with a broken, dotted line, because the positions of the 387th Infantry Division on Hill 188.5 had been partially breached, and some of the German defenders had pulled back closer to the patches of woods, toward where from all available evidence the German elements were being drawn, worn out by the fighting and weakened by the losses.

The neatly marked lines on Hill 188.5 (with the traditional understood lines of opposite trenches) on the night of 22-23 July probably did not exist. But from the documents it unambiguously and completely follows that the enemy was still occupying the woods west of Hill 188.5.

Over the day of fighting the 387th Infantry Division lost 60 men killed and 181 men wounded or missing-in-action. The losses of the 340th Infantry Division amounted to 91 men (22 killed and 69 wounded or missing-in-action).[23]

It is difficult to determine the total losses of our units on this day, since the casualty lists of many of them are missing. It is known that on this day, the units lost in killed alone: 26th Tank Brigade – 24; 148th Tank Brigade (only for the two tank battalions) – 38; 49th Tank Brigade – 6; 118th Tank Brigade – 2; the 1st Guards Tank Brigade – 5; and the 167th Rifle Division – 68 men (according to the Consolidated Database of the Memorial Foundation, which is working to identify and count all the Soviet dead from the Second World War), for a total of 143. According to the 38th Army's journal of combat operations, the losses of the 167th Rifle Division over the two days of 21 and 22 July amounted to 271 killed and 960 wounded in the 615th Rifle Regiment; 150 killed and 600 wounded in the 520th Rifle Regiment; and 50 killed and 145 wounded in the 465th Rifle Regiment, which was operating in the second echelon, lost as a result of German bombings. This totals to 471 men killed and 1,705 men wounded.[24] I have no precise data for the 27th Tank Brigade, 104th Separate Rifle Brigade, separate artillery regiments of Operational Group Chibisov, the 89th Tank Brigade, or the 284th, 340th and 193rd Rifle Divisions.

The German 387th Infantry Division on the day of 22 July was defending with its final remaining strength, and the division command was constantly asking VII Army Corps for help. It is worth citing excerpts from the VII Army Corps' journal of combat operations and reports from the 387th Infantry Division here.

> Morning report of the 387th Infantry Division:
> 0615. The enemy attack, which started in the evening southwest of Bol'shaia Vereika, was repulsed. Under the cover of darkness between 30 and 40 tanks managed to penetrate into the depth of the defenses in a southwestern and partially in a southeastern direction [evidence of the 148th Tank Brigade's foray – I.S.]
>
> Even before dawn, a portion of the tanks turned back again to the north. Information in greater detail about the situation is still lacking. Probably the switch positions, which our

22 NARA, T-314, roll 353, fr. 001081-1082.
23 NARA, T-314, roll 354, fr. 000726-727.
24 TsAMO, F. 202, op. 5, d. 258, ll. 1-2.

units occupied yesterday afternoon, are still fully in our possession, despite the breakthrough of the enemy tanks.

The 417th Infantry Regiment and the 559th Panzerjäger Battalion have been sent on a march in the direction of Zemliansk with the aim of setting up a blocking position on the northern outskirts of Terny. The defensive capability of the given position is very low, since the 417th Infantry Regiment after the heaviest fighting in the [Voronezh] bridgehead still hasn't received replacements.

Daily report, 1630:
The enemy attack in the strength of 41 tanks, which began early in the morning along the Bol'shaia Vereika – Somovo road, has been repulsed. A subsequent attack in the strength of two battalions from Lebiazh'e to the south was stopped at 1130. At the present moment the enemy is conducting a fresh attack out of Lebiazh'e to the south, about which detailed information is still lacking.

The forward line of defense has been pulled back to the main line of resistance in the right-hand sector as well. The enemy tanks that broke through in the night have partially been destroyed, and partially retreated to the north. 7 enemy tanks are still located west of Kaver'ia – Sivertsevo [remnants of the 148th Tank Brigade's 89th Tank Battalion – I.S.]. Today a total of 29 hostile tanks have been knocked out. The weather: Sweltering; a thunderstorm is imminent.

Evening report, 2140:
At the given moment, the enemy attack that began in the afternoon south of Bol'shaia Vereika and Lebiazh'e has been repulsed. The enemy is attacking with major infantry forces (in one company's sector, up to 400 or 500 attacking Russians) and tanks, with the support of artillery and mortars. Several enemy tanks managed to break through the infantry's positions and reach the Bol'shaia Vereika – Somovo road. A gap has been formed between Churikovo and the Bol'shaia Vereika – Somovo road.

On the whole our units are continuing to hold the previous line of defense. In the course of the day, so far up to 35 tanks have been knocked out. The tanks in the area west of Kaver'ia and Sivertsevo, which were mentioned in the previous report, have been destroyed. The division's final reserves have been committed to battle. On the line Terny – Zemliansk, a blocking position has been prepared by units of the 168th Infantry Division.

Weather: Because of a heavy downpour, the roads in places are impassable.

At 1040 the commander of the German Second Army General von Salmuth arrived at the command post of the VII Army Corps. The corps command briefed him on the situation, stressing the absence of reserves in order to repel the Russians' continuing attacks. The situation was becoming serious. The army commander was informed of the deep penetration toward Medvezh'e by a portion of the Russian tanks, true, without any accompanying infantry, which significantly eased the struggle with them. Groups of infantry and the I and IV Battalions of the 387th Infantry Division's artillery regiment had been assigned to block the 148th Tank Brigade's tanks; the latter in their firing positions near Kaver'ia not only had to repulse the attack of our units from the northwest, but also had to pivot in order to fire at the tanks that had broken through to the south. Then the III Battalion of this artillery regiment was removed from its firing positions near Skliaevo-5 and transported to the area of Hill 187.9. It was the crews of this artillery battalion that positioned their guns around the parked tanks of the 89th Tank Battalion and knocked out and set ablaze its final tanks.

Obviously, the following report is also connected with the 148th Tank Brigade's actions during the nighttime raid:

> On the night of 21-22 July enemy tanks attacked and reached the Langsdorf Woods [the patch of woods southeast of Lebiazh'e, which on the German side took on the surname of the commander of one of the 387th Infantry Division's infantry regiments], from where they split up and attacked in three directions: toward Somovo, toward Bol'shaia Treshchevka and along the high road. [Such was the name given to the track running along the hills to Medvezh'e. Puzzled by such actions, it plainly never occurred to the Germans that the tanks in reality hadn't split up, but had lost their bearings – I.S.] The firing positions situated on the northeastern outskirts of Bol'shaia Treshchevka were overrun by the enemy. Guns of the 7th Battery of the 387th Artillery Regiment were destroyed. Because almost all of the communication wires had been cut, the commander of the 387th Artillery Regiment issued an order for two reconnaissance groups headed by officers to clarify the situation. The tanks had managed to split the 541st and 542nd Infantry Regiments along the high road.

This report confirms the 148th Tank Brigade's breakthrough in the direction of Medvezh'e, but it isn't at all clear who overran the German firing positions at Treshchevka. Judging from the chronology of events, it was tanks of the 148th Tank Brigade, but there is no mention in any of the brigade's documents of a battle at Treshchevka, not to mention about the guns that were destroyed there. Even Commissar Golovin, who subsequently told of heavy German losses, didn't say a word about a battle at Bol'shaia Treshchevka and the German guns destroyed there. Possibly, the report is talking about attacks by the tank brigades of the 1st Tank Corps.

Further there follows an explanation that is important for understanding the course of combat operations, which also confirms the withdrawal of the 167th Rifle Division from the southern slopes of Hill 188.5: "The further advance of the infantry, which was following behind the tanks, managed to be stopped, and it was effectively struck with fire during its retreat."

Summing up the result of the combat operations on 22 July, the headquarters of the VII Army Corps' artillery wrote:

> Throughout the day, the enemy incessantly attacked out of Bol'shaia Vereika. I Battalion of the 108th Artillery Regiment destroyed 2 tanks and managed to take one as a trophy. The artillery is providing support for the infantry's actions, despite the large shortage of ammunition. The ammunition still available is brought to the front with the help of all of the regiment's available trucks and two trucks that belong to the division. Given a sufficient amount of ammunition, the artillery might have supported the infantry to an even greater extent and put a fuller stop to the enemy offensive.
>
> The artillery batteries are receiving the order to remain in their firing positions in order to serve as a bulwark for the retreating infantry. During the fighting with alternating success, the artillery batteries remained in their positions, even though in some places they were left abandoned by the retreating infantry. The commander of the 541st Infantry Regiment Colonel Langsdorf headed to the positions of the 387th Artillery Regiment's 8th Battery, and together with it continued to hold the line of defense. [Here the multiple scenes described in our literature come to mind, in which a commander with a pistol in his hand stops the fleeing men and organizes resistance to the foe, inspiring the shaken soldiers by his personal example. As we see, something similar happened on the German side – I.S.]
>
> The defensive fighting demonstrated the enormous value of artillery and its significance as a brotherly type of force for the infantry. The explicit order to remain in their positions,

> despite the fact that the enemy was already nearing them, gave the infantry the necessary buttress and served to prevent a Russian breakthrough.[25]

The high activity of the Luftwaffe again told on the outcome of the battle, which the enemy command noted with satisfaction: "Despite the bad weather, the Luftwaffe was effectively included in the battle."[26]

In his turn, Group Chibisov's chief of staff Colonel Pilipenko stated: "The savage, mass unobstructed bombings by German aircraft of the combat formations of our units is having a harmful effect on the infantry's morale and undermining its steadiness on the defense."[27]

In the documents of the 2nd Air Army, the combat operations of our aircraft in the area of operations are noted only on the evening of 22 July: Six Yak-1 fighters of the 221st Fighter Aviation Division at 1910 over the area of Somovo engaged nine JU-88 and, as described in the document "foiled the bombing of our forces and in aerial combat shot down 2 Ju-88, which fell in the Bol'shaia Treshchevka, Somovo, Malaia Treshchevka area. There were no losses."[28]

Next we read:

> 23 Il-2 of the 227th Ground Attack Aviation Division together with fighters of the 205th Fighter Aviation Division flew 45 individual sorties to the areas of Lomovo, Spasskoe, Gubarevo, Endovishche and Semiluki.[29]

Judging from the cited material, the 1st and 2nd Tank Corps received none of this air support. The 244th Bomber Aviation Division, which was based in Michurinsk, flew no combat missions because of poor meteorological conditions.

The final mentions of the activity of our air force in this area relates to the period of time between 1930 and 2015, when 12 Aerocobras "were covering the attacking tank groups in the Somovo – Mevezh'e area."[30] By this time, we no longer had any intact tanks in the Medvezh'e area. However, unaware of this, the pilots reported actions by our tanks units in this area. Obviously, it was on the basis of these arriving reports that the future chief of staff of the 38th Army (into which Group Chibisov was later converted at an order from the Briansk Front), Group Chibisov's chief of staff Colonel Pilipenko, even on the next day reported that "the 2nd Tank Corps at 0700 on 23 July according to information from an air force spokesman was located in the area of the Russko-Gvozdevskie heights and the northeastern outskirts of Medvezh'e."[31] The last report on 22 July that contains a reference to Soviet air support states, "In the Zemliansk area a group of Aerocobras engaged 6 Ju-88 covered by 6 Me-109 in aerial combat; 1 Me-109 was shot down and fell within friendly lines. The group of bombers was scattered …"[32] Thus in the daytime aircraft of the 2nd Air Army essentially did not appear above the battlefield, which again left our ground units without any air support.

In the evening on the basis of the reports from subordinate divisions, the command of the German VII Corps began to sum up the preliminary results of the combat actions on 22 July.

25 NARA, T-314, roll 342, fr. 001081-1082.
26 NARA, T-314, roll 353, fr. 000401.
27 TsAMO, F. 202, op. 5, d. 258, l. 8.
28 TsAMO, F. 2 VA, op. 4196, d. 14, ll. 89-90.
29 Ibid.
30 Ibid.
31 TsAMO, F. 202, op. 5, d. 251, l. 8.
32 TsAMO, F. 2 VA, op. 4196, d. 14, ll. 87-89.

From the 340th Infantry Division they were reporting that "the enemy attacks, conducted in little strength, were driven back."[33] However, the situation in the 387th Infantry Division's sector didn't generate the corps command's optimism:

> At 2145 the commander of the 387th Infantry Division reported to the corps commander that the division's situation was extremely serious. The infantry is badly worn out and the artillery has fired off the majority of its shells. Because of the heavy downpours from thunderstorms, little ammunition has been brought up.[34]

As we see, not only the infantry divisions of Group Chibisov were experiencing a crisis with artillery shells. Only a heavy rain had to pass through an area, and all the supply trucks of the German divisions would become immobilized in the mud.

Alarmed by the situation, the commander of the VII Army Corps decided to attach the 221st Pionier [Engineer] Battalion and the only reserve battalion of the neighboring 340th Infantry Division to the 387th Infantry Division. In addition, he passed operational control of the entire 559th Panzerjäger Battalion to the 387th Infantry Division (and not just one company, as had been the case the evening before).

Fifteen minutes after receiving the report from the commander of the 387th Infantry Division, the commander of the VII Army Corps reported to the commander of the Second Army General von Salmuth about the serious situation facing the 387th Infantry Division and again requested the 9th Panzer Division's support. In addition, General Hell reported that according to the statements of Russians who had come into German lines, a possible Russian offensive on the Don River should be expected in the area of Novozhivotinnoe. At 2230, as was written in the document, "the commander of the 9th Panzer Division was brought up to speed regarding the situation that had developed."[35]

At 2300 General von Salmuth called General Hell and informed him that the 9th Panzer Division was being made subordinate to the corps and that 23 July was marked as the day when it would go on the attack. Regarding the division's combat task, he was examining two possible options:

1. In the event that the Russians broke through, an attack from the south.
2. If instead the 387th Infantry Division could hold its line until the arrival of the 9th Panzer Division, the latter would attack out of the 340th Infantry Division's sector with the aim of eliminating the enemy penetration by an enveloping attack from the north.

If the 385th Infantry Division arrived by that time, then it would also become subordinate to the VII Corps and attack from the south. The 168th Infantry Division if possible would not shift to the north, but remain facing the east, so that in the event of the Russian offensive across the Don, some German units would still be present in this sector. After this, the corps commander brought the commander of the 387th Infantry Division up to speed on the situation and obligated him to report continuously on changes in the situation, since the actions of the 9th Panzer Division depended on whether or not the 387th Infantry Division could hold its line.[36]

33 NARA, T-314, roll 353, fr. 000402.
34 Ibid.
35 Ibid.
36 Ibid.

At 2330 the commander of the 9th Panzer Division received an order to shift his division quickly to the Zemliansk area. The II Battalion of the 102nd Artillery Regiment, which was supporting the German units within the Voronezh bridgehead with fire from the western bank of the Don River, was returned to the 9th Panzer Division. In place of the division's III/102nd Artillery Regiment, it was given the II/71st Artillery Regiment from its direct subordination to Second Army headquarters. In order to centralize the leadership over all of the available artillery, the commander of VII Army Corps' artillery returned from the Voronezh bridgehead to corps headquarters. The commander of the Second Army's reserve division (the 385th Infantry Division) received an order to move to the Novoseliabnoe – Dolgoe – Livenka – Poganets area by 23 July.

As we see, the enemy command both at the corps and army level began hastily to reinforce the threatened sector by shifting available reserves and units pulled out of quiet sectors of the front to the breakthrough sector. But what was the Soviet command doing? Lieutenant General Chibisov together with a small group of officers was directing the operation from his command post in Lukino. However, his full headquarters was still back in Slepukha. There, however, in addition to their leadership over the combat operations, the staff officers were busy with completely different matters. The point is that simultaneously with the start of the operation, a reorganization process began in Briansk Front's operational group. The operational group was being transformed first into the 4th Army, and then the 38th Army. On 20 July, on the eve of the operation's launching, the 38th Army headquarters, which had been previously disbanded on the Southwestern Front, arrived in Elets Station. On 21 July (that is to say, after the start of the fighting!), the headquarters of the arriving army began to take control over the formations "out of the hands of Lieutenant General Chibisov's operational group."[37]

At the commander's order, the field command of the army headquarters moved to Slephuka, where it began to organize a command post in the place of the disbanded 5th Tank Army headquarters. Thus, the newly-arrived headquarters (which is to say, the brains of the army!) had to enter into the course of the operation without any familiarization with the totally new theater of combat operations or with the forces that were to come under its command, at a time when combat operations were already moving at full speed. The chief of staff also changed. Leadership of the headquarters passed from the hands of Colonel Kalganov to the hands of Colonel Pilipenko.

The latter subsequently remarked: "One of the reasons for the failure was the fact that the headquarters of the divisions had never worked with the headquarters of the army, which had arrived at a time when events were already running at a feverish pace, which had not been part of the operation's elaboration, which had not taken part in organizing cooperation, and was inadequately provided with command resources and means."[38] Thus, the 38th Army headquarters became not a command organ, but a transmission link between the commander of the operational group and Briansk Front headquarters. In this sense, literally according to the bitter irony of fate, the history with the former 5th Tank Army's operation was being repeated.

By the evening of 22 July, when it became increasingly obvious that the attacks of the second day of the offensive had failed, Chibisov, who prior to this had been hounding Liziukov's tank brigades over the latter's head, ordered that he be summoned to his command post. This order caught the 2nd Tank Corps commander in Bol'shaia Vereika, where he issued his final instructions before setting off. The commander of the 27th Tank Brigade Captain Luchnikov states that Liziukov received the summons to the command post of the operational group at 2100.[39] As the crow flies, it was just a bit more than 12 kilometers from Bol'shaia Vereika to Lukino,

37 TsAMO, F. 1657, op. 9005, d. 39, l. 9.
38 TsAMO, F. 202, op. 5, d. 258, l. 10.
39 TsAMO, F. 202, op. 50, d. 1, l. 305.

where Chibisov's command post was located, and approximately 18 kilometers along a back road. Having set out to the command post, Liziukov and Assorov arrived at Chibisov's command post only by around 2200 (obviously because of the muddy roads after the rains). They returned to Bol'shaia Vereika only at 0700 the next morning.[40] Accordingly, they spent all night and the early morning at Chibisov's command post, which is to say, around 8 hours.

What did they talk about there? What did they discuss with Chibisov? What was this conversation, the final one in their lives, with their superior like? Alas, we don't know the precise answers to these questions. The meeting's contents aren't reflected in the documents, and those individuals who took part in it or were present at it didn't leave behind memoirs. However, knowing the incendiary situation of those days, the wording of Chibisov's orders to Liziukov, and the past sad experience of their relationship, one can assume with a great deal of confidence that against the backdrop of the offensive's failure to this point, this conversation, to put it gently, was not pleasant.

However, setting aside the personal aspects of the meeting that took place, as well as the possible (or probable) accusations on the part of the operational group's commander and the excuses of the 2nd Tank Corps' commander, we'll attempt to reproduce logically the contents of the discussion and the information that might lay at the basis of decisions taken that night regarding the 2nd Tank Corps' further actions.

Liziukov by nightfall already knew that some of the tankers of the 148th Tank Brigade had returned from the German rear without their tanks. In particular, the 148th Tank Brigade's chief of staff Major Mikhalev had returned with his crew. From his tale, the death of the brigade commander Lieutenant Colonel Mikhailin and many other tankers became known, as well as the fact that the tanks of the 260th Tank Battalion that had set off for the Kaver'ia area had been destroyed back in the early morning hours of 22 July. However, the crew members that had come back could say nothing about the fate of the 89th Tank Battalion, which had slipped past the battle involving the 260th Tank Battalion and had penetrated further in the direction of Medvezh'e.

Undoubtedly, Liziukov reported to Chibisov what he knew from the stories of the returning tankers. On his part, early that morning (probably, he had received the first messages about this from the aviation units on the evening before) Chibisov had received important information about the possible location of the 89th Tank Battalion, which he made known to Liziukov. The "air force spokesman" (as he had been called in the document) reported to Chibisov that according to the reports from the air crews, our tanks had been spotted in the area of the Russko-Gvozdevskie heights and on the northwestern outskirts of Medvezh'e.[41] That meant that the 89th Tank Battalion had actually carried out its assignment and was located in the enemy rear. There was still no contact with it, but it was completely obvious that 24 hours after setting off on the raid, the tank battalion was in urgent need of assistance.

In addition, a deep penetration of the German defenses had to be exploited quickly, and by strengthening the 89th Tank Battalion that had broken through, develop its success into one of the entire 2nd Tank Corps, and perhaps of the entire operational group as well. The only thing left to do was to advance along the already "beaten" path. The brigades of the 2nd Tank Corps were to do this, and one result of the meeting was that now the corps commander and commissar would join the attacking tank brigades and personally direct the fighting.

The operational group of the army's headquarters knew by nighttime that the 104th Separate Rifle Brigade was digging in along the line it had achieved and was firmly covering the left flank of the advanced units on the line along the Bol'shaia Vereika River. On the right flank of the 2nd Tank Corps, the 1st Tank Corps' 49th Tank Brigade and 1st Motorized Rifle Brigade were engaged

40 TsAMO, F. 202, op. 1, d. 1, l. 304.
41 TsAMO, F. 202, op. 5, d. 251, l. 8.

in battle south of Lebiazh'e, and reportedly had pushed forward with tanks to the southern fringe of the woods west of Hill 188.5. In the center, two regiments of the 167th Rifle Division according to a report from the division's headquarters by 2200 had made a further advance than all the other units and had reached the southern fringe of this patch of woods, a ravine west of Kaver'ia, and a fork in the road 2 kilometers south of Hill 188.5.[42] From this report it was apparent that the bottleneck between the two patches of woods had already been passed, and the conditions for the introduction of the 2nd Tank Corps onto open, rolling terrain without any tank obstacles had been created.

Of course, Liziukov had definite justifications not to trust too much what he was hearing at the command post regarding the situation that had developed by that night. From the reports of his units he knew that his tank brigades and the 2nd Motorized Rifle Brigade, which were operating with the 167th Rifle Division, were meeting resistance and being subjected to heavy fire on that very same Hill 188.5, which, if the reports from the headquarters of the 167th Rifle Division were to be believed, had already been passed by its units. But it was difficult for him to try to prove that the information from the 167th Rifle Division headquarters was mistaken and didn't correspond to reality. Chibisov might again begin to suspect that he lacked sufficient resolve and was incapable of forcing his subordinates to carry out an order, and was more likely to believe the gallant reports of a division headquarters that was "spearheading" the offensive than the commander of the 2nd Tank Corps whose tanks were "lagging behind the infantry" and who already had a tarnished reputation.

However, the fighting was continuing that night, and having been separated from their units by Chibisov, the commander and commissar of the 2nd Tank Corps were in a situation where they could judge the changes in the situation only according to the information from officers of the 38th Army's operational group. They, in turn, were receiving the information from subordinate units and hadn't had the time or the possibility to check it. Nevertheless, in the documents at the operational group's headquarters, the reports received from the units were already being treated as completely credible. One of the latest reports to arrive before Liziukov and Assorov left Lukino was a fresh report from the headquarters of the 167th Rifle Division, excerpts from which are presented a bit below. In order to draw a conclusion that there were no longer any natural obstacles with an organized enemy anti-tank defense left in the path of the 2nd Tank Corps, this second report, arguably, was decisive.

Later, having finally realized what the bravura reports were really worth regarding an advance and, supposedly, the forward lines that had been reached by the divisions, the chief of staff of the 38th Army (formerly of Chibisov's operational group) would write with indignation:

> Impermissible laxness, lack of discipline and the absence of a sense of responsibility in the headquarters of the divisions, perpetrated while the headquarters of the Front's operational group was in command of the troops, led to disregard of the demands of the army headquarters and **almost to absolute ignorance of the situation at the front, which prevented a correct, timely response to the course of the operation** [emphasis the author's].[43]

However, this occurred only later … while on that early morning the army headquarters, without verifying the report that had just come in, presented it to Liziukov at face value.

42 Ibid., l. 6.
43 TsAMO, F. 202, op. 5, d. 258, l. 10.

At 0600, the headquarters of the 167th Rifle Division reported that the two forward regiments of the division on the right flank had reached the southwestern fringe of the woods south of Hill 188.5 and were at a "fork in the road on a nameless hill 4 kilometers west of Kaver'ia"[44], while on the left flank they had seized the ravine and the patch of woods southwest of Churikovo and with forward units had reached a "watershed" on a hill to the southeast.[45] From this it seemed that the evening report had been fully confirmed and over the night the infantry of the 167th Rifle Division had not fallen back, but had pushed forward, and the path for the 2nd Tank Corps as far as the turnoff toward Medvezh'e had now been cleared.

With this "reliable" piece of information, Liziukov and Assorov headed back to Bol'shaia Vereika from Chibisov's command post, in order to get the 26th and 27th Tank Brigades moving as quickly as possible toward the 89th Tank Battalion that was "fighting at Medvezh'e". Not "fight their way through" nor break through an enemy defense, but as was written in the document, "to move out along the route"[46], as if talking about a simple forced march to a designated area.

None of them yet knew back then, that this "route" would soon become fatal for them …

44 TsAMO, F. 202, op. 5, d. 251, l. 8.
45 Ibid.
46 TsAMO, F. 202, op. 50, d. 1, l. 304.

8

The 2nd Tank Corps, 23 July 1942

On the morning of 23 July 1942, after the decision was made that Liziukov and Assorov would personally lead the corps on the attack from within a tank, the 2nd Tank Corps command turned out to be in three different places geographically, and in essence – in various hands. The corps commander and commissar were to direct the upcoming fighting of the 26th and 27th Tank Brigades to breakthrough to Medvezh'e, where, as they had been informed at the headquarters of Operational Group Chibisov, a far-advanced tank battalion of the 148th Tank Brigade was fighting (they didn't know that all of its tanks had already been destroyed). The 2nd Tank Corps' chief of staff Colonel Nagaibakov, while Liziukov and Assorov had been away at the meeting with Chibisov, had become the most senior commander in the corps and was executing overall leadership over it; he was located in Sedelki (at least at the moment when the morning operational summary had been generated).[1] However, the operational control over the corps' remaining units (after the destruction of the 148th Tank Brigade) was in the hands of the 2nd Tank Corps' chief of operations, Lieutenant Colonel Pupko at the command post in Surikovo. Nagaibakov expected that he would stay in contact with Liziukov through Pupko, once General Liziukov went on the attack.

However, the corps' observation post in Surikovo, which Liziukov had personally established in this village back on the eve of the offensive, on 20 July, had in fact become the 2nd Tank Corps' actual command post. On that day, he and Commissar Assorov, having taken along a small operational staff group, left the headquarters in order to be closer to the front, and set up an observation post on the northern outskirts of this abandoned small village in the steppe. Liziukov had brought along radiomen and a radio that was mounted in an American Bantam jeep (a visible result of the ever-expanding supplies via Lend-Lease in 1942). During the first two days of the operation, Pupko plainly didn't experience any large operational difficulties: in actual fact, the impulsive Liziukov was himself directing the battle; he had been restlessly driving around the different troops, appearing here and there, making decisions and issuing orders. It was left to the chief of operations to transmit these decisions and orders to the subordinates, while not carrying any personal responsibility for them. In addition, there was also still the headquarters back in Kreshchenka, where Nagaibakov remained with the rest of the staff to assist Liziukov, so Pupko's functions in directing the corps' fighting weren't the most important.

True, in the advanced observation post, the operational command group repeatedly had to experience bombings and artillery shelling which occurred in Surikovo much more often than at the forward headquarters in Kreshchenka, which was further from the front (or even Sedelki, where the chief of staff of the 2nd Tank Corps wound up on the morning of 23 July, which was even more remote from the front). The Luftwaffe was in particularly furiously bombing the area

1 TsAMO, F. 38 A, op. 9005, d. 35, l. 48.

of the bridges across the Bystrik Creek here, because of which, incidentally, German bombs hit almost the entire village, including its northern outskirts, where the observation post was situated. Nevertheless, thus far the operational command team somehow remained unscathed from all this, sheltering in slit trenches and root cellars. The jeep with the radio somehow also remained undamaged, even though there was almost not a single tall bush or tree around it, under which it could be safely hidden from the pitiless and predacious gazes of the brazen Nazi pilots. Once the forward units of Group Chibisov reached the Bol'shaia Vereika River and forced a crossing of it, the situation at the observation post became a little easier; the German bombings and artillery barrages shifted in order to follow the attacking troops to the south, and Surikovo wound up in nearly the second echelon ....

However, a new complication arose at the observation post on the morning of 23 July: Liziukov's decision to lead the tank brigades personally into a breakthrough toward Medvezh'e meant that there was no one left to direct the fighting of the 2nd Tank Corps' other units [chiefly the 2nd Motorized Rifle Brigade, 12th Reconnaissance Battalion and the corps' artillery] other than the chief of operations – Lieutenant Colonel Pupko. It would seem that this should be the task of the chief of staff Colonel Nagaibakov, who was both senior in post and in rank; however, the latter, judging from the available evidence, declared categorically and peremptorily that according to the received order, he was supposed to remain at the headquarters and "move it up only in the wake of the infantry's advance."[2] Thus it somehow happened that without even changing his location, Pupko suddenly wound up now not as the diligent executive officer with General Liziukov at the observation post, but as the senior commander at a corps' forward command post with all the consequences flowing from this – including the responsibility of making decisions. He plainly wasn't ready for this turn of events.

By the summer of 1942, the 2nd Tank Corps' 43-year-old chief of operations had been serving in the Red Army for 20 years, having started his service at the end of the Russian Civil War as a Red Army private in a signals battalion, and later as a copyist (a record clerk) in an army's logistics department. Later, after a two-year long-term leave of absence in civilian life, he again returned to the Red Army, this time intending to make it his career. His service regularly alternated with studies: first in the school of the All-Russia Central Executive Committee, then in a series of military-political courses, and lastly in the Stalin Military Academy of Mechanization and Motorization. At the beginning of 1937, the academy graduate returned to active service as the chief of staff of a tank brigade in Smolensk. Soon there began sweeping purges in the Red Army, in the course of which some Red Army commanders lost not only their posts, but also their lives, while others, as happened in the case of Pupko, quickly rose in both rank and postings, replacing those that had been weeded out. If it took him 16 years to rise from a Red Army private to senior lieutenant, he had a meteoric rise over 4 years through his next three ranks and became a lieutenant colonel, now serving in 1940 in the Directorate of Combat Training of the Armored Forces.

It was in this post that the war found him. For the entire first year of the war, Pupko as before served in the Directorate in a desk position and knew nothing of the battles underway from personal frontline experience, but indirectly, from others. In the process he knew much more, judging from everything, than he could have learned from official sources.

In April 1942, Lieutenant Colonel Pupko's long-standing service in the Directorate of Combat Training of the Armored Forces came to an end. The wholescale process of forming new tank corps needed masses of cadres, and Pupko was appointed as chief of the 2nd Tank Corps' Operations Department. However, throughout the spring and early summer of 1942, the 2nd Tank Corps was in the rear and took no part in the fighting. So Lieutenant Colonel Pupko also had no need to

2 TsAMO, F. 38 A, op. 11353, d. 14, l. 127.

direct an operations department in a combat situation. It was with this "combat experience" that he in fact met the combat actions that started on 10 July.

It seems that the first days of combat made a painful impression on the lieutenant colonel, who had long held office duties and who had never served at the front. Alas, personal observation was visibly confirming for him a lot of what he had learned about the course of the war previously through his service posts and connections, and the impressions of what he had witnessed, accumulating on what he had heard previously from others, became such a major irritant to him that he could no longer contain this thorn within himself, and he began to speak out when others would more sensibly hold their tongues. Obviously the incautious (and repeated) statements about that which was troubling him served as the reason why the 2nd Tank Corps' Special Department took him under secret monitoring soon after his arrival at the front. Using its favorite, simple and reliable tools – the network of informers spread throughout the Red Army – the diligent officers of the Special Department quickly learned of the views of the 2nd Tank Corps' chief of operations and the types of conversations he was leading within the circle of his service peers.

Very quickly the deputy chief of the Special Department had enough such information that he considered it necessary to inform the command about the information he had obtained. The report that he wrote to them is of great interest to us, since it is definite food for thought about Pupko's personality and gives us a better understanding of both his unembellished views regarding what was happening, which was not just a facade, and how the actions of the lieutenant colonel were assessed from the side. On 20 July 1942, right on the eve of the offensive, the deputy chief of 2nd Tank Corps' Special Department Senior Lieutenant of State Security Teterev reported to the chief of the 2nd Tank Corps' NKVD Special Department and the 2nd Tank Corps' commissar:

> According to materials in the NKVD Special Department of the 2nd Tank Corps Lieutenant Colonel Pupko is politically and morally unreliable. This is characterized by the following information. When speaking of the reasons for the defeat of our forces on the Kerch Peninsula, Pupko declared: "The Germans have been getting the better of us, because they have excellent generalship and we don't, since our generals don't know how to organize an adequate defense or offense; with us it is always: 'Someone shouted "Enough defending, we must learn how to attack!"' and because of this it turns out that our army doesn't know how to attack or defend." Later Pupko, continuing, announced in the conversation: "However the commanders are obviously building reserves well in the rear, but all this is wishy-washy, wishy-washy I say! What indeed might come from such an arrangement of the troops and reserves?! Nothing good! We have no defensive depth, but that doesn't really matter, since the point is you can't defy the enemy's power and equipment when you don't know how to attack or defend. Thus one can't rely on the forward units. It is necessary to form a defense and shock units here."
>
> Such a statement leads to the conclusion that Pupko doesn't believe in the power of the Red Army or in its equipment.
>
> On 11 July, brigade commander Lieutenant Markov was dismissed from command of the 2nd Motorized Rifle Brigade due to far-fetched information … and Lieutenant Colonel Pupko was made the brigade commander. As a result of a tank attack by the 148th Tank Brigade with the support of the 2nd Motorized Rifle Brigade, the enemy that was holding the opposite end of the bridge in Bol'shaia Vereika was dislodged and retreated. The outcome of the fighting on 11 July was on the side of the 2nd Motorized Rifle Brigade; the enemy began hastily to retreat, and accordingly it was necessary to pursue him doggedly and keep the enemy from digging in along a new line. However, Lieutenant Colonel Pupko decided not to pursue and stopped for the night; accordingly he showed cowardice and failed to carry out the assignment to the end. The NKVD Special Department of the 2nd Tank Corps believes

> that Lieutenant Colonel Pupko cannot serve any longer as the chief of the 2nd Tank Army's Operations Department and that it is necessary to dismiss him from the post and transfer him to a less responsible position.[3]

From the documents it isn't clear whether or not Assorov read this report, and even if he did read it, whether or not he had time to react to the arriving "signal". It is possible that on the eve of the offensive, and particularly once the fighting started, he didn't have the time or, more likely, the desire to summon the chief of the Operations Department and go into a lengthy, detailed discussion of Pupko's views and whether or not they reflected what was reported by the NKVD. It also isn't clear whether Liziukov himself learned of the "signal" against Pupko; he was fully absorbed with preparations for the offensive and with the first two days of fighting. One thing is inarguable: Lieutenant Colonel Pupko remained in his post on both 21 and 22 July. Nevertheless, I have no doubts that the chief of the NKVD Special Department, who wasn't burdened with operational or organizational matters, did read Teterev's report, since reading and taking measures in response to such "signals" was in fact an inseparable part of his duties. However, his authority was clearly insufficient to remove the untrustworthy Pupko from his post. This would require Liziukov's approval, and in the midst of an operation that wasn't starting well, General Liziukov plainly wasn't up to this.

One way or another, but for whatever reasons, on the morning of 23 July the chief of the 2nd Tank Corps' NKVD Special Department wasn't at corps headquarters, but was in fact at the command post in Surikovo together with Pupko, and I think that this wasn't a coincidence. The politically suspect Lieutenant Colonel had plainly prompted the *special* attention of the 2nd Tank Corps' Special Department. The chief of the 148th Tank Brigade's NKVD Special Department was also here, who possibly was reporting to his superior about the situation of affairs in the brigade and sharing his *special* thoughts on the subject of the offensive's failure and the death and disappearance of a significant number of its tankers.

The presence of the Special Department officers at the command post could hardly have given Pupko any confidence. More likely it was the opposite: under their gloomy gazes, the responsibility that had unexpectedly fallen on his shoulders became even more of a burden, if not to say a torment. As the senior commander at the forward command post, he was supposed to act, and to demonstrate activity …

The situation, alas, was complicated by the fact that Pupko, judging from the documents, didn't receive any concise instructions about organizing the combat of the units that remained under his command, and without these directives everything amounted to demonstrating his own initiative, which the chief of operations was experiencing plain difficulties in showing …

From the documents it is possible to draw the conclusion that prior to the fighting on 23 July, Liziukov and Assorov never dropped by the corps' forward command post in Surikovo. Having left Lukino, judging from the available evidence they traveled to the corps headquarters in Kreshchenka before heading on to Bol'shaia Vereika, from which point they were supposed to move out together with the attacking 26th and 27th Tank Brigades. Thus, on the third day of the battle, Pupko remained "alone" at the forward command post, without the usual orders from the command staff, but under the watchful gaze of the Special Department officers. Of course, most of all he needed contact with the commander, and he requested it from his radiomen. However, they were unable to make contact with Liziukov, despite the fact that the radio-equipped KV tank of the corps commander was just several kilometers from Surikovo.

3 TsAMO, F. 8 gv TK, op. 1, d. 224(b), l. 143.

Then there occurred an event that totally severed any possible communications between the forward command post and Liziukov, and almost cost Pupko his life. At 0930, at a time when radio communications with Liziukov's KV, which was moving out of Bol'shaia Vereika, became even more critical, the Luftwaffe struck the forward command post of the 2nd Tank Corps in Surikovo. It is difficult to say whether this was a deliberate strike or whether it was just a coincidence. It is possible that after two days of stay by the corps headquarters' operational team in Surikovo (the headquarters of the 118th Tank Brigade and the 167th Rifle Division's command post were also located here), the enemy aerial reconnaissance, observing the intense movement of vehicles, communication wires and a significant quantity of servicemen from rear elements, identified the likely location of a Russian command post in the village on the elevated, woodless bank of the Bystrik Creek, after which there followed a surprise attack against it by bombers, and then a second strike.

As a result, Pupko's sole radio was smashed (most likely, this happened to the vehicle as well), and a radioman was wounded. To boot, so were both chiefs of the Special Departments, and a T-60 tank that was located at the forward command post was hit and left burning. Pupko himself went unscathed, but after the second airstrike he decided not to test fate any further and opted to change his location urgently. Soon, the group of operational staff officers that he headed set out to a patch of woods several kilometers north of Surikovo: a little further from the front and a little closer to the corps headquarters. At 1000 the operations chief wrote his first and final report to the headquarters of Group Chibisov – a brief note with information about the bombing, the command post's change in location and the lack of contact with Liziukov, which he was "continuing to try to establish" ....[4]

The insufficient knowledge of the situation given all the responsibility that had suddenly fallen on him; the separation from friendly troops and from the headquarters; and the Luftwaffe's double attack on the command post plainly had such an effect on the chief of 2nd Tank Corps' Operations Department that he, clearly at a loss of what to do from all that was happening, asked the corps' chief of staff about what the operational command team should do next.[5]

Having received a query such as that one, Chief of Staff Nagaibakov and Headquarters' Commissar Moskalev traveled to the new command post in order to "lecture" Pupko. Having found him in a ravine overgrown by a copse of trees, without a radio and without any sort of communications other than runners, they decided to expand the new command post (later Nagaibakov wrote in his report that he "converted an observation post into a command post"[6]) and supplied Pupko with radios for communications up and down the chain of command. In order to do this, it was necessary to transfer signalmen and radios from the corps' headquarters location in Sedelki (approximately 10 kilometers north of the new command post) and/or from the former command post in Kreshchenka (also approximately 10 kilometers from the new command post, but now to the east). Moreover, obviously having decided after the conversation with the shaken Pupko that he needed command oversight and a "guiding hand", Nagaibakov and Moskalev decided to restage the entire old command post from Kreshchenka to the new command post in the copse of woods.

Partially this decision corresponded to an order from Liziukov himself, who had sent one of his signal officers "to the corps" the evening before. With this verbal order, Liziukov was instructing the staff officers to go to the 26th Tank Brigade's location in Malaia Vereika and "handle the

4 TsAMO, F. 38 A, op. 9005, d. 19, l. 40.
5 TsAMO, F. 38 A, op. 11353, d. 14, l. 127.
6 Ibid.

preparations for combat".[7] True, the remaining leadership of the 2nd Tank Corps didn't make it to Malaia Vereika; under the artillery barrages and bombings by the German aircraft that were swarming over the battlefield, the chiefs restricted themselves to just a cautious movement toward the front to the ravine near Surikovo. Anyway, the given order wasn't put down on paper, gave no precise schedule for carrying out the movement, and they hadn't heard it from the commander in person. In any event, they *began to carry out* the directive they'd received; however, in the meantime, in the present conditions, they'd been compelled to stop on their way to the front ...

The transfer got underway. They rolled up the signals antennae and communications wire in the place where they'd become settled in the village, and began unrolling them in the copse of trees in the ravine. Vehicles began rolling across fields and along country dirt tracks. Time passed. The copse of trees and ravine became filled with staff officers and those who surrounded them: communications troops and officers, security, intelligence agents and men of the headquarters company. The improvised headquarters and command post had to be fed, guarded, and provided with communications. At the new command post, arriving radios were switched on, and their operators began to seek contact with Liziukov, who had gone into battle. Alas, with no success ...

At 1330 Nagaibakov composed a combat dispatch to the headquarters of Group Chibisov. In it, he wrote confidently that "the 148th Tank Brigade is engaged in battle in the Sviridov area" (which is to say, on the northern approaches to Medvezh'e, where at that time there remained only the brigade's knocked out and burned out tanks, and the surviving crew members hiding in the grain fields), while three of its tanks were "in the area of a patch of woods 1 kilometer southwest of Kaver'ia" (these were more likely the destroyed tanks of the 260th Tank Battalion from the group of the now dead brigade commander Mikhailin). Further he wrote that the 26th Tank Brigade was breaking through to Hill 195.8 and had arrived again on the southern slopes of Hill 188.5, while the 27th Tank Brigade was fighting in the area of the southern slopes of Hill 188.5, and at 1150 (obviously a time given in a brigade report) "was making progress". He added that "Major General Liziukov is with the 27th Tank Brigade on the southeastern slopes of Hill 188.5."[8] True, he hadn't learned about this from the corps commander.

Most likely, a report from General Liziukov's signals officer Senior Lieutenant Vafin served as the basis for Nagaibakov's message. On that day, given Liziukov's failure to show up at the command post in Kreshchenka, where the 2nd Tank Corps commander had personally told Vafin he would return on 23 July, Vafin traveled to Bol'shaia Vereika "to find out about the general".[9] In this frontline village there were a lot of various elements and military servicemen, but nowhere did the signals officer find Liziukov and Assorov among them. Leaving behind his vehicle, he headed out on foot to look for the 2nd Tank Corps commander and commissar and passed through the entire village to the bridge across the river. Vafin opted not to cross to the opposite side, to the slopes of Hill 188.5, where in essence the battlefield began, but he decided to make contact with the 27th Tank Brigade by radio and inquire about whether Liziukov was there. The radio contact with the brigade, judging from everything, proved to be reliable (Vafin was just several kilometers from the 27th Tank Brigade), and he soon received a reply from the tank brigade. They assuredly transmitted to Vafin that Liziukov was with them in his tank. Having heard this report, Vafin stopped his search for the general, returned to Kreshchenka, and chances are reported what he had heard to Chief of Staff Nagaibakov.

Having composed and sent his daily written report to the headquarters of Group Chibisov via a liaison officer, Nagaibakov could now focus on essential tasks to organize the work of the new

7 TsAMO, F. 202, op. 50, d. 1, l. 300.
8 TsAMO, F. 38 A, op. 9005, d. 19, l. 41.
9 TsAMO, F. 202, op. 50, d. 1, l. 300.

command post. First of all, it was necessary to establish reliable technical communications with the subordinate units, just as with the higher command, but this proved quite difficult to do. It is more accurate to say that the establishment of technical communications became altogether the chief of staff's major problem. From the analyzed documents the impression forms that the change in location of the forward command post and the headquarters of the 2nd Tank Corps on the morning of 23 July turned into a crisis of command and control for the entire corps command in Liziukov's absence. The old telephone line was now useless, and there was still no telephone connection in the new command post. Speaking generally, radio communications with higher headquarters experienced a total collapse. On the day of 23 July, the 2nd Tank Corps didn't send a single encoded message to higher headquarters, not even a brief radio signal that would confirm the presence of an operating radio.[10] (In comparison, the headquarters of Katukov's neighboring 1st Tank Corps sent four coded messages on 23 July, not to mention signals to confirm an operating radio.)

Possibly, this disheartening failure in communications was connected with the inexperience and insufficient qualifications of the radio operators, who were unable to establish contact from the new command post (in contrast with the former command post and headquarters, which had been situated on hilltops in Sedelki and Kreshchenka, the headquarters was now located in the spurs of a ravine that was overgrown with woods). In addition, there was a shortage of operating radios themselves in the 2nd Tank Corps. At the very end of June, the corps had 4 RSB radios and 1 RAF radio, which, incidentally, needed repairs.[11] Just before Group Chibisov's operation, several radios of the 2nd Tank Corps were not working and needed repair.[12] At the least, one authorized radio of the 2nd Tank Corps became a combat loss by the morning of 23 July during the German airstrike on the forward command post. Thus, speaking of the communication means available at the headquarters of the 2nd Tank Corps on 23 July, one can speak confidently only about 3 radio sets of the 509th Separate Signals Battalion, which had been attached to the tank corps for the duration of the operation.[13] On various occasions the command staff of this battalion wrote about the inadequate training of the radiomen, both before and after those combat actions, thus one can hardly be surprised by the fact that it was difficult for them to handle their assignments in the challenging conditions that had arisen. After the relocation to the new command post, one can say figuratively (and perhaps even literally) that they were "below the mark". Moreover, it is fully possible that the frightening events of the morning airstrike on the command post at Surikovo became a reason for the extremely cautious use of radio sets, when command staff concerns about disclosing the location of the new command post were evidently more important than creating optimal conditions for the work of the radio sets.

It is impossible here to exclude as well the suspicions that the Germans used radio direction finding to locate the position of the command post in Surikovo, because of which it was subjected to two airstrikes, and accordingly, there was the threat that the Germans would use radio direction finding and launch another airstrike against the new command post, with all the consequences flowing from this. One should also probably look to this for an explanation of the striking radio silence that fell over the 2nd Tank Corps' command post on 23 July. The Luftwaffe's superiority in the sky and the plain results of this superiority on the ground eloquently spoke to the fact that there could be no talk about the safe operation of the corps' radios so close to the front.

10 TsAMO, F. 202, op. 52, d. 21, ll. 149-150.
11 TsAMO, F. 202, op. 52, d. 35, l. 40.
12 TsAMO, F. 202, op. 52, d. 21, l. 133.
13 TsAMO, F. 509 obs, op. 21661, d. 3, ll. 21-22.

Thus, excessive use of the radios, which would have regularly generated transmissions over the airwaves and thereby disclosed their location, might in these conditions be costly not only to them, but also to the entire command post. It was much more tranquil to keep the radios silent and rely on an old, reliable means of communication that was safe from the cunning adversary – runners. As they say, a little further from sin. Again, it was also impossible to guarantee that the secret messages that traveled across the airwaves would remain inaccessible to any listening codebreakers of the *Abwehr* ... and why subject the 2nd Tank Corps' "brains of command and control" to risk, if the higher headquarters of the operational group was just located 5-6 kilometers away? A liaison officer could reach that by car in just 20 minutes.

Was this a wary fear of radios, a deplorable lack of skill among the radio operators, or some other factor? It is difficult to say unequivocally. However, a fact remains a fact: the radios of the 2nd Tank Corps, which hadn't seen too much use even before this date (in the first two days of the operation), on 23 July fell completely silent over Briansk Front's radio networks. There was not a single contact. In vain, the Briansk Front radiomen kept calling the 2nd Tank Corps on this day. They didn't catch any signals from "Zephyr" (the call-sign of the 2nd Tank Corps[14]) over the airwaves. The headquarters of Operational Group Chibisov also stopped hearing signals from "Zephyr".[15] The leadership of the headquarters and command post of the 2nd Tank Corps that had settled into the frontline ravine beneath the copse of trees were keeping total "radio silence", or else absolutely refused to communicate by radio.

In general, without the firm resolve, energy and decisive orders of Liziukov and Assorov, the activity of the 2nd Tank Corps' headquarters and command post in operational leadership over the troops began to ebb quickly. With the departure of the corps commander and commissar, the emotional intensity, which had been maintained in the disciplined exertion of their nearest circle in the first days of the operation, inevitably also dissipated. The decision of the general and commissar to lead the corps' shock group into a breakthrough toward Medvezh'e to a great extent removed responsibility for the course of this battle from the corps headquarters, leaving chiefly support duties to it. If the corps commander and commissar were personally handling the fighting of the tank brigades from a position directly within the combat formations, then how could and why would the corps headquarters sitting in the rear interfere with their decisions? After all, everything is more visible to the commander up among the combat units than to one who remains in the rear.

Moreover, judging from the available documents, the chiefs remaining "at the corps" most likely understood "supporting the battle" to mean keeping the shock group supplied with fuel, ammunition and food, rather than organizing and leading the combat operations of the 2nd Tank Corps' other units in order to facilitate the breakthrough by the 26th and 27th Tank Brigades and carry out the overall operational task.

To a certain degree, this vagueness was prompted by the decisions of Liziukov himself, who didn't leave behind concise and detailed guidance to his, alas, not very energetic subordinates, much less any written orders (which, it seems, they needed most of all) regarding precisely what they were to do in his absence. Obviously, hoping for their complete understanding of their role and duties in operational work, and their energy and resourcefulness in seeking and reaching independent decisions, he was unable or didn't have time to realize that it was much more comfortable for them to follow word for word a superior's instruction, than the spirit of his plan not printed on paper.

14 TsAMO, F. 202, op. 52, d. 21, l. 146.
15 TsAMO, F. 202, op. 5, d. 233, l. 3.

In truth it must be said that the 2nd Tank Corps commander didn't even have time to go into his plan of battle or the tasks for the other units with his staff. Alas, any sort of detailed on-the-fly conferences with the chief of staff or the operations department before he left are out of the question. Liziukov had increasingly become inclined to take rapid, impulsive decisions, preferring not to discuss them, or at least to make them known to his subordinates; it seems he considered such discussions a needless waste of time, and there remained increasingly less time for him to achieve success and, at last, exonerate himself for his recent failures.

The combat possibilities of the brigades were also perceptibly melting away, one of which was moreover in a difficult position in the enemy rear and in need of urgent help. Another day or two of such little progress under German fire and airstrikes, and the tank corps would totally lose its ability to break through. Recognizing that the offensive was already on the verge of crisis and on the third day of the operation it was necessary stake everything on the play of a card in order to achieve success, Liziukov went into battle himself, trying to influence its outcome, and with a final do-or-die effort, nevertheless carry out the task he'd been given.

However, the same couldn't be said about the corps commander's immediate subordinates at the corps' new command post. Camouflaged in the ravine, it seems they were enjoying a respite both from the Luftwaffe's attention and the harassment of their tireless commander, and simply waiting for when their commander would accomplish the task assigned to the corps. While patiently waiting for Liziukov to achieve a combat success and for the infantry to make headway, only after which they were formally to move the headquarters forward, the chiefs remaining at the corps' command post didn't even bother to disturb the subordinate units. A surprising apathy, if not to say passivity, gripped them on this day in the absence of corps commander and commissar.

The 2nd Motorized Rifle Brigade received 700 replacements[16] (which is to say more than a full-strength battalion and almost 10 times more than the casualties suffered in the first two days of fighting[17]), but didn't even make an attempt to attack in virtually the same sector where the forward 26th and 27th Tank Brigades were supposed to operate. On the evening of 23 July Nagaibakov, Pupko and Moskalev coolly wrote to the operational group headquarters that the 2nd Motorized Rifle Brigade was occupying the northeastern slopes of Hill 188.5, as if this passive occupation was the only thing the brigade could do after receiving such an impressive number of replacements.[18] According to a political report, for the 2nd Motorized Rifle Brigade the entire day of 23 July consisted of … reconnaissance patrols, a sporadic exchange of rifle fire, and enemy airstrikes.

The political report continues:

> In the headquarters company, company commander Lezhnev, military commissar and deputy political commander Zavgorodny and the signals platoon were making repairs to an old signals network and rolling out a new one. A captured radio was repaired. The driver of a fuel truck Comrade Cherednin out of patriotic impulses wrote: "Onward to the west!" and "Death to the German occupiers!" All the men of the fuel and lubrication supplies group followed his example.

That's all of the day's important events, which the chief of the brigade's Political Department thought necessary to mention when describing the combat work of the 2nd Tank Corps' sole rifle unit.

16 TsAMO, F. 393, op. 9005, d. 35, l. 47
17 TsAMO, F. 8 gv TK, op. 1, d. 224(b), l. 36, 40.
18 TsAMO, F. 393, op. 9005, d. 35, l. 47.

(It is worth mentioning that according to the information of a signals officer of the 167th Rifle Division, which is confirmed by personal observations from an observation post by the commander of the 2nd Rifle Battalion of the 104th Separate Rifle Brigade, units of the 167th Rifle Division were located on the line of Hill 188.5, and not south of there, as the previously received divisional reports stated.)[19]

The 2nd Motorized Rifle Brigade's 462nd Artillery Battalion and the 27th Tank Brigade's anti-tank battalion were occupying firing positions on the northwestern outskirts of Bol'shaia Vereika and also took no part in the fighting of the corps' tank brigades. In particular, a battery commander detailed the third day of fighting as follows: "No losses. The men were fed on time, but the meals were of low quality; there were cases when the soup had gone completely sour. The political attitudes and morale of the personnel are healthy."[20]

The 2nd Tank Corps' 12th Separate Reconnaissance Battalion, which consisted of 20 armored transports and 12 armored cars[21], spent the entire day standing idle in an area not far from the new command post, as if it was a security battalion, and not the corps' reconnaissance battalion.

In the 148th Tank Brigade, a composite combat group consisting of 2 KV and 10 T-60 was formed out of the tanks that remained operational. It would seem that these 12 tanks could have strengthened the planned attack of the 26th and 27th Tank Brigades toward Medvezh'e, but the brigade received an order from corps' headquarters to move these tanks out behind the forward tank brigades ... only once the sun set.[22] In addition, at 1400 the 2nd Tank Corps' Intelligence Department informed the brigade about the movement of 20 hostile tanks from the direction of Gnezdilovo toward Bol'shaia Vereika (it is difficult to say what lay at the basis for such a report. According to German records, the nearest panzer group of a similar number was located many kilometers away from Bol'shaia Vereika and in the directly opposite direction from Gnezdilovo), which also plainly influenced the already rather timid decision of the corps headquarters about the use of the 148th Tank Brigade's tanks.

The political chief of the 26th Tank Brigade, the very same one that was supposed to fight its way forward for 15 kilometers through the German rear areas to Medvezh'e, wrote about something quite the opposite on this day: "The rifle companies of the motorized rifle battalion occupied a defense together with the tanks; the mortar company and anti-tank battery are positioned on the northern outskirts of Malaia Vereika ... Food for the men was brought up prior to an enemy airstrike, and with the onset of darkness, lunch and dinner were distributed. Public readings of newspapers were conducted in the tank battalions among the crews, and in the motorized rifle battalion, among the squads. Conclusion: a healthy condition, no amoral manifestations."[23]

The motorized rifle battalion commander of the 27th Tank Brigade, which was supposed to go into a breakthrough together with the 26th Tank Brigade, on the evening of 23 July reported: "The battalion operated in the third echelon together with a tank battalion and occupied a defense on the northern outskirts of Bol'shaia Vereika. Losses: 2 men wounded; no loss in materiel."[24]

The military commissar of the 27th Tank Brigade's 436th Tank Battalion at the same time reported: "1 T-34 and 1 T-60 are situated on the defense on the northern outskirts of Fomina-Negachevka and Kreshchenka [which is to say, more than 10 kilometers from the brigade's combat area – I.S.]. There is no command or headquarters at all in the battalion, because the battalion

19 TsAMO, F. 393, op. 9005, d. 35, l. 41.
20 TsAMO, F. 27 tbr (3109), op. 1, d. 9, l. 155.
21 TsAMO, F. 8 gv TK, op. 1, d. 224(b), l. 159.
22 TsAMO, F. 148 tp, op. 1, d. 3, l. 39.
23 TsAMO, F. 8 gv TK, op. 1, d. 224(b), l. 161.
24 TsAMO, F. 27 tbr (3109), op. 1, d. 9, l. 158.

commander, deputy commander and senior adjutant have been wounded, while the battalion adjutant has been transferred to the 239th Tank Battalion."[25]

The remaining tanks of this tank battalion had been transferred to the brigade's 2nd Tank Battalion for participation in the fighting. However, the adjutant of the 2nd Tank Battalion didn't report any combat whatsoever. From the battalion's rear command post in Kreshchenka, he wrote, in particular: "2 KV and 1 T-34 are in the process of towing a KV that got stuck at the crossing site in Bol'shaia Vereika. ... The personnel have been fed with one hot meal. Tonight, food will be delivered to the tanks at the front."[26]

The brigade's anti-aircraft battery, after the loss of 2 heavy-caliber DShK machine guns and the death or wounding of 6 anti-aircraft gunners from a bombing on the evening before was removed from its firing positions at Bol'shaia Vereika and pulled back into the rear. On 23 July it was located northwest of Kreshchenka and, as written in a report, "was covering units of the 27th Tank Brigade from the air", although it was guarding only the brigade's headquarters and immediate rear.[27] The hostile "vultures" never attacked the brigade headquarters or rear area, the battery did not engage in combat, and judging from the reports, never even once opened fire at enemy aircraft, "wisely" conserving the remaining 938 37-mm shells in the battery for the extent of several days.[28]

At the same time, the composite tank battalion of the 27th Tank Brigade (the 239th Tank Battalion), the brigade's sole element that wound up at the front a little more than 10 kilometers from the "vigilantly inactive" anti-aircraft battery in the rear, was experiencing one savage bombing attack after another. Cowering in a narrow copse of trees in a ravine, the battalion, for the majority of the crews of which this was their combat baptism (they had arrived in the brigade as a march replacement the evening before), spent the entire day desperately digging into the earth and seeking some sort of shelter beneath the chopped-up crowns of the mutilated trees against the enemy bombers that were circling like vultures above the battlefield.

Many of the crews, unable to endure the "breathtaking" howl of the Ju-87's dive sirens, the whistle of the falling bombs and the heavy, earth-shaking explosions of the bombs completely climbed out of their tanks and went through the bombing lying prone beneath their protecting hulls.[29] In these conditions, they were plainly giving no thought to any sort of attack. (One can only imagine the inner torments of the novice tankers from the batch of replacements, who almost as soon as they had arrived in the brigade had been thrown into this furnace, and what they must have been thinking about such a combat baptism that they were receiving ...).

The battalions of the 26th Tank Brigade wound up in a similar situation, the tanks of which were huddled up against the oak trees mutilated by shell fragments in this very same wooded ravine. The brigade's anti-aircraft battery, judging from the available information, had also wound up somewhere far from the battlefield and was covering whatever, but it wasn't the tankers at the front .... Thus, under the alternating airstrikes and artillery barrages, the day of 23 July stretched on for the elements of the 26th and 27th Tank Brigades that had set out to breakthrough to Medvezh'e.[30] (In these circumstances, the bravura report of the political chief of the 26th Tank Brigade about the public readings of newspapers to the crews and squads sounds almost surreal to me.) Yet both

25 TsAMO, F. 27 tbr (3109), op.1, d. 9, l. 151.
26 TsAMO, F. 27 tbr (3109), op. 1, d. 9, l. 157.
27 TsAMO, F. 27 tbr (3109), op. 1, d. 9, l. 156.
28 TsAMO, F. 27 tbr (3109), op. 1, d.9, l. 169, 187.
29 TsAMO, F. 202, op. 50, d. 1, l. 302.
30 From the recollections of the commissar of the 26th Tank Brigade's 270th Tank Battalion A.S. Kunilov, and indirectly confirmed by the intelligence summary of Briansk Front's headquarters that was in turn taken from a primary source (a prisoner interrogation), it follows that his tank wound up during the attack 3 kilometers northwest of Kaver'ia, which is to say, just to the southeast of this very same grove of trees.

the 26th and 27th Tank Brigade, according to the conception of the 2nd Tank Corps commander, were supposed to be attacking, and not spend the day taking shelter in a woodlot.

However, where were Liziukov and Assorov? It seems on this day that no one had certain knowledge of this. At the corps headquarters they believed he was somewhere up front, with the tank brigades that were striving to reach Medvezh'e. But in these brigades themselves? It turns out that even there no one could give a precise answer to this same question. When Liziukov's signals officer Senior Lieutenant Vafin was informed over the radio from the 27th Tank Brigade that the corps commander was somewhere among them in his tank (the comparison and analysis of documents allows us confidently to speculate that this took place already after the 27th Tank Brigade left Bol'shaia Vereika), this answer doesn't fully correspond to fact, or more accurately, strongly didn't correspond to it, but the one who gave the response, judging from the available documents, didn't know this for certain. It can be said definitively that at the moment he gave his answer to Vafin, he didn't have Liziukov in his sight.

But why did Vafin nevertheless receive a confident answer that Liziukov was with the 27th Tank Brigade? In my view, this is connected with the fact that someone of the brigade command, who in fact received Vafin's question via the radio operator, based his answer not on the factual situation at that moment, but on what happened early that morning. The individual who gave the answer knew well (or had personally witnessed) that before the battle itself, Liziukov had arrived in the 27th Tank Brigade in his tank and announced that he would follow the brigade's combat formations as they advanced. Thus he was confident that General Liziukov even now (at the moment of Vafin's query) was somewhere in a tank in the area of the brigade's operations, since he himself had decided to move out behind the 27th Tank Brigade (and how could it be otherwise?).

The situation, in which the tanks of the 26th and 27th Tank Brigade wound up in, scattered along a wooded ravine, with the artillery shelling and airstrikes that the crews were experiencing and which were almost fully preventing the movement of men between the slit trenches and craters undoubtedly hampered any searches on foot for Liziukov. In addition, Vafin didn't give the radio operator who was speaking with him (or the officer that was summoned to answer the question) any task to find the corps commander straight away and without fail, and also didn't ask to pass any information to him. He only asked them where General Liziukov was located, to which he received a clear answer. Neither the radio query nor, even more so, the received answer implied a need for any searches.

However, the oddities of this day didn't end with this. The reply to Senior Lieutenant Vafin, became one of the last, if not the very last radio message from the composite tank battalion of the 27th Tank Brigade that was taking shelter in the woodlot. At some point subsquently, the battalion's radios for some reason "quit working" – all at once.[31] The battalion was no longer able to receive or transmit radio messages.

According to the combat report of the 239th Tank Battalion, 18 T-34 and 5 KV took part in the battle on 23 July.[32] (Two T-34 tanks of the brigade's 436th Tank Battalion had already been attached to the composite battalion.) Documents state that already by 1 July, radios had been mounted in all the tanks of the 27th Tank Brigade. At the very least, some of the replacement tanks that had arrived in the brigade should have been equipped with authorized radios (for example, the KV tank that had arrived as a replacement, in which Liziukov went into the battle, had a radio).

Accordingly, the number of tank radios in the 27th Tank Brigade's composite battalion that was sheltering in the patch of woods was significant. Yet suddenly they all at once stopped working? It

31 TsAMO, F. 3109, op. 2, d. 3, l. 26.
32 TsAMO, F. 27 tbr (3109), op. 1, d. 9, l. 251.

is possible, of course, that some of the radios in the tanks might have actually been knocked out by the nearby explosions of falling bombs -- but all at once? It is strange … However, a subsequent search through the documents allowed an approximate solution to this surprising paradox and to suggest that the reason for this simultaneous "refusal to work" of all the radios should more likely be sought in something other than technical matters.

On the roster of the 27th Tank Brigade's composite tank battalion, the commander of which was a *Deputy of the Supreme Soviet*[33] Major Pavlenko[34], was a Lieutenant Kovalevsky, who was the battalion's communications chief. When he found out that all of the battalion's radios had stopped working, Kovalevsky hurried to report to Pavlenko that he had a spare working radio in his staff car, which could be switched on in order to restore the tank battalion's communications, if all the other radios had stopped working. However, the reaction of the battalion commander to this suggestion by Lieutenant Kovalevsky was completely unexpected. The battalion commander *ordered* Kovalevsky *not to let anyone know that he had a working radio*, and judging from available evidence, forbade it from being switched on.[35]

After such an exchange between the battalion's communications chief (who in that situation might fully expect praise and recognition for the prudent foresight he had shown, and not such an order …) and the battalion commander who must have given him a piercing gaze, it must be thought that a wordless scene had taken place. A battalion commander would hardly deign to explain to a lieutenant *why* the latter shouldn't say a peep about his working radio – a fixed gaze with a significant implication probably preempted the need for any and all explanations.

Indeed, Lieutenant Kovalevsky must have gaped in surprise, if not astonishment. He understood clearly that he was personally responsible for the battalion's uninterrupted communications in battle, especially when the battalion had become, in essence, the 27th Tank Brigade's sole striking fist. A lack of communications in such a situation would be his, Kovalevsky's, own dereliction of duty, if not a military crime. Consequently, the brigade's chief of communications would have launched an inquiry against him as a matter of course for concealing a working radio.

However, the battalion commander's order at the front had a much stronger effect on Kovalevsky than his concerns about a later possible inquiry. In the woodlot thinned by explosions, among the smoking shell craters reeking with cordite and the overturned clumps of black earth and splintered trunks of trees, Pavlenko's order plainly sounded much harsher, and given with such an accompanying gaze, Kovalevsky didn't even begin to protest. He knew that the brigade's chief of communications was far away, and possible troubles from him would come later, whereas the battalion commander, who had ordered him to keep silent about the working radio, was, as they say, "here and now". As a result, this radio was not put to use.[36]

33 Ed. note: The Supreme Soviet was ostensibly the pinnacle in the Soviet hierarchy power, but this was more on paper than in actuality, since the deputies of the Supreme Soviet served as a rubber stamp for Stalin's decisions. However, such a political post was a position of high status and merited the esteem and respect of surrounding people, and undoubtedly increased the "authority" of Pavlenko in the eyes of his peers and even the command.

34 TsAMO, F. 27 tbr, op. 1, d. 5, l. 210.

35 TsAMO, F. 3109, op. 2, d. 3, l. 26. In the order to the brigade, it isn't stated when precisely such a command was given, but from a comparison with other documents and facts, it follows that this was on 23 July 1942.

36 But how are we to understand why the battalion commander gave the battalion's chief of communications such a strange order? It is hardly possible to treat this as anything other than the battalion commander's plain unwillingness to have radio communications available, or to say more accurately, to be in contact. It is completely obvious that a commander who might have strived to restore a lost connection wouldn't have issued such an order, and would absolutely have used the chance that had fallen to him. Major Pavlenko not only didn't use it, but hurried to hide the fact, and demanded the same from his subordinate.

Why did this happen? In order to try to understand this, let's analyze the situation in which Major Pavlenko found himself together with his subordinates late that morning. Having come under an airstrike and anti-tank artillery fire on Hill 188.5, the composite tank battalion of the 27th Tank Brigade veered to the left from the axis of attack, shrank across a road, and then took cover in the patch of woods east of it, where the tanks of the 26th Tank Brigade were already located. Both tank brigades stood in this wooded ravine and went through the alternating airstrikes and barrages. Time passed, and yet not one tank brigade or the other made an attempt to exit the woods and resume the attack, and instead opted to remain in place in uncertainty and inactivity. Gradually, then, the avoidance of fire increasingly became an avoidance of battle, especially when considering the fact that the combat task given by the corps commander hadn't been carried out, nor had the tank brigades even attempted to do so.

All this, of course, threatened severe consequences, blowups and even blistering castigations from the corps commander and commissar themselves, who were supposed to be advancing in the wake of the 27th Tank Brigade. However, gradually it became clear that neither Liziukov nor Assorov were with the brigade. Nor were they with the neighboring 26th Tank Brigade. The corps commander's and commissar's tank was not among the tanks sheltering under the trees, and no one could say whether or not they had moved out at all, and if they did, when and behind whom?

Judging from everything, after such a "discovery" a definite vacuum of authority arose in the brigades of the 2nd Tank Corps that were standing side-by-side. With Liziukov or Assorov absent, no one in the "shock" grouping that was declining to advance was willing to take the responsibility to make a decision about what to do next. The "sly old dog" (according to Liziukov) commander of the 26th Tank Brigade Colonel Burdov was reluctant to show initiative and take control over the battle. It was harder to determine who was in charge in the 27th Tank Brigade, and it had no clear unified leadership at all. Formally the 30-year-old Captain Luchnikov was commanding the brigade, but in the absence of the former commander Lieutenant Colonel Mikhailin (who had been appointed to command the 148th Tank Brigade prior to the offensive and who'd been killed on the raid the day before), he was only the temporarily acting commander. His chief of staff Lieutenant Colonel Gorodetsky was senior to him by two full ranks and was 7 years older than Captain Luchnikov, and judging from their further appointments, had more experience and was better-prepared than the unexpectedly appointed acting commander. However, Gorodetsky was back at the headquarters in Kreshchenka and didn't take part in the raid with the tanks.

Major Pavlenko, who was commanding the composite tank battalion of the 27th Tank Brigade, which is to say factually all of the brigade's tank elements, was also senior to Luchnikov in both age and rank, and by his influence (a member of the Party-Soviet bureaucracy, an honorable "servant of the people", and deputy of the Supreme Soviet) totally overshadowed the captain, who was little-known outside the confines of the brigade. Perhaps, the tankers paid more attention to his word than they did to Luchnikov's orders. (At the very least, judging from the "story" with the radio, Pavlenko's order had such weight for Kovalevsky that he made no attempt to check it with the formal brigade commander, who was in that very same grove, and obediently concealed the working radio, just as he was told to do, for which he subsequently "paid" for this with 10 days of arrest.)[37]

Located in the "aura" of his well-known and influential subordinate (whom approximately a week later Luchnikov willingly put up for nothing more and nothing less than … the title "Hero of the Soviet Union"[38]), Captain Luchnikov, if not being too timid to do so, at the very least restrained from stepping into the role of "commander-in-chief" of the shock group, glancing at

37 TsAMO, F. 3109, op. 2, d. 3, l. 26.
38 Check the award list; TsAMO, F. 33, op. 682524, ed. khr. 408, l. 185.

his neighbor Burdov, who was senior in rank, and at his own battalion commander Pavlenko. Yet formally Pavlenko was subordinate to Luchnikov, who according to regulations and the current situation was supposed to make some sort of decision as the acting brigade commander. Yet all of them in the absence of their direct superior recovered from the shock of the unsuccessful "movement along a route" and were now *tenaciously holding* the salvational patch of woods, refusing to leave it under German fire and airstrikes in order to climb the totally exposed hill. A resumption of the attack in the present conditions plainly seemed a hopeless matter to those frontline veterans who had already "gotten a smell of gunpowder", if not a fatal one. What the totally unseasoned replacements were experiencing and thinking, one can only guess.

At the same time, Burdov and Luchnikov, and even Pavlenko clearly understood that by continuing to remain in the patch of woods, they were not carrying out the order to attack, which no one had yet cancelled. So why then in these circumstances did they need radio contact? They could expect nothing good to come from a working radio. It was one thing to write a note with the appropriate wording and to send it off with a runner over many kilometers and wait long hours for a response, but a different matter to be instantly accessible to higher command and to answer its threatening questions concretely and at once: "What line have you reached?", "Why have you stopped?", "Who gave you the right not to carry out an order?", "Immediately advance!" Radio contact in those circumstances became a type of hook, by which higher command could "yank" the recalcitrant subordinates at any second.

In general, the impression forms that those commanders who had wound up in a "command vacuum" and now stood as the leadership of the brigades began simply to wait out that desperately hard day and hope for some saving turn of affairs for everyone, which would allow them both to obey the order *and* to avoid crawling out again onto the open field under German bombs and anti-tank fire. After all, the Soviet pilots who had been ordered to chase the Luftwaffe away from the battlefield had gone missing somewhere, and the artillerymen hadn't done their job to suppress the hostile anti-tank artillery. If they had failed to provide adequate support for the offensive, then why must the tankers follow orders to the letter?

Of course, if Liziukov and Assorov had shown up in the wooded ravine, they would have quickly forced the brigades to get moving and to resume the attack. Their resolve, drive and unquestionable authority would undoubtedly have had the proper effect on the subordinates, even in the face of the completely unfavorable combat conditions, the unsuppressed enemy anti-tank batteries and the unopposed bombers. But the commander and commissar weren't with the brigades, and in the perception of the commanders taking shelter among the shattered trees, the sense of self-preservation (given the very real danger of death in renewed attacks) was plainly stronger than Liziukov's order that had arrived that morning, but which wasn't now buttressed by Liziukov's willpower and personal drive.

So the brigades stood idle, the commanders waited, and morning gradually stretched into daytime. The Luftwaffe, which was pinning down the actions of virtually all our units in the sector of the operation, regularly, just like a watchman, appeared in the sky above the front and again and again made the troops hug the earth under their falling bombs. However, the brigades sheltering in the woods had very few losses either in tanks or in personnel. Nevertheless, prudently apprehending both the Germans and his higher command, Major Pavlenko for all that managed to get in harm's way. In one of the barrages or airstrikes, he received a concussion[39], and the composite battalion of the 27th Tank Brigade was left without a commander [given Captain Luchnikov's unwillingness to take charge]. (In the operational summary of the battalion and brigade for 23 July, it is written that Major Pavlenko was wounded. It is also worth noting the

39 TsAMO, F. 33, op. 682524, ed. khr. 408, l. 185.

totally atypical distribution of casualties in the composite battalion: while standing idle in the wooded ravine, seven of the command staff were wounded simultaneously, only two of the junior command staff, and not a single enlisted man.[40]) Over the entire day of 23 July, the 27th Tank Brigade lost, according to reports, one KV and one T-34 left burned out, and one KV tank with a damaged turret. The entire brigade lost three men killed.[41] In the documents there is no mention of the losses of the 26th Tank Brigade, in which 24 T-34 tanks went into battle that morning.[42] However, according to the summarized report from the 2nd Tank Corps' chief of staff it turns out that on that day the 26th Tank Brigade lost 1 T-60 light tank burned-out.[43]

If you will, the sole, solitary attempt at active operations of those brigades that were sheltering in the patch of woods on the morning of 23 July was a commanders' conference, which was attended by the commander of the 26th Tank Brigade Colonel Burdov, the temporarily acting commander of the 27th Tank Brigade Captain Luchnikov, and the military commissar of the 148th Tank Brigade Senior Battalion Commissar Lesnoi. Having consulted with each other, they made the decision to conduct a reconnaissance-in-force and launch an attack … on the morning of 24 July.[44]

Thus, avoiding enemy fire (and combat itself), almost 50 tanks of the 2nd Tank Corps' 26th and 27th Tank Brigades stood motionless throughout the entire day in the sanctuary of the wooded ravine.[45] The early morning attempt to break through to Medvezh'e ended almost as soon as it began, and wasn't repeated. Nevertheless, obviously on the basis of the vague and general wording of the brigades' notes and reports, which concealed what was actually happening at the front, the 2nd Tank Corps headquarters sent an operational summary to the headquarters of Operational Group Chibisov, which informed that the brigades "had reached", "approached" and/or "were occupying" specified lines in the offensive sector (a fine Russian word, *zanimat'* [to occupy]: it can mean "standing without movement", but it can also be understood as "making an advance and reaching a new place or area").[46]

The flowery political reports from the units played a definite role in the mistaken interpretation of the events and unreliable assessments of the operational situation; as a rule, these were written in headquarters that were distant from the front. For example, the political chief of the 27th Tank Brigade, the tanks of which had stood motionless in the patch of woods for the entire day of 23 July and didn't even fire at the enemy[47], described this day in the major key:

> The brigade conducted offensive combat actions against the German forces. By the end of the day, it had advanced 6-7 kilometers to the southeast of Bol'shaia Vereika [in fact, the tanks, having covered 3-4 kilometers, had only approached the German front – I.S.] There was particularly fierce fighting for a patch of woods that had been fortified by the Germans, which lay 2-3 kilometers south of Bol'shaia Vereika [by 23 July the Germans had already withdrawn from these woods to the south, and thus the brigade didn't have to fight for them on this day – I.S.]
>
> Especially healthy attitudes were shown by tankers that had already participated in several battles. We have 6 such crews. The remaining 12 T-34 tanks are going into battle for the first time, which arrived in the brigade on 22.7. The men are especially satisfied by the fact that we

40 TsAMO, F. 27 tbr (3109), op. 1, d. 9, l. 251.
41 TsAMO, F. 27 tbr, op. 1, d. 5, l. 210.
42 TsAMO, F. 8 gv TK, op. 1, d. 224(b), l. 161.
43 TsAMO, F. 393, op. 9005, d. 19, l. 63.
44 TsAMO, F. 202, op. 50, d. 1, l. 307.
45 TsAMO, F. 202, op. 50, d. 1, l. 301.
46 TsAMO, F. 393, op. 9005, d. 35, l. 47.
47 TsAMO, F. 202, op. 50, d. 1, l. 302.

> struck the enemy flank, and thereby assisted the Voronezh Front. Soldiers of the motorized rifle brigade expressed dissatisfaction, declaring: "We must follow the tanks in the advance, there, where combat is occurring, but here on defense you only hide from enemy aircraft" [the soldiers didn't know that the tanks didn't fight for most of the day, and were also taking shelter from the enemy aviation – I.S.].[48]

Similar political reports with obligatory mentions of successes and a healthy political attitude and morale, where considerations of propaganda were much more important than the reliability of the operational information, came in from other units as well. Yet at the camouflaged 2nd Tank Corps command post/headquarters in the rear area patch of woods, it seems that no one bothered to check whether everything they were reporting "from the spearhead of the main attack" was real, whether or not the brigades had reached the lines indicated in the reports, or whether the corps commander and commissar were actually up among the combat formations ….

48 TsAMO, F. 8 gv TK, op. 1, d. 224(b), l. 100.

9

23 July 1942 on the front of Operational Group Chibisov

Early on the morning of 23 July, a brief and accusatorial directive arrived at the headquarters of Briansk Front from the General Staff of the Red Army:

> According to available information, the 2nd Tank Corps' headquarters has become separated from its units. It did not direct the crossing of the units over the Bol'shaia Vereika River on 22.7. It doesn't know where its units are and is deliberately reporting unreliable information. The tank brigades are operating indecisively and are not exploiting the success of its neighbors to increase the offensive's momentum. It is categorically necessary to move up the tank corps' headquarters closer to the brigades, to demand more initiative from the tank commanders, in order to exploit each gap in the enemy's defense with the aim getting the motorized and tank units on the flanks and rear of it.[1]

Chances are that soon this directive became known in the headquarters of Operational Group Chibisov in Lukino as well. It is difficult to say whether it received this directive prior to the departure of Liziukov and Assorov from there, and if so, whether they also knew about its contents. The directive from the General Staff became one more reason, if not a signal, to take the harshest measures against the guilty parties. Incidentally, even without this directive Chibisov had plenty of other reasons to rebuke the command of the 2nd Tank Corps and especially its commander. Doubtlessly, he didn't refrain from giving a number of these rebukes to the corps commander and commissar in the course of the nighttime meeting on the eve before.

(Chibisov's irritation and fault-finding toward Liziukov is known both from eyewitness testimony and from documents. It is possible to cite a report received by the headquarters of the operational group from the commander of the 104th Separate Rifle Brigade as one example of this, which might have "poured oil onto the flames" and become yet another reason for strengthening Chibisov's entirely negative attitude toward Liziukov. In it, when reporting on the course of the fighting on 21 July, the commander of the 104th Separate Rifle Brigade informed that units of the 2nd Tank Corps gave almost no help to his brigade, operated indecisively, and entered Bol'shaia Vereika only after that village had already been liberated by the 104th Separate Rifle Brigade, adding "the report sent to you that supposedly the 2nd Motorized Rifle Brigade took Bol'shaia Vereika was a lie and didn't correspond to reality." The commander of the 104th Separate Rifle Brigade ended his report to Chibisov with a request "to order an investigation of this matter.")[2]

1 *General'nyi shtab v gody VOV, Tom 23: Materialy i dokumenty* [The General Staff in the years of the Great Patriotic War, Volume 23: Materials and documents] (Moscow: Terra, 1999), p. 256.

2 TsAMO, F. 38 A, op. 9005, d. 19, l. 24.

Yet now they were reporting from Moscow about the slow and irresponsible actions of the corps command!

In addition, it should be said that together with the harsh assessments of his subordinate's actions in the received directive, Chibisov could also see a rebuke toward himself. Who else but he was supposed to control them and demand greater initiative? However, since the beginning of the operation the commander of the operational group had not at all rested on his laurels and moreover, had not been idle when overseeing the operation. As for the command of the 2nd Tank Corps, here he had in fact gotten a jump on the directive received from the General Staff, having summoned both the corps' commander and commissar to his command post on the evening of 22 July. In the course of that meeting with Liziukov and Assorov, Chibisov found out directly from the commanders about the situation of affairs in the tank corps, the course of the fighting and the plans for 23 July, just as he informed them of the latest operational information and personally issued them an order that conformed to the situation.

True, after their departure from his headquarters, there'd been no success in making any contact with them, and where the corps commander and commissar were now located, and how the combat of the brigades headed by them was going, were a matter of conjecture. Given their resolute and capable leadership from a point directly among the combat formations, it was fully possible to anticipate that the shock force of the 2nd Tank Corps was already nearing the area of Medvezh'e to link up with the tank battalion of the 148th Tank Brigade that had broken through to that place the day before. Moreover, units of the 167th Rifle and 118th Tank Brigade, according to reports, by morning had already broken through the narrow throat of the field lying in between the two patches of woods that the enemy had been defending (which they had totally been unable to do the day before) and had advanced along the hills, thereby securing the 2nd Tank Corps' access to operational space. A dash across the enormous fields toward Medvezh'e with the possibility of sweeping maneuvers, unconstrained by natural obstacles, and the bold bypassing of enemy points of resistance would now be fully possible for the 2nd Tank Corps.

With no direct contact with Liziukov, the headquarters of the operational group had to rely upon the reports from the 2nd Tank Corps headquarters. From these written reports it followed that although the staff had been unable to communicate with Liziukov directly, it appeared from an earlier message that he together with the 27th Tank Brigade had that morning pushed forward to the southern slopes of Hill 188.5. In the corps headquarters' evening operational summary, there had been no mention at all of either Liziukov or Assorov, from which the conclusion could be drawn that the headquarters also didn't know anything definite about where they were. However, judging from the lines reached by the brigades, it turned out that they still hadn't reached Medvezh'e.

Of course, the several messages received from the 2nd Tank Corps headquarters about the situation as it had been several hours before couldn't give the headquarters of Group Chibisov either a complete picture of the current situation or allow an efficient response to the received information. The change in location of both the command post and the headquarters led to a temporary collapse of wire communications with them, leaving the headquarters of the operational group one means of communication with the 2nd Tank Corps – the radio. However, for some reason or another, the radio operators in the headquarters of the operational group had stopped hearing the call sign ("Zephyr") of the 2nd Tank Corps.[3]

True, the scheme for the operational group's own radio communications was not beyond reproach, which leaves certain possibilities to explain "Zephyr's" silence. The scheme for radio communications worked out and distributed by Briansk Front's Signals Department was reworked in Operational Group Chibisov according to its own thinking. It is difficult to say why this

3 TsAMO, F. 202, op. 5, d. 233, l. 3.

happened and what advantages in its own scheme that the Group's radio specialists saw, but as a result of the revisions, there was at least one side effect: Up to five combat formations wound up tied to a single frequency, and their communications began to interfere with each other.[4] It is fully possible to assume that in connection with the change in location, the inexperience of the radio operators and the "crowding" on the frequency, "Zephyr" had been unable to "break through" to the operational group's radio – so far. Thus in the headquarters of the operational group, it seems that they didn't think the breakdown in the radio communications with the 2nd Tank Corps was any exceptional occurrence.

Thus, before the receipt of reliable information from Liziukov himself, at the headquarters of Group Chibisov they might only be able to make an approximate judgement on how the 2nd Tank Corps' attack was going. Waiting for word to arrive was all they could do.

The headquarters of Group Chibisov also had to wait for fresh operational information from other units. So thus far the headquarters primarily had to be content with the reports and very brief radio messages (if they had been sent) it had received the night before, and could inform the higher command about the progress of the attack only on their basis. Only toward evening on the basis of study, comparison and analysis of all the information that was arriving from the combat units might the headquarters staff obtain a more or less full picture of the course of the fighting and the successes achieved for the day (assuming those reports were credible). Then, the aggregated data could be passed on to Briansk Front headquarters. On the operation's third day, both the command of the operational group and the higher command of Briansk Front were still waiting for when the troops would carry out the first of the tasks facing the operational group and finally break through the enemy's defense. They were both waiting with increasing impatience ….

But how were events developing on that day for the rest of the operational group? Alas, the course of combat operations was showing with increasing clarity that expectations for any decisive turning point in the battle were still unfounded. As in the case with the 2nd Tank Corps, the offensive élan and combat activity of a significant portion of the operational group's forces began perceptibly to wane.

The 1st Guards Rifle Division's attack on the extreme right flank of the operational group in the Terbuny area was becoming increasingly unpromising and only needlessly lengthening the casualty lists. Over the three days of frontal assaults against the enemy's unsuppressed firing points, the division had lost around 600 men killed, wounded, missing or disabled for other reasons, not including the sick.[5] Obviously, considering that the division had partially carried out its assigned mission by pinning down the enemy with an attack on a secondary axis, and expecting nothing more to come of it, Chibisov in response to a query from the division commander ordered "a halt to offensive actions."[6]

On the front of the 104th Separate Rifle Brigade, which was attacking on the extreme left flank of the operational group, three of the brigade's battalions were occupying a defense along the northern bank of the Bol'shaia Vereika River, while the fourth was in reserve. Of the entire brigade, only one rifle company was engaged in combat on 23 July, striving to take Nizhniaia Vereika; it had taken one prisoner, but was subsequently counterattacked by enemy infantry and had fallen back to the northern outskirts of the village.

From the operational summary of the 167th Rifle Division it follows that the units of the division launched repeated attacks, but because its actions "were not covered from the air", over the

4 TsAMO, F. 202, op. 5, d. 233, l. 3.
5 TsAMO, F. 1 gv. sd, op. 1, d. 24, l. 276, 279, 286, 291.
6 TsAMO, F. 202, op. 5, d. 234, l. 48.

entire day they made no progress.[7] The thinned ranks of the division's regiments were digging into the fields in the area of Hill 188.5 and in front of the wooded ravine southwest of Churikovo (that same patch of woods where the tanks of the 26th and 27th Tank Brigade spent the entire day).

According to the 118th Tank Brigade's operational summary, on this day it made no advance, and instead spent the day in cooperation with units of the 167th Rifle Division repelling local counterattacks by the ... retreating enemy with fire from fixed positions (according to captured German documents, the German infantry amounted to various elements that were clinging to the switch line of defense and were not in the condition to launch counterattacks that day: they barely had enough strength to hold the front of the defense that was extending to the south). By evening, having captured a 75-mm gun, 3 motorcycles, 4 vehicles and having obviously inflicted other losses to the enemy, the brigade in return lost 3 KV tanks (two knocked out and one destroyed), 3 T-34 (knocked out) and 3 T-70 (2 burned out and one knocked out). In addition, it lost 5 men killed and 16 wounded. The brigade had 3 KV, 6 T-34 and 6 T-70 still operational.[8]

The 193rd Rifle Division, which was supposed to attack on the right of the 167th Rifle Division from Lebiazh'e to Bol'shaia Treshchevka, was burrowing into the earth in the fields and patches of woods under enemy barrages and airstrikes just a couple of kilometers outside of Lebiazh'e (the frequent enemy air raids had such an effect on the division command that in the morning operational summary of the 193rd Rifle Division, it reported to higher command that enemy aircraft were bombing the infantry's combat positions ... every minute).[9] In the division's regiments, it seems, there was no longer the strength or the zeal to attack the adversary. One of the division's regiments, as it was written in the operational summary by the chief of staff of the 193rd Rifle Division, fell back and took up a defense on the eastern fringe of the "Large" patch of woods under an attack by ... up to a company of German infantry. A different regiment, according to the evening operational summary, by the end of the day "reached" the very same fringe of woods that it had already reached according to the morning summary. A third regiment had with its right flank "reached the northern fringe of the "medium-sized" patch of woods south of Lebiazh'e, while its left flank had moved into the very same fringe of woods.[10]

Mind you, by this time there was very little left of the division's regiments. "Over the period of fighting from 12 to 23 July," wrote the 193rd Rifle Division's chief of staff, "the division has suffered heavy losses in personnel." (Beneath this typed report, the division commander Major General Smekhotvorov has added in pencil, "There remain 100-150 soldiers and commanders in each of the rifle regiments. Immediate replenishment is necessary.")[11] In his personal report to Chibisov, Smekhotvorov tallied up the results of the unsuccessful offensive: "As a result of three days of fighting, there remained 400-500 men in the division's units" and requested an urgent replenishment with 6,000-7,000 men.[12]

Senior Battalion Commissar Kuznetsov, a political instructor of Briansk Front's headquarters who'd been assigned to the 193rd Rifle Division, reported on the afternoon of 23 July 1942:

> From 0400 to 1600 the division was constantly being bombed by enemy aircraft and suffered large losses. The regiments have 80-120 active bayonets each. Over the day of 22 July alone, 1,600 wounded were sent to the division's medical sanitation battalion. Large numbers of wounded men are continuing to come in. In addition to dead and wounded, in the division

---

7 TsAMO, F. 393, op. 9005, d. 35, l. 45.
8 TsAMO, F. 393, op. 9005, d. 35, l. 42.
9 TsAMO, F. 393, op. 9005, d. 19, l. 35.
10 Ibid., l. 52.
11 Ibid, l. 35.
12 Ibid, l. 39.

> there are instances of individual soldiers fleeing from the battlefield. The division command has taken measures to detain them. Blocking detachments have detained approximately 100 men. Three men have been shot for fleeing the battlefield and abandoning their weapons. The active operations of the enemy's air force are paralyzing command and control over the division's units and has reduced the offensive zeal of the personnel.[13]

In the opinion of the 1st Tank Corps' command, by 23 July there was no longer any "offensive zeal" left in the 193rd Rifle Division.

It isn't surprising that in such a situation, the 193rd Rifle Division gave virtually no support to the 1st Tank Corps' attack, although according to the operation's plan, it was supposed to create a breach for the the 1st Tank Corps' introduction. Thus the tank brigades of the 1st Tank Corps were acting independently, without infantry support, and could only count upon its own small numbers of motorized riflemen to support the attack. The shortage or complete lack of shells also made the 193rd Rifle Division's artillery useless, which was noted with anger by Colonel Chukhin, the commander of the 1st Guards Tank Brigade that was cooperating with the rifle division.[14] The artillerymen of the 3rd Destroyer Brigade, which was equipped with 45-mm and 76-mm anti-tank batteries, also gave no support to the tankers; as before, they were positioned on the hills north of Lebiazh'e, received no order to advance, and essentially remained idle in the positions they had occupied before the attack (partially on 21 and 22 July) – "in the course of the day they didn't fire".[15]

In accordance with Katukov's plan, the 1st Tank Corps on 23 July was to continue its initial task to smash the opposing enemy in the Gremiach'e – Ruda – Somovo area, with the subsequent encirclement and destruction of the enemy knot of resistance in Malaia and Bol'shaia Treshchevka. The 1st Guards Tank Brigade was supposed to launch an attack toward Somovo. In his combat order, brigade commander Colonel Chukhin in particular had written:

> I am demanding the most decisive and impetuous actions of the units' commanders. Do not mill around in place. The enemy is withdrawing, covering the retreat with strong artillery and mortar fire. The capture of the Somovo, Bol'shaia Treshchevka, Malaia Treshchevka hub will secure the successful advance of Briansk Front's entire operational group. Mount the infantry aboard the tanks. I demand personal leadership over the fighting from the unit commanders in their combat machines, directing the combat from a point immediately behind the combat formations of their battalions ... Conduct the attack at top speed and the enemy will roll back to the south.[16]

Unfortunately, the available archival documents of many of the units are very sparing in details of those July battles. Mostly, they contain just a few lines about attained lines of advance, losses and captured booty (if there was any), the number of "active bayonets" and the availability of serviceable materiel over the day. Even more important in these circumstances are the few (alas) tales of participants in the fighting. One such story is contained in the "chronicle" of the 1st Tank Corps, written by military commissar and journalist Iu. Zhukov. It directly touches upon the fighting for Somovo based on the recollections of one of its participants – the 20-year-old Lieutenant Vladimir

13 TsAMO, F. 202, op. 36, d. 129, l. 448.
14 Archive of IRI RAN, F. 2, section 1, op. 36, d. 13, l. 43.
15 TsAMO, F. 3 ibr, op. 1, d. 1, l. 12.
16 TsAMO, F. 1 gv. tbr, op. 1, d. 6, l. 73.

Bochkovsky, who arrived in the tank brigade shortly before the offensive after graduating from a tank school. For him, this battle was the first in his life:

> The 1st Guards Tank Brigade was attacking Somovo; the 2nd Tank Battalion of Major Ivan Nikiforovich Boiko, a level-headed and composed Ukrainian to whom Lieutenant Bochkovsky was subordinated, was ordered to bypass the village from the north. However, intense German tank fire from the outskirts halted the battalion, which had been pushing its way through a field of tall sunflowers. The Nazis own situation wasn't the best: our artillery had set the village on fire, huts were in flames, and the tanks that were taking cover among them caught fire.[17] One way or another, the battalion's attack faltered. Two of our tanks were destroyed. The remaining tanks scattered as they moved away: the inexperienced tankers didn't feel confident and were performing incompetently.
>
> Volodia Bochkovsky also felt fear, but overcame it through force of will. Noticing a balka that led to the village, he turned his machine into it and approached the outskirts stealthily. There he discovered an entire battery of 23-mm automatic anti-tank guns [Judging from the documents, the enemy didn't have such guns; most likely, these were 20-mm autocannons – I.S.], which were firing furiously at our machines through the field, which was planted with tall sunflowers – the lieutenant recalled this because the shells were scything through the sunflowers, and their heavy blossoms were pelting the earth like a hail shower.
>
> He centered the crosshairs of his optical sight on one of the cannons. A shot … it fell short! He raised the crosshairs – another short! The German gunners spotted Bochkovsky's tank, and their shells began drumming against its strong armor. Inside the tank there was a terrible ringing, sparks were flying, and splinters painfully stung the face and arms.
>
> The experienced driver-mechanic Sergeant Moshkirev couldn't endure this, and disregarding all the regulations of discipline, coarsely swore: "Are you just going to fuck around here awhile longer, Lieutenant? What did they teach you at the tank school?" At this moment the gun loader Sergeant Riabov figured out what was happening and suggested "Check the sight!" Bochkovsky glanced at the sight and bit his lips in annoyance: the sight had been set on the machine-gun setting. He quickly switched it to the ballistic setting for the main gun, again centered his crosshairs on a cannon … and fired! Through the dispersing cloud of smoke Volodia caught sight of the cannon's wheels flying through the air – this was his first hit in combat.
>
> A second targeted shot, and a second cannon's operating lifetime was cut short. The German artillerymen became demoralized and began to run off in different directions. Now there followed an order to the driver-mechanic: "Forward!" Several minutes later, the remaining three cannons were being crushed beneath the tracks of the T-34 – Moshkirev had excellent skill in such matters.

17 Putting it gently, I have large doubts about this assertion. In the first place, the tanks were not fuel trucks, which could easily ignite from huts burning nearby. In the second place, the German tankers were likely not fools and wouldn't sit with their arms crossed and watch as their machines began to burn. Most likely, they might have driven away from any huts that were enveloped in flames. Thirdly, there was no way Iu. Zhukov could have personally seen the German tanks catching fire from the huts. Lieutenant Bochkovsky, who at the moment was outside the village, also could hardly have seen this. In the fourth place, burned-out tanks would have simultaneously become irrecoverable losses, which on the one hand would have noticeably decreased the number of combat-ready Panzers, and on the other hand, would have increased the number of "write-offs". Neither one nor the other is evident in the German documents. Therefore, the "observation" of a massed number of German tanks catching fire from the burning huts in Somovo is most likely a creative figment of Iu. Zhukov's imagination, who sincerely wanted to believe that this had in fact happened.

> Bochkovsky's spirits soared. He issued an order: "We're going to burst into the village!" Moshkirev accelerated. Nazis were tumbling out of the huts: "Russian tanks!" Bochkovsky was conducting rapid fire at them, now from the cannon, now from the machine guns, almost without aiming – most important now was to create as much crashing sounds and thunder as possible, in order to increase the panic among the fascists.
>
> Suddenly Bochkovsky caught sight of a German tank directly in front of him. What to do? It was already too late to fire – the tank was too close. "Ram it!" Moshkirev adroitly maneuvered and inflicted a heavy blow with the full mass of the T-34. A terrible crashing sound rang out. The German tank, lighter, flipped over. But at the same moment Moshkirev's engine died ... Agonizing seconds of waiting: would the engine catch or not? It started! Now at full speed out of the village to link back up with friends .... Bochkovsky's tanks sped away through the southern outskirts, setting a course directly toward the positions of the brigade's 1st Tank Battalion, and from there to the command post of his own 2nd Tank Battalion, which was positioned in some woods.
>
> Around were machines that had come out of the battle – his machine was already considered missing! – and tankers crowded around his tank. They began to count the pockmarks in the armor from the German shells – 57 hits. Yet not a single penetration – the armor of the T-34 is strong! True, there was nevertheless damage to the tank – the sight was knocked out, the driver-mechanic's hatch was jammed and the main clutch was slipping, but all this was repairable.
>
> Major Boiko and his political deputy Major Ishchenko attentively listened to the report of the young lieutenant with the grimy, scratched face, endorsed his actions, and concluded: this fellow had passed his first combat test, and he would go far, if everything went well. So Boiko told Bochkovsky: "I'm appointing you platoon commander."

Undoubtedly, the battle can be acknowledged as the successful combat baptism of Lieutenant Bochkovsky. His tank crew inflicted substantial damage to the foe and returned to the battalion's position intact and unharmed. However, on the whole the attack of the 1st Guards Tank Brigade was unsuccessful, since the tankers were unable to take either Somovo or Hill 228.5, so the assigned task remained unfulfilled. By 1600 according to the brigade's combat diary, the brigade's tank battalions were located in the area of Hill 210.9 about a half-kilometer south of Gremiach'e, together with two companies of the motorized rifle battalion. After the unsuccessful attacks, the rifle battalions of the 1st Motorized Rifle Brigade were also digging in on the approaches to Gremiach'e.

The 49th Tank Brigade was also operating in this area. Before the battle, this brigade was equipped with 41 T-34, 10 T-60 and 10 T-70; 4 76-mm guns; 5 mortars; 4 anti-tank rifles; 4 heavy and 20 light machine guns; 135 PPSh submachine guns; 468 rifles and carbines; and 94 pistols and revolvers. The personnel of a motorized rifle battalion numbered 383 men; that of the anti-tank gun battery – 52 men; that of the sapper platoon – 30 men; and scouts with the headquarters company – 42.[18]

The brigade suffered its first losses even prior to the start of the offensive. On 21 July, one T-34 on a reconnoitering mission was knocked out and burned up together with its entire crew. Four T-34 tanks and three T-70 light tanks were out of commission at the start of the operation and required repairs. (One of the political instructors assigned to the 1st Tank Corps from Briansk Front's Political Department viewed the reasons for the decrease in the number of combat-ready

18 TsAMO, F. 49 tbr (3109), op. 1, d. 5, l. 54.

tanks through his customary "political lens", and with his Bolshevik directness reported to the command with assessments and conclusions that corresponded to those times:

> The personnel of the 49th Tank Brigade, who arrived with the tanks from the [Nizhnyi] Tagil factory, showed poor and even criminal conduct. Owing to the insufficient work conducted with the crews before they went into battle, of the 10 tanks in the 253rd Tank Battalion, 4 were unserviceable and stood around for two days, but thanks to the intervention of the chief of the Political Department, two tanks were returned to service. There were incidents when before a battle 3 tanks of the 49th Tank Brigade sank into the mud at a crossing site and were rendered non-operational. These facts were investigated by the Special Department, and the guilty parties in the deliberate bogging of the tanks will be turned over for trial in front of a tribunal. In addition, decisive explanatory work was conducted among the men by the Party and political apparatus according to the directives given by me.[19]

The 49th Tank Brigade went on the attack with two tank battalions (according to an operational summary – 36 T-34, 8 T-70 and 11 T-60; it isn't clear from where it obtained another T-60, which wasn't counted among the brigade on 21 July[20]) and the motorized rifle battalion (367 men). At 0600, having moved out from Malaia Vereika and broken out across the field at Hill 188.5 (the same field from which approximately 50 tanks of the 26th and 27th Tank Brigades had veered off into the patch of woods several hours later, having come under fire and airstrikes), the tank battalions of the 49th Tank Brigade bypassed the large patch of woods southeast of Lebiazh'e from the south, advanced along the main road to Somovo and reached the fork in the road 3 kilometers south of Lebiazh'e; as was written in the brigade's account: "overcoming stubborn enemy resistance". In the process, this resistance was, judging from everything, no less than that which greeted the 2nd Tank Corps' 26th and 27th Tank Brigades a bit later: "massed enemy airstrikes and the surprise raking fire from well-camouflaged anti-tank guns along the fringes of woods."[21] Subsequently, already on the approaches to Somovo, it is possible that the 49th Tank Brigade actually ran into enemy tanks that were dug into the ground, as reported.

The 49th Tank Brigade attempted to develop the initial success and carry out its assigned task to seize Ruda and Gremiach'e together with the 1st Motorized Rifle Brigade, but was unable to do this. At 1545 after a multi-hour delay, a combat order from the headquarters of the 1st Tank Corps, which had been written at 1100, arrived in the tank brigade; it concerned an attack toward Hill 210.9 and Ruda that was ordered to begin at 1600. Thus, the brigade's command was left with only 15 minutes to prepare for the attack and pass the order along to the subordinate battalions. In addition, the 1st Tank Corps' chief of staff informed the brigade commander that the enemy was retreating to the southwest, and that the 1st Guards Tank Brigade that was operating nearby had already taken Somovo. Based on this untrustworthy directive and not knowing the true situation of affairs, the tankers of the 49th Tank Brigade went on the attack toward Ruda and came under flanking fire from German anti-tank guns positioned in the Somovo area. As a result, several tanks were lost and the attack again ended in failure.[22]

Over the day of fighting, the 49th Tank Brigade lost 4 men killed and 42 wounded, as well as 3 T-34 tanks knocked out and 3 destroyed. Another five T-34 tanks were knocked out of action because their cannon's recoil mechanism refused to work. By the end of the day the tanks of the

19 TsAMO, F. 202, op. 36, d. 132, l. 50.
20 TsAMO, F. 49 tbr (3163), op. 1, d. 5, l. 61
21 TsAMO, F. 49 tbr, op. 1, d. 9, l. 25.
22 TsAMO, F. 202, op. 36, d. 132, l. 50.

49th Tank Brigade returned to the southwestern slopes of Hill 188.5 (obviously to the southwestern fringe of the large patch of woods) in order to top up with fuel and replenish ammunition.

That afternoon practically on the heels of the 49th Tank Brigade, the 89th Tank Brigade went into battle. Throughout 21 and 22 July this brigade had been held in the reserve of the 1st Tank Corps at first in Kamenka, then in Lomovo, and with the exception of one tank battalion that was operating together with the 340th Rifle Division, had taken no part in the fighting. On the morning of 23 July Katukov received an order from Chibisov to move the 89th Tank Brigade out of his reserve and to commit it into the fighting on that same day.[23] Katukov had to carry out the received order, but did decide to leave 5 T-34 tanks and 3 T-60 tanks of the 89th Tank Brigade in his reserve.

The remaining tanks, together with an anti-tank gun battery and groups of the motorized rifle battalion loaded aboard five of the tanks, set out in two tank battalions to Malaia Vereika and by 1400 were assembled in the jumping-off area for the attack. According to Katukov's combat order, the 89th Tank Brigade was to bypass Bol'shaia Treshchevka from the east and attack toward Erofeevka and Malaia Treshchevka with the subsequent task to destroy the center of enemy resistance in Somovo and Bol'shaia Treshchevka together with the 1st Guards Tank Brigade. Subsequently the 89th Tank Brigade was supposed to cover the left flank of the 1st Tank Corps and establish tight connection with units of the 2nd Tank Corps.[24]

On the march from Lomovo to Malaia Vereika, the brigade's 202nd Tank Battalion came under an attack from enemy bombers, as a result of which 1 man was killed and 6 wounded, including the battalion commander himself, who was thus knocked out of action even before the start of the battle. After assembling in Malaia Vereika, five T-34 and seven T-60 scouted in the direction of Hill 188.5, Bol'shaia Treshchevka and Erofeevka.[25] Then the brigade's main forces went into action. At 1600 both tank battalions of the 89th Tank Brigade (according to the 89th Tank Brigade's account, 3 KV, 3 T-34 and 16 T-60 went into battle[26]) with submachine gunners of the motorized rifle battalion mounted aboard them launched an attack directly across Hill 188.5 and the combat formations of the 167th Rifle Division that were digging in there.

For the rifle division's units, just as for the 2nd Motorized Rifle Brigade, this was already the third opportunity over the course of the day to make use of a tank attack in order to make an advance, but just as on the preceding two occasions, the infantry either didn't move out behind the tanks or were immediately separated from them by enemy fire. Advancing across the field toward the neck of fields between the two patches of woods, the tanks of the 89th Tank Brigade passed within direct eyesight of the 26th and 27th Tank Brigades of the 2nd Tank Corps that were taking cover to the left in the wooded ravine, but they made no move to support the attack of their neighbor and never left their cover in the ravine. In this same area were tanks of the 118th Tank Brigade, which also refused to move out in support of the 89th Tank Brigade's attack. The startling lack of coordination among the units of the operational group continued to reduce all of the efforts in the one and same sector of attack to nothing. Considering this sorrowful detail of those desperately hard days, when the command of units that were fighting side by side could reach no agreement at all about even the most basic cooperation and with aggravation blamed neighbors for the lack of success, while the command proved unable to nip the flagrant discord in the actions of their subordinates, one can hardly be surprised by the piecemeal attacks of this day.

23 TsAMO, F. 1 TK, op. 1, d. 4, l. 12.
24 TsAMO, F. 89 tbr, op. 1, d. 2, l. 28.
25 TsAMO, F. 89 tbr, op. 1, d. 3, l. 28.
26 TsAMO, F. 89 tbr, op. 1, d. 2, l. 28.

Of course, those units standing in the area of Hill 188.5 had their own commands and were not subordinate to the commander of the 89th Tank Brigade that just went into the attack. However, each one had an order for the offensive that they had received prior to this, which they were supposed to carry out. Taking advantage of the 89th Tank Brigade's attack on this same axis, they might have linked up with it and joined their forces in one combined thrust, in order to carry out together the one and same initial task to breach the German defenses! However, such a theoretical possibility proved hopelessly remote from its implementation in practice, and instead of 80 to 90 tanks, supported by hundreds (if not thousands) of infantrymen, only 22 tanks with 24 submachine gunners went forward (four tank riders each were mounted on only the KV and T-34 tanks).[27]

As soon as the 89th Tank Brigade went on the attack, it, just like all our units during their previous attempts, was also subjected to an enemy airstrike, as a result of which the soldiers of the motorized rifle battalion dismounted and failed to keep up with the tanks. However, in spite of the continuing bombing runs and artillery barrages, the tanks ultimately broke through the narrow strip of field between the two patches of woods, reached the open and relatively flat steppe south of it and began to advance across the fields in the direction of Bol'shaia Treshchevka. Alas, the infantry was no longer with them, and the further they receded from friendly units, the tankers, just as had been the case with the 148th Tank Brigade the evening before, could not count upon the assistance of anyone else. This circumstance plainly had an effect on the commanders of the tank battalions (one of whom had stepped into command of the 202nd Tank Battalion just before the attack itself after the wounding of the previous commander during the approach march) and their subordinates, the actions of which became increasingly less confident.

In the end, instead of an impetuous envelopment of the enemy strongpoint in Bol'shaia Treshchevka from the east, both of the 89th Tank Brigade's battalions approached it from the north, halted, and began firing at the German positions from fixed positions. An attack toward Erofeevka and Malaia Treshchevka with the aim of linking up with the 1st Guards Tank Brigade, and the encirclement and destruction of the enemy opposing the brigades never in fact took place. To a great extent this happened because of the constant attacks by enemy aircraft, which although they failed to inflict heavy losses to the battalions in tanks, strongly constrained their actions, forcing them to endure long periods of bombing attacks. As a result, the battalion commanders were either unable or lacked the combat experience to exploit the maneuverability of the tanks and became bogged down in an extended positional battle with the enemy's unsuppressed anti-tank artillery, in a situation that was plainly to the advantage of the Germans. The Soviet tank crews opted not to close with and attack the enemy's camouflaged and dug-in anti-tank guns head on.

At 2000 in the evening the tankers, apparently, also had to engage in an exchange of fire with German tanks, which had moved out from the direction of Somovo and were threatening the 89th Tank Brigade with a flank attack. Until the sun went down, the battalions exchanged fire with the enemy and then, having expended their ammunition and taken losses (the brigade's documents do not indicate how many or what type), fell back with the onset of darkness to the area of the southern fringe of the large patch of woods in order to refuel and take on more ammunition.[28] Thus, the 89th Tank Brigade had failed to carry out the day's assigned task.

The 1st Guards Tank Brigade, which according to Katukov's plan was supposed to encircle and destroy the enemy in the area of Bol'shaia and Malaia Treshchevka together with the 89th Tank Brigade, in fact proved unable to take Somovo by day's end. At about 2000 in the evening, according to the 1st Tank Corps' operational summary, the 1st Guards Tank Brigade was struck

27 TsAMO, F. 89 tbr, op. 1, d. 2, l. 28.
28 TsAMO, F. 89 tbr, op. 1, d. 3, l. 28.

in the flank by approximately 20 German tanks from the direction of Bol'shaia Treshchevka.[29] Judging from the available evidence, both of the opposing tank groups traded fire at long ranges, but didn't enter close combat and eventually moved off in different directions: the German tanks to the west along the road to Somovo, and the 1st Guards Tank Corps' tanks to the southeast, toward the woodlot at Lebiazh'e.

After this event, the fighting subsided. Thus the pincers of the 1st Guards Tank Brigade's and 89th Tank Brigade's enveloping attack failed to close around the German knot of resistance in Bol'shaia and Malaia Treshchevka. Over the day of fighting the 1st Guards Tank Brigade lost 10 men killed and 6 wounded; 4 T-34s were left burned out by anti-tank artillery fire and 2 one-and-a-half ton trucks from aerial attacks. Units of the brigade were able to seize a German prime mover and a truck that was carrying ammunition, as well as an anti-tank gun, a mortar, 5 machine guns and 3 bicycles. At 2000 the brigade had 28 T-34, 9 T-70 and 18 T-60 still operational.[30]

The day of 23 July 1942 ended for the command of the 1st Tank Corps with disappointing results: even after three days of fighting, the corps' units still had been unable to carry out the operation's task set for them on the first day of the offensive. Although the tank corps on the whole had made a 4-6 kilometer advance, it had still not emerged in operational space and instead of the rapid pursuit of a fleeing foe it was being forced to batter its way through the German defense on the switch line. Meanwhile, little still was known about the course of the fighting in the headquarters of Operational Group Chibisov, since the latest operational updates arriving from the 1st Tank Corps corresponded with the situation as it stood on the evening of 22 July. Without any fresh information, the operational group's headquarters, in turn, was forced to note in a report to the headquarters of Briansk Front at 1100 that "information wasn't arriving" from the 1st Tank Corps.[31]

That same day, the commander of Operational Group Chibisov sent Katukov an urgent directive: "Immediately attack and destroy the enemy motorized column that is retreating from Zemliansk."[32] It is as if this directive went out in a vacuum; no report about executing it followed in response from Katukov, and from the documents of the 1st Tank Corps it follows that it wasn't even received for execution (indeed, how could the tankers have "caught" this retreating column, if it in fact even existed). No victorious communiques came from the 1st Tank Corps either about carrying out its previous task to breach the German defenses. Katukov's tank corps was silent ...

On this same day of 23 July (apparently closer to evening), Operational Group Chibisov's chief of staff Colonel Pilipenko sent the following message to the 1st Tank Corps:

> After a report from the Front headquarters, the Front commander expressed dissatisfaction with your slow actions and ordered immediately with your personal leadership from a tank in the combat formations to complete the destruction of the enemy in the Bol'shaia Treshchevka, Malaia Treshchevka, Somovo, Gremiach'e area. Report on the execution [of this order] to army headquarters and Front headquarters by the morning of 24 July. Confirm receipt. Report on steps you've taken.[33]

By that time Katukov, whom Rokossovsky had ordered to lead the corps in person from a tank among the combat formations, had been sick for the fourth day in a row and was located in the

29 TsAMO, F. 49 tbr (3163), op. 1, d. 5, l. 59.
30 TsAMO, F. 49 tbr (3163), op. 1, d. 5, l. 59.
31 TsAMO, F. 202, op. 5, d. 251, l. 8.
32 TsAMO, F. 202, op. 5, d. 258, l. 45.
33 TsAMO, F. 202, op. 5, d. 258, l. 41.

corps command post in Dolgoe, from where he was directing his units. Having received such a "signal" and angered by the unsatisfactory actions of the tank brigades, Katukov at midnight issued a strict order to the tank corps, in which he expressed his dissatisfaction with his subordinates:

> 1. Despite the insignificant enemy resistance on the Gremiach'e, Somovo line, the corps' brigades have not carried out their assigned tasks in the course of 48 hours. The units are performing criminally slowly, cautiously, with backward glances, advancing 1-2 kilometers in the course of a day, fearing it will come to no good. The enemy, exploiting the criminal slowness of our actions, has time to consolidate on new lines and to bring up artillery and tanks. Having a ten-fold superiority in equipment and personnel over the enemy, the brigades are afraid of decisive actions, and flailing around in place, are suffering losses from enemy artillery fire and aviation.
>
>   Command, control, and communications haven't been organized; the brigades are often losing wire contact with me and taking no measures over several hours for timely reports, and are not using the radio and mobile means. I am noting the exclusively criminal attitude to questions of maintaining communications and timely reporting to me on the part of the commanders of the 1st Motorized Rifle Brigade and the 89th Tank Brigade.
>
>   Operational summaries, as a rule, are arriving with great delay, and in them there is no mention of enemy losses, or what has been captured or destroyed of the enemy. The units are not making progress and not reporting what sort of enemy faces them and what is holding up their advance. The political departments are sitting in the rear, ensconced in bunkers, do not show up among the units, don't know the situation and are not conducting explanatory work with the personnel.
> 2. Units of the 1st Tank Corps throughout the night of 23-24 July are to continue to fulfill their assigned tanks, covering the combat formations of tanks with infantry. At 0400 on 24 July, all the brigades are to launch a simultaneous attack and to seize the Gremiach'e, Ruda, Malaia and Bol'shaia Treshchevka area.
> 3. Launch the general attack of tanks and infantry from the occupied line at 0400 on 24 July. I am warning the brigade commanders about the promptness of the start of the attack with all forces, paying no heed to possible enemy airstrikes. Conduct the thrust of the brigades' main forces on the attack at maximum speeds, disregarding enemy resistance, under the covering fire or your own artillery, mortar and machine guns, as well as tank units assigned to fire from fixed positions. Combat reconnaissance must precede the attack of the main forces, and move 500-700 meters out in front. With the combat reconnaissance, determine weak points in the enemy's system of defense, envelop his flanks and emerge in his rear. With a concentrated attack of the main forces staged in three echelons, destroy the enemy's equipment and personnel. Upon carrying out the task, fortify the occupied areas until the arrival of the rifle units and secure them with combat reconnaissance in the direction of future operations.[34]

As is apparent from the order, the ill Katukov (in the heaviest period of his illness), although not located in person at the front, was aware of the events, and from the reports and summaries from subordinates passed judgement on the course of the brigades' combat operations as a whole, and on the reasons for their lack of success. According to an account that was put together later, the corps' forward command post, consisting of a group of staff officers, from 22 July was located

34 TsAMO, F. 1 TK, op. 1, d. 2, l. 50.

on the western outskirts of Lebiazh'e, headed by the corps' chief of staff and military commissar.[35] Located literally just several kilometers away from the fighting brigades and alongside their headquarters, they were able to obtain first-hand information about the course of the battle. It should be noted however that the operational summaries and orders show that on 22 and 23 July they were signing these documents in the corps headquarters in Dolgoe. In any case, the 1st Tank Corps command was well-informed about the changes occurring at the front and the condition of the subordinate forces, and from the documents it follows that the corps headquarters regularly at 2000 put together an operational summary of the day for higher command.

However, on 23 July the operational group headquarters not only failed to receive an operational summary from the headquarters of the 1st Tank Corps by 2100, it in fact didn't receive any sort of operational messages from the corps command at all, something that a corresponding note in the documents of the operational group speaks about eloquently.[36] This seems even stranger, given the fact that technical communications between the headquarters of the operational group and the headquarters of the 1st Tank Corps were never broken. Moreover, both headquarters were located in neighboring villages literally just a kilometer apart, and a liaison officer could even deliver the necessary piece of paper from Dolgoe to Lukino on foot (if there was no longer any trust in the radio or telephone), not to mention the possibility of quickly delivering it by car or motorcycle.

Arguably, it is only possible to explain such a strange absence of operational information from the 1st Tank Corps at the headquarters of Group Chibisov by the fact that this information was *never even sent*, even though the headquarters of the 1st Tank Corps was experiencing no shortage of operational information. Obviously, the point is that while anticipating a breakthrough of the enemy's defenses by the corps' brigades to be just around the corner, the headquarters of the 1st Tank Corps in the meantime refrained from submitting summaries that spoke only of defeats and failures, which unequivocally meant that the task had so far not been carried out, and which no matter how they were written would more likely point to the failures of the tank corps, not its successes.

One way or another, one thing remains inarguable: the headquarters of Group Chibisov had a totally vague notion regarding the course of the 1st Tank Corps' combat operations for 23 July, and on the night of 23-24 July remained ignorant both about their results and about whether it had carried out (or failed to carry out) its own orders. More knowledge of what was happening, in addition to its operational strand, might also have cast light on a different matter, which subsequently would always remain something of a mystery. On 23 July 1942, a knocked-out KV tank was discovered by "a scout of the 1st Tank Corps" (more likely, this was a crew of one of the 89th Tank Brigade's tanks), on the turret of which was a dead man with four bars on his collar, which corresponded to the rank of regimental commissar. True, the scouts never climbed into the tank, made no effort to investigate and continued to move on, and neither the command of the 1st Tank Corps, nor the command of Operational Group Chibisov, nor their neighbors from the 2nd Tank Corps learned about the scout's discovery at the time …

* * *

35 TsAMO, F. 1 TK, op. 1, d. 4 , l. 10.
36 TsAMO, F. 202, op. 5, d. 251, l. 8, 12.

Addendum

From the recollections of the former commissar of the 26th Tank Brigade's 270th Tank Battalion

A.S. Kunilov

I was the commissar of the 270th Tank Battalion. My battalion was the guide battalion. We passed through Bol'shaia Vereika, Malaia Vereika and reached the fringe of some woods. However, there was a gateway between the woods and the enemy had deployed an anti-tank gun there. We had to destroy this gun in order to allow the entire tank corps to pass. At high speed we broke through there and "opened" this gateway [...]

The battalion commander was Filatov. We had one company up front and the other trailing behind. I, as a commissar, agreed with the commander that I would move with that company. In front of us was a field of sunflowers, although the blossoms had all been sliced off, so that only the stems remained. I was advancing with an open hatch. In front I saw a man running about 50 meters ahead of us. I weighed the situation and thought it was too soon for our infantry. I asked the driver-mechanic: "Do you see him?"

– "I see him," he replied.

– "Well, then, step on it."

The man turned around and raised his hands. The driver-mechanic wanted to run him over, but I could see that this wasn't an ordinary soldier and shouted at the driver, "Stop!" He braked, and the German took off at a run. We started after him. Coming up to him, I pulled out a Nagan revolver and fired a shot at him – a miss. The second shot also missed. Then he fired at me from a pistol. I next grabbed a submachine gun and fired a burst, and shouted "*Hände hoch*!" Then he raised his hands. I climbed out of the machine and asked: "Where are the *Deutschen soldaten*?" He replied, "All around."

I gave him a cuff and then asked again where the German soldiers were. He then replied, "*Nicht verstehen*." Now the driver-mechanic said, "Let me shoot him, Comrade Commissar." As soon as the German heard the word "commissar", he immediately straightened up and started to give me all sorts of photographs. As soon as we walked over to my machine, a [German] cannon started firing at me. I began to shoot and ordered the driver-mechanic to correct the fire. I fired 5 shells, and the third shell knocked out this cannon. At this the German, who turned out to be a captain, rose and said, "*Gut, gut, Rus*'".

I steered the tank into a ravine, and here Ju-87s dropped 8 bombs on me, but the German captain was beneath the tank at this time, lying there and shaking like a leaf. He kept saying only, "*Raketen, raketen*", which meant he wanted us to fire a flare, since white flares were his signal to his own guys. Then I seated him on the floor of the machine and took him to the brigade command post. He turned out to be an artilleryman, with 10 years of service in the army, and he had graduated from a German higher officers' school. He was 32 years old and his name was Rudolf Steik.[37]

A Briansk Front intelligence report continues this story:

A captain and battery commander with the 387th Artillery Regiment (387th Infantry Division) who was captured on 23.07.42 in the area of Kaver'ia revealed: the 387th Infantry

37 Archive IRI RAN, F. 2, section 1, op. 118, d. 3, l. 145.

> Division was formed in January 1942 in Austria, and arrived at the Eastern Front in the Kursk area on 10.06.42. The 541st Infantry Regiment, to which his battery was attached, between 13 and 23.7.42 lost 50% of its personnel killed or wounded. The 387th Infantry Division is part of the VII Army Corps. The 387th Infantry Division includes the 541st, 542nd and 543rd Infantry Regiments, the 387th Artillery Regiment, the 387th Medical Battalion, the 387th Anti-tank Battalion, the 387th Signals Battalion, a sanitary company, an engineer company, a bakery, a platoon to slaughter cattle and a mobile transport column. The commander of the 387th Infantry Division is Major General Jahr; the commander of the 387th Artillery Regiment is Colonel Geruch, and the commander of the 541st Infantry Regiment is Colonel von Langsdorf.
>
> The 387th Artillery Regiment consists of a headquarters and 3 battalions; the 1st and 2nd Battalion each has two batteries with 4 105-mm guns in each. The 3rd Battalion consists of two batteries, each with 4 150-mm heavy howitzers. In addition, in the month of May the 387th Artillery Regiment received two batteries of multi-barreled rocket launchers (8 75-mm).[38]

From data on the losses of the German 387th Infantry Division it follows that on 23.7.42, one of the division's officers did go missing.[39] Chances are that this officer was in fact the above-named Captain Rudolf Steik. However, recently uncovered new documents give us more accurate information about this military prisoner and his place of capture. One file contains a transcript of his interrogation. It states, "Captain, commander of the 2nd Battery, I Battalion of the 387th Infantry Division's 387th Artillery Regiment Rudolf Schenk, 1905 year of birth [...] On 23.7.42 the military prisoner was located at an observation post 3 kilometers northwest of Kaver'ia. Two guns of his battery were destroyed by the fire of our tanks, and then his communications line was severed. He sent two couriers to repair the break, when he was encircled by 4 of our tanks and taken prisoner."[40]

Political reports from the 1st Guards Rifle Division show the effects of the war on the civilian population:

> 18.7.42 ... In the course of the day political workers and especially assigned agitators of all four rifle regiments conducted work with the population in the sector of defense regarding an evacuation from the frontline area. General meetings were held. Fifty percent of the population in certain villages, as for example in Apukhtino and Davydovka expressed their willingness to evacuate voluntarily and had already partially abandoned their homes and departed, but a large part of the population doesn't wish to evacuate and is trying to remain in their homes by any means, offering resistance. Many residents are hiding in the rye and bushes, hoping in the evening or at night to return again to their huts. Many have begun to cross to the western bank of the Olym River. The crying and wailing of women is frequently audible. Many seniors and women with children declare: "Take all of our cattle away from us, shoot us, but we won't go!" In Griaznovka, one howling woman cursed Soviet power, after which she was arrested. Evacuation in all the villages is being conducted with the use of force. Many explain their unwillingness to leave with the fact that they've already been evacuated once and left abandoned to fate. However, the German air force subjected them to a bombing and they

38 TsAMO, F. 202, op. 12, d. 146, l. 355.
39 NARA, T-314, roll 354, fr. 726-727.
40 TsAMO, F. 202, op. 12, d. 499, l. 1096.

> returned to their former residence. Nevertheless, the evacuation is going well wherever there has been success in mobilizing a large number of vehicles.
>
> 21.7.42 … Evacuation is proceeding with the use of compulsory measures. In the villages of Griaznovka and Davydovka, and in other villages, the peasants' cattle are being rounded up and driven away. The people trail behind the cattle. Those who are resisting with particular stubbornness are forcibly removed from the villages in vehicles and farm wagons. The women are leaving with wails and tears, demonstrating their great dissatisfaction ….
>
> 22.7.42 … Eight families that stubbornly resisted evacuation still remain in Afrosimovka. This village is located in direct proximity to the front, and whenever force is used against the stubbornly resisting, the women beat the children so that they all start crying, while the women are themselves crying, so a great commotion is raised. The enemy at this time starts a heavy fire from machine guns and mortars.

Another political report from the 1st Guards Rifle Division focused on the situation with supplies:

> The question of armor-piercing incendiary shells, as well as of armor-piercing composite rigid shells for the 45-mm guns, is particularly acute in the division. There is a shortage of mortar shells of all calibers, particularly 82-mm shells. In Group Chibisov, artillery supply officers announced that they don't expect an improvement in the supply with these ammunition types. The situation stands poorly with the supply of oats and flour. There is no oatmeal at all, and only a single day of flour supply remains. The lack of transport continues to remain a great complication for the division; I request assistance. Twice I have requested typed agitation leaflets for the German soldiers from the 7th Department of Briansk Front headquarters, but the leaflets with typed material still haven't been sent.[41]

41 TsAMO, F. 1 gv. sd, op. 1, d. 24, ll. 270, 279, 290.

10

Operational Group Chibisov's reserve enters the fighting

From the very outset of the operation, the offensive on the right flank of Operational Group Chibisov developed very slowly. It is more accurate to say that it was stopped almost as soon as the units operating there went on the attack, even before reaching the enemy's main belt of defenses. Time after time the rifle companies and battalions rose to launch an attack, but again and again they came under withering mortar and artillery fire, as well as traversing bursts of German machine-gun fire that cut men down. Fierce airstrikes were regularly added to all of this, and our units at the front practically had nothing at all with which to oppose the bombers. No decisive thrust forward took place; the bullets and shell fragments were remorselessly mowing down the attackers, and the attacks collapsed almost as soon as they started.

Against this backdrop of overall failure, tankers of the 203rd Tank Battalion together with soldiers of the 340th Rifle Division's 1244th Rifle Regiment were able to achieve a sole success – a breakthrough to Hill 213.8. However, even this success didn't develop into anything more: after reaching the crest of the hill, the offensive stalled even here. Having lost 3 tanks knocked out and 2 tanks destroyed, the tankers went over to a defense, while the infantry hastily began to fortify a small section of the captured German trenches. Having reached the crest of the hill, the regiment's rifle battalions came under a heavy crossfire from the front and both flanks, which together with the intense artillery barrages and airstrikes put a halt to their further advance.

The breakthrough by the tanks of the 1st Guards Tank Brigade across Hill 181.8 on the evening of 21 July didn't at all lead to the "liquidation" of the German node of resistance there, as was mistakenly reported in the account from the 1st Tank Corps command. The tanks overran the German trenches on the hill and then pushed on to reach the northern outskirts of Lebiazh'e, but after their departure the enemy sheltering in the trenches "came to life" and just as before continued to put up bitter resistance to our rifle units, preventing them from taking the hill. After the retreat of the tattered battalions of the 387th Infantry Division's 542nd Infantry Regiment from their positions toward the Bol'shaia Vereika River, the enemy strongpoint on Hill 181.8 became a cornerstone of the enemy's line of defense on the right flank which stubbornly held out under the attacks of Group Chibisov's units, thereby limiting the breach in the German line.

For the entire day fighting went on as well for the elongated patch of woods to the northwest; the men of the German combat outposts that had fallen back regrouped in these woods. A combat dispatch from the 340th Rifle Division at 1500 on 21 July states that by this time the 1142nd Rifle Regiment had seized this patch of woods, but from subsequent reports it is clear that this information was mistaken, since combat continued for this patch of woods throughout the night and the entire following day. The attempt to bypass to the east of the woods also failed because of heavy enemy fire from Hill 181.8.[1] Moreover, according to the operation's plan, this hill was located

1 TsAMO, F. 340 sd, op. 1, d. 24, l. 212.

on the boundary line between the 340th and 193rd Rifle Divisions. Having encountered strong enemy resistance there, the right-flank regiment of the 193rd Rifle Division exploited the advance made to the east by the 167th Rifle Division and used an outflanking maneuver from the northeast to reach Lebiazh'e, leaving the German strongpoint on its flank on Hill 181.8 unsuppressed, which was noted by the command of the 340th Rifle Division. (Only on the third day of fighting, after our rifle elements had broken into the patch of woods and then had to abandon it due to a German counterattack, was the 340th Rifle Division's 1142nd Rifle Regiment "forced to take Hill 181.8 with fighting" and finally overcame the German resistance here.)[2]

During the fighting, a gap appeared between the 340th and 284th Rifle Divisions, which in the opinion of the 340th Rifle Division's command occurred because the 284th Rifle Division "didn't attack".[3] However, in fact this gap appeared in part because of the decisions of the 340th Rifle Division command, which on the night of 21-22 July withdrew the right-flank 1140th Rifle Regiment "that had suffered heavy losses from flanking fire coming out of the woods" from the western slopes of Hill 213.8 and inserted it in between the 1144th Rifle Regiment in the center and the left-flank 1142nd Rifle Regiment. Striving to guard the division's right flank against any surprises, the commander of the 340th Rifle Division issued an order to the now right-flank 1144th Rifle Regiment together with the 1244th Destroyer Artillery Regiment that had been attached to the division to defend stubbornly along the lines it had achieved with a front facing to the south and southwest and to "screen the woods" north of Vysochkino – an enemy strongpoint that was located in the neighboring 284th Rifle Division's sector of attack, but which was also preventing the right flank of the 340th Rifle Division from advancing.

Back on the evening of 21 July, the commander of the 340th Rifle Division Colonel Martirosian in his report to Chibisov persistently asked him to give "instructions to the commander of the 284th Rifle Division about making contact" with the right flank of the 340th Rifle Division, which speaking in a different language meant forcing his neighbor "that hadn't attacked" to at least shift his units several kilometers to the east in order to close the gap between it and his division.[4] However, reports that were arriving from the 284th Rifle Division testified that the units of the division, which had been greatly weakened in the preceding fighting and yet were extended along a lengthier front than those of other divisions, were hardly capable of carrying out the disgruntled requests of an angered neighbor.

Seeing only his own point of view, Martirosian hardly knew, or more accurately, refused to get off his perch in order to find out that even before start of the fighting, there were less than a couple thousand "active bayonets" and a miserly quantity of armaments and equipment in the 284th Rifle Division, which was well below table strength in these categories, as well as a grievous lack of ammunition (as has been noted previously, because of the lack of high-explosive and shrapnel shells, the division's artillery had to fire armor-piercing shells at the enemy's firing positions and infantry, involuntary expending their reserve of these shells in some sort of "firing at swallows").[5]

In distinction from all the other divisions of Group Chibisov that took part in the offensive, the 284th Rifle Division had no armor support at all, and yet had been expected to attack along its entire front. It is not surprising that the 284th Rifle Division's part in the offensive was more

2 Ibid.

3 Ibid.

4 TsAMO, F. 340 sd, op. 1, d. 24, l. 196.

5 The political chief of the 284th Rifle Division reported on 22.7.42: "The lack of rifles, machine guns, mortars and transport, which slows the bringing up of ammunition and food and the evacuation of wounded, continues to reflect on the course of the fighting. There is no footgear or uniforms to replace those that have become worn out. In addition, the division's elements lack up to 100 political workers. I ask to hasten the dispatch of political workers to the division in accordance with my requests." (TsAMO, F. 202, op. 36, d. 129, l. 34.)

nominal than real, about which even its results eloquently speak, despite the vigorous tone of the divisional reports: by the end of the day, judging from these reports, the division's regiments had reached ... virtually the very same lines from which they had in fact launched their attacks.

Given these circumstances, Chibisov considered it impractical, even if it was at all possible, to expand the 284th Rifle Division's sector of attack to the east and thereby further extend the thin regiments, which even without this were already stretched to the limit: Batiuk's rifle division (the 284th) was at the end of its strength. On the other hand, Chibisov also refused to extend the front of the 340th Rifle Division to the right given the situation that had arisen. The visible advance of the tank corps on the left together with their supporting rifle divisions, as well as the regrouping of the 340th Rifle Division's 1140th Rifle Regiment to the left that was already underway, led Chibisov to believe that Martirosian's 340th Rifle Division would achieve the line on the Sukhaia Vereika River that had been designated for it by an outflanking of the enemy from the left, even if it hadn't been able to achieve its objective with a frontal attack. For this it was necessary to increase the force of its pressure on the left flank, without dispersing its strength on other sectors.

The reports from the 340th Rifle Division on 21 July also spoke to Chibisov in favor of the 340th Rifle Division's visible success on its left flank; according to these reports, its 1142nd Rifle Regiment by 1500 on 21 July had taken the elongated patch of woods, and by 2000 was already tied up in fighting for the triangular patch of woods. In actual fact, these reports didn't provide a reliable basis for an accurate assessment, since by nighttime the elements of the 1142nd Rifle Regiment that had surged ahead had already fallen back from the lines they had reached earlier in the day, but judging from the documents, Chibisov wasn't aware of this.[6] According to captured German documents, the "Russian infantry" only managed to break through to the triangular-shaped patch of woods on 22 July, but after a Luftwaffe airstrike, they had abandoned it and fallen back to the east and southeast.[7]

In addition, it was becoming increasingly apparent with the 340th Rifle Division's shift to the left that the unsuppressed enemy strongpoint in the woods north of Vysochkino that still hadn't been taken was beginning to loom menacingly over the 340th Rifle Division's right flank. Considering the poor condition of the 284th Rifle Division and the results of its attack on the first day of the operation, it was hardly worth expecting that its weakened units would be able to eliminate this firmly embedded German splinter on its left flank, or even make some sort of substantial advance at all. In the reports from the division there were regular appeals to replenish the units with men, weapons and transport, for which the command of Operational Group Chibisov lacked the needed resources. However, the problem that had arisen due to the faltering of the offensive in the sectors of the 340th and 284th Rifle Divisions had to be resolved somehow, and as quickly as possible, which would improve the prospects of the entire operation.

Obviously, it was these thoughts that prompted the decision of Chibisov not to be limited to half-measures while searching for forces in order to plug the gap between the 284th and 340th Rifle Divisions, but to resolve this problem in a cardinal fashion and to launch here a powerful auxiliary attack against the enemy. Such an attack might also assist the offensive of the tank corps on the main axis to the east, while also simultaneously eradicating at last the German knot of resistance north of Vysochkino that was strongly hindering the advance of the operational group's units.

On the second day of the offensive, the commander of the operational group Lieutenant General Chibisov believed that the time had come to commit his reserves, and to throw not "crumbs" of reinforcements on the teetering scale of the battle's outcome, but the heavy weight of a fresh rifle

6 TsAMO, F. 340 sd, op. 1, d. 24, l. 194, 196, 211.
7 NARA, T-315, roll 2120, fr. 000738.

division – more than 12,500 men, plus the attached 201st Tank Brigade. On the morning of 22 July he signed a combat order to the commander of the 237th Rifle Division about moving out the units entrusted to his command to the Lomovo area.[8]

* * *

The 237th Rifle Division was typical of the wave of rifle divisions that formed in the winter and spring of 1942, when on the doorstep to the summer battles at the decision of the *Stavka*, the creation of reserve formations began in the deep rear of the country. The directive about forming the division had been issued back at the end of November 1941, after which there followed an order to the Siberian Military District dated 3 December 1941, according to which the division's forming up process began in Novosibirsk Oblast. On 15 December, the personnel began to arrive in the new division, which received the numerical designation of the 455th Rifle Division. On 13 January 1942, the division was relabeled as the 237th Rifle Division and the 835th, 838th and 841st Rifle Regiments joined it, as well as the 891st Artillery Regiment and an entire host of smaller units and elements. Colonel Tertyshnyi was appointed in command of the division; Colonel Burmanov became his chief of staff (although in July 1942 this post was occupied by Major Marol'), and Senior Battalion Commissar Prokof'ev became its commissar.[9]

On 15 February 1942 Colonel Tertyshni celebrated his 44th birthday. In his biography there was a lot similar to the biographies of a whole host of his command peers: a primary education of several years of schooling, hard work as an adolescent, then service in the Red Army as a young man. The Russian Civil War was at its very height, when on 10 April 1919 the 21-year-old Ukrainian Petr Tertyshni (according to his social origins a "worker from a peasant family" as he subsequently declared) voluntarily joined the Red Army. As a soldier of a railroad battalion and then a Red Army private of a rifle regiment, he fought on the Deniken and Polish fronts; when peace finally arrived, he decided to remain in the army and make military service his career. Thus began his long path up the steps of the career ladder, upon which after almost 20 years of service he had risen from Red Army private to colonel. Over this period of time he had shed his old habits in courses at a division headquarters (1921), before entering the Kiev Consolidated Military School (in 1925), while in 1937 he finally completed his basic education, having passed non-resident courses for the 7th grade. Two years later, he completed middle school.

Fortunately, the purges in the Red Army associated with searches for enemies of the people bypassed him. At their very height he was serving as a deputy commissioner on a Soviet control commission with the Soviet of People's Commissars for the Far East District. In 1938, he rose to the rank of colonel and in January 1939 went to serve in the headquarters of the Khar'kov Military District. It didn't fall to his lot to participate in the military conflicts or "liberation campaigns" in the pre-war epoch. From December 1940 he was studying in the *Vystrel* [Shot] courses to improve the command staff. When war threatened, he served for a short time as a military commandant on the city of Novgorod's Military Command Board, after which in July 1941 he received command of the 1004th Rifle Regiment of the then-forming 305th Rifle Division.

Thus, having served since 1930 in purely staff positions or on a Soviet control commission (his last combat-related post prior to this was – company commander), Colonel Tertyshni immediately entered the Great Patriotic War as a regiment commander, having behind him the combat experience of a Red Army private, a rich term of army service in the turbulent 1930s and an education of unclear breadth and depth. He, like very many other commanders of the Workers'

8 TsAMO, F. 237 sd, op. 1, d. 26, l. 25.
9 TsAMO, F. 1518 (237 sd), op. 1, d. 7, l. 1.

and Peasants' Red Army during that desperately hard period at the start of the war had to learn and gain experience already in the course of fighting and the bitter retreats; for this "tutelage" on their own mistakes and those of others, their soldiers had to pay with their blood and lives. The regiment entered combat at the end of August 1941 and as part of the 305th Rifle Division fought at Novgorod. In November 1941 Tertyshnyi was appointed deputy commander of the 3rd Tank Division that had been pulled back into the reserve (by that time there was not a single tank left in the division), and then at the beginning of December 1941 he received appointment to the post of commander of the 237th Rifle Division that was forming up in Siberia and was sent to remote Novosibirsk.[10]

By 15 February 1942 the 237th Rifle Division had been essentially fully-staffed with personnel and then went through a month-long program of training. On 31 March the division received its combat banner at a ceremonial parade, and on 22 April its command received an order to restage to Vologda, where the 237th Rifle Division re-assembled at the beginning of May and joined the 2nd Reserve Army. The division's units began receiving their weapons only at the beginning of June 1942.

The stay in Vologda ended on 6 July 1942, when Tertyshnyi received an order to move the division to a new area by railroad. On 7 July the division's trains were moving to the south and by 13 July they had arrived and unloaded at Lipetsk Station, after which the 237th Rifle Division joined the 3rd Reserve Army. On the following day the division was transferred to Voronezh Front's 60th Army, and here it received an order to march to the front. On the afternoon of 14 July, units of the division were marching to the southwest.

It was the middle of a hot summer, and tall plumes of dense clouds of dust accompanied the regimental columns. Because of an acute lack of horses and motorized transport (alas, a typical feature of virtually all the reserve rifle divisions that were then moving toward the front on the Don River), the soldiers not only had to carry their own weapon and gear, but also heavy machine guns, mortars, anti-tank rifles and the ammunition for them. At dawn on 15 July, having marched approximately 45-50 kilometers, the division's units assembled in the Nikol'skoe, Vorob'evka, Russkaia Lazovka area and set to work on fortifications for a line of defense. (Local residents recalled that "the soldiers were so exhausted that they were collapsing and falling asleep in the dust on the roadside.") On the next day the commander of the 237th Rifle Division received an order to move to the Voronezh River to the area of the village of Glushitsy, which prompted another march on foot for an additional 20-25 kilometers.

The regiments hadn't yet had time to assemble there, when another order followed to pivot the division in almost the opposite direction (from the south to the northwest) and to cross the Don River at Kon'-Kolodez' and Khlevnoe: the 237th Rifle Division had been shifted from Voronezh Front's 60th Army to the Briansk Front. The division's combat journal literally dedicated just two lines to the river crossing: On 17 July the crossing began, while on 18 July the units of the division had primarily completed it – a sparse, perfunctory entry. However, we still have the possibility of picturing the conditions in which the division's units crossed the broad and full-flowing Don River back then.

There were no bridges across the river in either Khlevnoe (more accurately, in Dmitriashevka) or in Kon'-Kolodez'. Only a low-capacity ferry traveled from bank to bank in Dmitriashevka; it had already been considerably riddled by bullets and shell fragments from the regular "visits" of the Luftwaffe. Kon'-Kolodez' lacked even this. There was no way this sole ferry could transfer a full-strength rifle division with all of its weapons, equipment, and transport quickly to the opposite bank. So if the artillery, vehicles and wagons would have to wait for their turn to cross aboard the

10 This information was taken from the service card of P.V. Tertyshnyi.

ferry, then the overwhelming majority of the division's men had only one way to cross to the west bank of the river – by swimming, with their weapon, gear and personal items. In other words, each was on his own resources, and had to cross by demonstrating resourcefulness and native wit or ... drown, but they were to carry out the order at any cost. A former nurse of the 237th Rifle Division E.I. Platonova decades after the war wrote about what it was like back then. As a testimony to the men and women, I will cite a lengthy excerpt from her memoirs:

> When they told us that a big river was in front of us, which we would have to cross by swimming, many soldiers lost heart. After all, not all of them knew how to swim, and those who could swim had doubts. No one had ever tried to swim while carrying a load, and here you had all of the soldier's property: a backpack that holding a greatcoat, boots, grenades and bullets. All of this would immediately sink a soldier to the bottom of the river as soon as he entered the water. The command was in a hurry, there was no time to wait. So they crossed; some on rafts, some in boats, some clinging to logs, others to wood doors.
>
> The soldiers were floating, hurrying as best they could to the opposite bank. Fountains of water were rising here and there in the river from exploding shells. Some shells struck a target, smashing the raft or boat and killing or wounding the soldiers; and everyone who was in the boat or on the raft would sink to the bottom, and this was happening across the entire river. So many bodies were floating in the river, who was counting them? Or else you'd see a cluster of drowned men floating along the river, and your entire body gets stiff in paroxysms of fear. Who knew their family names? On what lists would they be entered? Missing in action? But they weren't missing; they had drowned and there would be no lists for them.
>
> In our sector, where our battalion crossed, thick ropes had been stretched across the river in several places. The river's current was swift, and if you became separated from the rope, to which you were clinging with one hand, then you had to look to where the current was taking you and grab on to another rope. If you didn't, the water would begin to spin you around like in a whirlpool. There were not many who could swim well and rely upon their own strength.
>
> Having placed my carbine and backpack, in which my greatcoat and nursing bag were stuffed, on a raft, I asked the platoon commander to deliver it to the opposite bank, while I took hold of a rope with my hand, entered the water, pushed off from the bottom, and began to swim. Before the war I was considered a good swimmer; several times I had swum across the Moscow River and back again without resting. Every 3 meters, there was a soldier paddling along while holding the rope. I was calm and confident that my comrades wouldn't allow me to drown and would help me keep my head above the water. I was approaching the middle of the river, where the current was faster and more turbulent. Fascist aircraft appeared in the sky overhead and rained bombs down upon us. It is frightening to wait out a bombing while sitting in a trench, but even more frightening in a river, when your entire body is exposed [It must be said, that in the documents of the 237th Rifle Division that I studied, there was no mention of any artillery barrages or bombings when crossing the Don River. To be sure, though, there was also no report about the process and results of the river crossing – I.S.]
>
> Several soldiers that were sitting in boats were wounded by the near explosion of bombs. The boats were flipping over by the blast wave; soldiers were drowning or floundering like kittens, trying to keep their head above the water, but the load that was on some soldiers quickly dropped them to the bottom or else the men were quickly carried by the river's current toward us or past us. Someone grabbed me from behind with one arm wrapped around my neck and the other over my shoulder. I couldn't hold his weight; the rope slipped out of my hand and I started to sink to the bottom. The soldier that was clinging to me let go, but I

could feel his body above my head. I was running out of oxygen and had to make it back to the surface.

I opened my eyes and took a look into the translucence of the water. Sinking quickly, I felt my feet hitting the river bottom, when suddenly a stout drowned man rose up in front of me; his arms were outspread as if trying to catch a victim. His rifle was hanging on his waist belt; it was what had dragged him down and prevented him from swimming to the surface. I crouched, gave an energetic thrust from the river bottom, and shot to the surface underneath the outstretched arm of the drowned soldier. I was hungrily gulping air with my open mouth, but started swimming with all my might toward the riverbank. Having calmed my breathing, I glanced around and saw that the riverbank was nearby. Soldiers were standing up to their chest in the water, catching the weakened, swimming soldiers and hauling them to the bank, then immediately turning back for others. That's how soldiers dragged me out on to the riverbank. Many went missing during the soldiers' crossing of the Don River, but who is guilty in this? The war.[11]

(Likely, it is also worth adding to this the organization of the river crossing itself, and the haste, when people being driven by a strict order drowned because of the elementary lack of boats, rafts and flotation devices).

Judging from the recollection presented above, the 237th Rifle Division suffered its first losses even before entering combat, leaving behind some of their dead soldiers in hastily-dug graves along the banks of the Don River, while others were lost forever in its dark, deep waters.[12] After the ordeal of the river crossing, the division's units assembled in the Dmitriashevka area, then moved out to the west and began to prepare another line of defense along the eastern bank of the Nega Creek. According to the initial plan, the 237th Rifle Division was supposed to be made subordinate to the 5th Tank Army, but at the moment of its regiments' crossing of the Don River, that tank army had been disbanded, and the division joined the reserve of the quickly-formed operational group of Briansk Front. On 21 and 22 July, units of the 237th Rifle Division (except for its artillery regiment, which was attached to the 167th Rifle Division) continued to build a new line of defense in the Kreshchenka, Posel'skoe, Don area. It was here that Chibisov's order about moving up to the front found the division.

Having received the packet from the signals officer at 1430 on 22 July, the division commander Colonel Tertyshnyi, chances are, was shocked when, having read the order, he learned that the division entrusted to him was supposed to move out from its occupied area … at 1130 (which is to say, three hours ago!) and re-assemble in the Lomovo area. Including the time needed to prepare for the march, it turned out that Chibisov's order was late by five or six hours.[13]

Carrying out the order, the 237th Rifle Division on the afternoon of 22 July left the line of defense they had been working on since the day before and started a march to the west. Once again the company and battalion columns became choked with dust as they marched across fields and along dirt roads connecting the villages, while transporting the majority of their authorized weapons in the already accustomed fashion – on the shoulders of their soldiers. No matter how the commanders of their elements spurred them on, the excessively burdened soldiers were simply

11 *Voenno-istoricheskii arkhiv* [*Military History Archive*), No. 9 (2009), pp. 86-87.

12 In the available data on irrecoverable losses in personnel of the 237th Rifle Division, there is no mention of those killed, drowned or missing while crossing the Don River. One comes across only a report of one soldier who died while on march and was buried "on the left bank of the Don River."

13 TsAMO, F. 237 sd, op. 1, d. 26, l. 25.

unable to march faster than 5-6 kilometers an hour. In addition, the Luftwaffe began to appear in the sky once again, frequently forcing the marching troops to scatter off the road and drop to the ground, and wait for when the enemy aircraft would fly away, which significantly reduced the average speed of the march. As a result, there was no way to offset the multi-hour delay in receiving Chibisov's order by means of the soldiers' feet, and by the time designated in the order – 1800 – the rifle division still hadn't arrived in the jumping-off area. Only later that night did the hot, dust-covered, shuffling men of the rifle regiments finally begin to assemble in their designated areas.

The division's artillery regiment (which had been attached to the 167th Rifle Division) didn't even begin to move out to the jumping-off area that night, because it had been pulled out of the fighting only at the end of 22 July, and now had to make an approximately 10-kilometer march to its new firing positions in the gathering twilight and darkness. With this the day of 22 July came to an end.

Thus, Chibisov was unable to introduce the reserve rifle division into the fighting on the second day of the operation, so its attack was postponed to 23 July. Considering the new reality, the operational group commander even before the end of 22 July issued an order for an attack on the next day, and set H-hour for the attack at 0700 on 23 July. However, as was the case with the preceding order, the commander of the 237th Rifle Division received this order only after many hours had passed, at 0340 on 23 July.

(One can only be perplexed about by such "haste" in delivering the most important operational orders of the high command to the subordinates. It was just 6-7 kilometers between the headquarters of the operational group in Lukino and the headquarters of the 237th Rifle Division in a grove northwest of Lomovo, but the absence of radio or wire communications with a division on the march, plus the established regimen of the essential hand delivery of the official "paper" to the subordinate headquarters led to the fact that the liaison officer that was carrying the secret packet spent hours wandering around in the night searching for the appropriate headquarters, and arrived there only just before sunrise.)

The sky to the northeast was already beginning to grow light and only a little more than three hours were left before the designated H-hour for the attack, but the division command still had to assemble the regiment commanders, give them their tasks, allow them time to assign tasks to their battalion commanders (and further along down the chain of command), and take a multitude of other imperative steps to organize the forthcoming attack – and all this over the remaining time, which would be barely enough for the suitable attack preparations of a cohesive, experienced formation, whose commanders had already been in battle with their units and knew their business well. Here, however, we're talking about the organization of the very first battle of a totally green division and command staff, the majority of which didn't even have any frontline experience! What then might come of an inadequately prepared attack in such circumstances? Division commander Tertyshnyi had a lot to think about …

In his entire 22-years of military service, the division's upcoming combat baptism, and that of the division commander himself, perhaps, would become the most significant milestone not only of his career as an officer, but of his entire life. The fate of thousands of his subordinate men now depended on his actions, and the responsibility for the decisions he now took was very great. He clearly understood that the division's units didn't have time to prepare for the upcoming attack as they should.

The H-hour of 0700 first of all meant that the rifle regiments would be forced to attack without the necessary artillery support, because the 237th Rifle Division's artillery regiment hadn't even managed to take up its firing positions by the hour designated for it in the order, not to mention to conduct the necessary reconnaissance, firing calculations and registration of targets. So far there had been no success in establishing contact with the attached 201st Tank Brigade, and the commander of the 237th Rifle Division didn't even know precisely where it was located.

By midnight the division command had only been able to make contact with its neighbor on the right, the 284th Rifle Division and to receive from it the initial, general information about the enemy and the situation.[14] However, this information was totally inadequate for a detailed workup of a plan of battle, especially because there had been no possibility to examine the German forward edge, let alone do any detailed study of it or conduct elementary reconnaissance with the command staff. Yet after all, such reconnoitering was absolutely essential at least so that the commanders could familiarize themselves with the totally unfamiliar ground and orient themselves on the battlefield so as not to stray from their designated axis of advance.

The division's supply situation remained a headache for the 237th Rifle Division's command. This primarily concerned the supply of ammunition and food. Whereas the "dedicated soldier" might be able to do without the latter, there was no dedication that could offset a lack of shells and mortar rounds, yet here things were standing quite badly. The chronic shortage of motorized transport, deepened in the preceding days by the lengthy marches and the unsatisfactory supply of fuel and lubricants led to the fact that the division's supply train stretched back all the way from Dmitriashevka to Lipetsk, because the rear services simply could not bring up all of the division's belongings at once. They were forced to return for the supplies they had left behind – and the further the division moved away from the station of unloading in Lipetsk, the longer its tail became.[15]

After coming out of the battle on 22 July, the division's 691st Artillery Regiment had just three-fourths of an authorized combat load of ammunition, which was completely insufficient for an effective artillery preparation and for supporting the infantry in the course of the attack. The mortar elements didn't have a stockpile of shells, and obviously could "rain down" on the enemy's heads only that small number of shells that they had brought along in their batteries' wagons (in the corresponding notes of the document about the reserve of 50-mm, 82-mm and 120-mm mortar shells available in the division by 23 July, instead of numbers, there are only meaningful dashes).[16]

Considering the circumstances and reasonably believing that the division needed more time in order to properly prepare for the attack, Tertyshnyi mustered his courage and asked the operational group commander to postpone the attack until 1500. By the morning of 23 July, when this query was received, almost 24 hours had passed since Chibisov's decision to commit his reserve into the fighting (and thus far it had not been committed, and its entrance into the fighting was being delayed even longer); nevertheless, the headquarters and commander of Operational Group Chibisov listened to the arguments of the 237th Rifle Division's commander and allowed him to postpone the attack for 8 hours.[17]

Making use of this reprieve, the command of the 237th Rifle Division rolled out a hasty preparation of the units for battle. The regiment and battalion commanders were able to reconnoiter the terrain and identify landmarks for guidance. A plan of attack and the organization of the combat formations were worked out, after which the tasks were given to subordinates (in the divisional account it was written that even "the small elements of the units knew their task and conducted the corresponding preparation"[18]). By morning the batteries of the 691st Artillery Regiment began to take up their firing positions. Finally, close to noon contact was established with the 201st Tank Brigade that was attached to the division; its tanks were standing in a ravine southwest of Lomovo.

14 TsAMO, F. 237 sd, op. 1, d. 26, l. 25.
15 Ibid.
16 Ibid.
17 TsAMO, F. 1518 (237 sd), op. 1, d. 7, l. 3.
18 TsAMO, F. 237 sd, op. 1, d. 26, l. 26.

During a joint meeting, division commander Tertyshnyi and tank brigade commander Taranov discussed all the questions of cooperation. Much was done over the remaining time before the new H-hour; however, the reserves of ammunition could not be seriously replenished, and thus the attack had to begin without the desired reserve of 2-3 combat loads of ammunition, but with only what the batteries had on hand …

The artillery of the 237th Rifle Division opened fire at 1430 on 23 July, starting a 30-minute preparation before the attack. Considering the short time given to the preparatory fire and the amount of available ammunition, one could hardly say that the 30-minute barrage by the division's artillery before the attack swept away the German positions. Most likely, it encouraged the soldiers before the attack and had a greater effect on morale than any practical significance. At 1500 the infantry rose on the attack and units of the 237th Rifle Division entered their very first battle.[19]

According to the devised plan, the division attacked with two regiments up front and the third regiment (the 841st Rifle Regiment, minus its 3rd Battalion, which was still back at the division's old area of dislocation in the Kreshchenka area[20]) in the second echelon. On the right, supported by two battalions of the 691st Artillery Regiment, was the 835th Rifle Regiment with 10 "Matilda" tanks and 10 T-60 light tanks of the 201st Tank Brigade attached to it. The regiment was supposed to attack to the south toward Hill 212.9 and Chibisovka, and had the task to break the enemy's defense in the sector between the Perekopovka – Chibisovka road and the eastern fringe of the patch of woods north of Vysochkino (true, one of the two artillery battalions had in fact not yet moved into its firing positions and the attack had to begin without it[21]).

On the left, in the sector running from the fringe of this same patch of woods to Hill 213.8, the 838th Rifle Regiment was attacking, supported by one artillery battalion of the 691st Artillery Regiment. The regiment was supposed to break through the enemy's defense and seize the southern slopes of this hill (something that the right-flanking regiment of the 340th Rifle Division had been unable to do over the first two days of the operation). The division's overall objective was to reach the southern bank of the Sukhaia Vereika River in the sector between Chibisovka and Pavlovka-2.

With the start of the attack, the enemy opened heavy artillery and mortar fire on the attackers, which began to inflict painful losses to them. The division's two full-strength regiments in the first echelon were squeezed into a sector of attack that amounted to just 3-4 kilometers. With a third regiment following them in the second echelon, the attacking infantry of the 237th Rifle Division was advancing in dense combat formations, presenting a juicy target to the German gunners.

Despite the casualties, both regiments began gradually to push ahead, unflinchingly closing with the enemy's forward edge. True, it was difficult to say precisely where this forward edge ran. Even the commanders didn't know its precise outline.[22] Thus, periodically dropping to the ground under fire and aerial attacks and rising on the attack once again, the attacking battalions passed the southern slopes of Hills 212.9 and 199.8, left behind the sanctuary of the gullies and ravines in the upper reaches of the Bystrik Creek and reached the foot of Hill 213.8 and the nameless hill to the west of it. In their path they encountered trenches, foxholes and communication trenches that had either been abandoned by the Germans, or had no present relationship at all to the current German front line. The infantry in the attacking battalions plainly didn't observe any withdrawal of large groups of Germans in front of them …

Upon reaching the northwestern slopes of Hill 213.8 and the foot of the nameless hill to the west, the enemy resistance began to increase. German fire from the patch of woods north of

19 Ibid.
20 TsAMO, F. 1518 (237 sd), op. 1, d. 7, l. 6.
21 TsAMO, F. 1518 (237 sd), op. 1, d. 7, l. 5.
22 TsAMO, F. 1518 (237 sd), op. 1, d. 7, l. 4.

Vysochkino and from the hill north of these woods was particularly hindering the attacking battalions. Bursts of machine-gun fire that were sweeping the slopes of the hills added to the artillery and mortar shelling. Gradually, a growing gap appeared at the boundary between the two attacking regiments, in the center of which was that very same German knot of resistance in the woods north of Vysochkino, which had frustrated the attacks of the 284th and 340th Rifle Divisions in the first two days of the offensive and had never been taken by them. Having run into particularly fierce resistance in the area of the nameless hill and woods, the right-flank 835th Rifle Regiment began increasingly to swerve to the west, while the 838th Rifle Regiment diverged to the east of its initial direction of attack.

Moreover, having reached the western slopes of the nameless hill (with an elevation of 220 meters), the battalions of the 835th Rifle Regiment during the attempt to advance along the road to Chibisovka began taking increasing flanking fire from the right, thereby placing them under a crossfire. Casualties rose, and the initially successful advance faltered. The regiment became pinned down, lacking the strength to overcome the enemy's destructive fire coming from the front and both flanks. In order to suppress the enemy's positions that were firing into the flank of the 835th Rifle Regiment from the area of Hill 214.6, the regiment commander Lieutenant Colonel Kogotkov decided to pivot his right-flanking battalion to the west in order to attack this enemy knot of resistance that was hampering the regiment's advance. This hill was actually in the neighboring 284th Rifle Division's zone of responsibility, but the 237th Rifle Division's 835th Rifle Regiment now had to fight for it. On this subject the commander of the 237th Rifle Division would later write with irritation and annoyance: "The 284th Rifle Division located on the right not only failed to make a demonstration attack (not to mention that it was more useful for it to launch an actual attack), but on the contrary, from the morning of 23 July, the withdrawal of small units from the forward edge to the rear was visible."[23]

In general, the command of the 237th Rifle Division assessed the actions of its neighbors in a most critical fashion. The 340th Rifle Division located on the left, as they believed, "also made no attempt to attack". As a result, "the enemy, taking advantage of the passivity shown on both flanks, had the possibility to concentrate manpower and firing means against the division's attacking units".[24] The attached 201st Tank Brigade also received harsh criticism from the command of the 237th Rifle Division; in their opinion, "it did not carry out its assigned task to any extent" and its actions "amounted to no more than just a demonstration".[25]

To say how the command of the 201st Tank Brigade evaluated the course of the battle together with the 237th Rifle Division isn't possible, since in the brigade's documents related to its participation in Operational Group Chibisov's offensive there are mostly just general phrases. However, in the files of the Briansk Front there is a document, the authors of which came to a conclusion opposite that of the 237th Rifle Division's commander regarding the 201st Tank Brigade's performance. Workers of the operational group's Political Department (of the future 38th Army) that had been assigned to the 237th Rifle Division reported: "The advance of the 201st Tank Brigade was not timely supported by the infantry elements."[26] There you have it – just try to figure out who fought well and who didn't. Judging from everything, this was even difficult for the higher command to do after receiving such directly contradictory reports, which incidentally all shared one common characteristic: they spoke highly of their own merits, while blaming their neighbors for failures.

23 TsAMO, F. 237 sd, op. 1, d. 26, l. 28.
24 Ibid.
25 Ibid.
26 TsAMO, F. 202, op. 36, d. 162, l. 15.

Whoever's fault it was, the 237th Rifle Division's attack also went far from smoothly. Once the battalions of the 838th Rifle Regiment reached the slopes of Hill 213.8, the artillerymen and mortar crews that were supporting the regiment due to inexperience or a lack of awareness of the situation, began to fire on their own troops, bringing down their scarce large-caliber artillery and mortar shells on the regiment's forward elements.

The commander of the 691st Artillery Regiment's 2nd Artillery Battalion until the end of the battle never once visited the commander of the 835th Rifle Regiment that he was to support. Reliable communications between the units didn't exist, reports arrived at headquarters with large delays or didn't come in at all, which didn't give the senior commanders the possibility of following changes in the situation and make timely decisions of one sort or another.[27]

Once the battalions of the 835th and 838th Rifle Regiments ultimately overcame several kilometers of the enemy's advanced positions and had driven in his combat outposts, they became tied up in fighting in the German's main defensive belt. At this point the supporting artillerymen and mortarmen had nearly exhausted their scarce supply of shells. As a result, the infantry was left without artillery and mortar support at perhaps the most decisive moment of the battle, when the conclusively pinned down Soviet rifle companies in front of the finally revealed German front line were unable to raise their heads because of the heavy incoming fire, but now there was nothing with which to suppress or knock out the enemy's firing positions.[28]

In distinction from the account of the 237th Rifle Division's command, which saw the main reasons for the failure to carry out its tasks in the poor actions of its neighbors and objective factors (the unpunished enemy airstrikes, the lack of ammunition, the dissatisfactory situation with supplies, etc., which no doubt did play a role and substantially affected the outcome of the battles), the political workers that were assigned to the division reported with Bolshevik directness on something that was not reflected in the division's documents:

> The main shortcoming is the poor work of the headquarters. The reconnaissance was working very poorly; the division command lacked necessary information about the enemy that was operating in the division's sector. Reconnaissance was neglected even during the course of the battle. In the 838th Rifle Regiment there was no sort of leadership in the headquarters, nor any command post. The elements operated independently. Communications and the exchange of information between the regiments were lacking, as well as the mutual support of the elements. The flanks at the very outset of the battle were exposed. Cooperation between the different arms was absent.
>
> In the 838th Rifle Regiment, when the regiment commander was issuing a combat order, the anti-tank artillery battalion commander properly asked him to give the battalion its task, but received the reply: "You are attached, but not subordinate to me. Decide for yourselves what you are to do!" As a result, the battalion did nothing during the battle. There is a separation of the rear services and a lack of supply with ammunition and food. There is an irresponsible attitude toward the fulfillment of a combat task, especially in the 838th Rifle Regiment on the part first of all of the regiment commander Major P. and the commissar, Battalion Commissar D.[29]

By the evening of 23 July, the 237th Rifle Division's attack everywhere had sputtered out under intense enemy fire. The final attempt to break the enemy's resistance and make progress was

27 TsAMO, F. 1518 (237 sd), op. 1, d. 7, ll. 4-5.
28 TsAMO, F. 393, op. 9005, d. 19, l. 45.
29 TsAMO, F. 202, op. 36, d. 162, l. 15.

undertaken on the left flank of the 835th Rifle Regiment, when its 1st Rifle Battalion, striving to eliminate the stubborn enemy pocket of resistance in the woods north of Vysochkino that was hindering the regiment's advance, went on the attack toward its western fringe.

We read in the division's document:

> The commander of the 1st Battalion of the 835th Rifle Regiment [Senior Lieutenant Iushenkov – I.S.] and his headquarters particularly stood out in the fighting. Having broken through to the western fringe of the woods, the group encountered enemy fire coming from out of the woods, where a group of German officers was ensconced. The combat started with grenades and ended in hand-to-hand fighting, as a result of which the enemy group was partially destroyed, while the survivors fled in panic, abandoning weapons and documents.[30]

Nevertheless, Senior Lieutenant Iushenkov and his group didn't succeed in driving the Germans out of this patch of woods, the pocket of resistance wasn't destroyed, and the soldiers who had penetrated to this woodlot wound up in semi-encirclement there and were compelled to retreat.

On the right flank of the 835th Rifle Regiment, its other battalion that had drifted into the 284th Rifle Division's sector, fought until evening on the eastern slopes of Hill 214.6, but was also unable to eliminate this German knot of resistance. By the end of the day, when twilight began to descend on the battlefield, the 835th Rifle Regiment had made a greater advance than all the other units of the 237th Rifle Division, and attacking along the road, had penetrated approximately 1.5 kilometers into the enemy's forward edge of defense, enveloping the German-held patch of woods north of Vysochkino from the west (in the course of the fighting, soldiers of the 835th Rifle Regiment seized 5 prisoners and 58 bags of rice.[31] One can only conjecture about other damage done to the enemy). However, having achieved this line, the exhausted regiment came to a stop. Moreover, soon the enemy launched a counterattack, and the forward elements of the 835th Rifle Regiment began to pull out of the penetration as it was being swept with fire from three directions.[32]

The division's first battle left an indelible trace in the recollections of the former nurse of the 835th Rifle Regiment E.I. Platonova:

> The fascists' offensive on the Voronezh front was fierce. Enemy aircraft hung in the sky for entire days. Having dropped their death-dealing load on us, they would depart to get refueled, but in their place new ones would appear. It was possible to go insane from such bombing. In addition to all this, they were firing at us from artillery and mortars, and sparing no shells.
>
> We had a lot of wounded and killed. On the battlefield it was as if a terrible slaughter had taken place. The rye in the field was above your knees. Evening came. Like a lizard, I was dragging a severely wounded soldier to a safe place. There was only an empty socket in place of his left eye; his lower jaw was broken and lying on his neck, exposing a long, bloody tongue, from which saliva was constantly dripping together with the blood. His arms and legs were wounded. The wounded soldier was a beefy man, softly groaning. I didn't have the strength to carry him, but meter by meter I pulled him along, digging into the earth with my feet.
>
> It was July so the days were long; our soldiers were retreating, unable to withstand the enemy fire. In the distance there was a burst of automatic weapons fire; I glanced in that direction and froze. Fascist soldiers in helmets were moving across the field in black overalls

30 TsAMO, F. 1518 (237 sd), op. 1, d. 7, ll. 4-5.
31 TsAMO, F. 1518 (237 sd), op. 1, d. 7, l. 5.
32 TsAMO, F. 393, op. 9005, d. 19, l. 45.

> with their sleeves rolled up to their elbows, finishing off our wounded soldiers with gunshots. Leaving behind my wounded soldiers, I crawled away like a lizard off to one side, came across a bomb crater, and flat on my face dropped into it face first. I had to remain in that uncomfortable position as if I had fallen and died.
>
> The next burst of gun fire rang out quite nearby. Death was looming behind my shoulders and everything inside me froze. There was a flash of light above my head and immediately a short burst of automatic weapons fire rang out. The bullets flew above my head, humming, and drilled into the ground without touching my head. Then I could hear as the footsteps receded into the distance. It became quiet, the sun had set and it was dark, and with difficulty I took a seat on the bottom of the crater. I was shivering from the fear I had experienced, and then started to hiccup. I had no strength to stop them. My whole body was trembling all over. Soon it would be dawn; I had to crawl back to friendly troops, but in which direction? Where were they now?
>
> Climbing out of the crater, I began to crawl around it and suddenly came across a corpse. I began to search it with my hand. I ran my palm along the head and one finger found an empty socket instead of an eye. I ran my palm further down the face to the mouth and there was no lower jaw. This was my wounded soldier, but now he was dead, finished off by a fascist. From his body I found which way I needed to go, and I began crawling in that direction, paying heed to any rustling noises.[33]

It was quite difficult for the command of the 237th Rifle Division to assess the situation as it stood on the night of 23-24 July and the results of its first battle. On one hand the division had failed to carry out its assigned task fully and hadn't reached the southern bank of the Sukhaia Vereika River, but on the other hand, as the commander and his headquarters staff believed, it had broken through the enemy's defense, inflicted heavy losses to the Germans, and made a successful advance of several kilometers, which was rather significant in order to develop the achieved success on the next day. There were no doubts among them that they would have to resume the attack in the morning.

The forward edge of the enemy's defense had finally been determined accurately, everywhere the German outposts had been driven in, and now the regiments were close enough for a decisive thrust into the first line of German trenches. True, the condition of the regiments at the end of the first day of fighting remained largely unclear to the division headquarters. Reports from them were arriving late, and were extremely sporadic and not very informative. To a great degree this was connected with the fact that the regiments themselves still had little information about the condition of their subordinate units.

Toward the end of the day the commander of the 841st Rifle Regiment (minus one battalion) that was operating in the second echelon submitted a combat report to division headquarters, which stated that the regiment had lost 26 men killed, 60 wounded and 23 missing in action over the day of fighting, but in turn had destroyed "more than a company of infantry" and had knocked out 2 enemy machine guns and 2 mortars.[34] But the losses of the two forward regiments were unknown to the division's command. Regarding the 838th Rifle Regiment, in the 237th Rifle Division's combat journal it was written: "Information on the combat activity of the 838th Rifle Regiment was scarce. Over the entire day the regiment commander sent only one short report, in which he indicated the combat formation adopted by the regiment; other information

33 *Voenno-istoricheskii arkhiv*, No. 9 (2009), pp. 82-83.
34 TsAMO, F. 1518 (237 sd), op. 1, d. 7, l. 6.

wasn't supplied by the report, since the headquarters, failing to show adequate leadership over the fighting couldn't have it."[35]

The situation with ammunition was prompting the most serious unease among the command of the units, if not to say – alarm. The majority of the artillery and mortar shells had been fired off, and no resupplies had been brought up. Whether the trucks were wandering around somewhere in the night, or whether they hadn't yet left the division's designated stockpiles wasn't clear, but the division's rear supply areas were empty, and the prospects for their replenishment were murky.

A similar situation had developed with food supplies: the division's soldiers had gone into battle hungry, and came out of it (those who had been fortunate) with grumbling stomachs, because the chiefs responsible to provide the "porridge and cabbage soup" for some reasons unknown at the front had been unable to provide the companies with a hot meal. The long march the day before, the digging of trenches that night and the exhausting battle on the following day required the extreme exertion of the division's personnel. The men had to replenish their energy primarily by consuming water and dried bread, "compensating" the insufficient calories with the endless soldier's patience, the commander's shout and (or) the inspiring talks of the political instructor.

The conscientious Red Army soldier was supposed to endure all of this, shouldering all the burdens and deprivations heaped upon him, and he, already accustomed to this by his past Soviet life, in which he had already shouldered much and endured, for the most part didn't even dare to complain or grumble openly (many from back in their civilian lives well understood to what this might lead ...). However, no "Bol'shevik consciousness" could replace food for the exhausted men, and by the end of the first day of battle a lot of the soldiers were plainly experiencing not a high sense of pride for the division's combat baptism that they had received, but a traitorous fatigue in their legs. (The division's horses also had to go hungry because of a lack of fodder, but they were still able to find for themselves at least some forage in the fields and meadows.) Army-level political workers sent to the 237th Rifle Division later established that on 23 July the division had not been provided with food; for example, the soldiers of the 835th Rifle Regiment each received 100 grams of bread for the entire day![36]

One hundred grams of bread ... for young, healthy men, who had to shovel cubic meters of earth, go on the attack, smite the enemy and dig in once again. It has long been known that good nutrition raises the soldier's spirits, and together with this, the combat morale of his unit. A well-fed soldier also fights better. Alas, needless to say, there was none of this in the 237th Rifle Division's first battle. However, the situation didn't change even after the fighting subsided. The soldiers didn't receive a hot meal and in place of dinner, they were forced to rummage through their own pockets and backpacks for crumbs of bread or sugar, in order somehow to trick their gnawing hunger. Such an "organization" of provisions had a most pernicious effect on the mood in the companies, especially against the backdrop of fatigue, the murderous enemy fire and the casualties they'd suffered.

It is no coincidence that the political workers assigned to the division, having learned about the facts of such a crying shame, demanded that the chief of the 237th Rifle Division's Political Department immediately hold the negligent and undisciplined members of the rear services accountable, the actions of which according to the standards of those times could be fully characterized as "wrecking".[37]

35 TsAMO, F. 1518 (237 sd), op. 1, d. 7, l. 4.

36 TsAMO, F. 202, op. 36, d. 162, l. 4.

37 Ibid. [Translator's note: "Wrecking" was an oft-used accusation in the Soviet Stalinist society against "enemies of the people" who were working to undermine socialist construction in the country.]

However, the rear command had its own "truth", which neither the assigned political workers nor even the command of the 237th Rifle Division itself could eliminate: the division lacked the transport to ensure the uninterrupted flow of supplies (while there was yet again not enough fuel and engine oil for those available vehicles). After the latest march, the division's rear services hadn't been able to bring up and timely deliver everything necessary for the units in their new dispositions.

(The truth, most likely, was somewhere in the middle: the shortage of fuel and transport were doubtlessly aggravating the already considerable difficulties, which the 237th Rifle Division was experiencing in those days, but to this could be added the lack of administrative abilities, obtuseness and even bungling of the rear chiefs, who in such a complex situation proved incapable of making proper use of the available resources and means to carry out their responsibilities in an appropriate manner. As a result, once again the Red Army soldiers had to pay for the sins and incompetence of the command staff.)

Even before the combat wound down for the day, it had become clear at division headquarters that a new matter was adding to the already existing difficulties and problems: the large number of wounded. They were arriving at collecting points from all the combat units, but the division was unable to evacuate them through its own efforts because of the very same problem with the lack of fuel and transport. Even at 2000 on 23 July, the chief of staff of the 237th Rifle Division alarmingly reported to Operational Group Chibisov's headquarters: "The division has not been supplied with artillery rounds for the DA and RA [divisional and regimental artillery – I.S.] and 82-mm and 120-mm mortar shells, or else with food and fodder because of the lack of gasoline and engine oil. There is no way to evacuate the wounded. At least 20 ambulances are needed."[38] By nighttime the number of wounded was increasing and they all remained in the division's collecting stations. Just as there was no way to bring up scarce shells and mortar rounds to the front, there was also no way to evacuate the wounded to the rear (It is a good thing the division was attacking; but what if it suddenly had to retreat?).

If the difficulties with logistics were well-known to the division command, it had only a very approximate notion of the operational situation as it existed at the front that night. At day's end the division command had received a message from the commander of the 835th Rifle Regiment. The mood of the regiment commander was far from optimistic. Lack of confidence and alarm emerged from the clutter of written phrases:

> After your departure [chances are that Colonel Tertyshnyi had visited the regiment command post during the battle – I.S.], the 1st and 3rd Battalions ran into a fortified area, suffered enormous losses, and the neighbor on the right retreated. My elements are holding out in small groups. Cartridges and shells have been exhausted. The introduction of the second echelon didn't help. I am taking measures to save the remnants of personnel and equipment. I request that you move out at least one battalion of the division's second echelon to my sector by morning; otherwise, a catastrophe is threatening me.[39]

Then one more note from the same regiment commander was brought to Colonel Tertyshnyi, which was either an affirmation of fact or a prayer for help: "To the division commander – 835th Rifle Regiment. Flanks are exposed." There was not a word more. What was Tertyshnyi supposed to do, having read this note? What measures should he take?

38 TsAMO, F. 393, op. 9005, d. 19, l. 45.
39 TsAMO, F. 1518 (237 sd), op. 1, d. 7, l. 4.

That night he unexpectedly received a directive from the chief of staff of Group Chibisov, Colonel Pilipenko, in which the latter informed him that at Chibisov's order the 841st Rifle Regiment was being withdrawn from the 237th Rifle Division into the operational group's reserve.[40] Thus, at the stroke of a pen Tertyshnyi was suddenly deprived of his second echelon. At the same time, the division's task remained unchanged (in this same directive, Pilipenko informed Tertyshnyi about Chibisov's order to seize Vysochkino and subsequently attack toward Malaia Vereika on 24 July), but now he had only two regiments with which to carry out this order, both of which had already fought on 23 July and had suffered considerable losses.

Having received on the one hand an unequivocal confirmation of his continued combat task, while having on the other hand been deprived of his full-strength regiment, Tertyshnyi fell into an even more difficult predicament, which incidentally left him with no choice: he could not give an order about going over to a defense on favorable lines, but in the morning was to resume the discontinued attack. Plainly, it was for this reason that he didn't give authorization to the 835th Rifle Regiment to withdraw, despite the desperate note from the regiment commander about exposed flanks. Such a withdrawal would have meant that at dawn, the battalions that had already been weakened by casualties would have to attack again to seize the ground that they had already taken with such difficulty on the first day of the attack. Having read the murky messages from the 835th Rifle Regiment's commander, Tertyshnyi might have also fully believed that the excessively nervous and shaken regiment commander was simply unable to deal with the stress of the first day of fighting, had panicked, and playing it safe just in case, was surreptitiously requesting reinforcements. However, with the stripping of the 841st Rifle Regiment from the 237th Rifle Division, the division commander was no longer able to reinforce or replace the 835th Rifle Regiment with his second-echelon regiment.

One way or another, after reading all the reports he had received, Tertyshnyi opted not to take any extreme measures, having decided to leave everything as it was with no adjustments. The officer responsible for writing the division's journal of combat operations, plainly striving to present the command's decisions in the best possible light and not to get the division commander in trouble described the situation that had developed as follows:

> Division commander Colonel Tertyshnyi had no decisions in the morning, because no full-fledged information had come in from the units over the night; losses and the combat strength were unknown and it was very difficult to ascertain them; all ammunition had been expended; and the lack of transport, fuel and lubricants had led to the fact that a large number of wounded that hadn't been evacuated were accumulating in the medical stations … [..] A large gap has formed between the combat formations of the attacking regiments: their flanks could not be covered, and there were no communications between them, which raised the threat of a possible enemy counterattack at the boundary between the regiments and an expansion into the depth. The adoption of decisions for instilling order in the combat units themselves, in the combat formations and in the rear areas was necessary. It was necessary to organize cooperation, necessary to connect the flanks of the regiments, to organize the evacuation of the wounded and to replenish the stockpiles of ammunition. In the course of the night the commanders of the units and the headquarters of the regiments didn't take the appropriate measures to bring order to the combat units. The battalions didn't fortify themselves on the achieved lines; the personnel didn't dig in adequately; the reconnaissance of the enemy opposite the forward edge was poorly organized; ammunition was not brought up

40 TsAMO, F. 202, op. 5, d. 258, l. 56.

> during the night; and an entire number of elements weren't fed. In this situation, the division commander made no decision.[41]

It is strange to read such an explanation for the actions, or more accurately, the striking inaction of the division commander. Who else but he was supposed to be the first to take the most decisive measures to bring the units back into order and rigorously demand the same of his subordinates? But from the unusually diplomatic description of the situation that had developed (obviously, the officer who wrote it didn't forget for a minute about *whom he was writing*), it turns out that the division commander had nothing at all to do with it! He, it seems, had to wait patiently for when his subordinates themselves would figure out how to resolve all the problems, so that he, at last, might make some sort of decision on the basis of a situation that had been clarified and corrected by them. However, they didn't decide, they didn't clarify and they didn't report, and it follows that he couldn't do anything! Therefore, everything proceeded of its own accord, in a haphazard manner, with no sort of decision required, and thus everything was left in such a chaotic situation until morning …

Nightfall found the forward units of the 237th Rifle Division on the lines they'd been able to reach during the day with such difficulty and large losses. Having the assignment to resume the attack on the morning of 24 July, they weren't pulled back to their jumping-off positions and remained quite close to the enemy's forward edge. However, neither the shouting of superiors, nor the danger of artillery barrages, and not even the inevitable combat on the coming day were able to force the haggard and hungry men to dig in as they should, and with the arrival of the night, the soldiers helplessly drifted off to a heavy, hungry sleep in the fields and on the hills that their elements had reached that day …

41 TsAMO, F. 1518 (237 sd), op. 1, d. 7, l. 6.

11

At the command post of the 2nd Tank Corps on the night of 23/24 July 1942

On the evening of 23 July, a personal encoded message arrived for Liziukov at the headquarters of the 2nd Tank Corps from the Commander-in-Chief of Briansk Front Lieutenant General Rokossovsky.[1] In the absence of the corps commander, it was received by the Chief of Staff Nagaibakov. The received message forced him to get moving: to sit and wait until Liziukov returned to the command post had become impossible; he had to be found. Assuming that he was somewhere in the 26th or 27th Tank Brigade, Nagaibakov summoned the corps' intelligence chief Major Ivanovsky and ordered him to go to the brigades, find Liziukov, and hand him the message from the Front commander; simultaneously he was to report to General Liziukov on the steps that the corps headquarters had designated for the night to replenish the units with ammunition and fuel, and "on the spot familiarize himself with the actual situation in the brigades".[2]

Ivanovsky drove off. The regime of totally avoiding use of the radio being observed in the 2nd Tank Corps was contributing to the fact that in the corps headquarters that evening they were unable to say precisely in which tank brigade Liziukov was located. Thus Ivanovsky set out to the front to search for Liziukov in both brigades.

Meanwhile, Nagaibakov busied himself with putting together a combat order for the 2nd Tank Corps for 24 July. On his own, he couldn't write anything particularly new in the order: the units were to carry out the task they'd been given the day before and to continue the offensive. In essence, the chief of staff's order was a formality, since no one had cancelled Liziukov's previous order and it remained in effect. However, in the absence of the corps commander Nagaibakov obviously considered that such a formality would not at all be superfluous for himself ….

As with many of his other orders and reports, the chief of staff of the 2nd Tank Corps didn't trust the dubious radio, which might be heard by more than a few ears, but entrusted it to good, reliable paper, which only the addressee could read. Together with the order, Nagaibakov decided to compose an office memo to Liziukov personally, but since he didn't know the tank brigade with which the general was located, he wrote the note twice, for both brigades simultaneously, after which he summoned a liaison officer, Captain Veniukov, and entrusted the secret documents to him. At 2300, once night had already settled over the surroundings, Veniukov set out to cover the 10-plus kilometers to search in the darkness for the tank brigades and the corps commander.

A period of anxious waiting began. On the threshold of combat on the following day, Colonel Nagaibakov issued the necessary orders to supply the units with ammunition and fuel; the order itself had already been sent to the troops. The endless routines of staff business were winding

1 TsAMO, F. 38 A, op. 11353, d. 14, l. 127.
2 TsAMO, F. 38 A, op. 11353, d. 14, l. 128.

down, and it seemed everything necessary had been done for the coming day, so that he could allow himself to catch his breath. The latest 24-hour period of the war was approaching its end. Yet no cessation or end to this terrible war was in sight … Having exhausted himself over the day, the chief of staff of the 2nd Tank Corps went to sleep. Indeed, it wasn't *his* job to sit around all night without sleep, waiting for reports. He wasn't a young soldier, able to shoulder such duties; those years had already passed ….

We will also take a breather. Let's talk a bit about the past of Colonel Izmail Akhmetovich Nagaibakov.

By the summer of 1942, the nearly 47-year-old (short two months) chief of staff of the 2nd Tank Corps was the most senior officer by age of the tank corps' commanders. He had spent the greater portion of his life in the army, and moreover had started his military career back when officers still wore epaulets.[3] A native of the city of Shadrinsk in the Perm Krai, the young Tatar Izmail came from a family of clerical workers (in the space regarding social origin in his application form, the puzzling, vague answer "Miscellaneous" has been written); he studied in school and in 1914 graduated from the Tashkent Cadet Corps, at which point, he correspondingly began his military service. The First World War was underway, and the 18-year-old youth was sent to the Konstantinovka Artillery School, which he completed according to an accelerated one-year program in 1915 before being appointed to the mounted artillery, in which he served right up to December 1917.

In January 1918 the 22-year-old officer of the Russian Army Izmail Nagaibakov abruptly changed his life and began service in a new army, in new units that at times are surprising in their names: in the Muslim Red Guards Regiment of the city of Petrograd; in the International Mounted Detachment of Tersk Oblast; and in a separate mounted-mountain battery of the Azerbaidzhan SSR. The Russian Civil War was going on, and the assistant regiment commander, deputy chief of staff, platoon leader and assistant commander Nagaibakov served and fought in several posts and on several fronts: opposite General Shkuro, opposite Denikin, and in 1920 against the "Basmachi", the term given to those who opposed Soviet rule in the Muslim territories. After the Russian Civil War ended, he went through courses for the improvement of the command staff prior to becoming an instructor in these and similar courses, before serving in combat-related positions and study in the Frunze Military Academy between 1926 and 1929.

With such a solid educational background and service record in the army, the Academy graduate Nagaibakov continued his assured rise up the service ladder: in 1929 – chief of staff of an artillery brigade; in 1931 – chief of staff of an artillery school; in 1935 – rifle regiment commander; and finally, from January 1937 – chief of staff of a rifle division.

Well, and then … then the shocking exposure of a plot involving high-ranking military officers flashed across the entire country, the heads of "enemies of the people" rolled across the Chekist scaffold, and the crowds frozen with fear began to roar with public hatred. Meanwhile the best "friends of the people" – the NKVD investigators – began tirelessly and diligently to unravel a serpentine tangle of countless plots throughout the entire Red Army, the threads of which, as it seemed, insidiously permeated its entire structure from top to bottom. Then soon, exposed by the successfully tested arsenal of means of the investigate suite, there began to flow incriminating evidence from the persons under investigation pointing to their friends, superiors and peers, dragging more and more newly-revealed participants into a fatal whirlpool of repressions of this insane and bloody spectacle. … Indeed, this was not the best of times to be occupying the post of chief of staff of a division.

3 From its origins right up until the spring of 1943, the "egalitarian" Red Army dispensed with the old Tsarist army's signs and titles of rank, including epaulets.

Well, what could one do? The commanders of those years scarcely had any options. Observing how remorselessly "enemies of the people" were being purged from the Red Army and arrested (or worse), the military officers had nothing else to do but to serve and hope that, the dreaded NKVD wouldn't come for them, because they weren't enemies … and keep a watchful eye on subordinates, service peers and superiors.

In the autumn of 1938, the clouds began to gather over Nagaibakov as well, since it turned out that the *entanglements of a plot* stretched even to his 85th Rifle Division located in the provincial Cheliabinsk. The thunderclap came on 2 November 1938, when he was dismissed from the Red Army. (Many military men back then knew well what might follow this. Likely, this struck the soul of the former colonel as well, who was dismissed pursuant to a *political article of the law.*) On 14 November, having properly allowed him to become tormented by the ordeal of waiting, to weaken psychologically and to become ripe for arrest, *they* came for him ….

For all one knows, if this had happened a year earlier, the life path of the future chief of staff of the 2nd Tank Corps might have been terminated by an executioner's bullet in a Chekist torture chamber.[4] However, the bacchanalia of repressions, which pitilessly wiped out commanders of the Workers' and Peasants' Red Army on a never before seen scale for a year and a half, by the end of 1938 was nevertheless in decline. Indeed, it was hardly possible to continue to consume your own command cadres in such wild numbers. The year 1939 arrived, and with it a "thaw" and a portion of the previously arrested military men returned to the Red Army (and to life …). Moreover, in the summer of 1939 the Red Army for the first time in many years got a "real taste of fighting" on the Khalkin-Gol River, before engaging in the large-scale "liberation" of eastern Poland, and there were the expectations that it would soon have to do even more fighting and *liberating*. The Red Army was growing from month to month, and cadres, according to Comrade Stalin's apt expression, decided everything, so they were needed in ever greater numbers. In these circumstances, some of those sitting under investigation or the already sentenced military "plotters" were forgiven their sins and returned to the rapidly growing Red Army. Possibly, this happened as well in the case with the suspect Nagaibakov.

The Winter War with Finland had already started, when on 21 December 1939, after 13 months and one week of a prison stint, the case regarding the accusation of Nagaibakov as belonging to an anti-Soviet Trotskyist organization was dropped, while he, accused under Article 58, a political article with four sub-points, for which many in that time had simply been sentenced to prison camps or "the highest form of punishment" [execution], received a "ticket" to freedom. To the chief of staff, it was like a gift for the recently pardoned New Year's celebration.[5]

At the beginning of February 1940, they restored Citizen Nagaibakov to the Red Army, gave him back his military rank, and as if nothing had ever happened, sent him as an instructor to the Frunze Academy. However, chances are that the more than a year spent in jail, with all the revelations to him of the true nature of the *striking* Bol'shevik investigation techniques and the prospects of a death sentence by shooting, became for Colonel Nagaibakov an endless nightmare and left an indelible scar in his soul. With this scarring prison lesson (don't needlessly wag your tongue; carry out instructions; avoid initiative …) he obviously also emerged with a suspicious eye toward his relative freedom.

4 Translator's note: The height of the Stalinist purges occurred in 1937-1938 during Ezhov's tenure as NKVD chief (up until December 1938), which resulted in a terrifying surge in executions around the country, perhaps numbering in the hundreds of thousands. It is quite likely that Nagaibakov would have been shot, had he been arrested earlier.

5 After the cancellation of Christmas by the Bolsheviks as a "bourgious holiday", Stalin decided that the Soviet citizens needed a holiday in that season of the year, so New Year's Day became the holiday in the Soviet Union for exchanging gifts and holiday greetings.

In September 1940 Nagaibakov was sent from Moscow to Kazan' to assume the post of assistant commandant of an infantry school, then in April 1941 he was transferred to the post of deputy chief of a tank school, also in Kazan' (it is striking how many military training facilities there were at the time in the Soviet Union!). He was serving in this post when the war broke out and remained in it for almost its entire first, hardest year. In May 1942 Colonel Nagaibakov was on a training assignment with the 148th Tank Brigade, which was located in the reserve of the Briansk Front, and already in June 1942 he became chief of staff of the 2nd Tank Corps. Over a year of wartime, he hadn't spent a day at the front.

In this respect, he was a match with the 2nd Tank Corps' operations chief Lieutenant Colonel Pupko, who had also arrived in the acting army only in the spring of 1942. True, there followed for both of them three days of offensive fighting as part of the 5th Tank Army and the tank corps' retreat back beyond the Don. This summed up the combat experience in the Great Patriotic War of both the chief of staff and chief of operations prior to the current operation. Such was the immediate command circle that Liziukov inherited when he was demoted to take command of the 2nd Tank Corps. Indeed, he was supposed to conduct the tank corps' deep offensive operation with their assistance. They also were supposed to be the leading and organizing force in the tank corps now, when the corps commander and commissar were not at hand …

However, let's return to the command post of the 2nd Tank Corps. The fourth day of the operation – 24 July 1942 – had arrived. Major Ivanovsky returned to the command post at 0200. Chief of Staff Nagaibakov was sleeping. The information that Ivanovsky brought back with him was disquieting: he had been unable to locate Liziukov and Assorov in the tank brigades, just as he was unable to find anyone who might be able to tell him where they'd been that day or where they might be now. All of this lack of knowledge was becoming increasingly strange, if not to say alarming. Nevertheless, Ivanovsky decided not to waken the sleeping chief of staff, but instead delivered his news to the operations chief Lieutenant Colonel Pupko, informing him at the same time that the commissar of the 27th Tank Brigade was organizing a search for the corps commander and commissar. That last piece of information, apparently, completely satisfied Pupko, and the calm and deliberate course of the night at the command post of the 2nd Tank Corps continued undisturbed.

That night a directive arrived for the absent Liziukov from the chief of staff of Operational Group Chibisov Colonel Pilipenko, who was still far from understanding the situation that had developed in the 2nd Tank Corps: "To the commander of the 2nd Tank Corps. By a *Stavka* directive, the Voronezh Front's air force is covering the actions of your corps. Report your location. On the morning of 24 July units of the Voronezh Front will initiate a crossing at Semiluki with the task to link up with you."[6]

Who was now to carry out this directive? The on-duty staff officer had difficulty determining where he should now send it. He couldn't pass it to Liziukov, because he didn't know where he was located, nor was he able at the same time to say where the corps commissar was … Pilipenko's directive lay on a table and remained unanswered.

Another two hours passed, and dawn was approaching. Nagaibakov rose at 0400, and only then was he briefed about Ivanovsky's report. Having heard it, the chief of staff summoned both Pupko and Ivanovsky. When they arrived, he angrily asked the operations chief why the latter hadn't reported to him right away about Ivanovsky's arrival. In his defense, Pupko said that he didn't want to disturb the sleeping Nagaibakov, since steps had already been taken to find General Liziukov. Judging from everything, satisfied by the scolding he had given and the news that a search for Liziukov was underway, Nagaibakov didn't issue his subordinates any additional orders regarding the organization of searches.

6 TsAMO, F. 202, op. 5, d. 334, l. 47.

Around this same time, the liaison officer Captain Veniukov, who'd been sent by Nagaibakov late in the evening, returned to the command post. His report was just as discouraging as Ivanovsky's information. Veniukov reported that Liziukov and Assorov were not with either the 26th Tank Brigade or the 27th Tank Brigade.

Most likely, after these words an oppressive silence settled over the command post. Almost 24 hours had passed since the corps' commander and commissar had been last seen in Bol'shaia Vereika, but so far, as it turned out, no one could definitively say where they were. The confident report that they were directing the combat of the 26th and 27th Tank Brigades (which Nagaibakov had reported to the headquarters of the operational group the day before) proved to be unreliable – they weren't there, but where, then, might they be? Perhaps they had made their way through to the 148th Tank Brigade near Medvezh'e? However, over all this time not a single radio message had arrived from that tank brigade or from the missing commanders, and none of them had established contact with the command post. (True, there was no radio contact with them either…)

However, why would they have made their way through to Medvezh'e alone, leaving both tank brigades behind? Perhaps they had already returned? But where had they gone? To the headquarters' old location in Kreshchenka? Perhaps they were driving around somewhere among the units? Yet then why in this case had they not made their location known over all this time, and why had no one seen them anywhere? Had they driven off to visit a neighbor? Why? Indeed, why again had they not kept the command post informed about where they were, and what should the corps headquarters do next? Was it really normal to plan such extended and "secret" visits to some place unknown? Then where were they?

These or other similar questions undoubtedly rose in the minds of the staff officers of the 2nd Tank Corps with increasing acuteness on that early morning. It would seem that the moment had arrived when all the alarming information that had already been received by the headquarters would oblige Nagaibakov, as the senior commander present, to recognize the situation as an emergency. The more than strange disappearance of the corps commander and commissar for such a lengthy amount of time, the failure to make contact with them which could not be explained by any sensible reasons, and the complete ignorance of the headquarters about their possible location was demanding not only the initiation of active searches with their own means, but also the need to inform higher command about the situation.

However, Nagaibakov, obviously hoping that nothing bad had yet happened, didn't perceive what was happening as a "ChP" [*chrezvychainnoe proisshestvie* -- "extraordinary occurrence" that can mean an accident, foul up, emergency, or some terrible misfortune], and moreover, didn't hurry to report about this to superior headquarters. Indeed, what command loves it when it receives word of a "ChP", and what if suddenly Liziukov and Assorov reappeared somewhere (perhaps in the 148th Tank Brigade …), and in what embarrassing position would he place himself, as well as the corps commander and commissar, by raising this false alarm? Indeed … dumbfounded by such a panicked report the higher command, having learned about the staff confusion over the "missing" Liziukov, wouldn't be slow to retort: "What, have you lost your mind there? What's going on there, if you can't find each other? Why didn't the corps headquarters know where its commander and commissar were located, and yet falsely reported that they were with the 26th or 27th Tank Brigade, where it turns out they weren't after all?" – all of these menacing questions would be directed primarily at him, the chief of staff.

One way or another, Nagaibakov made no effort to inform the operational group headquarters about the suspicious disappearance of the corps commander and commissar. He also opted not to take any sort of emergency and large-scale measures to organize searches (including alerting the neighbors), nor did he take charge of them personally by driving to the forward 26th and 27th Tank Brigades in order to obtain a detailed explanation of the situation on the spot and to assume leadership over these searches.

Moreover, another question immediately arose in Liziukov's absence: Who now was to direct the battle of the forward tank brigades (and in essence, of the entire corps, since its other units in fact had not yet attacked)? The answer to this, of course, was Nagaibakov as the chief of staff … but he was not at all prepared for such a turn of events. He plainly had no desire to drive to the front, to where the tank brigades were sheltering in the wooded ravine under artillery barrages and bombings, and personally direct the fighting of their combat formations.

Should he send the operations chief to take charge of the brigades' attack? Nagaibakov also rejected such a commander candidate, if he at all looked at it seriously. In his eyes, Pupko was demonstrating plain confusion, a lack of initiative and incompetence, which was completely impermissible for an officer in his post, and moreover was incompatible with the task that had now arisen. In Nagaibakov's opinion, as things now stood Pupko was incapable of directing the offensive of the corps' forward brigades.

Having wound up in such a prickly situation right before the start of the fourth day of the operation, when the corps commander and commissar were absent, when he didn't want to take responsibility for the forward brigades' fighting and couldn't assign leadership of it to Pupko, Nagaibakov decided that it was best (*and safer …*) to give this responsibility to the commander of the 26th Tank Brigade Colonel Burdov. He would take unified command over both tank brigades and lead them on the attack.

Having reached this decision, Nagaibakov sent Burdov the corresponding order and simultaneously handed liaison officer Captain Veniukov the order to both tank brigades to initiate a search for Liziukov. Having received the new instructions, Veniukov for the second time in a row on that sleepless night set off on his 10-kilometer route to the tank brigades, from where he had just arrived. It was already becoming light …

Subsequently, clearly understanding how great the responsibility that now rested on him, Nagaibakov, when writing the explanations demanded of him, presented his actions and decisions in the following manner:

> In view of the fact that I'd been wounded in the head by shell fragments in the fighting on 13.7 and rejected evacuation only in view of the serious situation at the front, and in this condition couldn't be in a tank, nor could I at the command post entrust leadership of the fighting to Lieutenant Colonel Pupko, whom after the battle we dismissed from the headquarters and reduced to deputy brigade commander; thus I assigned direct leadership over the fighting of the 26th and 27th Tank Brigades to the commander of the 26th Tank Brigade Colonel Burdov, who was with the combat formations and knew well the situation directly facing the brigades, while I myself led the entire corps from the command post until the end of the battle. Simultaneously I sent an order to the commander of the 27th Tank Brigade and Colonel Burdov via liaison officer Captain Veniukov about searching for General Liziukov, since I didn't have a single tank.[7]

In what fashion did the tank brigade commanders carry out the order received from the command post regarding the searches for Liziukov and Assorov? The acting commander of the 27th Tank Brigade Captain Luchnikov, having learned at 0200 that "general's location is unknown" (although according to the earlier reports from the headquarters of the 2nd Tank Corps, Liziukov was with this tank brigade), at dawn on 24 July sent two light T-60 tanks out along the supposed route taken by Liziukov's KV tank. However, having come under fire, they didn't get far and didn't

7 TsAMO, F. 38 A, op. 11353, d. 14, l. 128.

find the general's tank.[8] The commander of the 26th Tank Brigade Colonel Burdov, who'd been made "commander-in-chief" of the 2nd Tank Corps' composite tank grouping by Nagaibakov, judging from the documents, undertook no separate searches of his own at all, obviously believing in the new circumstances that the foray by the two T-60 tanks from the 27th Tank Brigade *was the reconnaissance of the entire grouping entrusted to him*. With this brief, feeble effort, the searches came to an end.

The sun rose. Both tank brigades had already spent almost 24 hours in the wooded ravine close to the front that was now shattered by bombs and shells. The night had brought some relief from the barrages and bombings and had given the exhausted crews the opportunity to close their eyes and drift into a troubled sleep for at least a certain amount of time. However, with the arrival of morning, the tank brigades were to go over to some sort of active operations. Now, with Colonel Burdov's official appointment as overall commander of the tank grouping, the vacuum of authority that had unexpectedly been created the day before disappeared, when in the absence of Liziukov and Assorov the tankers had sidestepped into the wooded ravine and never resumed the attack. In the new circumstances, Burdov specifically now bore the responsibility for any such cowering; thus, he could not remain inactive. He had to undertake something, or at least schedule it …

Early on the morning of 24 July, dutifully fulfilling the role designated to him as overall commander of the composite group, he gave a verbal order for an attack in the direction of Medvezh'e. H-hour was set for 1000. But *for the meanwhile* the tanks stood idle. The 26th and 27th Tank Brigades remained hunkered down in the wooded ravine and undertook no offensive actions. Nevertheless, though factually remaining in place, the wary commander of the composite tank group was formally carrying out his order – after all, he had set a time to attack, but *the attack had to be prepared properly…*

Approximately at this same time, the chief of staff of the 2nd Tank Corps Nagaibakov put together his next report to Operational Group Chibisov's headquarters. Located at the corps command post, many kilometers away from the totally idle 26th and 27th Tank Brigades, he wrote:

> Units of the corps after the fighting in the Kaver'ia area by 1900 were concentrated in an assembly area, a wooded ravine 2 kilometers southwest of Churikovo, in order to replenish fuel and ammunition. Because of the traffic jams at the bridge across the Bol'shaia Vereika River in the Malaia Vereika area, the machines carrying the fuel and ammunition were late. The refueling process ended at 0600 on 24.7.42. Upon the completion of refueling, the corps' units quickly started to implement their tasks. Liziukov and Assorov are not here. I've appointed the commander of the 26th Tank Brigade Colonel Burdov as my deputy. For the second time I'm sending out instructions to confirm the execution of the order. I request sapper support for the crossing site over the Bol'shaia Vereika River in the vicinity of Malaia Vereika.[9]

"Quickly started to implement their tasks" … judging from these words, the chief of staff of the 2nd Tank Corps didn't know that the commander he had put in charge of the composite tank grouping was not carrying out his assignment as Nagaibakov imagined it at all; that in the wooded ravine at the front so distant from the command post, which the chief of staff never bothered to visit in order to satisfy himself that everything was going as he had reported, the commanders were anything but hurrying to carry out their tasks quickly …

8 TsAMO, F. 202, op. 50, d. 1, l. 304.
9 TsAMO, F. 38 A, op. 9005, d. 19, l. 63.

It is also worth noting Nagaibakov's careful and laconic formulation that "Liziukov and Assorov are not here." This "not here" can be understood and interpreted very broadly, and no unmistakable alarm signal follows from it. At the same time, by this time this was already not the entire truth, since an honest assessment of the situation would require the addition of "and we don't know where they are" after "not here", and information that searches had produced no results, that there'd been no contact with them, and that they hadn't been seen by anyone in almost 24 hours. However, the cautious and cagey Nagaibakov didn't add any of this (and indeed how could you write such? This would line you up for a tongue-lashing from higher command …), and limited himself only to the general statement of the fact that the corps commander and commissar were absent; nothing more.

At the end of his report, Nagaibakov provided information on the losses of the corps in materiel for 23 July (the 2nd Tank Corps lost 1 KV, 1 T-34 and 1 T-60 burned out, 1 KV knocked out and another KV stuck at the crossing site), and asked the headquarters of the operational group for air support in order to knock out the enemy's anti-tank defense system, and listed the areas where according to his information the German anti-tank guns were located that were hindering the tanks' advance.[10]

Having put together his next report to higher command and having handed it to a liaison officer for delivery, having appointed Burdov in overall command of the composite group of the 26th and 27th Tank Brigades (let him carry out the task, and face the inquiry …), while having simultaneously instructed him and his subordinates to search for the missing Liziukov and Assorov, the chief of staff of the 2nd Tank Corps might fully believe that he was conscientiously carrying out his service obligations, doing everything possible for this, while the headquarters under his leadership was keeping full control over the course of the battle and was ready, once the corps commander indicated this, to move up behind the attacking infantry and tanks. However, meanwhile there was no such advance, and the corps headquarters accordingly *had to stand pat.*

While waiting for the next reports to come in from the units, and having given all the requisite orders, Nagaibakov might even take a rest. The deliberate pace of the morning at the corps command post in the overgrown ravine continued undisturbed. The front had stopped 10 kilometers to the south, but soon the distant sounds of increasingly heavy fighting began to carry from the southwest. Then the rumble of gunnery, the hollow thumps of bomb explosions and the muffled howl of dive sirens (it is fully possible that the distant specks of dive bombers, diving on their targets, could have been seen in the sky from the hills near the corps' new command post) began to shift to the north. Meanwhile to the south, there where the 1st and 2nd Tank Corps were supposed to be attacking, it seemed nothing similar was happening.

Next information came in at the command post of the 2nd Tank Corps from the 1st Tank Corps that up to 100 German tanks had broken through in the Lomovo, Lebiazh'e, Kamenka area and were attacking to the north. The intelligence chief of the 2nd Tank Corps Major Ivanovsky immediately composed his own intelligence summary, which reflected the information that had been received from their neighbor.[11] However, a glance at a map while doing so was adequate to understand the gravity of the developing events: whereas Lebiazh'e was on the corps' flank, Lomovo and even more so Kamenka were already beyond the flank, almost in the 2nd Tank Corps' rear! However, there was no way Ivanovsky could make any decision to retreat without authorization, which would also derail the carrying out of the order issued previously by Nagaibakov. However, at that point all the doubts and uncertainty were dissipated by an order arriving from

10 Ibid.
11 TsAMO, F. 202, op. 50, d. 1, l. 306.

the Operational Group Chibisov headquarters: Chibisov was demanding the immediate removal of the 2nd Tank Corps from the front and its movement to the Murav'evka – Dolgoe area.

Having received such an order, Nagaibakov wrote his own order and sent it off to the brigades via the very same liaison officer, Captain Veniukov, who set out for the third time on his 10-kilometer path to the front. Veniukov arrived at the wooded ravine where the 26th and 27th Tank Brigades were located at 1030, and handed the order to Burdov. By this time, the brigades according to Burdov's order should have already been attacking toward Medvezh'e for the last 30 minutes, but they hadn't moved out and had made no advance thus far.[12] Then the order arrived ... now they had to cancel the *planned* attack, and whether anyone wanted to or not, fall back. An order is an order, and as they say, you don't discuss it, but carry it out!

So both tank brigades, the commanders of which had spent more than 24 hours in the wooded ravine and had been totally unable to prepare and launch a decisive attack, were operationally removed from their occupied position, and by 1120 they'd already fallen back 12-14 kilometers from their line of departure for the attack to the rear line of defense. This they accomplished in just 50 minutes, having left behind both their travails in the wooded ravine and the unsearched fields surrounding where their knocked-out tanks remained standing. In the process, the search for the missing corps commander and commissar was postponed for an indefinite amount of time.

12 On the basis of a political report from the 26th Tank Brigade it is possible to assume that the commander of the 26th Tank Brigade, at the very least, sent ahead a reconnaissance-in-force, as had been decided upon the previous evening. Judging from everything, the reconnaissance group consisted of the brigade's most experienced tank crews, including that of Lieutenant Komarov, which had distinguished itself in previous fighting as part of the 5th Tank Army. We read in the report:
Lieutenant Komarov's crew, the driver-mechanic of which was Senior Sergeant Eremin, broke into the enemy's forward edge of defense and destroyed 4 anti-tank guns and a mortar battery, and crushed more than 30 Nazis beneath the tank's tracks. Lieutenant Komarov and turret machine-gunner Kniazev finished off some of the Germans that remained alive in their trenches with shovels. Seven Germans were killed and 4 were taken prisoner. Lieutenant Komarov was wounded in the arm. As a result of this hand-to-hand combat in this battle Junior Lieutenant Gagarin's crew destroyed 3 cannons, 1 tank and killed up to 30 men. Gagarin himself and his driver-mechanic distinguished themselves.
Finished them off with shovels ... a savage scene, but in war anything and everything happened. To what degree of hatred must the tankers have reached, in order to act in such fashion? To this one must add genuine fearlessness, resolve and a perceptible feeling of superiority over the defeated foe, in order to climb out of tank, enter close combat and perform with such malice, daring and aggression that the once confident and arrogant Wehrmacht soldiers lost any will to resist and raised their hands in front of the enraged "Ivan". Yet such "Ivans" in the second year of the war were becoming fierce and capable of beating the German, and increasing in numbers in the Red Army.
Subsequently the driver-mechanic of tank commander Eremin recalled this episode: "We received an order to defeat the enemy submachine gunners [sic] in a patch of woods. We were to take this patch. Our platoon under the command of Senior Lieutenant Koluchev was the guide platoon. He was a very brave fellow. When we approached the woods, the battalion stopped, while with three tanks we surged ahead, entered the woods, and there we found the German trenches with infantry in a wood clearing. My hatch was open. The first trench was sandy. When we closed upon the second trench, the tank commander climbed out of the tank, grabbed a shovel, and simply began to shatter the Germans' heads with it. That's how he killed 7 men. I sent the turret machine-gunner in order to ask the commander to get back into the tank, but he also started to smite the Germans. With the butt end of his gun, he killed 8 men and brought 6 prisoners to the tank, which we took back to the brigade commander. We crushed a lot of Germans there back then." [Archive IRI RAN, F. 2, section 1, op. 118, d. 8, l. 2]

12

A review of the enemy's actions on 22 and 23 July 1942

On the morning of 22 July, the commander of the 9th Panzer Division General Baeßler received an order from the headquarters of the Second Army about making immediate preparations for a march to the Zemliansk – Malaia Vereika area.[1] As he might have fully expected after receiving the briefing on the previous day about the Russian breakthrough in the sector of the VII Army Corps, there followed the decision by higher command to re-activate the panzer division again in order to eliminate the latest crisis northwest of Voronezh. Like a fire brigade, the panzer division was being thrown into battle already for the third time in less than three weeks .... However, as is known orders are not for discussion, and Baeßler, well-disciplined after his years of service, "snapped to attention" and answered his superior "*Jawohl*!"

The panzer division's multi-thousand strong personnel went into motion. The long-awaited assignment of train seats to the men striving to get to Germany on leave,[2] which began that morning according to lists at headquarters[3], plainly had to stop, and chances are that leave was cancelled for some because of the arriving order. Liaison officers were immediately dispatched to the VII Army Corps and 387th Infantry Division in order to become familiar with the situation and to return with briefings for the headquarters. Soon, orders for the schedule and organization of the march went out over the radio.

However, not everyone was ready in the panzer division for the march. In distinction from the command of the Second Army, which from "on high" believed that the 9th Panzer Division was ready to carry out any order given to it after its period of rest, the chief of the division's rear services immediately rang the alarm bell. According to his calculations, the division simply didn't have enough fuel for a march and subsequent combat operations in an area 30-35 kilometers from its current location! Moreover, the time had come to change the oil in the new tanks, new halftracks and vehicles with new engines (as they say, war is war, but engine oil must be replaced on schedule ...), but the division still hadn't received the engine oil for this, despite its timely-made request. Because of the rains, the delivery of fuel to the division's 11th Panzer Grenadier Regiment was being delayed.

The persistent logistics chief made a second request to Second Army headquarters about allocating fuel and engine oil to the 9th Panzer Division, threatening the command that in the opposite

1 NARA, T-315, roll 541, f. 001109

2 NARA, T-315, roll 538, fr. 001387.

3 Surprisingly, in the *Wehrmacht's* units, it was considered possible to send men on leave even at the height of combat operations considering this important to support the combat spirit in the units. Commanders of the Red Army could only dream about any planned leaves from the front, while for the simple soldier this was beyond even mentioning. The war went on not for life, but to death, and the military servicemen (and women) of the Red Army were expected to fight without any leaves of absence until the very end – victorious, hospitalized, or in their graves.

case, he couldn't guarantee the combat-readiness of the units entrusted to his care. To his relief, at 1100 a supply train carrying fuel and lubricants for the division finally arrived in Kastornoe, including 370 metric tons of gasoline and 50 metric tons of diesel fuel.[4] Having learned of this, the supply chief immediately dispatched a column of trucks to Kastornoe with a combined carrying capacity of around 150 metric tons.

However, having received the fuel and lubricants, the column again experienced delays on its return to the division due to the poor condition of the roads, overcoming with difficulty the over-saturated black earth of the Voronezh – Kursk region (this means a lengthy column of trucks that were slowly crawling along muddied village roads – but where was our air force, in order to turn these slowly crawling trucks and their metric tons of fuel into blazing bonfires and thereby deprive the foe of fuel?). In view of the anticipated intensive fighting, a request was sent to the supply chief of the Second Army about obtaining additional ammunition, because the amount of which available in the division's units was plainly inadequate in the assessments of the division's supply chief. By nighttime, the fuel in fact hadn't yet arrived in the 9th Panzer Division, so the armored armada helplessly continued to remain in its assembly area. Only its forward units, which had obtained fuel taken from that still lingering in the division's machines, set out on the march on 22 July.

The reserve 385th Infantry Division (which had only two infantry regiments instead of the normal three), which the Second Army command planned to use together with the 9th Panzer Division in order to relieve the VII Army Corps, at the decision of the headquarters of Army Group "B" had actually been passed to the control of the Second Army on 21 July, so it immediately received an order to shift to the VII Army Corps' area of operations. However, all sorts of delays and procrastinations in the regiments with the preparations for moving out led to the fact that the division didn't set off on the march until 2200 on the evening of 21 July, and from the Volovo, Volovchik, Nizhnee Bol'shoe area moved to the east with a forced march. The regimental columns, unaffected by the presence or absence of fuel, albeit moved more slowly than the panzer grenadiers loaded aboard trucks, but in the end made more progress than the immobilized 9th Panzer Division left without fuel. Marching throughout the night and following morning, the 385th Infantry Division hurrying to the front of the VII Army Corps reached the areas of Verkhotop'e, Matveevka, Petrovskoe and Naberezhnoe by noon, while a forward detachment with a battalion of anti-tank artillery arrived in Novosel'skoe.[5]

No matter how the officers drove the soldiers exhausted by the march, the division's delay in moving out and the poor roads (an eternal German complaint!) slowed the column's progress, as a result of which the infantry units reached the designated areas only by lunch time instead of early morning, and chances are the exhausted foot soldiers immediately collapsed into the thick roadside dust. With a 14-hour march the 385th Infantry Division had covered approximately 40 kilometers, but it still had at least 30 kilometers to go before it could reach the expected combat area.

Meanwhile, for the second day the command of the VII Army Corps had to repel increasingly ferocious Russian attacks with only its available forces. The situation was greatly eased by the Luftwaffe support, but even it was unable to put a complete stop to the Russians' increasing pressure. By the morning it became known that in the course of the latest attack, Russian tanks had broken through the line of defense of the 387th Infantry Division during the night. The alarmed and perplexed staff officers of the division were reporting that some of the tanks had turned back, while the rest, "the smaller portion, without escorting infantry, had penetrated to the southeast to a depth of 15 kilometers."[6] (How could the bewildered German staff officers have known that most

4 NARA, T-315, roll 541, fr. 000471.

5 NARA, T-315, roll 2193, fr. 000244.

6 NARA, T-314, roll 353, fr. 000401.

of the 148th Tank Brigade had banally and annoyingly lost its bearings in the expansive fields at night, while the other tank brigades had simply given it no support?) According to a report from the division, the Russian tanks that had broken through had been cordoned off for subsequent destruction.

The desperate breakthrough by the vanguard of the 148th Tank Brigade, which had turned into both a success and a tragedy for its tankers, became for the enemy such a signal event that traces of it were left not only in the reports of the VII Army Corps, but also in the journal of combat operations of the General Staff of the OKH, thereby becoming an unwitting documentary monument to our fallen tankers in the captured documents. In the operational summary of the *Wehrmacht* for 23 July 1942 it was written: "Southeast of Elets, the enemy in strength of up to a regiment attacked our positions. In the process some enemy tanks were able to advance up to 20 kilometers to the south."[7]

In order to strengthen the division, the command of the VII Army Corps had subordinated to the division (in addition to the single company that had been attached the day before) all of the remaining elements of the 559th Panzerjäger Battalion[8], which at that moment consisted of 8-10 heavy 75-mm anti-tank guns (it is fully possible that it was just these anti-tank guns, which had fortuitously just arrived in the 387th Infantry Division, that were sent straight away into combat together with several assault guns of the 201st Stürmgeschutz [Assault Gun] Battalion, which had been attached to the 387th Infantry Division, against the 148th Tank Brigade's 89th Tank Battalion that had broken through to the Medvezh'e area).[9] At 1040 the commander of the Second Army General von Salmuth arrived at the command post of the VII Army Corps in order to discuss the situation and the possibility of launching a counteroffensive. The hypothetical question of using the 9th Panzer Division and 385th Infantry Division was finally resolved and became the basis for working out a practical plan; however, this scheme was being strongly affected by the factor of the ever diminishing combat capability of the 387th Infantry Division that had faced the brunt of the Russians' main attack. Whether or not this division could hold out until the arrival of the 385th Infantry Division and 9th Panzer Division became the decisive factor in the development of the counterattack plan.

At 2145 on 22 July, the commander of the 387th Infantry Division General Jahr reported to commander of VII Army Corps General of Artillery Hell that the division's situation was critical: the infantry was thoroughly worn out and the artillery had fired off most the last round of its ammunition, but because of the heavy rains, the delivery of more ammunition was being delayed and couldn't make up for the high expenditure.[10] Over the day's combat the division had lost 241 soldiers and officers (2 officers and 58 soldiers killed, and 2 officers and 167 soldiers wounded, plus 12 soldiers missing in action).[11] Although these casualties were in fact substantially fewer than those incurred on the previous day, over the two days of fighting the division had already lost over 700 men from its combat elements, which raised the question: How much longer could its regiments hold out given the intensity of the fighting and such a level of losses?

Having heard the alarming report from the commander of the 387th Infantry Division, the VII Army Corps' commander decided to reinforce the division with the corps' 221st Pionier [Pioneer] Battalion and a reserve battalion from the 340th Infantry Division that was positioned adjacent to the 387th Infantry Division. Of course, the engineers were needed by the corps to carry out their

7 *Stalingrad 1942-1943: Stalingradskaia bitva v dokumentakh* [*Stalingrad 1942-1943: The Battle of Stalingrad in documents*] (Moscow: Biblioteka, 1995), p. 14.
8 NARA, T-314, roll 353, fr. 000401.
9 NARA, T-314, roll 354, fr. 000256, 000210.
10 NARA, T-314, roll 353, fr. 000401.
11 NARA,T-314, roll 354, fr. 726-727.

own direct responsibilities (and to throw them into battle as simple infantry was too wasteful), and the decision to commit the sole reserve battalion of the neighboring 340th Infantry Division meant leaving its division commander without any reserve at all in the face of increasing pressure on his own front. However, it seems the commander of VII Army Corps simply had no choice.

Having issued the corresponding orders, General Hell immediately contacted the commander of the Second Army General von Salmuth and in his turn reported to him about the critical situation facing the 387th Infantry Division, and again requested the urgent support of the 9th Panzer Division for his army corps. In addition, Hell reported to Salmuth that according to the testimony of prisoners and deserters, the Russians were preparing an offense on the Don at Novozhivotinnoe, and thus he had to take into consideration this threat as well.[12]

At 2230 the 9th Panzer Division's commander was again briefed regarding the situation that had developed, and a half hour later the commander of the Second Army General von Salmuth called the headquarters of the VII Army Corps and informed General Hell that the 9th Panzer Division was under his operational control, and on 23 July it was planned that it would launch a counterattack. In the process von Salmuth clarified that in connection with the division's combat task he was leaving open two possible options:

1) In the event that the Russians broke through in the sector of the 387th Infantry Division, the 9th Panzer Division should attack from the south and thereby restore the broken front.
2) If in case the 387th Infantry Division was able to hold its occupied front until the arrival of the panzer division, the 9th Panzer Division instead should launch a flank attack out of the sector of the neighboring 340th Infantry Division with the aim of cutting off and destroying the Russian units that had penetrated.

Subsequently the discussion touched upon the question of using infantry divisions in the counterattack. Von Salmuth directed that if the reserve 385th Infantry Division was able to reach the operational area in time, it should also become subordinate to the VII Army Corps and launch an attack from the south. The 168th Infantry Division, the first units of which the day before had been replaced within the Voronezh bridgehead by the 57th Infantry Division and had crossed over to the western bank of the Don, should if possible not push its front to the north but remain facing to the east, so in the event of an enemy offensive across the Don at least some German units would remain in this sector (directly on the bank of the Don, the 323rd Infantry Division's 594th Infantry Regiment was defending in the sector between Khvoshchevatka to Gubarevo). The corps commander then informed the commander of the 387th Infantry Division of the decisions and directed him to report continuously on the situation, since the actions of the 9th Panzer Division would depend on the situation of his division.[13]

At 2330 the commander of the 9th Panzer Division received an order to shift his division to the Zemliansk area quickly. In the expectation of looming combat and in connection with the request of the 9th Panzer Division's commander, the II Battalion of its 102nd Artillery Regiment was returned to the division from Artillery Group "Don", which was supporting the defense of the German units on the northern front of the Voronezh bridgehead with fire from the western bank of the Don River. Baeßler was unsuccessful in getting the III Battalion returned to him, because the defense of the German "land" front in the Voronezh bridgehead, which was cracking under the pressure of Soviet attacks, required constant artillery support, and the loss of one more heavy

12 NARA, T-314, roll 353, fr. 000401.
13 NARA, T-314, roll 353, fr. 000401.

artillery battalion would have excessively weakened the fire of Artillery Group "Don". Nevertheless, in place of III Battalion of his own 102nd Artillery Regiment, the 9th Panzer Division was given II Battalion of the 71st Artillery Regiment out of the Second Army's reserve. The stressful day in the headquarters of the VII Army Corps ended with the receipt of an order that subordinated the 385th Infantry Division to it; on 23 July, this division was to arrive with its main forces in the Novosel'skoe, Dolgoe, Livenka area.

One can judge how the day of fighting went on the front of the 340th and 387th Infantry Divisions from the reports of the VII Army Corps:

> 387th Infantry Division: Early in the morning, an enemy attack conducted with the support of 41 tanks along the Bol'shaia Vereika – Somovo road was repulsed [At the headquarters of the 387th Infantry Division, they obviously took the idle tanks of the 26th and 27th Tank Brigades in the wooded ravine near Hill 188.5 for this "support" – I.S.]. Yet another enemy attack with the forces of up to two battalions, conducted from the direction of Lebiazh'e to the south, was stopped at 1130. At the given moment the enemy is repeating the attacks from the direction of Lebiazh'e and Bol'shaia Vereika to the south. More detailed reports regarding this are still lacking. The forward positions on the right were also withdrawn to the main line of defense.
>
> The enemy tanks that broke through during the night were partially destroyed, while another portion of them turned back to the north. Seven enemy tanks are still continuing to remain in the area to the west of the Kaver'ia and Sivertsevo villages. [This report speaks to the fact that by 1630, the tanks of the 148th Tank Brigade's 89th Tank Battalion had not yet been destroyed and still remained on Hill 187.9 – I.S.]. Today a total of 29 enemy tanks were knocked out.
>
> The 340th Infantry Division: The enemy offensive that was reported this morning has been driven back. The enemy attacks along the entire line of defense in the course of the morning were repulsed. The weather: sweltering; a thunderstorm is possible.[14]

The evening report at 2140 stated:

> 387th Infantry Division: The enemy offensive south of Bol'shaia Vereika and Lebiazh'e that was reported in the afternoon has been brought to a stop at the present moment. It is being conducted with major infantry forces (in the sector of one company, from 400 to 500 attacking Russians), with the support of tanks and unusually heavy fire support of artillery and mortars. Several enemy tanks managed to overrun our infantry and reach the Bol'shaia Vereika – Somovo road [as we can see, the offensive's artillery support targeting Hill 188.5 given by units of the 167th Rifle Division and 2nd Tank Corps, even when conducted by quite limited forces and scarce ammunition, seemed to the headquarters of the 387th Infantry Division to be "unusually heavy" – I.S.]. A breach in the defense has formed in the sector between Churikovo and the Bol'shaia Vereika – Somovo road.
>
> On the whole, our units are continuing to hold their lines. In the course of the day up to the present moment, a total of 35 enemy tanks have been destroyed. The Russian tanks positioned west of Kaver'ia and Sivertsevo, which were mentioned in the previous report, have been destroyed.
>
> The division's final reserves have been committed into combat. A new defensive line has been prepared through the efforts of units of the 168th Infantry Division along the Terny

14 NARA, T-314, roll 353, fr. 001338-1340.

> – Zemliansk line. The 201st Stürmgeschutz Battalion [the machines of which, obviously, took direct part in the fighting with the 148th Tank Brigade's 89th Tank Battalion on Hill 187.9 – I.S.] has 6 operational assault guns. Because of the heavy rain, in places the roads are impassable.[15]
>
> 340th Infantry Division: From the morning the enemy is undertaking further attempts to attack with tanks and infantry along both sides of Hill 213.8. The attacks have been suppressed by the fire of artillery and infantry guns. The enemy is digging in on Hill 212.9. After 1300 from this hill there was an attempt by weak Russian forces escorted by 3-4 tanks to make progress to the south. The Russians were pinned down in a grain field several hundred meters short of the main line of defense. After 1500, there was a movement of tanks, trucks and infantry to Lebiazh'e. The village of Lebiazh'e has been fully occupied by the enemy, with particular strength in its eastern portion. The Luftwaffe launched strikes at an aggregation of tanks and infantry in a ravine south of Lebiazh'e and the triangular patch of woods and partially drove them out from there. Field works are being thrown up on the hills close to Lomovo. The enemy is plainly increasing in strength in Lebiazh'e and to the east of the village.
>
> South of the village of Ozerki, attacks by Russians in strength of up to a company, unsupported by tanks. The enemy was pinned down as a result of our intense artillery fire. High activity in the air. On the right flank in the right-hand sector, an attack of infantry with the support of tanks was stopped at 1545 with the help of dive bombers. Around 1300 one German bomber was shot down by 8 enemy fighters to the west of the southern outskirts of Lomovo. At 1515, Novopavlovka was bombed. Information at 1545. Repeated attacks by Russian bombers on the left flank. Figures for the day: 4 deserters, 5 prisoners.[16]

On 22 July, the losses of the 340th Infantry Division amounted to 22 soldiers and non-commissioned officers killed, 57 wounded and 12 missing in action.[17]

Having received the order to march shortly before midnight on 22 July, the commander of the 9th Panzer Division wound up in a very awkward position: the motorized supply column sent to Kastornoe still hadn't returned with fuel, but the division was already supposed to move out somehow. In expectation of the arrival of the supply column, the unit commanders allocated their remaining fuel first of all to their forward units, so that they could at least begin the march at dawn. The panzer regiment without serious fuel "infusions" could not get very far.

The motorized supply column still hadn't arrived by dawn. Waiting no longer for it, the forward units of the 9th Panzer Division at 0400 set out on the march with the fuel that they had at that moment. The first fuel trucks arrived from Kastornoe only around 0800, after which it finally became possible to move out all of the panzer division's units. Having filled the tank engines with dozens of metric tons of the scarce fuel, almost 100 panzers of the 9th Panzer Division and several dozens of armored halftracks started their engines and set out on the march. They were followed by a large multitude of the most diverse vehicles of support and accompaniment. To the satisfaction of the 9th Panzer Division's supply chief, even more trucks carrying the Kastornoe fuel managed to catch up with the division, and by evening he managed to create a reserve of 30 metric tons of fuel at a forward distribution point in a patch of woods northwest of Zemliansk. However, the "voracious" panzer regiment expended so much fuel during the march that it required an additional 40 metric tons of fuel – and this didn't include the multitude of other vehicles.

15 Ibid.
16 NARA, T-315, roll 2120, fr. 001083.
17 NARA, T-314, roll 353, fr. 000726-727.

To the relief of the anxious supply chief, by evening another column with 170 metric tons of fuel caught up with the division, but it immediately became clear that because of possible leaks (the barrels were only partially full), up to 10% of this amount of fuel had been lost.[18] Thus, so far the division had been supplied with the necessary amount of fuel, but there had been no success in creating substantial reserves for it in the expectation of upcoming combat actions, and therefore, in the future the division's supply with fuel would have to count upon "just in time" deliveries.

Meanwhile, the 9th Panzer Division's column was approaching the front. The 9th Panzer Division's sapper battalion sent out ahead began to lay down two bridges and arrange two fords across the Sukhaia Vereika River at Novopavlovka and Spasskoe. While still on the march, the panzer division received a briefing from the headquarters of the Second Army, which informed that the division would have to be ready to enter the fighting already on the afternoon of 23 July. Its task was also set: with an attack toward Somovo, to penetrate along the road to the northeast to the relief of the 387th Infantry Division, and in particular of its encircled 542nd Infantry Regiment. At 1130 the 9th Panzer Division officially became subordinate to the VII Army Corps.[19] General Baeßler immediately flew off in his Storch liaison aircraft to the corps' command post.[20]

The corps command gave him a detailed assignment for combat actions in the breakthrough area. Over the morning hours, the situation was continuing to deteriorate. The Russians were stubbornly attacking in the entire breakthrough sector, forcing the right flank of the 387th Infantry Division to retreat, and with tanks and infantry were increasingly pressing the center of the 387th Infantry Division; by noontime, the VII Army Corps' defense, putting it figuratively, was beginning to come apart at the seams. All these events placed the German command's preferred option of launching a flanking counterattack to envelop the Russians under the threat of becoming a no-go, because if the 387th Infantry Division couldn't hold out until evening, the 9th Panzer Division instead of a flank attack would have to save it from complete destruction and would have to plug the hole in the front with its panzers in place of the infantry.

Thus, forced to search hastily for some sort of decision and to improvise on the march, the command of the VII Army Corps leaned toward a compromise option: to activate the division's panzer regiment in an attack from Somovo to the northeast, in order to ease the critical situation of the 387th Infantry Division, but with the calculation that the entire panzer division would manage to cross the Sukhaia Vereika River by nighttime and be ready to launch the planned flank attack on the morning of the following day in the Novopavlovka, Spasskoe area. Such a plan required that the panzer regiment, without becoming tied up in prolonged fighting, would be able to exit the combat after a brief attack and even before nightfall move out toward a new jumping-off area and occupy it by the morning of 24 July.

Soon, however, it became clear that the instructions from the headquarters of the Second Army that had been received that morning were already outdated, because the village of Somovo, which had initially been planned to use as the jumping-off area for the attack, was itself being threatened by a Russian penetration (a consequence of the offensive by Katukov's 1st Tank Corps). A company of the anti-tank battalion was immediately sent to Somovo (which was then followed by the entire battalion), and shortly thereafter a battalion of the 11th Panzer Grenadier Regiment was sent to the same place.[21]

Meanwhile, in addition to the commander of the 9th Panzer Division, the commanders of the 340th and 387th Infantry Divisions arrived at the command post of the VII Army Corps. There,

18 NARA, T-315, roll 541, fr. 000472.
19 NARA, T-315, roll 541, fr. 001110.
20 NARA, T-315, roll 538, fr. 001387.
21 NARA, T-315, roll 541, fr. 001110.

General Hell held a detailed discussion with them regarding the plan for the upcoming counterattack. Having received the approval from von Salmuth, the Second Army commander, General Hell made the ultimate decision to stick to the compromise plan of actions, even though it was quite risky. On the one hand, a brief, violent attack by the panzer regiment might be insufficient to guarantee that the staggering front of the 387th Infantry Division could be maintained. On the other hand, there was the danger that the panzer regiment wouldn't manage to pull out of the combat in time, and then the full attack by the entire panzer division on the following morning would be substantially weakened (the enticement of an effective flank attack was too great to be rejected, even with the risk of the collapse of the 387th Infantry Division's front).

Having adopted this decision, General Hell meanwhile attempted by every means to create at least some sort of switch position in the rear of the 387th Infantry Division in the event that a Russian breakthrough nevertheless occurred. Therefore he issued an order to the commander of the 168th Infantry Division, which had been withdrawn to the western bank of the Don River, to form a single, reinforced composite battalion from each of his 417th and 442nd Infantry Regiments (these regiments were simply incapable of anything more after the heavy fighting in Voronezh) and to send them on a march to be at the disposal of the 387th Infantry Division for taking up switch positions north of Dolgovskoe and Bol'shaia Treshchevka.[22] Judging from all the available evidence, it was with these hastily-assembled composite battalions that the tankers of the 1st Tank Corps' 89th Tank Brigade had to engage in battle.

In order to strengthen the 385th Infantry Division that was approaching on the march the commander of VII Army Corps attached one battery of the 201st Stürmgeschutz Battalion to it. Meanwhile, the 9th Panzer Division received the 560th Panzerjäger Battalion (on 18.7.42 – 16 heavy anti-tank guns) that had been assigned to VII Army Corps by the Second Army.[23]

With the aim of helping the engaged units of the 387th Infantry Division repulse the attacks by the Russian tanks that were breaking through to the south, the commander of the approaching 385th Infantry Division Major General Karl Eibl received an order to advance his anti-tank battalion, which consisted of 19 75-mm and 6 50-mm anti-tank guns, as quickly as possible to the sector of the 387th Infantry Division's front.[24] Together with the division's forward detachment, which had been busy with combing through a patch of woods in the zone of the division's disposition, the anti-tank battalion arrived at the front and took up firing positions. Major General Bergen, the commander of the reserve 323rd Infantry Division that was moving out toward Voronezh received a similar order. A portion of his anti-tank battalion had been urgently taken from the march and unexpectedly received an order to move more than 30 kilometers to the north from the 323rd Infantry Division's axis of movement, in order to take up firing positions near Kaver'ia, thereby strengthening the defense of the 387th Infantry Division.[25] Thus, decisively and rigorously using every available possibility, the command of the VII Army Corps began quickly to augment the strength of the corps' anti-tank grouping, having increased its numerical strength by approximately 50 heavy 75-mm anti-tank guns in the course of two days.

By 1700 an imposing grouping of the 9th Panzer Division consisting of the 33rd Panzer Regiment, a battalion of the 11th Panzer Grenadier Regiment and the anti-tank battalion had gathered in Somovo; it was being supported by two artillery battalions that had been attached to it. Having assembled in the jumping-off area, the 33rd Panzer Regiment went on the offensive together with the panzer grenadiers and accompanying anti-tank guns along the general

22 NARA, T-314, roll 353, fr. 000406.
23 NARA, T-314, roll 354, fr. 000243.
24 NARA T-314, roll 2193, fr. 000246; NARA T-315, roll 2199, fr. 000649.
25 NARA, T-315, roll 2038, fr. 000434.

direction of the Somovo – Bol'shaia Vereika road and soon "reached Hill 210.9 without meeting any resistance."[26] General Baeßler drove out to an area northeast of Somovo in order to observe the battle from a hilltop that had already been taken by the German panzers.[27]

The panzer regiment's further advance was met by intense flanking fire from "Russian infantry" (plainly the 193rd Rifle Division) and "savage fighting that arose in separate sectors", in the course of which as the 9th Panzer Division command believed, 12 enemy tanks were knocked out.[28] By 1835, judging from the 9th Panzer Division's operational map, the shock grouping had passed the fork in the road leading to Lebiazh'e, where a portion of its force was left behind in order to screen the flank with a front facing north, while the tanks continued to advance. Within a short time, they reached the southern fringe of the large patch of woods south of Lebiazh'e and the fork in the road leading to Bol'shaia Vereika, "thereby significantly easing the 387th Infantry Division's situation."

The encircled 542nd Infantry Regiment, which on the day of 23 July had taken up an all-round defense in the patch of woods south of Lebiazh'e, was able to replenish itself with ammunition, water and food, and to evacuate its wounded men. No less important was the effect on morale that the tankers of the 33rd Panzer Regiment had on the infantrymen, who had spent the day under the fire from units of the 167th and 193rd Rifle Divisions, the 1st and 2nd Motorized Rifle Brigades, and the 89th Tank Brigade that had been besieging them in the woods. Putting it figuratively, the soldiers of the 542nd Infantry Regiment were able to catch their breath, when they had seen their own panzers that evening instead of the Russian tanks that had isolated them and were sweeping the patch of woods with fire. The day of combat had again cost the division heavy losses: 54 men were killed (one of them an officer), 104 wounded (including four officers), and 2 went missing in action (one of them an officer) – altogether, 160 men.[29]

The absence of any mention in the Soviet documents about a combat with tanks of the 33rd Panzer Regiment in the area of the southern patch of woods, and the accompanying markings on the 9th Panzer Division's operational map, gives evidence to the fact that the positions of the 167th Rifle Division and the 118th Tank Brigade by the evening of 23 July were significantly to the north of the patch of woods and the road fork.

Having carried out the assignment and having concentrated in an assembly area by around 1900, the 33rd Panzer Regiment and the panzer grenadier battalion began to carry out the second part of the plan by moving into a jumping-off area for the outflanking attack on the morning of 24 July. Wasting no time, the panzer regiment turned around, and having again left behind the encouraged men of the 542nd Infantry Regiment to their uneasy fate, moved out in a thundering armored armada back toward Somovo, which it reached by 1950.[30]

The division's regrouping for the attack on the next morning went smoothly and was completed by nightfall. Two reinforced infantry battalions were formed in the neighboring 340th Infantry Division, which were to follow behind the attacking tanks of the 33rd Panzer Regiment and secure the left flank of the attacking 9th Panzer Division. On 23 July 1942, the 340th Infantry Division had lost 37 killed, 129 wounded (two of them officers) and 3 missing in action, for a total of 169 men.[31]

The 385th Infantry Division by the end of 23 July had managed to reach the jumping-off positions at Novopavlovka only with one regiment; the other regiment was assembling in the Dolgoe,

26 NARA, T-315, roll 541, fr. 001110.
27 NARA, T-315, roll 538, fr. 001387.
28 NARA, T-315, roll 541, fr. 001110.
29 NARA, T-314, roll 354, fr. 726-727.
30 NARA, T-315, roll 542, fr. 000014.
31 NARA, T-314, roll 353, fr. 000726-727.

Livenka, Kazinka area 10-12 kilometers from the Sukhaia Vereika River and its last units arrived in Dolgoe only at 2300. A forward detachment moved out toward Gremiach'e in order to screen to the east and south.

A staff officer accurately noted in the *kriegstagebuch* (journal of combat operations):

> The movement went smoothly. The division commander received a verbal order from the command of the VII Army Corps for the next day. The division's tasks for the offensive were discussed at a conference of all the commanders around 1800. During a personal meeting with the participation of the commanders of all three involved divisions, the plans were amended. The "freewheeling" dispensation of the tasks [by the corps' command] created a lot of bother for the division. The division commander and his operations chief returned from the 340th Infantry Division's command post only after midnight.
>
> The enemy air force throughout the day and night conducted attacks by solitary aircraft or in small groups. Several horses were killed. The division headquarters shifted from Berezovka to the woods 500 meters northwest of Livenka. The road conditions after the morning's rains were still very poor that night, although in the course of the day some improvement was seen. The unit commanders and the chiefs of the departments of the division headquarters sent their congratulations to the division commander on the occasion of his birthday.[32]

(None of his peers who congratulated their chief on his 51st birthday suspected that this would be his last birthday and the cavalier with the Knight's Cross with Oak Leaves and Swords General Eibl would suffer an absurd death and be killed in the frigid January of the German grand retreat just six months later, when disoriented Italian soldiers in the heat of the moment or out of fear mistook his car as a vehicle of the attacking Red Army and blew it up with grenades from an ambush position).

In the 9th Panzer Division on the evening of 23 July, the restless supply chief again expressed his anxiety to the command. Having no decisive word in the reaching of operational decisions, he was approaching the upcoming operation with his own thoughts, which plainly didn't include the combat actions of an entire panzer regiment on the planned day of march. Facing the need to make corrections to his calculations regarding fuel consumption literally on the move, the supply chief was compelled on the following day to furnish the panzer regiment (which had launched the swift attack out of Somovo and returned) with another 10 metric tons of fuel, but did not lose a chance to report on the occasion that already more than half of the 397.2 metric tons of fuel that had been designated for the 9th Panzer Division for conducting the counteroffensive had been supplied, and this quantity had already been almost fully consumed![33]

For the 9th Panzer Division's command, the excess consumption of fuel was undoubtedly justified by the operational results achieved. The compromise plan adopted by the commander of the VII Army Corps was going well, and the units had managed to extricate themselves from combat and had taken up their jumping-off positions for the flank attack. Thus, the division command had every right to believe that the day of 23 July had ended with good results for the 9th Panzer Division. However, the overall successful day had been darkened by an absurd incident.

The panzer regiment's counterattack had succeeded in easing the situation of the 387th Infantry Division, and the regiment's commander Colonel Walter Rödlich had every right to be satisfied both with his tankers' actions and the results. The regiment had crushed all the resistance it had encountered in its path, had taken up its designated area, and was ready for the new combat task.

32 NARA, T-315, roll 2193, fr. 000246.
33 NARA, T-315, roll 541, fr. 000472.

After completing the counterattack that had relieved the encircled 542nd Infantry Regiment, the victorious colonel climbed out of his tank and set off in a car back to headquarters, in order to take part in the planning for the next day's flank attack. However, fate had prepared something quite different for him.

On the way back to headquarters, the colonel's driver lost control on the road made slippery by the rains; the car skidded off the road and overturned into a ravine together with its passengers. As a result, Rödlich received fatal injuries and died on the eve of the division's planned flank attack! This was a shocking and inglorious death of an experienced officer and one of Hitler's obedient and brave war dogs, who had earned the Knight's Cross and had taken part in many battles and skirmishes, but who died so incongruously.

On this same day, as captured documents testify, Colonel Rödlich was buried with full military honors at a "cemetery of fallen heroes" in Zemliansk.[34] (It seems that in the 9th Panzer Division they thought of Zemliansk as a new German fiefdom in the depths of Russia, where the carefully tended graves of the *Reich*'s fallen heroes would now and forever be located as an example for future generations. But just as in the later case with General Eibl, the subordinates of the commander who had just been buried with honors didn't know that within six months there would not even be a trace left of the departed brave commander's grave).

Having learned of what had happened, the commander of the 9th Panzer Division General Baeßler was quickly forced to appoint a new commander for the panzer regiment on the night before the offensive, which of course might negatively affect the command and control over the troops at a most unsuitable moment. Indeed, the dreadful car crash could not have created anything other than heartburn in the division headquarters. Perhaps the incongruous death of Knight's Cross recipient Major Rödlich, the commander of the 33rd Panzer Regiment, was also a bad omen for several of the senior officers of the division, which spoke to them about the difficulty of the upcoming battles and let them know that their own fate might at any moment turn tragic ...

Nevertheless, having tossed aside any possible premonitions (if in fact there were any), the command of the 9th Panzer Division energetically prepared the troops to carry out the order that had been received and to go on the attack. Subordinate to a single will, the machinery of the panzer division worked like a well-oiled mechanism. The tanks and halftracks fully topped up with fuel (seeing the scale at which fuel was being expended, the supply chief quickly began to compose a priority request to the headquarters of Second Army for the supplemental deliveries of fuel and lubricants[35]), ammunition was taken aboard, the men were fed and decorations were awarded (1 Iron Cross 1st Class, 23 Iron Crosses 2nd Class, 26 Tank Battle Badges in silver and 21 General Assault Badges[36]), the command post was shifted closer to the front, routes of advance were reconnoitered and marked, fords and bridges were prepared, and even collection points for prisoners and captured equipment were planned. After reaching the departure lines for the attack, the tank crews and panzer grenadiers were left with only several hours of precious sleep.

At dawn on 24 July, the 9th Panzer Division was assembled for the planned counterattack at the western base of the Russian salient. On the panzer division's left flank, the battalions of the 340th Infantry Division were ready for the offensive, but the 385th Infantry Division had failed to arrive on the right flank at the designated time, and the attack had to begin without it.

34 NARA, T-315, roll 541, fr. 001110.
35 NARA, T-315, roll 541, fr. 000472.
36 NARA, T-315, roll 538, fr. 001387.

13

24 July 1942

The sun had barely emerged above the horizon when a German airstrike hit the positions of the 237th Rifle Division, followed by a second and a third. True, in comparison with the previous massed aerial attacks, fewer enemy aircraft participated in these attacks – only 9 to 12 bombers each, but they repeatedly bombed the area occupied by the division's regiments (as well as their neighbors), flew back to their bases to refuel and rearm, and then returned to deliver another strike. The howling sirens of the bombers that were diving on their targets, the enervating whistle of the falling bombs, and the earth-shaking explosions among the infantrymen in the fields that were hugging the earth rocked the division's combat formations with the deafening roar of a brazen, unpunished bombing.

With the sunrise, German artillery and mortars also opened fire on the division's units. The soldiers were scrambling to dig trenches, burrowing into the earth, when once again they were subjected to an airstrike, now for the fourth time.

Then observers watched as the dark silhouettes of tanks began to appear one after the other among the waving crops on the hillcrests out in front of them. Their number swelled as they openly maneuvered across the field and arrayed for battle. The soldiers in the forward elements of the 237th Rifle Division's 835th Rifle Regiment soon counted approximately 40 black turrets above the waving rye in the field. A heavy, ominous rumble carried from that direction ....

Then more tanks began to appear in the distance, which were also advancing in the direction of the positions occupied by the 835th Rifle Regiment. They also shook out into a combat formation on the hills within direct sight of the entire regiment. Soon two panzer groupings, the total number of tanks in which according to the observers' counts began to reach a frightening 100, formed on the enormous, open field, which was split north to south by the Zemliansk highway[1].

One can only imagine this formidable sight, to which hundreds of soldiers, commanders and political workers of the 237th Rifle Division's 835th Rifle Regiment (and obviously a number of other units) involuntarily became witnesses. In front of their eyes, the enemy's armored armada was arraying itself in the field, and its intentions were completely obvious. Yet this entire, confident assembly of this horde of German tanks on their jumping-off line was neither struck by massed, intense Soviet artillery fire, nor were the panzer grenadier units targeted by Soviet aircrafts. For the most part, our aircraft never appeared above the battlefield, while the divisional artillery had few or no shells left.

Thus, the unhurried assembly of dozens of German tanks and their deployment for combat, as well as the approach of infantry that appeared in the distance and were coming up in support, took place in a morning silence, undisturbed by any thunder of the 237th Rifle Division's artillery fire. Meanwhile, the soldiers of the 835th Rifle Regiment, for the vast majority of which this was only their second day at the front, gazed upon this spectacle from their hastily dug positions ...

1 This highway is not in use today.

What were they thinking about back then? We don't know, but with the mental image of what was happening, it isn't difficult to guess what sort of chilling effect this had on the green, hungry and exhausted men of the rifle battalions, who were already dispirited by the heavy losses of the preceding day. Obviously, for many of the soldiers it was an unendurable test of morale and a deadly torment to see what sort of a dauntingly large, pitiless and remorseless force that was being assembled against the regiment.

The deployment of the hostile armor grouping on that morning could also be seen from the positions of the neighboring 284th Rifle Division, and with an experienced glance its commander Lieutenant Colonel Batiuk, who by that time was already a battle-seasoned veteran, noted its openly intimidating nature, observing, "All of the enemy's actions were designed to affect morale."[2] Then having completed its assembly on the jumping-off line, the tidal wave of German tanks began rolling toward the 835th Rifle Regiment from two primary directions: from the west out of the area of Hill 214.6 and from the south out of Novopavlovka.

One can judge the further events on the basis of two primary sources: the 237th Rifle Division's journal of combat operations, and the after-action report written by the division's command about the conducted operation. In its report to higher command, the command of the 237th Rifle Division reflected on the course of the battle as follows (with all the characteristic aspects of presenting what happened and treating the command's own decisions and actions that were inherent to such documents):

> At 0920 the enemy tanks closed right up to the forward edge of defense and penetrated the combat positions of the 835th Rifle Regiment's 3rd Battalion. By 1100 the battalion refused its left flank 800 meters back in the direction of a patch of woods 3 kilometers to the northeast [sic – obviously to the northwest] of Lomovo. The enemy tanks reached the firing positions of the artillery and the ravine northeast of Hill 212.9. The artillery knocked out several tanks, yet one battery was overrun by enemy tanks; the remaining batteries were able to conduct a fighting withdrawal. By 1100 the enemy tanks had managed to break through to the southern slopes of Hill 217.8, where they struck two battalions of the 841st Rifle Regiment, which was located in the commander's reserve in the second echelon.
>
> The regiment with its own means knocked out 25 tanks and upon the receipt of an order to retreat was forced to fall back to the north under the pressure of superior enemy forces.[3]

Likely, it would have been more accurate and honest to write "we believe that the regiment knocked out", since a report about knocked out enemy armor isn't a guarantee that this was actually the case. In addition, given the shortage or complete absence of shells that the command of the 237th Rifle Division had reported previously, it turns out that regiment's "own means" consisted primarily of anti-tank rifles and anti-tank grenades, which supposedly knocked out 25 German tanks at once.

In the division's war diary, a much fuller and more detailed picture of the fighting on 24 July is given. Moreover, the events are described with enviable directness and honesty (with the exception of the actions of the command, where the language of the assessments, for understandable reasons, is couched). This makes this document an important source in our research, which allows us to avoid retelling and/or reconstructing the events on the basis of meager and uninformative data, but to present them with a sufficiently detailed documentary description (the style of the original document has been preserved):

2 TsAMO, F. 79 gv. sd, op. 1, d. 6, l. 18.
3 TsAMO, F. 237 sd, op. 1, d. 26, l. 26.

The enemy, having assembled during the night on the line Spasskoe, Novopavlovka, woods 2.5 kilometers north of Vysochkino, "Rogataia" (meaning "with horns") woods, in the morning went on the offensive, having Perekopovka, Ozerki and Kamenka as its primary axis of attack.

Unable to withstand the blow of the enemy's attacking units, the forward units of the 835th Rifle Regiment began to retreat into the depth of their combat formations without orders. Up to five battalions of [German] infantry, escorted by up to 100 tanks, began to exert pressure on the 835th Rifle Regiment, and the regiment began to retreat, at first covering it with fire, before going into disorderly flight.

Thanks to a coincidental convergence of events, a staff officer of the division's operations department had been sent to the village of Kamenka in the headquarters' second echelon; he spotted the regiment's disorganized flight, shot several of the fleeing men, made a quick situational decision and took up an area of defense on Hill 207.2 and Hill 217.8 [on the 1:500 meter map – I.S.], where the regiment's retreating elements began to rally.

After the 835th Rifle Regiment fell back, passing with its left flank through the right flank of the 841st Rifle Regiment, the entire mass of enemy tanks and infantry fell upon two battalions of the [latter] regiment. The first frontal attack was repulsed and the enemy, suffering losses, began to envelop the battalions from the flanks, having left behind a small screening force in front. Up to 60 tanks were hurled against the 841st Rifle Regiment by the enemy. The enemy's second attack was driven back, just like the first attack. After regrouping, the enemy went on the attack for the third time. The battalions became fully encircled on Hill 212.9; the regiment's headquarters was located in some woods lying 2 kilometers to the northeast of Hill 212.9

The battalions fought valiantly, repulsing the enemy onslaught. The enemy infantry launched repeated attacks, but each time they were forced to pull back to their jumping-off position. The fighting became one of close combat; the fiery ring of tanks kept constricting [two battalions of Katiusha rocket-launchers of the 66th Guards Mortar Regiment made their own contribution to this situation of chaotic fire; upon receiving information that the enemy had reached the area of Hill 212.9 and the woods northeast of there, at 1120 and 1140 they launched a strike against this area, pouring 276 rockets on the heads of everyone located there – I.S.[4]].

The battalions were struggling bravely, refusing to take a step back, yet by the end of the day the enemy had the advantage. In the course of the fighting the battalions had suffered enormous casualties. Of the two full-strength rifle battalions, only 200 men came out of the fighting. The commanders and commissars of both battalions were killed in the battle [...].

When the enemy began to outflank the battalions, the regiment headquarters' communications with the battalions were cut and they couldn't be restored until the very end of the battle. Having lost communications and control over the fighting, the regiment commander Major Dudkin faced the matter of taking some sort of decision, but the absence of reserves and the 3rd Rifle Battalion, which continued to remain in the Kreshchenka area, didn't suggest anything sensible to the regiment commander, and the first decision he made was to withdraw the small specialized units (attached to regiment headquarters) to the rear and to send the chief of staff Senior Lieutenant Kazachenko to division headquarters with a request for help [the division headquarters by that time was located in a small patch of woods east of Kamenka, 4 kilometers to the northeast of the location of the 841st Rifle Regiment's headquarters – I.S.].

4 TsAMO, F. 66 gmp, op. 1, d. 1, l. 93.

The small, specialized units began a planned, orderly withdrawal, but were spotted by enemy aircraft and came under their attack; the moment when the column of elements began to scatter was discovered and spotted by the regiment's assistant commander of the quartermaster service Supply Officer 3rd Class V., who without reflecting on the overall situation and course of events, created a panic in his own wagon train and in all the rear elements, and the trains began a panicked flight in various directions; naturally, they were all drawn to the Don River, to the area of the recent crossing, where they gradually began to re-cross the Don River [on the morning of 24 July, it was more than 20 kilometers as the crow flies from the division headquarters to the closest bridge across the Don – I.S.]

The small, specialized elements, having received an order to retreat, had no indicated assembly area, and thus a caravan of wagons and men stretched to the rear. Having lost control over the battalions and direction over the battle once the tanks had encircled the regiment's combat formations and reached the immediate vicinity of the command post, the regiment headquarters scooted away and began a hasty retreat to the rear, leaving the remnants of its battalions to fate [...].

The contact between the division headquarters and the headquarters of the subordinate regiments was unreliable, and thus word and reports about the counterattack launched by the enemy were late in arriving; basically, the enemy counterattack was detected at the moment when enemy tanks arrived in the immediate vicinity of the command post and were located just 300-400 meters from it. [It is striking. It turns out that the division command post had no telephone or radio contact with the units and runners hadn't managed to reach it in time, so the command of the 237th Rifle Division had no clear knowledge that the enemy had gone on the offensive; had overrun the division's right flank; was encircling its reserve regiment; nor did it have any idea that dozens of German tanks were closing upon its location – I.S.]. The shift in the command post's location began directly under enemy tank fire and aerial attacks. No alternate command post had been designated [...].

At the moment that the enemy tanks moved out, the artillery had no shells and there was nothing with which to repel the enemy attack. The division headquarters had no accurate information about the situation on 23.7 or on the night of 23-24.7. Thus the division commander opted not to make any decision with the onset of the day of 24 July. The situation required analysis. [This is how the division's staff officer who wrote these lines uniquely treats the confusion and surprising passivity of the division command – I.S.]

After the enemy launched the counterattack, the commander of the 201st Tank Brigade for unknown reasons and without corresponding orders for this withdrew his tanks beyond Murav'evka and Kamenka, thereby failing to render the appropriate assistance in repelling the enemy's counterattacks. [Also striking is the matter of cooperation between different types of forces, or more accurately the question regarding how the command of the 201st Tank Brigade, having at least 23 operational tanks, "supported" and "came to the relief of" the rifle division that was left without shells and had fallen into a predicament, which by orders the tank brigade was supposed to support.][5]

5 In a combat report from the 201st Tank Brigade, the fighting on the morning of 24.7.42 was depicted quite uniquely: "... the 237th Rifle Division, having abandoned its positions, began to retreat to the north. The 201st Tank Brigade, engaged in combat against superior enemy forces, inflicting damage to them in personnel and equipment. With the approach of artillery, it pulled out of combat and by 1240 began to re-assemble in the patch of woods south of Point 204.0 and bringing itself back into order." (TsAMO) It isn't clear from the text whose artillery had approached (from documents it follows that no reinforcing artillery units approached the battlefield that morning, and the only artillery that was taking on the enemy's attack was the 237th Rifle Division's own artillery batteries, as well as some of those of the 284th Rifle Division) and why, accordingly,

Let's turn now to the testimony of one of the direct eyewitnesses to the fighting on 24 July – the former nurse of the 835th Rifle Regiment E.I. Platonova:

> Early in the morning everything began once again. Aircraft bombed incessantly, bombs and shells were exploding everywhere, and the soldiers were shaken and began to retreat. The commanders went hoarse, shouting at the soldiers and issuing orders, but no one wanted to die, so that's why they were retreating to the rear. The fear of death was stronger than orders. Catching sight of the fleeing infantry, the artillerymen were cursing them roundly.
>
> Under the onslaught of German tanks and the intense fire of artillery, mortars and machine guns, we were retreating kilometer after kilometer. Fascist aircraft were bombing our rear areas.
>
> Our ammunition stockpile had been camouflaged in a small patch of woods. Enemy aircraft dropped several bombs on it. The sound of an explosion of unbelievable power carried from the woods. Uprooted trees were tossed through the air for several meters. In the woods, everything was burning and exploding. I was running along the road, trying to catch up with a wagon that was loaded with ammunition. Another explosion rang out in the woods; the horse reared up, wild with fear, and immediately took off into the field like a bobcat.
>
> I dropped to the earth. Raising my head, I saw a motorcyclist who was driving along the road in the same direction that I'd been running. Rising from the ground, I started after him at a run. The road led into a shallow swale. The man on the motorcycle disappeared into it; suddenly, there was a powerful explosion rang near the road in the low ground up ahead, and the blast wave knocked me flat to the ground. Several seconds later, I jumped up and started running along the road down into the swale. The man riding the motorcycle was quietly coasting to a stop, but trailing some sort of rope behind him. Coming up to him, I got a better look and blanched in horror. The man's abdomen had been ripped open by a fragment of the exploding shell, and all of its contents had spilled out onto his knees, and from his knees onto the ground. His intestines were stretched along the ground, and he had been rolling forward simply from inertia. I was struck by a wave of nausea. I grabbed my stomach and took off at a run into the field as if chased by hounds. Once in the field, I fell to the ground and began sobbing. The rye was standing waist-high, but it wasn't going to bring satisfaction to anyone. Soon, very soon, soldiers' boots and German tanks would be crushing it. I was lying on the ground and crying out of helplessness and rage – how long would such go on?[6]

Despite the fact that the command of the 237th Rifle Division recognized the extent of the threat only when German tanks were nearing its command post, and knew nothing about the situation around it, the Briansk Front Commander-in-Chief Rokossovsky was aware that the enemy counteroffensive had started, and judging from his memoirs, he knew about it even before the command of Operational Group Chibisov did (it is possible that on his drive to Operational Group Chibisov's command post, he personally witnessed the retreat of disorganized groups of infantry and/or the tanks of the 201st Tank Brigade that were heading to the rear). In his memoirs he describes the meeting with Chibisov at the operational group's command post, and although he gives no date for it, from the general context of the passage and a comparison with documents it follows that this meeting may well have taken place on the morning of 24 July 1942:

this was considered a respectable reason to abandon the battlefield at a critical moment, when the German tanks were pitilessly crushing and destroying the 237th Rifle Division's infantry, and head to the rear.

6 *Voenno-istoricheskii arkhiv*, No. 9 (2008), pp. 83-84.

> General N.E. Chibisov had assumed command of the 38th Army[7] just recently; before this he had been the deputy commander of Briansk Front. According to our information, his posting was unquestionable and he was commanding the army irreproachably. His deliberate, arguably even phlegmatic nature bothered me somewhat. An army commander should react to everything more promptly. However, this was the character of the man, and it wasn't so simple to change him.
>
> I unwillingly recall an incident during the heated fighting near Voronezh. Located in the 38th Army's disposition, I found out that the enemy had shoved our units back with a surprise attack in one of the sectors. This really concerned me and I had to head to the army's command post. I found the army commander at a table, upon which a samovar was whistling merrily. Chibisov was in fine spirits. To my question about whether he knew the situation on his flank, the army commander calmly replied that he still hadn't fully ascertained the situation, but was confident that nothing in particular had happened there. So he invited me to have a cup of tea.
>
> This literally Olympic calm in such an alarming situation outraged me to the depth of my soul and compelled me to have a sharp conversation with him. It had its effect. The army commander energetically got to work.[8]

As we see, it was only after the sharp words of the Front commander that Chibisov began to take the enemy's actions completely seriously. After familiarizing himself with the situation, he decided to remove the 2nd Tank Corps from its front at Bol'shaia Vereika and to withdraw it urgently to the rear to the Murav'evka – Dolgoe – Hill +3.0 [thus was the designation given to an ancient burial mound in the area] line, behind which the operational group headquarters was located in Lukino.

This decision placed the operational group's further offensive in doubt, since it cut the strength of its shock tank grouping almost by half, but seemingly Chibisov had no other choice. His last remaining substantial reserve – the 237th Rifle Division's 841st Rifle Regiment – was itself under enemy attack and by this time had already been drawn into the fighting (in essence – it had been overrun; German tanks had furiously crushed the barely completed and even yet unfinished trenches and were mercilessly slaughtering the infantry on the barren hilltop…). Thus, other than the 2nd Tank Corps that had been hastily removed from the front, Chibisov no longer had any other major combat-ready units that he could send to counter the attacking enemy tank grouping or at least organize a new line of defense in its path.

For his part, having learned of the enemy's offensive and the retreat of the 237th Rifle Division (regarding the scale of the disaster that had come to the division, neither Chibisov nor Rokossovsky, and not even the division command was yet aware at the time), the Briansk Front Commander-in-Chief took urgent steps to reinforce the operational group.[9] For this purpose he decided to use the 7th and 11th Tank Corps, which at that moment were in Briansk Front's reserve some 35-40 kilometers from the combat area, resting and replenishing after their fighting as part of the 5th Tank Army. Rokossovsky made the decision to send the 7th Tank Corps to the front even before

7 Here Rokossovsky is mistaken, because the operational group was officially transformed into the 38th Army only after the completion of the operation.

8 K.K. Rokossovsky, *Soldatskii dolg* [*Soldier's duty*] (Moscow: Voenizdat, 1988), p. 131.

9 If you will, the first step on this path was the decision to transfer the 150th Tank Brigade to the area of the operational group's actions; on the morning of 24 July it was located several kilometers south of Izmalkovo. Already at 1000, carrying out a coded order from the Briansk Front Commander-in-Chief, the brigade's tank battalions began loading onto railroad trains. (Website www.podvignaroda.ru, 150th Tank Brigade's journal of combat operations)

0800 on 24 July.[10] (It is possible that he had been planning to strengthen the attack of the 1st and 2nd Tank Corps with it; the offensive was running out of steam after three days of fighting.[11] It also can't be excluded that having received information about the major German panzer grouping that had moved up to the front and was assembling north of Zemliansk, Rokossovsky made a timely decision to take precautions and to reinforce Operational Group Chibisov with one more tank corps right away in order to counter the threat of an enemy counterattack.)

By directing both tank corps to the front, Rokossovsky was counting upon the fact that they would arrive in the jumping-off area in the afternoon and already by early evening could launch a strong counterattack against the enemy that had broken through. True, judging from the available evidence, Rokossovsky didn't have any precise information about the number of combat-ready tanks in the 7th and 11th Tank Corps[12], but on the basis of previous summaries and reports, he could fully assume that they had approximately 200 operational tanks, including almost 100 heavy and medium tanks.[13] The commitment into combat of such a powerful grouping might not only eliminate the threat of a further German breakthrough, but also lead to the destruction of the attacking German units.

At 1110 – 1130, Briansk Front's chief of operations Colonel Sidel'nikov at Rokossovsky's behest sent an order by telegraph to the commander of the 7th Tank Corps Rotmistrov to reach the new area not by 1800, as had been indicated in a preceding order, but by no later than 1400. At the same time a written order was sent by airplane to Rotmistrov. (Obviously somewhat perplexed by such compressed periods of time, the commander of the 7th Tank Corps had noted to Sidel'nikov: "Take into consideration that it is already 1130 and I must make a 40-kilometer march.")[14]

At 1155 – 1208 a similar order went out to Lazarev, the commander of the 11th Tank Corps. A liaison officer was also to deliver a written combat order to him by staff car. Sidel'nikov briefed Lazarev and informed him that "the direction of his actions" was the village of Vislaia Poliana, and the tank corps was to reach the Vislaia Poliana, Iakovlevo area no later than 1600. Lazarev, just as Rotmistrov had done 30 minutes before him, indirectly expressed doubt in the reality of the time schedule that had been set for him, declaring that he required three hours to assemble the corps (the 7th Tank Corps had received its first order to march at 0800 and was still in the process of assembling at 1130, 3 hours later) and two hours for the march. Thus, according to Lazarev's calculations, the 11th Tank Corps could not reach its designated area until 1700 at the earliest. However, Sidel'nikov seemingly shut his ears to Lazarev's calculations (indeed, he had no power to change the designated time) and repeated the time set by Rokossovsky, demanding that the tank corps move out as soon as possible. In response Lazarev telegraphed that "we are setting about to carry out the order", but at the same time again added, regarding the time schedule, "I've reported my calculations."[15] On this vague note, the discussions regarding the time set for moving out came to an end. Meanwhile, having received a report from Rokossovsky that the 7th and 11th Tank Corps were moving up to the front and that Rotmistrov's 7th Tank Corps, already subordinate to the operational group, was to arrive first, Chibisov decided to deploy it on the Kamenka

10 TsAMO, F. 202, op. 5, d. 489, l. 266.
11 TsAMO, F. 202, op. 5, d. 489, l. 265.
12 TsAMO, F. 331, op. 5041, d. 5, l. 45.
13 This follows from the summary information according to the following documents: TsAMO, F. 11 TK, op. 1, d. 284, l. 117; d. 50, l. 14; F. 62 tbr, op. 1, d. 19, l. 99; F. 87 tbr, op. 1, d. 5, l. 152; F. 3 gv tbr, op. 1, d. 22, l. 20; d. 24, l. 24.
14 TsAMO, F. 202, op. 5, d. 489, l. 266.
15 TsAMO, F. 202, op. 5, d. 489, l. 263.

– Murav'evka line and "to attack the enemy at 1800 in the direction of Hills 217.8, 212.9 and 214.6 with the task to destroy his units that have broken through."[16]

In the 7th Tank Corps on the morning of 24 July, they were waiting for motion-picture cameramen. In particular, in the 3rd Guards Tank Brigade they'd been readying for filming since 0800[17] (chances are the men were putting into order their uniforms, which had seen better days, and cleaning their boots and "polishing" their equipment). The cameramen did actually show up, but the arriving order for a march, obviously, ruined the entire plan of work they'd intended: instead of a carefully calibrated film for the newsreels, the tankers had to prepare to move out.

The units of the 7th Tank Corps set out on the march only around noontime (the motorized rifle battalion of the 3rd Guards Tank Brigade – at 1100, the 2nd Tank Battalion – at 1300), and having stretched out in lengthy columns that extended for many kilometers, they moved along dusty village roads to the south. The main movement route ran along the road connecting Kriukovo, Ol'shanyi Kolodez' (with a bridge across the Snova River), Verkhniaia Kolybel'ka and Kamenka. The 7th Tank Corps was supposed to arrive in Kamenka no later than 1400, but already soon after moving out on the march it became clear that this wasn't possible: the columns were moving too slowly. For example, the 3rd Guards Tank Brigade's 1st Tank Battalion (the brigade's main shock force consisting of 14 KV tanks) only reached the Snova River at Ol'shanyi Kolodez' by 1430.[18]

From that point on, the time schedule set by Rokossovsky began to fall completely apart at the seams. On the path from the Snova River, the forward units of the 3rd Guards Tank Brigade received a totally new task – to assemble in Verkhniaia Kolybel'ka and take up a defense there. By 1700 the 3rd Guards Tank Brigade's 1st Tank Battalion had deployed its 14 KV tanks on the southwestern outskirts of the village, and within an hour its motorized rifle battalion was standing on the defense in a field south of there, not having reached the endpoint of the march (Kamenka) either by 1400, or by day's end.[19] Only the brigade's 2nd Tank Battalion (5-7 KV tanks) managed to reach Kamenka by evening, but it took no part in the combat actions.[20]

The 62nd Tank Brigade, which was located further from the front than the other brigades of the 7th Tank Corps (in Panikovets beyond a bend in the Don River), conducted a march from Ol'shanyi Kolodez' through Pisarevka along a shorter route, but was nevertheless assembling in Kamenka only by 2200 (eight hours later than the deadline set by Rokossovsky), when it was already dark, and also didn't enter the fighting.[21] The 87th Tank Brigade and 7th Motorized Rifle Brigade also didn't enter the fighting. In fact, not a single one of the 7th Tank Corps' units took part in the fighting on 24 July. Thus, the counterattack planned by Chibisov with the forces of the 7th Tank Corps never took place, because the tank corps had failed to reach the jumping-off area in time. (The 11th Tank Corps set out on the march even later than the 7th Tank Corps – its 160th Tank Brigade, for example, moved out only at 1430.[22] Not subordinate to the operational group, the 160th Tank Brigade was in movement toward Dubrovskoe, but also didn't arrive fully in the jumping-off area in time. Only the forward 59th Tank Brigade had assembled in a patch of woods at Malinovaia Poliana.[23])

16 TsAMO, F. 202, op. 5, d. 251, l. 10.
17 TsAMO, F. 3 gv tbr, op. 1, d. 22, l. 20.
18 TsAMO, F. 3 gv tbr, op. 1, d. 22, l. 20.
19 TsAMO, F. 3 gv tbr, op. 1, d. 22, l. 35; d. 25, l. 10.
20 TsAMO, F. 3 gv tbr, op. 1, d. 24, l. 25.
21 TsAMO, F. 62 tbr, op. 1, d. 4, l. 14.
22 TsAMO, F. 160 tbr, op. 1, d. 15, l. 55.
23 TsAMO, F. 202, op. 5, d. 238, l. 491.

Meanwhile, how were events developing in the area of the German counteroffensive that had started that morning? Alas, the situation was deteriorating for the 237th Rifle Division, which had come under the unexpected concentrated attack of enemy tanks. We read in the division's journal of combat operations:

> The 838th Rifle Regiment with the sunrise on 24 July was continuing to carry out its assigned task to attack. The battalions made slow progress. Intense enemy fire was constantly hindering the advance. Having reached the southern slopes of Hill 213.8 with its forward units, the regiment was forced to dig in.
>
> In the afternoon, after the 835th Rifle Regiment abandoned its lines and retreated, the enemy with its entire force of tanks and infantry launched a counterattack against the battalions of the 838th Rifle Regiment. Unable to withstand the onslaught of the enemy's armored avalanche, the regiment began to retreat in the direction of Lomovo and further to the north. Two battalions were retreating along a ravine, and one along the crests of the hills west of the ravine. The regiment's retreat was being covered by one machine-gun squad of the 3rd Machine-Gun Company and a group of 17 submachine gunners led by Junior Political Instructor Barabanov. The withdrawal of the covering group was exceptionally difficult. Enemy submachine gunners [sic] were on the march and in hot pursuit, while the enemy air force was ceaselessly bombing the combat formations of the retreating battalions. Enemy tanks crossed the ravine and reached the southern slopes of Hill 199.8.
>
> The two battalions that were retreating along the ravine, having reached Lomovo, pivoted to the right and began to retreat in the direction of Surikovo and the woods north of there. The other battalion continued to retreat to the north and reached the hills north of Lomovo, where it was spotted by enemy aircraft. The battalion then came under the concentrated attack of aircraft, tanks and infantry. The battalion's combat formations became scattered and the elements began to make a disorderly retreat in the direction of Murav'evka and Verkhniaia Kolybel'ka. Taking advantage of the enemy's distraction, the other two battalions conducted an orderly retirement into the woods north of Surikovo. Barabanov's covering group took up a defense on the southern slopes of a hill north of Lomovo and held it until the morning of 25.7.42.
>
> After the assembly of the two rifle battalions in the woods, the enemy conducted an airstrike on the woods and subjected it to heavy bombing; the regiment commander Major P. was wounded. The battalions scattered and in small groups began to retreat to the north, after which they began to re-assemble in the Guliaevka, Verkhniaia and Nizhniaia Kolybel'ka area.[24]

This was 18-22 kilometers from the positions they had occupied that morning. Subsequently, in the summary account produced by the 38th Army's Political Department, officers of which spent time in the 237th Rifle Division, the reasons for the 838th Rifle Regiment's retreat were given as follows:

> An irresponsible attitude toward carrying out combat tasks, especially in the 838th Rifle Regiment on the part primarily of the regiment commander Major P. and commissar Battalion Commissar D. The commander of the 4th Department of the regiment's headquarters D. displayed cowardice and panic. Having arrived in the second echelon, he said: "Run away, they'll kill everyone here!"

24 TsAMO, F. 1518 (237 sd), op. 1, d. 7, ll. 6-7.

> In the 838th Rifle Regiment there was no leadership on the part of the headquarters whatsoever; there was no command post and the elements operated independently. At a critical moment of the battle, the staff officers scattered in flight. Junior Political Instructor Shch. of the 50th Anti-tank Battalion fled from the battlefield. The political instructor of a signals company Junior Political Instructor K. fled beyond the Don River together with the company commander and chief of signals of the 838th Rifle Regiment, where they remained separate from the elements for 4 days.[25]

The 237th Rifle Division headquarters' own account continues:

> The firing positions of the 691st Artillery Regiment and the supporting group of infantry from the 835th Rifle Regiment were subjected to intensive bombing from the air and an attack by enemy tanks. The 1st Battery was completely smashed, having lost all of its materiel and a significant number of its horses. The men of the battery together with the rest of the unit retreated to the northern outskirts of Kamenka. The batteries of the artillery regiment suffered losses from enemy aircraft, retreated to the rear, and began to reassemble north of Murav'evka and Kamenka. The losses in equipment and horses in the regiment reached one-third, after which the 691st Artillery Regiment had to be reduced to two artillery battalions.
>
> The training battalion was occupying defensive positions on Hill 217.1. Affected by the general nature of the retreat and the enemy onslaught, it spontaneously began to retreat in the Dolgoe, Murav'evka direction. The battalion commander for unknown reasons left by car to search for his rear services and returned to the battalion only on the next day. The battalion's companies were left by themselves. [...].
>
> After the chief of staff of the regiment [the 841st Rifle Regiment – I.S.] arrived to seek help, the division commander issued an order for the machine-gun battalion to go to the aid of the regiment, but the distance of its separation from the division headquarters didn't permit a timely delivery of the order – the aid didn't show up in time.[26]

This is another surprising thing: at that time the headquarters of the 237th Rifle Division was just several kilometers from the combat area, and the "distance of its separation" from the machine-gun battalion, which didn't allow a timely delivery of the order, can be explained by the fact that the battalion, which was supposed to be closer to the front than the division headquarters, by that time was already somewhere far from both the front and the headquarters.

The retreat of the 237th Rifle Division from its occupied line unavoidably exposed the flanks of the neighboring 284th and 340th Rifle Divisions, which thereby came under the threat of envelopment and a German attack from the rear. Here's how the commander of the 284th Rifle Division Lieutenant Colonel Batiuk saw the course of the fighting in his sector:

> The enemy by 0650 on 24.7.42 had assembled up to 100 trucks with infantry in the woods south of Hill 218.7; up to 30 trucks with covered beds in the Il'inovka area; and an aggregation of trucks in Spasskoe and in the woods north of Vysochkino (it was impossible to establish the exact number). At 0705 the enemy launched a counterattack in the direction of Hill 214.6 with up to 70 tanks in the first echelon. At the same time, one and a half battalions of infantry went on the attack out of the eastern fringe of woods south of Hill 218.7 in the direction of Perekopovka, while up to two battalions of infantry attacked out of the woods

25 TsAMO, F. 202, op. 36, d. 162, l. 4.

26 TsAMO, F. 1518 (237 sd), op. 1, d. 7, ll. 6-7.

> south of Hill 214.6 and Spasskoe in the direction of Hill 214.6 and along the road with the support of aviation, strong artillery and mortar fire [...] and rocket launchers, which targeted the combat positions of the units, especially the artillery.
>
> The bulk of the tanks out of the area of Hill 214.6 and Hill 213.8 headed in the direction of Hill 212.9 and Lomovo in order to envelop the division's left flank (by striking the 237th Rifle Division's sector), leaving up to 50 tanks on the axis of Hill 214.6 (opposite the 1045th Rifle Regiment's sector), and reached the area of Hill 212.9 and the vicinity of Lomovo with up to 40 tanks by 0845. At 1110 up to 200 enemy tanks were attacking in three echelons out of the areas of Lomovo and Hill 212.9 in the direction of Kamenka, but upon reaching Hill 217.8 and the southern portion of Ozerki, the attack was stopped by the fire of neighboring artillery (a portion of the tanks turned back to the south and southwest, while the rest remained on Hill 212.9 and south of there, with up to 10 tanks, 6 concealed vehicles and up to a battalion of infantry in the southern portion of Ozerki).
>
> At 0800 the 237th Rifle Division, without offering any resistance [this phrase is underlined in the text – I.S.], was fleeing in the direction of Kamenka, completely exposing the left flank and rear of the 284th Rifle Division, and made no attempts to regain its lines or to render fire support.
>
> The units of the 284th Rifle Division, offering stubborn resistance, were continuing to hold their occupied line running from Hill 218.7 along the northern slopes of Hill 214.6 to Point 44.0 on the road lying east of Hill 214.6. Only by 1400 was the left flank pushed back to a line along the southwestern outskirts of Ozerki under the onslaught of a large number of tanks and enemy motorized infantry and by the impact of the wildly fleeing units of the 237th Rifle Division. [...] The 1045th Rifle Regiment ... by the end of the day fell back to the line running from the woods north of Hill 214.6, through "K" [Kolodez'] to the southwestern outskirts of Ozerki. [...] Our losses: 20 men killed, more than 150 wounded, and 16 missing in action. Three guns were knocked out, each of which is under repair (a total of 8 guns are under repair).[27]

Now let's turn to the documents of the 340th Rifle Division that was positioned on the 237th Rifle Division's left flank:

> Enemy bombers escorted by fighters on the morning of 24.7.42 were bombing and strafing the division's combat formations, hindering the units' advance. At 0415 on 24.7.42, the units of the division launched an attack toward Hill 213.8, Khrushchevo and Gremiach'e, but under the attacks of enemy aircraft suffered losses and the attack bogged down. At 1000 the enemy in strength of 50-70 tanks with motorized infantry and submachine gunners [sic] broke through the front of the 237th Rifle Division on the right, and its units, materiel and wagons fled in disorder, exposing the flank of the 340th Rifle Division. As a result, the tanks, motorized infantry and submachine gunners [sic] wound up deep on the flank and rear of the division. Having committed anti-tank means [the 1244th Destroyer Anti-tank Artillery Regiment and the artillery regiment of the 4th Destroyer Brigade[28] -- I.S.] and the engineer and training battalions, the division is stubbornly fighting with the enemy that started their attack from the front and has outflanked the division.[29]

27 TsAMO, F. 38 A, op. 9005, d. 19, l. 70.
28 TsAMO, F. 340 sd, op. 1, d. 24, l. 213.
29 TsAMO, F. 340 sd, op. 1, d. 91, ll. 437, 441.

In a combat report at 1300, the 340th Rifle Division headquarters reported:

> We have deployed blocking detachments with the task of defending and detaining everyone on the line: crossroads north of Hill 208.8 and Hill 204.0, Surikovye Vyselki. The division's command post has moved from Lomovo to its alternate location – the woods 2 kilometers south of Hill 204.0. A company of [enemy] submachine gunners [sic] and tanks has broken through to the area of the small patch of woods 2 kilometers southeast of Hill 213.8. The 1144th Rifle Regiment is stubbornly defending its occupied line and with its flanks has started a gradual withdrawal to the line of Hill 208.8.
>
> I have decided for the 1140th and 1142nd Rifle Regiments to defend stubbornly on the occupied line, while the right-flank 1144th Rifle Regiment is to protect the artillery that is occupying Hill 199.8.[30]

A later report on the same day states:

> Wire communications with the division's units and the Front's auxiliary command post have been broken; contact is being maintained by radio and runners. Until 2030 radio communications with the units functioned normally, but the regimental radios have been silent since 2030. More than 4,000 soldiers of the 237th Rifle Division and partially of the 193rd Rifle Division have been detained by our blocking detachments, but without their command staffs; many lack weapons and ammunition. [In the award list compiled by the chairman of the 340th Rifle Division's military tribunal, it is written about Military Advocate 3rd Class Chekhov: "On 24 July 1942 during the panicked flight of the 237th Rifle Division and other units, Comrade Chekhov honorably carried out the division commander's order to detain those fleeing from the battlefield." – I.S.]
>
> [...] At the end of the day, the tanks and submachine gunners [sic] broke into Lomovo, having shoved back the engineer and training battalions to the line of woods north and northeast of Surikovye Vyselki. The enemy's further advance to the east was stopped by the commitment of the division's anti-tank rifle units and the 1142nd Rifle Regiment on the line: woods west of the northern portion of the Surikovye Vyselki, Point 144.3".[31]

The 340th Rifle Division's evening report stated:

> At 1600 on 24.7.42, the enemy took the village of Lomovo. By 1700 the neighboring 193rd Rifle Division on the left initiated a retreat, and since 1800 the division has been fighting in semi-encirclement. The 1142nd and 1144th Rifle Regiments are fighting, having taken up an all-round defense along the northern slopes of Hill 213.8 and the lengthy patch of woods to the east of there. The 1140th Rifle Regiment is on the left. The 911th Artillery Regiment and 511th Separate Mortar Battalion are in firing positions among the units. The engineer battalion is engaged in combat for the northeastern portion of Lomovo and Hill 208. The training battalion has taken up a defense in the area of the division's command post.
>
> The enemy is continuing the offensive, subjecting our units to ceaseless aerial attacks. Our units are taking casualties. A preliminary check of the personnel shows that not more than 100 men are present in the 1st Rifle Battalion, around 150 men each are with the 2nd and 3rd Rifle Battalions, and 200 men are with the mortar battalion. In the other elements of this

30 TsAMO, F. 38 A, op. 9005, d. 19, l. 66.
31 TsAMO, F. 340 sd, op. 1, d. 24, l. 215.

> rifle regiment, the losses amount to 40-50%. Heavy losses also in horses. The 1144th Rifle Regiment's horse-drawn 45-mm and 76-mm batteries have lost almost all their horses. The 1142nd Rifle Regiment over 23 and 24 July has lost 45 horses.
>
> Four hundred and thirty-nine men have arrived at the medical-sanitation battalion over the course of 24.7, of which 131 are from units of our rifle division. In connection with the loss of a large number of political workers in the fighting, especially company-level political instructors, I request your assistance by sending more political workers. We are having significant difficulties in the matter of bringing up ammunition because of the lack of transport. I request your assistance by delivering ammunition to the division with the army's transport. [As in the case with the 237th Rifle Division, the lack of transport created substantial difficulties in keeping the divisions supplied, which thereby affected their combat capabilities – I.S.][32]

As can be seen in these documents, despite the difficult situation in which the 340th Rifle Division found itself, the consequences of the German panzer attacks were nevertheless not as catastrophic as they'd been in the case of the 237th Rifle Division (of course, one must consider here that it was the 237th Rifle Division, not the 284th and 340th Rifle Divisions, that received the enemy's main attack); the considerable significance in this is the fact that in distinction from its green, unseasoned neighbor, the 340th Rifle Division was already a veteran unit that had become forged in fighting, having fought since December 1941. In fact, a location for an auxiliary command post had been designated in its sector, and the command and control over the units was resilient. When wire communications were lost, the units switched to radios, and thus the division command retained control over its units almost until the end of the battle. On its front, there was no manifestation of the disorderly retreat of entire elements, and its regiments retained their combat capability. Having refused its right flank, the 340th Rifle Division with its main forces remained as before in the isthmus between the Sukhaia Vereika River and Bystrik Creek.

Even so, it was becoming increasingly obvious that the German counteroffensive was beginning to envelop not only the 340th Rifle Division, but all of the units of Operational Group Chibisov located between the Bol'shaia Vereika River and Bystrik Creek. The Germans were hovering on their flank and rear and were threatening to disrupt or even cut their flow of supplies.

However, what was the 2nd Tank Corps, which had been hastily withdrawn from the front and sent to cover the Murav'evka – Dolgoe – Hill +3.0 line, doing all this time? The corps was in position, waiting to meet the enemy tanks with fire. However, the German tanks didn't approach this line and didn't appear in the optical sights of the gunlayers. Only the 148th Tank Brigade, which was located 3-4 kilometers southwest of the other brigades, "exchanged artillery fire with the enemy."[33] The tense, nervous hours of waiting dragged on. Heavy fighting was going on out in front; the tankers of the 26th and 27th Tank Brigades could clearly hear its distant rumble (judging from the map, it was possible for some in the 148th Tank Brigade to even see it!), but the villages and hills occupied by them remained relatively quiet. The tank corps didn't budge from place. At this time, German tanks were mercilessly crushing the remnants of the 237th Rifle Division, stamping out the last pockets of organized resistance and putting to flight its dispirited soldiers, who were unable to withstand such a "combat baptism", just 5-7 kilometers to the southwest (for the 148th Tank Brigade, just 2-3 kilometers).

Seemingly, if Chibisov had decided to advance the 2nd Tank Corps to the relief of the dying 237th Rifle Division, the approximately 60 combat-ready tanks remaining in its brigades (according to the operational summary of the 2nd Tank Corps headquarters, at 0700 that morning the corps

32 TsAMO, F. 340 sd, op. 1, d. 91, l. 441.
33 TsAMO, F. 148 tbr, op. 1, d. 3, l. 39.

had 9 KV, 30 T-34 and 22 T-60 in service[34]), if unable to put a full stop to this cruel slaughter of this inexperienced, unseasoned rifle division, which had never previously seen action, might have at least eased its fate, enabled the division to make an organized withdrawal, or ultimately diverted the enemy onto itself and spared hundreds of the riflemen from death and imprisonment! By this time, so many servicemen of the 237th Rifle Division were fleeing in disorder through the positions of the 2nd Tank Corps and these very same villages of Dolgoe, Lukino, Murav'evka and the fields around them that the extent of the 237th Rifle Division's destruction was becoming increasingly clear, and urgent assistance to it was completely imperative ...

Chibisov, however, decided not to commit the 2nd Tank Corps to the 237th Rifle Division's relief. Possibly, in such a murky situation he was afraid of being left without his final reserve, preferring to keep it at hand on the defense rather than sending it to counter the German tanks that had broken through, which would have resulted in a meeting clash with an unforeseeable outcome and just as unknowable consequences. In any case, Chibisov opted to hold the 2nd Tank Corps on the line it occupied, like an armored shield for the operational group's headquarters and command post (in addition, that afternoon Chibisov ordered the 118th Tank Brigade as well to be removed from the front and re-assembled south of Murav'evka).[35] Instead of assistance ... he sent authorization for a withdrawal to the division commander Tertishnyi, which the latter received at 1400.[36] Incidentally, by that time the division's chaotic retreat was already well underway, even without his authorization.

I cannot read the further description of events from the 237th Rifle Division's journal of combat operations without a feeling of heartburn and bitterness. Ultimately the despairing commander of the 237th Rifle Division, who had lost command over his units and control over the course of events, began personally to request assistance from Chibisov. It is possible that Tertyshnhyi had learned that the tanks of the 2nd Tank Corps were standing literally just a couple of kilometers away from his new command post, and they might have been able to strike the Germans and ease the situation of his shattered division.

By that time, the 118th Tank Brigade (14 combat-ready tanks: 1 KV, 9 T-34 and 4 T-70[37]) had come up and linked up with the left flank of the 2nd Tank Corps, and the 7th Tank Corps was on the march, so therefore Chibisov apparently decided at last to commit the armored shield of the 2nd Tank Corps; however, not all of it – just a single tank brigade. The commander of the operational group finally issued an order to the commander of the 2nd Tank Corps to attack the enemy with the forces of the 26th Tank Brigade, in order thereby to give the battalions of the 841st Rifle Regiment, which were still shedding blood and fighting in isolation on Hill 212.9, an opportunity to come out of encirclement. However, it isn't clear who was supposed to carry out the order. Liziukov was missing; perhaps its chief of staff Nagaibakov? But that morning he had given command of the tank corps to Burdov ... but had Chibisov himself confirmed this decision? It wasn't clear.... Nagaibakov, as the chief of staff was supposed to do, handed Chibisov's order to Burdov. As it turned out, Burdov, the nominal commander of the 2nd Tank Corps, was now supposed to give the order to attack the enemy either to himself, because he was still in fact the commander of the 26th Tank Brigade, or to one of the commanders selected by him.

Having wound up in such a contradictory situation and plainly taking advantage of the continuing command confusion, when Liziukov was absent and Nagaibakov was now his interim subordinate chief of staff, Colonel Burdov (possibly in the presence of staff officers from the 237th Rifle

34 TsAMO, F. 202, op. 5, d. 238, l. 787.
35 TsAMO, F. 118 tbr, op. 1, d. 47, l. 21.
36 TsAMO, F. 237 sd, op. 1, d. 26, l. 26.
37 TsAMO, F. 118 tbr, op. 1, d. 47, l. 21.

Division or even the division commander himself) "categorically refused to carry out the order", pointing out that "… the time was late (past 2000) and it was getting dark.".[38]

Amazing – over an hour before sunset, the simultaneous commander of the 26th Tank Brigade and the 2nd Tank Corps, openly ignoring the order given to him by Nagaibakov (and to the latter, by Chibisov, who was playing it safe in the situation), in response to a desperate request from the 237th Rifle Division's commander, unceremoniously announces that it is getting late, and the tank brigade would not advance.

There are not any words for this … although there is a supposition. Of course, over the several preceding days of that stomach-churning operation, Burdov had more than once had the opportunity to convince himself that nighttime operations of the tank brigades wouldn't lead to anything good, and that darkness for the tankers was just as hostile as the accursed Germans. However, to speak about falling darkness at shortly after 2000 on a July evening – in that situation? It is strange. Incidentally, recalling how the commander of the 26th Tank Brigade had behaved in the preceding days with such guarded wariness, it is possible to assume that the reference to the oncoming night before the sun had even set was also a demonstration of this extreme caution, but in essence, it was a justification for not going on the attack against the German panzers.

The fact that Chibisov, judging from all available evidence, made no reaction to what it would seem would be a flat refusal to carry out his order is also surprising. The brigade never went into action under the excuse of "late evening", and no one showed any responsibility for the crisis, except for the 237th Rifle Division commander who was requesting relief. It is also possible that Chibisov, who never checked whether his order was being carried out, in fact didn't know about Burdov's refusal. Moreover, by that time neither the 7th Tank Corps, nor the 11th Tank Corps that had set out later, had arrived at the front, as Chibisov was expecting, and so the 2nd Tank Corps and the 118th Tank Brigade remained his sole shield and reserve. Nagaibakov also made no attempt to force Burdov to carry out the order. Indeed, how could he? After all, just that morning he had appointed Burdov in command of the 2nd Tank Corps – hence *it was for Burdov in fact to decide, since he now shouldered all the responsibility….*

The sun was setting, and the 389th day of the war was coming to an end. On Hill 212.9, the fighting was over. No one came to the relief of the encircled battalions of the 841st Rifle Regiment. Under the security of the German tanks now standing by the hill, the German infantry was combing over the battlefield, which was pitted with entrenchments, riddled with shell craters, and covered by blood-soaked and flattened corpses. German soldiers were prodding prisoners toward the road, gathering or finishing off the wounded, collecting the piles of rifles everywhere (or else simply breaking them on the ground with the blow of a buttstock); medics were carrying away or driving away the wounded and dead, and officers were counting up the captured loot. Those of our soldiers who were unharmed or only lightly wounded and who managed to break out from that deadly pocket were retreating alone or in small groups to the north, getting away from the place of the recent massacre …

Left without help and under the threat of a German attack upon its command post, the command of the 237th Rifle Division for the second time that day shifted its location, and conclusively losing all threads of command and control, moved to the northeast in the direction of Verkhniaia Kolybel'ka. Toward the end of the day, virtually the entire division was retreating to the north, northeast and east: the rear echelon, the supply trains, those elements that hadn't taken part in the fighting, and the remnants of its shattered and roundly-beaten units. Just the 835th Rifle Regiment alone, which had been brushed aside by the enemy at the very start of the battle, took up a line on the western slopes of Hills 207.2 and 217.8 by the end of the day with a portion

38 TsAMO, F. 1518 (237 sd), op. 1, d. 7, l. 7.

of its battalions.[39] Thus for the 237th Rifle Division, the second day of its brief combat history had come to an end.

Just the day before, a fresh, full-strength, fully-equipped reserve division was at the disposal of the commander of Briansk Front's operational group – more than 12,500 men. Just 24 hours later, this division no longer remained combat-capable, and one could only guess how many "active bayonets" still remained in the 237th Rifle Division's fragmented elements that were scattered around the area. Alas, the introduction of the reserve division into the battle, which was ultimately supposed to break the enemy's resistance and decide the outcome of the battle in the favor of Operational Group Chibisov, unexpectedly turned for Chibisov not into a decisive success, but a dispiriting failure of his operational scheme and a need now to rally its broken units that had fled to the rear.

Nevertheless, plainly expecting that the division could be reassembled over the night, brought back into order, and committed into the battle on the next day, Chibisov wrote the following in a report to the headquarters of Briansk Front at 1800 on 24 July:

> According to a report from the division commander, the 237th Rifle Division after a disorderly flight is holding the Ozerki, Hill 208.8 line. In the report at 1600, the commander didn't know the exact location of the division. The division's disposition is being ascertained. Forty [German] tanks that were operating opposite the division's front began a withdrawal to the south and southwest around 1500 according to the information from the chief of staff of the 284th Rifle Division, who was observing the action. The division is being brought back into order.[40]

From the headquarters of the 284th Rifle Division, Chibisov also received word (which he then passed on to Rokossovsky) that the enemy had been stopped in front of the woods north of Hill 214.6, and that around 14 knocked-out and burned-out German tanks remained there, while "at 1300 the enemy tanks in a total number of up to 30 began a withdrawal in small groups toward Spasskoe from Hill 214.6 [which is to say from the right flank of the attacked 237th Rifle Division – I.S.]."[41]

Regarding the position of the 340th Rifle Division Chibisov wrote that the regiment commander had decided to leave one regiment on the Hill 199.8 – Hill 213.8 line (that is to say, to pivot its front to the west because of the enemy breakthrough in the sector of the 237th Rifle Division), but was to re-occupy its former position with the other two regiments. Concerning the other divisions of the operational group, Chibisov confidently reported that "the army's units in the sector of the enemy tanks' breakthrough were continuing to carry out their assignment to liquidate the penetration, and in the remaining sectors were continuing to hold their occupied lines."[42]

How was the situation developing on the operational group's front that hadn't been hit by the enemy counteroffensive? With the withdrawal of the 2nd Tank Corps from combat, followed by the 118th Tank Brigade, the operational group's offensive on the left flank virtually ground to a stop. In addition, having witnessed their tanks withdrawing from the front, the infantry of several rifle units felt vulnerable and began to fall back. The 104th Rifle Brigade withdrew to the north

39 TsAMO, F. 1518 (237 sd), op. 1, d. 7, l. 6.
40 TsAMO, F. 202, op. 5, d. 251, l. 10.
41 Ibid.
42 TsAMO, F. 202, op. 5, d. 251, l. 10.

from the line of the Bol'shaia Vereika River, leaving behind only combat outposts on the northern bank of the river in the area of Malaia and Bols'shaia Vereika.[43]

The 167th Rifle Division, according to a report to the operational group's headquarters, "suffered significant losses from incessant enemy bombing."[44] The division command subsequently remarked, "Small groups of submachine gunners [sic], making their way into the grain fields, woodlots and ravines, were keeping the units constantly under fire. The intensity of the fire and bombing attacks grew. The units were hugging the ground and the offensive was weak [according to other documents, the 167th Rifle Division didn't make any headway at all – I.S.]."[45]

After the withdrawal of the 118th Tank Brigade and the majority of the 2nd Tank Corps, they left behind sectors of the front that were plainly unoccupied by our units. Small enemy units quickly took advantage of this and occupied them, before moving on into the Soviet rear. Two surprise encounters with them in the rear of our forces were obviously connected with this. The commander of an anti-tank battery of the 27th Tank Brigade Lieutenant Razvodovsky reported to brigade headquarters:

> On 24.7.42, at an order [the battery] was to take up a position on the fringe of a large, elongated patch of woods behind Bol'shaia Vereika. On the march, the battery ran into a meeting battle with the enemy at a distance of 50-100 meters and destroyed 2 vehicles, 2 anti-tank guns and up to 100 enemy soldiers and officers. The morale of the men is high, which was shown in the meeting engagement during the sudden enemy attack; the battery timely deployed, no one wavered, and 2 anti-tank guns and 2 vehicles were destroyed and up to 100 enemy soldiers and officers were killed at pointblank range.[46]

It seems strange here that given such a catastrophic outcome for the foe as a result of this encounter (judging from the report, the battery had no losses), Razvodovsky didn't report any captured prisoners, any documents from the German dead, or any captured loot, from which one can conclude that the place of combat wasn't scrounged, and most likely, the battery itself hastily abandoned this area. The estimate of the damage done to the enemy, at least with respect to the number of men killed, seems here to be plainly exaggerated, which German documents also confirm. How the Germans wound up at Bol'shaia Vereika with two vehicles and two anti-tank guns, considering that the bridges across the Bol'shaia Vereika River suitable for motorized transport were at that moment in the rear of the 167th Rifle Division, and what the real losses inflicted on the enemy were, one can only guess.

The second unexpected encounter also happened to an anti-tank battery, but it was not at all of a victorious nature. A 3-metric-ton ZiS-5 truck with a driver and three escorts was bringing food up to the battery's firing positions, and in the vicinity of Bol'shaia Vereika … ran into Germans. How they got there one can also only guess. The outcome of this unexpected encounter was tragic: apparently, the Germans stitched the truck with a burst of machine-gun fire and immediately brought an end to its ill-fated trip. One man was killed on the spot and a second was wounded (he, chances are, managed to escape so he could report on what happened, otherwise no one in the tank brigade would have known about it), while the other two men went missing in action and plainly became prisoners. As it happened, the battery's food went to the Germans.[47]

43 TsAMO, F. 38 A, op. 9005, d. 35, l. 78.
44 TsAMO, F. 202, op. 5, d. 251, l. 10.
45 TsAMO, F. 202, op. 5, d. 334, l. 64.
46 TsAMO, F. 27 tbr (3109), d. 9, l. 164.
47 TsAMO, F. 202, op. 1, d. 251, l. 10.

Two regiments of the 193rd Rifle Division remained on the line stretching from the overgrown ravine 1 kilometer to the east of Gremiach'e to the mid-sized patch of woods south of Lebiazh'e, while its third regiment fell back to the southwestern outskirts of this village.[48] Pinned down by aerial bombings and artillery and mortar barrages, weakened by losses, and demoralized by the entirely unsuccessful outcome of the fighting in its quite brief combat history, the units of the division suspended active operations.

Disturbed that the units of the operational group's left flank might waver because of the Germans' appearance on their flank and rear and trigger a retreat without orders, Chibisov sent them a threatening warning: "To the commanders of the 193rd and 167th Rifle Divisions and the 104th Rifle Brigade: Stubbornly hold the occupied line. Not one step back. Explain to the entire staff that an abandonment of the occupied positions without an order will be viewed as betrayal of the Motherland."[49]

Other than the 340th Rifle Division, which was still trying to attack, but had been forced to detach forces to counter the enemy breakthrough on the front of the 237th Rifle Division, the only other formation of Operational Group Chibisov that was still continuing active operations was the 1st Tank Corps. Its commander – Major General Katukov – ordered his tank corps on 24 July to launch a simultaneous attack at 0400 and to take the Gremiach'e, Ruda, and the Malaia and Bol'shaia Treshchevka area.[50]

Early on that morning, the units of the tank corps went on the attack but ran into stubborn resistance across the entire attack sector. Systematic airstrikes by the Luftwaffe were restricting the actions of the tank units and kept the infantry hugging the ground. The attacks by the brigades collapsed and the overall offensive stalled. By 1600 only a few of the T-34s of the 1st Guards Tank Brigade managed to break through to the outskirts of Somovo; the rest of the tanks remained in the area of Point 210.9. The tankers were plainly reluctant to go on the attack against unsuppressed enemy anti-tank guns. The 1st Guards Tank Brigade lost 3 men killed, 6 wounded (including its chief of staff) and 2 missing in action. Two T-34 tanks and one 76-mm gun were knocked out.[51] (According to the operational summary of the 1st Tank Corps at 2000 on 24.7.42, the brigade lost 3 T-34 destroyed and 1 blown up on a mine; 24 T-34, 9 T-70 and 12 T-60 remained operational.)[52]

The 49th Tank Brigade conducted an attack in the direction of the village of Ruda, but had no success and was unable to carry out its order. A report on the combat actions of the 49th Tank Brigade notes: "By 1800 4 tanks reached Ruda; the remaining tanks were forced to retreat and to take up their previous positions. The motorized rifle battalion, having lost over 70% of its personnel over the period of the preceding fighting, was also cut off from their advancing tanks."[53] By 2000 in the evening, 10 T-34, 6 T-70 and 8 T-60 remained serviceable in the brigade.[54]

The 89th Tank Brigade, separate from the other brigades of the 1st Tank Corps on this day, again attacked toward Bol'shaia Treshchevka. In the course of the fighting by 2000 in the evening the tanks of the brigade had approached the patches of brush north and northeast of the village, but made no further headway and by the end of the day they had fallen back to their jumping-off positions along the southeastern fringe of the woods lying 2 kilometers south of Hill 188.5.[55] In

48 TsAMO, F. 202, op. 1, d. 251, l. 10.
49 TsAMO, F. 202, op. 5, d. 334, l. 58.
50 TsAMO, F. 1 TK, op. 1, d. 2, l. 50.
51 TsAMO, F. 1 gv tbr, op. 1, d. 11, l. 10.
52 TsAMO, F. 49 tbr, op. 1, d. 5, l. 62.
53 TsAMO, F. 64 gv tbr (3163), op. 1, d. 11, l. 9.
54 TsAMO, F. 49 tbr, op. 1, d. 5, l. 62.
55 TsAMO, F. 89 tbr, op. 1, d. 3, l. 30.

the course of the day's fighting the brigade lost one 76-mm gun, 3 T-34, 4 T-60 and 1 KV, and 17 men killed and 18 wounded. The brigade had 5 KV, 7 T-34 and 19 T-60 still serviceable.[56]

The 1st Motorized Rifle Brigade was fighting for Gremiach'e together with the left-flank regiment of the 340th Rifle Division. The chief of staff of the 1st Motorized Rifle Brigade Major Solov'ev reported on the morning of 24 July:

> Units of the brigade at 2320 on 23.7.42 after a 10-minute artillery preparation conducted an attack toward Gremiach'e. They were met by strong fire from the eastern outskirts; in addition, the approaches to the eastern outskirts had been mined, as a result of which the units fell back to the jumping-off line. The brigade commander ordered a second attack to be made at 0830 on 24.7.42. Between 0530 and 0630, and from 0645 to 0815, the combat formations and brigade command post were subjected to intensive aerial bombings by enemy heavy bombers [sic – the Luftwaffe had no operational heavy bombers] and dive bombers. Officers of the command staff lost communications with the units. Telephone communications were constantly interrupted. The radio sets in the units weren't working. Our radio set isn't making contact with yours because the previously assigned frequency for contact with your radio set isn't correct. We ask that you supply us with the frequency for the work of the radio sets.[57]

A former commander of an artillery battery in the 1st Motorized Rifle Brigade wrote in his memoirs many years later about those battles (I am presenting an abridged version of the text):

> I began to deploy my battery between the villages of Lebiazh'e and Gremiach'e in order to support the attack of the 49th Tank Brigade, which had been dawdling for a long time at the village of Malaia Vereika. Katukov probably didn't anticipate that the Germans in this area would offer such tenacious resistance and that the enemy air force would be so active, or else he probably would have asked the Front headquarters to cover the troops with at least a dozen fighters. When crossing the river, our units lost a lot of men and equipment. German aircraft were continuously "hovering" in the air; in groups of three to five aircraft they dove and released bombs on our positions.
>
> My battery was in low ground between two balkas, while the observation post was on a low hill in the rear of the defending rifle battalions. The combat would die down, before flaring up again. For two days in a row our 461st Separate Artillery Battalion didn't abandon its positions, and the cannonade on the Sukhaia Vereika River never quieted. There were moments when the battery fired so intensively that the gun barrels became red hot. I was concerned: another hour or two of such firing and the barrels would begin to burst. There was not even time to grab a bite to eat. The soldiers, sticking a lump of sugar in their mouths and grabbing a swallow of water from their canteens, would again go into action.
>
> It was hot July weather, the sun was beating down mercilessly, and the crews became worn out from the heat and fatigue. In the course of the fighting, we had to switch firing positions and the location of the observation post many times. Continuing to fire, I was thinking all the time: "When would this damned 'carousel' come to a stop?"[58]

56 TsAMO, F. 49 tbr, op. 1, d. 5, l. 62.

57 TsAMO, F. 19 gv mekhbr., op. 1, d. 6, l. 462.

58 P.M. Devidov, *Na sluzhbe y boga voiny* [*In service of the 'God of War'*] (Moscow: Iauza- Eksmo, 2007), pp. 101-102.

Not a single brigade was able to fulfill Katukov's order and the 1st Tank Corps remained practically on those same lines that it had reached on 22-23 July. On the evening of 24 July, Operational Group Chibisov's chief of staff informed the tank corps of the high command's dissatisfaction: "Malinin [a general and delegate from Briansk Front's headquarters who was subordinate to Rokossovsky – I.S.] is asking why Katukov is spending the entire day spinning his wheels in place and has failed to carry out his assignment; what sort of enemy is in front of the 1st Tank Corps and in what strength?"[59] In the headquarters of the operational group, they had no detailed information on the course of the fighting in the 1st Tank Corps' offensive sector. In his report to the headquarters of Briansk Front at 1045, Chibisov wrote directly that "information isn't arriving from the 1st Tank Corps", while at 1800 he wrote nothing at all about the combat actions of the 1st and 2nd Tank Corps, nor anything about the 201st Tank Brigade, as if they weren't part of the operational group.[60]

In sum, judging from this report, nothing particularly bad had happened on the operational group's front. After the undertaken counterattack, according to arriving reports from the units the enemy had suffered heavy losses in men and equipment and had begun to withdraw the still-operational tanks, while the operational group's troops were restoring the position. In his confident and optimistic assessments, the commander of the operational group, seemingly, was departing from the fact that the enemy's counter-attack had ceased.

Somehow in his summaries and reports, however, it went unremarked by Chibisov that the village of Lomovo in the rear of his operational group had for the most part been taken by the Germans and not won back; that in addition to the 340th and 387th Infantry Divisions that had been activated against the operational group, the fresh 385th Infantry Division had suddenly been detected at the front on the basis of prisoner testimony; and that the large number of knocked-out and destroyed German tanks was based solely on the reports from the units (which was impossible to verify), because the battlefield remained in enemy hands.

* * *

On the day of 24 July one more episode was chronicled in the 2nd Tank Corps, which against the backdrop of all the dramatic events occurring in the tank corps and operational group went almost not (or totally not) noted by a command that was pre-occupied by the course of the heavy fighting. However, we can't pass it by in our study.

That evening, an unexpected visitor arrived at the headquarters of the 2nd Tank Corps: for some reason, a military feldsher of the 26th Tank Brigade with the last name of Mussorov had been persistently trying to arrange a meeting with the corps' chief of staff. Nagaibakov, exhausted by everything that had happened over the day and by the responsibilities that he was suddenly bearing, was probably at the very least perplexed or even irritated by such a strange visitor from some medical-sanitation platoon or other, who for some reason wanted to speak personally with him, a colonel, distracting him from the multitude of most pressing matters …

What sort of business could a brigade's military doctor's assistant have with Colonel Nagaibakov, who was responsible for an entire corps? Why did he come to him over the heads of all his superiors, in crude violation of all the basic procedures based on regulations?

However, once Nagaibakov heard from Mussorov the reason for his visit, it doubtlessly became clear to him why a simple military medical assistant had hurried to meet him, ignoring both the regulations and his direct command. Unexpectedly, Nagaibakov learned about that which none

59 TsAMO, F. 202, op. 5, d. 334, l. 59.
60 TsAMO, F. 202, op. 5, d. 251, l. 10.

of his subordinate brigades and staff had so far been able to ascertain, despite all the efforts and orders, and at last partially drew open the dark curtain of secrecy over the strange disappearance of the 2nd Tank Corps' commander and commissar. Mussorov informed Nagaibakov about what might have happened to Liziukov and Assorov.

The military feldsher's story had such an effect on the chief of staff of the 2nd Tank Corps that he immediately set aside all his official duties, took a seat in a car, and hurried the driver through the night for dozens of kilometers, hastening to follow the thin investigative thread that had been laid out by Mussorov for traces of the missing general …

14

25 July 1942

Among the accessible archival documents of the TsAMO, I wasn't able to find a single informative combat dispatch, report, order or operational summary from Operational Group Chibisov to the headquarters of Briansk Front for 25 July 1942. There is almost a complete break in what had been prior to this a relatively full and sequential flow of information to higher headquarters (I only managed to find one hand-written, unsigned note, the authors of which probably had some connection to the headquarters of the operational group). Thus a diligent investigation and analysis of the events on 25 July, especially with respect to the decisions and motivations of the command, are connected with definite difficulties, since the lack of necessary primary sources forces us to rely on secondary information and suppositions wherever there are no documents. Nevertheless, the general course of the fighting on 25 July is relatively clear.

Over the night of 24-25 July and on the early morning hours of 25 July, Chibisov had to make a decision about the fighting on the fifth day of the operation. The overall task of the operational group was to regain its lost positions and to resume carrying out its previously assigned orders. By the morning of 25 July, Chibisov could finally put the 7th Tank Corps into motion, which had by then fully assembled in its jumping-off area. The 2nd Tank Corps, which had adopted a defensive posture on the previous day, and the 201st Tank Brigade, which had fallen back behind Murav'evka, could also be given offensive tasks. In order to strengthen the attack of the tank units with infantry, Chibisov was counting upon using the 237th Rifle Division, the command of which was supposed to have rallied its retreating units over the nighttime hours, brought them back into order, and finally to have restored command and control over the division. The operational group also needed air support from the air force and protection from the enemy's brazen bombing attacks. In the final combat message for 24 July, clearly understanding (yet again …) how important this matter was, Chibisov (or his chief of staff) wrote: "I request the more active cooperation of the air force in the destruction of the opposing enemy (then, having given some thought to his words, he struck out this direct, demanding expression and changed it to a more circumspectful one: "I request the augmentation of the air force in order to destroy the opposing enemy.")[1] Chibisov most likely didn't know the capabilities of the air force that was supporting the operational group, but over the past several days of the operation, he had every basis to be dissatisfied with its activities.

Obviously, believing that the crisis was passing and that he now had sufficient force under his direction not only to repel the enemy offensive, but also enough to conduct a powerful counterblow, Chibisov decided to return the 118th Tank Brigade, which had been hastily pulled out of the front the day before, to its previous sector. The brigade commander received a corresponding order, and at dawn the 118th Tank Brigade moved out from Dolgoe to return to Malaia Vereika, having the assignment to attack together with the 167th Rifle Division and "to assist the division in taking Erofeevka."[2]

1 TsAMO, F. 202, op. 5, d. 251, l. 10.
2 TsAMO, F. 118 tbr, op. 5, d. 334, l. 69.

On the evening of 24 July and the night of 24-25 July, there was an entire series of orders from the command of the operational group to its subordinate units. At 0050 there followed an order to the commander of the 284th Rifle Division to go on the attack at 0500, and having taken Spasskoe, to regain its previous position, while coordinating its actions with the commander of the 7th Tank Corps.[3]

At 0100 on 25 July, the chief of staff of the operational group Colonel Pilipenko issued a separate combat order to the commander of the 237th Rifle Division: "By dawn take up a line along Hill 212.9, Hill 217.8 and the woods south of there, and at 0500 on 25 July go on the attack with the 2nd Tank Corps; having taken Vysochkino, regain the previous position. Coordinate actions with the commander of the 2nd Tank Corps."[4]

Five minutes later there followed an order to the commander of the 340th Rifle Division: "At 0500 on 25.7.42, go on the attack and take Khrushchevo and Gremiach'e, thereby regaining the previous position."[5]

The commander of the 193rd Rifle Division was ordered to go on the attack at 0500 and take Somovo and Bol'shaia Treshchevka, while the commander of the 167th Rifle Division was "to go on the offensive with the 118th Tank Brigade in the direction of Erofeevka and to take it"; the commander of the 104th Separate Rifle Brigade received the task "to go on the attack and seize Churikovo and Kaver'ia".[6] At 0130 there followed an order to Katukov, the commander of the 1st Tank Corps: "Break through in the direction of Ruda and Malaia Vereika. At 0500 on 25.7.42, attack the enemy that has broken through in the direction of Vysochkino and Spasskoe."[7]

The overall scheme of the operational group's commander was to destroy the enemy units that had broken through with the forces of the 7th Tank Corps and an attack in the direction of Hill 217.8, Hill 212.9 and Hill 214.6, while 1st Tank Corps's attack to the west and the arrival of its tanks on the banks of the Sukhaia Vereika River at Novopavlovka and Vysochkino would isolate the enemy from the bridges, sever the German supply line, and create the threat of the encirclement of the enemy's shock grouping.

From an operational point of view, the situation in the operational area by the morning of 25 July had become quite tense, and the commands of both sides were nursing the potential possibilities for launching an attack into the flank and rear of the enemy, but also facing the possibility of being subjected to just such an attack themselves. Much depended on who could more quickly turn the potential possibilities into a real success, while simultaneously parrying the enemy's possible attack. However, perhaps to an even greater degree this depended on the troops who in fact were to implement the command's plan on the battlefield.

The dawn on 25 July caught the 237th Rifle Division scattered all over the map: From Kamenka and Ozerki in the west, to Khlevnoe and Kon' Kolodez' in the east, already on the left bank of the Don River. However, the majority of its units were located in the vicinities of Murav'evka, Lukino, Dolgoe, and Verkhnaia and Nizhnaia Kolybelka.

By morning the 841st Rifle Regiment's chief of staff returned to the regiment, which had been smashed the day before, but the regiment commander and the commissar were not among the groups of soldiers. The regiment commissar showed up only in the middle of the day, while the regiment commander never appeared at all. As was subsequently determined, he "had wound up with the supply trains on the other side of the Don River in the Kon' Kolodez' area, and then

3 TsAMO, F. 202, op. 5, d. 334, l. 74.
4 TsAMO, F. 202, op. 5, d. 334, l. 69.
5 TsAMO, F. 202, op. 5, d. 334, l. 70.
6 TsAMO, F. 202, op. 5, d. 334, l. 71, 72, 73.
7 TsAMO, F. 202, op. 5, d. 334, l. 76.

crossed over to Khlevnoe" and didn't return to the regiment until 27 July.[8] The shattered groups of servicemen that had retreated from the front plainly lacked leadership, which undoubtedly told on the coming events. In the conditions such as they were, one couldn't begin to speak of an attack toward Vysochkino, as the order from the operational group's chief of staff had demanded.

A fragment of a summary report from the 38th Army's Political Department (of the recently former Operational Group Chibisov) gives a few lines to the situation in the 237th Rifle Division in those days: "During the fighting, Party-political work was weakened. Meetings on the results of the fighting were not held, political information was absent, and heroic actions were not propagandized. Certain political workers, rather than bringing about order and heightening discipline showed confusion and in isolated cases even panic."[9]

According to the 237th Rifle Division's war diary, the division commander Colonel Tertyshnyi at dawn decided to take up a defense on Hills 217.8 and 208.8 (from which follows that he had no clear picture of the situation, since both hills were already in enemy hands, and in order to take up a defense there, he was first going to have to win them back from the Germans).[10] However, it was hardly possible to do this, because according to his own account, Colonel Tertyshnyi had extremely few troops at hand.

We read in the account: "At 2000 [on 24.7.42 – I.S.], I made the decision for the 835th Rifle Regiment to occupy a defense on the southern outskirts of Kamenka and the brushy area, and for the training battalion to extend the line from the brushy area to the patch of woods southwest of Point +3.0. At 2300, according to information received about the condition of the 835th and 841st Rifle Regiments [for some reason Colonel Tertyshnyi made no mention of his division's 838th Rifle Regiment, as if it wasn't part of his division – I.S.], it was hard to escape the conclusion to withdraw them instead to the Guliaevka, Hill 202.9 area with the aim of bringing them back to order, which in fact was done."[11] That is all. With this elliptical, diplomatic statement, the participation of the 237th Rifle Division in Operational Group Chibisov's operation, according to the official account of the division's command, comes to an end.

However, what stands behind this strange expression about the conclusion to withdraw that was "hard to escape"? In order to understand this, let's turn from the command's official account to the division's journal of combat operations (which, as they say, was for internal use only), the entries in which in fact clarify what happened with the units of the 237th Rifle Division on 25 July, which the division commander didn't dare mention:

> In the course of the night, wagons and remnants of the battalions of the 838th and 841st Rifle Regiments that had come out of the battle, as well as the intact 3rd Battalion of the 841st Rifle Regiment, were accumulating in Murav'evka. [By that time the 3rd Battalion had moved to Murav'evka from the Kreshchenka area. One can only imagine what tales its men were hearing from those soldiers of other units that had survived the slaughter, and what effect these tales had on the morale on the completely unseasoned soldiers of the reserve battalion before the next battle – I.S.] In addition, several tank brigades were located there – the congestion of men and machines was extraordinary.
>
> Around 0500 approximately 15 enemy heavy bombers [sic] conducted a raid against Murav'evka and subjected the crowded troops to a bombing attack. Under no one's control and lacking a unified command, the men began to scatter alone and in small groups in every

8 TsAMO, F. 1518 (237 sd), op. 1, d. 7, ll. 6-7.
9 TsAMO, F. 202, op. 36, d. 162, l. 15.
10 TsAMO, F. 1518 (237 sd), op. 1, d. 7, l. 9
11 TsAMO, F. 1518 (237 sd), op. 1, d. 26, l. 27.

> direction, moving primarily in the direction of Verkhniaia Kolybel'ka. The bombs dropped by the aircraft landed in a concentrated pattern, but off to one side of the crowded troops, and thus the casualties were insignificant, but the panic was appalling.[12]

The panic was appalling …

When reading military documents, I often think about what the troops, commanders and political workers had to experience, about the trials and defeats through which they had to pass, in order ultimately to emerge victorious in this terrible war. How desperately difficult and bitter were those summer days of 1942! I try to imagine the scenes that are described in the reports and what was going on back then in those places: the roar of low-flying aircraft; the deafening bomb explosions; the chaos and fear of the soldiers fleeing from the village and of those frightened local residents hiding in the root cellars, who seeing what was happening, might have expected the arrival of the Germans from day to day; and the exulting, malicious joy of the enemy pilots, who watched the "Ivans" scattering down below them.

Alas, for the men of the units of the 237th Rifle Division that were remaining in Murav'evka, that diabolical morning bombing, it seems, became the last drop that overflowed the cup of trials that fell to their lot. Dispirited by what was happening, demoralized by the defeat and the shocking losses they had suffered, the hungry and exhausted men simply could not endure this latest crushing blow to their nerves – it was already beyond their inner strength. As a result, the division's battalions were disintegrating into separate, widely scattered groups of armed (or else now totally unarmed) Red Army soldiers, and ceased to be combat-capable military units. (In general, the staff officer who was keeping the journal had to have a lot of citizen courage in that turbulent time, to write about everything so openly and honestly). Thus, there was no infantry left in the 237th Rifle Division to support the attack of the 2nd and 7th Tank Corps on the morning of 25 July.

Such were the conditions in which the tank corps began their attack. Chibisov was planning to launch a simultaneous, concentric attack with the 7th and 2nd Tank Corps: the 7th Tank Corps was to attack from the northwest across Hills 217.8 and 208.8 toward Lomovo, while the 2nd Tank Corps was to attack from the northeast out of the Dolgoe area.

The brigades of the 7th Tank Corps went on the attack around 0800. Rotmistrov decided to launch the main attack toward Hill 217.8 with the heavy 3rd Guards Tank Brigade, behind which the 7th Motorized Rifle Brigade was to advance echeloned to the right. The 87th Tank Brigade received the task to screen the right flank of the corps' main forces to the west and to attack Hill 214.6. The 62nd Tank Brigade remained in the corps commander's reserve.

Moving out from the southern outskirts of Kamenka, the tanks and motorized rifle battalion of the 3rd Guards Tank Brigade began slowly climbing the low gradient toward the northeastern slopes of Hill 217.8. Out in front, 16-18 KV tanks (it is impossible to give a precise number of attacking tanks in the 3rd Guards Tank Brigade on the basis of the available documents, just as it isn't possible to say whether the light T-60 tanks took part in the attack) were advancing like a powerful armored shield. German anti-tank guns opened fire at the tanks as they approached the hill, and a stubborn battle unfolded on the expansive field.

The tall KV tanks were easy to spot among the vegetation, and the crews of the dug-in and camouflaged German anti-tank guns took advantage of this, sending shell after shell toward the approaching machines. For their part, the tankers could only search with great difficulty for the guns that were firing at them from out of the waving rye, but for the time being the thick armor of the KV tank was protecting them from nearby explosions and even direct hits by German

12 TsAMO, F. 1518 (237 sd), op. 1, d. 7, l. 9.

shells, which left impressions on the tanks' turrets and hull, but were unable to penetrate the armor. Having determined where the enemy's line of defense ran on the hill and the approximate firing positions of the anti-tank guns', both of the brigade's tank battalions and the motorized rifle battalion began increasingly to envelop the flanks of the enemy unit, which proved to be exposed. Meanwhile, German tanks seen on the adjacent hill when the KV tanks of the 3rd Guards Tank Brigade reached the southern slopes of Hill 217.8 refused battle and began to retreat to the south and southeast.[13] This was obviously interpreted by the Guardsmen as a sign of the enemy's fear to take on their menacing armored vehicles in open combat.

Acting with increasing confidence and boldness, the tankers and motorized riflemen began to overrun the enemy trenches on Hill 217.8, crushing and shooting up the anti-tank guns and "prying" the German infantry out of the trenches. Most likely, it was during this stage of the fighting that the crews of the German anti-tank guns were able to knock out several tanks, taking advantage of the fact that the KV tanks that were enveloping and attacking them were exposing their flanks to them. However, not a single one of these tanks received critical damage or burst into flames, and to one or another extent they were able to keep fighting. Meanwhile, the aggression of the tankers and motorized riflemen didn't slacken, and with tracks and fire they were wiping out any enemy soldiers and artillery crews that they came across. The German soldiers that had been resisting stubbornly up to that point wavered ….

Obviously, having seen with despair that the fire of their anti-tank guns had thus far not destroyed a single heavy Russian "monster", nor did it seem that they had inflicted any fatal damage to them; seeing that they were now fully encircled and would simply be crushed and destroyed on this ill-fated field and that no help was coming and would hardly show up in time, the German soldiers behaved in accordance with their conceptions of their duty and common sense. Believing that they had done everything possible and that further resistance in the situation would lead inevitably to their deaths, they sensibly began to raise their hands and in an organized manner ("In the same way they had been fighting before this", said one war veteran that I knew when reading this portion of the manuscript, "the vermin surrendered!")[14]

The very same thing happened later in the woods south of Hill 217.8 that the Germans were also stubbornly defending; there, too, resistance ceased and they surrendered. Here as well the orderly Germans displayed a conduct that was surprising for the Slavs, who were unaccustomed to *just such* discipline. (In similar situations the soldiers of our shattered elements were nevertheless marked by desperate "disorder". In fact, some in fear and hopelessness would raise their hands, while others, completely disdaining any wisdom, would fight to the very end even in a hopeless situation. There were also those who even having suffered a harsh thrashing and defeat would make every effort to break out of encirclement, even after they'd been unable to do this as part of shattered elements. Incidentally, the Germans also had such men, but about this later in the text. However, in the captured documents relating to these battles, I didn't come across any sort of examples of an organized surrender of Red Army troops, led by their commanders.)

On the afternoon of 25 July, the fighting for Hill 217.8 and the woods south of there ended with the total and unconditional capitulation of the enemy. This was a genuine success of the 3rd Guards Tank Brigade, and a well-deserved, glittering victory! In the battle, the cooperation of the tank crews and motorized riflemen allowed them not only to inflict a resounding defeat to the

13 TsAMO, F. 202, op. 36, d. 162, l. 1.

14 One of the German prisoners taken in this battle under interrogation explained the behavior of the German soldiers in the following fashion: "25.7.42 at dawn on the front of the division's actions, Russian tanks appeared. A platoon commander of this division *Unter-offitsier* Aurath ordered his soldiers not to retreat, but with the approach of the Russian tanks, to surrender voluntarily, which in fact was done." [TsAMO, F. 202, op.12, d. 499, l. 1079.]

enemy, but also to achieve this with very few losses. In the course of the battle the entire brigade lost 4 men killed and 8 wounded. Six KV tanks were knocked out (one of them, for example, had a damaged torsion bar and rocker; another's main gun, mantlet and armor covering the engine compartment had been damaged; a third KV, obviously in the heat of the battle for the woods had toppled upside down into a ravine).[15] All of the damaged tanks were repaired. After seizing and mopping up the hill, under their own power or by tow they began to head back to the brigade's field repair shops.

The total number of German prisoners taken in this action varies to a surprising extent in the Soviet documents. One can offer a definitive number that is closer to the truth only after gathering and comparing the available sources. In the 3rd Guards Tank Brigade's war diary, it is stated that the brigade took 122 prisoners.[16] In the evening report of the 7th Tank Corps at 1600, the number of prisoners fell to "up to 100".[17] In a political report of the operational group (named as the 38th Army in the document) for 26 July, it is indicated that more than 200 prisoners were captured on Hill 217.8[18], in addition to 60 Germans captured on the morning of 24 July.[19] (This is clearly a mistake on the part of the political workers who failed to investigate the matter, because the 7th Tank Corps didn't conduct any combat operations on the morning of 24 July, or even on the entire day of 24 July, and was located 40 kilometers from the combat area.) In a different political report for 28 July, the number of prisoners falls to 124 men.[20] Finally, in the 38th Army's journal of combat operations, it was written that "on Hills 217.8 and 208.8 [units of the 7th Tank Corps didn't actually reach the latter hill – I.S.], two battalions of the 10th Panzer Grenadier Regiment were smashed and 55 prisoners were taken", but just a little below that entry there is another that states "... over the period of combat on 25.7.42, 100 prisoners were taken by units of the 7th Tank Corps", which is plainly based on the evening report from the 7th Tank Corps at 1600 that evening.[21] In a combat report from the 7th Tank Corps at 2200 on 25 July, the number of prisoners rose to 180.[22]

Reports from the headquarters of the 7th Tank Corps served as the basis for estimates of the number of German soldiers and officers killed in that battle. The command of the 3rd Guards Tank Brigade believed that it had killed "more than 600 enemy infantry"[23] in the battle (which shows that no one bothered to conduct an accurate count of the enemy corpses, even though the battlefield remained in our hands), while the corps command went even further – already by 1600 it believed that it had destroyed two battalions in the battle.[24] In the Operations Department of the operational group's headquarters, they considered that "up to two destroyed battalions" was quite a lot, and cautiously transferred them to the "defeated" category, but the Political Department decided that two destroyed battalions wasn't enough, and wrote that an entire motorized regiment had been routed.[25]

In the 3rd Guards Tank Brigade they also believed that they had destroyed "11 enemy tanks, 45 vehicles, 5 artillery guns, 12 anti-tank guns, 8 mortars, 14 heavy and 28 light machine guns,

15 TsAMO, F. 3 gv tbr, op. 1, d. 10, l. 24; also see d.24, l. 24.
16 TsAMO, F. 3 gv tbr, op. 1, d. 10, l. 24.
17 TsAMO, F. 38 A (445), op. 9005, d. 19, l. 76.
18 TsAMO, F. 202, op. 36, d. 162, l. 1.
19 TsAMO, F. 202, op. 36, d. 162, l. 1.
20 TsAMO, F. 202, op. 36, d. 162, l. 7.
21 TsAMO, F. 38 A, op. 9005, d. 39, ll. 11-12.
22 TsAMO, F. 202, op. 5, d. 238, l. 450.
23 TsAMO, F. 3 gv tbr, op. 1, d. 10, l. 24.
24 TsAMO, F. 38 A (445), op. 9005, d. 19, l. 76.
25 TsAMO, F. 202, op. 36, d. 162, l. 7.

1 prime mover, 4 motorcycles, 3 heavy caliber machine guns, 1 anti-tank rifle, 1 bunker and 2 radio sets."[26]

If the data was quite contradictory regarding the number of killed and captured enemy soldiers, just as in the case with the destroyed enemy equipment, then the captured booty was accurately counted and mentioned in various documents with an enviable degree of agreement (in various combinations). We will present them, since against the backdrop of the heavy and unsuccessful fighting, these data demonstrably and eloquently speak to the success achieved, which encouraged both the troops and the command, and might have been taken as some sort of portent of new victories.

Thus, in the course of the fighting for Hill 217.8 and the woods south of there, the 3rd Guards Tank Brigade seized: a 105-mm howitzer, 1 anti-tank gun, up to 7,000 shells, 14 cases of ammunition, 100 hand grenades, 2 radio sets, 23 light and 10 heavy machine guns, 2 field kitchens, up to 3 metric tons of food, 3 battalion mortars (of which two were inoperable), 12 cases of 82-mm mortar rounds [obviously of the German 81.4 mm caliber – I.S.], 61 cases of 50-mm mortar rounds, 13 machine pistols, 74 rifles, a scissors telescope, 13 binoculars, 2 optical sights, and loads of infantry gear.[27] As was written in the journal of combat operations of the 3rd Guards Tank Brigade's motorized rifle battalion, "...intact scrounged weapons were immediately put to use against the enemy. The captured [German] arms were collected and turned over to the brigade's artillery supply unit. [From this it follows that at least some of the collected weapons were of Russian models which had simply been lying about abandoned on the battlefield, which isn't surprising given what had taken place here in the preceding days – I.S.].[28]

In this same document there is a description of the battalion's combat (although the time given in the war diary for the start of the attack and the capture of the hill and woods contradicts other sources):[29]

> 0800: The battalion attacked Hill 217.8 together with tanks ... and fully took it by 0845, while in the process capturing 35 soldiers and officers [there were no German officers there, according to other documents – I.S.]. At 0900 it took the eastern and northern fringes of the woods lying 1 kilometer south of the hill. When taking possession of the patch of woods, 33 soldiers and officers were taken prisoner and a food stockpile was captured. The battalion continued to fight its way forward to the southern fringe of the woods. Ten soldiers and junior officers were captured.
>
> 1200: Continuing to carry out its assignment, the battalion and tanks drove the enemy out of the woods, taking full possession of them at 1200, while taking 44 soldiers and officers prisoner [probably, summing these groups of prisoners provided the source for the 122 prisoners given by the 3rd Guards Tank Brigade's journal of combat operations – I.S.].[30]

---

26 TsAMO, F. 3 gv tbr, op. 1, d. 10, l. 24.

27 TsAMO, F. 3 gv tbr, op. 1, d. 10, ll. 22, 24, 25, and political reports of the 38th Army for 28 July 1942.

28 TsAMO, F. 3 gv tbr, op. 1, d. 25, l. 35.

29 For example, the order to attack Hill 217.8 arrived in the brigade's 1st Tank Battalion only at 0800. The hill itself, according to the brigade's journal of combat operations, was taken at 1200 (according to the 1st Tank Battalion's combat diary, at 1600) and the woods south of it at 1500. According to the combat report from the 7th Tank Corps' headquarters, Hill 217.8 was jointly taken by the 3rd Guards Tank Brigade and the 7th Motorized Rifle Brigade already by 0745. However, this is dubious, considering how both the combat diaries of the 3rd Guards Tank Brigade's units (relative to time) and the 7th Motorized Rifle Brigade's map of the action both give the brigade's positions at 1200 on 25.7.42 only on the western slopes of Hill 217.8.

30 TsAMO, F. 3 gv tbr, op. 1, d. 25, l. 35.

The 38th Army's political reports also provide details of the combat for Hill 217.8 and the woods to the south of it:

> Junior Lieutenant Astakhov's crew demonstrated valor and heroism in this battle. He destroyed up to a platoon of fascist infantry; smashed a command post in which up to 12 officers were located; destroyed a wireless station and several telephone sets; and shot up a truck carrying a field kitchen. Comrade Astakhov himself, having exited his tank, shot several resisting Germans with his Nagan and captured 7 prisoners. Battalion Commissar Tret'iakov, the military commissar of the 2nd Battalion, was operating as part of this crew. [...]
>
> Guards Senior Sergeant Vaisberg of the 1st Tank Battalion's 2nd Tank Company particularly distinguished himself. Fluent in the German language, Vaisberg through one German prisoner gave commands to the German soldiers, which they carried out and surrendered together with their weapons. The German fiends fear our menacing tanks; seeing them, they were throwing down their weapons and surrendering. On 25.7.42 the soldiers of one German platoon numbering 30 men killed their commanders [I must confess that I find this hard to believe – I.S.], raised our leaflets with offers of safe conduct through our lines on bayonets, and surrendered together with a junior officer. The captured soldiers declare that they were recently brought up to this sector from the deep rear of the Briansk direction in order to replenish the battered German units.[31]

The dozens of German prisoners taken in the fighting on 25 July gave our command a rare opportunity for those times not only to identify and learn the composition of the enemy's divisions at the front, but also to interrogate and check the statements of many servicemen of one unit simultaneously, to get an insider's look at the enemy, and to learn about the moods and morale of the German soldiers. The report continues:

> From the testimony of the prisoners it has been established that the enemy's 9th Panzer Division is operating in the breakthrough sector, consisting of the 10th and 11th Panzer Grenadier Regiments, the 59th Kradschützen [Motorcycle] Battalion, and the 33rd Panzer Regiment, which has up to 80 tanks. [...] From the 60 men captured by the 7th Tank Corps' units it has been established that all of the prisoners come from the 5th Company, II Battalion of the 9th Panzer Division's 10th Panzer Grenadier Regiment. Among the prisoners are one *Oberfeldwebel* (a platoon commander), 8 *Unteroffizier*, 4 *Obergefreitor*, 39 *Gefreiter* and 6 *Soldat*. By nationality 3 are Germans and the rest are Austrian. Their battalion was formed up in Vienna. According to age, the majority is comprised of young men of 20-24 years of age, but there is one born in 1907 [35 years old] and one born in 1923 [19 years old].
>
> According to their social category the overwhelming majority of them are small landholders, handcraftsmen, millers, carpenters, village merchants and petty venders. There are a few qualified factory workers. The majority of the prisoners have served on the Eastern Front since the start of the war [1941]; some have been wounded since the start of the war with the USSR and have been on medical discharge at various times between February and July 1942 inclusively. This group of prisoners, consisting of almost an entire company, in their words voluntarily surrendered, although they had no other choice.
>
> According to prisoner testimony, battalion commander *Major* Voss was severely wounded and has been sent to the rear; company commander *Leutnant* Schroeder was with them in the combat sector, but what happened to him at the final moment, they don't know (probably, he

31 TsAMO, F. 202, op. 36, d. 162, l. 7.

> was killed). In addition to them [the prisoners], the company had not more than another 20 men, some of whom were killed, others wounded, and some fled according to the prisoners.[32]

Prisoners from the 9th Panzer Division were also taken on that day in the sector of the 87th Tank Brigade. The brigade commissar reported:

> In the middle of the day two prisoners were taken, an *Obergefreiter* and a *Soldat*. They told us (and our intelligence information confirms it) that the enemy has up to 6 divisions in the corps' combat sector, 2 of which are panzer divisions. The prisoners were from the 11th Panzer Division [sic – actually the 9th Panzer Division's 11th Panzer Grenadier Regiment] and the 10th Panzer Grenadier Regiment. According to their statements, panzer divisions have one regiment of tanks and two regiments of motorized infantry. The infantry represents a variety of nationalities: Czechs, Romanians, Magyars and others. The prisoners declared that the divisions are battered and are fighting unwillingly, and that they themselves, these two men, surrendered without combat.[33]

The success of the 3rd Guards Tank Brigade in the combat for Hill 217.8 was total and undoubted. The tankers by right were feeling like victors, counting up the rich harvest of loot and sending prisoners to the rear. However, in this victorious euphoria, the brigade's combat task to launch an attack toward Lomovo, and not simply crush the foe on Hill 217.8, somehow faded into the background. Meanwhile, the tankers and motorized riflemen of the brigade, celebrating their well-earned victory, stopped on Hill 217.8, fortified the lines they had taken, and from fixed positions exchanged fire with the enemy that had fallen back to Hill 212.9 and hastily dug in there.

Over the approximately 3-hour battle with the German company that was ultimately crushed, the tanks expended a lot of ammunition and fuel (according to Rotmistrov's report at 1600, up to two combat loads of ammunition and one refill of fuel),[34] and it was necessary to replenish them. Rotmistrov informed the headquarters of Operational Group Chibisov that once the tanks were replenished with ammunition and fuel, the brigade would continue to carry out its assigned task after 1800. At the same time, the command of the 7th Tank Corps, believing that their corps had already done a lot to fulfill their assigned order, complained about the actions of the neighboring 2nd Tank Corps, which "weren't visible" and *asked* the commander "to force the units of the 2nd Tank Corps to move out and to destroy the enemy's Lomovo grouping in cooperation with them."[35]

Of the brigades of the 7th Tank Corps, in essence only the single 3rd Guards Tank Brigade took part in combat prior to noontime. Rotmistrov was keeping the 62nd Tank Brigade in reserve and the 7th Motorized Rifle Brigade was in the process of moving onto the western slopes of the hills south of Ozerki. After 1200, the 87th Tank Brigade went on the attack toward Hill 214.6, but ran into the organized resistance of hostile anti-tank guns and fell back to its jumping-off positions in the ravine south of Perekopovka. As was written in the brigade's political report: "The attempts to find weaknesses in the enemy's defense yielded no results"; educated by the experience of past battles, the tankers were plainly reluctant to launch a pell-mell, frontal attack into the teeth of the German guns and altogether refused to do so. In the combat action the battalions seized the

32 TsAMO, F. 202, op. 36, d. 162, l. 1.
33 TsAMO, F. 87 tbr, op. 1, d. 5, l. 156.
34 TsAMO, F. 38 A (445), op. 9005, d. 19, l. 76.
35 TsAMO, F. 38 A (445), op. 9005, d. 19, l. 74.

2 prisoners mentioned above, and lost in return 1 man killed and 5 wounded. Two tanks were knocked out, which were evacuated to the rear.[36]

According to a report from the headquarters of the 7th Tank Corps, throughout the day the Luftwaffe was bombing and strafing the 7th Tank Corps' combat formations in groups of 15-20 aircraft, but at 1545 our own air force unexpectedly struck our forward units, inflicting "damage, which is still being ascertained".[37] At 1600 Rotmistrov decided to detach one battalion from his reserve 62nd Tank Brigade and gave it the task to screen the actions of the 3rd Guards Tank Brigade and 7th Motorized Rifle Brigade from the direction of Lomovo.[38] However, for some reason instead of a battalion, only one company (6 T-34 and 3 T-60) moved out pursuant to Rotmistrov's order, which having reached the wooded area south of Hill 217.8, from fixed positions exchanged fire with "retreating enemy units". The 7th Tank Corps' offensive had sputtered to a stop; its command was plainly waiting for when the neighboring 2nd Tank Corps would reach Lomovo.

The line that the 2nd Tank Corps was occupying on the evening of 24 July was separated from the northern outskirts of Lomovo by approximately 6 kilometers. The tank corps' offensive, according to a combat report from the headquarters of the 2nd Tank Corps, began at 0730 with the forces of 4 KV, 25 T-34 and 16 T-60.[39] The 26th Tank Brigade went on the attack, bypassing to the west of a ravine that ran to the northwestern outskirts of Lomovo. The pace of the brigade's attack was stunning: the 26th Tank Brigade covered 4 kilometers … in 8 hours and by 1530 this super-cautious attack reached the eastern slopes of Hill 217.8, where it became engaged in combat with "dug-in enemy tanks and infantry" [if this report is true, then it turns out that the 26th Tank Brigade was fighting the tanks and infantry of the 3rd Guards Tank Brigade, which were already occupying the hill by this time – I.S.].[40]

The 27th Tank Brigade with the attached 4 remaining KV and 3 T-60 tanks of the 148th Tank Brigade, attacked toward Lomovo to the east of the ravine, closing on its northern outskirts across a broad field, edged by several patches of woods. The enemy was silent. The brigade's tanks were approaching the northern fringe of the woods at Hill 208.8, when suddenly it unexpectedly took fire from close range. The political report from the 27th Tank Brigade preserved the details of this sharp battle and brought the names of its heroes to us:

> On 25 July, from out of a patch of woods 4 kilometers southwest of Murav'evka, the enemy was conducting intensive mortar and artillery fire against our attacking units. Junior Political Instructor Comrade Khripkov with 3 tanks began combing through the woods with fire. When our tanks approached the woods and destroyed an enemy mortar battery [whether this battery was in fact destroyed is unknown, since our tanks never entered the patch of woods, but only fired into it – I.S.], suddenly 8 German tanks appeared from out of the woods at a range of 50 meters. Our 3 tanks joined combat. One heavy German tank was destroyed and the remaining fell back into the woods, but at this moment two of our tanks burst into flames.
>
> In the burning tanks driver-mechanics Liubanenko and Sobolev were moving in our direction in order to find cover. All of the soldiers and commanders who were watching the movement of the burning tanks were thinking that they were moving of their own accord, but our driver-mechanics were handling them. All the hair on Liubanenko's head was scorched, but

36 TsAMO, F. 87 tbr, op. 1, d. 5, l. 254.
37 TsAMO, F. 202, op. 5, d. 238, l. 450.
38 TsAMO, F. 38 A (445), op. 9005, d. 19, l. 76.
39 TsAMO, F. 202, op. 50, d. 7, l. 498.
40 TsAMO, F. 202, op 50, d. 7, l. 498.

> with this selfless act he saved the crew, because it was impossible to clamber out of the tanks – heavy fire from machine guns was coming out of the woods at a range of 50 meters.
>
> Junior Political Instructor Comrade Kuzennyi, who had previously destroyed 3 German tanks, with two of our own tanks rushed to bail out Comrade Khripkov. His tank rammed a heavy German tank, striking its flank, and thereby forced the remaining [tanks] to disappear into the woods. The companies' military commissars, Communists Kuzennyi and Khripkov displayed courage and heroism in this action. The tanks were burning, flames were towering high above the tank, and one figure could be seen through the flames climbing out of the tank a minute later with a machine gun and dispatch case. It was Junior Political Instructor Khripkov. His hair and eyebrows were scorched, but he had saved a machine gun and documents. In this unequal battle, 2 German heavy tanks, a mortar battery, and 4 trucks with their loads were destroyed, and up to 40 German infantry killed. Our losses: 5 T-34, 2 KV and 2 T-60. One T-34 was towed back to the field repair station. Ten junior command staff and Red Army soldiers were killed, and 31 wounded.
>
> The situation with respect to the German aircraft was worse [than the tank battle just mentioned in the report]. They were incessantly bombing our units. There were casualties and the loss of equipment due to the bombers. Worst of all was the fact that often it was necessary to lay prostrate in slit trenches, instead of fighting [the brigade's anti-aircraft battery had been left behind in the vicinity of Verkhniaia Kolybel'ka, 10 kilometers distant from the combat units, remaining unengaged for the third day in a row; in essence, it was covering only the brigade rear areas and itself.[41] – I.S.] One positive was the fact that in comparison with the large number of bombs being dropped, we had relatively few losses. This is developing fearlessness among the personnel toward the German bombers.[42]

The 2nd Tank Corps' sole motorized rifle unit, the 2nd Motorized Rifle Brigade, was occupying defensive positions behind the woods south of Murav'evka. We read in the brigade's political report:

> We dug standard trenches. All day long, the area of defense was subjected to enemy aerial bombings. A new batch of replenishments numbering 589 men from the 17th Cavalry Division arrived and was introduced into 448th and 450th Motorized Rifle Battalions. Political meetings were held in the units to report information from the Sovinformburo and the *Krasnaia zvezda* newspaper for 22 and 23 July.[43]

Despite the solid batch of replacements received on 24 July, the 2nd Motorized Rifle Brigade took no part in the corps' offensive on 25 July and didn't even have such an order. In connection with this it is strange to read the complaints of the 2nd Tank Corps' chief of staff that "the infantry didn't go on the attack in the wake of the tanks, didn't consolidate lines, and the tanks are operating alone out in front of the infantry and suffering losses from artillery fire and aerial attacks."[44]

The impression forms that Nagaibakov didn't consider his own 2nd Motorized Rifle Brigade as infantry and wasn't counting upon it in any way for the offensive. Who, then, was he counting upon? Further lines of his report make this obvious: the infantry that was to follow the tanks

41 TsAMO, F. 27 tbr, op. 1, d. 9, l. 161.
42 TsAMO, F. 8 gv tbr, op. 1, d. 224 (b), l. 106.
43 Ibid., l. 154.
44 TsAMO, F. 202, op. 50, d. 7, l. 498.

(which, by the way, was one of the official and primary tasks of a tank corps' motorized rifle brigade) were the men of the 237th and 340th Rifle Divisions. But what condition were they in at this moment?

We've already discussed the woeful condition of the 237th Rifle Division. During the afternoon of 25 July, through the efforts of the remaining commanders and political workers in its units, as well as the organization of blocking detachments on the roads leading to the rear[45], separate groups of men from the division's regiments were gathered and took up a defense: the 841st Rifle Regiment's 3rd Rifle Battalion (the only unit that hadn't suffered heavy losses in the preceding fighting) on the line between Hills 204.0 and 199.0; "a small group of little elements" of the 838th Rifle Regiment in the second echelon 1.5 to 2 kilometers north of Lomovo (judging from the analysis of other documents, this statement seems mistaken)[46]; and remnants of the 835th Rifle Regiment on the southeastern outskirts of Kamenka.

For the third day in a row, the personnel of the 835th Rifle Regiment was on hunger-inducing bread rations: the soldiers had received only 100 grams of bread on 23 July, nothing at all on the 24 July, the day of the heaviest fighting with German tanks, and on the afternoon of 25 July they were each given a 100-gram piece of bread.[47] During the preparation for the 25 July attack, it was discovered that the regimental battery had only 36 shells and simply couldn't provide adequate artillery support to the infantry with respect to either the intensity of the barrage or the duration.[48] The outcome of the rout that occurred on the previous day continued to tell upon the condition of the division's units on 25 July as well. As a result, neither the 835th Rifle Regiment, nor any other regiment of the 237th Rifle Division could launch the attack on 25 July that had been planned by the command of Operational Group Chibisov, neither on that morning nor at any other point that day.

The 340th Rifle Division faced a similar situation with artillery support. The chief of staff of the 2nd Tank Corps Colonel Nagaibakov asserted in a summary report: "The division's artillery provides inadequate support to the tanks' advance with fire. According to a member of the 340th Rifle Division, their shells are running out. The division's heavy artillery regiment has taken almost no part in combat operations and even hasn't been fully deployed into firing positions." In a separate combat dispatch, Nagaibakov complained:

> During the approach of the corps' units right up to the village of Lomovo with the aim of scouting the enemy, heavy fire was opened at the tanks from enemy tanks (heavy and medium) that were positioned in woods. As a result, there were losses: 4 KV, 3 T-34, and also killed and wounded men. The 340th Rifle Division didn't follow the tanks, choosing instead to hold fast in some woods. … Offensive actions by tanks alone, without infantry, will lead to a great wastage in tanks".[49]

---

45 A worker of the Briansk Front's Political Department reported: "On 24.7.42 three workers from the army's Political Department were sent to restore order and discipline in the division. In the course of 24 and 25.7 they helped the command take up a new defensive line and increased discipline and organization. They organized blocking detachments to detain fleeing groups and individuals. In the course of 24 July, up to 200 men were returned to the forward positions, and on 25 July – more than 100 men." (TsAMO, F. 202, op. 36, d. 162, l. 4.)

46 TsAMO, F. 1518 (237 sd), op. 1, d.7, l. 9.

47 TsAMO, F. 202, op. 36, d. 162, l. 4.

48 TsAMO, F. 202, op. 36, d. 162, l. 4.

49 TsAMO, F. 38 A (445), op. 9005, d. 19, l. 77.

Judging from the documents of the 2nd Tank Corps, the 201st Tank Brigade, which had fallen back to Murav'evka on 24 July, failed to join the 2nd Tank Corps' tanks in the fighting on 25 July and no traces of its combat activity on that day could be found in the documents. As a result, only the tank brigades of the 2nd Tank Corps conducted the attack toward Lomovo from the north, which had no success and weren't even able to close upon Lomovo. That afternoon, angered by the lethargic actions of the 2nd Tank Corps, Chibisov sent an impatient, prodding order to the corps' command:

> According to a message from the 193rd Rifle Division, up to 40 enemy tanks at 1500 were in movement from Lomovo and Lebiazh'e. The 2nd Tank Corps is to hasten the destruction of the enemy in the Lomovo area and with a decisive attack toward Hill 181.8, conclusively crush the enemy attacking toward Bol'shaia Vereika. Your actions are criminally slow. I demand energetic actions and the fulfillment of the task.[50]

However, no matter how much Chibisov kept demanding, the 2nd Tank Corps's actions were never energetic; moreover, the attacking enemy was neither conclusively crushed nor defeated. Even the northern outskirts of Lomovo remained inaccessible to the tank corps, so there could be no talk at all about its ability to take Hill 181.8 with a decisive attack from out of the southern outskirts of Lomovo. For the remaining corps command, this was simply an overwhelming task.

By evening on 25 July, leaving behind the cautious, temporizing Burdov in the ravine at Dolgoe, Nagaibakov withdrew the headquarters of the 2nd Tank Corps 10 kilometers to the rear and located it in the village of Sedelki, from which the offensive had started 5 days before, and thus wound up significantly further from the front than even the operational group's headquarters. In this peaceful new location for his headquarters, Nagaibakov was able by 1700 to give a detailed account of his observations and thoughts:

> According to intelligence information from the 2nd Tank Corps and 340th Rifle Division, altogether approximately 100 enemy tanks are operating in the Ozerki – Lomovo sector. Approximately 30 of these tanks are in the vicinity of Hill 217.8. There are approximately 50 tanks with motorized infantry in the village of Lomovo, and 18 tanks are striving to break through the combat formations of the 340th Rifle Division 2 kilometers south of Lomovo in the direction of Surikovo. According to information from the 340th Rifle Division, a group of enemy submachine gunners [sic] has infiltrated into Surikovo. A patrol has been sent out from the 12th Separate Reconnaissance Battalion to check the latter information.
>
> The enemy tanks are being cautious, not moving out into open terrain, obviously being preserved for counterattacks and active operations. [...] There is a request for our air force from the morning of 26.7.42 to ensure the prolonged exposure of the enemy tanks assembled in Lomovo [to attacks]; to increase the fighter activity, preventing the frequent and continuous bombings by the enemy's air force; to ascertain with aerial reconnaissance the enemy's grouping and its intentions; to order the rifle divisions to advance behind the tanks and to consolidate achieved lines; and overnight, the replenishment of the 340th Rifle Division with ammunition.[51]

Having learned that the 2nd Tank Corps' offensive was "failing to gain traction", the command of the operational group demanded that Rotmistrov, the commander of the 7th Tank Corps,

50 TsAMO, F. 202, op. 5, d. 334, l. 64.
51 TsAMO, F. 202, op. 5, d. 238, l. 452.

help his neighbor "whip the foe with an attack from the rear".[52] However, the 7th Tank Corps was literally standing frozen on the line of its initial success, proudly counting up the captured booty and enemy losses, and leisurely replenishing the brigades with fuel and ammunition, and not budging from its position. At the same time, its command was nonchalantly reporting to the operational group that "the attacks of the 2nd Tank Corps have been repulsed and enemy tanks are counterattacking"[53] and that the 2nd Tank Corps needed a prodding …

The impression forms that while the operational group's headquarters came to a decision regarding this "prodding", the command of the 7th Tank Corps, clasping its victorious laurels, was waiting jealously for when its slow and indecisive neighbor would finally carry out its share of the overall task and take Lomovo. It proved totally unable to do this, so the 7th Tank Corps remained as if ossified. The hour of 1800 came and went – the deadline by when Rotmistrov claimed the brigades would complete the process of refueling and loading ammunition and resume the offensive.[54] However, the corps made no attempt to get going, and the refueled and replenished brigades were still positioned on the lines they had seized in the day's combat. From fixed positions, they were merely trading fire with an enemy that was answering apathetically.

In the evening, of the entire 7th Tank Corps (around 110 operational tanks, of which approximately 50 were KV and T-34 tanks), only two attempts at active operations were noted. The 3rd Guards Tank Brigade's motorized rifle battalion, carrying out a verbal order from the brigade commander, joined battle for possession of Hill 212.9 at 2030, but because the tanks "lagged behind" (which should be read as "failed to support"), the battalion's attack fell apart under enemy fire. The actions of a tank battalion of the 62nd Tank Brigade could be termed a second attempt, about which the brigade commissar wrote:

> At 1800 one tank company consisting of 6 T-34 and 3 light T-60 tanks for communications set out along the route Kamenka – woods southeast of Lomovo with the task to seize the woods … and to open fire at Lomovo from there. Having reached the patch of woods and taking position to the left of it, the tank company commander Captain Sotnikov opened fire at Lomovo and sent back a message that the path to Lomovo was clear. In reality, the enemy was occupying this patch of woods with strong anti-tank defenses. The 27th Tank Battalion with the motorized rifle battalion mounted on the tanks moved out toward Lomovo. On the approach to the woods, they were greeted by intense, organized enemy anti-tank fire and were forced to fall back, losing 1 T-60 and 1 T-34 knocked out in the process; one forward [tank] had a penetrating shell hole in the turret.[55]

With this, the battalion's active operations came to an end. Having observed this sortie, the commander of the neighboring 3rd Guards Tank Brigade Colonel Vovchenko sarcastically reported to the commander of the 7th Tank Corps Major General Rotmistrov: "The 27th Tank Battalion with the motorized rifle battalion [on] the tanks made a ceremonial march along the road to Lomovo past Hill 217.8 without reconnaissance or security. At 2130 they passed the northern patch of woods and approached Lomovo. They were fired upon from the western outskirts of Lomovo and from Point 199.8."[56]

52 TsAMO, F. 38 A (445), op. 9005, d. 19, l. 75.
53 Ibid., ll. 75-76.
54 Ibid., l. 76.
55 TsAMO, F. 62 tbr, op. 1, d. 4, l. 10.
56 TsAMO, F. 3 gv tbr, op. 1, d. 14, l. 23.

Nighttime arrived. The 7th Tank Corps as before continued to stand stock still on the line it had seized, ready to intercept any attempts by the hated foe to win back even a clump of the Soviet land that had been lost by them. However, the defeated foe did not even try to make an attempt, having cowardly pulled back its tanks to some place, and was licking his wounds. This, judging from all the documents, was the leitmotif of the many discussions being led by the political instructors and agitators regarding the results of the recent fighting. With the nightfall (by 2330), the 3rd Guards Tank Brigade's units received an order "to halt and to dig in on the line that had been reached [where the tank brigade had already been standing for many hours in a row – I.S.] and to remain there until the morning of 26 July, after which it was to turn over its sector of defense to the 7th Motorized Rifle Brigade."[57] Starting at 02:30, the tank battalions successively began pulling back to the outskirts of Kamenka after turning over their sectors.

With this order, the 7th Tank Corps' offensive that had factually stopped earlier that day was officially halted. The fighting in the area to the northwest of Lomovo had completely subsided by nighttime. However, by evening, the rumble of battle was intensifying somewhere on the distant hills beyond Lomovo, toward where the pressure of the German offensive had been gradually but irresistibly shifting throughout the day.

* * *

Even on 25 July, Katukov's 1st Tank Corps showed little reaction to the enemy offensive that had begun on the front of the 237th Rifle Division back on the morning of 24 July, which by the evening had plainly revealed the intent to envelop the operational group's shock units, including the 1st Tank Corps. Fighting on the flank, and then in the rear of the 1st Tank Corps had been going on for more than a day, but the tank corps was continuing its attacks on the same axis, as if there was no enemy offensive at all.

Arguably, this can be explained by the Chibisov's lack of desire to divert the 1st Tank Corps from its current mission, much less withdraw it from the lines it had achieved with such difficulty. The removal of the 2nd Tank Corps from the front had *already* greatly weakened the penetrating power of the operational group's tank grouping, and the withdrawal of the 1st Tank Corps in these circumstances would have signified a total end to the entire offensive operation, since the infantry of the rifle divisions had already limply stopped in front of the enemy's second line of defense, and only Katukov's tankers were still trying to attack. Therefore, other units would have to deal with the enemy's breakthrough.

In addition, Chibisov decided that Katukov might contribute to this with an attack on the southern bank of the Bol'shaia Vereika River at the very base of the German panzer salient that was wolfishly extending to the north, while at the same time making no withdrawal with the 1st Tank Corps and even continuing to press the attack on its current axis of advance. According to Chibisov's scheme, the coordinated actions of the 1st, 2nd and 7th Tank Corps were to become that "chisel", which might dislodge the enemy's armored wedge that had been driven into the front of the operational group. In connection with this, the offensive axis of the 1st Tank Corps in its current area was only slightly shifted to the west, while as before the main vector of its efforts remained to the south and southwest.

This might explain why the task of the 89th Tank Brigade remained unchanged, even after the enemy had seized Lomovo and had reached the Surikovo hills in the deep rear of the 1st Tank Corps. The 89th Tank Brigade for the third day in a row had been conducting unsuccessful battles for possession of Bol'shaia Treshchevka, which were very similar to one another in their scheme

57 TsAMO, F. 3 gv tbr, op. 1, d. 22, l. 20.

and pattern: Under aerial bombings and artillery barrages, escorted (or not accompanied at all) by a small number of riflemen from the brigade's motorized rifle battalion, the tanks would close upon the outskirts of the village and stop there to exchange fire with enemy anti-tank artillery batteries, refusing to attack the enemy head-on, but also making no attempt to outflank this knot of resistance. In the evening, the tank battalions would fall back for refueling and to take aboard ammunition. With each passing day, the 89th Tank Brigade's penetrating power fell, the offensive actions became increasingly sluggish, and ultimately the 89th Tank Brigade went over to a defense on the line it occupied. By the evening of 25 July, the brigade had only 2 T-34, 11 T-60 and just one KV that were still combat-capable.[58]

Just as the 89th Tank Brigade lacked the strength to break through to the south at Bol'shaia Treshchevka, the brigades that were operating without it lacked the strength to break through at Somovo, Ruda and Gremiach'e and reach the bridges at Vysochkino. The 49th Tank Brigade, having shifted the axis of its attack from Ruda to Gremiach'e in order to cooperate with the 1st Motorized Rifle Brigade, was able by the end of the day, after bitter fighting, to enter this village, but the brigade was no longer in a condition to penetrate further to Vysochkino.[59]

The 1st Guards Tank Brigade, left without the support of the 49th Tank Brigade on its right, was also unable to break the enemy defensive line at Somovo, halted its attacks, and by 1700 fell back 5 kilometers from the combat area to the western fringe of a patch of woods with the map inscription "Mel".[60]

An hour or two later, the men in the tank brigades noticed that units of the 193rd Rifle Division were abandoning their positions and retreating to Lebiazh'e. Seeing this massed retreat, the command of the 49th Tank Brigade organized a blocking detachment out of command staff, political workers, the headquarters' platoon and Special Department officers and began to detain the fleeing infantry, putting a stop, as it was written in the brigade's report "to the panicked flight of units of the 193rd Rifle Division."[61]

It isn't possible to say exactly what happened in those hours to the 193rd Rifle Division, because there are no operational summaries or reports from the division for the days 24-28 July among the documents of Operational Group Chibisov or Briansk Front (save for one scarcely informative note at 0300 on 25 July), but considering the situation and the condition of its units at that moment, it is possible to assume that command and control over them had become disrupted or totally lost, and their uncontrolled flight began after the rumble of combat became increasingly audible in their rear and quickly spreading rumors made it clear that the Germans were outflanking (or had already outflanked?) our forces, and the division might quickly wind up encircled.

In addition, at the order of the commander of the 193rd Rifle Division Major General Smekhotvorov, the division's artillery regiment pulled out of its firing positions due to a lack of shells and began to head to the rear, which might have been taken by the soldiers and officers of the other units, who didn't know the reason for the withdrawal, as the "disorganized retreat" of a frightened neighbor.[62] The breakthrough by the enemy's tanks also forced the removal of the 396th Artillery Regiment's 152-mm howitzers that had been supporting the 193rd Rifle Division from their firing positions in the area of the Surikovo hills, which had further weakened the artillery support for the 193rd Rifle Division's units.

58 TsAMO, F. 202, op. 50, d. 14, l. 245.
59 TsAMO, F. 3163 (64 gv tbr), op. 1, d. 11, l. 9.
60 TsAMO, 1 gv tbr, op. 1, d. 11, l.17.
61 TsAMO, F. 3163 (64 gv tbr), op. 1, d. 11, l. 9.
62 TsAMO, F. 202, op. 36, d. 129, l. 460.

The unauthorized retreat of the 193rd Rifle Division unavoidably exposed the right flank of the adjacent 167th Rifle Division. Its command reported:

> At 1800 on 25 July, observers in the command post spotted the retreat of units in the sector of the 193rd Rifle Division, while simultaneously the increasing roar of battle was approaching from the direction of Lomovo toward Surikovo. The enemy brought up tanks and motorized infantry, and by the end of 25 July had reached Surikovye Vyselki. The 340th Rifle Division has retreated, and there has been no information about the 193rd Rifle Division's situation. Army headquarters has supplied no information whatsoever; the neighbor on the left – the 104th Rifle Brigade – was still holding Bol'shaia Vereika. The rear areas of the 167th Rifle Division have wound up exposed to the enemy from the right.[63]

By evening the situation in the 167th Rifle Division had become critical. One of its regiments (the 465th Rifle Regiment) was shifted to Surikovo in order to block an enemy attack to the east. Meanwhile the two other regiments still had to hold their positions in the area of Hill 188.5, Lebiazh'e, Malaia Vereika and the southwestern outskirts of Bol'shaia Vereika, because the division command had received no order to withdraw. By this time, enemy panzers and panzer grenadiers that had broken through to Lomovo and Surikovye Vyselki [the Surikovo settlements, which lay on either side of a stream that flowed south into the Bol'shaia Verieka River north of Surikovo itself] were already in the division's rear and were threatening to cut off its line of communications.

The enemy that before this had been holding solidly on the defensive also began actively to probe the positions of the division's elements that were still occupying their sectors. In the daytime, the 118th Tank Brigade was finally removed from the positions it was occupying and left the 167th Rifle Division's sector. The 177th Anti-tank Battalion was shifted to Surikovo and also parted from the rifle regiments. Elements of the 520th Rifle Regiment withdrew into the patch of woods that the tank brigades of the 2nd Tank Corps had left the day before. Finally, on the evening of 25 July, men in the units of the 167th Rifle Division witnessed the tank columns of the 1st Tank Corps retreating toward Lebiazh'e and the bridges at Malaia Vereika. Units began to pull out of the bridgehead on the southern bank of the Bol'shaia Vereika, which had been seized with such difficulty and won at such a cost in blood; arguably, this spoke much more eloquently than anything else to the soldiers about the offensive's failure ....

On the basis of the available documents, it is difficult to say who started the general retreat. The people who wrote them were inclined to blame their neighbors for failures, while emphasizing the achievements of their own units and elements. The command of the 167th Rifle Division in its own report to higher command asserted that the division's units remained on their lines until the morning of 26 July, but the command of the 1st Tank Corps saw the actions of its neighbor on the left (as well as its neighbor on the right) in a completely different light. Corps commander Major General Katukov informed the headquarters of Operational Group Chibisov: "Units of the 193rd and 167th Rifle Divisions on the afternoon of 25 July 1942, having no firm orders or leadership from the headquarters of the divisions, began a disorganized retreat to the northeast."[64]

The chief of staff of the 1st Tank Corps Major General Kravchenko, who in distinction from Katukov wrote with much less restraint, allowed himself to speak out much more disparagingly. Refusing to stand on ceremony with the reputation of the command of the neighboring rifle divisions and showing no restraint in his choice of words, he wrote in the corps' operational summary:

63 TsAMO, F. 202, op. 5, d. 334, l. 66.
64 TsAMO, F. 38 A (455), op. 9005, d. 19, l. 94.

> At 1800 on 25 July, the enemy launched an energetic attack from Point 213.8 toward Lebiazh'e; the defending units of the 340th Rifle Division scattered, and thereby exposed the right flank of a brigade [the 1st Motorized Rifle Brigade; in his operational summary, Kravchenko repeated almost word for word the statements from the operational summaries of this brigade – I.S.]. By this time, the enemy had also attacked out of Somovo toward Bol'shaia Vereika. The defending units of the 167th and 193rd Rifle Divisions scattered in flight, exposing the left flank of the brigade. At 2000 on 25 July, units of the brigade were fighting on the southern outskirts of Gremiach'e, [while] together with the 49th Tank Brigade detaining fleeing units of the indicated divisions...[65]

According to Kravchenko it turns out that all of his neighbors ran away, and only the 1st Tank Corps was in fact fighting.

Here it comes to mind how Kravchenko, plainly flaunting his significance and status as the *chief of staff of the 1st Tank Corps*, and failing to restrain himself in the presence of his subordinates and the instructor from the headquarters of Briansk Front who had just arrived at the corps, had already prior to this publicly declared that "the all the other units are worthless and everyone should be shot", including in this all-encompassing "everyone" the commander of the 340th Rifle Division Colonel Martirosian, who in his opinion "must absolutely be shot"![66] Unfortunately, it must be said that instead of a feeling of combat comradeship and mutual assistance, a certain portion of the command staff of the 1st Tank Corps had more a feeling of disdain, if not to say outright contempt with respect to the infantry that was fighting side-by-side with it. This, unfortunately, affected the mutual assistance of the tankers and infantrymen in battle, as well as the effectiveness of joint combat operations of the tank and rifle units on the whole.

Katukov reported that at 1900, the tank corps' brigades were entirely continuing to fight on the lines they occupied, but at the very least, this wasn't true for the 1st Guards Tank Brigade, since already by 1700 the brigade had abandoned the battlefield at Somovo and had retreated to the patch of woods at Lebiazh'e. By the same time, the 49th Tank Brigade and 1st Motorized Rifle Brigade had retreated from Gremiach'e, which they had occupied according to previous reports.

By 2000, assessing the situation that had developed, the commander of the 1st Tank Corps faced a difficult choice. No one had cancelled Chibisov's order for the offensive, and formally Katukov was obliged to continue to carry it out. However, in fact the offensive had already sputtered out, the offensive possibilities of the tank corps had been exhausted, and the rifle units supporting it had all begun to retreat. Moreover, from the analysis of the situation, the highly experienced commander of the 1st Tank Corps could see that the situation was becoming menacing, since the enemy's appearance on the flank and rear of the operational group was fraught with the most calamitous consequences for his tank corps.

All the while, the headquarters of Operational Group Chibisov remained silent and wasn't giving Katukov any instructions, even though it follows from his messages that he had been reporting over the radio every 3-4 hours about the situation at the front.[67] However, it isn't clear whether his radio messages were being received there. Katukov had no wire communications with Chibisov by the end of 25 July (from Chibisov's orders to the commander of the 2nd Tank Corps to appear at a meeting of the Military Council in Bol'shaia Poliana, one can assume that on 25 July the headquarters of the operational group had been shifted 13 kilometers to the west from Lukino, which had become too proximate to the front, to a point behind the line of the Kobyl'ia Snova

65 TsAMO, F. 202, op. 50, d. 15, l. 245.
66 TsAMO, F. 202, op. 5, d. 251, l. 51.
67 TsAMO, F. 38 A (445), op. 9005, d. 19, l. 92.

River, which was being screened by troops[68]). Over the extent of the entire day of 25 July, when the command post of the 1st Tank Corps relocated to Surikovo, it was subjected to aerial bombings 14 times, "as a result of which the telephone line was severed, there were losses in personnel, and only by chance did the radio remain undamaged."[69]

(As to the question of how complete and timely was the flow of information between the headquarters of Operational Group Chibisov and the command of the 1st Tank Corps, Katukov's explanations stand in contradiction to other documents. On that same day of 25 July, the operational group's chief of staff stiffly rebuked the chief of staff of the 1st Tank Corps: "For the last 48 hours you have reported nothing about the situation of the units, by which you are disrupting the work of the army headquarters and the Front headquarters. I am bringing to your attention your lack of discipline, and demand that you carry out the following: Supply information every other hour, and present a summary combat report for the day over the signature of the commander and commissar, taking into your calculations that it must arrive at army headquarters by 2100.")[70]

Considering the reports of the operational group's headquarters for 23 and 24 July, which instead of information about the actions of the 1st Tank Corps for those days contain only the dispassionate "Information didn't arrive", it is hard to escape the conclusion that either the headquarters of the 1st Tank Corps failed to keep the command of Operational Group Chibisov timely informed on 25 July as well, or the messages he sent simply failed to arrive at the operational group, although there was contact between them. According to a special report from the deputy chief of staff of the Briansk Front's Armored Forces Directorate Major Eizer, who on 25 July had been sent on special assignment to the 1st and 2nd Tank Corps with the aim of clarifying the situation with radio communications in them, "the headquarters of Operational Group Chibisov had a signals link with the headquarters of the 1st Tank Corps that was operating without interruption."[71]

Having wound up in such a double-edged situation and understanding that it was impossible to wait any longer, Katukov decided to take initiative into his own hands and at his own risk issued an order to his tank corps for a partial retreat. First the 1st Motorized Rifle Brigade (minus one battalion) and the 1st Guards Tank Brigade would withdraw from the bridgehead, and by dawn on 26 July they were to reach the area west of Posel'skoe and Kreshchenka and take up a line of defense along the hills facing to the southwest. Their withdrawal would be covered by the 89th and 49th Tank Brigades (plus the rifle battalion of the 1st Motorized Rifle Brigade).

Having issued such an order, Katukov sent another wireless telegram to Operational Group Chibisov's headquarters that went unanswered, this time with a coded message about the decision just taken, and duplicating it, sent a staff officer with the message to the operational group's headquarters just in case.

Units of the 340th Rifle Division as a result of the German breakthrough in the sector of the 237th Rifle Division, already by the evening of 24 July had wound up split into two groupings: the 1140th and 1144th Rifle Regiments still remained in the Hill 213.8, Khruschchevo area, while the 1142nd Rifle Regiment, the training and sapper battalions, as well as the division's headquarters and rear echelons had fallen back to the hills and patch of woods northeast of Lomovo. Having wound up in semi-encirclement, the 1140th and 1144th Rifle Regiments took up an all-round defense on Hills 213.8 and 181.8 and the woods between them, having deployed a portion of their battered battalions with a front facing to the north and west, now occupying the very same German trenches that they had stormed two days before. Wire communications between them

68 TsAMO, F. 202, op. 5, d. 334, l. 62.
69 TsAMO, F. 202, op. 5, d. 238, l. 524.
70 TsAMO, F. 202, op. 5, d. 334, l. 68.
71 TsAMO, F. 202, op. 5, d. 233, l. 3.

had been cut, so contact was maintained only by radio.[72] All day long on 25 July the regiments fought, gradually falling back under enemy pressure into the valley of the Bol'shaia Vereika River at Lebiazh'e.

The 1142nd Rifle Regiment and the training and engineer battalions of the 340th Rifle Division came under a German armored attack in the morning: "The 1142nd Rifle Regiment and the training battalion in the course of the night were digging in on the new line, and from the morning they traded fire with the enemy, coming under a bombing and strafing attack by enemy aircraft in groups of 12-15 every 1-2 hours for 30-40 minutes each time. The ordered attack by our tanks of the 2nd and 7th Tank Corps toward Lomovo wasn't conducted [as we see, absorbed by their own heavy combat, the commanders and men of the 340th Rifle Division didn't even notice the attack made by the 7th and 2nd Tank Corps toward Lomovo – I.S.]".[73]

Around 1500, observers from elements of the 1142nd Rifle Regiment, which was digging in on the elevated bank of a stream that flowed through Surikovye Vyselki saw German tanks and motorized infantry that were emerging in clouds of dust on the hills to the west on the opposite bank of the stream. Soon after a brief softening attack by fire, they went on the attack, and a fierce battle erupted in the valley of the stream. By this time a portion of the 118th Tank Brigade's tanks were located in the 1142nd Rifle Regiment's defensive area, which also joined battle, supporting our infantry.

This is how the battle was seen in the headquarters of the 340th Rifle Division:

> … tanks of the 118th Tank Brigade, being in the defensive area of the 1142nd Rifle Regiment, tried to attack, but having lost 3 tanks, fell back. The enemy twice went on the attack with tanks against the 1142nd Rifle Regiment, but having lost 3 tanks in the first attack and 2 in the second, withdrew; only with a third attack at 1600 did the Germans break through the left flank of the 1142nd Rifle Regiment, overrunning a battery of anti-tank guns and one piece of the regimental artillery (the regimental artillery battery had only one shell left). The 3rd Rifle Battalion was forced to retreat. Up to 40 tanks with submachine gunners [sic] broke through and continued to advance to the northeast.[74]

Nevertheless, having broken through to Hill +3.0, the enemy tanks and infantry were soon compelled to fall back again. This happened, most likely, because the remaining tanks of the 118th Tank Brigade and the 167th Rifle Division's 465th Rifle Regiment had hurried to the point of combat. Having heard (or hearing about) the enemy breakthrough into the rear of their units, their commanders made a joint decision to move out a rifle regiment that was reinforced with tanks to the threatened axis. As a result of the ensuing counterattack, the forward German units that had advanced 3 kilometers beyond the stream abandoned the bridgehead they had taken under the fire of the approaching 465th Rifle Regiment and 118th Tank Brigade and fell back again to the hills to the west of the stream, where according to observers, they began to regroup to make another attack. Here's how the subsequent events were chronicled by the 167th Rifle Division:

> The division command decided: The 465th Rifle Regiment, which was located in the second echelon, was moved out toward Surikovo and was to arrive north of Surikovo in order to screen the right flank. At 2000 on 25 July, the enemy assembled up to a regiment of infantry and 30 tanks in the area of Point 144.3 in readiness to counterattack the 465th Rifle

72 TsAMO, F. 340 sd, op. 1, d. 24, l. 215.
73 TsAMO, F. 340 sd, op. 1, d. 24, l. 215.
74 TsAMO, F. 340 sd, op. 1, d. 24, l. 215.

> Regiment, which was occupying a defense. The division command decided: With an attack by the 465th Regiment's 3rd Rifle Battalion from the hills south of Surikovo and by the 118th Tank Brigade's motorized rifle battalion from the hills north of Surikovo to strike the enemy, preventing him from deploying for a counterattack.[75]

There are no details of the ensuing clash in the documents of the 167th Rifle Division. In the account it is only stated that the regiment destroyed 11 hostile tanks, after which "the remaining tanks fell back with the infantry to Surikovye Vyselki."[76]

A political report from the 118th Tank Brigade discusses a tragic episode of that battle:

> On 25 July when issuing orders to repel the attack from the direction of Surikovo, discussions were held with the soldiers and crews by the company and battalion military commissars about the tasks in the upcoming battle. In this battle on 25 July, the commander of the 2nd Tank Battalion Hero of the Soviet Union Captain Plotnikov was killed in action. Here are the circumstances of Captain Plotnikov's death:
>
> Comrade Plotnikov was given an order by the brigade command in the observation post of the 167th Rifle Division to guide the tanks headed by chief of staff Senior Lieutenant Sergeev into battle and to return to the observation post. Comrade Plotnikov didn't follow the order and took a seat in a tank himself. Moreover, instead of following the order, which was to repulse the enemy attack with fire from place and maneuver, Captain Plotnikov's tank surged forward by itself and crossed the bridge into Surikovo, where his tank was hit and set ablaze. Plotnikov was severely wounded.
>
> The crew exited the burning tank and began to retreat. Plotnikov was dragged out of the tank by driver-mechanic Petrovsky, but Petrovsky was wounded in both legs. The remaining crew members – turret gunner B. and radio-operator gunner B. abandoned their badly wounded commander and got away. Despite his leg wounds, driver-mechanic Petrovsky attempted to carry Plotnikov from the battlefield. Immediately, as soon as this became known, an armored transport was sent out with the commander of the reconnaissance platoon and submachine gunners, but they were unable to break through to them. The body of Comrade Plotnikov remained behind enemy lines. The crew members were arrested and turned over for trial. Work was conducted around this episode on the question of protecting a commander in battle. The entire personnel expresses contempt for the cowardice displayed by the crew and is demanding their harsh punishment.[77]

Unsurprisingly, in this tense and murky situation, the regrouping of the 167th Rifle Division's 465th Rifle Regiment to the north to counter the German attack was taken by the neighboring 104th Rifle Brigade as the start of a retreat by the entire division. Having received a corresponding message about this, Chibisov wrote the headquarters and commander of the 167th Rifle Division, "According to a message from the 104th Rifle Brigade, the 167th Rifle Division is seemingly retreating to the hills north of Malaia Vereika. I demand that you stubbornly hold Hill 188.5 and maintain tight contact with the right flank of the 104th Rifle Brigade on the northern outskirts of Churikovo and with the 193rd Rifle Division. At the command post of the 193rd Rifle Division, help defeat the enemy's army."[78]

75 TsAMO, F. 202, op. 5, d. 334, l. 66.
76 TsAMO, F. 202, op. 5, d. 334, l. 66.
77 TsAMO, F. 118 tbr, op. 1, d. 47, l. 21.
78 TsAMO, F. 202, op. 5, d. 258, l. 63.

By the end of the day, the combat on the line of the stream flowing through Surikovye Vyselki had subsided. Our troops were occupying positions on the eastern slope of the valley, the Germans – on the western slope. It was dusk and night was approaching. With the arrival of darkness, "enemy submachine gunners" – as was written in the report from the command of the 167th Rifle Division – "began to signal from Surikovye Vyselki."[79] Colored flares soared into the night sky from a village that had been seized by the enemy, concealing within them an evil, ominous meaning for many of our soldiers, who were observing them from the quiet, dark hills and fields. To whom and why were the Germans signaling? No one knew exactly. However, one glance at a map in the headquarters of the units that were huddled together in Lebiazh'e and Malaia Vereika was sufficient to understand: the spearhead of the German armored wedge, which for the second day in a row had torn apart Operational Group Chibisov, only had to advance another 10-12 kilometers in order to link up with its infantry in Bol'shaia Vereika. The flares soaring into the July nighttime sky were already visible from that village.

By the end of 25 July, the encirclement of units of Operational Group Chibisov in the Lebiazh'e area had become a genuine threat …

79 TsAMO, F. 202, op. 5, d. 334, l. 66.

15

A review of the enemy's actions, 24-25 July 1942

The VII Army Corps' counteroffensive envisioned an attack by the 9th Panzer Division out of the Novopavlovka, Spasskoe area in the direction of Hills 219.9 and 217.8 with a subsequent swing to the east and an advance along a lengthy arc to the north around Lomovo toward Hills 187.4 and 191.3 east of Bol'shaia Vereika, where the panzer division would link up with the 387th Infantry Division that was attacking from the south. The 385th Infantry Division in cooperation with the 9th Panzer Division was to attack on its right flank in the direction of Hill 213.8, advancing along a shorter arc to the south of Lomovo in order to seize the crest of the hills west of Bol'shaia Vereika, thereby sealing the inner ring of encirclement. The 340th Infantry Division detached two reinforced battalions, which became subordinate to the 9th Panzer Grenadier Brigade [consisting of the 10th and 11th Panzer Grenadier regiments of the 9th Panzer Division] and were to attack in the direction of the woods north of Hill 214.6 and subsequently toward Hill 212.9 in order to cover the left flank of the attacking 9th Panzer Division. Unquestionably, the 9th Panzer Division played the main role in the conceived operation.

On 24 July, after 8 days of rest and the repair of equipment that had been knocked out of action in the battles with the 5th Tank Army, the 9th Panzer Division was again ready to carry out offensive assignments. True, thus far during the German summer campaign the division hadn't received a single new tank, and despite the well-functioning and effective work of the repair services, the numerical strength of its tank park was falling steadily due to irrecoverable losses. Having started Case Blau on 28 June with approximately 150 panzers, the division over 12 days of active combat operations had lost 39 tanks irrecoverably, and by 14 July, taking into account that in the course of the fighting a lot of machines were knocked out and/or temporarily out of service due to mechanical problems, the panzer division had reached its lowest number of operational tanks – 55.[1]

During the period of rest in the rear, the repair elements were able to return a significant number of disabled machines to service, and by the end of 22 July the 9th Panzer Division had 96 operational tanks (5 Pz-I[2], 22 Pz-II, 64 Pz-III, 8 Pz-IV and 2 command tanks without guns).[3] Of these 96 combat machines (in reality – the 94 that had guns), only the Pz-III and Pz-IV had any chance to oppose the Soviet anti-tank artillery and tanks, but only 8 of them had the long-barreled 75-mm gun, which was comparable to the combat effectiveness of the 76.2-mm gun that equipped the T-34 and KV tanks, as well as a lot of the anti-tank batteries.

Understanding well the limited capabilities of their tanks in combat with Soviet tanks and anti-tank guns, the German command was compelled to plan the tactical use of their panzer elements

1 NARA, T-314, roll 353, fr. 000983.
2 The number of Pz-I tanks is often not even mentioned in the reports, because by this time as a rule they did not take part in combat operations as part of the panzer regiment, but were used as tow vehicles or for carrying out other auxiliary tasks.
3 NARA, T-315, roll 541, fr. 000710.

carefully and meticulously, and couldn't allow itself to do what the Soviet tank commanders did all too frequently. Frontal attacks by the panzers against unsuppressed anti-tank guns and tanks had to be avoided by all possible means, since such use might lead only to significant losses without yielding the desired tactical effect, not to mention the inflicting of commensurate damage to the enemy.

Inherently inferior in both a qualitative and quantitative respect to the tank units of Operational Group Chibisov, the command of the 9th Panzer Division on the one hand had to conserve their tanks in order to preserve its main attacking force, and on the other, it had to hurl them into battle in order to fulfill the orders given to the division. These strict demands and severe limitations dictated the need to use the tanks en mass and in close cooperation with other types of troops, the main task of which was to suppress the enemy's anti-tank means and to secure for their tanks the freedom of maneuver on the decisive axis. With such tactical considerations, which flowed from the realities of the given situation, the 9th Panzer Division entered the battle.

Early on the morning of 24 July, the division's panzer regiment crossed the Sukhaia Vereika River over scouted fords and bridges that had been laid down the day before, and in view of the elements of the 237th Rifle Division that had arrived there on the evening of 23 July, began to assemble on the hills opposite their front line. The 10th Panzer Grenadier Regiment, the anti-tank battalion and the motorcycle battalion were following behind the 33rd Panzer Regiment (the 11th Panzer Grenadier Regiment remained on the southern bank of the river, in order not to clog the roads for the forward units). Then, after airstrikes and a barrage by artillery and mortars, the 33rd Panzer Regiment went on the offensive in the direction of Hill 212.9.

No matter how powerful the attack by the 80-90 tanks of the 9th Panzer Division and no matter how catastrophic were its consequences for the regiments of the 237th Rifle Division, the Germans' attack still didn't go easily and quickly. The 9th Panzer Division's journal of combat operations unambiguously speaks about the bitter resistance given to the panzer regiment: "A large quantity of anti-tank guns initially hampered the advance, and now and then numerous enemy tanks, launching flank attacks, attempted to check the offensive."[4]

Such assessments by the headquarters of the 9th Panzer Division, judging from everything, weren't totally accurate or entirely reliable. The anti-tank guns of the 237th Rifle Division that were hindering the advance of the hostile tanks were in the area of Hill 212.9, not at all in large numbers. In addition, as we recall, the artillerymen lacked shells. The anti-tank battalion of the 237th Rifle Division, according to the testimony of prisoners captured by the 9th Panzer Division, had 3 batteries of four 45-mm anti-tank guns and one anti-tank rifle company with 36 anti-tank rifles.[5] To be sure, there was also the regimental artillery, but the number of guns in it, judging from everything, wasn't large.

The mention of the numerous Russian tanks, which supposedly now and then launched flank attacks, and thereby hindered the offensive, is completely doubtful. On the morning of 24 July the only tanks, which might have made such attacks, were the totally few tanks of the 201st Tank Brigade, which quickly retreated toward Murav'evka (according to the report by the command of the 237th Rifle Division, they took no part at all in the battle). It is difficult to say whether the overly cautious German tankers were being too wary, pricking their ears at each gun report and taking the knocked-out tanks from past battles that were standing on the fields as operational ones. However, it is obvious that they advanced on high alert, only in the wake of strikes by the Luftwaffe and artillery, probing the positions of the anti-tank guns, suppressing them with concentrated fire, and only then resuming the advance.

4 NARA, T-315, roll 541, fr. 001111.
5 NARA, T-315, roll 541, fr. 0012228.

Having received a report of stubborn resistance, the division commander added another artillery battalion to the fire support for the 33rd Panzer Regiment and issued an order to the 11th Panzer Grenadier Regiment to join the battle quickly and reinforce the division's shock grouping.[6] Arguably, this was the decisive moment: the 237th Rifle Division could no longer withstand such pressure; as a consequence its front was breached, the command post came under threat, and the units began a poorly organized (or totally disorganized) retreat from their positions.

In the wake of the tanks, the accompanying panzer grenadiers surged up the hill, followed by infantry of the 340th Infantry Division's reinforced battalion, while a second battalion prior to this had driven the weak elements of the 284th Rifle Division out of the woods north of Hill 214.6. The 9th Panzer Division's left flank was thereby covered for the subsequent attack toward Hill 217.8. Nevertheless, the resistance put up by the 284th and 237th Rifle Divisions and the bitter fighting compelled the command of the 9th Panzer Division to acknowledge that the counteroffensive was developing with difficulty and that the division's strength was insufficient to count upon the achievement of a quick success. In the analyses of the reasons for such a state of affairs that were written in the journal of combat operations, there is a certain degree of nostalgia over past successes and recognition of the fact that the achievement of new victories over the stubborn and increasingly stronger Red Army was becoming increasingly more difficult:

> One detail of the situation consisted in the fact that [on this occasion] not only were superior enemy forces opposing us, which were arrayed in a deeply-echeloned defense [It is impossible to call the defense of the 237th Rifle Division such, and indeed, the 237th Rifle Division had no superior force opposite the 9th Panzer Division – I.S.], but also in the fact that our own combat power in comparison with that which we had possessed during the 13 July 1942 offensive was significantly lower (minus two artillery and three mortar battalions). Thus, the initial conditions for a greater success than before had shifted in an unfavorable direction.[7]

To this it is worth adding that the 13 July counterattack by the VII Army Corps had been launched by two panzer divisions – the 9th and 11th – whereas now the 11th Panzer Division was no longer subordinate to the corps or the army. The 11th Panzer Division had been called back to Army Group Center, the command of which was showing concern for its front and was persistently demanding mobile reserves.

Having taken Hill 212.9 and brought up the infantry of the 10th Panzer Grenadier Regiment, which by this time had joined with the 11th Panzer Grenadier Regiment, the 33rd Panzer Regiment launched the second stage of the offensive and attacked Hill 217.8. The division's war diary notes:

> The enemy's defensive line ran along the line: Hill 208.8 – 217.8 – southern outskirts of Ozerki. The enemy now and again launched counterattacks with the participation of tanks and infantry, so our attack made slow progress. Here it is necessary to note as in the preceding battles that the situation of our tanks, which are clearly inferior to Russian tanks in their rate of fire and armor penetrating capabilities, was not in our favor. Only owing to particularly skillful command and control and the superb use of forces and means were we able to achieve a certain balance of success [the panzer division's staff officers who produced these *particularly skillful* praises to the command plainly didn't suffer from modesty – I.S.].[8]

6 NARA, T-315, roll 541, fr. 001111.
7 NARA, T-315, roll 541, fr. 001113.
8 NARA, T-315, roll 541, fr. 001112.

This entry on one hand confirms the fact of the stubborn resistance of the 237th Rifle Division's 841st Rifle Regiment on the hill, but on the other hand prompts the usual doubt in the numerous counterattacks with tanks as seen by the headquarters of the 9th Panzer Division. Judging from the Soviet records, the defending side hardly had any tanks at all. Around 1100 the tanks of the 33rd Panzer Regiment reached the ravine south of Hill 217.8 and approximately 30 minutes later broke through to the hill, where savage fighting with dug-in Russian infantry erupted. The German staff officer gave the resistance its due: "The fighting went on with great difficulty in the tall grain and sunflower fields, in which the enemy was defending with great skill."[9]

The "mopping up" of the seized area, which the infantry of the 10th and possibly the 11th Panzer Grenadier Regiments conducted under the cover of tanks, required several hours. The slowing of the pace of the offensive and the stubborn resistance, which the 9th Panzer Division broke with difficulty, prompted a reaction similar to that of the Soviet commanders on the part of the panzer division's command – complaints about a neighbor: "The division had the task to advance stubbornly, while receiving no support from the 385th Infantry Division, the attack of which quickly stopped only after making little progress."[10]

After seizing the high ground, the units of the 9th Panzer Division began to conduct a regrouping. Having turned over responsibility for defending the sector extending from the woods north of Hill 214.6 to Hill 212.9 to the 340th Infantry Division, the commander of the 9th Panzer Grenadier Brigade, under whose command the two attached reinforced battalions of the 340th Infantry Division were operating, assumed control of the 33rd Panzer Regiment and gave an order to the commander of the 10th Panzer Grenadier Regiment *Oberst* Borawicz to head the assault group in an attack to outflank Lomovo. The assault group included two panzer battalions of the 33rd Panzer Regiment (one panzer battalion was left together with a battalion of the 10th Panzer Grenadier Regiment at Hill 217.8 in order to cover the flank and rear of the assault group) the 10th Panzer Grenadier Regiment (minus its I Battalion) and the 59th Kradschützen Battalion. Having carried out the first stage of the offensive plan, the 9th Panzer Division command was expecting that the units of the 385th Infantry Division would finally support it once the division's assault group had pivoted to the east; by plan, the infantry division was supposed to form the inner ring of encirclement on the 9th Panzer Division's right flank. However, the infantry was still nowhere in sight ...

At this time, the 385th Infantry Division's attack was experiencing a genuine crisis, if not to say a total collapse. Problems and difficulties began in the division even before launching the attack. Of its two regiments, only one had been able to assemble in the jumping-off area by the designated time; the other regiment was late and on the morning of 24 July it was still 10-12 kilometers from the designated line. The artillery units were also lagging behind. A battery of assault guns (numbering 7 StuGs) attached from the 201st Sturmgeschütz Battalion had also not arrived in time.[11] Thus, the 385th Infantry Division's attack began with only its 539th Infantry Regiment. Offering justifications, cautiously complaining at the higher command, and grumbling about its neighbor (the three totally typical characteristics in the explanations given by Soviet headquarters), the headquarters of the 385th Infantry Division viewed what was happening in its own way:

> The 385th Infantry Division received an order to attack initially with its available 539th Infantry Regiment out of a jumping-off area northeast of Novopavlovka along the high ridgeline east of Hill 213.8 and to seize it. The attack by the 9th Panzer Division was at such a

9 NARA, T-314, roll 353, fr. 000407.
10 NARA, T-315, roll 541, fr. 000112.
11 NARA, T-314, roll 353, fr. 000407.

> distance that it was unable to facilitate the 385th Infantry Division's advance in any way. The division's initial plan consisted in attacking with one regiment south of Vereika, and the other regiment north of Vereika, and to pinch off the place of breakthrough by means of a side-by-side attack. Given the strength of the opposing infantry, it was vital that the division conduct combat actions in linked combat formations. However, the higher command's plan went further [than this], so the division had to send its forward regiment into battle, without permitting it to rest after the two days' of a forced march.[12]

Just as the 539th Infantry Regiment reached Hill 213.8, it came under heavy fire from the front and southern flank, and already at the outset of the attack, it ran into the fierce resistance of units of the 340th Rifle Division on the line of Hill 213.8 and the woods east of it [the Crocodile woods]. In addition to the lack of forces, the regiment's command made tactical miscalculations and oversights: "It had been planned to conduct the attack with the forces of the 539th Infantry Regiment and the reinforced battery of assault guns strictly to the east, in order to bypass to the north of the Triangular and Crocodile woods [the elongated patch of woods east of Hill 213.8]. However, at the recommendation of the troops in their positions, despite the strictly formulated order to the division, the 539th Infantry Regiment staged the attack so far to the south that it was stopped already at the Triangular woods [a very strange explanation and no less surprising basis not to follow the order that had been received – I.S.]."[13] As we see, the right-flank regiment of the 340th Rifle Division with the artillerymen of the 1244th Destroyer Anti-tank Artillery Regiment (20 45-mm anti-tank guns at the start of the battles[14]) confidently repulsed the attack that had been launched by the 385th Infantry Division's 539th Infantry Regiment, quickly pinning down the infantry that was unescorted by tanks in the field and holding their positions that had been swung back en echelon to the west.

As soon as it became known to the commander of the 385th Infantry Division that the 539th Infantry Regiment had run into stubborn resistance and was pinned down in the field by enemy fire, he ordered to cease the attack in order to avoid excessive losses and decided to regroup his forces for a second attack by sending the 537th Infantry Regiment, which had come up by this time, to the left and by shifting the overall direction of the division's attack further to the north. However, as the 385th Infantry Division's war diary notes, "this scheme could not be implemented, because the corps gave the division a new order." The 9th Panzer Division "had become stuck" northeast of Lomovo, having encountered major enemy forces, and because of the flanking fire from two directions it was unable to continue the attack to the east. For this reason, the 385th Infantry Division "was given the immediate task to seize and mop-up the village of Lomovo. For this purpose, the division moved out the 537th Infantry Regiment, leaving the 539th Infantry Regiment on its occupied line. Later, it was planned to continue the offensive to the southeast, having gathered all the units together."[15]

The VII Army Corps' journal of combat operations provides an interesting opportunity "to see" what was happening through the eyes of the staff officers and how the German command was assessing the situation that was developing in front of the corps:

> The corps commander and chief of staff left the corps headquarters [in Biakhteevka on the Veduga River, 4 kilometers to the southeast of Kondrashovka – I.S.] at 0400 and took position

12 NARA, T-315, roll 2193, fr. 000247.
13 Ibid.
14 NARA, T-315, roll 541, fr. 001236.
15 NARA, T-315, roll 2193, fr. 000248.

in the corps' forward field command post at the headquarters of the 340th Infantry Division [in a ravine north of Malaia Vereika – I.S.]. [...] The impression has formed in the division that the enemy was retreating from the battle with the 9th Panzer Division. This opinion isn't shared in the corps. [...] The attack by both divisions was conducted with the effective support of all of the Luftwaffe's available aircraft! [...]

From early morning the enemy was attacking the eastern front of the 387th Division on the Don River. Here the enemy succeeded in crossing the Don River in five places with small groups. In the course of counterattacks, everywhere the enemy was driven back across to the opposite bank. Only west of Novozhivotinnoe did the Russians in small detachments managed to hold out in two rectangular patches of woods 2 kilometers west and 2 kilometers northwest of Novozhivotinnoe. However, the enemy's further attempts to cross the Don were blocked by fire.

At 0900 the *Führer's* adjutant Major Engels arrived in the corps headquarters. He had received an assignment to form an opinion of the situation on the Voronezh front. The chief of staff briefed him on the situation and the corps' intentions, at which point the adjutant flew off at 0930 to the corps' forward field command post. Here the corps commander described the combat actions to him [and informed, that] up to this moment, the units had suffered very heavy losses. One can draw a conclusion regarding the ferocity of the fighting just by the fact alone that the corps, since 10.7.42, had knocked out 536 enemy tanks. During these battles almost half of the heavy anti-tank guns had been knocked out.

The corps' divisions have a sector of frontage that extends for approximately 25 kilometers. In order to ensure a successful defense in the future, a minimum of 3 divisions are necessary on the corps' northern front and in addition to have one panzer division as a reserve in the rear. [The *Führer*'s head might have become spinning from all such requests that he was receiving from one sector or another of the enormous Eastern Front – where was he to find all these reserves?! Germany's resources were not limitless, and already he likely recognized this better than anyone; the "Thousand-Year Reich" was already struggling to keep up with the war's demands, and this would become even more problematic in the nearest future. Incidentally, placing no particular hope on the *Führer*, but plainly striving in any event to strengthen the troubled sector of the new front by at least a bit, the Second Army command gradually shifted the S.S. 1st Motorized Brigade from the LV Army Corps' sector of defense to the area of the VII Army Corps' operations, although without making it directly subordinate to the VII Army Corps. On 24 July the S.S. brigade was already concentrated at the Nizhniaia Veduga River[16] – I.S.]

The corps' defensive capability was greatly suffering from the difficulties in keeping supplied with ammunition, because of the muddy roads caused by the frequent rains. The corps commander also believes that the strength of the air force present in the given sector is insufficient. The enemy, in his words, often has air superiority here.

[If only our commanders, who were complaining about the Luftwaffe's activity, could have heard this assessment; General Hell, judging from everything, had simply "been pampered" by the effective support his corps had received from the air during the fighting with the 5th Tank Army, when not just 12-15 bombers had taken part in the strikes, but 30-40. However, the Luftwaffe was no longer able to guarantee such a high number of aircraft in the VII Army Corps' sector of operations. Its point of main efforts was ceaselessly shifting to the south, following the troops that were attacking toward the Caucasus and Stalingrad. On the other sectors of the Eastern Front,

16 NARA, T-314, roll 354, fr. 000217.

the *Wehrmacht* had to be satisfied with the few Luftwaffe units that remained there, and had to be increasingly accustomed to doing without aerial support in their own battles. This fate was inevitably awaiting the VII Army Corps as well. In a not too distant future operation, the "insufficient" support of just 12-15 bombers for each raid would seem to many to be the "glory days", which they could only dream about returning – I.S.]

The VII Army Corps' war diary continues:

> Next Major Engels flew off to the 57th Infantry Division as well, and from there returned to the Second Army via the corps' command post.
>
> Since the attack by the 385th Infantry Division on its former axis doesn't promise success because of the powerful flanking [fire] out of Lebiazh'e, the corps has decided to alter the division's direction of attack. The division is receiving the order to attack together with the 537th Infantry Regiment, which will arrive by noon, and will go on the attack with the support of the battery of assault guns that has arrived toward the woods located 2 kilometers east of Hill 213.8, then pivot to the north toward Lomovo, and only then along the Bystrik Creek in the direction of Bol'shaia Vereika to the southeast.
>
> Between 1000 and 1100 signs appeared that the enemy at the point of breakthrough on the left flank of the 387th Infantry Division is withdrawing his forces. With the help of reconnaissance on the ground and from the air, the retreat of enemy forces has been observed. However, the given assumption has not been confirmed.
>
> Around noon, the Russians renewed attacks here in strength of up to a regiment to the southwest and west. According to the intelligence obtained from intercepted radio communications, the enemy still has the task to seize Somovo today [This was completely correct. It follows that the Germans had figured out how to decode the radio messages that were being sent out over the airwaves, unless, of course, the Soviet headquarters that were sending them weren't transmitting them in open text – I.S.]. The Russians have managed to shove our units even further to the south. Units of the 542nd Infantry Regiment have wound up cut off by enemy tanks in the woods 3 kilometers southeast of Lebiazh'e.
>
> The situation of this regiment has remained unclear for a long time. At times the division has come to the opinion that the elements that have been encircled here have already been lost. [This note testifies to the fact that everything wasn't going so smoothly with the Germans either concerning radio communications. Having no contact, the regiment's exhausted and depleted battalions were ensconced in a tight defense in the woods, and were only hoping that help for them would arrive like it had on the previous day. It is worth noting that despite the difficult situation, they were continuing to offer stiff resistance, and all the attempts by our units to dig them out of these woods on 24 July were unsuccessful. – I.S.]
>
> The enemy managed to break through to Gremiach'e; however, they were shoved out of the village again by the forces of the units of the 340th and 387th Divisions that were located here. A few tanks passed south of Gremiach'e to the southeast, however here a portion of them were knocked out and the rest were forced to turn back.
>
> Thus, the 340th Infantry Division didn't have the necessary organ of leadership (a headquarters) that might have been able to exert unified control over composite group in the switch position near Gremiach'e, so at an order from the corps, Blocking Group "Meyer" was formed from the elements positioned there under the command of the chief of the corps' engineering service, which was subordinated to the 340th Infantry Division.[17]

17 NARA, T-314, roll 353, fr. 00408.

Complaints about the difficulties and the ever increasing Russian forces are found as well in the 9th Panzer Division's war diary, and moreover, among the units that were opposing them at Lomovo the Germans "detected" units that were not even there at all: "The Russians are defending with the 237th Rifle Division, the 89th Tank Brigade, units of the 340th Rifle Division, the 118th Tank Brigade, the 923rd Rifle Brigade and units of the 13th Cavalry Regiment."[18] The latter two units were not anywhere near Lomovo; they weren't even part of Operational Group Chibisov.

The 9th Panzer Division's war diary also presents a clear image of the course of the fighting in VII Army Corps' main sector of operations:

> The complexity of the assigned task is determined by the quantity of the enemy's opposing forces. The division went on the attack under the conditions of a constant threat from the flank. The reinforced II Battalion of the 10th Panzer Grenadier Regiment was holding Hill 217.8 and thanks to its selfless efforts was covering the flank, and then the rear of the division. After repulsing an enemy attack by major forces, the division's offensive developed slowly and with great difficulty. In particular, the I Battalion of the 10th Panzer Grenadier Regiment that was attacking on the right flank in a ravine southwest of Lomovo ran into stubborn enemy resistance.
>
> The panzer group conducted an outflanking maneuver across Hill 208.8 in order to bypass Lomovo to the north and to attack the enemy from the rear. The attack was supposed to begin with a strike by dive bombers that had been designated at 1630. Because of some problem, the reason for which remains unknown even at corps headquarters, this airstrike didn't take place. In the process, the division lost valuable time for the attack, and went in motion at 1630 without the promised air support. With stubborn fighting, the units advanced to the western outskirts of Lomovo. At the same time, the 385th Infantry Division that had been brought up also fought its way to Lomovo.
>
> The enemy resistance, which was especially strong in the northern portion of Lomovo, was finally broken thanks to the 9th Panzer Division's attack. The large amount of loot, especially guns, and the large number of enemy dead (in the sector of the I Battalion of the 11th Panzer Grenadier Regiment, approximately 400 killed enemy soldiers) – all this is proof of the severity of the fighting, which ended with the taking of Lomovo. The panzer units were withdrawn to the area south of Hill 212.9 in order to refuel and take on ammunition. The reinforced 10th Panzer Grenadier Regiment is securing the Hills 208.8 and 217.8. The reinforced 11th Panzer Grenadier Regiment and the 59th Kradschützen Battalion are defending the Lomovo area.[19]

The 385th Infantry Division's combat diary supplements the picture of the combat on 24 July:

> A battery of assault guns was attached to the 537th Infantry Regiment and the support of bombers targeting the northern portion of Lomovo was promised. The attack began at 1600. Overcoming strong resistance, the regiment at 1800 took the low ground east of Hill 199.8, after which, with an impetuous attack, it seized Hill 199.8 with an assault at 1900 and reached the western outskirts of Lomovo. At 1945 forward units of the regiment penetrated to the eastern end of the village and were fighting their way to its northern outskirts. A further attack along the valley of the Bystrik Creek to the southeast couldn't be continued in the evening. At 2100 the division halted the regiment's attack after it took firm possession of the western half of Lomovo.

18 NARA, T-315, roll 541, fr. 001113.
19 NARA, T-315, roll 541, fr. 001113.

A detachment was covering the division's rear near Gremiach'e, and counterattacking, threw back an enemy attack. There had been concern in the division, whether an enemy attack south of Vereika into the 385th Division's rear through Gremiach'e could be stopped, because the available anti-tank means there were not at all comparable with the number of tanks that the Russians had. [Unfortunately, the concerns of the 385th Infantry Division's command were groundless, because neither the 1st Tank Corps as a whole, nor any of its brigades received a task to alter the direction of attack to the northwest and to launch an immediate attack into the flank and rear of the enemy grouping that had penetrated to Lomovo, but instead continued to follow the order to attack to the southwest – I.S.]

As noted above, at an order from the corps, Blocking Group "Meyer" was formed from the 221st Pionier Battalion, the forward detachment of the 385th Infantry Division, and the units of the 340th and 387th Infantry Divisions that were positioned along the Bol'shaia Treshchevka, Somovo, Gremiach'e line (including the anti-aircraft and artillery units located there). The division's order for 25 July demanded a continuation of the offensive, but one battalion of the 537th Infantry Regiment was to remain in the Lomovo area and to mop-up the village and the valley of Bystrik Creek.

The German air force was very active. In addition to constant aerial reconnaissance, it frequently attacked the woods east of Hill 213.8 and Lomovo. The enemy's air force also conducted raids. Three Russian aircraft were shot down by fighters. Three assault guns from the battery of the 201st Stürmgeschutz Battalion that was attached to the division were knocked out because of mines.[20] The quantity of loot still hasn't been determined. From the troops there were reports of 20 prisoners and 4 deserters. Our units, particularly the II Battalion of the 539th Infantry Regiment, suffered heavy losses. With the start of the attack, the division's forward command post was set up in the low ground at Hill 208.9. The division commander spent the day among the troops.

At the end of the first day of fighting, the division has wound up extended along 11 kilometers of a front that faces south, east and north. The assignment for the next day for a continuation of the offensive between the Vereika and Bystrik Creek demanded a strict concentration of all the division's strength, but this is contradicted by the corps' demand to leave sufficient security forces in Lomovo in order to cover the right flank of the 9th Panzer Division. Bitter enemy resistance should be expected on the coming day as well. In the course of the night, a regrouping of force took place for the preparation of the attack, which again deprived the already exhausted enlisted personnel of rest.[21]

The losses in men of the VII Army Corps' units on 24 July amounted to:

20 According to a report from the battery commander, all three assault guns blew up on German mines: two during the attempt to make a stealthy advance along the hollows southwest of Lomovo, and the third during an attempt to evacuate one of the disabled assault guns. The hollows, as potentially dangerous avenues for the stealthy approach of Russian tanks, had been mined as a precaution by the German infantry units [obviously, the 340th Infantry Division] that had previously been positioned there, but in the chaos of the battle and the back and forth of the movements, no one had thought to warn the commander of the arriving battery of *Stürmgeschutz* about them. As a result, he didn't know about this "surprise", and for the German crews the disablement at the start of the battle of nearly half of their available seven StuGs on mines left behind by their own infantry was a genuine wake-up call. (NARA, T-315, roll 2199, fr. 000839.

21 NARA, T-315, roll 2193, fr. 000248-250.

9th Panzer Division: 34 killed (including 2 officers), 226 wounded (including 14 officers, two of which remained on active duty);[22]
340th Infantry Division: 20 killed, 124 wounded (including 2 officers), 31 missing;
387th Infantry Division: 46 killed (1 officer), 66 wounded (2 officers), 5 missing;
385th Infantry Division: 18 killed (1 officer), 175 wounded (8 officers), 1 missing.[23]

Altogether, 118 men were killed, 591 wounded and 37 went missing in action, for a total number of 746 casualties. Of these, a certain portion of the wounded, perhaps 10%, remained on active duty.

During the day of 24 July, the commander of the 542nd Infantry Regiment reached the decision to abandon the woods south of Lebiazh'e, where for 2 days his isolated regiment had occupied an all-round defense, and ordered a break out in order to link up with the rest of the division. That night, the battalions pulled out of their positions and in an organized fashion, bringing out their wounded, broke out without serious losses to the 387th Infantry Division's new sector of defense at Bol'shaia Treshchevka. The absence of any mention in the Soviet documents about combats with the enemy in the vicinity of the woods on the night of 24-25 July speaks to the fact that the Germans' departure remained practically undetected by our units, since the ring of encirclement by our rifle units was the weakest at the southern portion of the woods.

The task of the VII Army Corps' assault group for 25 July remained as before: to conduct a unilateral envelopment of the enemy and to encircle the Russian units that had penetrated to Lebiazh'e. In his characteristic manner to lead the combat actions from a position among the units' combat formations, the commander of the 9th Panzer Division General Baeßler at 0430 drove to the forward command post 1 kilometer south of Hill 212.9, where in the course of a short conference with the commander of the panzer grenadier brigade *Oberst* Hülsen, he gave him an order to attack together with the 33rd Panzer Regiment and supporting units in bypass of Lomovo across Hill 208.8 toward Surikovye Vyselki. However, barely had he managed to issue the order, when his command of the panzer division unexpectedly came to an end: a fragment of an exploding shell struck him in the left knee and immediately and irrevocably terminated his participation in the operation that was underway (and possibly could have ended his life, had it struck him a bit higher).

This was the second wounding in his military career (he had received his first wound in August 1914 in the First World War). Baeßler was given first aid and within 30 minutes he was delivered to a small hospital. On the next day they took him by ambulance to the airfield in Kursk, from which point he was carried by a Ju-52 to a rear hospital in Kiev.[24] He never returned to the 9th Panzer Division. After recovering from his wound, he became the commander of the 14th Panzer Division, then after service in the reserve, he received a transfer to the Western theater of combat operations, where he oversaw the construction of defensive fortifications. A little more than a year later he would be the commander of the 242nd Security Division, with which he entered the fighting in Normandy against the Allies. He received his third severe wound in August 1944 on the Western Front; this one he wouldn't survive, and he would die in a Vienna hospital in November 1944. In January 1943, for his successful command of the 9th Panzer Division, Baeßler had been awarded the German Cross in Gold.

In order to prevent a crisis in command at a critical moment of the battle, *Oberstleutnant* Hülsen, the commander of the 9th Panzer Division's panzer grenadier brigade, assumed command of the

22 NARA, T-315, roll 541, fr. 001431.
23 NARA, VII Army Corps, T-314, roll 354, fr. 726-727.
24 NARA, T-315, roll 538, fr. 1387.

9th Panzer Division. Having issued an order to the elements of his assault group with an explication of their tasks, he was forced to return urgently to the division command post in Dmitrievka, in order to take a detailed look into the situation now at the level of the entire division. The commander of the I Battalion of the 10th Panzer Grenadier Regiment *Oberstleutnant* Brassert assumed command of the assault group.[25]

The tasks of the 385th Infantry Division for the operation's second day was set as follows: "Attack south of the valley of the Bystrik Creek to the southeast, seize the high ground at Bol'shaia Vereika in order to pound it [the village] with the fire of artillery and heavy infantry weapons, and then attack to the south through Vereika and destroy the encircled enemy."[26]

The 385th Infantry Division's 539th Infantry Regiment was supposed to attack on the right, and its 537th Infantry Regiment on the left. Their task included a joint attack to seize and mop up both patches of woods east of Hill 213.8 and then to take and hold a sector of the Vereika River.

The daily log of the 385th Infantry Division provides an interesting opportunity to follow the chronology of the battle and to see how the combat operations at the division and regiment level were organized:

> 0025. From the corps they reported that dive bombers would continuously deliver airstrikes against the Dolgoe area and the woods right up to Surikovye Vyselki, as well as the valley of the Bystrik Creek as far as Bol'shaia Vereika.
>
> 0510. The first report from the 537th Infantry Regiment about the launching of the attack. The attack is developing successfully.
>
> 0600. Over the radio it was demanded that the 539th Infantry Regiment report on the start of the offensive.
>
> 0633. The 539th Infantry Regiment reported that a regrouping was underway.
>
> 0650. The corps was made aware of the start and development of the offensive.
>
> 0700. Both regiments were required to submit targets for the air force immediately. [Oh, only if such an offer had been presented to the units of Operational Group Chibisov – I.S.]
>
> 0702. The division requested the support of dive bombers at the Triangular and Crocodile patches of woods. Malaia Vereika and Lebiazh'e were named as subsequent targets.
>
> 0705. A report from an aerial reconnaissance flight about the situation.
>
> 0715. An announcement from the corps: the commander of the 9th Panzer Division has been wounded. The corps is giving special significance to the fact that the division's offensive should keep pace with that of the 9th Panzer Division. The division commander reported to the corps that the 537th Infantry Regiment, pursuant to its orders in the sector, has wound up under the threat of a flank attack from the direction of the Crocodile Woods.
>
> 0722. Briefing of the 9th Panzer Division's headquarters with our situation. It was made aware that the offensive of the left flank regiment [the 537th Infantry Regiment] had been stopped by an order from the division and would be resumed only after a strike on the patch of woods by dive bombers [as we can see, the command of the 385th Infantry Division didn't want to take the woods "at any cost" and drive the regiment into an attack against the defense of the two regiments of the 340th Rifle Division, which was fraught with the danger of heavy losses, preferring instead to "crush" it with the summoned dive bombers. – I.S.]. The engineer battalion received the assignment to mop up the valley of the Bystrik Creek.

25 NARA, T-315, roll 541, fr. 001114.
26 NARA, T-315, roll 2193, fr. 000250.

0745. The assault gun battery has managed to reach the road to Bol'shaia Vereika and was stopped there by heavy fire. All of the battery's assault guns have been knocked out. The III Battalion [obviously, of the 537th Infantry Regiment – I.S.] has received an order to dig in.

0752. A report from the 537th Infantry Regiment … the enemy is abandoning Lomovo.

0800. The 537th Infantry Regiment has reported on 50-60 German tanks north of Lomovo and is requesting artillery support against an attack by Russian tanks.

0802. The 385th Artillery Regiment has been informed of the enemy attack and was ordered to support the 537th Infantry Regiment with fire [it can only be guessed when and where, and what sort of attack, moreover with tanks, was spotted by the regiment – I.S.].

0805. The corps has announced that from 0830 to 0840, a strike by dive bombers will be conducted against the Triangular and Crocodile Woods. The regiments were immediately informed about this [most likely, to hasten the spreading of recognition sheets for the Luftwaffe at the forward positions – I.S.].

0815. The 539th Infantry Regiment requested artillery fire on the Crocodile Woods after the airstrike.

0830. The regiment is requesting an attack by dive bombers against the northern portion of Lebiazh'e, since the road leading out of Lebiazh'e to the south is not exposed to artillery fire.

0845. Report to the corps: not a single assault gun is combat-capable any longer. In the best case, one can only count upon the fact that three of the assault guns will be repaired on 26.7.42.[27]

0852. The 537th Infantry Regiment "has bogged down" in front of the enemy's numerous tank forces [?? – I.S.].

0900. The engineer battalion has been ordered to equip the close assault groups being formed in the regiments with all the means available in the division (mines, anti-tank magnetic shaped charge mines, hand grenade bundles), since the supply of these is of particularly important significance for today's combat.

0900. A report from the division commander to the commanding general. All of the assault guns have been knocked out. Heavy enemy resistance is expected in the Triangular and Crocodile patches of woods. A request for the allocation of anti-tank guns. Close assault groups have been formed. The division commander is proposing the use of dive bombers against the tanks. The corps command has been informed that the combat capability of the personnel is falling due to heavy fatigue.

The commanding general briefed the division commander regarding the situation in the 9th Panzer Division, agreed with the division commander's proposals, and asked to inform the personnel of the following: "The *Führer* has shown his personal interest in the combat actions of the VII Army Corps, having sent his personal adjutant to the [Second] Army, since the future success of the operation on the southern front depends upon the outcome of the VII Army Corps' offensive." [Here one can't help but recall Liziukov's appeal to his subordinates before the offensive, when he declared that the corps was

27 According to a report from the battery commander, one assault gun was hit in the flank by a round fired by a Russian tank or anti-tank gun and became consumed in flames, while the three remaining assault guns were rendered non-operational due to mechanical breakdowns: two because of a failure with the gun's recoil mechanism, and one because of problems with the electrical firing trigger, after which all three assault guns were withdrawn for repairs. (NARA, T-315, r. 2199, fr. 000839).

carrying out a special government assignment. As they say, the analogy is self-evident – I.S.]

0930. An order from the VII Army Corps' chief of artillery regarding an artillery barrage on the Crocodile Woods, since the infantry will attack the patch of woods immediately after the artillery preparation.

0935. The 539th Infantry Regiment reported that it went on the attack at 0845. A report has arrived that the airstrike by the dive bombers was successful.

1000. A report from the 385th Artillery Regiment: with the forces of the II Battalion of the 539th Infantry Regiment, the Triangular Woods have been taken. There was no enemy resistance.[28]

As we can see, it was only after artillery and aerial attacks that the units of the 340th Rifle Division's 1140th and 1144th Rifle Regiments that were defending in the area of the patch of woods were compelled to retreat, and the 385th Infantry Division was able to advance. However, its advance again quickly came to a stop under the fire from our units, and the usual reports about difficulties and deprivations began to fly up the channels of command. *Oberst* Meyer, the commander of the blocking group, reported that he'd been totally unable to take Hill 210.9. From the 385th Artillery Regiment, they were passing along word that 5 German tanks had been knocked out by Russian artillery fire. The 537th Infantry Regiment reported the lack of ammunition and that all of its battalion commanders were casualties …

Concerning the resumption of the offensive, the commander of the 537th Infantry Regiment announced that the regiment could advance only when the resistance by the Russians weakened. The 385th Infantry Division, which had become bogged down around mid-day in part because its men were "totally exhausted", was waiting for when the 9th Panzer Division would advance, the tanks of which were finally supposed to crush the stubborn Russians.

Around 0700, the 9th Panzer Division's assault group went on the attack. However, its main force – the 33rd Panzer Regiment – was already not fully intact: because of the need to protect the division's extended flank and rear, one of its panzer battalions numbering 20-25 tanks had been left behind not far from the western outskirts of Lomovo. The two other panzer battalions advanced along the high ground north of Lomovo. To the left of them, a battalion each of the 10th and 11th Panzer Grenadier Regiments were attacking; on the right, the 59th Kradschützen Battalion was advancing along the valley of the Bystrik Creek.

Progress was slow. Because of flanking fire and attacks launched from the north (primarily by the 2nd Tank Corps), increasingly the assault group had to detach units to screen its northern flank. Initially, the security in this direction had been assumed by the I Battalion of the 10th Panzer Grenadier Regiment, which was occupying a patch of woods on Hill 208.8, but later by the other two panzer battalions, under the protection of which only the remaining three battalions of the shock group [a battalion each of the 10th and 11th Panzer Grenadier Regiments, plus the 59th Kradschützen Battalion] were able to advance. A reconnaissance patrol sent out in advance reported back that Surikovye Vyselki, and in particular the commanding heights, were occupied by "major enemy forces".[29] Obviously, this was how the German scouts viewed the units of the 1142nd Rifle Regiment and the training and engineer battalions of the 340th Rifle Division with their anti-tank guns, as well as the units of the 3rd Destroyer Anti-tank Artillery Regiment.

Seeing that the assault group's forces were beginning to thin out, the command of the VII Army Corps ordered the 340th Infantry Division to assume the protection of the sector between Hill

28 NARA, T-315, roll 2193, fr. 000258-260.

29 NARA, T-315, roll 541, fr. 001114.

208.8 and 212.9 (leaving the forward positions on Hill 217.8 for the 9th Panzer Division), in order to free the mobile units of the 9th Panzer Division in order to put fresh wind into the faltering offensive. However, even as this process was underway, Rotmistrov's 7th Tank Corps launched an attack toward Hill 217.8 and overran a company of the 10th Panzer Grenadier Regiment that had been left there as a screen. The 9th Panzer Division's journal of combat operations confirms the debacle that occurred there, which became an unprecedented, crushing defeat in the previously victorious history of the division's fighting in the summer of 1942: "On Hill 217.8, enemy tanks succeeded in overrunning the 5th Company of the 10th Panzer Grenadier Regiment that was positioned there, partially wiping out its personnel, after which the remnants of the company were ultimately annihilated by the enemy infantry that attacked after the tanks. Only 8 soldiers have returned to the battalion.[30]"[31]

What happened on Hill 217.8 became a genuine shock not only for the grenadiers of the 5th Company of the 10th Panzer Grenadier Regiment that were overrun by the Soviet tanks (some in a very literal sense of the word), but also for the entire command of the 9th Panzer Division. At the most critical moment of combat actions, after the shock grouping had already pivoted for an attack to the east, and the screening of its attack became important as never before, in its rear, one of its covering elements was genuinely annihilated. The Russians now had complete possession of Hill 217.8, and now there was no longer any advantageous defensive line left between the enemy tanks and the rear of the entire grouping at Lomovo in order to cover the lines of supply that had become instantly vulnerable. Only the single panzer battalion that had been left behind near Lomovo now remained in the path of the major Russian tank grouping approaching from the north. The panzer battalion's tanks were not up to the task of opposing the heavy Russian tanks, if the enemy launched a massed armor attack against the western outskirts of Lomovo, followed by waves of accompanying infantry.

The German command might have simply recoiled at the thought of such a development in the course of the battle, well imagining what sort of debacle might await the 9th Panzer Division's assault group given such a massed tank attack from the rear. The operational crisis that arose as a result of the destruction of the 9th Panzer Division's screen on Hill 217.8 arguably became a real moment of truth in the entire operation and presented the German command with a devilish predicament: Should the offensive to the east be continued as planned, or should the offensive be suspended or even cancelled in order to redirect the forces of the assault group to counter the threat from the rear?

By this time, German aerial reconnaissance had doubtlessly detected the movement of the 7th and 11th Tank Corps' tank columns toward the operational area, and the command of the VII Army Corps had every justification to fear that having been drawn into heavy fighting in almost every direction and being left without reserves, the 9th Panzer Division might not withstand the massed attack of Russians from the exposed flank and rear, which was fraught not only with the panzer division's heavy defeat, but also the collapse of the VII Army Corps' entire operation, especially since the corps itself no longer had any substantial reserves.

30 A list of the 9th Panzer Division's losses allows the clarification of the approximate number of German prisoners that were taken in the battle with the 3rd Guards Tank Brigade on Hill 217.8. The missing-in-action on that day amounts to 77 men, from which it is possible to conclude that the report of 55-60 prisoners mentioned in the Soviet documents is closer to the truth, and not the reports of 100 or 200 prisoners. The comparison between the German and Soviet documents also provides the basis for another supposition: the enemy lost 15-20 men that were killed in action in the battle for Hill 217.8 against the tanks of the 3rd Guards Tank Brigade and the brigade's motorized rifle battalion.

31 NARA, T-315, roll 541, fr. 001114.

On the other hand, the Russians' strange pause after the destruction of the 9th Panzer Division's covering element on Hill 217.8 and the absence of any signs of a rapid and decisive buildup of forces and means at the point of breakthrough gave the divisional and corps command hope that a further deterioration of the situation could be avoided, and the destruction of the screening company wouldn't develop into a crushing defeat of the entire 9th Panzer Division.

Facing such a sharply complicated operational situation and the need to react to the changes in it as quickly as possible, the German command was forced to reach a critical operational decision, upon which the fate of the entire operation now depended. In essence, this decision boiled down to a choice between risk, which carried with it the most heavy potential consequences, but still allowed a chance for the operation's success, and a rejection of risk with the aim of saving the panzer division, but at the same time precluding this success. There was no third path here: either it was necessary to operate with a barely covered "spine", having thrown all the remaining forces forward, or to abandon the counteroffensive totally in order to parry the threat to the assault group's flank and rear.

In this dramatic situation, where faith in their own troops (and I would say, a sizeable amount of self-assurance) plainly superceded concerns that the situation might develop according to the worst scenario, the 9th Panzer Division command decided to continue the offensive at whatever the cost and achieve its designated objectives. In this connection, the shift of the sole remaining reserve, a battalion of the 11th Panzer Grenadier Regiment, which was to have been used to cover the northwestern approaches to Lomovo on 25 July, was cancelled, and instead the battalion was sent to reinforce the assault group.

With heroic pathos, the author of the journal of combat operations used only the selfless actions of the German panzer grenadier company to explain the "miracle" at Lomovo rather than the banal mistakes and miscalculations of the Soviet command, and concluded: "Owing to this company's dogged resistance to the very end, the rest of the II Battalion of the 10th Panzer Grenadier Regiment managed to consolidate on a new defensive line along the northern lip of a ravine to the south of Hill 217.8 and held this line, repelling repeated attacks by the enemy's tanks and infantry. Owing to such selfless actions by the soldiers of the company, the division's rear was covered. At the cost of their own lives they guaranteed the success of the division's offensive."[32] Commenting on this excerpt, it must be said that the 9th Panzer Division's rear remained safe primarily not because of the selfless actions of the soldiers of the 5th Company. While they did offer resistance, they proved unable to stand against the heavy KV tanks and later in fact surrendered en masse, but because of the uncoordinated and indecisive actions of the 7th and 2nd Tank Corps, the leadership of which proved unable to exploit the tactical success of the 3rd Guards Tank Brigade and develop it into an operational success by striking the overextended units of the 9th Panzer Division from the rear, the opportunity was lost.

While the German command could cover the 9th Panzer Division's rear with just a single panzer battalion, committing all the rest of its force to the resolution of offensive tasks, the Soviet tank commanders indecisively dallied in front of the German blocking detachment, and having barely advanced, adopted a defensive posture, fearing the threats of counterattacks. The ponderously slow and indecisive actions of the command of the 7th and 2nd Tank Corps, given the significant quantitative and qualitative superiority over the enemy in tanks and their inability to use it, unquestionably became the main reason for the halt of the counterattack toward Lomovo almost as soon as it had started. Meanwhile, the destruction of the German company didn't lead to the collapse of the 9th Panzer Division's offensive.

32 Ibid.

However, with the benefit of hindsight it would be incorrect and unjust to believe that this is the fault of the Soviet commanders alone and to question how they could act so irresolutely. It is known today how thin and brittle the German covering screen was, but the commanders of Operational Group Chibisov didn't know this (to a great extent due to the shortcomings in the organization of reconnaissance or to its complete absence), and thus they had certain justifications to assume that the adversary was strong and might be able to launch unexpected counterstrokes anywhere. The headquarters of the units of the operational group time and again requested information from aerial reconnaissance, but received it only sporadically, which cannot be said about the German command, which with the help of reconnaissance aircraft regularly "peered" into the Soviet rear and had the opportunity on-the-fly to discover the movement of major forces and to include this information when directing their own forces.

Going *va banque*, the command of the 9th Panzer Division directed the division's assault group toward the decisive fulfillment of the offensive's tasks and the grouping's soonest possible emergence on the hills east of Bol'shaia Vereika. With the aim of liquidating the continuous threat from the flank, "which could not be eliminated even with the help of tank attacks and airstrikes", the I Battalion of the 10th Panzer Grenadier Regiment received an order to attack and take the woods northwest of Surikovye Vyselki.

Having repulsed the feeble attacks by the 2nd Tank Corps' brigades on the northern outskirts of Lomovo and having deployed panzer grenadiers and anti-tank guns there, the two remaining battalions of the 33rd Panzer Regiment initiated a regrouping, in order to resume the offensive to the east. Here, however, the next painful blow on this day was waiting for the 9th Panzer Division. Directed to support the panzer division's offensive, German bombers arrived over the target area and without checking the situation on the ground, unexpectedly released their bombs over their own forward units, forcing them to forget immediately about any offensive and to take cover from the explosions that were shaking their positions in shellholes and slit trenches … The mistake was made clear only after frantic signaling from the ground and angry radio messages, but the attack was totally disrupted, and taught by bitter experience, the German elements now were taking a concerned glance into the sky with the approach of any aircraft.[33] The subsequent events have been described in the 9th Panzer Division's war diary:

> Close to evening the II Battalion of the 11th Panzer Grenadier Regiment managed to reach the eastern outskirts of Surikovye Vyselki, while at the same time the 59th Kradschützen Battalion arrived at the western bank of a stream that runs through the same village. After reconnoitering the area and the discovery of a ford across the river, the 33rd Panzer Regiment was able to break through to Hill +3.0. This bold breakthrough could be described with the phrase "as a battle through the midst of enemy forces". Having come under flanking fire from enemy tanks and in constant combat contact with enemy tanks, and ultimately winding up under the threat of an attack from their own dive bombers, the attacking troops had to acknowledge that they were not in a condition to hold the narrow salient they had created in the Soviet lines and were compelled to fall back, because the panzer grenadiers didn't have the possibility to follow directly behind the tanks.
>
> The division's situation became precarious. Taking into account the latest alarming reports from the sector of defense on Hill 217.8 and the constant threat to the flank from the direction of the patches of woods located northeast and northwest of Surikovye Vyselki, as well as the significant losses in personnel (among the casualties were two commanders of two

33 NARA, T-315, roll 541, fr. 001115.

> artillery battalions),[34] a decision was reached regarding whether there was a need to shift the division to a defensive posture. A continuation of the offensive in the conditions when the arrival of fresh forces wasn't anticipated would mean the prolonging of combat in the circumstances of a constant threat from the flanks, the danger of encirclement, and losses in tanks in the combat against vastly superior enemy forces. Only the skillful leadership over the forces and the special selflessness of the men might, given the known conditions, bring about the battle's successful resolution. Without hesitations, the division made the decision to continue the offensive. For the night, an order was issued about organizing the security of the assembly area.[35]

What can be said here? The heroic characterizations given to one's own actions while rendering faceless the countless masses of the unheroic enemy, was inherent to the documents of both sides. If however you attempt to get a look at the true correlation of forces between the two sides hiding behind the phrases about "special selflessness", then it turns out that the Russian adversary didn't have any overwhelming superiority in force in that battle; with respect to the number of tanks, the 118th Tank Brigade, the only one of all of Operational Group Chibisov's tank units that took part in the fighting at Surikovye Vyselki, was considerably inferior to the two panzer battalions of the 33rd Panzer Regiment. Meanwhile, the Germans had overwhelming superiority in the air, which frequently had a decisive influence on the course of combat operations. On this day, according to the summary of the Second Army, the Luftwaffe conducted 357 individual aircraft sorties in the operational area.[36] It is a different matter that the 9th Panzer Division was acting with much greater effectiveness than the numerous, but uncoordinated units of Briansk Front's operational group.

The outcome of the battle at Surikovye Vyselki on the evening of 25 July, which ended with the forced withdrawal of the 33rd Panzer Regiment's tanks that had broken through to Hill +3.0 to the western bank of the stream, meant that VII Army Corps' assault grouping still hadn't carried out their offensive tasks even on the operation's second day. The 9th Panzer Division's faltering offensive also didn't facilitate an advance by the 385th Infantry Division; after seizing the patches of woods, its regiments again encountered stubborn Russian resistance and halted under the fire coming from the hills northwest of Malaia Vereika and Lebiazh'e.

The failure to conduct a brief, effective offensive operation also disrupted the calculations of the 9th Panzer Division's supply chief regarding keeping the units supplied with fuel. Already on 24 July he was compelled to make a new request for an additional 150 metric tons of fuel, of which only 100 metric tons had arrived in Kastornoe. The dispatched trucks were barely able to bring up enough fuel to "satiate" the hundreds of engines in the panzer division's numerous vehicles; just one panzer regiment alone could consume 50 metric tons of fuel over each day of combat operations. Having no knowledge when this prolonged "lightning" operation would finally end, and how much fuel the panzer division would actually need, the supply chief in any case made another request to the Second Army on 25 July for another 150 metric tons of fuel …

The need for ammunition of all types was also growing, the delivery of which also came via the railroad to Kastornoe. The troops were expending ammunition at such a rate that an acute deficit of certain types of ammunition was already noticeable. The supply of 75-mm shells was under

34 Only one of them, judging from the 9th Panzer Division's casualty lists, served in the division. The other commander, obviously, was from an artillery battalioin that had been attached to the 9th Panzer Division.
35 Ibid.
36 NARA, T-315, roll 354, fr. 000215.

special control; the delivery of 510 such shells was, for example, immediately made known to the panzer division's operations chief and the commander of its panzer regiment.[37]

In the 385th Infantry Division's account, the end and outcome of the fighting on 25 July was reflected as follows:

> The enemy's losses in tanks were heavy. In the evening, smoke from the burning Lomovo was intermingled with the black smoke rising from knocked out tanks that rimmed the horizon. The troops after almost inhuman exertions were completely exhausted. With the objective dangling right in front of their eyes, it seemed that they had become strained to the limit. However, the plea of the division commander, who ordered it to be made known to the men that he is fighting alongside them, forces each and every soldier to put up with his fatigue. Despite the enemy's bitter resistance, the line extending from the western part of Lebiazh'e to the western part of Surikovo was achieved. Taking advantage of the bright moonlight, the 537th Infantry Regiment also managed during the night to occupy a favorable jumping-off position for the attack on the following day.
>
> As for the results of the day, the following can be stated: despite the numerical superiority, all of the enemy's attempts to expand the sector of penetration, to strike the flank of our offensive and thwart it, suffered a failure. The designated envelopment of the Russian forces by the forces of the 9th Panzer Division and the 385th Infantry Division had significant success. The Luftwaffe played a major role in this success by substantially hampering the enemy, which was constantly introducing new forces into the battle.
>
> On 26 July, the outcome of the heated battle should be decided. The time has arrived to "reap the fruits" of the recent days of fighting. The units understood the full significance of these hours. Each man recognizes the direct connection between these battles and the overall course of our Ostheer's operation in the south. If the 9th Panzer Division succeeds in advancing just another 6 kilometers to the southeast, then the ring will close around the powerful enemy forces that have penetrated. True, given the correlation of forces this will still be insufficient for a "final resolution". Persistent attempts by the enemy to break out of the relatively weak ring of encirclement can be expected, which might lead to a new crisis.[38]

The losses of the VII Army Corps' divisions that were participating in the operation continued to grow. Over the day of combat on 25 July, the 9th Panzer Division lost 58 killed (including 1 officer), 192 wounded (including 8 officers, of which 2 remained on active duty), and 77 missing in action.[39] The 385th Infantry Division had 42 killed (including 1 officer), 265 wounded (including 15 officers), and 19 missing in action. The 387th Infantry Division had 31 killed, 54 wounded (including 1 officer) and 3 missing in action. The 340th Infantry Division had 11 killed (including 1 officer), 51 wounded (including 1 officer) and 1 missing in action. Altogether the casualties amounted to 804 men, of whom 142 were killed (including 3 officers), 562 wounded (including 25 officers) and 100 went missing in action.

At 2030, a radio message arrived at the headquarters of VII Army Corps from the 9th Panzer Division, reporting that the situation on Hill 217.8 had become extremely tense, and the division was requesting the transfer of additional forces to this place (which isn't surprising, because the 9th Panzer Division no longer had any reserves; all of its units had been activated). But how could the corps' command respond to this? It also had no reserves left (showing that there was a

37 NARA, T-315, roll 541, fr. 000472.
38 NARA, T-315, roll 541, fr. 000624.
39 NARA, T-315, roll 541, fr. 001431.

considerable amount of adventurism in the decisions of the German command when conducting this operation). So in order to at least somehow ease the situation of the 9th Panzer Division that had become lodged in the very midst of the enemy, the VII Army Corps command ordered the commander of the 340th Infantry Division, which was fighting alongside the panzer division, to scrounge up some reserves for the panzer division, taking them from its relatively quiet left flank.[40]

Meanwhile, plainly aiming to ensure that no undesirable hesitations and doubts arose in any of its subordinates about the possibility of leading the operation to a victorious conclusion, the Second Army command made an unambiguous, final declaration: "The army has made a firm decision to envelop and destroy the foe located in the breakthrough area northeast of Zemliansk. There are no signs that he can avoid encirclement from the northeast."[41]

40 NARA, T-315, roll 353, fr. 000415.
41 NARA, T-315, roll 354, fr. 000215.

General Aleksandr Il'ich Liziukov, commander of the 5th Tank Army, April 1942.

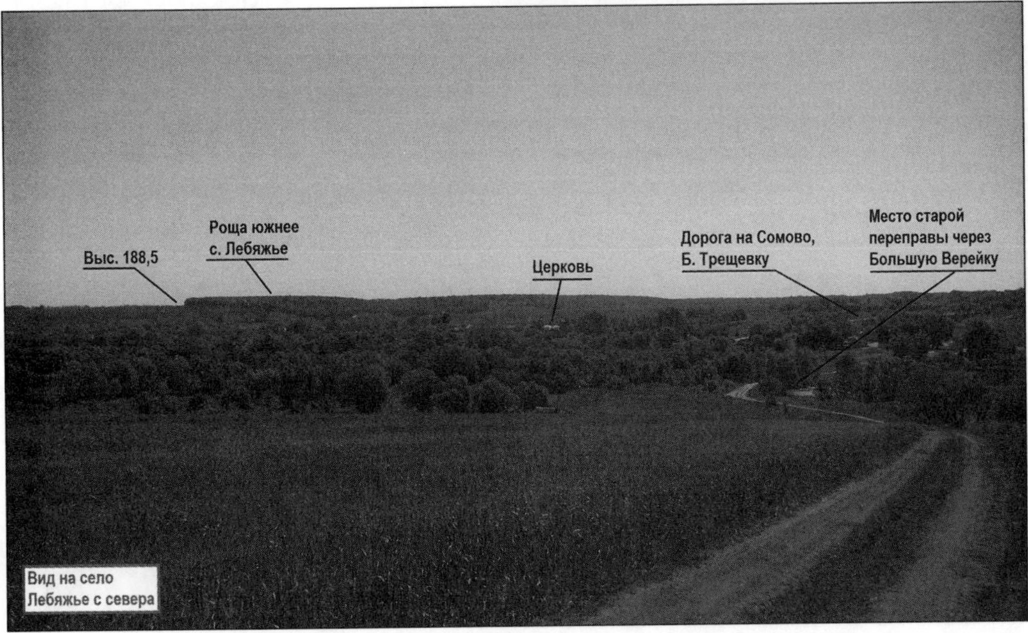

View toward Lebiazh'e from the north, as Soviet attackers would have seen it.

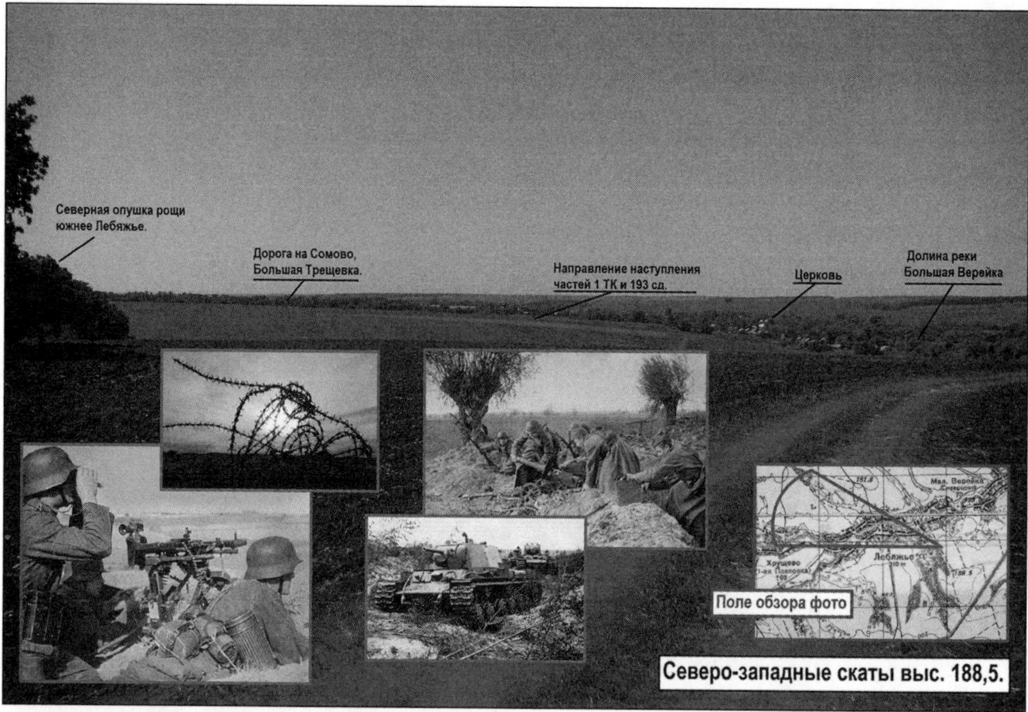

View toward Lebiazh'e from the German positions on the northwestern slopes of Hill 188.5.

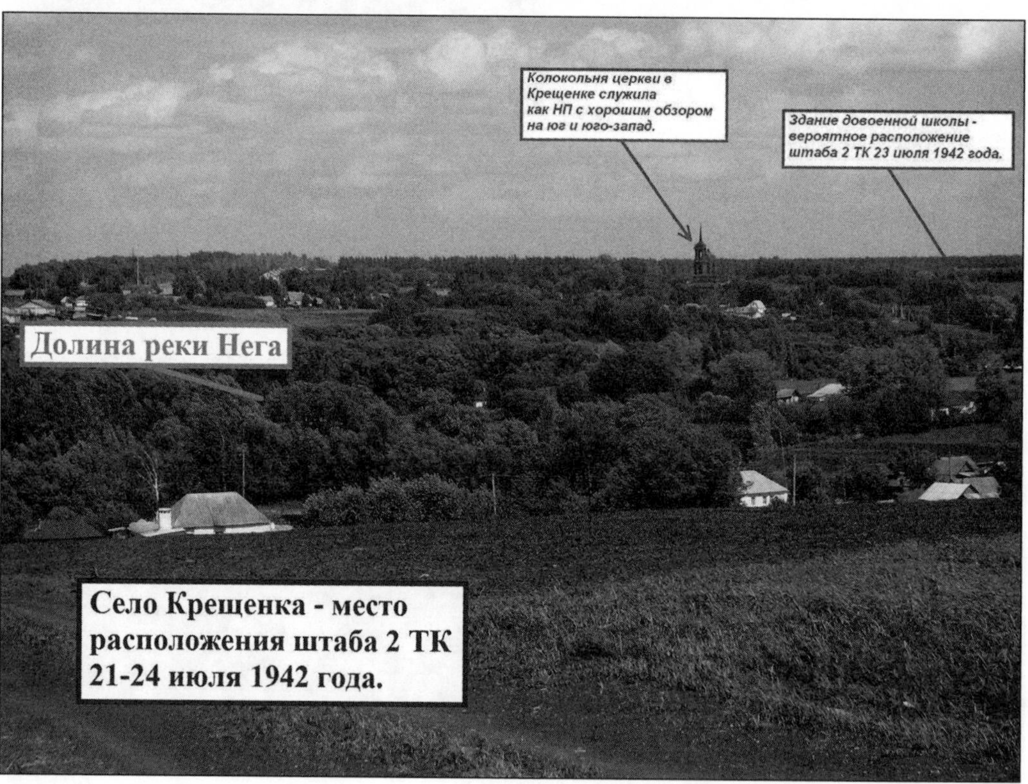

Location of the 2nd Guards Tank Corps' headquarters; a view toward Kreschenka from the west.

In this direction, Liziukov's tank ever closer to the German ambush on the morning of 23 July 1942.

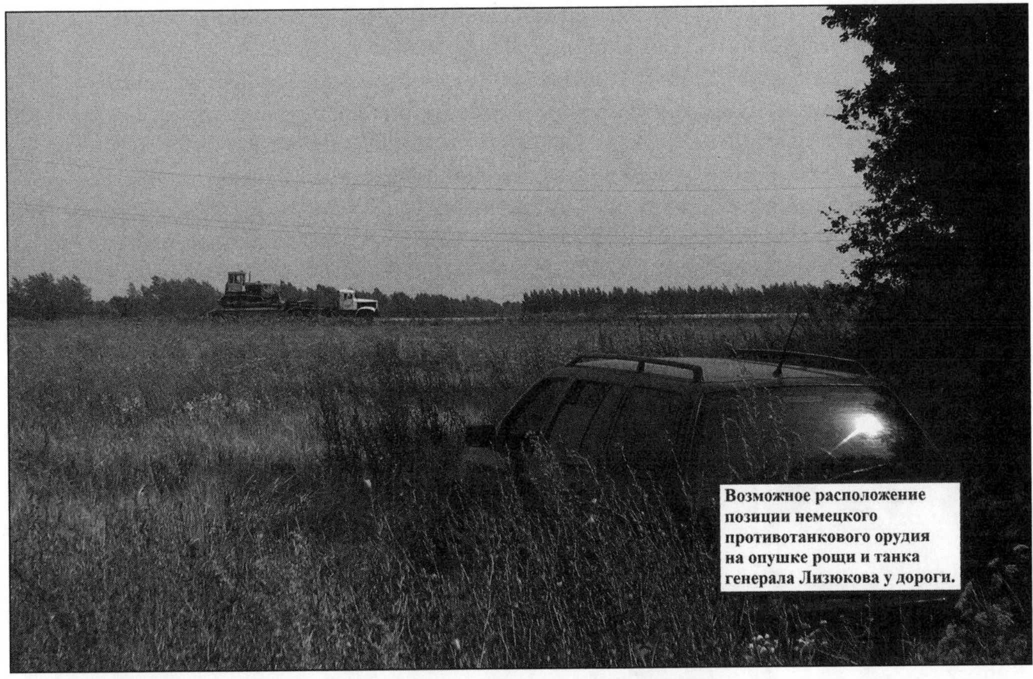
Возможное расположение
позиции немецкого
противотанкового орудия
на опушке рощи и танка
генерала Лизюкова у дороги.

A modern restaging of the ambush of Liziukov's KV tank; Note the close-range, flank shot that was available to the German anti-tank gun crew in the fringe of the woods.

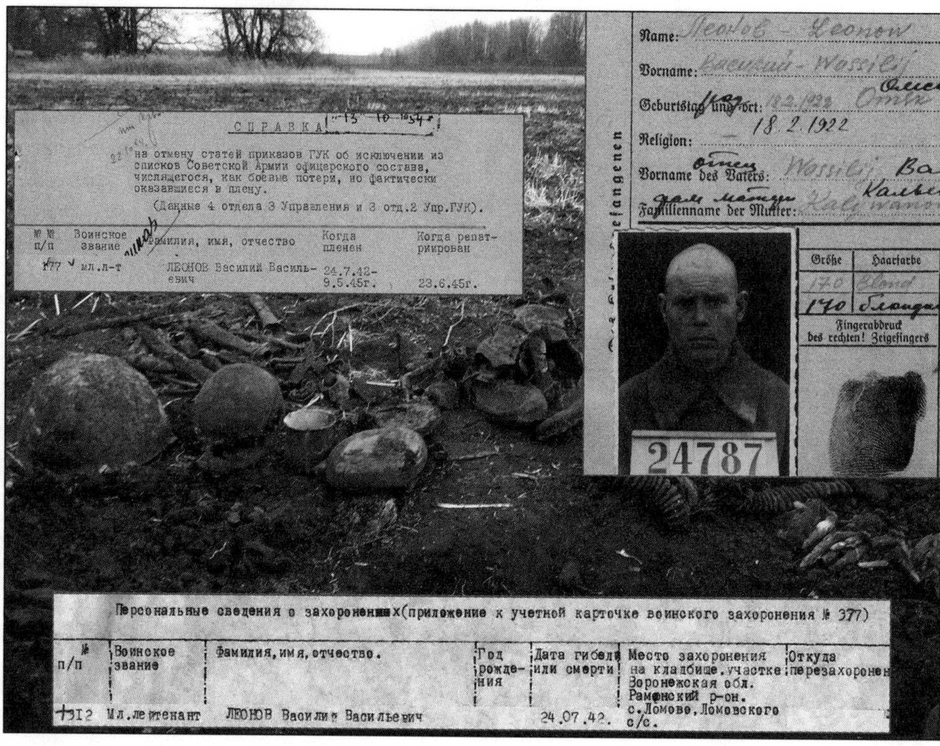

Hill 212.9, the place of Junior Lieutenant Leonov's first and last battle. Believed to be KIA, in fact he was taken prisoner and survived the war.

1 2 7 8 14 15 16 23 24 25

Personalkarte I: Personelle Angaben

Kriegsgefangenen-Stammlager: 1631

Beschriftung der Erkennungsmarke: Nr. 24787

Lager:

Name: Леонов – Leonow

Vorname: Василий – Wassilij

Geburtstag und -ort: 18.2.1922 Omsk / Омская обл.

Religion: – 18.2.1922

Vorname des Vaters: Wassilij / отец Василий

Familienname der Mutter: Kalywanowa / дам. матери Калыванова

Staatsangehörigkeit: Russe / СССР

Dienstgrad: U/LTN / младш. лейт.

Truppenteil: 841 J.R. / 841 стр. полк Komp. usw.:

Zivilberuf: Buchhalter / бухгалтер Berufs-Gr.:

Matrikel Nr. (Stammrolle des Heimatstaates):

Gefangennahme (Ort und Datum): 24.7.42. Lomowo / пленен 24.7.42 д. Ломово

Ob gesund, krank, verwundet eingeliefert: gesund / здоров.

Nähere Personalbeschreibung

Größe	Haarfarbe
170	Blond
170	блонд.

Besondere Kennzeichen: удл-01137

Fingerabdruck des rechten! Zeigefingers

Name und Anschrift der zu benachrichtigenden Person in der Heimat des Kriegsgefangenen: 16 / ... Omsk / r-n Kolotschinskij D. Pawlosohanka / Leonowa E.

24787

Wenden!

Junior Lieutenant Vasilii Leonov's prisoner identification card.

Excavation of military artifacts from July 1942.

16

26 July 1942

Later on the evening of 25 July, having received the alarming word about the enemy breakthrough and the retreat initiated by the rifle divisions, Chibisov decided to take the sternest measures and if he couldn't return the units to their previous lines, then at whatever the cost he would halt their retreat and create a new line of defense on a favorable line. Having announced his decision to his chief of staff, he directed him to prepare the corresponding orders for the division commanders, which his chief of staff did. One after another, three brief orders were written for the 193rd and 340th Rifle Divisions, and the 167th Rifle Division and 104th Rifle Brigade, all of which began with the same phrase: "On your own responsibility, the army commander has ordered you to rally your units and to hold the line firmly …."

Then there followed specific instructions. The 167th Rifle Division and the 104th Rifle Brigade were to defend the Surikovo – Bol'shaia Vereika line, but the order added "In the event of a forced withdrawal, occupy the Posel'skoe – Kreshchenka second and final line of defense, to which withdraw only with the authorization of the Military Council."[1] (The 104th Rifle Brigade received the task to defend on the front stretching from Bol'shaia Vereika to the Don River and if need be the second Kreshchenka – Fomina-Negachevka line.)[2] The 193rd Rifle Division was directed to "hold the Surikovye Vyselki – Murav'evka line firmly" and the second Murav'evka – Posel'skoe line, to which the division also might withdraw only with the authorization of the Military Council.[3] The 340th Rifle Division's commander was directed to take operational control of the 118th and 201st Tank Brigades and to defend the Dolgoe – Murav'evka – Dmitriashevskie Vyselki – Lukino line with the task to prevent an enemy breakthrough toward Verkhniaia Kolybel'ka. Chibisov also informed the commander of the 340th Rifle Division that in front of his division, the 7th and 11th Tank Corps would be implementing the enemy's destruction.[4]

Having written all these orders around 2300, the operational group's chief of staff Colonel Pilipenko handed them off to liaison officers, who immediately drove off in the night to search for their designated recipients. On the night of 25-26 July, in addition to the 7th Tank Corps that had already been made subordinate to Chibisov on the prior day, the Commander-in-Chief of Briansk Front Rokossovsky decided to reinforce Operational Group Chibisov with the 11th Tank Corps, which after the march on 24 July was now located in the Dubrovskoe area. At 0030 the 11th Tank Corps became operationally subordinate to the commander of the operational group.[5] With Rokossovsky's order, Chibisov also received control of the 119th Rifle Brigade, which had been resting and replenishing in Briansk Front's rear since 6 July.

Thus, when working out the plan of battle for 26 July, Chibisov could now commit 4 tank corps, 2 separate tanks brigades and one separate rifle brigade to the aid of the operational group's rifle

1 TsAMO, F. 202, op. 5, d. 334, l. 60.
2 Ibid., l. 77.
3 Ibid., l. 60.
4 Ibid., l. 61.
5 TsAMO, F. 202, op. 5, d. 35, l. 91.

divisions. In truth, not one of these units was now (or even had been) fully staffed and equipped. The 118th and 201st Tank Brigades and the 1st and 2nd Tank Corps had already suffered substantial losses, while the 7th and 11th Tank Corps had not been brought back up to full strength after the previous fighting. Nevertheless, between them all they had approximately 330 operational tanks, of which 135-140 were medium and heavy tanks.[6] A concentrated, coordinated attack by them might become crushing for the foe.

Operational Group Chibisov's command staff now had to devise a plan of battle in such a way as to make the best use of the tank formations in order to give a resounding check to the enemy that had broken through the front of the rifle divisions, which were now to go over to a rigid defense. By sunrise on 26 July, their overall defensive line was to run along a convex arc to the south: Ozerki, Kamenka, Point +3.0 [a different mound from the burial mound +3.0 northeast of Surikovo], Dolgoe, Murav'evka, Hill 199.0, Surikovye Vyselki, Surikovo, Bol'shaia Vereika, Don River south of Fomina-Negachevka.

After midnight, having received a message from Katukov regarding his decision to withdraw a portion of his 1st Tank Corps from Lebiazh'e to the area west of Kreshchenka and Fomina-Negachevka, Chibisov not only approved of this decision, but also issued an order to withdraw the entire 1st Tank Corps to the ridgeline along the road from Dolgoe to Nizhniaia Vereika. The brigades of the 1st Tank Corps were to strengthen the defense of the rifle units here, taking up positions in the second echelon in readiness to launch counterattacks. Simultaneously, the 1st Tank Corps with part of its strength was to launch an attack toward Surikovo and Lomovo at 0500, "destroy the enemy in the area of Surikovo and Surikovye Vyselki … and to fortify in the Surikovo area, preventing the enemy from advancing to the east."[7]

A liaison officer delivered Chibisov's verbal order to Katukov at 0400 on 26 July.[8] Having received Chibisov's authorization, chances are the commander of the 1st Tank Corps finally gave a sigh of relief and at 0545, now without a glance over his shoulder, issued his own order to withdraw to the Posel'skoe – southeastern outskirts of Kreshchenka line of defense, which the tank corps was instructed to occupy by 1100.[9] Based on the fact that the 1st Tank Corps would deploy on a new line with a front to the west and would meet a possible enemy offensive out of Surikovye Vyselki in its sector, Chibisov decided with the forces of the 7th Tank Corps to launch an attack against the German panzer grouping from the rear, thereby placing it between Rotmistrov's armored hammer and Katukov's anvil. The 2nd Tank Corps (a second "hammer") was supposed to cooperate in this task with an attack against the enemy's left flank, while Chibisov gave the 11th Tank Corps (yet one more "hammer") the task "to smash the enemy in the Surikovye Vyselki area with an attack along the Surikovo – Bol'shaia Vereika axis", and in the future "develop the attack across Hill 187.4 with the task to finish off the enemy that has broken through."[10]

Obviously, believing that he now had at his disposal plenty of strength to deal with the overreaching enemy at Lomovo and Surikovo, Chibisov also issued an order to the newly subordinate commander of the 11th Tank Corps. He was to detach a substantial group of tanks from the 11th Tank Corps (he eventually resolved upon 17 Matilda Mk-II tanks) for a reconnaissance-in-force together with the 21st Cavalry Division to probe Hill 218.7 at the boundary between the 284th Rifle Division and the 8th Cavalry Corps southwest of Perekopovka.[11]

6 There is not complete information on the number of operational tanks for all of the brigades on the morning of 26 July in order to give a precise number.
7 TsAMO, F. 202, op. 50, d. 14, l. 251.
8 TsAMO, F. 38 A (445), op. 9005, d. 19, l. 94.
9 TsAMO, F. 38 A (445), op. 9005, d. 19, l. 82.
10 TsAMO, F. 38 A (445), op. 9005, d. 39, l. 12.
11 TsAMO, F. 38 A (445), op. 9005, d. 35, l. 92.

Over the remaining hours of the night, the 1st Guards Tank Brigade and 1st Motorized Rifle Brigade were pulling out of the Lebiazh'e area and heading to the northeast. The movement went slowly in complete darkness. There were no well-worn roads in this direction, and the tanks and motor transport had to overcome ravines and stream crossings. To the north, the signal flares soaring above Surikovye Vyselki and Lomovo revealed that the forward enemy units were already looming over them. The march didn't go by without clashes. According to the 1st Guards Tank Brigade's war diary, "the trailing signal machines were knocked out before reaching the Surikovo area; the crews were wounded." Communications in the brigade became "intermittent".[12]

No matter how much the commanders kept hurrying their elements and despite all the efforts of the tankers and motorized riflemen, neither by 0300 nor even by 0500 did the 1st Motorized Rifle Brigade and 1st Guards Tank Brigade reach their jumping-off line. It goes without saying that the initial plan to attack the enemy at 0500 with the forces of the 1st Guards Tank Brigade proved impossible and was immediately forgotten (the chief of staff of the 1st Tank Corps made no further mention of it and offered no explanations, as if the 1st Guards Tank Brigade never had this task) – the brigades were able to reach their designated line only by 1100.

Dawn arrived and the sun began to emerge above the horizon. The day of 26 July 1942 was beginning. The forward elements of the 1st Tank Corps' two brigades, having covered approximately 10-12 kilometers over the night, were beginning to arrive at their designated lines, when suddenly in the west rose the thunderous sounds of heavy combat. A fierce battle had erupted in the area of Surikovye Vyselki, which was barely obscured by the nearby hilltops. An analysis of Soviet and German documents gives the following description of what was happening there.

Around 0700, a group of German bombers appeared in the sky above Surikovo and Surikovye Vyselki. Having shaken out into a combat formation, they began working over the forward edge of defense of our units along the line of hills on the eastern bank of a nameless brook that flows southward into Bystrik Creek. Once the bombers departed, enemy artillery and mortars opened fire on the positions of our units. The brief artillery preparation concluded with a furious barrage, after which dozens of German tanks began moving from the hills toward a ford across the stream in Surikovye Vyselki.

The Luftwaffe continued to pound the positions of our units, suppressing the fire of the anti-tank batteries and driving the infantry into trenches and foxholes. Under such cover, approximately 30-40 enemy tanks accompanied by up to a battalion of infantry quickly crossed the stream and began to climb the slope on the eastern side of the valley. Soon they sliced into the combat positions of the right-flank battalion of the 167th Rifle Division's 465th Rifle Regiment, the 118th Tank Brigade's motorized rifle battalion and the 340th Rifle Division's training battalion, which together with the 167th Rifle Division's 177th Anti-Tank Artillery Battalion were occupying the defenses here. Forced to join battle under the attacks of German bombers, the anti-tank battalion under the command of the 28-year-old Senior Lieutenant Voronin opened fire at the hostile tanks at almost point-blank range. A fierce combat between the battalion's artillerymen and the attacking tanks unfolded on the slopes of the broad field east of Surikovye Vyselki. The supporting German Stukas were laying down a path for the German tanks.

Quickly, the axis of the enemy's main attack became clear. The German tanks were lunging toward Hill +3.0, while on their way overrunning the artillery's firing positions and crushing the trenches and foxholes dug by our soldiers. Possibly, the gun crews of the 177th Anti-tank Artillery Battalion managed to knock out several tanks, but the concentrated and swift actions of the enemy assault grouping, together with the smooth, effective air and artillery support, inevitably had their effect, silencing the pockets of resistance on the exposed, level hilltops and quickly

12 TsAMO, F. 1 gv tbr, op. 1, d. 11, l. 17.

decided the battle's outcome. Two of the anti-tank battalion's guns were knocked out by bombs, two were crushed by tanks, and the battalion commander Senior Lieutenant Voronin was killed (together with a portion of the gun crews in their firing positions).[13]

From the political reports of the 118th Tank Brigade, it is possible to judge what happened on that morning on the line of defense at Surikovye Vyselki:

> On 26 July, the motorized rifle battalion joined battle. Occupying an area of defense of the northern and eastern spurs of a bushy ravine north of Surikovo and the burial mound labeled "+3.0" on the map, it was attacked at 0700 by 73 tanks and 15 motorcycles from out of the northeastern fringe of the Surikovo hills, and from out of Surikovo by two battalions of infantry. Our right flank was completely exposed.
>
> The tanks penetrated the battalion's defense. The battalion's fierce struggle with enemy tanks and infantry lasted for 40 minutes. The battalion displayed exceptional heroism. Not a single man broke and ran, even though the losses were heavy. Enemy tanks were flattening the area of defense under their tracks, but the soldiers and commanders resisted courageously, tossing grenades and Molotov cocktails at the tanks. The battalion set 10 enemy tanks ablaze and killed up to 400 Hitlerites. The battalion lost 50% of its men, 5 anti-tank rifles, 2 heavy machine guns, 4 mortars and up to 150 rifles and PPSh submachine guns.
>
> Senior Sergeant Mikhailiuk particularly distinguished himself in the battle; having applied for Party membership before the battle and showing exceptional bravery, he was the first to set a hostile tank ablaze with a Molotov cocktail, which inspired the other soldiers to destroy the tanks. Private and Komsomol member Kuz'min brewed up a tank and fell heroically in the battle. When a tank was directly approaching him, Deputy Political Instructor Semenov stood up at full height and with the cry "For the Motherland, for Stalin!" threw a Molotov cocktail and a grenade at the tank and destroyed it. [You begin to tremble when you picture this terrible scene in your mind: a roaring tank with clattering tracks, and a man standing up with hatred and fearlessness to meet it. We must never ever forget about such forefathers. – I.S.]
>
> The wounded Senior Sergeant Pronin, who'd already been wounded once before in the Patriotic War, refused to leave the battle while he still had the strength to continue to kill fascists. Privates Kamerin and Kuznetsov fell heroically on the field of battle; before the battle they had both received their candidate Party membership cards. Communists and political workers skillfully directed the fighting and inspired the men to struggle with the foe, leading by example.
>
> Across the entire battlefield you could hear the cries of the military commissar of a submachine gun company Junior Political Instructor Kubasov: "Kill the foe to the last breath! Burn the fascist tanks! Victory will be ours!" Kubasov himself was killed with a weapon in his hands. The 2nd Company's political instructor Comrade Baluev earned the soldiers' opinion in the battle, "With such a political instructor it is not even fearful to die!" Under a storm of fire he moved from foxhole to foxhole and with a Bolshevik word enflamed the hearts of the soldiers, calling upon them to hold their positions and mercilessly slaughter the Germans. Comrade Baluev was also killed in this battle. Junior Political Instructor Logachev, the secretary of the Komsomol Bureau, moved from one end of the battlefield to the other, stopping at every foxhole; by his personal example he was leading on the others.[14]

13 TsAMO, F. 202, op. 5, d. 334, l. 65.
14 TsAMO, F. 118 tbr, op. 1, d. 47, l. 30.

Unfortunately, the heroism and self-sacrificial stand by the soldiers and commanders of the 118th Tank Brigade, the 177th Anti-tank Artillery Battalion, the 167th Rifle Division's 465th Rifle Regiment and the 340th Rifle Division's training battalion only slowed, but couldn't stop the powerful and deliberate enemy onslaught. Having breached the defensive line of our units with a concentrated armored battering ram in the wake of their Stuka airstrikes, the forward German tanks burst onto Hill +3.0 already within 30 minutes of the start of the attack.[15]

At the start of the German attack, the commander of the 124th Howitzer Artillery Regiment Lieutenant Colonel Kolesnikov was located in his observation post on the hill together with his staff officers (his howitzer regiment was supporting the 167th Rifle Division). The German breakthrough was so swift and unexpected that they were caught in the observation post and came under an attack by German tanks, which began to crush and shoot the men trapped there. Lieutenant Colonel Kolesnikov and his artillery officers, who were unarmed against the tanks, were tragically killed in this terrible final battle.[16] Among them, artillery battalion commander Captain Nikitin, the regiment's chief of intelligence Lieutenant Petrash, and artillery platoon commander Lieutenant Koshchenik were killed.

The destruction of the observation post and the death of the howitzer artillery regiment's commander immediately led to the fact that the artillery battalions deployed in their firing positions several kilometers to the north were left "blinded" and "excluded" from the battle, while the regiment was leaderless. Having learned of the breakthrough by German tanks just several kilometers from them, the blinded battalions of the 124th Howitzer Artillery Regiment vacated their firing positions and began to retreat toward the Don River.[17]

The German breakthrough and the emergence of German tanks and panzer grenadiers near Hill +3.0 had a most adverse effect on the resilience of the rifle units that still remained in their positions, which the enemy didn't fail to exploit and to "roll up" their line of defense from the flank, threatening to enter their now exposed rear areas with the crushing tank steamroller. Soon the Germans launched a second attack in the south and began to attack out of Lomovo toward Bol'shaia Vereika along the Bystrik Creek, increasingly splitting apart the semi-encircled units of Operational Group Chibisov from the northwest.

After the emergence of the German tanks on Hill +3.0, tankers of the 1st Guards Tank Brigade's 2nd Tank Battalion under the command of Major Boiko joined battle with them. At this time, they were the only tanks of the entire tank brigade that had managed to take up a defense of the western spurs of the ravines west of Kreshchenka.[18] Having received a rebuff, the panzers didn't risk attacking the battalion of T-34 tanks and took up positions on the hill. After the initial powerful enemy lunge across the stream in Surikovye Vyselki, when the rifle units defending there were either overrun or brushed aside, the tankers of the 1st Guards Tank Brigade, arguably became at that moment the sole organized force that could stop the armored enemy wedge (according to Katukov's message, the 118th Tank Brigade's motorized rifle battalion helped repel the German advance from Hill +3.0 together with the tankers of the 2nd Tank Battalion).[19] The motorized riflemen plainly took courage under the shield of the arriving tanks.

In addition, in contrast with the previous, punishing strikes by the Stukas against our rifle units and artillery, the continued furious attacks by the German bombers didn't at all have such a ruinous effect on our tanks. In this respect, the aerial support received by the rapidly advancing

15 NARA, T-314, roll 353, fr. 000417.
16 TsAMO, F. 202, op. 5, d. 334, l. 15.
17 TsAMO, F. 38 A (445), op. 9005, d. 35, l. 92.
18 TsAMO, F. 38 A (445), op. 9005, d. 19, l. 94.
19 TsAMO, F. 38 A (455), op. 9005, d. 35, l. 94.

panzers was quickly losing its effectiveness. The Germans couldn't take the Guardsmen's tanks "by force", like they had treated the infantry, or spook them with howling dive sirens, while it was an extremely difficult task to strike a T-34 with a bomb even from out of a dive.

An apparent hitch now occurred in the advance of the German armored steamroller, and a shaky, unsteady equilibrium suddenly arose in the battle. Avoiding a gun duel and declining a direct clash with the T-34, which was superior to their tanks in firepower and armored protection, the commander of the German panzer grouping pulled his tanks back to a safe distance and evidently began to regroup his forces.

Continuing to hold to a rigid defense on the indicated line, the 1st Guards Tank Brigade's 2nd Tank Battalion prepared to repel a new enemy attack and was waiting, waiting for the arrival of the rest of the brigade (quite possibly, the crews realized they might not even have the time to wait for when this would finally happen ...). Tensions grew; the enemy was conducting long-range fire and sending out reconnaissance patrols, but ... never sent the tanks into an attack. Then, having left some of the panzers on Hill +3.0, the Germans withdrew the remaining machines somewhere. Meanwhile, they began to move up their anti-tank guns to the hill. At the same time, the sounds of combat began to spread both to the right and left of the battalion's line of defense.

Its commander, Major Boiko, was in a difficult situation. He couldn't extend his front; the tank battalion's strength was limited, but he also didn't have the authorization to abandon his screening line. Somewhere to the left, the brigade's 1st Tank Battalion was supposed to arrive in its positions, but even its front of defense wasn't unlimited. It could be outflanked, if it had no neighboring unit. Major Boiko needed support and help ...

However, what were the other three tank corps of Operational Group Chibisov doing at this time? After all, according to Chibisov's plan, they were supposed to launch a crushing blow against the enemy from the flank and rear, which might prove to be even more devastating now, when the German assault grouping had quite literally turned its back to them.

The 7th Tank Corps actually had gone on the attack at 0600 according to Chibisov's order, getting a jump on the active operations by the German panzer grouping at Surikovye Vyselki by an entire hour, and genuinely threatening to sever its supply line with its attack. Alas, with this achievement, the tank corps could do no more. Its 87th Tank Brigade, at the commander of the 7th Tank Corps Rotmistrov's order (possibly, at Chibisov's direction) was sent to attack Hill 214.6, 5 kilometers to the southwest of the axis of the main attack, and it took no part in the 7th Tank Corps' "decisive" attack.

Reporting to higher command on the fighting on 26 July 1942, the 87th Tank Brigade's military commissar wrote:

> At 0500 today, the brigade was assigned to attack Hill 214.6. The resulting attack has broken down. The enemy had mined the southern slopes of the hill and has strong anti-tank fronts on the forward edge of defense. In addition, the enemy in cooperation with aviation is subjecting our units to a mortar barrage [a strange barrier for tanks – I.S.]. Our units after attempts to attack went over to a defense for the rest of the day and conducted reconnaissance and observation of the enemy. Losses: 4 junior commanders and 2 enlisted men were killed, and 3 of the command staff, 2 of the junior command staff and 5 soldiers were wounded. Altogether, 15 men [sic] became casualties on this day. T-34 tanks: 4 were lost; one of them became disabled in the minefield and the others were knocked out. T-60 tanks: 2 were knocked out by bombing from the air. [Also lost:] Vehicles – 2, anti-tank guns – 1, anti-aircraft guns 1, and a field kitchen and an anti-aircraft machine gun. [...]
>
> Despite the fact that we have sent two requests to you for political staff for the brigade's motorized rifle battalion, to the present day we haven't received a single man from you. I ask you to hurry to satisfy our requests. Yesterday the motorized rifle battalion received 139

> replacements, but because of the lack of rifles, submachine guns and machine guns, it isn't possible to send them all into battle.[20]

Rotmistrov kept in reserve his 3rd Guards Tank Brigade, the only one in the entire tank corps having the heavy KV Tanks that had shown themselves so impressively on the day before in the destruction of the enemy covering detachment on Hill 217.8 (and suffered not a single irrecoverable loss during the entire battle). The brigade didn't go on the attack. Thus, from the very outset, the 7th Tank Corps launched its main attack with only half of its subordinate forces: the 62nd Tank Brigade and the 7th Motorized Rifle Brigade. Even here, though, the attacking force didn't reach half the corps' strength: following the example of his chief, the commander of the 62nd Tank Brigade left one of his two tank battalions in reserve.

As a result, the 7th Tank Corps launched the "crushing" attack on the main axis … with just one of its six tank battalions and only 22-25 tanks (of which approximately 15 were light T-60s) of the approximately 100 operational tanks it had that day. It isn't surprising that given such minimal tank support, the battalions of the 7th Motorized Rifle Brigade, which in essence were shouldering the main burden of the attack in these conditions, operated indecisively, glancing back for tanks, and instead of a dash forward, for the most part were digging in on the field under enemy fire. Two of the already few T-34 tanks of the 62nd Tank Brigade that were accompanying the infantry of the 7th Motorized Rifle Brigade were struck by "thermite shells" [as was written in the report – I.S.] and were left burning on Hill 212.9.[21]

At 1100 the chief of staff of the 7th Tank Corps wrote Chibisov reports that were far from victorious:

> The 62nd Tank Brigade and 7th Motorized Rifle Brigade [are attacking] out of the area of Hill 212.9 in the direction of Hill 213.8. Progress is slow; the infantry is advancing in short bounds before digging in, because heavy fire out of the area of Lomovo and Vysochkino are hindering them. The enemy air force continues to bomb and strafe the combat formations. The tanks are engaged with enemy tanks, which have reached the southern slopes of Hill 212.9. […] I request the movement of units of the 273rd Rifle Division [sic – obviously, he had in mind the 237th Rifle Division – I.S.] to Hill 217.8, as was your order yesterday. Cover the combat formations of the corps from the air with fighter aircraft. Establish through aerial reconnaissance whether or not fresh enemy forces are on the approach to Vysochkino.[22]

Over six-plus hours of such an offensive "into the rear of the enemy that has broken through", the 7th Tank Corps advanced several hundred meters and stopped on Hill 212.9 under enemy fire.

The 11th Tank Corps set out on a march at dawn, and having covered approximately 12 kilometers, by 0400 the head of the column was approaching Bol'shaia Poliana. However, the corps' units didn't assemble in the area of Kamenka for the counterattack until 1000, three hours after the start of the enemy's attack. It is true that according to Chibisov's order, the 11th Tank Corps was given a time for its assembly in its jumping-off area at Kamenka, but only "by the morning of 26.7.42", which was quite elastic as a concept.[23] Finally, the 11th Tank Corps did arrive at Kamenka and … began to move out to the east, gradually extending its brigades along a lengthy line of defense. Paradoxically, but in its combat report the chief of staff of the 11th Tank Corps

---

20 TsAMO, F. 87 tbr, op. 1, d. 5, l. 158.
21 TsAMO, F. 89 tbr, op. 1, d. 19, l. 100; also see F. 62 tbr, op. 1, d. 4, l. 20.
22 TsAMO, F. 38 A (445), op. 9005, d. 19, l. 91.
23 TsAMO, F. 38 A (445), op. 9005, d. 39, l. 12.

diligently writes about the brigade's combat strength and the positions that they occupied, but completely fails to mention any of the tank corps' offensive tasks to destroy the enemy in the area of Surikovye Vyselki, as if it hadn't received any such order at all from Chibisov!:

The corps' units assembled by 1000 26.7.42 and are occupying a defense in the areas:

> 53rd Tank Brigade numbering 4 KV tanks, 24 T-60 tanks and 69 motorized riflemen are defending the line: Lukino, southern outskirts of Dolgoe, (excl.) Murav'evka. The anti-aircraft battery consisting of 3 37-mm guns is covering the bridge in Kamenka.
>
> 59th Tank Brigade numbering 3 Mk II tanks, 5 T-60 tanks, 2 anti-tank guns and 50 motorized riflemen are occupying a defense along the southern slopes of Hill 200.2. Two directions for counterattacks have been prepared: the axis toward Lukino and the axis toward the southeastern outskirts of Anikeevka. For the reconnaissance-in-force in cooperation with the units of the 21st Cavalry Division, 17 tanks of the 59th Tank Brigade have been detached, which at dawn on 26.7.42 were engaged in combat in the direction of the woods 3 kilometers east of Ivanovka …
>
> 160th Tank Brigade consisting of 5 Mk II tanks, 18 T-60 tanks and 45 motorized riflemen are occupying a line of defense: woods south of Anikeevka, Posel'skoe, Pribytkovo …
>
> 12th Motorized Rifle Brigade numbering 210 motorized riflemen and 5 anti-tank guns is defending the Point 204.0, Point 199.0, Murav'evka area. The 8th Separate Reconnaissance Battalion numbering 3 T-34 tanks, 19 armored transports and 12 armored cars is assembled in the woods southwest of Point 192.4 and is scouting in the direction of Dolgoe, Lomovo, Pribytkovo, Bol'shaia Vereika, Malaia Vereika. The command post – woods southwest of Point 192.4.[24]

However, at the first glance the operational summary's paradoxical contradiction to the order previously issued by Chibisov, arguably, has a logical explanation. By the time the 11th Tank Corps arrived in Kamenka, Chibisov already knew about the enemy breakthrough at Surikovye Vyselki, and the number of enemy tanks that were operating there was becoming increasingly larger in the messages received from the units. Obviously, because Chibisov feared a pivot by the enemy's major panzer grouping to the north and the destruction of the rear areas of the operational group's rifle units by its forces, he rejected his initial plan to hurl the 11th Tank Corps into an attack and instead decided to strengthen the threatened direction with a hastily-created new defensive line.

This also explains the operational summary written by the 11th Tank Corps' chief of staff, which completely fails to accord with the previous task that had been set for the corps. Upon arriving at Kamenka, the 11th Tank Corps' command no longer had offensive assignments, but had received an order to assume a defensive posture instead. However, even a defensive task raised doubts in the 11th Tank Corps' headquarters about its ability to fulfill the order unconditionally because of its lack of strength. Ending the operational summary, the cautious chief of staff of the 11th Tank Corps wrote the following discomforting conclusion: "The corps, occupying a defense with a frontage of 10 kilometers and having an insignificant quantity of tanks and infantry under its command, given the extremely light density of artillery means (in view of its understaffing) cannot create a continuous defensive line, or moreover create a defense in depth. The most urgent staffing and equipping of the corps' units with personnel, materiel and weapons is necessary."[25]

So just what sort of *offensive tasks with decisive objectives* regarding the "final finishing off of the enemy that has broken through" could be given to the command of the 11th Tank Corps, after

24 TsAMO, F. 38 A (445), op. 9005, d. 35, l. 91.
25 TsAMO, F. 38 A (445), op. 9005, d. 35, l. 92.

such a conclusion and such a pessimistic-defensive tone? Judging from the operational summary, none at all …

The 2nd Tank Corps by the morning of 26 July was positioned in virtually the very same area to which it had fallen back on the morning of 24 July and was occupying a defense along the line Dolgoe and Point +3.0 which lay 2 kilometers to the west. The tank corps had 3 KV, 30 T-34 and 29 T-60 that were combat-ready.[26] As in the case of the operational group's other tank corps, the 2nd Tank Corps on the morning of 26 July had been given offensive tasks with decisive objective to destroy the German panzer grouping.

However, with the start of the German attack at Surikovye Vyselki and information received by the headquarters of Operational Group Chibisov about a breakthrough by the German tanks to the road running through the hills at Hill +3.0 (which in connection with this opened the possibilities of a rapid exploitation both to the northwest and to the southeast), the prior plans for the decisive destruction of an overextended, but *stopped* enemy immediately collapsed. The enemy clearly hadn't been stopped, and still holding the initiative, was again making the operational group's forces dance to his tune.

Having learned of the German breakthrough on the morning of 26 July, Chibisov made the decision to reject the risky option of a maneuvering battle, the twist and turns of which plainly neither he nor his headquarters would be able to follow with communications in that situation and position. Instead of offensive orders, he gave the tank corps much less risky defensive tasks (Chibisov, it is possible, also doubted whether the acting commander Burdov could confidently handle the corps in the complex operational situation of a meeting battle in the absence of the 2nd Tank Corps' commander and commissar, who had disappeared somewhere).

Thus, just as with the 11th Tank Corps, the 2nd Tank Corps received an order to assume a defensive posture. Its initial task on the line extending from Point +3.0 to the ravine 1 kilometer south of Dolgoe was "to check the advance of enemy tanks" and only then launch a counterattack with the aim of "destroying the tanks, artillery and infantry that have broken through".[27] West of the line designated by Chibisov, the 119th Rifle Brigade was to connect with the 2nd Tank Corps' right flank, while elements of the 3rd Destroyer Brigade that had fallen back out of Lebiazh'e were to connect with its left flank.[28] Together with the 3rd Destroyer Brigade, battalions of the 1142nd Rifle Regiment and the 340th Rifle Division's training battalion were digging in on the hills.[29] In front of them, on the general line Kamenka, Hill 217.8, Hill 208.8, the regiments of the 237th Rifle Division (or more accurately, what remained of them and had been able to be gathered over the last two days) were to be occupying a defense.[30]

Thus, on the morning of 26 July, the operational group command on the basis of reports it had received from the troops was busy not with a crushing counterblow, but with the organization of a multi-layered defensive line. In order to form this impenetrable line, the operational group command used practically all of its available forces, including two of the three tank corps located in the area. The commander of the 340th Rifle Division gave orders for this defense to his

26 TsAMO, F. 38 A (445), op. 9005, d. 35, l. 93.
27 TsAMO, F. 38 A (445), op. 9005, d. 35, l. 92.
28 TsAMO, F. 38 A (445), op. 9005, d. 35, l. 82.
29 TsAMO, F. 340 sd, op. 1, d. 91, l. 484. On this day the 340th Rifle Division's training battalion remained without its field kitchen or food reserves. As was written in reports, "As a consequence of a heavy bombing, the training battalion's food stockpile, which was situated in Murav'evka was destroyed. Twelve horses were killed, the kitchen smashed, and workers at the food stockpile were injured and killed." (TsAmO, F. 340 sd, op. 1, d. 91, l. 466.)
30 TsAMO, F. 237 sd, op. 1, d. 7, l. 11.

operationally subordinate 118th and 201st Tank Brigades (true, he so far hadn't been able to find the brigades anywhere).[31]

Late on the morning of 26 July, the multi-layered line of defense was occupied by the operational group's rifle, tank and artillery units, ready to battle the enemy tanks that had broken through. However, they weren't appearing … Hours passed, but the enemy wasn't approaching the line. Only that morning and later in the hazy heat of the day, the unsubsiding cannonade of a distant battle carried over the fields and patches of woods from somewhere much further to the south.

By noon the remaining tanks and the motorized rifle battalion of the 1st Guards Tank Brigade finally arrived and joined up with Major Boiko's 2nd Tank Battalion. They took up a line of defense along the upper reaches of the ravines west of Kreshchenka. Under their protection, the 1st Motorized Rifle Brigade arrived on the brigade's right flank and began to dig in. Next, the first elements of the 49th Tank Brigade began to arrive on the 1st Guards Tank Brigade's left flank. Three brigades of the 1st Tank Corps were urgently creating a new line of defensive front west and southwest of Posel'skoe and Kamenka, blocking the enemy's path to the east. (In the 1st Tank Corps' intelligence summary this episode was described as follows: "At 1300 22 enemy medium tanks emerged at Hill +3.0 out of Surikovo. With the fire of anti-tank artillery and tanks, the enemy was thrown back to its jumping-off position, leaving behind two burning tanks."[32])

However, the enemy wasn't attacking to the east. Having seized Hill +3.0, the German tanks turned to the southeast and began to fight their way along the road in the direction of Hill 187.4, overrunning and shooting up any nests of resistance they found in their path. This advance wasn't swift. The units that had wound up on the enemy's path (obviously, the 167th Rifle Division and a portion of the 118th Tank Brigade) were putting up stubborn resistance to the Germans. However, the German tanks and panzer grenadiers with increasing frequency veering from the road in order to outflank and crush the defensive positions in their path, penetrated along the 5-kilometer corridor of ground between the Bystrik Creek and the Nega River and by mid-day seized Hill 187.4, winding up just 5-7 kilometers from the front of the 387th Infantry Division along the Bol'shaia Vereika River. Only a narrow corridor to the east remained open of the "pocket" being drawn closed around Lebiazh'e by the enemy …

The enemy grouping's pivot and its emergence in the rear of the operational group's units that still remained in the Lebiazh'e – Bol'shaia Vereika area had the most pernicious consequences for the latter and to a significant degree determined the entire course of subsequent events. In the alarming and murky situation, given the shortage or even complete absence of reliable information, the disruption of communications, the rumors, the command that had gone missing somewhere, and the plainly increasing sounds of battle behind them, the ominous word "encirclement" began to be heard all around within the forming pocket.

Alongside the regular, impudent and almost totally unpunished aerial attacks by German bombers, this threat of encirclement, if you will, became the reason why our units, which hadn't even received the initial attack by the German tanks, wavered and began to retreat. This was happening both to the north and to the south of the area of the initial breakthrough by the enemy at Surikovye Vyselki, when even ordinary soldiers recognized that the "situation was bad", and this knowledge was goading the already retreating elements, even forcing those of them that hadn't yet received an official order to retreat to abandon their positions.

As a result, the Surikovo – Bol'shaia Vereika – Don River line that had been designated by Chibisov for a rigid defense began increasingly to break down and fall apart in the current of the

31 TsAMO, F. 38 A (445), op. 9005, d. 19, l. 80.
32 TsAMO, F. 1 TK, op. 1, d. 235, l. 70.

massed retreat that had started. It is extremely difficult to say where, when and what units engaged in combat operations on that line on that day, and at times even impossible, because the information in their documents is so vague, inarticulate and fragmentary. Their general characteristic is the finger-pointing at neighbors and the mention that "the units occupied a new line" on that day, but how the combat actions actually went remains unclear. The command of the 167th Rifle Division, for example, laid out its view of events as follows:

> [...] from the direction of Lomovo the enemy hurled up to 40 tanks and up to a battalion of submachine gunners [sic] toward Bol'shaia Vereika, having the likely objective to isolate the 465th and 520th Rifle Regiments. The location of the neighbor on the right [the 1142nd Rifle Regiment, the 340th Rifle Division's training battalion, and the 118th Tank Brigade – I.S.] was unknown, while the neighbor on the left [the 104th Rifle Brigade] was retreating toward Kreshchenka. The division command decided to withdraw the 615th and 520th Rifle Regiments to the Kreshchenka area and to go over to a defense on the Kreshchenka – Pribytkovo line.[33]

Yet here is how the command of the 167th Rifle Division's left-hand neighbor, the 104th Rifle Brigade, explained its retreat: "Units of the 104th Rifle Brigade, pursuant to an order from the army headquarters following the retreat of its neighbor on the right [the 167th Rifle Division] initiated a fighting withdrawal at 1300 26 July to the high ground south of Fomina-Negachevka."[34] From the 167th Rifle Division's report it happens that the 104th Rifle Brigade was the first to begin to retreat, but from the 104th Rifle Brigade's report it turns out that everything was on the contrary. At the same time, in its account the command of the 167th Rifle Division fails to say a single word about the banning of a withdrawal without the authorization of the Military Council, as if there had never been such an edict, while the 104th Rifle Brigade speaks of an order from the army headquarters (for a retreat), although judging from the final report of Operational Group Chibisov's headquarters, Chibisov never issued such an order.

The account written later by the operational group's headquarters allows a certain understanding of the overall course of events on that day, in which what happened is described as follows (the original style of the report has been preserved):

> [...] enemy tanks, reinforced with infantry, began to spread to the east, operating against the rear areas of the 340th, 193rd and 167th Rifle Divisions.
>
> The 340th Rifle Division, situated under the threat of encirclement, received an order to retreat, and without notifying its left-hand neighbor, began to withdraw, but with swift actions against the rear areas that put up almost no resistance, the enemy was given the possibility to take Surikovo and Surikovye Vyselki, thereby cutting off the path of retreat for the two regiments of the 340th Rifle Division that still hadn't been withdrawn and for the entire 193rd and 167th Rifle Divisions.
>
> The 167th Rifle Division and the 104th Rifle Brigade, having discovered the emerging threat of encirclement, conducted an immediate retreat to the second line of defense without the Military Council's authorization for this.[35] The retreat of the 167th Rifle Division and

33 TsAMO, F. 202, op. 5, d. 251, l. 15.

34 TsAMO, F. 202, op. 5, d. 251, l. 14.

35 As concerns the 167th Rifle Division, it is fully possible that in the division's headquarters, they still weren't aware at that moment of Chibisov's order from the evening before about a rigid defense of the Surikovo – Bol'shaia Vereika line and the banning of a withdrawal to the second line of defense without the Military Council of Operational Group Chibisov's authorization for this. An explanation contained within a coded

> 104th Rifle Brigade to the second line without the permission of the Military Council exposed the left flank of the 193rd Rifle Division, which gave rise to the possibility of the complete encirclement of the entire 193rd Rifle Division and the two regiments of the 340th Rifle Division ....[36]

It is worth noting that the more mobile brigades of the 1st Tank Corps were the first to withdraw from the closing pocket; judging from the documents, they were not involved in heavy fighting when coming out, but hurried to occupy the new line indicated for them. Of course, they were following an order that they had received from Katukov, but their withdrawal from their occupied positions and retreat to the east, which was left unexplained to the infantrymen, didn't at all inspire the rifle units that had been abandoned by them or fortify their combat spirits. In the eyes of the infantry left behind, the tankers had simply abandoned them and retreated from the battlefield ... Moreover, the total ignorance of the actions and orders of neighbors was not only at the level of the non-commissioned officers and enlisted men, but also among the command staff, including the unit commanders and their headquarters. The discordance in the command and control, the disruption in communications and the completely inadequate exchange of information affected Operational Group Chibisov's organization and course of the battle in the most negative manner.

Complaints about the inadequate or complete absence of operational orientation coming from the operational group's headquarters were heard in the statements of many commanders, but Katukov wrote to Chibisov about this most openly of all:

> I request your order to the operational group's headquarters in order to keep me more completely informed in an operational respect about the group's front, since the disposition of units and the enemy's actions in other sectors are completely unknown to me. All the information about our [neighboring] units and the enemy on the front Ozerki – Surikovye Vyselki – Bol'shaia Vereika – Nizhniaia Vereika I am receiving only with the assistance of my own scouts. [...] I ask that you take measures to establish more reliable communications with me.[37]

What could Chibisov say in response to this? That Katukov himself was without sin – a general who for most of the past two days had been keeping the headquarters of Operational Group Chibisov ignorant of his own actions?[38] That thus far on 26 July as well it had received nothing from him, and thus with no information even on the whereabouts of the 1st Tank Corps, the operational group's discouraged chief of staff had requested from Katukov, "Radio your location." We won't even guess.

However, the truth is that judging by the decisions, messages and orders of Operational Group Chibisov's commander, he didn't have the necessarily complete operational information either. The operational group's headquarters was experiencing increasing difficulties in gathering information for analysis, and the more complicated the situation at the front became, the greater problems it was having. Wire communications with a lot of the units had been severed. With radio communications, security matters often created complications and delays with the rapid coding and timely

telegram from the operational group's chief of staff from 2245 on 25.7.42 that was received in the division speaks to this. According to the document, it arrived in the division only ... at 1700 on 28.7.42 and was decoded within an hour. Accordingly, the headquarters of the 167th Rifle Division was unable to give a timely confirmation of the receipt of this coded telegram or, moreover, report on its implementation.

36 TsAMO, F. 202, op. 5, d. 258, l. 8.

37 TsAMO, F. 38 A (445), op. 9005, d. 35, l. 92.

38 TsAMO, F. 202, op. 5, d. 334, l. 68.

de-coding of the sent radio messages, while communications sent on paper with liaison officers arrived slowly due to the changing situation, not to mention that with the enemy breakthrough it had become even more difficult to send liaison officers, if not to say dangerous.

Chibisov didn't have his own reconnaissance aircraft. In order to receive some information from aerial reconnaissance, he had to appeal to Briansk Front's headquarters, which in the best case substantially delayed the receipt of the necessary operational information, and in the worst case didn't yield any at all (in the Front's headquarters, they might have a differing opinion about the priority of one or the other tasks for the reconnaissance aircraft, and might not at all consider requests from Operational Group Chibisov a matter of primary importance).

The lack of discipline in the headquarters of the subordinate units regarding the regular and timely delivery of reports and operational summaries became a headache for the operational group's command, which inevitably had an effect on the completeness and timeliness of its own summaries. To all of this was added the problem of the *reliability* of the reports received from below, which could not but affect the objectivity of the assessments of the operational group's command and the soundness of its own decisions.

On 24 and 25 July this problem became even more apparent, and reached its peak, arguably, by 26 July. Paradoxically, the more enemy tanks and manpower that the units reported destroying, the more there appeared on the battlefield on the next day. It was totally difficult to grasp what was happening in the vicinity of Surikovye Vyselki, and with how much force the enemy was attacking there. According to the arriving messages, the number of German tanks attacking the village was growing to simply frightening proportions![39]

From prisoners taken on the previous day it became clear that on the front of the operational group, the German 9th Panzer Division was attacking, having up to 80 operational tanks. In the prisoners' words (plainly translated with a mistake), it turned out that the 11th Panzer Division was operating there as well (in reality, the 11th Panzer Grenadier Regiment of the same 9th Panzer Division). However, already on the following day from Katukov's messages it followed that a Hungarian panzer division was also engaged in the battle, and it had up to 230 operational tanks![40]

Of course, Chibisov and his staff had certain justifications to assume that the real number of enemy tanks, possibly, was smaller, and that the information coming from the attacked units, probably, was exaggerated; but by how much? How many times over? To these questions, no one in the operational group's headquarters could give a precise answer. There remained only to give the subordinates an angry prod and constantly demand timely and correct summaries and intelligence from them. However, they were increasingly silent about what had been lost and instead reporting something vague and/or of secondary importance … It isn't surprising that on the morning of 26 July, the operational group's headquarters that had moved from Lukino to Bol'shaia Poliana began to experience an acute deficit of reliable reports on the course of the fighting and the situation at the front.

Arguably, it was precisely in these alarming hours, when there simply wasn't enough necessary information for decisive actions and orders, that Chibisov, in order to keep his hand "on the pulse" and give a proper jolt to his subordinate commanders, sent a coded message to his subordinates, which had no direct relationship to directing the course of the battle, but sharply reminded the commands of the units (in the conditions of the initiated retreat) of the responsibilities that rested upon them:

39 TsAMO, F. 11 TK, op. 1, d. 11, l. 88.
40 TsAMO, F. 38 A (445), op. 9005, d. 35, l. 94.

I am demanding from all the commanders of formations and units:

1. The preservation and collection of materiel and weapons.
2. The daily delivery of reports on the availability and expenditure of ammunition by 2400 and immediate reports on the loss and disablement of all types of weapons.
3. The turning in of all fired shell casings and canisters. I am warning in advance that ammunition will not be supplied without information on the expenditure of ammunition and the turning in of all fired shell casings.[41]

It is surprising at times to read the wartime documents. *Without the turning in of all fired shell casings, ammunition will not be supplied …* Well, it would still be understandable to demand this, if the troops were settled on a front that hadn't moved in some time, were engaged in positional battles and due to the turpitude or oversight of the commanders weren't turning in tons and tons of fired shell casings for smelting. However, in the circumstances of maneuvering combat actions, given the initiated retreat and the threat of encirclement?

Incidentally, if in fact the headquarters of the 167th, 193rd and 340th Rifle Divisions ever in fact received this coded message, it was plainly too late. The rifle units that were retreating into the valley of the Bol'shaia Vereika River were plainly not up to collecting the piles of shell casings that were lying about everywhere. They had completely different concerns …

Everywhere, the troops were on the retreat, abandoning their positions. After 1300, "from a ravine 3 kilometers northeast of Kreshchenka", the commander of the 1st Tank Corps appealed in a personal message to Rokossovsky, the Commander-in-Chief of the Briansk Front:

> According to information from my scouts, in Murav'evka and Dolgoe units of the 2nd Tank Corps, the 340th Rifle Division and the 193rd Rifle Division are retreating in disorder to Dmitriashevka. I've given an order to all brigades and to my headquarters to detain [the retreating men] and rally the troops on the line of their defense. I will lead everyone who was running toward Dmitriashevka into ravines and woods in the vicinity of Sedelki for their assembly; restore order; and I will report about this to Chibisov. […] The enemy is not so strong, whereas the infantry of the named divisions is behaving disgracefully and fleeing in panic. […] The headquarters of the operational group is keeping poor contact with me. The radio messages are not being received for some reason, and I'm compelled to send [liaison officers] in vehicles, which wastes time, and the situation is changing. I am not receiving operational information, which makes it hard for me to take correct decisions. […]
>
> Just in case, with the engineering battalion we're building a 60-ton bridge across the Don in Dmitriashevka and I'm simultaneously preparing it for demolition. The bridge will be ready tomorrow. I request that you give it air cover, because the enemy is always bombing a ferry that is conveying one single wagon. I will hold the front, and if my neighbors let me down and run away, I've decided to defend the Derezovka, Kreshchenka bridgehead with a front to the west, having the Don River at my back. I consider it necessary for the further operation to rally the rifle divisions and occupy my front with them, while keeping the corps as a shock group somewhere in the Dmitriashevka area and at this time repair equipment, primarily the tanks; I can't say anything more, because I don't know the situation, the plans, or the forces available to Group Chibisov and yourself.[42]

41 TsAMO, F. 202, op. 5, d. 258, l. 78.
42 TsAMO, F. 202, op. 5, d. 238, ll. 453-454.

Then, already from his new command post in Dmitriashevka, Katukov wrote a message to the headquarters of Operational Group Chibisov as well: "In the area of Dmitriashevka [which is to say, on the banks of the Don River itself – I.S.], a large number of disorganized rifle and artillery units and elements have gathered, which have retreated from the defensive lines. A group of commanders have been sent to this area in order to restore order and I will collect all of these arriving and retreating elements and will assemble them in the area of the woods 2 kilometers southwest of Verkhniaia Kolybel'ka. I request that you send your representative to these areas in order to find out the reasons for the retreat and to issue orders to these elements."[43]

There, in Dmitriashevka, Kutukov found the leaderless 124th Howitzer Artillery Regiment that had abandoned its firing positions that morning and had already covered the 10-12 kilometers to the Don River and was fully capable of beginning a crossing to its eastern bank. Still retaining his presence of mind, on the spot Katukov took decisive command of the howitzer regiment and placed it in firing positions in the ravines west of Dmitriashevka. Then, having learned that the regiment was really supposed to be supporting the 167th Rifle Division, Katukov "returned it to the direction of the 167th Rifle Division's commander."[44] (Possibly, if Katukov hadn't in the heat of the moment taken immediate control of the 124th Howitzer Artillery Regiment, the commander of the 167th Rifle Division might have subsequently found it on the eastern bank of the Don River.) The problem was, however, that Katukov didn't have contact with the 167th Rifle Division, just as he didn't with any of its neighbors, and he didn't know where it was located or what orders it was following.[45]

If to the east of the line of the Nega River, it was Katukov's problem, as the senior commander on the spot, to stop the disorganized retreat of the rifle units and return them to the line of defense that had been designated by Chibisov, then in the area of Lebiazh'e and Malaia and Bol'shaia Vereika, the troops would soon have nowhere to retreat. German tanks and panzer grenadiers had taken Hill 191.3, the final commanding height over the Bol'shaia Vereika area and were now blocking a retreat from the village to the east, and had then cut the final paths that led out of the pocket.

Quickly after this, the panzer group conducted a final dash to the southeast and reached the bank of the Bol'shaia Vereika River from the north, where it linked up at Skliaevo-3 with the triumphant German infantry that had already arrived there. The "cauldron" at Lebiazh'e was closed. Attempts to exit it were now met everywhere with fire from the commanding heights between the Nega River and the Bystrik Creek.

Of the three rifle divisions that wound up that morning in the valley of the Bol'shaia Vereika River, only the 167th Rifle Division, which was located further to the east than the others, managed to escape largely intact from the closing pocket (at the very least, a portion of its 520th Rifle Regiment wasn't able to get out before the pocket closed) and by 1700 it had taken up a more or less organized defense on the line of the western approaches to Pribytkovo and Kreshchenka.[46] The 193rd Rifle Division and two regiments of the 340th Rifle Division (the division's 1142nd Rifle Regiment and the engineer and training battalions already by 24 July had been engaged in fighting separate from the rest of its regiments) didn't manage to escape and wound up encircled in the Malaia Vereika – Lebiazh'e area.

True, their tribulations had already begun even before the final closing of the pocket, since the enemy already that morning had reached the hills both north and south of Lebiazh'e, squeezing

43 TsAMO, F. 38 A (445), op. 9005, d. 35, l. 92.
44 Ibid.
45 Ibid.
46 TsAMO, F. 202, op. 5, d. 251, l. 7.

the encircled troops like two fiery jaws of a vice. However, if the two experienced regiments of the 340th Rifle Division didn't waver under the enemy pressure and kept their combat capabilities, for the 193rd Rifle Division the encirclement had catastrophic consequences. Demoralized by the setbacks, heavy casualties, and the loss of command and control, the division's units were literally huddled together in Lebiazh'e and Malaia Vereika, winding up in a low land under a cross fire from the hills overlooking the valley of the Bol'shaia Vereika River.

Fearing a panicked flight and striving at least somehow to organize the retreat of his units, the 193rd Rifle Division's commander General Smekhotvorov blocked the path of the retreating tanks of the 49th Tank Brigade's 239th Tank Battalion (at Katukov's order, the 1st Motorized Rifle Brigade's 445th Motorized Rifle Battalion had also been attached to the 49th Tank Brigade[47]), which had been covering the rest of the tank brigade's withdrawal from combat and had the task of following behind its main forces to the Kreshchenka area. Threatening him with a weapon, Smekhotvorov began to shout that he would shoot the tank battalion commander if he continued to retreat and abandoned the infantry.[48] The tankers stopped in confusion. No references to the order they had received to exit the battle had any effect on the division commander, who was losing his composure. He announced that under his authority he was canceling all the orders they had received and was ordering them to cover the retreat of his division!

Thus, threatening to open fire, Smekhotvorov forced the tank battalion commander to stop all of nine of his tanks and the remnants of the motorized rifle battalion in order to cover his division's withdrawal.[49] In addition, just in case Smekhotvorov covered all his bases to prevent the tankers from retreating; as the documents testify, "by force of arms he took all the personal documents, including the Party membership card" from the tank battalion's assistant chief of staff for intelligence Captain Zemsky.[50] One can only guess in what tones of voice the discussion between the commanders went on that July morning – and all in the presence of the tank crews and in front of the eyes of dozens of soldiers.

Thus Katukov's tankers, not having any communication with its own command and now disobeying his order, unwillingly entered their final battle. This battle, however, had already been lost before it even started. The 193rd Rifle Division quickly disintegrated into a large crowd of milling men. A large quantity of the division's weapons, transport and gear was abandoned.

Meanwhile, having clear observation of Lebiazh'e and Malaia Vereika from the hills on both the left and right bank of the river valley, the enemy concentrated fire on the final pockets of resistance and began quickly to bring up anti-tank means to destroy the tanks of the 253rd Tank Battalion. Deprived of mobility and freedom of maneuver, they became relatively easy prizes for the enemy's anti-tank artillery. One after another, the remaining tanks of the 253rd Tank Battalion were knocked out and set ablaze. The majority of the tank crews were killed, and only a small portion of the surviving tankers began to make their way along the river's channel through the bankside bushes and vegetation toward the village of Bol'shaia Vereika in the hope of reaching friendly lines.[51] The fate of the 1st Motorized Rifle Brigade's 445th Motorized Rifle Battalion, which had been attached to the 49th Tank Brigade, also proved tragic. The headquarters of this rifle brigade reported: "As a result of the 49th Tank Brigade's retreat and the exclusive commitment of only the 445th Motorized Rifle Battalion's forces and means into the fighting, the 445th Motorized Rifle

47 TsAMO, F. 19 mbr, op. 1, d. 6, l. 152.
48 TsAMO, F. 202, op. 36, d. 132, l. 51.
49 Ibid.
50 Ibid.
51 Ibid. Also see the 1st Tank Corps' account of the conducted operation: TsAMO, F. 1 TK, op. 1, d. 4, ll. 8-16.

Battalion was completely destroyed – both men and the materiel. Only isolated survivors made their way out of the pocket."[52]

The plight of the encircled units was deteriorating by the hour. Their supply line had been cut, ammunition was running low, and there was no way to evacuate the wounded men to the rear.

At this time in the headquarters of Operational Group Chibisov, which in Bol'shaia Poliana was rather distant from the combat area, they were anxiously awaiting word about the course of the fighting. Somewhere in the afternoon, presumably between 1300 and 1500, it became known to Chibisov that after the German panzer grouping's breakthrough at Surikovye Vyselki, it didn't turn to the north or continue on to the east, where in accordance with his morning orders the 2nd, 11th and most likely the 1st Tank Corps (Chibisov still didn't know this) were occupying blocking positions, but had instead operated with its main forces to the southeast. Subsequent messages that the enemy had reached Hills 187.4 and 191.3 and had enveloped the entire Bol'shaia Vereika area spoke to the fact that the enemy, most likely, had no intentions (at least to this point) to develop the offensive to the north and attempt to breach the defensive line of the operational group's units in the Murav'evka, Dolgoe, Kamenka area. Likely, the enemy's main task was "only" to parry the operational group's offensive and encircle its vulnerable units across the Bol'shaia Vereika River.

In connection with this, it was becoming increasingly clear that the hastily created and occupied defensive line that included the tank corps was dooming them to inactivity, while the German tanks were chopping up the columns of the rifle units that were retreating from Lebiazh'e; smashing them, expressing it figuratively, having turned their backs to the 2nd and 11th Tank Corps that continued to stand immobile. Judging from his following orders, Chibisov reached this conclusion, or one very similar to it, on the afternoon of 26 July.

Finally having put together a more or less complete mosaic of what was happening from the arriving information and having discovered that the German pocket around the 193rd and 340th Rifle Divisions was about to snap shut, Chibisov decided that his morning defensive plan of battle no longer suited the current situation and that not only the 7th Tank Corps should be given offensive tasks, but also the other tank corps. With their joint attack they should be able to smash the overextended enemy from the rear, thereby freeing the rifle divisions that were trapped against the Bol'shaia Vereika River. In essence, Chibisov returned to his offensive plan of the day before.

Chibisov decided to remove the 2nd Tank Corps from the defensive line and throw it into battle with the task to strike the enemy in the rear, thereby assisting the 7th Tank Corps' attack, which according to messages from the corps commander was making little progress. In accordance with this order, the operational group's chief of staff sent an urgent combat directive to the 2nd Tank Corps: "The army commander has ordered upon receipt to execute an immediate attack against the enemy along the road from Kamenka to Hill 187.4 and Hill 191.3 with the task to destroy the enemy in this area. I am warning on the need for the immediate execution of this order."[53]

Precious time was passing. Both Chibisov and his headquarters staff knew full well that with each passing hour, the situation of the encircled and unsupplied units was becoming worse. Meanwhile it became clear that the 2nd Tank Corps couldn't set out on the attack right away (obviously, the corps command had requested at least some time to prepare for the attack and to give the subordinate commanders their orders). With a heavy heart, one must think, Chibisov granted a postponement of the attack until 1600.[54]

Then, having given a concrete time for the start of the 2nd Tank Corps' attack to take Bol'shaia Vereika, Chibisov decided to oblige the commander of the 193rd Rifle Division General

52 TsAMO, F. 19 mbr, op. 1, d. 6, l. 152.
53 TsAMO, F. 202, op. 5, d. 258, l. 77.
54 TsAMO, F. 202, op. 5, d. 258, l. 83.

Smekhotvorov to take command over all the units in the Lebiazh'e – Bol'shaia Vereika area, and also to brief him on the actions of the 2nd and 7th Tank Corps. Through his chief of staff Colonel Pilipenko, Chibisov sent Smekhotvorov a combat order:

> Consolidate under your leadership the units of the 340th and 193rd Rifle Divisions that remain in the vicinity of Hill 181.8. Make contact with the 1st Tank Corps that is located in the wooded area south of Lebiazh'e. Take operational control of the 1st Tank Corps. With reconnaissance, establish the location of the 167th Rifle Division in the Malaia Vereika, Bol'shaia Vereika area, link up with it, and having unified all of these units under your leadership, break out with an attack toward Surikovo and reach the Pribytkovo, Otskochinskie Vyselki, Posel'skoe area.
>
> Keep in mind that at 1600 on 26 July, the 2nd Tank Corps will cover your breakout with an attack out of the Dolgoe area in the direction of Hill 187.4. Also have in mind that units of the 1st Tank Corps are breaking through from the area south of Lebiazh'e toward Bol'shaia Vereika. In order to organize and give assistance to you, as of 1100 units of the 7th Tank Corps were fighting in the area of Hill 212.9. Choose a place for the breakout and the method of the units' actions according to the situation. Report by code a brief plan and [your] ideas for the breakout. Radio [upon] receipt of this order.[55]

From this document it follows that Chibisov didn't know the exact locations of the units he mentioned and was proceeding from already dated information. The 1st Tank Corps, which according to his briefing was in the wooded area south of Lebiazh'e, had already withdrawn from there that morning, so Smekhotvorov was no longer able to take control of it or even find it. The same thing can be said about the 167th Rifle Division, which with the exception of its lagging units had already by that time with its main forces made its way out of the pocket to the east.

Pilipenko attempted to communicate the directive he had received to the 193rd Rifle Division by radio (wire communications with it had already been severed), but the divisional radios were off-line …

The hour of 1600 came and went – the H-hour for the 2nd Tank Corps' attack. In the headquarters of Operational Group Chibisov in Bol'shaia Poliana, they began to wait for reports. An hour passed without a word. A second hour went by. The 2nd Tank Corps' headquarters was silent. A third hour passed with no news. What was happening at that time in the hilly area east of Bol'shaia Vereika, 20 kilometers from the operational group's headquarters? Was the 2nd Tank Corps routing the enemy? Had it encountered bitter resistance? What lines had it reached and did it help the rifle divisions escape encirclement? In the discouragingly long wait for messages, no one in the operational group's headquarters knew …

Obviously, it was in these anxious hours of waiting that Chibisov, having lost all patience, ordered a wireless message to be sent to the 2nd Tank Corps with the demand to report immediately on the situation of the corps' units and the lines reached by them. At his order, the same message was sent (for the second time) to the headquarters of the 1st Tank Corps, which had been silent since the morning and had disappeared to some place unknown.[56]

At this time, Chibisov's hope – the 2nd Tank Corps – hadn't met any bitter resistance and hadn't smashed the enemy, because over all this time it was still sitting in its jumping-off area and hadn't advanced. Not in the least. Only at 2100, likely after receiving Chibisov's harsh wireless message,

55 TsAMO, F. 202, op. 5, d. 258, l. 83.
56 TsAMO, F. 202, op. 5, d. 258, l. 79.

did the 2nd Tank Corps finally move out.[57] However, the 2nd Tank Corps' new command didn't see any fault on its own part for the multi-hour delay.

Subsequently, putting the explanation for the delay down on paper, the 2nd Tank Corps' chief of staff Colonel Nagaibakov stated the following: "The delay in time occurred at the fault of the chief of artillery made responsible by army headquarters for supporting the tanks, who failed to show up. The corps command was forced to take up the organization of cooperation and to search for the commanders of the artillery units."[58] Nagaibakov didn't clarify which artillery commanders the corps command was seeking or whether any were found, or whether it could have gone on the offensive without the aforementioned, but more than four hours were lost which couldn't be replaced.

Irritated by the prolonged silence of the 2nd Tank Corps' headquarters and the complete uncertainty regarding how the attack was going, and unsettled by the absence of radio communications with the 193rd Rifle Division, Chibisov ordered a wireless message for the commander of the 193rd Rifle Division to be sent through the headquarters of the 340th Rifle Division, now plainly discounting any timely relief for the encircled units from the 2nd Tank Corps: "In view of the loss of contact with the 193rd Rifle Division, immediately inform the 1044th Rifle Regiment the following: 'Smekhotvorov is to combine the units of the 340th and 193rd Rifle Divisions under his command. With the fall of darkness, break out in the direction of the southern outskirts of Ozerki. Keep in mind that the Hill 212.9 area is held by units of the 7th Tank Corps, which has been notified. Reach Hill 212.9 by 0300 on 27 July."[59]

Chibisov left the 11th Tank Corps on the defensive and gave it no offensive tasks. It can't be known whether or not he regretted that a portion of its tanks were conducting a reconnaissance-in-force on a secondary axis, considering the despondent message from its chief of staff Kalinichenko that the tank corps lacked the strength *even for a defense*; this diversion of strength on a secondary axis did him precious little good here, on the decisive sector of the front. … Indeed, quite likely the Matilda tanks that were now 15 kilometers from the area of decisive fighting would have been handy now, when it was necessary to organize a counterattack as quickly as possible by the operational group's tank units and free the encircled units. Chibisov opted not to risk the 11th Tank Corps' remaining tanks (4 KV, 8 Mk. II, 47 T-60 and 3 T-34) and kept the 11th Tank Corps on the line it occupied, obviously supposing that he should have at least some sort of mobile reserve.

The following was written in the 59th Tank Brigade's journal of combat operations about the reconnaissance-in-force that was conducted that day:

> At 1630 on 25.7.42, an order was received about readying 5 Mk. II and 10 T-60, as well as one submachine gun platoon for actions as part of a reconnaissance-in-force toward Hill 218.7. On 26.7.42, the reinforced reconnaissance group consisting of 5 Mk. II, 10 T-60, 28 submachine gunners, 4 mortars and a reconnaissance platoon engaged in combat on Hill 218.7, but in view of the complete absence of support from the 21st Cavalry Division, in cooperation with which the group was supposed to act, the tanks retreated, having received an order to withdraw from the combat, in view of the brigade's redeployment to a different area. In the

57 On the following day the 2nd Tank Corps' chief of staff wrote in an operational summary that the corps' attack had begun at 1900, but the brigade documents unambiguously state that in fact this happened later. Thus, according to the 27th Tank Brigade's operational summary, the brigade only received the order for the attack at 1930, and set out at 2000 (TsAMO, F. 27 tbr, op. 1, d. 5, l. 211). The 148th Tank Brigade didn't receive the attack order from the corps' headquarters until 2000, and accordingly moved out on the attack even later (TsAMO, F. 2 TK, op. 1, d. 224 (b), l. 114).

58 TsAMO, F. 38 A (445), op. 9005, d. 35, l. 96.

59 TsAMO, F. 202, op. 5, d. 258, l. 90.

battle, 1 Mk. II and 1 T-60 were lost. The T-60 tank was evacuated from the battlefield, but the Mk. II was left on the battlefield in view of the absence of tracks. During an attempt to repair it, the crew was killed by enemy fire. Among the tankers, 9 were killed and 3 wounded. Among the infantry and reconnaissance scouts, 20 were wounded and 3 killed.[60]

If you will, the only combat episode on the front of the 11th Tank Corps took place when the tankers of one of the brigades saw unknown tanks completely dissimilar to the Soviet T-34, KV, T-70 or T-60 tanks approaching their camouflaged positions. The brigade hadn't been notified about any shifting of their own units; based on the briefings they'd received, they were expecting an enemy attack along that axis, and thus seeing how the foreign tanks were closing upon their positions, they decided the tanks were German and opened fire at them. However, it turned out that these weren't attacking Germans, but the 201st Tank Brigade's Matildas of British manufacture, which were falling back to the rear; in the heat of the moment, the tankers of the 11th Tank Corps took their "non-Soviet silhouettes" as German tanks ...[61]

How this incident ended is unknown; the documents of the 201st Tank Brigade are sparse and thus it is extremely difficult to assess the brigade's combat activities in this period. I'd like to believe that the incident went by without any casualties, but with "just" a deep fright for both sides and the subsequent ill-tempered verbal fusillade by the crews of the 201st Tank Brigade at the "knuckleheaded" (most likely, here they used a totally different adjective back then), "blind" neighbors, who fired at them without checking first to see whether or not they were friendly.

Actually, the absurdity of what happened is surprising, considering that the 11th Tank Corps' 59th and 160th Tank Brigades were both equipped with Lend-Lease Matildas, so the silhouette of these British tanks should have been well-known. It remains only to assume that for the tankers of the 11th Tank Corps, who hadn't received prior notification from command, and who were plainly anxious about the coming battle and already on edge, what was more important was not the silhouette of the tanks, but the fact that they were approaching from the enemy's direction.

By the evening of 25 July, there remained only seven operational tanks in the 118th Tank Brigade (3 T-34 and 4 T-70).[62] As a result of the fighting on 26 July, the brigade withdrew to the northeast and was in need of replenishment with personnel and equipment. As was the case with the 201st Tank Brigade, Chibisov didn't give the 118th Tank Brigade offensive tasks, leaving it subordinate to the commander of the 340th Rifle Division (Chibisov still didn't know that the division headquarters couldn't find one tank brigade or the other and didn't know where they were located.)[63] Meanwhile, the commander of the 340th Rifle Division on his part didn't realize that the 118th Tank Brigade had retreated together with the 167th Rifle Division, and its commander was at that division's command post.[64] In turn, the 167th Rifle Division's commander failed to inform the headquarters of Operational Group Chibisov about the whereabouts of the 118th Tank Brigade, plainly not aware that the 118th Tank Brigade had already been re-subordinated to a different division.

At 2100 in the evening, the 2nd Tank Corps consisting of approximately 60 tanks (of which approximately half were T-34 tanks, plus a few KV tanks) and the motorized riflemen of the 2nd Motorized Rifle Brigade[65], as well as those of the tank brigades' motorized rifle battalions, moved

60 TsAMO, F. 11 TK, op. 1, d. 19, l. 163.
61 TsAMO, F. 202, op. 50, d. 1, l. 282.
62 TsAMO, F. 202, op. 50, d. 14, l. 270.
63 TsAMO, F. 38 A (445), op. 9005, d. 19, l. 80.
64 TsAMO, F. 118 tbr, op. 1, d. 42, l. 30.
65 On this day the 2nd Motorized Rifle Brigade was once again replenished with personnel. The 448th Motorized Rifle Battalion received 204 men, the 450th Motorized Rifle Battalion – 325 men. Taking into account

out of the Murav'evka – Dolgoe area and began to advance in an armored fist along the dirt road that ran along the hills toward Bol'shaia Vereika. Having covered approximately 5 kilometers, the tank brigades became engaged with the enemy in the vicinity of the burial mound, Hill +3.0. However, no fierce tank clash, for which possibly the tankers had been readied, resulted. Upon the approach of the 2nd Tank Corps, the German tanks opened up a delaying fire, but refused combat and began to withdraw. The chief of staff of the 2nd Tank Corps later characterized the combat action that took place as follows: "The tank battle that played out on the burial mound +3.0 at 1930 was fleeting. The enemy's tanks and submachine gunners [sic] quickly retreated toward Surikovo from here and other places."[66] Nevertheless, without first looking into what had happened and plainly failing to double check the initial "hot off the press" reports arriving from the brigades, the headquarters of the 2nd Tank Corps hurried to inform the operational group about 40 burning German tanks east of Surikovye Vyselki.[67]

The 27th Tank Brigade's military commissar, plainly concerned more with questions of propaganda than matters of an operational nature, characterized the enemy's withdrawal in a customary political style: "With great wrath, the tankers rushed into the battle, but the German [side] refused to fight. Having caught the sound of our tanks, he retreated beyond Surikovo. This made our tankers angry, but also once again demonstrated the certainty of our victory."[68] The 27th Tank Brigade's chief of staff, plainly unconcerned with matters of political propaganda, didn't write about the "certainty of victory", and when putting together the next operational summary, was much more "dry" and concise: "At 2000 the brigade's tanks went on the attack. At 2015 they reached the line of [Hill] +3.0, where they wiped out several submachine gunners [sic]. Losses: 1 killed, three wounded. In formation: 14 T-34, 4 KV, and 14 T-60. At 2300 the tank battalions reached the burial mound +3.0, and pivoted to face Surikovo."[69] In the course of the evening battle, only 1 T-34 of the 27th Tank Brigade was knocked out … by fire from the 26th Tank Brigade.

In his turn, the chief of the 26th Tank Brigade's Political Department reported:

> When following the motorized rifle machine-gun battalion to Surikovo at night, in the Surikovo area, deployed tankers of the 148th Tank Brigade fired at our mechanized column from machine guns: Tank No. 206, the commander's family name I haven't been able to ascertain. There were no casualties only because Comrade Kurbatov, a department secretary with the Party bureau, made his way to the tank at a crawl, climbed up onto the hatch, and forced the crew to cease fire.[70]

One can imagine the words Kurbatov hurled at the tankers, who unexpectedly opened fire at our units that were approaching the front in the night. The fire was absurd and senseless, the obvious reason for which was the uncertainty and nervousness of the soldiers, whose eyes could play tricks on them …

Unfortunately, the absurdity of that night didn't end on this. Having reached Surikovo, a group of soldiers from the motorized rifle machine gun battalion headed by the commander of the 1st Company and leading the battalion's main forces, went on patrol. The soldiers cautiously picked their way through complete darkness, when suddenly fire was opened at them. The company

---

the preceding replenishments, the 2nd Motorized Rifle Brigade's strength in personnel began to approach its table strength. (TsAMO, F. 2TK, op. 1, d. 224(b), l. 111.)

66 TsAMO, F. 202, op. 50, d. 14, l. 306.

67 TsAMO, F. 11 TK, op. 1, d. 11, l. 88 (49).

68 TsAMO, F. 2 TK, op. 1, d. 224 (b), l. 97.

69 TsAMO, F. 27 tbr, op. 1, d. 5, l. 211.

70 TsAMO, F. 2 TK, op. 1, d. 224 (b), l. 120.

commander (who was obviously leading the patrol) was wounded, a confused exchange of fire erupted, but the soldiers kept their cool and opened return fire at the muzzle flashes in the night. With the fire of several rifles and submachine guns, the firing position was ultimately suppressed, the gunfire stopped, and everything became quiet. The soldiers cautiously approached the firing position they had riddled with fire and discovered that the man who'd been firing at them had been killed outright. The scouts searched his body and discovered the documents of a driver-mechanic of the 148th Tank Brigade, Petrovsky.[71] Why he had opened fire at the scouts of the motorized rifle – machine-gun battalion had to remain unanswered; it was impossible to question him now, and useless to swear at him …

Alas, in those dark, unsettling hours, when our units wound up close to the German front at night, the nerves of many soldiers were stretched to the limit. The nerves of some men simply snapped.

Having received reports from the brigades, the chief of staff of the 2nd Tank Corps in the middle of the night wrote a combat report to the headquarters of Operational Group Chibisov:

> The task was carried out by 2400. The corps' units approached Surikovo without meeting heavy resistance. … I request that you inform the headquarters of the 193rd Rifle Division about our arrival in the Surikovo area for joint actions. The village of Surikovo itself is occupied [by the enemy] and being held by anti-tank guns and submachine gunners. I've decided at 0500 on 27.7.42, after working it over with artillery fire, to take complete possession of Surikovo.[72]

Having signed the document together with the headquarters' military commissar Moskalev, Nagaibakov handed it to a liaison officer and sent him into the night to search out the location of the operational group's headquarters, obviously fully satisfied with himself and with the results that had been achieved by the 2nd Tank Corps. But for some reason in his report it remained unmentioned that the day's task had been to destroy the enemy in the area of Hill 187.4 and Hill 191.3 at Bol'shaia Vereika, and not at all to reach and stop at Hill +3.0 that was 5 kilometers to the northwest of the objectives, and at that only after a 4-hour delay.

Meanwhile, the shock group of the 7th Tank Corps since mid-day had remained in the area of Hill 212.9 and exchanged fire with the enemy. At 1330, a movement of German tanks was spotted in the brigades. Deciding that the enemy was going on the attack with a force of up to 40 tanks and accompanying infantry, one brigade opened fire from fixed positions at the enemy's aggregation. The tanks took cover in folds of the ground and in the brigades the men believed that they had repulsed a hostile attack. With this, the activity in front of the 7th Tank Corps' sector came to an end, and a positional exchange of fire continued. The many hours of idling in place found its reflection in the documents of the 3rd Guards Tank Brigade:

> Prior to 1240 the battalion [the 1st Tank Battalion – I.S.] was in the brigade commander's reserve. At 1300 the battalion commander was summoned to brigade headquarters. The situation: 15 enemy tanks and artillery were attacking toward Hill 217.8. The task: the battalion was to organize an ambush in a ravine on the southern outskirts of Kamenka and was to be ready to repel the enemy's armored counterattack. The battalion continued to remain in place,

71 Ibid.

72 TsAMO, F. 202, op. 50, d. 14, l. 306.

> having sent out a group of submachine gunners for observation. Until evening the enemy showed no activity.[73]

Also:

> Up until 1200, the tanks stood on the southeastern outskirts [of Kamenka – I.S.]. At 1200, an order to the battalion [arrived] to advance to the hill south of Kamenka. The tanks remained on the hill until 2100 and received no order.[74]

Further:

> The battalion [the motorized rifle battalion – I.S.] couldn't carry out the brigade commander's order to disengage from combat and assemble on the southern outskirts of Kamenka because the replacing units of the 7th Motorized Rifle Brigade didn't show up. At 0900 the battalion was continuing to hold a defense on the achieved lines, reconnoitering the [German] defenses with small groups. An anti-tank gun crew and a machine-gun crew were wiped out by a patrol. The anti-tank gun and machine gun were brought back to the battalion. At 0940 the enemy struck [the battalion] with an intense barrage from artillery and mortars, and under the cover of the fire went on the attack in small groups. We joined in an exchange of rifle and machine-gun fire with the attacking enemy infantry. Because of the absence of recognition signals, our air force strafed us. ... At 2100 the battalion is occupying its former position. ... Our tanks have moved out ahead by 200-300 meters and opened fire at enemy tanks, which are standing on Point 44.0; 3 enemy tanks are burning [yet the distance to the target could not have been less than 2 kilometers – I.S.]. Our losses are 6 wounded.[75]

Only in the afternoon (at approximately 1400[76]), plainly recognizing that there was no way a "half-steam" offensive with just one and a half brigades could lead to success, the commander of the 7th Tank Corps Rotmistrov decided to commit another tank battalion from the reserve 3rd Guards Tank Brigade. He formed an assault group out of a tank battalion of the 62nd Tank Brigade and the brigade's motorized rifle battalion, plus the 3rd Guard Tank Brigade's tank battalion mounting a company of tank riders, and gave it the order to attack the enemy in the direction of Hills 212.9 and 213.8, stopping short of the woods southeast of Hill 213.8 in order to comb through it with fire from fixed positions, before advancing on to the southern outskirts of Lomovo. There it was to place fire on the village before returning back to an assembly point on Hill 217.8.[77]

Long hours passed before this decision was implemented. The battalions carrying out the order operated independently. The group consisting of the 27th Tank Battalion and the motorized rifle battalion of the 62nd Tank Brigade launched the attack at 1800, while the 3rd Guards Tank Brigade's 1st Tank Battalion set out on the attack along the very same route at 1900. The confusing description of the operation in the brigade documents, if you will, was worthy of its sketchy plan.

We read in the 62nd Tank Brigade's report:

73 TsAMO, F. 3 gv. tbr., op. 1, d. 22, l. 20.
74 TsAMO, F. 3 gv. tbr., op. 1, d. 24, l. 24.
75 TsAMO, F. 3 gv tbr., op. 1, d. 25, l. 36.
76 TsAMO, F. 62 tbr., op. 1, d. 4, l. 10.
77 TsAMO, F. 3 gv tbr., op. 1, d. 22, l. 20.

> At 1800 the tanks [9 T-34 tanks[78] -- I.S] reached the woods southeast of Hill 213.8 at high speed, meeting no resistance. The tank riders dismounted in the woods, and taking advantage of a downpour, quickly covered the distance between the woods and Lomovo, and reached its outskirts. The enemy had no large forces in Lomovo. Up to a company of enemy submachine gunners [sic], offering no resistance, fled and quickly took cover behind a hill. We had 5 men killed and 15 wounded, plus 15 missing in action.[79]

Altogether in the fighting on 26 July, the 62nd Tank Brigade lost 3 T-34 tanks destroyed.[80]

The 1st Tank Battalion of the 3rd Guards Tank Brigade reported:

> We set out at 1900 to carry out the assignment. The battalion successfully advanced. [The combat journal of the 3rd Guards Tank Brigade states that "... the 1st Tank Battalion met fierce enemy resistance in the vicinity of the southern slopes of Hill 212.9 and in a balka northeast of Hill 213.8."[81] – I.S.] The enemy, covered by mortar and artillery fire, began to retreat to the south. By 2400 the battalion had passed Point 212.9 and reached Point 213.8, and at 0120 launched its final attack to sweep through the woods lying 1600 meters to the east. Sensing the threat of the emergence of our units on their flanks, the Germans were compelled to abandon Lomovo [alas, on this matter the men of the 3rd Guards Tank Brigade were mistaken – I.S.]. Having combed through the woods, the battalion began to pull back to the assembly point on the southeastern outskirts of Kamenka. The battalion assembled [there] at 0530 with 13 KV and 1 T-34.[82]

The losses of the 3rd Guards Tank Brigade amounted to 4 men killed and 3 wounded (according to other data, 9 wounded[83]); 4 tanks were damaged, but returned to the assembly point under their own power. With this, the foray came to an end.

What objective was Rotmistrov pursuing when giving the order for this operation, and what was he trying to accomplish? This isn't easy to understand. Perhaps he was counting upon the possibility that the Germans would abandon Lomovo, once they realized that Russian tanks had emerged in their rear, and then the entire German front here would collapse? However, he didn't send rifle units into the attack with the tanks, other than the numerically insignificant companies of the motorized rifle battalion. Accordingly, he had nothing with which to hold the expansive area south of Lomovo, even in the event of success.

Was he trying to destroy the opposing enemy in this fashion in accordance with the order he'd been given by Chibisov? It is difficult to count upon such a result, if he was trying to achieve it with such meager forces, which were directed to "comb through" an unscouted patch of woods with fire, and bring fire to bear on a dark village at night. It also isn't easy to see whether or not he was satisfied by the outcome of such a strange attack. I was unable to find in the documents any commentaries by the 7th Tank Corps' command staff on this matter.

From the intent of this raid and the absence of any mentions about the need to connect it with an attempt by the rifle divisions to break out of the pocket, it is possible to assume that Rotmistrov didn't give such a task to the battalions before the attack. Most likely, by 18-1900, he didn't know about Chibisov's decision to use the offensive by the 2nd and 7th Tank Corps to go to the relief of

78 TsAMO, F. 3 gv tbr., op. 1, d.10, l. 23.
79 TsAMO, F. 62 tbr., op. 1, d. 4, l. 10.
80 TsAMO, F. 62 tbr., op. 1, d. 19, l. 100.
81 TsAMO, 3 gv tbr., op. 1, d. 10, l. 23.
82 TsAMO, 3 gv tbr., op. 1, d. 22, l. 20.
83 TsAMO, F. 3 gv tbr., op. 1, d. 14, l. 24.

the 340th and 193rd Rifle Divisions. As a result, both battalions of the assault group after reaching Hill 213.8 didn't continue the attack to the south toward Lebiazh'e, but rather pivoted to the north toward Lomovo, thereby failing to establish any contact with the encircled rifle units.

Only late that night, when the tanks of the corps' assault group were wandering somewhere on the distant, dark hills, did the commander of the 3rd Guards Tank Brigade Colonel Vovchenko receive a briefing from the 7th Tank Corps' headquarters about the need to aid the operational group's encircled rifle units in Lebiazh'e in breaking out. However, now he had only a very few combat-ready machines at hand in order to carry out this new task. He instructed the commander of the motorized rifle battalion to bring out the encircled units. At 0140 in the morning, Colonel Vovchenko sent him an order: "The commander of the motorized rifle battalion is to send out 3 groups headed by mid-level commanders to the woods east of Hill 213.8, link up with Chibisov's units, which are presently surrounded, and bring them out behind the tanks back to our lines. Commence the implementation [of this order] immediately. It is possible that our rifle units will emerge out of Lebiazh'e in the direction of Hill 212.9 and the southern outskirts of Ozerki. Keep this in mind."[84]

It isn't possible to say precisely whether or not this order was carried out. However, the fact that the rather detailed combat journal of the 3rd Guards Tank Brigade's motorized rifle battalion doesn't say a word about the departure and nighttime searches of groups of scouts with the aim of freeing the encircled units, leads one to think that Vovchenko's order remained unfulfilled and was set on the back burner until morning.

Late in the evening, the first information about the encircled units in Lebiazh'e and Malaia Vereika appeared in a combat message from the isolated headquarters of the 340th Rifle Division:

> According to information received at 1720 from Lieutenant Liunenko, a liaison officer of the 193rd Rifle Division, the path to the 193rd Rifle Division has been cut off by enemy tanks, which moved out of Surikovye Vyselki with 30-40 tanks and out of the northern outskirts of Bol'shaia Vereika (Hill 173.7) with 30 tanks. Together with the 193rd Rifle Division are the 1140th and 1144th Rifle Regiments of the 340th Rifle Division, from which at 0300 the commander of the divisional headquarters set off to make contact with the regiments and returned to division headquarters at 1000, who confirmed the situation of the 1140th and 1144th Rifle Regiments and their actions together with the 193rd Rifle Division. We have no information that these regiments have received the ammunition and rations that were sent by us ...
>
> So far the 201st Tank Brigade and 118th Tank Brigade have not been detected in the given area for the defense. According to Kalganov's information [he was a representative from the Operations Department of Briansk Front's headquarters – I.S.] the 201st Tank Brigade has been assembled in Pokrovskoe and has become subordinate to a different formation. According to the just-received information from the Political Department's assistant chief for the Komsomol Political Instructor Gor'ky, who arrived from the 1140th Rifle Regiment at 0900 today, the information regarding the encirclement of the 193rd Rifle Division and the 1140th and 1143rd Rifle Regiments is confirmed.[85]

Just 7-9 kilometers were separating the encircled units from the 2nd and 7th Tank Corps that were attacking to the south. However, neither corps carried out the task to assist the rifle units in breaking out of the pocket, and both had stopped for the night without making an effort to

84 TsAMO, F. 3 gv tbr., op. 1, d. 14, l. 21.
85 TsAMO, F. 38 A, op. 9005, d. 19, l. 65.

link-up (except for the 7th Tank Corps' tank-riding detachment, which totally unaware of the fact had covered more than half of these kilometers, but had returned).

That same evening, or that night, a signals officer from the 193rd Rifle Division made his way out of the pocket. The officer was brought to the headquarters of the 167th Rifle Division, which at the time had fallen back to the second line, and he delivered a note that he had been carrying. This note, by chance, became the sole surviving document of the 193rd Rifle Division from those desperate days. Hastily written on a scrap of paper, it stated:

> To the 167th Rifle Division's artillery chief. Kreshchenka.
>
> We are located [in] Malaia Vereika with the 540th Rifle Regiment. There are no other units. Ammunition is running low. A vehicle was sent for ammunition – it hasn't returned. We have one [artillery] battery. All the remaining artillery has been cut off. We request possible assistance. A signals officer. The decision is to take up an all-round defense [of the] Malaia Vereika – Lebiazh'e [area] until nightfall. [Signed] 193rd Rifle Division's chief of artillery.[86]

86 TsAMO, F. 202, op. 5, d. 251, l. 7.

17

A review of the enemy's actions on 26 July

By the third day of fighting, chances are that the stress on the two attacking divisions of the VII Army Corps was becoming excessive. The complete absence of reserves and the plain lack of available forces were constantly telling on their actions, and not only slowed the carrying out of their assigned tasks, but also threatened to undermine the entire conceived operation. Appeals to higher command for help with fresh units led to paltry results or went totally unanswered: the VII Army Corps command also had no reserves.

On the night of 25-26 July, searching for some way out of the growing crisis, the corps commander ordered the commander of the 340th Infantry Division to take everything possible from his left flank, "disregarding all else"[1] and shift them to the right flank, so as to free up the "bogged down" units of the 9th Panzer Division there and strengthen the division's increasingly weak shock fist with them. In a final, desperate lunge and with their last remaining forces, on the counterattack's third day the divisions were finally to break the Russians' stubborn resistance on their final remaining line of defense and encircle their grouping that had broken through.

In the given circumstances, time was working against the Germans. The excessively protracted operation had to be concluded as quickly as possible, and to end successfully with the elimination of the enemy penetration. In the opposite event, there was the risk that the reserve divisions that had been assigned to conduct the counterblow would be bled dry in extended positional fighting, in which case the VII Army Corps would not receive any relief on its front. There could also be no talk of leaving the 9th Panzer Division postured in a lengthy positional defense. The Second Army was demanding its quickest withdrawal from combat back into its reserve. There was also no confidence that the 385th Infantry Division would remain subordinate to the VII Army Corps much longer, and thus 26 July had to become the decisive day of the entire operation.

The 385th Infantry Division initiated active operations on the night of 25-26 July. In the subsequent fighting, its 539th Infantry Regiment was able to seize Hill 181.8 and by morning it had advanced along the hills for another 800 meters, winding up on the northern approaches to the village of Lebiazh'e. Its 537th Infantry Regiment was still located on the southwestern approaches to Surikovo. It was designated for the 385th Infantry Division to resume its attack at 0500. The 9th Panzer Division was to go on the attack an hour later.[2]

Carrying out the order from the corps commander, the new commander of the 9th Panzer Division *Oberst* Hülsen issued his own order to the panzer division, in which the division's objective was formulated with extreme clarity: "the destruction of the enemy in the Bol'shaia Vereika area". Regrouping his division's forces yet again, the division commander formed an assault group under the command of the motorcycle battalion's commander, an experienced veteran of the

1 NARA, T-314, roll 353, fr. 000416.
2 NARA, T-314, roll 353, fr. 000417.

Eastern Front who was widely known in the division – *Oberstleutnant* Görn. The group consisted of the 33rd Panzer Regiment (minus one tank battalion), the 59th Kradschützen Battalion, II/11th Panzer Grenadier Regiment, the 5th Battery of the attached 71st Artillery Regiment, the II Battery of the 50th Panzerjäger Battalion and II/102nd Artillery Regiment. The three remaining panzer grenadier battalions and panzer battalion were covering the division's flank, which now extended for many kilometers. A group under the command of the commander of the 10th Panzer Grenadier Regiment *Oberst* Borawicz, which was positioned on the division's extreme left flank, was waiting for units of the 340th Infantry Division to come up to replace it.

The subsequent events were presented in the 9th Panzer Division's war diary in the following manner:

> The regrouping of the division's forces went without hitches, so the assault group was able to arrive in the area of deployment on time. At 0600 Görn's group went on the attack. Constantly accepting battle, the group kept pushing ahead, setting up tanks screens on Hills +3.0 and 187.0. *Oberstleutnant* Görn now and then made personal appearances at the most difficult sectors of his group and by his personal example inspired the men to rush forward on the attack. [The *kampfgruppe* commander's actions so impressed the 9th Panzer Division command, and were apparently so effective, that on the next day the headquarters of the 9th Panzer Division sent a report to the headquarters of the VII Army Corps about "the stellar actions of the Cavalier of the Knight's Cross *Oberstleutnant* Görn."[3] – I.S.]
>
> Despite the enemy's numerical superiority, our tanks successfully advanced and shoved back the enemy's tanks [we'll stress once again that the 1st Guards Tank Brigade that engaged in battle with the two battalions of the 33rd Panzer Regiment had no numerical superiority in tanks – I.S.]. In pace with the development of the offensive to the south, the division's right flank now became exposed, because the 537th Infantry Regiment of the 385th Infantry Division "became stuck" in the valley of the Bystrik Creek 3 kilometers to the northwest of Bol'shaia Vereika and was unable to develop its own offensive.
>
> When examining the division's position on the whole, it is impossible not to note certain concerns … Just as before, the covering flank in the north was now and again subjected to enemy tank attacks, which were striving to break through our positions and encircle the assault groups. Thanks to the support of dive bombers, the covering flank was able to withstand [these attacks] and thereby liquidated this threat.[4]

Entries in the account of the 385th Infantry Division supplement the report from the 9th Panzer Division headquarters:

> The regiments went on the attack: the 537th Infantry Regiment at 0500, the 539th Infantry Regiment – at 0600. The difficult situation of the 9th Panzer Division was demanding an advance by the 385th Infantry Division before the 9th Panzer Division could be able to resume the offensive. The enemy threw every available force he had against the 9th Panzer Division's offensive – the threatening encirclement of it became obvious.
>
> The 537th Infantry Regiment's attack, which was subjected to fire from both flanks, required much effort; nevertheless, owing to the desperate courage of all the commanders and elements, the objective was reached even before noon. After taking the hill west of Bol'shaia

3 NARA, T-315, roll 538, fr. 001388.
4 NARA, T-315, roll 541, fr. 001116.

> Vereika, the enemy's positions were bombarded by artillery and mortars. Only a narrow passage remained at his disposal, in order to withdraw his forces.[5]

Another entry states, "Meanwhile, enemy columns numbering up to one division were spotted retreating to the east. Because of the excessively wide planned envelopment, and also because of the enemy's significant numerical superiority, the offensive slowed, and the division was unable timely to close the 'pocket'.[6]

The fighting on the line of hills north of Bol'shaia Vereika became a genuine drama for the 9th Panzer Division. Stubbornly advancing, taking losses, and increasingly forced to leave behind new covering screens to the east as it advanced, the panzer division's assault group ultimately reached a point so close to its objective, that the tank crews and the infantry accompanying the tanks could observe the Soviet units retreating out of the pocket, but at the same time were no longer able to stop it, so weakened had they become.

The German command and the reconnaissance aircraft circling overhead time and again were reporting that the Russians were slipping out of the closing pocket, but exhausted and worn down by their efforts, the ground troops were already unable to do anything and halted almost within direct eyesight of the positions of the 387th Infantry Division, with which they were supposed to link up. Although they were struck repeatedly by artillery fire and German aircraft, in the process thousands of soldiers and commanders from various units of Operational Group Chibisov made their way out through the narrow corridor to the east that still remained open.

Only after that, out of all of its units that were extended along a bulge that stretched for many kilometers, was the 9th Panzer Division able to detach a single combat-capable element to make the final lunge to link up with the 387th Infantry Division, and thus completed "the encirclement" with the forces of just one (!) tank company (8-10 machines). The efforts of the 387th Infantry Division to meet it were similarly limited. On the entire 12-kilometer front from Bol'shaia Vereika to the Don River, the 387th Infantry Division was able to detach for the attack ... two infantry companies of the 543rd Infantry Regiment that had been defending along the Don River. Nevertheless, they were able to cross the Bol'shaia Vereika River and push to the north for several kilometers: one as far as Hill 191.3, where it met a company of the 9th Panzer Division; the other along the western bank of the Don River as far as the hills opposite the Gorozhanka settlement.[7]

Incidentally, such a significant accomplishment by two separate German companies on a front of 12 kilometers was unsurprising. Advancing, they were no longer encountering any resistance, because the 104th Rifle Brigade that had been defending the line of hills north of Bol'shaia Vereika River that morning, under the influence of the retreat initiated by other units of the operational group, had already managed to fall back to the southern approaches of Fomina-Negachevka, abandoning their positions without combat. Toward evening, a momentous event occurred on the front of the 387th Infantry Division: its headquarters reported to the VII Army Corps that its units everywhere had returned to that line of defense that they had been occupying prior to the start of the Russian offensive on 21 June.[8] Thus, the breach created by Briansk Front's operational group in the positions of the VII Army Corps, which had cost our troops so much effort and so many casualties, had been eliminated.

Simultaneously with their arrival in the previous positions north of the village of Bol'shaia Vereika, units of the 387th Infantry Division from the south, the 385th Infantry Division from

5 NARA, T-315, roll 2199, fr. 001360.
6 NARA, T-315, roll 541, fr. 001116.
7 NARA, T-314, roll 353, fr. 001348.
8 NARA, T-314, roll 353, fr. 001348.

the north, and Blocking Group "Meyer" from the west conducted a concentric offensive toward the villages in the river valley in order to reduce the pocket, covered by the 9th Panzer Division on the outer ring of encirclement. It is interesting to note that having been unable to trap the main Russian forces in the pocket and having seen them escape, the command of the 9th Panzer Division was apparently so irritated by this "failure" that it didn't even notice that units of the 193rd Rifle Division and 340th Rifle Division hadn't had time to escape from the Lebiazh'e – Malaia Vereika area. On the evening of 26 July, the 9th Panzer Division received an order to secure a cordon, behind which the infantry divisions would be able to occupy the new (in essence – old) defensive positions on the entire former front of the VII Army Corps and work to restore them (in essence – resurrect them).

Occupied by two reinforced panzer grenadier regiments, the 9th Panzer Division's covering line ran from Hill 191.3 along the crests of the hills as far as Surikovye Vyselki, then turned to the west and stretched as far as Hill 208.8, to the east of where the positions of the overextended 340th Infantry Division began. The 9th Panzer Division's panzer regiment, with the exception of one company, was withdrawn behind this covering line where it could serve as a unique, mobile anti-tank reserve, ready to move out quickly to any threatened sector. However, until late in the evening there were no attacks against the screening line, and the infantry divisions could begin mopping up the entire encircled area.

Toward the end of 26 July, the 9th Panzer Division received an order to pull back to a shorter "nighttime" screening line that ran along the line of Hill 191.3, Bol'shaia Vereika, the Bystrik Creek and Hill 199.8, with the aim of economizing on force and creating more compact combat positions.[9] The launching of the 2nd Tank Corps' belated attack, which was late by many hours, largely coincided with the planned withdrawal of the 9th Panzer Division, and that's why the fighting in the vicinity of burial mound +3.0 was so fleeting. Conducting only rear guard combat actions, the units of the 9th Panzer Division made an organized withdrawal to the shorter line of defense and disappeared into the nighttime that was settling over Surikovo and the valley of the Bystrik Creek. In the 2nd Tank Corps, many took this withdrawal as a flight by a panicked enemy (let's recall the 27th Tank Brigade's political report). Nevertheless, no pursuit of the "fleeing" Germans was organized, the 2nd Tank Corps stopped, and the 9th Panzer Division's new, shorter line of defense remained undisturbed (the nighttime sally conducted by the 7th Tank Corps' two brigades wasn't even noted in the 9th Panzer Division's documents).

The outcome of the combat operations for 26 July was reflected in the 9th Panzer Division's war diary as follows:

> The main forces of Görn's *kampfgruppe* is pivoting around and starting to mop up Bol'shaia Vereika. Up to 800 prisoners were taken, among which was one division commander. A large quantity of various types of weapons was seized: all this signifies a visible success.
>
> The withdrawal of the units from the former sector and their occupation of a new defensive line with the aforementioned arrangement of forces went according to plan. In the course of the night, units of the division took up the shortened line of defense that had been designated for them. In the abandoned area, all of the recovered and seized weapons were gathered or rendered unusable. The enemy tanks that made an attempt to pursue were stopped at Surikovo and forced to retreat ... One order from the corps that arrived in the evening notes the special merits of the division, which had to carry the main burden of the fighting and

9 NARA, T-315, roll 541, fr. 001117.

which managed to conduct an offensive in the most difficult conditions. The merits of the command staff and personnel are worthy of each other.[10]

In connection with the completed encirclement and the restoration of the previous front line, the VII Army Corps command disbanded Blocking Group "Meyer", the units of which returned to their divisions, while the 221st Pionier Battalion was re-subordinated to corps command. On this same day, obviously, in response to the prior requests (if not a prayer …) that arrived from the headquarters of VII Army Corps for reinforcements from out of the reserves, the Second Army command finally took a step to meet the requests and rather tardily and belatedly reinforced the corps … with one battalion. The battalion came from the neighboring XIII Army Corps (in the future the Second Army command would increasingly have to rob Peter to pay Paul in order to patch up the cobbled-together fronts of its subordinate corp).

In the evening report, the VII Army Corps command alarmingly informed superior headquarters about the heavy losses in the 385th Infantry Division. The combat strength of III/537th Infantry Regiment by the end of 26 July amounted to 130 men per company (what then was its starting strength? – I.S.), while II/539th Infantry Regiment had 25 men per company.[11] The losses of the VII Army Corps' divisions for 26 July amounted to:

385th Infantry Division: 14 killed, 82 wounded (including 1 officer)
340th Infantry Division: 41 killed, 120 wounded (including 5 officers) and 24 missing in action
387th Infantry Division: 32 killed, 14 wounded, 2 missing in action.[12]
9th Panzer Division: 13 killed, 66 wounded (including 3 officers) and 1 officer missing in action.[13]

Altogether, 100 killed, 282 wounded and 27 missing in action, for a total of 409 soldiers and officers.

By the end of the day, the number of operational tanks in the 9th Panzer Division had fallen by 11 in comparison with the evening of 24 July and amounted to 85 tanks (5 Pz-1, 17 Pz-II, 59 Pz-III [24 with the short barrel and 35 with the long barrel] and 4 Pz-IV [1 short-barreled and 3 long-barreled]), from which one can assume that in the course of the fighting on 25 and 26 July, 15-20 tanks might have been knocked out (the number of operational machines also depended on the work of the division's repair services, which returned a certain number of combat machines to service, thereby offsetting the losses. Tanks also became knocked out of action due to purely mechanical reasons, although the majority of them in those days were most likely combat losses.)[14]

10 Ibid.
11 NARA, T-314, roll 353, fr. 001348.
12 NARA, T-314, roll 354, fr. 726-727.
13 NARA, T-315, roll 541, fr. 001432.
14 NARA, T-315, roll 541, fr. 000736.

18

27 July 1942

At 0500, even before the completion of the valiant but ill-defined foray by the composite detachment of the 3rd Guards and 62nd Tank Brigades, which began with unclear objectives and ended with uncertain results, the commander of the 7th Tank Corps Rotmistrov issued an order for the tank corps to go over to the defense.[1] The 7th Motorized Rifle Brigade and the 62nd Tank Brigade took up positions along the southern outskirts of Perekopovka, Ozerki, the southern slopes of Hill 212.9, the fringe of woods to the northeast, and the eastern slopes of Hill 217.8. Rotmistrov withdrew the 3rd Guards Tank Brigade to Kamenka, into his reserve, and the heavy KV tanks left the front. With this, the 7th Tank Corps ceased active operations.

From the morning of 27 July, the 11th Tank Corps continued to hold the positions it had occupied the evening before and received no offensive tasks. The tank corps' tanks stood in readiness to meet an enemy attack, but the Germans didn't make an appearance. The rifle units standing alongside the corps' tanks (the collected remnants of the 237th Rifle Division with the 201st Tank Brigade, 119th Rifle Brigade, 1142nd Rifle Regiment, the 340th Rifle Division's training battalion and the 3rd Destroyer Brigade) were digging into the ground. A relative calm settled over the Lomovo sector of the front, disturbed only by an occasional exchange of fire.

In the area northeast of Bol'shaia Vereika, the 1st Tank Corps, 167th Rifle Division and 104th Rifle Brigade were also digging into their occupied line, bringing their elements that had retreated back into order, and were preparing to repel a German attack. But the enemy, which had suddenly ceased any activity, made no appearance here either. Only the Luftwaffe, as before, periodically arrived over the battlefield and time after time bombed the units of the operational group that had gone on the defense, although even its activity began gradually to reduce.

Of Operational Group Chibisov's four tank corps, only the 2nd Tank Corps undertook active operations on the morning of 27 July and launched an attack toward Surikovo. In so doing, the 2nd Motorized Rifle Brigade assumed the main burden of the attack, while the tank brigades supported it with fire from fixed positions (and at that, not in full strength; for example, the 27th Tank Brigade's motorized rifle battalion was located in Verkhniaia Kolybelka and took no part at all in the fighting between 25 and 27 July[2]). But under artillery barrages and Luftwaffe attacks, the 2nd Motorized Rifle Brigade's advance increasingly slowed, and came to a complete halt before reaching the outskirts of the village. The enemy on the Surikovo line, which had fallen back from the hills the day before almost without combat, began to offer bitter resistance, plainly speaking to the fact that the Germans had no intention to retreat any further. The battalions of the 2nd Motorized Rifle Brigade were pinned down on the outskirts of Surikovo and began to dig in.

The tank brigades remained behind, supporting the motorized infantry with fire from place, but under the pitiless fire of German anti-tank guns from camouflaged positions, made no advance. By 1400, of the three tank brigades only the 148th Tank Brigade consisting of 4 KV and 12 T-60

1 TsAMO, F. 62 tbr, op. 1, d. 4, l. 10.
2 TsAMO, F. 27 tbr, op. 1, d. 9, l. 166, 167 and 169.

tanks remained on the approaches to Surikovo. The 26th and 27th Tank Brigades were pulled back to the rear and assembled as a "shock group" on the fringes of the woods southwest of Posel'skoe "with the task to destroy the enemy in the event of a German counterattack."[3] However, the enemy didn't go on the attack or the counterattack, and the tanks of the two tank brigades (4 KV, 24 T-34 and 22 T-60) remained inactive until evening itself. The infantry of the 2nd Motorized Rifle Brigade also remained pinned down in front of Surikovo until evening.

At 1600, at a time when the 2nd Tank Corps' attack had long ago faltered in front of Surikovo, having gathered its forces the 1st Tank Corps finally went on the attack. The 1st Guards Tank Brigade from its jumping-off positions atop Hill +3.0 attacked toward Hill 173.7, and after three hours, having advanced all of 1 kilometer, reached the upper reaches of the ravine north of Surikovo (which is to say, the very same lines that the 2nd Tank Corps had reached that morning, according to Colonel Nagaibakov's operational summary), where it ran into "intense artillery and mortar fire" and "continued a slow advance". By 2000, after four hours of fighting, the 1st Guards Tank Brigade took Hill 173.7, which the 2nd Tank Corps' 26th Tank Brigade … had left at 1400.[4] (One can only be surprised at such a lack of coordination in the actions of two corps that were fighting side by side, when a brigade of one corps must once again with fighting take a line that had been abandoned prior to this by a brigade of the other corps).

The 1st Motorized Rifle Brigade with the support of 9 tanks from the 49th Tank Brigade went on the attack toward Bol'shaia Vereika from the east, and after three hours reached Hill 187.4, where it met "strong artillery and mortar fire from the area of Bol'shaia Vereika and Hill 191.3". The rest of the 49th Tank Brigade took no part in the attack and remained in Kreshchenka. The brigades' attack bogged down on Hill 187.4 and made no further advance. That evening, bad news became known to the 49th Tank Brigade's tankers: all of the 7 tanks that had been stopped by the commander of the 193rd Rifle Division had been set ablaze by the Germans during the withdrawal from Lebiazh'e on 26 July.[5]

The 89th Tank Brigade, as the 1st Tank Corps commander's reserve, took no part in the combat and remained in the vicinity of a hamlet on the Don River (1 kilometer north of Sredniaia Dolina). Altogether, by evening the 1st Tank Corps had 3 KV, 36 T-34 and 28 T-60 that were combat-ready, but only 47 of them (a little more than half) took part in the attack on 27 July.[6]

Together with the 1st Tank Corps, the 167th Rifle Division went on the attack toward Bol'shaia Vereika. With its two first-echelon regiments, it approached the village and Hill 191.3, and in places also broke into the eastern outskirts of Bol'shaia Vereika, having reached the church and water mill with forward elements.[7] However, by nightfall the elements of the 167th Rifle Division fell back closer to the tanks of the 1st Tank Corps and were digging in on the southern slopes of Hill 187.4.[8] The 104th Rifle Brigade as before was defending on the line of the ravine lying 1.5 kilometers south of Fomina-Negachevka.[9]

With this, the combat actions of Operational Group Chibisov's units on the front of the enemy's penetration came to an end. To the west and north of the penetration, its troops had not undertaken any active operations. In its eastern sector, the attack by the 1st Tank Corps (and 167th Rifle Division) and the 2nd Tank Corps "at half-strength", having driven in the enemy's combat outposts, had cautiously stopped in front of the line along the Bystrik Creek and the village of

3 TsAMO, F. 38 A, op. 9005, d. 35, l. 102.
4 TsAMO, F. 202, op. 50, d. 14, l. 280.
5 Ibid.
6 Ibid.
7 TsAMO, F. 38 A, op. 9005, d. 35, l. 97.
8 TsAMO, F. 38 A, op. 9005, d. 35, l. 112.
9 TsAMO, F. 38 A, op. 9005, d. 35, l. 105.

Bol'shaia Vereika that was being fiercely defended by the Germans. Alas, a defeat of the enemy and a breakthrough to the operational group's encircled units didn't take place, and thus the encircled units had to rely upon themselves for relief. They would have to break out of the encirclement with their own forces ....

* * *

Starting from the morning of 26 July, the fate of the encircled units remained unclear to the command of the operational group. The initial word that arrived from them by nighttime confirmed the fact of the encirclement, but provided little information about their situation, intentions or combat capabilities. The radio messages that went out from the operational group's headquarters and were transmitted to the encircled grouping seemed to disappear in the air waves, since they received no response. In my diligent study of the archival documents of the units of the operational group and its headquarters, I was unable to find any mention of who took command of the encircled grouping, what actions he undertook, and how and when an escape from the pocket was organized. Rather, the available documents speak to the fact that from the very beginning, there was no unified command in the encircled grouping at all. Chibisov's decision to appoint the commander of the 193rd Rifle Division Smekhotvorov as commander of the encircled grouping either never reached him or was never carried out; possibly, it wasn't even the best choice. No centralized organization of the encircled units of the 193rd and 340th Rifle Divisions is discernible in the documents.

In vain, Chibisov sent a briefing on the situation to Smekhotvorov over the radio, as well as a proposal about the direction and timing of the breakout. He also was demanding that Smekhotvorov submit his own proposals on this matter. An organized breakout attempt by the encircled units on the night of 26-27 July didn't happen. It also didn't follow on the day of 27 July. An attempt never took place at all. The main reason for this, judging from the available evidence, was precisely the absence of any firm command and control over the encircled units.

This particularly concerned the 193rd Rifle Division. Remorselessly bombed by enemy aircraft, cut off by German tanks and having swiftly lost its combat capability, the division simply fell apart into separate, poorly connected or completely unconnected groups of armed or even totally unarmed men. The encircled regiments ceased to exist as combat units under unified command, capable of carrying out combat tasks and resisting an organized enemy.

German documents give evidence in favor of such a conclusion. Already on 26 July, there is no mention by them regarding the organized resistance of the encircled Soviet units in the Lebiazh'e area. Thus, alas, one cannot speak about the organization of any overall line of defense of the encircled units, just as one cannot speak of their investment by the enemy. The operational group's encircled units were cut apart and scattered across the fields by German combat groups on that day, or simply disintegrated of their own accord prior to this. According to VII Army Corps' journal of combat operations, the link-up between the units of the 387th and 385th Infantry Divisions that were attacking toward Lebiazh'e from the north and south occurred already at mid-day on 26 July, and by evening the area around Bol'shaia Vereika had already been "mopped-up from the enemy."[10] The very same facts follow from the documents of the 9th Panzer Division.

In the VII Army Corps' evening report after the announcement that "major enemy units had succeeded in retreating across the Bol'shaia Vereika River to the northeast", in particular it is stated: "After mopping-up the Lebiazh'e – Malaia Vereika area the 385th Infantry Division is occupying a new forward line of defense. There is no significant pressure on the part of the enemy

10 NARA, T-314, roll 353, fr. 000420.

against the 9th Panzer Division's outpost line. The obtainment of information regarding captured items and enemy losses is possible only after scouring the battlefield and putting the elements back into order."[11]

If you will, one must seek an understanding of what happened to the encircled units in this last phrase. Shattered by the enemy and having disintegrated without the cementing will of commanders, the units turned into tiny clusters of men concealed in the fields, ravines and patches of woods that were trying to make their way to the north through the German lines. In their turn, the German headquarters plainly hurried to announce that the battle had come to a victorious conclusion and that the pocket had been mopped up (a note by the 193rd Rifle Division's artillery chief, who was located in Malaia Vereika, which was written no later than the evening of 26 July, eloquently speaks to this). The enemy units had only had time to advance hastily along the roads and through the villages, but they didn't have either the time or the strength to sweep the enormous fields with their tall plantings, where primarily our trapped soldiers, commanders and political workers were hiding. Moreover, even the ring of the encirclement didn't exist in its traditional, Stalingrad understanding, with dug trenchlines facing each other and a watchful besiegement of the encircled units of the operational group. Again, the enemy lacked the strength for this. The encircled troops at Lebiazh'e and Malaia Vereika were separated from friendly lines only by a thin and intermittent line of German forces, which was being monitored by mobile German patrols.

There are practically no documents that show how our units made their way out of the pocket. In the reports of the 340th Rifle Division, it is only briefly stated, almost as an aside, that the personnel of the 1140th and 1144th Rifle Regiments that wound up encircled were making their way out of the encirclement in small groups from the morning of 27 July, and that a resupply for the emerging units with ammunition and food had been organized by the division.[12] A political report partially repeats this information, in which it is stated: "The 1144th is emerging together with units of the 193rd Rifle Division out of a wooded area northwest of Point 181.8 and Lebiazh'e and linking up to the division's remaining regiments in the Dmitriashevskie Vyselki, Anikeevka area. There is no information on the rear services of the 1144th Rifle Regiment's elements. Ammunition and food have been dropped on the routes of their movement."[13] Obviously, it was only possible to drop the ammunition and food mentioned in this report on friendly territory, as well as *only on the anticipated movement routes* of the small groups making their way out of encirclement, which prior to this, alas, could only count upon their own strength.

Excerpts from a special message from the military commissar of the 340th Rifle Division Senior Battalion Commissar Fukin to the chief of the Briansk Front's Political Directorate give some image of the situation within the pocket:

> The 1144th Rifle Regiment, like other units of the division, fighting in semi-encirclement 24-28.7.42 wound up cut off from their rear services, and in the course of 26-28.7.42 was deprived of the possibility of resupply with ammunition and food. Since this question became in essence decisive for the regiment, the regiment commander Lieutenant Colonel Buinovsky together with the regiment's commissar Baronov decided that Buinovsky would remain behind to lead the elements, while Baronov would make an attempt to reach the regiment headquarters and regiment's rear areas, which were also cut-off from the units, in order to secure the delivery of ammunition and food to the battalions that had fallen into difficult circumstances.

11 NARA, T-314, roll 353, fr. 001349.
12 TsAMO, F. 340 sd, op. 1, d. 24, l. 217.
13 TsAMO, F. 340 sd, op. 1, d. 91, l. 446.

On 27 July Military Commissar Baronov together with the regiment's chief of staff Solov'ev and the Special Department Agent Tolokno arrived at the divisional command post [this supports the argument that the German units didn't have a continuous ring of encirclement around the 193rd and 340th Rifle Divisions – I.S.], reported on the situation, after which the division commander and I issued an order to get ammunition and food to the regiment, which at the time was still located in the area southeast of Lomovo, at whatever the cost. Simultaneously, they were given a radio set, since the regiment's radio wasn't working. Baronov took every measure and directed food and ammunition to the regiment, but since it was almost fully encircled by this time, the transport couldn't advance because the route was being blanketed by intense mortar and machine-gun fire.

At the same time, the 1142nd Rifle Regiment was also in a difficult position [this is the regiment that didn't wind up encircled – I.S.] and was in need of urgent help for the men. The division commander gave Baronov a second task to organize everything possible in the rears of the 1144th Rifle Regiment and to send it all to assist the 1142nd Rifle Regiment.[14]

It isn't possible to give an accurate count of how many of the men of the 340th Rifle Division's regiments managed to escape the pocket and how many perished within it – the division's documents are silent on this matter. If you take as a basis a political report from the division's military commissar, who reported, for example, that the losses of the 1144th Rifle Regiment already on 24 July amounted to 40-50%; that 200 men remained in the mortar battalion; that the 2nd and 3rd Battalions each had 150 men and the 1st Battalion no more than 100; it is possible to assume that little was left of the regiment's combat elements after their emergence from the pocket.[15] (In the light of other data, it appears that the estimates of the units' losses given by the 340th Rifle Division's military commissar were nevertheless exaggerated).

I was unable to find any sort of documents of the 193rd Rifle Division for this period in the central archives of the Ministry of Defense. It is possible to assume with a great degree of probability that they were all destroyed just during these days, when the division was encircled. Thus it is even more impossible to say exactly how the division's breakout from encirclement went and how many men were lost in the process. Fortunately, a manuscript of the recollections of the 193rd Rifle Division's commissar, Nechaev, has been preserved, which is if you will the single source available on this matter in place of the division's documents. Despite its inherent shortcomings (the subjectivity of the assessments, the biased nature of the statements, and the chronological and geographical inaccuracies and mistakes), the manuscript is important first of all as evidence of a contemporary and eyewitness to those events, the story of whom allows us to "see" what was happening through the eyes of the 193rd Rifle Division's commissar and to get a better sense of those hard July battles of 1942:

The division's observation post was located in the center of the battlefield, in the valley of the village of Bol'shaia Vereika. On the right was a hill, covered with bushes and an early-growth forest. The 685th Rifle Regiment was occupying it. About 2.5 kilometers at an angle out in front was the ascent to Point 188.5. There the 883rd Rifle Regiment was fighting. From our vantage point, we had a splendid view of the terrain.

The 685th Rifle Regiment commander reported that the enemy was attacking his neighbor on the right, had deeply penetrated its combat positions with tanks, and it had been forced to retreat. Some of the elements fell back along a ravine in the direction of the Don,

14 TsAMO, F. 340 sd, op. 1, d. 91, l. 485.
15 TsAMO, F. 340 sd, op. 1, d. 91, l. 441.

through the combat ranks of the 193rd Rifle Division. The retreating men were exhausted, totally worn-out by the fighting. Fedor Nikandrovich [Smekhotvorov, commander of the 193rd Rifle Division] summoned their senior officer, who turned out to be the deputy division commander of our neighbor, and sternly demanded that he explain the reason for the retreat. He reported that he had an order from the division commander to retreat and that the enemy had struck them with a heavy attack by tanks and aviation. Where the enemy was now, he didn't know.

General Smekhotvorov listened to all the justifications, became enraged, and on the spot attempted to make contact with the commander (of the operational group). However, communications were still down and not working. Fedor Nikandrovich set down the telephone and said, "This is bad; the division's right flank is now exposed." He summoned the commander of the 895th Rifle Regiment and demanded that he move out part of his regiment to cover the division's right flank.

The retreat of the right-hand neighbor substantially affected the morale of the 193rd Rifle Division's troops. Many of our company and battalion commanders, observing the neighbor's retreat, became confused and didn't know what to do. The enemy launched brief attacks. The combat formations of the regiments became perceptibly disorganized, and communications with them was working intermittently.

Night and silence arrived. The enemy lay low and didn't undertake any combat actions prior to morning.

The commander of the 895th Rifle Regiment Major Vorozheikin reported: "Sergeant Mitkin of the 8th Company disabled a fascist motorcycle; and delivered a captured Fritz to regiment headquarters, as well as valuable documents of the German "Rheingold" Infantry Division [the enemy didn't have such a division in this sector – I.S.].

General Smekhotvorov ordered the regiment commanders to restore order in the elements and to take a roll call, send the wounded to the medical-sanitation battalion, replenish the elements with ammunition, and to give the men a meal. The deputy personnel officer Brigade Commander Romanov was sent to the 883rd Rifle Regiment and directed to ascertain the situation on the spot and to take necessary measures to enhance vigilance.

The division's chief of artillery Lieutenant Colonel I.Ia. Kudriavtsev heard Fedor Nikandrovich's essential orders. We then decided to visit the defensive positions near the division's command post. It was dark – we moved from company to company, foxhole to foxhole; the grass rustled beneath our feet, the fatigue was terrible, and in a low voice we shared our impressions of the day's battle. Our feet were failing us, we were stumbling now and then; I wanted to sit and have a smoke. Our throats had become dry; for two days we had received nothing to eat, but that didn't matter to us – there was no need for this. However, we were parched and badly wanted something to drink.

We approached a machine-gun position. The moon illuminated the crew. There was a strapping young soldier, his head resting on the machine-gun, as if embracing it, and next to him were two other men. They were all snoring sweetly. Bawl them out? But why? That day they had fought splendidly and their team commander had been badly wounded. It was clear that the preceding day of combat had exhausted them. They were heavily fatigued. We woke them up; all three jumped up, sensed their guilt, and didn't face us directly. They knew that to fall asleep in such a situation was a major crime. At any minute, this could result in a tragedy. What to do? You couldn't correct the matter with a shout. We directed their attention to the impermissibility of allowing everyone to sleep in such a situation. We demanded that they properly organize rest and observation of the ground and the enemy lying out in front of them.

We walked up to the positions of a mortar company. They had fought well that day, and in the evening had repelled an advancing enemy group with their mortar fire and had put them to flight. Taking advantage of the darkness and brief lull in the fighting, the soldiers were strengthening their positions, digging trenches and preparing places for their mortars. They were setting up machine guns. The political instructor among the troops Nikolai Gordilovich Noga, a 1st Military Technician, was here. He loved the mortarmen and was helping them with his words and actions.

It was after 0100. We proceeded further – the ground was almost monotonous: short grass in the swales, up to the knee on the knolls, and in places up to the belt. We encountered elements of the 883rd Rifle Regiment. We spoke with the officers. They appeared tired, but they spoke eagerly about their troops, how they had repulsed attacks, who of their soldiers and non-commissioned officers had distinguished themselves, how many knocked-out fascist tanks there'd been and by whom; we knew many of them – we ran into them repeatedly during the training exercises that had been conducted before the battle. Battalion Commissar Gurevich was now the acting commissar of the 883rd Rifle Regiment. Over a brief period in the fighting, he had studied the officers, non-commissioned officers and men. He spoke well about his closest assistants.

Party-political work had been properly organized and was being constantly conducted in the regiment through the efforts of the Communists and Komsomol members. Gurevich was simple in his communications with people; calm and well-groomed. His appearance spoke to the fact that he, a commissar, was completely confident in the regiment's men. Listening to Gurevich, I recalled how our train had stopped on its way to the front. The train crew was being changed. I was standing on the station platform. Gurevich walked up; at the time he was an instructor in the division's Political Department. He reported on the state of morale and the work that had been done on the journey. Standing next to him was an adolescent boy, about 14 years old – well-built, handsome, and wearing a sailor's striped shirt. A sentry on the train warned us that the train would be leaving in five minutes. Parting from the adolescent, Gurevich said, "Farewell, sonny, be happy, grow, you have your whole life in front of you! Give my greetings to Momma. We're going to the front to defend our Motherland against the fascist barbarians." The father embraced the son and kissed him three times. Gurevich didn't think at the time that he was parting from his son forever. A signal: to the cars! The train carrying the personnel of the 883rd Rifle Regiment set off to the west.

Gurevich spent the night in the regiment's combat positions. The artillery chief Lieutenant Colonel Kudriavtsev and I returned in the morning to the observation post. Brigade Commander Romanov arrived; General Smekhotvorov listened to our reports. He said that scouts had established that the enemy had conducted a regrouping during the night and brought up fresh forces. Probably, the Germans would soon go on the attack.

Our regiments, battalions and companies yesterday had fought courageously with the foe, not sparing lives. We had to consider that over the previous two days of fighting, we had lost a significant number of company and platoon commanders killed or wounded. We were short in non-commissioned officers and troops. There were no replacements. The regiment commanders kept reporting fresh information about the enemy.

Under enemy fire combat medic Pavlina Ivanovna Iuzhenko made her way to the observation post. She personally reported to the division commander: "Approximately at 0700, I was rendering aid to the wounded and to the right of the 685th Rifle Regiment's position I saw a column of tanks bypassing the village of Lebiazh'e and moving along a swale into the division's rear."

After midnight, at an order from their commanders, the army headquarters' assets pulled out of their firing positions and fell back to the second line without informing the commander of the 193rd Rifle Division. At 0800 from the direction of the 883rd Rifle Regiment's positions to the right of the division's observation post, five of our tanks were moving. General Smekhotvorov ordered me to detain them and find out where the tanks were going and why they were retreating. Having dashed approximately 400 meters, I stopped the lead machine. The second and third machines were each towing a disabled tank. The senior lieutenant opened his hatch, clambered out of the tank, presented a document and reported that he had an order from his commander to fall back to the second line, which lay about 6 kilometers behind us.

While we were talking, the enemy opened targeted fire. Shells exploded long and short of us. A cloud of smoke and dust rose into the air. Soon I returned to the observation post and reported in detail to Fedor Nikandrovich. He thought a bit and said, "It is hardly likely that the commander issued such an order to withdraw, and even if by chance there is such an order, why didn't we receive it?" He again attempted to contact army headquarters, but the attempt failed. Communications were still out.

The commander of the 883rd Rifle Regiment Botvenko reported: "The enemy has gone on the attack at the boundary between the 1st and 2nd Battalions and reached the regiment's command post, where we accepted battle. A mortar barrage knocked 6 men out of action of the headquarters group – 2 killed, 4 wounded. Among the wounded staff officers is Lieutenant I.G. Gapak."

Soon a second message arrived from Botvenko: The Germans had pushed forward another 300 meters or so. There were 13 people in the headquarters group: Major Buriukin [according to the consolidated data base of the Memorial project, Captain Semen Pavlovich Buriukin, the deputy commander of the 883rd Rifle Regiment, 193rd Rifle Division; killed in action on 26 July 1942], Regiment Commissar Gurevich, chief of staff Samsonov, political instructor Maratkanov, a young female combat medic, Senior Lieutenant Steblin, a signals officer, and six soldiers. I ordered Major Buriukin to take charge of the group and to break out to Malaia Vereika and link back up with the regiment's battalions. We would support the group's movement with fire.

It became increasingly difficult to hold our positions. The division's units had heavy losses in men and equipment. No replacements were arriving. The enemy seized the hills in the area, from which they could clearly see our combat positions. The ravine in which the command post was located was taking fire from all types of weapons. Tanks penetrated our defensive positions from the west. More tanks and motorized infantry were advancing from the direction of Zemliansk.

Assessing the situation and having no contact with higher command, the commander of the 193rd Rifle Division decided to withdraw the units out from under the enemy attack. Over the telephone he issued a verbal order: the units were quickly to turn the combat formations around toward the Don River. [It is strange to read this. As the crow flies, it is 18 kilometers from Lebiazh'e to the Don River. Perhaps Nechaev wanted to say "to the east"? – I.S.]

We were retreating: the command team and the training battalion. On the right was the 883rd Rifle Regiment, on the left – the 895th Rifle Regiment. In the second echelon, the 685th Rifle Regiment was covering the retreat. The chief of artillery was ordered to cover the retreat with the artillery fire from the 384th Artillery Regiment and the regimental artillery, to prevent the enemy from actively pursuing our units. Enemy aircraft were constantly overhead, bombing and strafing our combat formations. It was hard for our troops, but the adversary didn't seem powerful and menacing. The vanguard reached the designated line, failed to find any units of the left-hand neighbor, and was met by enemy fire.

The movement of tanks and motorized infantry from the direction of Zemliansk was spotted. In the afternoon, the enemy opened artillery fire. Our elements hadn't had time to recover from the artillery barrage, which lasted for 20 minutes, and restore order in the ranks, when tanks appeared that were advancing vigorously. Aircraft were covering them, and the enemy was squeezing the division's units from three directions.

The division's headquarters group was stopped by the enemy at a deep anti-tank ditch. The division commander ordered Brigade Commander Romanov and a group of trainees from the training battalion to delay the enemy, while the headquarters group shifted its movement to the left, toward Khlevnoe.

I was assigned to rally a group of wounded men and patients that were following behind the headquarters group. I walked back around 300 meters. I came across approximately 50 men. Taking advantage of the short halt, they were taking shelter in a ravine and distributing food that had hastily been prepared in the soldiers' mess kits, helping each other bandage the wounded, and re-wrapping their foot cloths. [Ed. note: Red Army soldiers wrapped their feet and ankles with a binding of cloth, rather than using socks]. They all looked exhausted.

My appearance cheered them up a bit. I explained the situation to them, put senior non-commissioned officers in charge, and demanded that they get their men out of the ravine as soon as possible and follow behind their regiments that were retreating to the second line of defense.

Approximately at 1500, Senior Lieutenant Steblin reported to me that Major Buriukin, the deputy commander of the 883rd Rifle Regiment, was breaking through the enemy-occupied village of Malaia Vereika, had knocked the Germans aside, and was advancing to link up with the regiment's battalions. The Germans were pursuing them with fire and infantry. The group was throwing back enemy attacks. In this action northwest of Point 188.5, the commissar of the 883rd Rifle Regiment Comrade Gurevich was mortally wounded in a ravine. Major Buriukin was killed at close range by a German sniper. The regiment chief of staff Senior Lieutenant Samsonov, a brave combat officer, assumed command of the headquarters group.

The Germans bounded forward. Stopped by the fire of our artillerymen, they camouflaged their tanks, organized an ambush, and deployed several guns to place direct fire. The enemy had a good view of the surrounding terrain. They spotted Samsonov's group at the moment it was climbing Hill 188.5 [Here Nechaev is plainly mistaken, because this hill was off to one side of the group's breakout direction and the 193rd Rifle Division's initial positions – I.S.] They opened mortar fire and wounded staff officer I.G. Gopak. Samsonov under the cover of fire from his group was moving toward some woods, which lay 300-400 meters away.

At this time Senior Political Instructor Maratkanov was mortally wounded. Rushing to Maratkanov's aid, the young female combat medic of the 883rd Rifle Regiment was killed. Chief of staff Senior Lieutenant Samsonov was wounded twice, and at the very edge of the woods was killed by the explosion of a series of mortar shells.

On 27 July the enemy tanks kept advancing, and in the vicinity of Surikovye Vyselki bumped into the artillery positions of the 384th Artillery Regiment. [Judging from captured documents, there were no German tanks at Surikovye Vyselki on 27 July; they had already fallen back behind the Bystrik Creek on the night of 26-27 July – I.S.] The 1st Battery (commanded by Senior Lieutenant Georgii Fedorovich Kulikov) fought courageously. A gunlayer was wounded; Kulikov took his position at the gun and personally knocked out three German tanks, while the rest of the battery slaughtered a platoon of submachine gunners [sic] that was covering the tanks.

One gun crew of the 384th Artillery Regiment (gunlayer Junior Sergeant Ivan Pavlovich Polunin) performed superbly when repelling the tanks; the crew knocked out two tanks. The battalion commissar, Chief of the Political Department Georgii Pavlovich Ovcharenko crawled up. He was agitated, sweaty, covered with grime and bleeding from the mouth. Having calmed down a bit, he said: "A fascist bullet split [my] lips and tore away half of a tooth. The sniper, plainly, was aiming at my head and hit a tooth", and added: "Here are two rifles. I scrounged them on the battlefield, choose either – it's serviceable."

I told the chief of the Political Department about our position and the situation in which the 883rd Rifle Regiment found itself, and about the heroic deaths of Comrades Gurevich, Buriukin, Samsonov, Maratkanov and our young Communists, which we knew well. I took our Russian Moisin-Nagant .30 cal rifle. It gave me good service and saved my life.

During my time of service in the army, I gained experience and learned to master a weapon – the skills of individual marksmanship. The 7th Vitebsk Infantry School, where I was a cadet; the 4th Volochaevsky Regiment, the 2nd Amur Division, the 56th Kuniavsky Regiment of the 23rd Khar'kov Division, and other units in which for a lengthy time I commanded a platoon or company, all instilled a love for marksmanship in me. There I mastered my ability to handle a weapon. Back then, each commander demanded excellent knowledge of a weapon and excellent marksmanship with a rifle, machine gun and revolver.

For a long time I recalled the evaluation target shooting sessions and how we prepared for them, and how difficult they were. Indeed, it was a holiday when my target shooting received an "Excellent" mark. I gripped a rifle firmly in my hands. The most important thing was that I believed it would never let me down in any situations.

I put the cartridge clips in my pockets. In short bounds we moved in the direction of the division headquarters group. I was hurrying to report to the division commander about the sorrowful events that occurred in the 883rd Rifle Regiment.

A wounded trainee of the training battalion crawled up to meet us. He reported that the headquarters group was locked in combat at an anti-tank ditch and that the enemy had brought up fresh forces. Deputy division commander Romanov had been badly wounded. It was impossible to drag Romanov off the battlefield – the enemy had zeroed-in on this spot, and with fire was preventing anyone from crawling over to Romanov. A long machine-gun burst chattered. We quickly settled into a spot like a dug-in emplacement and watched as an enemy motorized column appeared on the hill from the direction of Zemliansk. A battalion detached from the column, deployed into combat formation, and a line of fascists at full height began moving in our direction, closing the distance quickly.

We found cover and from our knees began conducting aimed fire. We fired at the infantry and the vehicles. The Germans unlimbered two guns from vehicles, bustled around them, and turned them toward us. They opened fire.

It was clearly visible that enemy tanks had broken through the thin line of the 883rd and 895th Rifle Regiments in three places. They were advancing slowly forward, firing at intervals. The regiments' companies were fighting independently, but they couldn't stop the enemy. The regimental artillery was firing at the tanks.

Georgii Pavlovich shouted that tanks were moving to the left of us and we had to retreat. We kept shooting; someone else shouted: "Tanks, tanks!" Somewhere quite nearby, a fascist heavy machine gun opened up. The bullets, like powerful shears, were clipping the trunks, branches and crowns of the young bushes and forcing us to hug the earth. We chose a moment, then darted about 200 meters and fell into a shallow washout, surprisingly overgrown with fragrant gray sage. A narrow village road ran beside it. I shouted for Ovcharenko. He didn't answer; apparently, he had run on ahead.

There was a rumble of motors; five medium tanks appeared, camouflaged with paint the color of ripened wheat. The hatches were closed and they were moving in a column. A line of 50 Germans, 25 each on either flank of the tank column, were at a distance of 200 meters; they were submachine gunners [sic], half of which were equipped with rifles. They were calling to one another, fearing to become separated from each other. Because of the tall grain, only their heads were visible. We had no anti-tank weapons. I was lying on my belly, my head toward the road; it became stuffy, sweat was trickling into my eyes, and my heart was pounding violently.

There I was in a woolen, khaki combat blouse, with collar insignias showing my rank: the four bars of a regimental commissar. On my sleeve, an epaulet with the "Hammer and Sickle" star. On my head, a fore-and-aft cap bearing a star. In my left chest pocket, my Party card, in the right pocket – my certification as commissar of the 193rd Rifle Division. On my belt was a holstered revolver with 7 bullets. I also had a rifle and two anti-personnel grenades. Khaki trousers and calfskin boots. My entire uniform was filthy, in places torn by branches and stones during the bounding movements and concealments.

Another long machine-gun burst cut through the air. My left leg below the knee suddenly felt as if it had been burned by red-hot iron. I felt something warm in my bootleg and my trouser leg became sticky; blood was oozing. I became alert, gripped my rifle more firmly, and laid the grenades out in front of me. I very much regretted that they weren't anti-tank grenades and a Molotov cocktail.

Watchful of mines, their tracks squeaking, the fascist tanks passed by in a column just 3 meters from my position. Everything happened quickly. It felt like a hammer was pounding in my temples. I decided: anything other than shameful captivity. Before the war, in the Red Army we were taught that the Red Army soldier in the most difficult circumstances is to carry out his duty to the end; justify the Motherland's trust; show no mercy in hand-to-hand struggle; and achieve victory. Only victory, there is no other way out. Be dedicated to the Soviet people, as well as to the Communist Party, of which I'd been a member since 1927, to your last breath.

There was a rustle in the grass. I tensed. A husky Red Army man crawled up to me and softly asked, "Comrade Commissar, are you alive?" I recognized him as a telephone operator with the signals battalion. He'd always been located at the division command post. He showed me his right hand, the wrist covered with blood, and said, "Just look, the fascist scum shot off two fingers just like a hatchet." I tore off the sleeve of my undershirt and bandaged his wound. At the same moment I thought to take off my boot and bandage my own wound, but decided against this: if removed the boot, I wouldn't be able to put it back on. I'd grit my teeth and bear it. The signalman helped me tighten a cord around my leg above the knee.

Soon, two men of the 883rd Rifle Regiment and three men of the 895th Rifle Regiment crawled up. Two of them were lightly wounded. I was very relieved not to be alone.

The first question: "What should we do, Comrade Commissar?" We decided to move out quickly in the wake of the tanks that had just passed by and follow them, before the enemy's second echelon arrived. We set off to the north, in the direction of Khlevnoe, toward where shells and mortar rounds were exploding. We passed the facilities of a machine and tractor station [Ed. note: In the Soviet communal system, the machine and tractor stations were rural agencies that owned and maintained all agricultural machinery, and provided tractors, farm machines and people to run them to the collective farms in the area.]. It became dark. We lost track of where the tanks had gone. On the way to the village, we passed vegetable gardens, but didn't encounter a single soul. We decided not to tarry; only forward. We belly crawled across the village street and kept moving. The night sky was bright. There was not a single dark cloud in the sky to obscure the moon's illumination, yet how we wanted the night to be dark!

We reached an expansive field, dropped to the ground and gave a listen. A German telephonist was issuing commands. We heard German speech and distinct laughter. Four guns had been set up into positions, but they were neither emplaced nor camouflaged. We couldn't see the crews.

We turned to the right and dropped into a shallow, dry ravine that had gradual rises and descents. I was frightfully tired. My pulse was beating with palpitations; I wanted something to drink. We stealthily advanced along the ravine about 300 meters, then stopped, dropped and gave another listen. From down below we could clearly see up above: on the edge of the ravine, there was some sort of shock of wheat or haystack. A fascist with a machine pistol on his chest appeared, playing a harmonica. We could hear gunfire off to the left; our regiments were trying to repel the German onslaught. I decided that the fighting was going on for the second line of defense. A second fascist appeared, singing something in a soft voice. One of my men whispered, "The swine are trying to chase away sleep and fear."

We prepared to take the fascists. Soon two more appeared. They were looking in our direction. I whispered to hold fire. We took a look around. Petrov said that it wasn't a haystack, but a camouflaged tank. The Germans detected our presence and let go a burst of submachine gun fire. We scrambled back along the ravine about 300 meters, and then dropped prone on the right-hand slope; the moon was faintly illuminating us. The signalman was softly groaning from the sharp pain of a wound. The Germans dropped mortar rounds along the ravine. Shells exploded nearby and showered us with sand and clumps of dirt and mud. We kept prone and quiet. It was pointless to get up and run. Ten minutes later, everything fell silent. Dawn was breaking.

I was terribly worried. My heart was pounding in my chest. It was weakness, not strength. Not even 24 hours had passed, and three times, it would seem, we had wound up in a hopeless position and only by simple chance had we avoided falling into the fascists' clutches. Here again we were lying under fire, and I was wondering what to do next.

Just 30 minutes or so of darkness remained. We clambered out of the ravine on our bellies. Several motorcycles roared by. The road was being patrolled. Out in front was a field of ripe, unharvested wheat. Beyond it was the dark mass of a forest. Friendly lines were somewhere nearby. I ordered Petrov: if necessary, cover the group with fire and quickly follow us. We took off, jumped out into the middle of the road, and simultaneously there was a "Halt! Halt!" followed immediately by a burst of automatic weapons fire.

We ran across the wheat field, paying no heed to the whistle of bullets, putting increasing distance between us and the Germans. The firing stopped. Within 15 minutes we had successfully covered the distance without a loss. We stopped and dropped. Right then and there, we found ourselves in another predicament. A village road ran along the other side of the grain field in which we were lying. It was just a stone's throw to the woods, and we needed their shelter like air. I don't know about you, but I feel safer in woods.

The August sun was climbing above the horizon. [Judging from the evidence, this was the morning of 28 July 1942 – I.S.] It was getting warm. My wound was throbbing. The signalman was moaning – his temperature had risen. Petrov was trying to soothe him, pulling burdock roots and advising to apply them to the wounded arm. [Ed. note: Burdock root has been used for hundreds of years in herbal medicine as a blood purifier and anti-inflammatory.]

On the left we spotted a tank, the barrel of its main gun pointed in the direction of the woods. Our guys were somewhere nearby. Unexpectedly, there was the sound of gunfire; I rose to one knee and saw several trucks about 800 meters away from us. The fascists had stopped and were conducting area fire with automatic weapons from the truck beds, combing the terrain.

A pack of sheepdogs with a yip retreated off to one side – downwind. The Nazis were operating boldly, cruising around through the crops in their vehicles like bastards. We hadn't had time to collect ourselves when the matter reached the point of hand-to-hand combat. Two motorcycles carrying 5 Germans soldiers speedily drove toward us from the direction of the tank. They stopped and leaped off the motorcycles. They advanced toward us, firing as they moved. We were returning their fire.

In front of me rose a huge young German, armed with a rifle, wearing a green tunic with rolled up sleeves, like a butcher; he was intoxicated, his bovine eyes bloodshot. The fascist advanced toward me, firing, his rifle leveled at my stomach. I was also firing at him. But it was some kind of marvel – neither of us was hitting our target. Everyone was shooting. I heard Petrov behind me shouting, "Oy, I'm dying". I glanced back. From behind I felt a powerful blow between my shoulders with the butt of a rifle – a second fascist had attacked me. I saw an explosion of sparks in my eyes, and twisting around, I fell on my back. In my right hand, I kept a tight grip on the stock of the rifle with its attached faceted bayonet, and somehow I quickly came to me senses just in time to be able with great difficulty to knock aside with my left hand the German's knife-like bayonet that was aimed at my chest.

The third time I failed in the attempt to deflect the thrust, and the bayonet freely entered the elbow of my left arm and buried itself into my forearm, when suddenly the German stumbled and dropped to his knees. As he quickly tried to stand back up, I struck him from my prone position with my right hand. The Russian faceted bayonet struck the fascist's left temple and slashed across his face, wounding his eye and nose. My adversary dropped the rifle that was sticking in my arm. Gushing blood, the German howled, shouted for someone's help, spun around in circles, and then fled in the direction of the tank.

I rose to my feet, put down my rifle, stepped onto the other rifle's strap, and pulled the Nazi's rifle out of my left arm. There were three cartridges in its magazine. With great difficulty I took aim with the German rifle, and as calmly as I could from a standing position fired three aimed shots at two fascists. The range was 100 meters. Both fascists dropped face-first to the ground. Then I jammed the German rifle's barrel into the ground. I picked up my own rifle, loaded my final clip into the Moisin-Nagant rifle, and headed in the direction of the woods.

Everything was mixed up, I couldn't remember which way was north and which way was south. My head was aching terribly. It seemed to me that I was going in the wrong direction. I needed something to drink. It was impossible to stop – I'd be killed. On my left was an immobile German tank, which had been knocked out by our guys the day before. No one fired at me. I came to my senses when I reached the forest fringe; I couldn't move my left arm. It was dangling and I couldn't move my fingers. The sleeve and pocket were filled with clots of dried black blood.

In a forest clearing, I found craters from the explosions of bombs and shells. The trees had been tossed around like matchsticks, torn up by their roots. I also found damaged and abandoned German rifles, machine guns, helmets, ammunition and bloody bandages. I went on ahead – my strength was leaving me. I took a seat on the trunk of a mutilated birch tree, tore the sleeve of my combat blouse along a seam and exposed the wound to the sun.

I quickly fell asleep. I don't know how long I slept, but at some point our aircraft flew overhead and dropped bombs on the German positions; I woke up from an explosion. Large forest flies had sensed the blood and were biting the wound. They were circling in swarms above my head.

We assembled in the woods, climbed onto a low rise that offered a good field of vision and fire, and caught the sound of German speech. We organized an all-round defense, taking into account our possibilities and the murky situation. Without any incendiary, inspiring speeches we each gave a vow not to be taken alive by the Germans and to fight to the last bullet. The vow was given thoughtfully; the men were firmly sticking together in the most difficult circumstances. The soldier Petrov didn't show up. He remained forever in the wheat field. To me it was such a shame that such a splendid Komsomol member, a combat soldier of the 895th Rifle Regiment, had been killed.

At 0100 there was a most intense artillery barrage. We were lying in the targeted sector. Dirt, tree roots, stones and fragments were thrown skyward by the shell explosions, and then fell back to the earth like hailstones and thudded on the ground. It was very difficult to determine who was firing: the enemy, or our side. The barrage continued for 20 minutes. Then it became quiet. I decided that we were between the lines. Three hours remained until daybreak. We decided to push on, in the attempt to reach friendly lines.

In a line, we began belly crawling in the opposite direction from the German speech we had heard. I was in the center. On the right and left flanks, some men crawled forward 200 meters and gave a signal – the soft, recognizable tapping of the Moisin-Nagant's folding rear-sight leaf against its steel plate. In this way, we cautiously moved forward another 800 meters. Then suddenly, the heart leaped with joy. Not far ahead, about 400 meters away, we could hear the sound of Russian speech and the clatter of soldiers' mess kits.

We discovered that one of the elements of our army was nonchalantly feeding the men breakfast right at the very front right under the enemy's nose. We went on. In a ravine was the field kitchen. Right in front of me, a senior sergeant literally rose up from out of the ground. It was Grisha Kutnevsky. We were old friends. Before the war we had served together in the 185th Rifle Division's 470th Artillery Regiment. From the very first days of the war, we took part in the fighting on the Northwestern Front. Now we were serving and fighting in the ranks of the 193rd Rifle Division.

Kutnevsky was taller than average and superbly built. He was physically powerful. A blond with blue eyes and sunny hair, he was a Komsomol member. Now, as if feeling guilty, he said, "Comrade Commissar, I've been looking for you. In the last 24 hours I've carried two wounded officers from the battlefield."

I asked him whether he knew where the medical-sanitation battalion was located. He responded affirmatively. "Take me there." To the right we could hear the sound of firing. The division's headquarters group was fighting off the enemy attacks. That evening General Smekhotvorov gathered his staff officers and his reserve trainees of the training battalion together with their commanders. He told them, "Likely, in the morning the enemy will resume the offensive in our direction and attempt to destroy us. I have no communications with the regiments. Liaison officers I have sent out haven't come back. I order you to be vigilant."

Before midnight, there were the sounds of Russian speech, coming from the enemy's side of the lines: "Attention! Attention! Resistance is useless. There are few of you left. Surrender, tomorrow it will be too late."

The division commander issued the order to continue onward. Everyone began creeping to the north, quietly eliminating fascist detachments on the way. They were dealt with quickly. The enemy woke up and opened up an indiscriminate fire, and an exchange of fire flared up. Morning was arriving quickly. Fedor Nikandrovich was moving in the column of Russian troops. He was annoyed by each pause in the actions. He kept commanding, "Onward, only onward!"

The cadets and staff officers kept advancing, suppressing enemy firing positions and taking cover in folds of the terrain. They gained separation from their pursuers. An enemy mortar shell exploded. Dozens of tiny fragments embedded themselves in the right side of the body, right arm, buttocks and thigh of Fedor Nikandrovich; he was lying on the ground, softly moaning. His adjutant Senior Sergeant Grigorii Kutnevsky crawled over to him. Together, they carried the commander into a sheltered spot. They placed him on a tank and delivered him to the tank corps' medical unit.

The time had come for my group to part. Wounded, I was going to the medical-sanitation battalion. The rest of my comrades headed back to their units. "Well, comrades", I said, "thank you for everything, but mainly for the fact that we didn't let down our division."

Soon, a radio operator and I were lying on an operating table of our medical-sanitation battalion. Three doctors were bustling about over us, focused on treating our wounds. They cleaned the wounds and stopped the bleeding. The radio operator was crying. I had lost a lot of blood and felt weak, and my head was aching. They did everything, and gave me a soldier's mug of some liquid to drink to fight off the shock. I gulped it down. Grisha brought some kasha and warned that I should only eat a little, or else I would have intestinal problems. I said my goodbyes to the radio operator, thanked my doctors profusely, and headed back to headquarters.

The chief of staff reported that at the decision of the army commander, the 193rd Rifle Division had been withdrawn from combat. They had pulled it back to a place in the army's second echelon, 4-5 kilometers behind the front. They were taking roll calls in the regiments and working to determine the losses in men and equipment. The ranks of the regiments, battalions and companies had thinned. We were particularly short in mid-level command staff. Many had been knocked out by wounds. Sergeants were now leading many of the platoons.

The bandaged commander of the 193rd Rifle Division Fedor Nikandrovich Smekhotvorov, who had just been brought there on a stretcher, was lying in the sanitary ward of the tank corps' medical unit 5 kilometers from the front. I was getting better and paid him a visit. I bent down over him. He happily exclaimed, "Pavel Il'ich, you're alive! In shipshape condition! What is with your arm? Are you limping?"

"It's just a trifle; I was wounded by a fascist shell fragment and bayonet," I replied.

"They also hit me with fragments. A mortar shell exploded right next to me; it's a miracle that I survived. Thanks to the troops – they brought me out under enemy fire and gave me first aid. They've decided to send me to a rear hospital aboard an airplane."

He was quiet for a moment, and then said: "Everything happened in the vicinity of Bol'shaia Vereika's anti-tank ditch. You remember, I ordered you to instill order among the wounded men and laggards, who were following behind the headquarters group? As soon as you disappeared into the bushes about 300 meters away from us, the danger was approaching by the minute. Fresh enemy motorized units were approaching from the direction of Zemliansk. The headquarters group had no anti-tank weapons. I had no contact with the artillery regiment. Communications with the regiments had been disrupted. I decided under the cover of the rest of the night to gain separation from the enemy. We began to fall back to the army's line.

(With these explanations by Smekhotvorov, the rapid collapse of the 193rd Rifle Division in encirclement is clearly discernible. The division commander, who had units with heavy weapons and thousands of soldiers and officers under his control back on 25 July already by the next day was hiding in the grain fields, trying to make his way out of encirclement like a common soldier, and was complaining that he had no anti-tank weapons or communications.)

Nechaev's manuscript resumes as General Smekhotvorov continues his story:

"There were 2 kilometers left to go. Just as soon as we moved out, the Germans immediately opened intense mortar, machine-gun and artillery fire, and the pre-dawn quiet was shattered. Mortar rounds and artillery shells were exploding all around me. I don't even recall the number of times I was tossed to the ground by an explosive blast. I have no memory at all of what happened next; right now I have constant ringing in my ears and my head aches."

Then he asked, "What's the situation in the division?"

> I told him in detail and handed Stalin's Order 227 to him. He read it attentively. He then stressed his following words: "We must stubbornly, to the last drop of blood, defend each meter of Soviet territory." He thought a bit more, then said, "In my opinion, you and I and our soldiers, our Communists and Komsomol members, did everything that our oath of allegiance demanded of us. Pavel Il'ich, take me to the division. I'll make it to the hospital in due time."

As we can see, General Smekhotvorov fought honorably and didn't want to lie around in hospitals. He was striving to get back to his division, but he was also plainly not inclined to self-criticism. The division commissar Nechaev also kept delicately silent about what he'd heard ….

Nechaev's manuscript continues:

> Discussions were useless. We appealed to the doctor. He didn't protest, and soon we arrived at the division headquarters. The combat collective gathered around us.
>
> That night, Fedor Nikandrovich's temperature rose; he was moaning. Doctors were summoned and they took the necessary measures. By morning he was feeling better and his temperature was down.
>
> It was 7:00 in the morning. The August sun was warming the clear skies. We summoned the unit commanders. Many of those arriving had light wounds and bloody bandages. They had refused to go to the medical-sanitation battalion. They replied, "The division commander and division commissar are at their posts, we will also be on duty." We began listening to brief reports from the commanders, unit commissars and service chiefs about the losses in men and equipment. The chief of the Political Department gave a report on the morale in the division. We determined that in the preceding fighting, we had knocked out or set ablaze more than 20 German tanks from all types of weapons. [Alas, the command of the 193rd Rifle Division that was encouraging itself on this matter was badly mistaken – I.S.] We ordered that those who had distinguished themselves in the fighting be put up for medals and Orders.
>
> The division commander made a thorough analysis of the dynamics of the division's battle and the fighting done by each soldier, and noted the positive and negative aspects. [Arguably, it would have been more useful had General Smekhotvorov thoroughly analyzed primarily not the "fighting done by each soldier" but his own actions as division commander, especially in the period of encirclement, as well as the actions of the unit commanders subordinate to him – I.S.]
>
> The conclusions were correct; Smekhotvorov emphasized the threat of the encirclement of the division's units by the enemy. The order to gain separation from the enemy was timely and necessary. He cited the names of many officers, who courageously conducted themselves in the fighting. Among those names he cited were Brigade Commander Romanov, Major Gurnichev, Major Buriukin, Senior Lieutenant Samsonov, Regiment Commissar Gurevich, Senior Political Instructor Maratkanov and Captain Kurilin. He said that comrades whose names he had given didn't return from the battlefield; they fell heroically on Voronezh soil; eternal glory to them! [Nechaev didn't know that Brigade Commander Romanov had been taken prisoner and that he was already being interrogated by staff officers of the 9th Panzer Division – I.S.]
>
> In the future battles we would get revenge against the fascist barbarians for our fallen comrades. We decided to report to the army commander about how heroically the division's troops had fought, how its regiments had been caught by enemy pincers, but how they had driven back attacks and gained separation from the enemy. The 193rd Rifle Division, although it had suffered considerable losses in men and equipment over many days of fighting, was still combat-capable and ready to enter battle.

It is understandable that the former division commissar was an interested party when writing his memoirs (as were, incidentally, many other authors of memoirs among the number of generals and political workers of the Soviet era), and was plainly striving to put the command's actions (as well as his own actions) in the most favorable light. It isn't surprising that in his recollections we see a multitude of examples of self-sacrifice and heroic actions by the soldiers, commanders and political workers of the 193rd Rifle Division (he, too, didn't make any blunders in a desperate moment), but we can't find a single critical comment addressed at the command, while the strikingly rapid collapse of the division into scattered, disorganized groups of men and the loss of all heavy weapons is presented as some sort of random misfortune, a bad convergence of circumstances, or the machinations of an "evil" adversary, all totally independent of the will and decisions of the 193rd Rifle Division's command.

So that the picture of what happened with the 193rd Rifle Division might become more comprehensible and clear, here it is worth offering different testimonial of another political worker – Senior Battalion Commissar Kuznetsov, who'd been assigned to the division as a representative of Briansk Front's Political Directorate. He reported on 31 July 1942:

> Exceptionally large losses in materiel … It is impossible to say precisely what happened with all the weapons. The overwhelming portion of them was left on the battlefield after the division initiated a retreat on the day of 26.7.42. There was no possibility to collect them and bring them off the battlefield, because the path of retreat had already been severed. A significant portion was abandoned by panic-mongers (especially side arms, rifles and machine guns). The weapons taken from wounded soldiers were not brought out, and a lot of weapons were knocked out of action and damaged in the course of the fighting …
>
> The military commissar of the division Regiment Commissar Nechaev came out on the morning of 30.7.42. He'd been lightly wounded in the leg by a fragment and also lightly wounded in the arm by a bayonet, and remained on duty. The chief of the division's Political Department has still not shown up, and the division's commissar is located in a hospital in Baranovo and will not be evacuated; he has more than 20 wounds, but they are all light with no damage to the bones, and will return to his post within 2 or 3 weeks. Of the 14 men who'd been previously assigned to bring him off the battlefield, 11 ran away. Three men carried him out on 28 July: Sergeant Kutnevsky, platoon commander Junior Lieutenant Rabinovich of the 895th Rifle Regiment, and the 895th Rifle Regiment's assistant chief of staff for the field postal service 2nd Technician-Intendant Vladchik.
>
> As before, the primary shortcoming in the division is the lack of exactingness and the poor work of the procuracy. In the heaviest days of fighting on 25 and 26 July, when the division essentially wound up alone and cut-off from the rest of the units, the investigators of the regimental procuracies fled; the procurator never in fact showed up at the command post and thus far not one has been convicted – not a single commander, although there are men who fled the battlefield without firing a shot ([such as] a regimental battery of the 685th Rifle Regiment). Having 110 rounds of ammunition, at the order of the battery's military commissar it abandoned its positions and fled to the rear as soon as German tanks appeared …
>
> The failure to take measures against the criminals is the primary evil in the division. I had a serious discussion with the division's procurator and military commissar on this matter; I told the latter directly that if there is no fundamental change on this matter alone, he himself might suffer serious consequences …
>
> Now conversations of the following sort are going on in the division, starting with the headquarters commanders and the division's Political Department, the commanders of units and right down to the sergeants and Red army privates: "We didn't fight badly and carried out our immediate assignment; we didn't retreat without an order, but our neighbor, the 340th

> Rifle Division, let us down and fled, which allowed the enemy to fall on us from the rear, and in this lies the entire reason for our failures." Although this was in fact the case [In reality the 340th Rifle Division didn't flee, but it was forced to pivot its right flank to the west and north because the neighboring 237th Rifle Division had been unable to withstand the attack by the German tanks and had begun to retreat in disorder, exposing not only the flank of the 340th Rifle Division, but of the entire grouping of our forces – I.S.], yesterday at a conference I proposed to everyone to stop these conversations; that it was better to get busy with eliminating their own combat disgraces and shortcomings, which are present in large number, and to turn their attention away from criticism of the neighbor toward their own sins. I let them know that higher command would deal with the neighbors.[16]

How many men remained in the 193rd Rifle Division after it came out of the encirclement? On 28 July, in the 38th Army's journal of combat operations (formerly, that of Operational Group Chibisov, and then of the 4th Army), it was written: "The 193rd Rifle Division has come out of encirclement in small groups and is assembling in the following places: in Nizhniaia Kolybel'ka – the 685th Rifle Regiment, which has 400 men after the period of fighting and the combat in encirclement; in Treshchevka – the 883rd Rifle Regiment with 100 men; the regiment's commander and commissar haven't emerged from the pocket and there is no information regarding them; in the vicinity of the Piatiletka State Farm – the 895th Rifle Regiment with 200 men."[17]

By 30 July, which is to say after several days of assembling, the regiments of the 193rd Rifle Division numbered: 685th Rifle Regiment – 804 men; 883rd Rifle Regiment – 648 men; and the 895th Rifle Regiment – 491 men; the division's artillery regiment, which had retreated before the other units because of the lack of ammunition and didn't fall into encirclement, numbered 879 men. Together with the rear services, 4,100 men remained in the 193rd Rifle Division (of which almost half were unarmed).[18] The losses in the division were catastrophic, including among the command staff. For example, according to archival data, over the period between 21 and 28 July 1942, which is to say over one week of combat operations, primarily in the fighting around Lebiazh'e, 311 men of the senior and middle command staff alone were killed or went missing in action, 1,141 men of the junior command staff, and 3,172 rank and file! The number of wounded men exceeded 2,800. Thus, the division's total losses amounted to almost 7,500 men.[19]

The chief of the 38th Army's Department of Cadres Colonel Iakimov reported shocking data on the 193rd Rifle Division's lack of command staff: "Division commander – 1, division chief of staff – 1, rifle battalion commanders – 5, commanders of the separate signals battalion – 1; deputy commanders of rifle companies – 26, of the machine-gun battalions and mortar companies – 10, of the submachine gun companies – 3, of the anti-tank rifle companies – 11; rifle platoon commanders – 96, machine-gun platoon commanders – 39, mortar platoon commanders – 57, submachine gun platoon commanders – 12, anti-tank rifle platoon commanders – 28, signals platoon commanders – 7; on-foot scout commanders – 3, mounted scout commanders – 3, engineer platoon commanders – 4, translators – 1, bandmaster – 1, divisional engineer commander – 1, regimental assistant chiefs of staff – 6, senior adjutants – 2, commanders of transport companies – 19, and a deputy commander for documentation. I request that you hasten the dispatch of command staff to cover the shortage.[20]

---

16 TsAMO, F. 202, op. 36, d. 129, l. 460.
17 TsAMO, F. 38 A, op. 9005, d. 39, l. 14.
18 TsAMO, F. 202, op. 36, d. 129, l. 460.
19 TsAMO, F. 202, op. 7, d. 72, ll. 450-451.
20 TsAMO, F. 202, op. 5, d. 258, l. 91.

After coming out of the encirclement and collecting the remnants of the division, it turned out that 40 men of the division's political staff alone were killed or missing in action. There was only 1 (!) man left in the headquarters of one rifle regiment, and no one at all remained in the headquarters of a second regiment![21] However, all this became clear only later, since the division's disintegration was so complete that on 26, 27, 28 and 29 July the 193rd Rifle Division was fully lost as a combat-capable combat unit to the command of the operational group. For several days, the command of Operational Group Chibisov had no knowledge of the condition or the exact location of the 193rd Rifle Division and no ability to give it combat tasks. Then, when it became clear that there could be no expectation of the emergence of any significant groups of personnel of the 193rd Rifle Division and that little was left of the division, the Briansk Front command made the decision to withdraw the 193rd Rifle Division into the deep rear for resurrection and refitting. Such was the sorrowful outcome of the fighting and the division's encirclement at Lebiazh'e.

Concluding this chapter, it is worth citing one more document that touches upon the 193rd Rifle Division. On 29 July 1942, Battalion Commissar Soroka, who'd been sent as the head of a group of political workers to search for and assemble elements that had left the front, reported to command about the results of their travels:

> Pursuant to your order about assembling the army's units that had retreated from the front, the following was verified by me in the area of Verkhniaia Kolybel'ka: the 193rd Rifle Division's 883rd Rifle Regiment [Ed. note: In his haste, here Soroka had written "838th Rifle Regiment; this regiment belonged to the 237th Rifle Division] and its commander and the regiment's commissar have been found in open foxholes in the Guliaevka area [more than 10 kilometers behind the front – I.S.], having taken up an all-round defense (in the words of the military commissar). He was told to establish contact with the division and army headquarters right away. On that same night, its location was reported to army headquarters. In the Verkhniaia Kolybel'ka, Solov'evka, Piatiletka, Guliaevka area, the following groups of Red Army men and commanders have been detained in the fields, vegetable patches, bushes and gullies and sent back to their units:
>
> 193rd Rifle Division's 685th Rifle Regiment: Battalion Commissar Ryzhkov and 8 armed Red Army men;
> 237th Rifle Division – 3 men of the division's engineer battalion;
> 838th Rifle Regiment – Lieutenants Rusanov and Samusin and up to 100 armed soldiers, including 1/3 of the submachine gunners. A second group of 100 men of this same regiment headed by a captain has been sent back to the unit.
> 340th Rifle Division's 1140th Rifle Regiment – Lieutenants Orlov and Sivokhin with 3 Red Army men;
> 340th Rifle Division's 1142nd Rifle Regiment – Lieutenant Demin and 8 submachine gunners with a field gun;
> 340th Rifle Division – Vdovin, a regiment finance officer, was supposedly searching for the regiment's field postal service together with 1 submachine gunner and 1 armed Red Army soldier;
> 49th Tank Brigade – Lieutenant Litvin and Captain Kaluzhsky became separated from their unit, failed to find it, stopped in the village of Verkniaia Kolybel'ka and began firing the tank's machine gun at a tree;

21 TsAMO, F. 202, op. 36, d. 129, l. 460.

193rd Rifle Division's 883rd Rifle Regiment – 5 Red Army soldiers have been detained and sent back to their unit;
340th Rifle Division's 1144th Rifle Regiment – Lieutenant Litvin, the commander of a machine-gun company, with 12 Red Army soldiers;
340th Rifle Division's 1144th Rifle Regiment – the commander of the 9th Rifle Company Lieutenant Churilov with 9 Red Army soldiers;
237th Rifle Division's 838th Rifle Regiment – Lieutenant Karpenko and an anti-tank rifle platoon of the 3rd Company of the 3rd Battalion with 10 armed soldiers and Senior Sergeant Anosov, platoon commander of the 9th Company with 19 armed soldiers.

In conversations Senior Sergeant Anosov showed a lack of discipline and made unhealthy statements, saying supposedly all commanders and commissars were running from the battlefield; that only they'd been left behind, and that he would have shot any commander or commissar if they had come across him there. When I ordered Anosov to follow me and instructed the lieutenant to send his [Anosov's] soldiers back to their unit, Anosov's soldiers rose and one demonstrably declared to me that they weren't going anywhere without their commander.

I was forced to give a more strict order for all of Anosov's soldiers to return to their unit under the lieutenant's command, and for Anosov and the soldier who had stated that they wouldn't go anywhere without their commander to be sent separately to the regiment's commander and commissar with an accompanying letter about their harmful attitudes. As was established through their own words, Anosov's and Karpenko's soldiers abandoned their positions without orders and headed to the rear.

In addition, up to 70 men of the 193rd, 237th and 340th Rifle Divisions intercepted by blocking detachments were sent by us back to their units. The entire 193rd Rifle Division was also discovered [The division had long ago ceased to exist as a whole – I.S.], and I ordered the division's remaining command staff to get in contact immediately with the army commander and to report on their location and combat strength. Later we ordered them to send out a group of submachine gunners to search for the division's wounded commander, who according to the soldiers was located in a gully northwest of Bol'shaia Vereika.[22]

As we see, not only in the 193rd Rifle Division were there groups of men who wound up separated from their elements and/or who fled from the front. They were also in other units.

22 TsAMO, F. 38 A (393), op. 9005, d. 45, l. 7.

19

The end of the operation

Documents, July 1942

a) Order to the Second Army, 26.7.42

Filled with pride, I was able to report to the *Führer* that after winding up the counteroffensive north of Zemliansk today, the second stage of the defensive battle for Voronezh has come to a victorious conclusion. Stalin threw the main forces of his reserves and a countless number of tanks on the attack against us here with the aim of reversing military fortune. Inflicting significant damage to the enemy, you frustrated these plans. Thanks to your courage our armies are now continuing their victorious march along the lower Don and in the direction of the Volga's mouth.

In bitter fighting, you, the soldiers of Group Blumm and of the VII Army Corps, displaying tenacity on the defensive and aggression on the offensive, obtained a decisive victory over the hordes of tanks, which moved out against us in such numbers as we've never seen before. Side by side with you, the soldiers of the ground forces, the flying units of the combat formation "North" and elements of the anti-aircraft artillery of the 153rd Flak Artillery Regiment contributed to this major victory, splendidly cooperating with each other and knowing no fatigue when carrying out their combat task.

With reverence I want to honor those who gave their lives for victory. Whatever is meant to be, will be. You've inspired in me a feeling of confidence in the fact that each new enemy offensive on the front of the Second Army will also be smashed, just like this one was smashed.

Hail the *Führer*!

Commander of the Second Field Army von Salmuth[1]

b) TRANSLATION (FROM THE RUSSIAN LANGUAGE)

Special Department — Top secret

NKVD [People's Commissariat of Internal Affairs]

118th Tank Brigade. To the chief of the army's NKVD Dept.

An urgent message

According to an order from the deputy commander of Briansk Front, the 118th Tank Brigade was pulled from the front at 2030 on 24.7.42. It assembled in a patch of woods 600 meters east of the fork in the roads on Hill 199.0 and in the northern fringe of the woods 200 meters southwest of Hill 199.0. The motorized machine-gun battalion and the anti-tank battery are positioned on the northern fringe of the woods east of Hill 199.0.

1 NARA, T-315, roll 2193, fr. 000289.

The tank battalions after the fighting will be assigned for repairs. The number of tanks suitable for combat: KV – 3, T-34 – 8, T-70 – 7. An accurate report on the combat operations over the period between 21 and 24.7.42 will be delivered tomorrow.

[Signed] The deputy chief of the NKVD Special Department Sr. Lieutenant Lavrushkov

c1) 9th Panzer Division
Division command post, 26.7.42

Summary results of prisoner interrogations
over the period from 23 to 25.7.42

The enemy soldiers taken prisoner in the division's sector over the given period belong to the following enemy formations:

49th Tank Brigade, 1st Tank Corps: 2nd Tank Battalion and motorized rifle battalion. Altogether in the brigade, there are 40 tanks (of which 20 are T-34, and the rest – T-60 and T-70). The tank brigade's initial composition included 10 heavy KV tanks as well, which were later transferred to the 89th Tank Brigade. The brigade was formed in the winter of 1941/42 at Oblivka Station in Rostov Oblast'. In March 1942 the brigade initially arrived in the city of Lipetsk, and then in the course of the next few months it was moved to Orel Oblast' via Borinskoe and Zadonsk. Here, in June 1942 it took part in combat operations.

On 30.6.42 the brigade was destroyed at Rapotkino Station; only 5 tanks remained undamaged. Next it was moved on 13 July 1942 to Strelets (Orel Oblast'), and here in the course of 5 days it was replenished with personnel and weapons. On 20.7.42 the 49th Tank Brigade arrived in the area of Ozerki together with the 89th Tank Brigade, where the latter was positioned in combat readiness, while the 49th Tank Brigade marched on to Lomovo Station, and here on 23.7 it had its first combat contact with the enemy.

The prisoners can't give any information on the location of the 253rd Tank Brigade [There was no such tank brigade in this area; plainly the prisoners were talking about the 49th Tank Brigade's 253rd Tank Battalion, and the Germans misunderstood what they were saying – I.S.]

The 237th Rifle Division's 841st Rifle Regiment: The 237th Rifle Division is subordinate to the 5th Tank Army and has the 835th, 838th and 841st Rifle Regiments, the 691st Artillery Regiment, the 5th Separate Anti-tank Artillery Battalion, a separate combat engineer battalion, a mortar battalion, and a battalion of anti-aircraft artillery. The commander of the 237th Rifle Division is Colonel Tertyshnyi; the commander of the 841st Rifle Regiment is Major Dudkin.

The 841st Rifle Regiment has 3 rifle battalions, a battery of 3 76-mm guns, 1 battery of 4 45-mm guns. A rifle battalion consists of 3 companies (170 men each), a machine-gun company (9 heavy machine guns), a mortar company and an anti-tank rifle company (16 anti-tank rifles). The 691st Artillery Regiment has three battalions, each of which consists of 3 batteries. Of this number, 3 batteries are equipped with 122-mm howitzers and 6 batteries have 24 76-mm guns. The 5th Separate Anti-Tank Artillery Battalion has 3 batteries, each with 4 45-mm anti-tank guns and one anti-tank rifle company with 36 anti-tank rifles.

The 237th Rifle Division was formed in the winter of 1941/42 in Stalinsk (Novosibirsk Oblast'). The personnel came from Red Army soldiers who'd been recently discharged from the hospital and elderly reservists (up to 45 years of age), as well as new conscripts who'd been born in 1923. The rank and file passed through a 3-month course of combat training on average. Among the officers' staff there are a large number of former reservists with higher education, who had never before served in the army; after passing a 3-month course of training, they graduated as lieutenants.

At the end of April 1942 the division was transferred to Vologda Oblast', from where it was then moved along railroads to the area south of Elets, where it unloaded on 13.7.42. Then the division marched on foot to the area of Lomovo Station, where it first made contact with the enemy. In the process, supposedly, the 841st Rifle Regiment suffered particularly heavy losses. Its 2nd Rifle Battalion was completely destroyed.

The 1144th Rifle Regiment belongs to the 340th Rifle Division: The 340th Rifle Division also includes the 1142nd Rifle Regiment, the 1143rd Rifle Regiment, and an artillery regiment with an unknown numeric designation. The 1144th Rifle Regiment has 3 rifle battalions. Each battalion has 3 rifle companies (of 120 men each), one machine-gun company, one anti-tank rifle company, and one anti-tank artillery platoon. The regiment also has a chemical platoon with 31 men. It is fully equipped with gas masks. The regiment is not equipped with poison gas or special weapons.

The regiment received replenishments in May 1942 in Okhlebnino (Tula Oblast'), after which it was activated on a frontline sector of this oblast'. Later the regiment arrived in Kaluga and then unloaded on 19 July south of Efremov, before being sent on foot to the area of Lomovo, where it first made contact with the enemy on 23.7.1942. The regiment's losses have been given as very heavy. For example, in the 6th Company as a result of the fighting on 24.7, only 18 men remained uninjured. For this reason the company was disbanded and its survivors were transferred to the 4th Company. Losses are particularly heavy among officers. The regiment commander has been killed, as has the commander of the 2nd Rifle Battalion.

c2) 9th Panzer Division, 26.7.42

Detected enemy formations in the period from 23.7 to 25.7.

During the attack conducted on 23.7 out of Somovo in the direction of Bol'shaia Vereika, the 9th Panzer Division was opposed by units of the 193rd Rifle Division and tanks of the enemy's 2nd Tank Corps. The 193rd Rifle Division arrived in Malaia Vereika on 12.7 and in the course of 12, 13 and 14.7 while engaged in combat suffered large losses. Up to 1,500 soldiers of this division were taken prisoner by units of the 9th Panzer Division.

The 2nd Tank Corps arrived in the area north of Bol'shaia Vereika and Bol'shaia Treshchevka at the beginning of July. The tank corps was smashed in the course of the fighting in the period between 10.7 and 14.7.

On 24.7 the 9th Panzer Division made combat contact with units of the 1st Tank Corps, or more exactly the 49th Tank Brigade and the 237th Rifle Division. In addition, the 193rd Rifle Division's training battalion, which has state of the art equipment, took full part in the fighting at Lomovo.

The 49th Tank Brigade took part in combat operations around Orel at the end of June 1942 and was smashed there. In the middle of July it was in Strelets and was fully replenished with personnel there in the course of 5 days. On 20.7 it arrived together with the 89th Tank Brigade in the Ozerki area. There is no more detailed information on the 89th Tank Brigade. Thus far, the 9th Panzer Division hasn't taken any Russians prisoner from the 89th Tank Brigade.

The 237th Rifle Division was formed up in the winter of 1941/42 in Stalinsk (Siberia). At the end of April the division arrived in Vologda. From there it was transferred in July to Elets, where it arrived on 13.07. The division then marched on foot to the Ozerki – Lomovo area and there had its first contact with the enemy on 24(?).07. The division is well-equipped, has up to date weaponry and well-trained men in ages between 19 and 45.

On 25.7 the [9th Panzer] division entered combat with the above-named enemy units, as well as the newly-appeared 240th [sic] Rifle Division. As follows from a captured order, the 118th Tank Brigade and the 512th [sic] Rifle Regiment of the 146th Rifle Division were also supposed to take part in the fighting; however, their presence wasn't confirmed. Based on suppositions, it is possible that the 118th Tank Brigade is directly subordinate to the Briansk Front command, and the possibility that the 512th [sic] Rifle Regiment was subordinate to the tank brigade isn't excluded.

The 340th Rifle Division received replenishments in May 1942 in Tula, and from there it arrived in Kaluga. On 19.07 this division was shifted to the area south of Efremov and then marched on foot to the Ozerki Station area [in the original, this is crossed out and replaced by "Surikovo" – I.S.] and to the west of there. The 340th Rifle Division's 1142nd Rifle Regiment appeared in the frontline sector of our 340th Infantry Division already in the middle of July [1942].[2]

d) Urgent to the OKH Headquarters

INTERROGATION SHEET OF A PRISONER-OF-War

Information on the individual (only in the case of exceptionally important testimony and no lower than a senior officer)

Name and Surname: Mikhail Romanov　**Nationality:** Russian

Rank: Brigade Commander　**Post:** commander of the 193rd Rifle Division

1) **Composition of the combat units and formations**

   Battalion, artillery battalion, regiment: 193rd Rifle Division consists of the 883rd, 895th and 685th Rifle Regiments and the 384th Artillery Regiment

   Higher formation: The division was subordinate to the command of a group of forces, the headquarters of which on 26.7 was in Murav'evka. The 167th and 340th Rifle Divisions were also subordinate to this command of a group of forces (probably, the 1st Tank Corps).

   Date and place of formation: The 193rd Rifle Division formed up in the winter of 41/42 in Sorochinsk (Chkalovskaia Oblast'). In May 1942 it initially arrived in Riazan' Oblast', and from there it was sent on around 10 July to the Lomovo area.

   Quantity and types of guns, mortars, tanks and similar: The 384th Artillery Regiment has three battalions and is equipped with 18 122-mm howitzers and 18 76-mm guns.

   Names of the division commanders and superior commanders: Until 11.07.42 the division commander of the 193rd Rifle Division was Major General Smekhotvorov. Due to illness he was replaced. Romanov arrived from the command reserve of the Voronezh Front. Until October 1941 he was the commander of the 277th Rifle Division, which was later destroyed at Piriatin.

   Table strength: The table strength of the division amounts to 13,000 men.

   Present strength: 13,000 men.

2 NARA, T-315, roll 541, fr. 001227 – 1230.

2) **Composition of the combat units and formations**
Composition of the soldiers according to age, place of residence and length of training: The personnel are of various years of birth. 50% are Russian, the rest – Azerbaizhanians, Kirghiz, Tatars and Kazakhs. The length of combat training amounts on average to 3 months.

3) **Replacements**
From what reserve regiment (or other unit) did the latest replacements arrive?
Over the last 2 months the division hasn't received any replacements.

4) **Arms and supplies**
Were there enough food, ammunition and uniforms available?
The division had a sufficient quantity of food, ammunition and uniforms.
Contents of letters from relatives:
The new from relatives was good.
Location of stockpiles of food, ammunition, fuel and similar:
Stockpiles of food and ammunition were located in Zadonsk.
Preparation for anti-chemical defense (poison gas, munitions and similar):
The division had available only passive means of chemical defense. Each soldier had a gas mask.
27.7.42 9th Panzer Division

e) **9th Panzer Division, 28.7.1942**

Summary results of prisoner interrogations
over the period from 25.07 to 26.07.42

As was already mentioned in the report from 15.07, the 193rd Rifle Division again appeared in the sector of the division's front. Testimony from the adjutant of the commander of the 883rd Rifle Regiment's 2nd Battalion contradicts the information given by the division commander Mikhail Romanov, according to whom the 193rd Rifle Division suffered only insignificant losses in the course of fighting on 12 and 13.7. In particular, the adjutant stated that he had heard a statement by his division commander that the division had lost 3,000 men on 13.7. Of this number, the 883rd Rifle Regiment's 2nd Battalion alone, which had a total strength of 900 service personnel, lost 550 men.

Over the accounting period, the following new enemy units were detected:

26th Tank Brigade: There is no information about its superior headquarters. The brigade consists of two tank battalions (one of which is the 270th Tank Battalion) and 1 motorized rifle battalion. The 270th Tank Battalion consists of 3 tank companies, each with around 100 men. Two companies are equipped with 10 T-34 tanks each and one company, accordingly, is equipped with KV tanks. The commander of the 270th Tank Battalion is Major Filatov.

The 26th Tank Brigade was formed in the winter of 1941/42 in Nizhnyi Tagil (the Urals). According to prisoner testimony, the brigade's personnel are made up of older age soldiers.

In March 1942 the brigade at first arrived in Elets, and from there it was later transferred to the south. On 19.07 it arrived in Bol'shaia Kamenka, where it first met the enemy. According to prisoner testimonies, the 270th Tank Battalion suffered major losses, primarily as a result of the Luftwaffe's activity. The battalion's remaining operational tanks were dug into positions in Kamenka on 24.7. On 25.7 five tanks received an assignment to attack to the south, and in the process all of them were destroyed.

The 167th Rifle Division: There is no information about its superior headquarters. It consists of the 520th, 465th and 615th Rifle Regiments, the 576th Artillery Regiment, the 180th Combat Engineer Battalion, and the 535th Chemical Defense Company.

The 465th Rifle Regiment consists of three rifle battalions and a submachine-gun company. The rifle battalions consist of 3 companies (of 160 men each), a machine-gun company, and a mortar company. The 180th Engineer Battalion had two companies (of 100 men each, the majority of soldiers of which are of older draft age).

The 167th Rifle Division was formed up in the period between February and April 1942 in the location of Sukholozhe (Sverdlovsk Oblast'). The majority of the men are new recruits. Among them are a large number of former workers of defense industry factories. The length of combat training was 3 months.

At the end of April the division arrived in Morshchansk, then in Lipetsk, and at the beginning of July – in the Kamenka area. In all of these places, the division's cantonments were busy with digging trenches. On 23.07 it was transferred to Lomovo, and here on 25.7 it took part in fighting for the first time.

The 118th Tank Brigade: Subordination unknown. It consists of two tank battalions of supposedly 40 tanks each of an unknown type and a motorized rifle battalion. The motorized rifle battalion consists of 4 companies (100 men each). The 1st Company is equipped with 8 light machine guns, 4 anti-tank rifles and 12 submachine guns.

The brigade was formed in April 1942 in the Urals from a number of soldiers who'd been discharged from hospitals, as well as a number of new recruits. The soldiers went through 3 months of combat training. In June the brigade was sent by railroad to Elets, and on 22 July it arrived in the Surikovo area. Here it first took part in fighting on 26.7.

The 104th Separate Rifle Brigade, which is supposedly subordinate to the 3rd Tank Army. It consists of four rifle battalions.

The brigade formed up in February 1942 in Gor'kov Oblast', and the personnel went through a course of training until the end of April. On 20 July it arrived in Novokreshchenka and here it had its combat baptism. The estimated losses were very high. The 4th Battalion was supposedly destroyed completely.

The 923rd Motorized Rifle Brigade: Subordination unknown. This brigade was supposedly formed on the basis of the 138th Guards Rifle Regiment, which was located in reserve near Briansk. It consists of 3 rifle battalions. The brigade arrived on ?.07 in the Lomovo area and here on 25.07 it first took part in combat.

The 445th Motorized Rifle Battalion likely belongs to the 1st Tank Corps' 1st Motorized Rifle Brigade. The battalion consists of three rifle companies, an anti-tank rifle company, a machine-gun platoon (6 heavy machine guns), a mortar battery (6 82-mm mortars). The battalion formed up in April 1942 in Moscow and went through combat training until the middle of June. Later it arrived in Lipetsk, and then was transferred on 20[?].07 to the Lomovo area. Its first contact with the enemy took place on 26.7.

The 13th Cavalry Regiment (of the 17th Mountain Cavalry Division). The 13th Cavalry Regiment's 1st Company has one anti-tank rifle platoon and one submachine gun platoon with 15 submachine guns. The regiment was formed in February 1942 near Moscow, and there it went through combat training until the month of July. On 24.07 the regiment arrived in the Surikovo area and supposedly took part in the fighting here.

The 1244th Guards Destroyer Anti-tank Artillery Battalion: Subordination unknown. It consists of 5 batteries, each with 12[?] soldiers of a crew and each with 4 45-mm anti-tank guns. The place of the battalion's forming is unknown. The last time the battalion received replacements was at the end of May, from the 26th[?] Reserve Artillery Regiment in Vodop'ianovo (Tambov Oblast'). On 16.7 the battalion arrived in Lomovo and here it took part in the fighting on 26.7. In the process it lost 4 guns.

The 811th Artillery Regiment, attached to the 340th Rifle Division (probably, the artillery reserve of the main command). It is equipped with 12 76-mm guns, approximately 18 122-mm howitzers, and 18 152-mm[?] long-range guns.[3]

* * *

At 2000 on 27 July, having carried out its assignment to screen the infantry divisions as they moved back into their old line of defense, the units of the 9th Panzer Division began to withdraw to the rear. Prior to this, in the course of the day the division's engineer-sapper battalion had repaired the bridges and crossing sites along the designated withdrawal routes.[4] In the growing dusk, the division's columns were moving along the dusty village roads to the south, leaving behind the infantry that was digging in along the hills. The 9th Panzer Division had completed its role in the operation: the Russian breakthrough had been liquidated, the infantry division's frontline had been restored, and the crisis on the front of the VII Army Corps had been eliminated. At the order of the Second Army headquarters, the 9th Panzer Division, just like a fire brigade that had done a fine job, was withdrawn to Orekhovo in the army's reserve for rest. Another "fire" had been extinguished, but the tendency was that it wouldn't be long until new fires broke out along the rickety front.

Just one panzer battalion of the 33rd Panzer Regiment received an assignment to stay behind in the area of Hill 191.3 east of Bol'shaia Vereika until the evening of 28 July, in order to cover the shift of one of the battalions of the 387th Infantry Division's 541st Infantry Regiment to this key defensive position. The losses of the 9th Panzer Division for 27 July amounted to 5 killed, 37 wounded and 1 missing in action (all were soldiers or junior officers).[5]

That same evening, at an order from the Second Army the company of the 201st Sturmgeschütz Battalion that was supporting the 385th Infantry Division's offensive was again returned to Group Blumm within the Voronezh bridgehead.[6] The 323rd Infantry Division's 594th Infantry Regiment was also returned to this group; prior to this, it had been defending the eastern bank of the Don River as part of the 168th Infantry Division. After the conclusion of the operation, the subordination of the anti-tank artillery battalions was also changed in accordance with fresh tasks. An

3 NARA, T-315, roll 541, fr. 001231-1234.
4 NARA, T-315, roll 541, fr. 001118.
5 NARA, T-315, roll 541, fr. 001432.
6 The grouping of German forces defending in Voronezh was named for the commander of the 57th Infantry Division that led it, Lieutenant General Blumm.

order from the Second Army confirmed that the VII Army Corps would continue to have the 340th, 385th, 387th and 168th Infantry Divisions.[7] Taking advantage of the calm settling over the front, the 387th Infantry Division's command finally was able to allow itself to withdraw one of the division's regiments into reserve (the 542nd Infantry Regiment was chosen, which had been substantially battered in the fighting).[8]

The day of 27 July was marked by a sharp decline in the combat activity of the troops, which was reflected in the reduced casualties. These amounted to 5 killed and 28 wounded in the 340th Infantry Division (in the VII Army Corps' report it was noted: "On the front of the 340th Infantry Division – a conspicuous calm)[9]; 25 killed and 121 wounded (4 officers) with 9 missing in action in the 385th Infantry Division; 36 killed and 21 wounded (1 officer) in the 387th Infantry Division.[10] Altogether there were 71 killed, 207 wounded and 10 missing in action in the four divisions of the VII Army Corps, for a total of 288. This, on a relatively quiet day of fighting!

The final episode of the 9th Panzer Division's participation in this operation was a nighttime clash at Hill 191.3, where the 33rd Panzer Regiment's panzer battalion, which had remained behind to provide security, and the infantry of the 387th Infantry Division's 541st Infantry Regiment repulsed an attack by an "enemy forward detachment with the support of tanks". Obviously, the 9th Panzer Division's casualties for 28 July were connected with this action: 2 soldiers killed and 11 wounded.[11] Already at 0900, pursuant to an order that had arrived, the panzer battalion left its positions on Hill 191.3 and set off on a march to the south, in order to catch up with the rest of the 9th Panzer Division. With this the 9th Panzer Division's participation in the VII Army Corps' operation officially came to an end, although in fact the VII Army Corps' command considered the operation completed back on 26 July, as noted by von Salmuth's order to the troops congratulating them on the success. It was on this day too that the first results of the fighting were added up; the VII Army Corps' journal of combat operations noted: "As a result of this second defensive battle in the area north of Zemliansk, 171 tanks were knocked out and 3,785 men were taken prisoner by the forces of the VII Army Corps."[12]

In a detailed account of the fighting between 21 and 26 July 1942, compiled by the headquarters of VII Army Corps on 28 July, the following information was provided:

> Over the period from 21.7 to 26.7 the enemy lost 2,643 men prisoner and 171 tanks knocked out [as we see, the number of prisoners in the account was reduced by more than 1,000 men in this account, but the number of knocked-out tanks remained the same – I.S.], as well as 21 guns, 61 anti-tank guns, 164 anti-tank rifles, 83 mortars, 201 machine guns and a large amount of combat equipment. On the field of battle, 5,500 dead enemy soldiers were counted [for a total of 8,143 irrecoverable losses in men – I.S.]. Our own losses were not insubstantial due to the severity of the fighting. Over the period from 21.7 to 23.7, the 387th and 340th Infantry Division's lost on the defense 286 men killed, 993 wounded and 171 men missing in action [for a total of 1,450 men – I.S.]
>
> The losses of the 9th Panzer Division and 385th Infantry Division during the offensive between 24.7 and 26.7 comprised 165 men killed, 872 wounded and 29 missing in action [1,066 men – I.S.]

7 NARA, T-314, roll 353, fr. 000421.
8 NARA, T-314, roll 353, fr. 001349.
9 NARA, T-314, roll 353, fr. 001349.
10 NARA, VII AK, T-314, roll 354, fr. 726-727.
11 NARA, T-315, roll 541, fr. 001432.
12 NARA, T-314, roll 353, fr. 000417.

> Given the great significance that the Voronezh bridgehead has for future operations in the southern sector of the Eastern Front, the corps anticipates new enemy attacks soon.[13]

On the morning of 28 July the VII Army Corps' infantry divisions, which were occupying the positions along the former front line from which they'd been driven by the Russian offensive, continued to dig into the earth and improve their "new" old defensive lines while bringing themselves back to order. Once again, the VII Army Corps, which had fought off the Russian attacks with the help of reserves of panzer and infantry divisions that had hurried to its support, as well with the powerful Luftwaffe support and the reinforcing anti-tank artillery battalions, went over to a solid defense …

The 9th Panzer Division's withdrawal from the screening line went so quickly and smoothly, that at first it wasn't noticed by the units of Operational Group Chibisov, and by inertia they continued to count dozens of German tanks in places where in fact there were now none. For a certain time, contact with the enemy was lost, and the reconnaissance detachments of Operational Group Chibisov, which was renamed first as the 4th Army and later as the 38th Army, conducted numerous probes with the aim of establishing where the suddenly departed Germans had gone, and where the German frontline now ran.

The chief of the 340th Rifle Division's Political Department reported: "Patrols of the reconnaissance companies, which moved out on the night of 27/28 July in the direction of Lomovo, by 0500 reached the northern outskirts of Lomovo with one group, where, having detected no enemy presence, they continued to scout the southern and southeastern outskirts of Lomovo. The second group reconnoitered Surikovye Vyselki. Throughout the day of 28 July, the enemy demonstrated no activity."[14]

Intelligence summaries from units of the 11th Tank Corps reported:

> At 1600 on 27.7.42: "At night [the night of 26/27 July – I.S] the tanks that were in the patch of woods west and east of Surikovye Vyselki left in an unknown direction …."
>
> At 0350 on 28.7.42: "I reached the village of Lomovo at 2000. In the process of scouting, I established through observation and the questioning of villagers that the enemy on the night of 26/27.7.42 crossed all of his forces to the southern bank of the river and took up a defense about 200 meters above the village. In conversation with the local population it became clear that the enemy began to leave the village for its defensive position in the daytime. The Germans are taking cattle from the population and forbidding the people to make any movements around the village. According to the peoples' information, the enemy has no tanks. At night the enemy is firing at Lomovo from mortars, especially focusing on the northern side of the village, where the roads approach the village. When returning from the village, the enemy spotted us and opened mortar fire at us and all the while shelled the vehicles that were parked in the woods next to Hill 208.8."
>
> 1000 on 28 July: "Route of reconnaissance: woods 1 kilometer north and northeast of Surikovye Vyselki, Burial Mound +3.0, villages of Surikovo and Surikovye Vyselki. With reconnaissance it has been established: the enemy has not been detected in the indicated direction. According to the statements of the population, on the evening of 26.7.42 the enemy tanks and motorized infantry withdrew from Surikovo in the direction of Lomovo. The enemy fell back from Surikovo with the onset of darkness."

13 NARA, T-314, roll 353, fr. 000912-915.

14 TsAMO, F. 340 sd, op. 1, d. 91, l. 449.

1030 on 28 July: "Under the pressure of our units on the afternoon of 27 July, on the night of 28 July the enemy fell back to the southwest to the Lomovo, Surikovo area and took up a defense to the south of Lomovo, to the left of Point 134.7 and to the right of Points 199.8 and 214.6. The enemy appears in the village of Lomovo only in the daytime and in small numbers, but at night withdraws to defensive positions. Mortar batteries are positioned 1 kilometer south of Lomovo, and are shelling all of Hill 208.8. At night the sharp rumble of engines, like those of tanks or tractors, was audible beyond Lomovo, but nothing has been established. The enemy was driven from the village of Surikovo by a motorized and mechanized unit of the 27th Rifle Corps (an obvious mistake, since this corps did not operate in the area at all. – I.S.). At 0500 on 28.7.42, there was no enemy in Surikovo. At 0400 on 28.7.42, in the area of Bol'shaia Vereika, the enemy was located 1 kilometer north of Bol'shaia Vereika. At 0400 28 July the enemy was keeping the woods south of Posel'skoe under frequent shelling, while mortars were shelling the road right up to the village of Murav'evka."

1800 on 28 July: "It has been established that the enemy's forward edge of defense runs along the northern outskirts of Bol'shaia Vereika with the presence of a small quantity of infantry. Sub machine gunners [sic] are scattered among the attics and lofts of the village's buildings. … There is no enemy in Surikovo. His forward edge of defense runs along the northern slopes of the hills lying south of Surikovo.

1900 on 28 July: "Along the entire extent of the route [Surikovye Vyselki – woods to the west – Lomovo – Surikovo], no enemy was detected. The enemy stockpiled up to 10 cases of ammunition in the middle of the village of Surikovye Vyselki. Another 200 meters beyond there stands a knocked-out German vehicle, which contained a letter that I've [previously] noted and a German-language book. We seized both. Along the valley of the Bystrik Creek and in the village of Surikovye Vyselki, rifles, helmets and up to 500 of our gasmasks lie about. In addition, from the bottom of the stream …. [the document's page ends here and there is no continuation – I.S.][15]

According to the information brought back by the patrols, the enemy had fallen back in a southerly direction to the main defensive belt. However, conclusions differed regarding this withdrawal. In the headquarters they suspected a fresh regrouping of hostile forces with the possible aim of resuming the active operations that had ceased. Indeed, judging from documents, the higher the level of Soviet command, the greater were these suspicions.

For example, the 62nd Tank Brigade's headquarters was reporting to its neighbors that an aggregation of 120 machines of the 9th Panzer Division had been detected in the area of Vysochkino, from which followed the conclusion that the enemy was conducting a regrouping for a new offensive.[16] An analogous conclusion was later drawn in the headquarters of the 340th Rifle Division as well. A report about an enormous number of German machines assembled opposite its front also arrived from the 1st Tank Corps. In an operational summary it was reported that "by the end of 27 July up to 200 enemy vehicles were unloaded in Bol'shaia Vereika, which were bringing up motorized infantry and ammunition."[17]

Early on the morning of 28 July (between 0600 and 0650), these suspicions were voiced in telegraph conversations between Briansk Front's operations chief Colonel Sidel'nikov and the deputy chief of operations Colonel Kalganov, who'd been assigned from Briansk Front's headquarters to the headquarters of Operational Group Chibisov (the 38th Army). Giving a briefing on the

15 TsAMO, F. 11 tk, op. 1, d. 239, l. 71.
16 TsAMO, F. 11 tk, op. 1, d. 239, l. 73.
17 TsAMO, F. 38 A, op. 9005, d. 35, l. 112.

situation, Kalganov reported: "On Chibisov's left flank, at Chibisov's order the establishments [a code word used by the Soviet command for "units"] are standing in place today. The enemy has not shown any activity today since daybreak. Within an hour I'm expecting the return of my liaison officers, who will bring back updated information on the situation from Lazarev, Mel'nikov, Martirosian and Katukov [that is to say, the commanders of the 11th Tank Corps, 167th Rifle Division, 340th Rifle Division and 1st Tank Corps respectively – I.S.]. I will immediately transmit this information to you and bring it back with myself."

Next Sidel'nikov asked Kalganov a direct question: "Can active enemy operations be expected in the first half of the day today? Is there any information or any signs that active operations have started?"

Kalganov replied:

> It is necessary to expect active operations this morning. All the establishments were briefed with respect to this yesterday evening. The arrival of enemy motorized infantry in Bol'shaia Vereika serves as the basis for possible enemy actions. Up to 200 vehicles arrived in this place yesterday. Yesterday evening, Katukov's establishment approached Surikovo. Katukov's chief of staff reported that the enemy wasn't occupying Surikovo and that they [the 1st Tank Corps] also didn't occupy it because this place is situated in a deep valley. Yesterday evening, more precisely at 2300, Katukov was ordered to secure Surikovo, and if it wasn't advantageous to remain there, to move onto the hills south of it and dig in there. How this was carried out – the information will be brought back at 0700; I've dispatched liaison officers.

Sidel'nikov again asked the question that was troubling him: "Are there any signs of active operations? Acoustic or other signs? Are enemy aircraft operating?"

Kalganov clarified: "One and half hours ago there were no audible signs or enemy aerial activity in the given sector. There is now disruptions in wire communications with Katukov. I cannot say at the given moment whether or not these are signs. From my area, no aerial activity is discernible."

With the understanding that Kalganov was going to head back to Sidel'nikov at 0800 and having preliminarily given him the expected information on the matter, the chiefs of the operations departments terminated their discussion.

Yet in the headquarters of Operational Group Chibisov (the 38th Army) and in the distant headquarters of Briansk Front, an alarming ambiguity arose on the subject of whether or not the Germans would launch a new offensive on the army's front. The Briansk Front's Military Council just in case sent a telegram to the army headquarters about digging in on the occupied line.[18]

Morning passed, the day began, and there were no signs of an enemy offensive. Tension in the operational group's headquarters began to subside, and in the afternoon General Chibisov decided that there would be no fresh German offensive. The crisis, judging from everything, had passed. Obviously, his decision to withdraw the worn-out and battered 2nd Tank Corps into the army reserve was connected with this assessment. At 1500 the corps' chief of staff Colonel Nagaibakov issued an order for the corps' movement into the army reserve and for its withdrawal to the Alekseevka, Griboedovo, Korovkino area.[19] The new commander of the 2nd Tank Corps Colonel Burdov, who'd been appointed to the post by Colonel Nagaibakov, makes no appearance in the corps' documents over all the time after his appointment, leaving all the documentation of decisions, including orders, to his chief of staff, as if it was Nagaibakov, not he, Burdov, who was the commander of the 2nd Tank Corps.

18 TsAMO, 38 A, op. 9005, d. 39, l. 15.
19 TsAMO, F. 3109 (27 tbr), op. 1, d. 9, l. 181.

The 11th Tank Corps remained on the line it had occupied back on 26 July and was continuing to defend it. The corps' chief of staff reported at 1400:

> The 59th Tank Brigade has 7 Mk-II and 14 T-60 tanks, and no motorized infantry. The 53rd Tank Brigade: 5 KV, 3 T-34 and 24 T-60 tanks, and 69 motorized riflemen. The 160th Tank Brigade: 9 Mk-II, 13 T-60. The 12th Motorized Rifle Brigade has 265 men and 5 anti-tank guns. Fifty-five replacements have arrived. Losses from airstrikes over 27.7.42: 2 trucks with ammunition burned-out, 1 transport vehicle and 1 ambulance damaged; 1 dead and 5 wounded. The 8th Separate Reconnaissance Battalion has 18 BTR, 13 armored cars; 3 T-34 tanks have been transferred to the 53rd Tank Brigade.
>
> The 193rd Rifle Division is not combat-effective. The 72nd Guards Mortar Regiment is in firing positions in the Ozerki area ... the 396th Howitzer Artillery Regiment is in the Sedelki area. In the course of the day, the corps' formations were not subjected to enemy aerial attacks. The corps occupied and is holding the Dolgoe, Hill 204.0, 199.0, Posel'skoe line. From the morning with the aim of improving our positions, [the corps] has moved out with rifle units to the northern outskirts of Lomovo, Surikovye Vyselki, Surikovo line. At 1400 the infantry's forward units reached the Hill 199.0, woods north of Surikovye Vyselki, hill southwest of Posel'skoe line. The 12th Motorized Rifle Brigade is few in numbers, and the 340th Rifle Division needs refitting. Time is necessary to bring the 193rd Rifle Division back into order. The tank brigades are each presently equipped according to table strength with 20% of their heavy tanks, 15% of their medium tanks and 80% of their light tanks. The corps as a whole ... can defend the occupied line and perhaps conduct active operations with a limited objective.[20]

The 167th Rifle Division together with units of the 1st Tank Corps' 49th Tank Brigade and 1st Motorized Rifle Brigade was conducting local fighting to improve the forward positions in the area of Hill 191.3. In the division's documents there are no mentions of this combat. According to a German account, "the enemy was attacking the combat outposts, in particular on Hill 191.3. The attacks were driven back with the help of powerful and effectively directed artillery fire. With the onset of darkness the forward positions on Hill 191.3 were abandoned under the cover of the artillery fire and shifted back."[21]

The VII Army Corps' war diary clarifies a number of details: "Around mid-day the enemy again attacked Hill 191.3 with major forces. This time up to 2 battalions attacked with strong artillery support. The attack bogged down under our artillery fire."[22] Nevertheless, it was in this battle that the hero of the 387th Infantry Division's recent defensive fighting was killed – the 541st Infantry Regiment's commander, Colonel Langsdorf, who'd been noted for his bravery in the corps' documents. The VII Army Corps' combat journal dryly reports his death without offering any details. However, unexpectedly I was able to find traces of the colonel's death in Soviet documents.

In a 1st Tank Corps' intelligence summary I came across a comment that undoubtedly speaks to this incident: "According to information from the 104th Separate Rifle Brigade it has become known that at 1430 on 28.7.42, during an artillery preparation by our forces, a German colonel and lieutenant were killed by submachine gunners in Bol'shaia Vereika. According to documents found on their bodies, it has been established that Colonel Guldendorff [this, apparently, is how they messed up when translating Langsdorff's surname – I.S.] is the commander of the

20 TsAMO, F. 340 sd, op. 1, d. 22, l. 193.
21 NARA, T-314, roll 353, fr. 001085.
22 NARA, T-314, roll 353, fr. 000422.

387th Infantry Division's 545th Infantry Regiment [in reality, he commanded the 541st Infantry Regiment – I.S.], and the lieutenant was his adjutant. On a map they were carrying it has been marked that the headquarters of the 545th Infantry Regiment is in Kaver'ia, the headquarters of the 387th Infantry Division is in Dolgoe [a different Dolgoe, this one south of the Bol'shaia Vereika River], while the headquarters of the 385th Infantry Division is on the northern outskirts of Sivertsevo – Kaver'ia."[23]

As we see, the courageous German colonel, who performed superbly during the heaviest defensive fighting of the 387th Infantry Division between 21 and 25 July and passed through it without a scratch, was killed together with his adjutant in the division's final and not so important battle as the operation was winding down.

A similar incident happened in the 27th Tank Brigade's sector. Its commissar reported, "... an *Oberleutnant* was killed, whose documents with maps and family letters were taken by me. Everything has been forwarded to the 2nd Tank Corps."[24]

Of the four tank corps of the operational group (which was now known as the 4th Army), an offensive task was given to only one on 28 July – the 7th Tank Corps. Heading a grouping of his tank corps and the attached 284th and 237th Rifle Divisions, the 119th Rifle Brigade and the 201st Tank Brigade, Major General Rotmistrov received an order to break through the enemy's defense north of Spasskoe and Vysochkino and, if you will, with one final desperate effort of this operation in a narrow sector was to reach the Sukhaia Vereika River and destroy the opposing enemy in the Novopavlovka – Chibisovka area.

The attack began at 1800 and continued throughout the evening and night. The 7th Tank Corps' tank brigades penetrated the German frontline and reached the approaches to Spasskoe and Novopavlovka and the woods east of there, but the infantry of the rifle units that were following behind the tanks became pinned down even before reaching the German frontline. By morning, the tanks were compelled to withdraw from the battle for re-fueling, since the tank brigades were unable to hold the breakthrough area without infantry. On the morning of 29 July, the Luftwaffe again made an appearance above the battlefield, and as if making up for the hours lost over the night, pounced upon the grouping's attacking units with redoubled strength.

A general staff officer located with the 7th Tank Corps Major Krasov reported:

> On 28 July at 1700 the 7th Tank Corps consisting of a group of forces of the 4th Army, went on the attack. The task: attack the enemy in the direction of the southwestern outskirts of Perekopovka, Spasskoe, Vysochkino, Point 213.8 with the assignment to destroy the enemy on the axis of attack and cut off his retreat to the Sukhaia Vereika River.
>
> On 29 July under the effects of a strong attack by enemy aircraft and artillery and mortar fire, the attack was stopped. The corps' units went over to a defense ....
>
> The shameful actions of the 237th Rifle Division's infantry must be noted. Given the slightest attack by enemy aircraft, they ran away in panic, as happened on 29.7.42 when they fled from Hill 199.8 to Kamenka. In fact, there were in general a lot of shameful incidents in this division. I've already reported to you in code about the commander of the 237th Rifle Division Colonel Tertyshnyi's failure twice to carry out a combat order from the headquarters of the 7th Tank Corps. On 28.7.42 staff documents and 3 fascist flags (resembling pennants) were taken. On 29.7.42, 7 men of the 340th Infantry Division were taken prisoner. They didn't reveal anything significant in their interrogations.

23 TsAMO, F. 1 tk, op. 1, d. 235, l. 69.
24 TsAMO, F. 2 tk, op. 1, d. 224(b), l. 97.

> Today on 29.7.42 the enemy aircraft are rife above our combat formations with growing strength. Our air force is absent. I also will report that under the attacks of enemy aircraft, the motorized riflemen of the 7th Tank Corps' 87th Tank Brigade and 7th Motorized Rifle Brigade scattered in flight. Steps have been taken to reassemble them.[25]

The 3rd Guards Tank Brigade was operating together with the 62nd Tank Brigade to the east of a Zemliansk tract in the general direction of a hill in front of the woods north of Vysochkino. The brigades attacked in two united combat groups: on the right, consisting of 12 KV, 8 T-34 and 11 T-60 with the motorized rifle battalion of the 62nd Tank Brigade, and on the left, 12 KV, 6 T-34, 10 T-60 and the motorized rifle battalion of the 3rd Guards Tank Brigade.[26] Altogether, the attacking grouping numbered 59 tanks, of which 38 were medium and light tanks. Such a high concentration of KV tanks in the attack – 24 machines simultaneously – arguably had never been created anywhere else over all the days of the operation.

In the 3rd Guards Tank Brigade's combat diary, the course of the battle is reflected as follows:

> With tank fire, the enemy infantry was put to flight. The brigade approached the western and eastern fringes of the woods, but had no success. The infantry, operating on the right, didn't support the brigade and failed to reinforce the line occupied by the brigade. As a result of this, the brigade's tanks had to withdraw. As a result of 16-hours of bitter fighting, the brigade lost 5 KV tanks destroyed and 2 KV tanks knocked out; 21 men burned up in their tanks, 2 were killed and 2 wounded [judging from all the available documents, this total didn't include the losses of the motorized rifle battalion – 2 killed and 22 wounded – and partially, the losses of the 2nd Tank Battalion – 9 killed, 6 wounded and 10 missing in action – I.S.]."[27] The brigade's motorized rifle battalion seized 7 76-mm guns [apparently, abandoned by the Soviets], of which 4 were inoperable and 3 serviceable, as well as 6 light machine guns and a lot of shells, cartridges and 35 rifles.[28]

The 62nd Tank Brigade went on the attack at 1800 from its jumping-off area 1 kilometer south of Hill 217.8:

> An infantry platoon of the motorized rifle battalion, without meeting any resistance, occupied Lomovo [the scale of one infantry platoon's actions in a village that extended for more than 5 kilometers is astonishing – I.S.] and cleared the road of mines. Tanks and infantry, overcoming heavy artillery and mortar fire, advanced and by 1900 reached the valley between Point 217.8 and Hill 212.9. The enemy concentrated all of his firepower on the assault groupings, putting into action two batteries of 6-barreled rocket launchers [Nebelwerfers] and forced the infantry, which was taking significant casualties, to hug the ground, yet despite this the woods 1 kilometer north of Vysochkino were taken by 2245 [this assertion contradicts German documents – I.S.]. The tanks by this time were running low on ammunition, and the pace of the attack slowed, since only those tanks that still had some ammunition were taking part in the fighting. Brigade commander Guards Major Gumeniuk ordered Battalion Commissar Eliseenko to bring up more shells, which were delivered by sunrise on 29 July.[29]

25 TsAMO, F. 202, op. 5, d. 373, l. 53.
26 TsAMO, F. 62 tbr, op. 1, d. 4, l. 29.
27 TsAMO, F. 3 gv. tbr, op. 1, d. 10, l. 24.
28 TsAMO, F. 3 gv. tbr, op. 1, d. 25, l. 37.
29 TsAMO, F. 62 tbr, op. 1, d. 4, l. 30.

The 62nd Tank Brigade's documents highlight the conduct of the commander of the 27th Tank Battalion:

> From the very start of the fighting, a young Communist and commander of the 27th Tank Battalion Captain Volkov stood out. Before the attack, when giving the company commanders their assignments, Comrade Volkov told them, "Comrade commanders, follow my example! Onward to destroy the foe!" Going on the attack in a T-34 tank, Comrade Volkov destroyed 4 enemy tanks. As a result of the heavy stress and heat in the machine, Volkov was nearly overcome by the fumes, but he refused to leave the machine while he still had ammunition. While refueling his machine, Comrade Volkov refreshed himself before going back on the attack.[30]

However, the tank brigade's documents clearly blame the infantry for the attack's failure:

> The tanks began to be pulled back to take on more fuel and ammunition; simultaneously with this, the infantry abandoned their occupied lines and began to retreat in the tanks' wake. Measures taken to stop the retreat had no substantial success, because the enemy, taking advantage of the slackening fire and confusion, rallied and under the cover of mortar and artillery fire and support by bombers, which began to show high activity, pushed forward and met our tanks with intense anti-tank fire.[31]

As a result of the action, the 62nd Tank Brigade lost 14 men killed, 69 wounded and 11 missing in action. One T-34 was destroyed, and 6 T-34 and 6 T-60 were knocked out.[32]

The 87th Tank Brigade, which was attacking toward Spasskoe west of the Zemliansk tract, also complained about the infantry's "poor conduct":

> Fire support from the infantry of the 7th Motorized Rifle Brigade, which was operating with the tanks, was necessary; however, one portion of the infantry retreated, while the rest became pinned down on Hill 214.6 and failed to support the tanks. As is obvious, the troops of the 7th Motorized Rifle Brigade weren't motivated to carry out the combat task and not only failed to carry it out, they stymied the fulfillment of the combat task by the tankers. In the Spasskoe area as soon as dawn broke the tanks were subjected to intense fire from anti-tank guns and were compelled to fall back with losses to the northern slopes of Hill 214.6 and take up a defense there.

The document continues: "6 enemy soldiers, 4 rifles, a light machine gun and an anti-tank rifle were captured. Our losses over this time: 13 killed, 24 wounded, 4 missing in action. We lost 10 T-34s, of which 4 were burned out, 1 became disabled in a minefield, and 5 were knocked out; and 5 T-60s, of which 2 were burned out, 1 became disabled by mines, and 2 were knocked out."

This political report also preserved for us the charged atmosphere of those most difficult days, and the condition and mood of the tank crews:

> The morale is fine. For 18 hours, the tankers, engaged in combat with the fascists, did not leave their machines. At the end of the battle, many men climbed out of their machines, stupefied by the combat, but properly managed to come back to their senses, rise to their feet,

30 TsAMO, F. 62 tbr., op. 1, d. 19, l. 102.

31 Ibid.

32 TsAMO, F. 62 tbr, op. 1, d. 4, l. 30.

> and the first thing to come out of their mouths was "Eh, damn it, it's too bad the infantry didn't support us; we would have given them [the Germans] even more fire! Eh, they didn't want to leave our own (Soviet) ground."
>
> One wounded driver-mechanic declared: "We fought; we battled yesterday evening, last night and this morning. The only thing which was left was for 200-300 men with submachine guns and light machine guns to prevent the enemy from bringing up new groups of artillery into the village; Spasskoe would have been ours, and our task fulfilled. It's a shame, such a shame, that the fighting we conducted today didn't bring good results! The Germans were holding out stubbornly, we were crawling up to their bunkers and shouting "Surrender!" but they didn't surrender; we were wiping them out with grenades, crushing them in their trenches with our tracks. Burning hatred for these vultures ignited in our breasts; even though it was possible to take more than 100 of them prisoner, our tankers took only 6, and the rest were killed![33]

The losses of the German 340th Infantry Division, which received the main attack by the 7th Tank Corps' grouping, over two days of fighting (28 and 29 July) amounted to 69 killed (4 officers), 200 wounded (2 officers) and 18 missing in action. The 385th Infantry Division over the two days of fighting lost 10 killed (1 officer) and 26 wounded. The 387th Infantry Division lost 27 killed (2 officers), 39 wounded (3 officers) and 1 officer missing in action.[34] Altogether for the three divisions: 106 killed, 265 wounded and 19 missing in action, for a total of 390 men.

In the headquarters of the 237th Rifle Division, however, they didn't see any participation of the 7th Tank Corps' tanks in the attack, as if they hadn't been there at all:

> At 1800 the attack began. The enemy began to retreat to the south to a previously-prepared line, from where in fact he stopped the regiments' attack. The intensity of the fighting was light; in places the enemy didn't accept battle and retreated to the south. That's how it was in the 841st Rifle Regiment's sector until the regiment reached Hill 199.8, where it first ran into enemy fire.
>
> On the line of Hill 217.8 and Lomovo, the division's right flank shoved back the enemy and with the onset of darkness reached the following line: the 835th Rifle Regiment's 1st Rifle Battalion – Point 220 2 kilometers east of Spasskoe; the 2nd Battalion – north of the woods, north of Vysochkino; the 3rd Rifle Battalion – the scrub brush east of Point 44.0 on the main road. The 841st Rifle Regiment is at the western upper reaches of the ravine southwest of Point 199.8 and along the ravine in the hills. The 838th Rifle Regiment is in the brushy ravine west of Hill 199.8. The artillery is in firing positions 1 kilometer north of Hill 217.8.
>
> At 0600 on 29.7.42, an order was received about going over to a defense on the achieved line. With the sunrise, the enemy began to assemble infantry and tanks [all of the 9th Panzer Division's tanks had already left this area more than 24 hours before this – I.S.] opposite the division's left flank, and with the sunrise, receiving cover from aircraft, went on the attack against the 841st Rifle Regiment. Unable to withstand the onslaught, the regiment began to retreat to the north without orders and wasn't able to stop until it reached the northern slopes of Hill 217.8.
>
> By the end of the day, the remnants of the scattered battalions and special elements numbering 400 men with 2 heavy machine guns, 4 anti-tank rifles, and 1 76-mm gun and 1 45-mm

33 TsAMO, F. 87 tbr, op. 1, d. 5, l. 162.
34 NARA, T-314, roll 354, fr. 726-727.

gun at an order from the division commander were pushed forward to the southern slopes of Hill 199.8, where they took up a defense.

The enemy attack had been so intense and unexpected that the regiment headquarters, the command and the command staff were unable to stop the current of retreating troops. The men were running from the battlefield in panic, and the measures taken by the command staff to stop the retreating elements weren't crowned with success. Disdaining death and taking every measure to halt his battalion, the commander of the 3rd Rifle Battalion Lieutenant Nikolai Vasil'evich Kozhukhov fell bravely in the battle. ...[35]

Angered by the failure, the commander of the 7th Tank Corps Rotmistrov was even more categorical in his critical assessments of the 237th Rifle Division's actions, when soon after the battle he reported to the army commander:

I will report that according to the group's Order No. 019 at 1700 on 28.7.42 the units and formations that were part of the group went on the offensive with the general task of smashing the enemy in the Perekopovka, Vysochkino, Lomovo area and reaching the line of the Sukhaia Vereika. As a result of a stubbornly developing offensive on the evening and night, by 0300 on 29.7.42 units began to emerge at the Sukhaia Vereika River. The 284th Rifle Division was engaged in fighting on the line of the southern fringe of the woods south of Point 218.7, Hill 214.6; the 7th Motorized Rifle Brigade had reached Hill 214.6; and the 87th Tank Brigade had entered Spasskoe. The 3rd Guards Tank Brigade and 62nd Tank Brigade had taken the woods north of Vysochkino and were combing through them with their motorized rifle battalions. The 119th Rifle Brigade was advancing behind the 3rd Guards Tank Brigade and 62nd Tank Brigade, and with one battalion had reached the lettering "Novopavlovka" [on the map]; in fact, only the 237th Rifle Division due to exceptionally poor command and control and the division commander's lack of desire to carry out the group's order was held up on the line of the ravine southwest of Point 199.8.

At 0530 on 29.7.42, the combat positions of the group's units were subjected to the first savage bombing by 50 enemy heavy bombers and an enemy artillery and mortar barrage. Such a working over with fire especially affected the 237th Rifle Division, which, by the way, was subjected to it least of all. The division began to retreat, bringing along with it some of the soldiers of other units as well. The lack of command and control in the 237th Rifle Division didn't give the division commander the opportunity to catch the moment of retreat in time and to take control of the troops.

The intelligence chief of the 7th Tank Corps Captain Bogachev, who'd been sent by the group's headquarters in order to determine the line that had been reached by the 237th Rifle Division, saw that the 237th Rifle Division was fleeing to the north and had already partially passed through Lomovo. Captain Bogachev found the division command in Kamenka in complete ignorance of the real situation, and took the division commissar and chief of the Special Department to Point ..., east of Kamenka, where soldiers of the 237th Rifle Division were gathering. Here the division commissar took decisive measures, shooting several of the fleeing men on the spot. The group's headquarters had to exert much effort in order to restore elementary order and hold the main forces on the Lomovo line.

Repeated, uninterrupted bombing attacks and the withdrawal of the infantry because of the bombings forced the group's command to reject a continuation of the offensive and to go over to the defense. As a result of the fighting, 5 tanks and prisoners of the 340th Infantry

35 TsAMO, F. 237 sd, op. 1, d. 7, l. 12.

> Division were captured [Rotmistrov doesn't report exactly what sorts of tanks were captured. Judging from captured German documents, there were no longer any knocked out, or even more so, serviceable German tanks in this area – I.S.]. The tank corps lost 6 KV and around 10 T-34 tanks either burned out or knocked out [Rotmistrov makes no mention at all of the lost T-60 tanks – I.S.]
>
> Conclusions: In order to restore the 237th Rifle Division to combat condition, it is immediately necessary to appoint a different division commander and, apparently, re-examine the leading command staff of this division …."[36]

Alas, in this final battle of the operation, Operational Group Chibisov (the 4th Army) repeated again and again many characteristic features of those unsuccessful battles: enemy aerial superiority over the battlefield, which in a most catastrophic manner affected the infantry of the rifle units that had no cover from the air; the lack of coordination between the infantry and the tanks; the incapability of the tank units alone to convert a breakthrough of the enemy's positions into a general offensive success, and as a consequence, the failure of the troops to carry out assignments.

The results of the first combat operation in which the recently-formed 237th Rifle Division happened to take part, were disquieting:

> The losses in the division's units as a result of the fighting from 23 to 30.7.42 reached enormous dimensions; the personnel of the division became equal to the following – instead of 1,136 men of the command staff, there are 780; instead of 2,752 men of the junior command staff, there are 1,684 left; instead of 8,990 rank and file – 5,770. Instead of 2,113 horses, there are 1,382 horses – 137 mounts, 437 artillery draft horses, and 772 draft horses. Available rifles – 5,554, out of 639 submachine guns – 455. There are 67 light machine guns, 30 heavy machine guns, 110 anti-tank rifles, 12 122-mm howitzers, 48 82-mm mortars, 30 50-mm mortars, and 16 radios of all types.
>
> The 835th Rifle Regiment had 1,680 men, 1,225 rifles, 1 heavy machine gun, 16 light machine guns, 130 submachine guns, 31 anti-tank rifles, 4 76-mm guns, 4 45-mm guns, 3 120-mm mortars, 15 82-mm mortars, 5 50-mm mortars and 5 radios.
>
> The 841st Rifle Regiment had 1,143 men, 251 horses, 742 rifles, 3 heavy machine guns, 3 light machine guns, 64 submachine guns, 4 76-mm guns, 2 45-mm guns, 5 120-mm mortars, 12 82-mm mortars and 6 50-mm mortars.
>
> The 838th Rifle Regiment had 2,088 men, 275 horses, 1,335 rifles, 6 heavy machine guns, 17 light machine guns, 25 anti-tank rifles, 106 submachine guns, 3 76-mm guns, 6 45-mm guns, 6 120-mm mortars, 17 82-mm mortars and 15 50-mm mortars.[37]

Becoming increasingly aware of the critical condition in which the 237th Rifle Division found itself as a result of the fighting, the division commander Colonel Tertyshnyi appealed to the commander of the 4th Army (the operational group) Lieutenant General Chibisov in a personal message:

> The 237th Rifle Division between 23 and 29.7.42 was engaged in intense fighting with the enemy; the latter, seeing the activity of the division's units, over all these days from early morning until late in the evening was employing aircraft, which constantly bombed the unit's combat formations. As a result of the systematic bombing from the air, as well as the

36 TsAMO, F. 38 A, op. 9005, d. 42, l. 20.
37 TsAMO, F. 237 sd, op. 1, d. 7, l. 12.

> concentrated artillery and mortar fire on the enemy's part in the division's sector, the rifle regiments have heavy losses in personnel, including two regiment commanders (of the 835th and 838th Regiments) who've been wounded. The majority of the battalion and company commanders have also been killed or wounded. [...]
>
> The resulting difficult situation with the circumstances described above compels me to report to you that the division over the next 2-3 days cannot carry out assigned operations. In the course of 2-3 days it is at least necessary to choose men from the rank and file for the posts of platoon and company commanders, and to choose individuals from among the command staff for the posts of battalion commanders. To the posts of regiment commanders, the following have been temporarily assigned: for the 835th Rifle Regiment, deputy regiment commander Major Naumov, who has very little military education and totally lacks command experience; for the 838th Rifle Regiment, the commander of the anti-tank battalion Captain Komashev, a vigorous commander, but he has no experience in the organization of battle for rifle units and, correspondingly, no military education. I will report the losses in personnel for 29.7.42 inclusively by the evening of 30.7.42. I request: in the next 2-3 days, don't give the division any offensive combat tasks, as long as the situation doesn't compel this.[38]

Tertyshnyi said nothing about the commander of the 841st Rifle Regiment, but even before receiving the division commander's appeal, Chibisov in fact reported about the command style of his (Tertyshnyi's) subordinate:

> The commander of the 841st Rifle Regiment Major D. on the second day of the battle, toward the end of the day of 24 July abandoned his regiment and wound up beyond the Don River in the area of Kon' Kolodez'; he returned, apparently only after having come to his senses, only on the night of 27/28 July, and at the given moment is not fully directing the regiment's fighting. On the night of 28/29 July, the regiment was engaged in offensive fighting, but the regiment commander Major D. back in the evening left for the 3rd Battalion and failed to direct the fighting from his own command post. [...] It is necessary to bring the commander of the 841st Rifle Regiment Major D., who in point of fact abandoned his regiment on the battlefield, to responsibility – to turn him over to trial in front of a military tribunal.

How could Chibisov respond to Tertyshnyi's message? Practically all of the units of the former operational group were in a woeful condition as a result of that unsuccessful operation and the terrible losses, but the inexperienced rifle divisions (the 193rd, 237th and 167th Rifle Divisions) that found themselves promptly thrown into the furnace of war particularly suffered. This fate also befell to the veteran 340th Rifle Division. Only the 284th Rifle Division and 104th Separate Rifle Brigade wound up somewhat off to one side of the main fighting and therefore suffered fewer losses. However, the condition of the 284th Rifle Division also left much to be desired: after the fighting at Kastornoe and its emergence from encirclement, the division's ranks were extremely thin, and although it had retained its combat spirit, the division was in need of rest, replenishment and replacements.

Virtually all of the army's tank units were in need of rest for the men and the replenishment of materiel. The troops had completely exhausted their offensive capabilities, and its commander (just like the Briansk Front command, which had followed the course of the operation with even greater skepticism), arguably understood this better than anyone else. By the end of 29 July, the army's forces everywhere had gone over to the defense.

38 TsAMO, F. 38 A, op. 9005, d. 42, l. 18.

Serious changes in the 4th Army's composition were also ripening. Back on 28 July in telegraph discussions with the headquarters of the 4th Army, Briansk Front's operations chief Colonel Sidel'nikov had reported on the decision of the Front Commander-in-Chief Lieutenant General Rokossovsky to withdraw several of its rifle divisions in order to bring them back up to strength. The representative of the Briansk Front headquarters Colonel Potapov, who'd been assigned to the army's headquarters, was telegraphing: "Chibisov's outfit is in extreme need of rebuilding, while the tank formations must bring their materiel back into order. There is nothing with which to replace [the units and formations], only through the arrival of new outfits, but they are arriving very slowly, and in any case, it is impossible to pull a single rifle outfit out of the battle prior to their arrival. We now have even tank outfits carrying out the role of rifle outfits."[39]

When it became clear that the enemy had no intentions (or strength ...) to undertake any new active operations, and once new Red Army units began arriving at the front, a regrouping of forces began. The first to depart from the 4th Army and Briansk Front was the much-suffering 193rd Rifle Division, the remnants of which moved by a march to Dolgorukovo Station on 1 August. The 284th Rifle Division followed it. The 119th Rifle Brigade was pulled back into the Front's reserve. The tank corps (except the 11th Tank Corps) pulled out of the front and headed to the rear. New units were hurrying to take their place at the front: the 240th Rifle Division, the 229th and 248th Rifle Brigades, and the 86th and 96th Tank Brigades. They were fresh, fully outfitted and eager for battle, just like their now departing predecessors had been several weeks ago. The ravenous front that was hungering for troops needed fresh blood again. In order for the Red Army to keep on fighting, it was repeatedly necessary to commit thousands of new lives, mountains of weapons, tens of thousands of tons of supplies and enormous material resources of a country that was totally engaged in war ...

It was in this period of relief in place of some units by others that a genuinely profound event took place in the 4th Army, which had just been formed from Operational Group Chibisov. By the way, it became well-known across the entire enormous front that stretched for almost 3,000 kilometers from the Bering Sea to the Black Sea, and continues to linger in the national conscience. The People's Commissar of Defense's Order No. 227, the famous "Not one step back!" order, arrived at the front.

In the remaining units, which still had to ponder the experience of the recent fighting, and in the bloodied and battered divisions that were leaving the front, which had taken a full swallow from the bitter cup of experiences that had befallen them, and in the fresh, unseasoned brigades that were moving up to replace them, and in the seasoned 240th Rifle Division, a lot of similar processes were taking place on these days of 30-31 July 1942. A representative from higher headquarters was arriving in the units and elements, carrying an envelope that had been sealed with sealing wax. At the designated time, the command gathered and assembled all the men, and having unsealed the envelope, pulled out of it a copy of an order from the USSR People's Commissar of Defense, which had been printed in thousands of copies. After the order "Attention!" rang out, the soldiers, commanders and political workers of the Red Army that had gathered in wood clearings and patches of woods, on fields and in ravines, and in villages and cities heard earthshaking words that had never been uttered before, words that contained such a naked, bitter truth:

> The foe is hurling more and more fresh forces to the front, paying no regard to his heavy losses, and is creeping forward, penetrating into the depth of the Soviet Union, capturing new areas, pillaging and plundering our cities and villages, and raping, robbing and killing the Soviet people. Fighting is underway in the Voronezh area, at the Don, and to the south

39 TsAMO, F. 202, op. 5, d. 489, ll. 239-240.

> at the gates of the Northern Caucasus. German occupiers are lunging toward Stalingrad, to the Volga, and want at any cost to seize the Kuban', the Northern Caucasus with their oil and grain riches. The foe has already taken Voroshilovgrad, Starobel'sk, Rossosh', Kupiansk, Valuiki, Novocherkassk, Rostov on the Don, and half of Voronezh. A section of the troops on the southern front, yielding to panicmongers, abandoned Rostov and Novocherkassk without serious resistance and without an order from Moscow, coving their banners with shame ...

The soldiers were hearing heavy, bitter phrases and keeping silent. What were they thinking about? What thoughts came to mind that echoed in the conscience? What were their hearts and souls aching about? The war was rolling ever further into the country, like a sinister steamroller, and the bitterness of the latest bloody failure on the Don expanses only increased the sense of gravity from all that was happening. The country stood on the verge of collapse.[40]

But something else, painful and vexing, was completely clear: it was no longer possible to fight as they had done before; it was time to put an end to the shameful retreats – to win, or else to die. No other choice was given to the country or the people! The fate of the Motherland and their fate now depended on everyone and each person ....

* * *

Documents and recollections, July-August 1942

Even as the operation wound down and in its immediate aftermath, both sides were digesting lessons to be drawn from it and began to turn their attention to its consequences:

> To the commanders of the Briansk Front's tank corps and separate tank brigades, and to the commander of the army, 27.7.42
>
> a) The latest period of combat operations of the Front's tank forces has demonstrated that there is an entire array of shortcomings in command over the tank units and formations. These primarily include:
>   1. If command and communications exist before the tanks move out from their jumping-off positions, then after they move out on the attack, command and communications with them, as a rule, cease. Separate tank units, and sometimes entire tank formations, operate uncontrolled by higher headquarters; resolve combat tasks of

40 In his memoirs, the writer Konstantin Simonov, who in those July days happened to be at the headquarters of Briansk Front and became an unwilling witness to what was happening around him, wrote about his reaction to Order No. 277 in that situation:
We had to pay a visit to a member of the Front's Military Council, and we were waiting outside his hut, and while we waited, the secretary of the Military Council brought and allowed us to read a copy of Stalin's July order about the fact that there was nowhere to retreat further and that it was necessary to stop the foe at any price.
Utkin and I were sitting on log well in the village, and we sat there silent for an entire hour, stunned after reading the order. I really came back to myself only several days later in Moscow. All these days it seemed to me that the hands of time had stopped. Before this, the war was winding up like a ball of string, like a ball of misfortune; later, in December '41, this ball of string seemingly began to unravel, but later it again began to tighten up again, like a ball of new misfortunes. Then suddenly, when I read this order, everything seemed to stop. Now, life's movement was presented in the future as some sort of leap – either make the leap, or die! We sat and remained silent. Later we dropped by the Military Council member who had returned. Then just as silently as before, we went our separate ways to our own huts. (Konstantin Simonov, *Raznye dni voiny* [*Various days of the war*], Vol. 2 (Moscow: Molodaia gvardiia, 1978), p. 157.

local significance; and sometimes exit the battle under their own authority, abandoning tanks to the enemy.

2. Marches are being organized with exceptional carelessness; the proper discipline is lacking, and frequently complete arbitrariness reigns on the march.
3. There is no systematic, reliable operational information both from below to above and from above to below. Very seldom is intelligence data obtained with combat. In the majority of cases it is obtained through observation and goes unchecked.
4. Decisions in the process of a changing situation are being taken hastily, on the basis of haphazard, unverified intelligence.
5. The order to introduce the tank units and formations is being issued without taking into account the element of time – hastily, often without documentation. The fulfillment of orders is not being monitored, while those guilty of not carrying out an order are not being brought to responsibility. Cases of the introduction of formations in a piecemeal manner are frequent (2nd Tank Corps, 21 and 22 July). Radio means of command and control over the tank units and formations in battle are seldom used.
6. The headquarters of the tank corps and brigades are keeping higher headquarters informed about the situation, their decisions, unit actions, and the availability of operational combat machines with large interruptions and delays (7th and 11th Tank Corps, 118th Tank Brigade).
7. The operational groups of the headquarters of corps and brigades are remote from their units and in essence are not directing the course of the battle and do not know the situation on the battlefield. Take, for example, the 1st Tank Corps headquarters; in the period of 23-27 July, the entire headquarters was 20 kilometers distant from the operating units of the brigades. All this speaks to the fact that there is still not the proper operational efficiency in the leadership over the combat actions of the units and formations, and this leads to the main shortcomings in their combat activity.

I categorically demand:

1. The commanders of tank formations and units are to take the most serious, decisive measures in questions of handling communications and the flow of combat information with the units under their command.
2. The operational groups of the headquarters of the tank corps and brigades are to be in the area of the second echelons of the subordinate, acting combat units, from where they are directly to lead their combat operations.
3. The tank formation commanders are obliged to take decisive measures independently, and to achieve constant, mutual contact and due coordination with rifle, artillery and similar units, which are operating on their directions.
4. I am warning that in the future the lack of proper leadership over the combat activity of subordinate units and formations; the lack of reliable, constant communications with them; and the lack of timely, accurate information on the part of the tank headquarters at all levels will be viewed as the unwillingness of the corresponding commanders and commissars to carry out their direct responsibilities, and strict measures to correct this will be taken.

Commander-in-chief of the Briansk Front Lieutenant General Rokossovsky
Front Military Council member Brigade Commissar Shabalin
Deputy commander of the Front's armored forces Colonel Sukhoruchkin

b) The interrogation of Russian prisoners of war, captured on 29.7.42 by the forces of the 340th Panzerjäger Battalion, the III Battalion of the 695th Infantry Regiment and the 605th Flak Battalion

The seized prisoners belong to the 237th Rifle Division's 835th and 841st Rifle Regiments.

During the operation of reconnaissance patrols on 29.7.42, one junior lieutenant and a sergeant major from the 835th Rifle Regiment and one junior lieutenant and one lieutenant from the 841st Rifle Regiment were taken prisoner in the area of Hill 220.

The 835th Rifle Regiment in recent days was retreating and took up defensive positions in a patch of woods, from where on 28.7 it was to conduct an attack toward an unknown village [either Spasskoe or Vysochkino], where it was supposed to dig in again. The 841st Rifle Regiment (as seen from the German side) was attacking in the sector on the right. Eight to ten tanks (one T-34 and the rest KV) also participated in the attack; the majority of them were knocked out by the enemy. Further in the rear they didn't see any anti-tank artillery at all, but they saw 8 50-mm mortars. During the attack there were significant losses from German mortars and rocket launchers, while at the same time no one of the higher command was visible. Thus combat morale is particularly low. Rations: soup, bread, millet and other types of porridge; butter and jam, which could be spread on the bread, is absent, as is tobacco. Senior officers (the commanders of battalions and regiments) eat separately in the rear; other officers eat together with the men. They didn't see a Katiusha rocket-launcher; they only heard their use two days ago. Several days ago they saw 8 German soldiers being interrogated back in the regiment headquarters. Supposedly Austrians. General order: take the German prisoners away to the rear. The majority of soldiers are equipped with gas masks.

They have seen and read German leaflets (partially only in the German language). On the whole during the movement to the front and particularly from the moment of combat deployment in the given sector of the front, the delivery of food was poor and thus the morale is low; in the rear as well, where there is not enough labor and machinery. The delivery of ammunition is also organized poorly. The opinion of the German soldiers: "Better dressed, more cleanly washed, and first of all, a better system of communications". Radio sets are only at the regiment headquarters (set up in a light automobile). Discipline from the moment of combat introduction has dropped because of the bad rations. Common statements were such: "At first adequate rations have to be provided and only after that would the execution of orders follow. The lower officers' staff can do nothing about this, because they must live together with the soldiers."

Senior officers stay in the rear. Four days ago a batch of 84 replacements arrived from the 401st Reserve Rifle Regiment in Achinska (Siberia). Approximately 200 men lagged behind on the road. After a single, brief period of training, the soldiers head to the front. Commander – Captain Garbushin. Location of the 237th Rifle Division's headquarters – Krasnaia Poliana.

The 841st Rifle Regiment, commander of the 8th Battalion Senior Lieutenant Kozhukhov: The regiment had a table and actual strength of 717 men before the first battle. Approximately in the middle of July, the 237th Rifle Division became part of the 2nd Reserve Army of the Moscow Military District. After the days of recent fighting, only 158 men of the 1st and 2nd Battalions remained uninjured; thus on 28.7 the 3rd Battalion was introduced into the battle, which prior to then had been in the army's reserve. During the attack on the evening of 28.7, no particular task was given; only the axis of attack was designated.

Significant losses came as a result of mortar and machine-gun fire, partially also from a barrage by their own (Russian) mortars. The left flank was supposedly covered inadequately. They didn't see artillery and tanks. (Supposedly there was a report about the 127th(?) Tank Brigade.) He saw only one mortar company, which was supposedly having particular problems with the delivery of ammunition. Military servicemen are of various ages (approximately 40% born in 1923) and various origins (approximately 20% from Siberia's industrial regions). Food supply from the moment of entering the front is particularly bad because of poor delivery. The distribution of ammunition is also poorly organized. In Murav'evka, supposedly an ammo stockpile was blown up as a result of a raid by dive bombers. They read German leaflets; he didn't see prisoners.

c) To the chiefs of staff of the 1st, 7th and 11th Tank Corps, 31.7.42
The Commander-in-Chief has called attention to the following:
In the combat intelligence reports from the group's headquarters, the headquarters are allowing crude distortions, bordering on a direct lie. The combat experience of the last 10 days demonstrated that the headquarters are not at all busy with the analysis of occurring events, encumbering themselves with a pile of unchecked or dated intelligence and then passing them along to higher headquarters as something new. Times are not given or are incorrect, the assessment spur-of-the moment or not objective. Some of the intelligence on the enemy, arriving during the battle, was plainly calculated so as to frighten higher headquarters and compel it to take measures in support of the reporting unit. If the reports on the enemy are compiled over a single day of combat on 24, 25 or 26 July, then it turns out that the number of the foe's attacking tanks amounted to 300-400 machines. For example, the number of tanks attacking Surikovye Vyselki counted successively on one and the same day came to 40, 70, 110 and 150 tanks.

The quantity of enemy vehicles in Bol'shaia Vereika was set at 200 machines, which had assembled there in the blink of an eye. A column of 200 vehicles extends at a minimum for 5 kilometers, and the jamming of all of Bol'shaia Vereika's streets with such a number of vehicles is totally improbable, given the situation as it existed there.

On 26 July the 1st Tank Corps headquarters reported 40 burning enemy tanks east of Surikovye Vyselki. Eyewitnesses were found, and this proved to be a lie. It is awkward to give a number of "destroyed" enemy machines that exceeds the number that showed up on the field of battle. A similar disorientation is prompted by the lack of monitoring, lack of specificity and vagueness given to the tasks set for reconnaissance and observation. Having received a report, the staff doesn't ponder the subject matter or quality of the material; do not peel away the subjective, often incompetent and unwarranted assessments; and without checking, mechanically submits everything to its commander and higher headquarters.

2. In its summary for 30.7.42, the 7th Tank Corps headquarters rewrote its intelligence tasks according to the instructions of the field service staff. There, the biographical particulars of prisoners were given, but not the numerical designation of their units or elements or where and when they were captured; in other words, there is no information that would cast light on the enemy's position, his strength and means, unit boundary lines, flanks and similar.

In this same summary report, the number of individual enemy bomber sorties for 30.7.42 above the 7th Tank Corps is 100, which yields 1,000 dropped bombs. This hogwash is served up at a time when higher headquarters was directly observing the events as they occurred. In this same summary, the enemy is indicated in the area of the 237th Rifle Division's second echelons (the woods west of Lomovo).

On the part of the 7th Tank Corps headquarters there was a case, when the number of their own lost tanks was set "at around 6". This [vague] style is suitable on the scale of many months of fighting and for directions, when in reports they must handle thousands of vehicles, hundreds of kilometers and groups of armies, but it isn't suitable for the number "6" on the scale of a tank corps. One can assume that 3 of the 6 tanks had been abandoned on the battlefield and the headquarters, weighing the chances for their recovery, decided just in case to write "around 6". Given a success, this number is confirmed as "3", but given a failure, this number will be reliable.

3. The headquarters are maintaining in intelligence reports and summaries that the enemy is continuing to throw up field works, deploy obstacles, etc. In the operational summaries, there is no information at all about any responding actions by our artillery and mortars to these enemy measures. This creates the impression that headquarters are calmly contemplating the enemy's construction of obstacles against the operations of our forces in the future, while having the full opportunity to hinder the foe and disorganize his work.

The Commander-in-Chief has given an order:

1. Activate reconnaissance on every sector and conduct it constantly.
2. Check the information brought back by patrols, the entire system of observation from the front line, and the positions of combat outposts. In order to verify the scouts' information, organize search groups of select scouts with the aim of taking prisoners.
3. Exchange intelligence with neighbors, which are mutually monitoring the acquisition of data.[41]

d) Headquarters of the German Second Field Army, 5.8.1942
Commander-in-chief of the Second Army

Soldiers of the army!

You have conquered land, in which a rich harvest of grain has ripened, in which forage for our horses is growing in abundance, and in which there are enough milk cows to satisfy our army's need in protein.

In order to prevent us from taking advantage of these Soviet riches, they (the Soviets) have driven away labor and draft animals. Each is to help ensure that we can timely gather the harvest of the conquered country. After the victory by arms, let there follow a no less important victory in the agricultural battle. Be filled with pride for the fact that the Fatherland will have no need to draw upon any of its own meager agricultural reserves before the next harvest. Be filled with pride for the fact that the fruitful soil, which you have soaked with your blood, will yield a harvest that in the next year will liberate us and our close ones of any concerns in subsistence. Take part in this with your own hands!

41 TsAMO, F. 11 tk, op. 1, d. 11, l. 88 (49).

Not a single man should now take a holiday, not a single horse should be idle. It is necessary to draw all Russian peasant men and women to work to gather the harvest. I know that different urgent work also is in store. It is necessary to throw up defensive works. The repair of roads and bridges and the procurement of fuel cannot tolerate delays.

Now, however, the struggle for the harvest stands in first place! Let each man consciously appreciate his responsibility in front of the Fatherland and his close ones.

Everyone to the harvest!

Convey this down to the company level.

e) Order to the units of the 2nd Tank Corps. Isaevka, August 1942

I am announcing a decree of the 4th Army's Military Council from 1 August 1942 about the organization of the harvesting of grain and the evacuation of the population, material valuables and livestock from a frontline zone of 30 kilometers.

1. Calculate the belt of the 30-kilometer zone within the boundaries: from the front – the troops' combat line; from the rear: Dolgorukovo, the course of the Snova River to its confluence with the Don. Round up all of the large and small livestock belonging to the collective farmers and individuals into herds, and drive them to areas no closer than 30 kilometers from the front. Expropriate the livestock from those who don't desire to evacuate the livestock beyond the zone, record the expropriation, and give them a receipt. Create herds from a portion of the expropriated livestock in the units with a view to provide 15 days of rations. Turn over the surplus livestock to the divisional herd ….[42]

f) From documents of the 106th Rifle Brigade:

In Ivanovka we encountered a horrible scene. Several days before our troops entered, the Germans had rounded up 30 collective farmers and brutally martyred them. A formal note has been drawn up about the Germans' evil deeds. On 28.7.42 in the village of Ivanovka, at the order of the commandant, 30 adult collective farmers and their children were drawn up on the village square. They were all family members of Red Army servicemen. They were all tied up and turned face to face; hay was piled up around them, saturated with kerosene, and set ablaze. When burning people began to leap out from roaring flames, soldiers chased them down and stuck them with bayonets, while sneering at them; they gouged out eyes, ripped open stomachs and crushed heads. They tossed little kids back into the fire. All 30 people were killed …

The Germans set up a post in the square and fastened a board to it. In the interim, an order was nailed to the board, announcing that in return for helping partisans, their families and the families of Red Army servicemen would be executed; for violation of the blackout – execution; for failure to carry out the plan of procurements – execution. There followed a long list of crimes punishable by death. The Germans were pitiless.[43]

42 TsAMO, F. 30 gv. mbr, op. 1, d. 1, l. 23.
43 TsAMO, F. 106 sbr, op. 1, d. 1, l. 80.

g) From an article written by the commissar of a rifle battalion of the 284th Rifle Division's 1047th Rifle Regiment, Junior Political Instructor Maksimov about the fighting between 23 and 27 July 1942 for the division's collection of articles. August 1942:

On 28 July, the very same task was given – to reach the southwestern fringe of the woods and take up a defense behind the river. This time, previous mistakes were taken into account: We belly-crawled and with quick, short bounding movements under intense machine-gun and mortar fire reached the woods, hit the Germans in the flank and drove them out of the woods. Here it is necessary to note the exploits of individual comrades, like the commander of the medical platoon Leonid Zykin, who led his platoon directly at the front, in the first line; he himself brought out 47 wounded men from under enemy fire and gave them aid. Armed with a submachine gun, more than once he was forced to silence a German cuckoo in the woods.

The light machine gun of a machine gunner refused to fire; Zykin also helped here. He brought in the machine gun and said, "Comrade Commissar, let's fix the machine gun so it can kill more fascists." Together we quickly disassembled and cleaned the machine gun, and 3-5 minutes later the machine gun was again sending out destructive fire at the fascists.

Medical instructor Comrade Spichan is fearless, energetic, and mindful of the patient's word. He brought 57 wounded soldiers and commanders out from under the fire of fascist machine guns and mortars, and never parted from his self-loading Tokarev rifle. About 800 meters away, a German sniper spotted the location of our command team and didn't allow them to raise their heads. Comrade Spichan spotted the sniper's position and with accurate shots silenced the sniper, which gave the command team the opportunity to shift to a new command post.

Medic Leliain – is the very image of a fearless Siberian. Under a storm of mortar fire, Comrade Leliain gave aid to the wounded; he brought 46 soldiers and commanders out from under enemy fire. All the soldiers loved him for the fact that he runs over to a wounded comrade in time, and once there, like a mother, asks the wounded man where he is hurting and how he is feeling, and soothes the wounded with his own tender words. [...]

One evening, German propaganda in the Russian language came from their side of the lines; they were trying to persuade our soldiers to come over to their side and promising to feed them well; but when we drove them out of the woods, they left behind their own unfinished dinner – it was only a watery puree of peas, while we were eating meat until our bellies were full. Our soldiers answered their propaganda with spite, laughter and gunfire, and the loudspeaker conveying Goebbel's propaganda fell silent.

h) From a political report of the 62nd Tank Brigade dated 2 August 1942:

Communist Political Instructor Comrade Spitsin in his presentation said:
The submachine gunners are operating not badly, but it is necessary to point to a shortcoming in the tanks' actions; in particular, the fact that the tanks are stopping in order to conduct fire, and standing immobile in one place for a long time instead of energetically maneuvering. Meanwhile the enemy anti-tank artillery is firing at our tanks, easily shooting them up and setting them on fire. This can be avoided by the tanks' maneuvering, and great damage can be done to the enemy with much fewer losses, than was the case in our unit and other units.

Senior Sergeant Volokov said:
I personally killed two Germans in one battle; I believe this is too few for me, and in the next battle I'll kill more. Simultaneously I want to point to the shortcomings in the actions of our infantrymen. Individual cowards and panic mongers begin to flee encirclement, so they say, carrying away others with them. This is disgraceful! With fewer forces we must beat the enemy's superior forces. The main thing is more resolve, more responsibility for each clump of Soviet soil, which the Motherland has entrusted us to defend!

i) From the recollections of a military surgeon of the 340th Rifle Division K. Boldin:

Toward evening I went over to take a look at German prisoners. They were situated in a garden, on the grass. The evening was chilly; they were huddled against each other, but weren't losing their cheerfulness. They were content that the war for them was now over. They were feeling confident that if they hadn't been shot up to this point, they wouldn't be shot.

The next morning, having evacuated all the wounded, we drove off to Ol'shanyi Kolodez'. We were surprised that they had moved us back approximately 25 kilometers from the frontline, but ... we weren't protesting – here it was possible to live and work! We were cleaning and washing our accommodations, setting up the operating and bandaging wards, receiving the first wounded and ... then we received an order to move to Novo-Pokrovskoe, somewhat closer to the front. We were upset – we'd prepared everything and were counting upon at least a couple of hours of rest.

Novo-Pokrovskoe is a large, dreary, dusty village. They assigned a hut to us in which it was possible to fit only two tables. I went to complain to the battalion commander – he promised to "think up something". In the morning the operating ward was moved into a school, while the bandaging facilities moved into a church. There were a lot of military units around us. Tanks were at a creek, quite nearby. The neighborhood had little to go for it; the entire day German airplanes were in the air and struck intact neighboring villages so heavily that columns of dust and smoke were rising into the sky.

Somehow in the evening I was despondently eating a sorry bit of soup. Suddenly, there was a fearsome roar of engines just above the rooftops – two airplanes, one behind the other, and a third higher, at an altitude of 500-600 meters. Several seconds later I heard the sound of a machine-gun burst, and a cloud of black smoke rose into the sky. Two "Messerschmitts" came back. Ours had been shot down.

I hopped into truck with K. Ia., nurses tossed me bandages, splints and my medical kit. We took off at high speed in the direction of the smoke coming from the burning airplane. A motorcyclist caught up with us, heading to the same place. On a hilltop was the wreckage of two more planes with stars – these had been shot down previously. The smoke column was rising from a field of rye. Some ambulance was also heading there. We drove blindly through the still unharvested rye. Smoldering wings, ammunition belts, pieces of the engine, fuselage and cockpit were lying about. The downed aircraft had plowed into the earth. Fragments of it were scattered to a distance of 60-70 meters from where it hit. The pilot wasn't visible. Thinking that he had become pinned in the cockpit, we took a look into it – no, he wasn't there! Then collective farm girls came running, waving their hands and shouting: "Here he is!"

We ran over to the place. A strapping blond pilot in an oil-soaked flight suit was lying on the ground. His face and arms were a little burned, particularly his left shoulder. Scorched skin ran like a band around his wrist, where his watch had been. Plainly, the watch band, soaked with aviation fuel, had been burning there, until it burned away completely. The pilot was conscious, but he couldn't rise. He was complaining about pain in his rib cage and in the vicinity of his tailbone. It turned out that he had managed to bail out with a parachute; the parachute opened, but it didn't have enough altitude to open fully, and he struck the ground heavily. He was swearing up a storm. He stopped only long enough to recall, that he had already shot down two Germans in recent days: "When I get back from the hospital – I'll settle with them!"

[...]

About 28-29 July we began to work in Bol'shaia Kolybel'ka. Our accommodations were spacious. The pharmacy was given a separate building. They housed the nurses in huts of peasants, which gave the nurses a good chance to receive supplemental food from the sympathetic owners. Young potatoes had matured (from school garden that had been abandoned by the teachers), and we added them to our table, along with an almost unlimited quantity of cucumbers. Milk began to appear frequently, and there began to be even leftover bread. A period of good weather had settled in, and I slept under an apple tree in an orchard.

We observed several dogfights above Kolybel'ka. In one of them, three of our aircraft were shot down. Everything happened so quickly – a short machine-gun burst, a tongue of flame, smoke ... and an aircraft went plummeting to the earth. Sometimes pilots managed to bail out with parachutes, but then had to figure out how to remain intact – the Messerschmitts were firing at the descending pilot with their machine guns. They even killed one pilot that way. Once, a dogfight developed directly overhead at an altitude of 600-700 meters. Our airplane was striving to get away (as it turned out, the pilot had been wounded), but failed in the attempt. Beyond the village, at a low altitude, the "LaGG" caught fire. We rushed there in the division commander's Soviet model M-1 car, but we didn't find the fighter. They delivered the pilot to us at the medical-sanitation battalion a little later. He had managed to land his fighter and smother the flames. He was lucky to be alive!

In the first days of August, an Uzbek, Sergeant Atamurzaev, arrived with seven wounds in the lower abdomen. He was a calm and composed fellow. Several hours after the surgery, I dropped by to check on him; he was already awake and called, "Chief, come here!" With a smile he showed me a row of healthy, strong teeth, and gazing at me with his big, dark eyes from beneath his bushy eyebrows, said "Thanks, dear man!" in a characteristic Uzbek accent. I asked how he was doing. "Just fine!"

His stitches were removed 10 days later, and on the 12th day we discharged him in good health, on his feet. Together with Atamurzaev, three other "stomach" patients had survived. They now had a little longer to live! The point was that it was now warm, and there were no vitamin deficiencies. I could let the men rest for an extent of 10-12 days and keep them under a corresponding regime of constant monitoring. This made all the difference!

Possibly, the German were right to situate their hospitals (they had no medical-sanitation battalions) no closer than 30 kilometers from the front, but they had vehicles to transport the wounded, not half-starved horses.

The division's offensive was not crowned with success – we advanced 1.5 kilometers, took Lomovo, and dug in there. To the south, we abandoned Rostov, Feodosiia, Maikop. The Germans were nearing Stalingrad. Stalin's Order was received: "Not one step back!" It was read and explained in all the companies. Afterward, all we talked about was how to stop the foe ...

20

Liziukov's Fate

Now that the last page of the final chapter about Operational Group Chibisov's operation on the west bank of the Don River has been turned, the time has come to return to one of this book's most important questions: "What in fact happened to the commander of the 2nd Tank Corps, Hero of the Soviet Union Major General Liziukov and the 2nd Tank Corps' commissar Regimental Commissar Assorov?" Where did they go missing on 23 July 1942; and how can we track what happened to them? These questions and the full drama of General Liziukov's fate will be the focus of this chapter.

In fact, at the end of July 1942, the question of General Liziukov's fate for the higher Soviet command was to a great extent a complete mystery. There was a lot both puzzling and contradictory in his disappearance, but the fact of his previous service under the command of General Vlasov, who had gone over to the German side, and the dramatic circumstances of the 5th Tank Army's unsuccessful operation under his command were further complicating this puzzle, and all sorts of rumors and conjectures were swirling around it. But now, from the height of the passing decades and on the basis of archival documents, memoir literature and recollections, it is possible to say what happened with a great deal of likelihood. Indeed, if in Chapter Nine about the fighting on 23 July the events were viewed from the vantage point of the tank brigades that were hunkering down in the wooded ravine and that of the 2nd Tank Corps headquarters positioned in the rear, here the discussion will cover what most likely happened with the corps commander and his commissar after they climbed into the KV tank and left on their foray.

I'll remind the reader that in the fighting on 23 July, Liziukov was most likely focused on prodding the two remaining tank brigades of his tank corps to follow into a breakthrough that had supposedly been created by the heavy tank brigade, which had already set out. From his perspective, it was possible to conclude that the 148th Tank Brigade's attack on 22 July along the road to Somovo had created a breach in the German defenses, into which it was now possible to commit the rest of the 2nd Tank Corps. At 0700 on 23 July, after their nighttime summoning to General Chibisov, the commander of Briansk Front's operational group, Liziukov and Assorov arrived in Bol'shaia Vereika.[1] The order to attack and reach the Medvezh'e area had been issued by Liziukov back on 22 July, but in connection with his summoning to his superior commander, the attack had been postponed. Now Liziukov was intending to go on the attack together with the tank brigades and direct the fighting from a point directly among their combat formations. He decided not to employ the corps' motorized rifle brigade; it had already suffered heavy losses, and thus only the tanks were to go on the attack toward Medvezh'e.[2] He took no submachine gunners along with him.

The evening before, Liziukov had directed the commander of the 27th Tank Brigade to prepare a KV tank and crew for him and to park it next to the church. It was in this tank that he was in fact planning to fight his way through to Medvezh'e, and from inside it he planned to control the tank

1 TsAMO, F. 202, op. 50, d. 1, ll. 304-305.
2 Ibid. Also, see F. 148 tp, op. 1, d. 3, l. 40 and F. 8 gv TK, op. 1, d. 224 (b), ll. 106, 110 and 113.

corps' battle.[3] In the morning Liziukov and Assorov arrived in the 27th Tank Brigade. Liziukov ordered the brigade commander to begin moving out as soon as possible, and notified him that he would be following the brigade's tank column in his tank.[4] At this time, the corps' two tank brigades were positioned on the southern outskirts of Bol'shaia Vereika, which they had reached on the evening of 22 July and where they had spent the night while waiting for the corps commander's return. The first to move off in the direction of Hill 188.5 was the 26th Tank Brigade; the 27th Tank Brigade was to move out behind it. Quickly the tanks of the brigades climbed the steep southern slope of the river valley and disappeared from view over the crest of the hill.

For some time Liziukov remained behind in Bol'shaia Vereika. Then, around 0900, having issued the necessary orders and having left behind his chief of staff, Liziukov set out in his tank to catch up with the tank brigades. The general's KV rolled across the Bol'shaia Vereika River over the bridge, reached the road to Hill 188.5 and began to climb the hill. After the downpour of the previous evening, the dirt road had only begun to dry out in the morning sun and the KV tank's tracks were churning through the mud. Out in front was a prolonged slope, and vision was restricted to several hundred meters.

Here is the time to make an important clarification. All the tank crew members of the KV tanks (50 men altogether) and their 10 KV tanks had arrived in the 27th Tank Brigade from Cheliabinsk as part of the 12th and 13th March Companies on the very eve of the offensive – 20 July 1942. They were new guys in the brigade, and had never previously participated in any combat operations as part of the tank brigade, but already on the day after their arrival in their new unit, they went into their first combat. The KV tank that had been prepared for Liziukov at his order by Captain Luchnikov (the acting commander of the 27th Tank Brigade) was a relatively new one, which had left the ChTZ [Cheliabinsk Tractor Factory] in the beginning of January 1942 and bore the factory number 43686. According to its roster, its crew consisted of:

1. Junior Lieutenant Nikolai Evseevich Ivonin (platoon commander and also the tank commander).
2. Sergeant Major Ivan Fedorovich Zhludin (senior driver-mechanic).
3. Sergeant Major Evgenii Aleksandrovich Suslov (gunner)
4. Senior Sergeant Aleksei Ivanovich Puzikov (radio operator).
5. Sergeant Sergei Iakovlevich Mozhaev (junior driver-mechanic).[5]

From the analysis and comparison of available documents, it is possible to draw the reasonable conclusion that the tank's assigned gunner – Sergeant Major Suslov – was not part of the KV crew in the fighting on 23 July. Obviously, having received the order to prepare a tank for Liziukov, Captain Luchnikov foresightedly "removed" the gunner from the tank in order to free a place in the KV tank's turret for the general. When Commissar Assorov on the evening of 22 July in Kreshchenka also decided to join Liziukov, the assigned tank commander was also removed from the crew in order to free a place in the tank for him, as Liziukov's liaison officer later testified. Accordingly, Junior Lieutenant Ivonin was also not part of the KV crew in Liziukov's last battle on 23 July. Thus on the morning of 23 July, the following men were most likely in KV No. 43686, in which the commander and commissar of the 2nd Tank Corps went into battle:

3 Ibid.

4 TsAMO, F. 202, op. 50, d.1, ll. 307-309. Further evidence regarding the subsequent events has been taken from this same file and corresponds to the same endnote information.

5 TsAMO, F. 27 tbr, op. 2, d. 3, l. 16.

1. Major General Liziukov
2. Regimental Commissar Assorov
3. Senior driver-mechanic Sergeant Major Zhludin
4. Radio operator Senior Sergeant Puzikov
5. Junior driver-mechanic Sergeant (according to Colonel Sukhoruchkin's report, Senior Sergeant) Mozhaev

Sergeant Major Zhludin was driving the tank. The radioman/machine gunner Puzikov was sitting beside him on his left. Three men were positioned in the turret: Liziukov, Assorov and junior driver-mechanic Mozhaev, who was carrying out the duty of the gunloader. Liziukov, probably, was sitting in the tank commander's seat. In case of battle, Assorov and Mozhaev were to conduct the fire from the cannon and machine gun, although Assorov likely had little experience as a gunlayer. However, Liziukov plainly had little intention of getting tied up in battle in his command tank, and if Assorov took his seat in the gunner's place, then he apparently did this due to his high rank. It wasn't for a regimental commissar to sit upon boxes of shells, as the loader in the KV tank crews often had to do!

The delay in Bol'shaia Vereika led to the fact that Liziukov moved out to follow the tank brigades almost 90 minutes later. Over this interval of time, the tank brigades might have gone far ahead, and having reached the narrow corridor between the patches of woods that restricted tank movement, might have turned to the southeast and even now be advancing along the high ground toward Medvezh'e. True, over the time while Liziukov and Assorov were in Bol'shaia Vereika, there was fighting going on in the hills to the south that they could not see, but the sounds of it plainly carried to the village. The opponent was clearly offering resistance and (so it seemed) striving to block the advance by the tanks of the brigades to the south. However, Liziukov knew well that approximately 50 tanks had gone on the attack, and believed that with a unified armored fist they could penetrate the enemy's defenses in the corridor between the woods and enter a breakthrough.

He didn't know, though, that the battle that had started at 0800 had not gone well for the tank brigades or that they had been struck by Luftwaffe attacks and the withering fire of enemy anti-tank artillery. Seeking to escape the barrage of fire and air attacks, first one, and then the second tank brigade diverged from the axis of advance, pivoted to the left, and had taken cover in a wooded ravine not more than 500 meters from the now emptied road. The corps' offensive had faltered from its outset; both tank brigades were now sitting side by side in the patch of woods, waiting out the airstrikes. Some of the crews, unable to withstand the howl of dive bombers and the nearby bomb explosions clambered out of their tanks and took shelter beneath them…[6]

Having driven our tanks into the wooded ravine and having blunted their advance, the German Stukas flew away. After the 26th and 27th Tank Brigades vacated the road to Somovo, the enemy's anti-tank artillery fire also subsided. A lull had settled over the battlefield. Just at these very minutes, Liziukov's KV tank climbed the road leading up the hill and emerged on the extensive plain between the woods.

In front of the eyes of the crewmen sitting in the KV tank, there opened the vista of a road leading to the south and an expansive field with still smoking shell craters and knocked-out tanks, many of which had been left standing here since the 5th Tank Army's failed offensive. However, neither Assorov, nor Liziukov, nor anyone else of the KV's crew observed *moving tanks* on the road or in the field. Of course, some of the tanks that had set out earlier that morning on the attack might have been knocked out and left in the field, but neither the corps' commander nor the commissar who were observing the field could assume that *all of the tanks had been knocked out* as

6 TsAMO, F. 202, op. 50, d. 1, ll. 307-309.

a result of the fighting. In fact, they were completely correct, because the brigades' losses in that battle had been inconsequential. Only the conclusion regarding what they were seeing was incorrect. Observing an empty road out in front of them and the lack of any movement in the field, Liziukov and Assorov plainly decided that the 26th and 27th Tank Brigades had broken through and were already exploiting a breakthrough deeply into the German defenses. They didn't know that there was no movement on the hill because the *brigades had turned off to one side and were hunkering down in a wooded ravine.*

Looking back from the vantage point of today, it is difficult to understand why the brigade commanders and the corps commander were operating so disjointedly that morning, to the point of a flagrant absence of cooperation. Many of the 2nd Tank Corps' command tanks were already equipped with radio sets by July 1942, and in the documents one comes across mentions of radio messages between Liziukov and the brigade commanders in the preceding days of fighting. However, on this fatal morning, located less than 1 kilometer from each other, the corps commander and the brigade commanders were literally separated by a solid wall of a communication breakdown, which grew to an eternity for Liziukov. (Incidentally, recalling the story about how the actual commander of the 27th Tank Brigade, whose radio had gone silent, had reacted to a suggestion by the signals commander to use his functioning radio, it is perhaps not worth being surprised at this …)

The general's lone KV tank was moving along the road past the brigades that were sheltering in the wooded ravine practically within direct eyesight of them, but no one attempted to stop it, and judging from later interrogations, no one even noticed it. Moreover, as we recall, in response to the radioed query from Liziukov's signals officer about the general's location, made when there were no chiefs of the 2nd Tank Corps left in Bol'shaia Vereika, they had reported from the 27th Tank Brigade that General Liziukov was with them![7] There were radio sets in the brigades, but subsequently no one could recall that the corps commander had tried to contact anyone over the radio. (I'm increasingly inclined to believe that from a certain point in time, the available radios in the brigades weren't even switched on …).

The radio airwaves were jammed with the sounds of excited German speech. In the headquarters of various German units, they were reporting on the approach of tanks, requesting air support, sending urgent orders about the regrouping of available forces and requesting reinforcements, but in the airwaves of the 2nd Tank Corps and its brigades, there was apparently just a crackling silence. Alas, just like in the Napoleonic Wars more than a century prior, the most reliable and frequently used means of communication in the Red Army was still the courier.

Liziukov's fatal mistake was the fact that he didn't double check to see whether the tank brigades that had moved out on the attack were carrying out his order, and whether or not they had actually advanced along the road. He was confident that the 26th and 27th Tank Brigades were engaged in combat out in front of him, while he, as was set by his order, was following behind them under their reliable cover. However, in fact after the brigades' pivot into the wooded ravine on the left, there was no longer any screen out in front of Liziukov, and with each passing minute the corps commander's tank, which had rolled past his brigades, was receding ever further from them in the direction of the enemy …

(I assume as well that one of the reasons for such a total lack of caution, which is difficult to explain at first glance, was Liziukov's and Assorov's mistaken confidence that units of the 167th Rifle Division had already driven the enemy beyond the southern tip of the woods by that morning. This followed directly from a briefing by the operational group's headquarters, which became known to the 2nd Tank Corps' commander and commissar early on the morning of 23

7 Ibid.

July, when they were still at Operational Group Chibisov's headquarters in Lukino.[8] This briefing was based upon an unverified report from the 167th Rifle Division's headquarters regarding the division's successful advance and, supposedly, the lines occupied by its units, which didn't quite correspond to reality or didn't even correspond at all to it.)[9]

However, Liziukov and Assorov didn't suspect the nearby danger that was threatening them. In the 2nd Tank Corps' decisive battle, they were hurrying to catch up with the tankers and to take the place of a commander and commissar in the combat formations of the units entrusted to them. For Liziukov, this was the last chance to regain the confidence of the higher command, and to purge all of the painful and bitter failures of the recent weeks with a decisive victory. He had staked everything on this operation, and without any doubts, was spoiling for a fight.

It was now shortly past 0900. Time was pressing, and Liziukov had no intention of pulling off the designated route, in order to check just in case upon the location of the brigades that were nowhere in sight. In his mind, they were out in front … Accelerating after the extended climb up from the river valley, the general's KV tank steadily and confidently headed to the south …

On the morning of 23 July elements of the 387th Infantry Division's 542nd Infantry Regiment and their anti-tank guns were defending in the woods south of Lebiazh'e.[10] There are grounds to believe that they had been strengthened by several anti-tank guns from the panzerjäger battalion subordinate to the VII Corps headquarters. The major portion of the German anti-tank artillery was obviously concentrated near the northeastern fringe of the woods. It was these anti-tank guns that had greeted the tanks of the 26th and 27th Tank Brigades that were climbing the hill with intense fire, forcing them to swerve increasingly to the left from the axis of advance.[11]

However, because of aspects of the lie of the ground, a significant portion of the road from Bol'shaia Vereika to Somovo remained outside the zone of effective fire from the enemy anti-tank guns in the woods, while the beginning of the road was completely outside the field of vision from the woods. Thus Liziukov's tank wasn't fired upon and most likely hadn't even been spotted from the northeastern fringe of the woods. It was only once the KV tank emerged on the section of road atop the hill that the KV tank became visible from the eastern fringe of the woods. The expansive field here sharply narrowed to the east, and the southern spur of the woods approached almost up to the road. It was here that the narrow, 1,000 meter neck between the two patches of woods began in the upper reaches of the ravines that were inaccessible to tanks, after which there opened an expansive field to the south, where tanks could conduct wide-flanking maneuvers around any knots of resistance. There can be little doubt that it was precisely on this tank-vulnerable axis that the enemy in fact concentrated his remaining anti-tank guns in the area of the woods.

In the southern portion of the woods near Lebiazh'e, by the morning of 23 July there was most likely just a pair of 50-mm anti-tank guns, the crews of which were being covered by groups of infantry. There is documentary evidence of this. For example, a 1st Tank Corps intelligence summary noted that two platoons and two anti-tank guns in firing positions had been detected in the southern fringe of the woods.[12]

On the basis of the analysis of available documents, it is possible to assert what happened next with a great deal of confidence. Approximately 3 kilometers from Bol'shaia Vereika, Liziukov's KV tank reached the eastern slopes of Hill 188.5, where it appeared in the field of vision of German observers. It is possible to assume that they were initially puzzled, when they saw a single Russian

8 TsAMO, F. 202, op. 5, d. 251, l. 8.
9 This flows from a comparison and analysis of both Soviet and captured German documents, which will be discussed below.
10 NARA, T-314, roll 353, fr. 000398-400.
11 TsAMO, F. 202, op. 50, d. 1, l. 340.
12 TsAMO, F. 1 TK, op. 1, d. 235, l. 75.

tank, totally unaccompanied by other tanks or infantry, confidently rolling along the road toward them without a single shot being fired. This was even more unbelievable, because the Russian tank attack by that time had been stopped at the front, and fighting had subsided.

The field of vision here exceeded 1.5 kilometers, and from that distance it was difficult to recognize the type of tank that had appeared. Soon, however, the German artillerymen undoubtedly determined that the enemy's most menacing tank – a heavy Russian KV tank – was approaching them.

It is worth noting how coolly the German anti-tank gun crew waited for the tank to draw near, in order not to reveal their position prematurely, but to wait for the right moment in order not to miss. The Germans simply didn't have any great choice in the means to counter the KV tank! The sole, sufficiently effective ammunition in the arsenal of a German anti-tank gun crew was the armor-piercing, discarding sabot 50-mm shell, which had a super-hard projectile made of tungsten carbide, or, as our tankers called it back then, an armor-piercing "slug".[13]

The supply of these shells (because of their limited production and the costliness of tungsten) was extremely limited in the standard allowance of ammunition for the German anti-tank guns, and so the gun commanders conserved them for special, emergency cases. There is no doubt that having spotted an approaching heavy Russian tank, the commander of the German 50-mm anti-tank gun decided that this was the right moment and ordered the use of the most effective shell of all those available to him against the KV tank.

However, even at this, the Germans plainly had no assurance that the 50-mm shell could penetrate the frontal armor of a heavy KV tank, and thus even positioned close to the road, the German crew had no intention to open fire at its front from a distance, but to remain concealed in anticipation for when the KV tank would pass them and present its flank at point-blank range. Although the gun was doubtlessly well-camouflaged and dug in, and rose less than a meter above the ground, nevertheless the road was so close to its position that it might have been spotted from the tank! It was necessary to have strong nerves and self-possession in order to keep quiet and concealed as the heavy KV tank approached. The Germans waited and kept quiet. Meanwhile the tank, without stopping, kept approaching closer and closer, and possibly its crew members weren't keeping careful watch of the surrounding terrain, confident that the fighting had already passed here …

The German infantry supporting the anti-tank gun also prepared for combat and tensely watched the heavy tank as it approached them with clattering tracks and a roaring engine. For Liziukov and the members of his crew, these were the last seconds of the deceptive silence reigning over the field and their steady movement along the road, as they thought "right on the heels of the corps' main forces". For all but one of them, these were also the final seconds of their lives.

Close to the southern spur of the woods, the tank was supposed to turn to the left and advance in the direction of Medvezh'e, where according to Liziukov's calculations his tank brigades were to enter combat. Most likely, Liziukov's tank at this moment was located somewhere in the vicinity of the modern-day road fork on the main road to Bol'shaia Vereika. It is possible that the tank had even begun to turn, and as a result of this maneuver that was unexpected to the enemy, exposed its right flank to surprise, close-range fire from the woods even sooner than anticipated. In these seconds, the commander of the German anti-tank gun apparently decided that it was impossible to wait any longer and that it was necessary to act, or the tank would slip away. The KV tank was now so close to the gun that the gunlayer was now quite able to distinguish separate parts of it in

13 M. Postnikov, *Bronezaschita tiazhelykh tankov KV i IS, 1941-1945* [*The protective armor of the heavy KV and IS tanks, 1941-1945*] (Moscow: Eksprint, 2006), p. 24.

his gunsight, and could fire without any lead or the need to make any corrections for target speed or range … In short, he couldn't miss.

Having waited for several agonizing and nervous minutes, while staying totally concealed, and ultimately having waited for the best possible moment, the commander of the German crew gave the order to open fire ….

The camouflaged German anti-tank gun in the patch of woods unexpectedly opened fire at the KV from point-blank range. The shell struck the tank practically at a 90 degree angle and apparently penetrated the armor; then the hull was struck by another shell, then a third …

Studying various materials and publications about Liziukov's last combat action, I came across the opinion that his tank was supposedly knocked out by a German heavy 88-mm Flak gun, shellcasings of which were found by modern-day searchers in the fringe of the woods. However, putting it gently, this version is dubious.

The use of heavy 88-mm Flak guns for anti-tank defense was a forced measure of the German command. The Germans preserved these expensive guns and sought to use them only in the depth of their combat positions. It was impossible to call the heavy Flak guns a close-combat anti-tank weapon. In close combat they would to a great extent throw away their advantages, and in return become an easy target for enemy tanks, mostly because of their large size, which made it extremely difficult to conceal them on the battlefield. Their superiority was in accurate, long-range fire, and not in the possibilities of camouflaging them and using them for ambushes.

After the fighting on 21 and 22 July and once our tanks had reached the southern bank of the Bol'shaia Vereika River, the enemy withdrew the bulk of his heavy anti-tank weapons to the main line of defense in front of the villages of Somovo and Bol'shaia Treshchevka, where the tanks of Katukov's 1st Tank Corps repeatedly attempted to break through. The breakthrough by one of the tank brigades of Liziukov's 2nd Tank Corps (the 148th Tank Brigade) to the Medvezh'e area also forced the German command to detach a portion of the heavy anti-tank artillery to that place in order to combat those tanks that had broken through. Thus, by the morning of 23 July, all of the heavy Flak guns, which might have been used for anti-tank defense (there were already too few of them as it was!), had most likely already been withdrawn into the depth of the German defenses.

Because of the terrain conditions that offered an extremely limited view to the north and the obvious relative immobility of the large 88-mm gun, in the event of a rapid approach by enemy tanks from the opposite side of the woods (by that time our tanks had already broken through to Somovo and might quite simply encircle the entire patch of woods), it no longer made any sense to use the 88-mm Flak guns for an anti-tank defense here. They themselves might have been destroyed by Russian tanks emerging on their flanks and rear.

However, even if one assumes that for whatever reason one of these guns might have been left in the patch of woods and not withdrawn to the rear, then even in this case the Germans most likely would have used it in a different manner. Taking advantage of its long-range accuracy and stopping power, *the enemy artillery crew would absolutely have attempted to hit the KV tank when they first spotted it, at a distance. To wait until the KV tank approached more closely would have been not only unnecessary in that situation, but even dangerous.*

So, finally, one more argument: The consequences of a hit by a heavy 88-mm shell, fired from close range with an initial velocity of almost 1 kilometer/second, would have been quite different for the KV tank. The explosion of such a shell within the tight confines of the tank most likely would have meant the death of the entire tank crew, and possibly the detonation of the on-board ammunition. In this case, we hardly would have been able to learn how General Liziukov was killed, because no surviving eyewitnesses among the crew would have been left.

It is possible that General Liziukov and Regimental Commissar Assorov didn't even have time to recognize what had happened. The projectile's kinetic energy when fired from such close range was such that they were immediately left badly wounded or killed on the spot by the exploding fragments and flaking pieces of armor. At the very least, from junior driver-mechanic Mozhaev's story it follows that after the shell struck the tank, Liziukov didn't show any signs of life. True, there was no explosion within the turret. In addition, there was no detonation of the on-board ammunition or conflagration, which is one more indirect confirmation that the KV tank's turret was struck by an armor-piercing discarding sabot shell that didn't have any explosive materials.

The senior driver-mechanic sitting at the tank's control levers was also killed instantly or left severely wounded. It is possible that this was because the tank was immediately struck by a second, then a third armor-piercing slug[14] -- the Germans hurried to plant one or two more shells in the KV tank from close range, fearing that one alone wouldn't be sufficient! They had to finish off the tank! Mozhaev himself was wounded by a fragment, but was nevertheless able to open a hatch and get out. Catching sight of him, the Germans opened fire at him, but were plainly too slow. Bullets struck the armor, but only one of them hit him before he rolled off into the rye and started to crawl away from the knocked-out tank.

The radio operator began to clamber out of the tank after Mozhaev, but a German machine gunner and (or) riflemen were now at the ready and didn't give him any chance to get away. The radioman was cut down by a hail of bullets and killed on the spot, just as soon as he emerged from the tank.

The entire combat, or more accurately the targeted fusillade of fire from out of ambush, quickly ended. Having struck the tank and becoming convinced that the KV's crew had apparently been put out of commission, the German gun commander ordered to cease fire. He then gave an order to the infantrymen that were supporting the gun to move out onto the road and investigate the knocked-out KV tank.

It didn't take them much time to cover the distance separating them from the knocked-out tank. Through the rye field, with their weapons at the ready, they quickly reached the immobile KV.

At this time, Mozhaev, the twice-wounded and sole surviving member of the entire crew, made a dash away from the tank. One can imagine the entire horror and tragedy of those terrifying seconds for him. The only source of salvation from close-range fire was the knocked-out KV tank. Its immobilized body rose above the rye and was still screening Mozhaev from enemy bullets, concealing him from the field of view of the German infantry approaching from the opposite side of the tank. However, it was completely clear to him that the Germans would soon come looking for him, and if they caught sight of him in the field, he wouldn't be able to get away. Seconds were deciding everything, during which he had to get as far away as possible from the tank and then drop down into the rye. No sooner and no later. Fate had given him precious little time for all this.

So, ignoring the pain and leaving behind a bloody trail from the bullet and shell fragment that had struck him, Mozhaev, rising and falling, scrambled further into the rye. Very likely, at the time he was stifling his pain and groans. He clearly knew that *death was snapping at his heels together with the approaching fascist troops.*

Based on the research materials, the twice-wounded Mozhaev had time to stagger and crawl only a short distance from the tank before the enemy soldiers arrived at the knocked-out KV. Seeing them, Mozhaev froze and hid in the rye. His situation was simply desperate, but it is completely obvious that even in these terrifying circumstances he didn't lose heart and composure. He didn't go crazy with fear and didn't cower in the rye, wishing not to be seen or heard, focused only upon not being spotted. No, he turned his face toward the foe and watched what happened next.

Possibly, he was prepared for a last battle and had readied his sidearm – a Nagan with 7 bullets, which equipped the crew members (according to the recollections of tankers, the Nagan was

14 This is according to materials of the FSB archive, from which the author received an official reply.

usually kept in the boot and not in a holster, which might have caught on something when exiting the tank). It would seem that in this hopeless situation, the bleeding tanker might only hope for the mercy of the victors! However, Mozhaev had no intention of surrendering. He, of course, wanted to live and most likely feared death, like any mortal man, but while struggling for his life, *he didn't shed his honor and didn't lose his worth* – the value of a true Russian soldier.

So, despite the Death dressed in German uniforms that was stalking nearby (the enemy troops, having talked among themselves, were likely scanning the field around the tank), he didn't lose the will to resist, didn't succumb to panic, and didn't stand up in the rye with upraised hands …

No! Lying among the crushed stalks of grain in his increasingly bloody combat blouse and having no way to bandage his wounds, Mozhaev (as I can picture it) was quietly gripping his Nagan with bloody fingers and from under his eyebrows peering at what was happening. Obviously, *he was ready to die, but not to surrender to the adversary*. … I bow my head before his courage!

Does Mozhaev's story prompt trust? In my view – yes. There is no basis to suspect him of false testimony, since he made no attempt to justify himself and put his actions in a favorable light. Let's give it a thought: being the sole eyewitness, Mozhaev, for example, could have said that Liziukov was killed instantly when the projectile hit the tank, which would have meant that there was no longer any sense in trying to drag him away. Such a version of the events would have spared him any questions about General Liziukov's further fate. He could have said that he exchanged fire with the Germans until his last bullet, and then made an effort to drag the general from the tank, but being wounded, lacked the strength to do so. He could have thought up an even more dramatic scene, that the Germans were chasing him and firing at the place where he was hiding in the rye, and thus he barely managed to evade the pursuit and didn't see what happened next. He also could have said that he was wounded, lost consciousness, and thus he didn't see or didn't know anything.

He had no need to justify himself or feign his wounds; they spoke eloquently for themselves, and if he had offered any such excuses, no one would have made any inquiries about what happened in fact. But Mozhaev spoke about what he saw. What need did he have to think this all up? For the command, there was nothing good in his story; on the contrary, Mozhaev was reporting the worst possible news and gaining no advantage from this. His story is simple and guileless, and it is possible to explain this primarily by the fact that Mozhaev made no attempt to contrive anything, and simply spoke the truth.

Ultimately, if he had felt guilty and feared investigation by the Special Department with all the consequences flowing from this, he could have surrendered. Then the "specialists" of the NKVD couldn't have touched him with their interrogations, and then we wouldn't have ever known about what happened with General Liziukov. However, Mozhaev was a genuine soldier and remained faithful to his military oath and to the Motherland. He didn't surrender, and despite the wounds he had received, began to make his way back to friendly lines, where he in fact told about the death of the 2nd Tank Corps commander.

It is characteristic that an official investigation later conducted by Colonel Sukhoruchkin from the Briansk Front headquarters considered it necessary to bring the command of the 26th Tank Brigade to responsibility and was highly critical about the inactivity of the 2nd Tank Corps headquarters, but he didn't utter a single word of rebuke toward Senior Sergeant Mozhaev, although had he considered him guilty of something, he could have simply turned him over to trial by a military tribunal. The investigation of Liziukov's death took place over the very same days when Stalin's famous Order No. 227 was being read out to the troops at the front, which demanded that the command staff take the harshest measures in order to keep order and discipline in the troops. In the spirit of the order, the attitude toward such crimes as the abandonment of a combat sector by the troops or fleeing from the battlefield changed sharply in the Red Army. Nevertheless, even in this changing situation, Sukhoruchkin didn't find anything suspicious in the actions of the wounded driver-mechanic.

Senior Sergeant Sergei Iakovlevich Mozhaev became the sole eyewitness to the death of Liziukov's crew. The death of the commander and commissar of the 2nd Tank Corps happened practically in front of his eyes. However, their tragedy didn't end on this ...

According to Mozhaev, the German soldiers approached the tank, climbed aboard it, and glanced in the hatches. The dead Liziukov and Assorov remained in the turret. The enemy soldiers entered the turret hatch, cut off the commander's map case, pulled the documents out of it, and started to glance through them.[15] Having glanced at the field around the tank, they made no effort to search for Mozhaev ...

Thus, fate saved him from death, as if compelling him at whatever the cost to report the news about what happened with the corps' commander and commissar. The weakening Mozhaev slowly crawled back to friendly lines through the fields of rye grain that had been flattened by tanks, riddled with craters, and strewn with corpses. After the wounds he had received, he took an agonizingly long time to reach friendly lines (probably losing consciousness in the process and lying oblivious for hours), and wound up in the medical-sanitation platoon of the 26th Tank Brigade only on the next day – 24 July 1942.

Only then, apparently realizing that he didn't have time to report on everything he had seen to higher command (his condition became critical, and he had to be sent to a hospital), he decided to tell a medical attendant, Mussorov, about what had happened, and asked him to report as quickly as possible about this to the command, which Mussorov in fact did, when he appeared at the headquarters of the 2nd Tank Corps that evening. Mussorov's story about what he had heard from Mozhaev for the first time partly opened the curtain of mystery over Liziukov's and Assorov's fate for Nagaibakov, and became a genuine "ChP" for the rest of the corps' command staff.

As soon as Nagaibakov learned about what had happened, he decided that same evening to drive dozens of kilometers in order to find Mozhaev – the sole eyewitness, who could directly tell him about what had happened with Liziukov and Assorov. Nagaibakov found out that Mozhaev had been sent to a hospital in the village of Baranovka (4 kilometers from the Khitrovo railroad station, and approximately 50 kilometers from the 2nd Tank Corps headquarters over village roads), and decided to head there to find him.

Alas, by the time the chief of staff of the 2nd Tank Corps arrived in Baranovka, Mozhaev was no longer there. They had sent him on to a rear hospital, so Nagaibakov didn't get to question him in person. Nevertheless, he found out the number of the medical train, and learned also that the train had been sent along the railroad "in the direction of Tambov". Nagaibakov made no effort to drive that far, obviously considering it impossible to abandon the units of the 2nd Tank Corps that were engaged in battle for that long in the absence of the corps' commander and commissar. Nevertheless, as was to be expected from an executive officer in charge, Nagaibakov passed along the information he had obtained to higher command and reported that he had managed to make it known to three important addressees simultaneously: a representative of Briansk Front's Political Directorate, a representative of the Front's Special Department, and a military commissar of Briansk Front's Department of Armored Forces Senior Battalion Commissar Ognev. After this, the higher command finally learned about what had happened, and the flywheel of an official investigation began to spin.

At the same time from the analysis and comparison of documents one can draw the conclusion that investigators were sent to track down Mozhaev. They quickly found him in the hospital and questioned him, and his written testimony (or that written on his behalf) lay at the basis of both the investigation pursued by the Special Department and Colonel Sukhoruchkin's final report.

15 TsAMO, F. 202, op. 50, d.1, ll. 304-305.

That is to say, the wounded Mozhaev's evidence wasn't at all lost, and his eyewitness testimony (and not Mussorov's retelling of it) in fact did become the primary source for the subsequent reports on Liziukov's death, which unquestionably enhances its value and eliminates the possibility of distortions in retellings by secondhand sources, plain examples of which can be found in a number of books of a memoir or journalistic nature.

Unfortunately, the information passed along by Nagaibakov to higher command didn't prompt immediate, extraordinary and all-encompassing measures to ascertain all the circumstances surrounding what had happened or a search for any supplementary information. It took too long for this information to pass up the chain of command and be "digested", and the fragment of time between the night of 24/25 July and the morning of 26 July that was decisive for any searches on the location was irretrievably lost.

Obviously, this was primarily connected with the difficult situation in the operational group, when its front had been breached as a result of the German counterattack and German tanks had made a deep penetration into its lines, winding up in dangerous proximity to Chibisov's headquarters. The operational group's command found itself facing a genuine operational crisis and was compelled to take extreme measures to resolve it. In these circumstances, the question regarding the fate of Liziukov and Assorov faded into the background and was plainly not the most important for either the operational group's command, which was simply over its head in the flow of events that were engulfing it, or for the Briansk Front headquarters, which took a long time to rouse itself after the alarm bell.

After Mussorov's report about Mozhaev's story, the chief of staff of the 2nd Tank Corps Nagaibakov and the other officers in the corps' headquarters (if he had briefed them about what he had heard from Mussorov) wound up in a delicate situation: how trustworthy was Mussorov's news? Did it offer sufficient grounds to believe that Major General Liziukov had been killed? But since they didn't have any other information about the fate of the missing Liziukov, they had to rely upon only what they had heard from the medical orderly. Liziukov's tank hadn't been spotted, his body hadn't been found, and none of the other members of the crew, except for the wounded Mozhaev, had returned.

During the day of 25 July and the morning of 26 July, when there was still a chance to search the battlefield for the missing general, the 2nd Tank Corps had already left the Bol'shaia Vereika area, fallen back by 10-12 kilometers to Murav'evka and Dolgoe, and at an order from the commander of Operational Group Chibisov had conducted an unsuccessful attack toward Lomovo. In fact, by the morning of 26 July it had totally gone over to the defense. In that period of one and a half days, realistically only the brigades of the 1st Tank Corps, in particular the 89th Tank Brigade, units of the 167th Rifle Division and the 118th Tank Brigade might have been able to investigate the battlefield, but they didn't conduct any special, purposeful searches for any traces of the commander and commissar of the neighboring tank corps because they didn't receive any order to do so, nor were they even aware of Liziukov's and Assorov's disappearance. Doubtlessly, if such an order had been given to them in time, there wouldn't have been much murkiness left in the case of Liziukov's death. However, this didn't happen; they didn't receive any queries from the 2nd Tank Corps over these one and a half days, and thus the proffered chance to clarify many of the facts surrounding what had happened and to recover and bury the dead crew members in Liziukov's tank was irretrievably missed.

Meanwhile, the investigation of the "ChP" exceeded the scope of the 2nd Tank Corps headquarters and came under the control of the Briansk Front's Department of Armored Forces. A study of the facts surrounding what had happened was conducted, but it was already impossible to organize a detailed survey of the location: the area of the 2nd Tank Corps' combat on 22-24 July was now behind German lines. However, the investigation conducted by Briansk Front headquarters nevertheless yielded its results.

It was in this period, plainly in response to a query of Briansk Front headquarters to the commands of all the units that conducted combat operations alongside the 2nd Tank Corps, that a report was received from the headquarters of the 1st Tank Corps. It stated that during the fighting south of Bol'shaia Vereika, scouts had spotted a knocked-out KV tank on the battlefield. They approached it, but didn't glance inside the tank. The scouts said that they had seen the body of a dead tanker hanging from the turret, and this tanker had 4 bars on his collar ....

This was already saying a lot and was confirming Mozhaev's tale, making him much more trustworthy that it seemed at first: four bars signified a regimental commissar, and at this time and in that area the body could only have been that of the missing Regimental Commissar Assorov. This confirmed with a high degree of probability that the scouts had seen on that day the very KV tank in which Liziukov had set out from Bol'shaia Vereika on that ill-fated morning.

Further information from the scouts of the 1st Tank Corps might have provided, arguably, even weightier grounds to confirm that the commander of the 2nd Tank Corps Major General Liziukov had been killed. Approximately 100 meters from the tank, in the field of rye, they discovered (as was written in the document) "the corpse of a Red Army man". In the pocket of the dead man's overalls, they found a booklet bearing Liziukov's name listing items of his uniform and assigned military equipment...[16]

Judging from the documents available in the archive, this evidence became known to the individuals who were investigating the circumstances of General Liziukov's disappearance only toward the end of July 1942. In Briansk Front headquarters, there was not any reliable information about where General Liziukov was buried. Moreover, the materials received in the course of the investigation didn't provide any basis to believe that the body of the 2nd Tank Corps' commander had even been committed to the earth. From the words of the people who had heard the story of the only eyewitness, as well as on the basis of information returned by the 1st Tank Corps' scouts, only the fact that General Liziukov had been killed emerged. But was it possible to confirm even this with absolute confidence?

In reality, if this question is approached exclusively from the point of view of formal logic and only the available facts are taken into account, then it is necessary to acknowledge that Colonel Sukhoruchkin had no indisputable proof of Liziukov's death. In view of the fact that the head of the "Red Army man" that had been found in the rye field not far from the tank had been crushed, it was impossible to make a visual identification of the body. Thus, the only basis to assume that the scouts had found the body of General Liziukov was the booklet found in the pocket of the dead man. However, how weighty can this piece of evidence be considered?

Analyzing the documents and pondering those facts known to us today, it is impossible not to note the questions that arise in the process, to which now it is difficult to give an unambiguous answer. We'll try to go into more detail regarding these existing contradictions and ambiguities.

In Colonel Sukhoruchkin's report, it was written that scouts from the 1st Tank Corps had found Liziukov's booklet *on the corpse of a Red Army man*. Is it possible to talk here of a mistaken expression in the text of the report, assuming its author was simply using the most common term for designating a serviceman of the Red Army? Or was the conclusion that this was the corpse of a Red Army soldier made by the scouts who found the body? However, if this is the case, then why did they decide that the dead man was a Red Army soldier? They could have asserted this judging only on the basis of the body's appearance and the uniform it was wearing.

16 Ibid. Translator's note: The exact term in Russian for this booklet is *veshchevaia knizhka* ("clothing booklet" or "property booklet"), which listed all of an officer's army-issue belongings (uniform items and military equipment) and allowances. It has no direct equivalent in the U.S. Army or the English language. I have chosen to use the word "property booklet" or simply "booklet" elsewhere in the book.

It is known that Liziukov donned overalls and wore simple soldier's boots whenever he took a seat in a tank[17], which was the case on that day, when he planned to link up with the tank brigade that had marched off into the breakthrough. Thus it is natural that our scouts might have seen not a general's tunic on the body, but overalls without any signs of rank. However … it is hardly likely that sitting in the tank, Liziukov had put on a pair of overalls over his naked body or underwear. Most likely, he was wearing the overalls over his field uniform, *which had insignia of rank.*

In this case the scouts might have easily established the identity of the corpse, had they simply opened the overalls and taken a glance at the collar insignia. We'll recall that the scouts noticed a dead tanker with four bars on his collar dangling from the turret, which allows one to establish that this was Regimental Commissar Assorov. It is hard to imagine that having found a booklet with the name of Liziukov on the body of the corpse they found in the field that the scouts wouldn't have then checked the corpse more thoroughly and identified the rank of the dead man from the insignia he was wearing. However, other than the booklet, the scouts didn't report any other confirmation of the identity and rank of the dead man. From this one can draw the conclusion that they didn't find any signs of rank on the uniform of the dead man, *because there weren't any*. Why?

Major General Liziukov had been awarded the Gold Star of the Hero of the Soviet Union and other honors, which should have been on his field tunic. If we assume that he had donned the overalls over it before taking a seat in the tank, then after his death General Liziukov's medals might have been discovered beneath the overalls. However, as was the case with any signs of rank, the scouts didn't say a word about any decorations found by them on the dead man's uniform. This means that there weren't any medals either. Judging from all this, it is possible to speak only about two possible versions of what happened.

The first version is that the discovered body wasn't the body of General Liziukov, but was really the body of a Red Army soldier. However, then the question arises: How did General Liziukov's booklet wind up in the possession of this Red Army soldier?

The second version is that the scouts *in fact* found the body of the dead general, but on his uniform there were no insignia that would have allowed one to say, at the very least, that the dead man was a member of the command staff. Why?

I think one of the possible explanations for this might be the following: after Liziukov's death, the German soldiers cut off all the decorations and signs of rank from his tunic (or else removed his entire general's tunic as a trophy), so our scouts didn't find them under the general's overalls.

However, even in this case a question remains. Even if all the medals and signs of rank had been cut off by the Germans, the general's tunic itself would have been left under the overalls … Most likely, the scouts would have recognized the Red Army tunic of a member of the command staff. One war veteran from Voronezh A.P. Shingarev in a conversation with me, immediately declared, "Just from the uniform alone, even without any signs of rank, I would have immediately recognized whether this was a Red Army soldier or an officer."

Does this mean that there was also no tunic beneath the overalls? If so, then must one allow that the enemy soldiers made no effort to cut off the signs of rank and medals, but simply removed the tunic from the dead man together with all its insignia and honors, and carried it off?

There is another possible explanation for a "Red Army man" in the form of a dead general, suggested to me by a journalist from Krasnoiarsk, Denis Trufanov: heading into combat, Liziukov, like many other highly-ranked officers often did, might not have donned his general's tunic and service breeches, but instead soldier's trousers tucked into tarpaulin boots and the blouse of a Red Army soldier, possibly without even any signs of rank. Thus, the scouts called the general's body

17 A. Krivitsky, *Ne zabudu vovek* [*I will never forget*] (Moscow, 1963), p. 237.

that of a "Red Army man". (The 2nd Tank Corps' intelligence chief Major Ivanovsky claimed in 1943 that once before a battle, Liziukov gave him all of his personal documents; however, an entire number of instances in the stenograph of his recollections about Liziukov's death prompt definite doubts in the accuracy and credibility of his words.)[18] However, in that case why is there not a single mention of the medals left behind by him in the documents and recollections? It is hard to assume that before a battle he would have removed all of his decorations from his general's tunic, only to have them by all means on a soldier's blouse …

Unfortunately, re-reading the spare lines of a report yet again, it is now only possible to conjecture about all of this. Of course, military documents are an important source in our search, but alas, one cannot ask any questions of this source … Only the scouts who found the body might have been able to answer all of these arising questions. Yet even if they were in fact questioned in the immediate aftermath of the events during the recording of their story, the details that interest us today, unfortunately, would still remain murky to us more than 70 years after what happened. The materials of the Special Department's investigation are still classified, and ordinary scholars have no access to them.

In conclusion, if you will, it is necessary to discuss one more strange circumstance, which is now also hard to explain. According to Mozhaev, General Liziukov was killed or badly wounded while still in the tank. He was still in it, because later Mozhaev watched as the German troops climbed the tank and removed the general's map case that contained documents and maps; thus the assertion that after the shells hit the tank, Liziukov remained unharmed, climbed out of the tank, and was killed only after this contradicts Mozhaev's eyewitness account. However, if this is so, then how did Liziukov's body wind up 100 meters away from the tank, where the 1st Tank Corps' scouts found it? Did someone drag it that far, then abandon it?

If this was the case, then possibly this was done by the German soldiers themselves, who climbed into the tank and from the documents, signs of rank and medals, realized that this was an important Russian officer, after which they decided to deliver his body to their superiors. However, having dragged the body approximately 100 meters, they decided for some reason to drop it and as proof of their victory, decided to take his general's tunic with all of its medals and the map case that contained the documents.

It is also possible to assume that as a result of the shells' hits, Liziukov was not killed, but only badly wounded and rendered unconscious. The enemy soldiers believed that he was dead, when they cut off and removed his map case. Later the general regained consciousness and managed to get out of the tank and crawl away from it by approximately 100 meters before dying.

However, it is impossible to crawl with a crushed head, which means he could have received such a devastating injury only on the spot where his body was found in the field. However, the scouts didn't report about any other wounds or injuries that they found on the body, from which it follows that the only wound on the Red Army soldier found not far from the tank was in fact the damage to the head, which is incompatible with life. However, perhaps the Red Army scouts didn't attentively and thoroughly examine the dead man's body, or having seen the crushed head, paid no attention to other wounds? Questions remain ….

I think that in July – August 1942 during the thorough analysis of all the circumstances surrounding the disappearance of the 2nd Tank Corps' commander, certain doubts arose in the minds of several Special Department investigators and officers, if not to say *suspicions* …

Hypothetically, it was fully possible to assume that the corpse wearing the overalls without any signs of rank, found by the scouts, wasn't the body of General Liziukov, while the identification booklet in his name was deliberately left in the overalls, so that anyone who found the body would

18 Nauchnyi arkhiv IRI RAN, fond 2, razdel 1, op. 118, d. 4, l. 51.

conclude that the general was dead. What if this was an artfully done staging of the body with the aim of throwing off an investigation?

It is fully possible to understand some of these doubts even today, if you approach what happened with that distrust and paranoia that was rampant in our country back in the pre-war period, and later became an inseparable part of the war years. The greatest concerns in those days, arguably, were prompted not by the supposition that General Liziukov was dead, but that he instead became a prisoner …

Moreover, for the officers and investigators of the Special Departments, who were called upon to seek out and reveal any and all enemy spies, counter-revolutionary elements and traitors in the Red Army's units (and who had to show constantly the need for their work), the fact of the disappearance of a commander was to come under careful scrutiny and might fully lead to an investigation, where the main question was: What if a commander who was missing in action had possibly gone over to the enemy?

Unquestionably, as a result of the *special nature* of their work, the 2nd Tank Corps' chief of the Special Department and the workers of Briansk Front's Special Department could not have failed to examine such a possibility. We'll try to analyze the thoughts that might have directed them during a possible examination of the case of a missing general along the line of *their agency*, and how convincing their justifications might have been to believe that "*not all was clear in this case*".

General Liziukov disappeared at a most difficult and tragic time for him. The commander of the 2nd Tank Corps and Hero of the Soviet Union was by the end of July 1942 essentially in a complete fall from grace. The offensive by the 5th Tank Army, which he had commanded and upon which the *Stavka* had placed such high hopes, had ended in failure. His army was disbanded, while Liziukov was demoted to the post of a tank corps commander. For many it was obvious that the commander of the 5th Tank Army would shoulder most of the blame for the operation's failure to destroy the German Voronezh grouping. The *Stavka*'s frosty directive about the 5th Tank Army's unsatisfactory actions[19] and failure to carry out a personal order from the Supreme Leader to take Zemliansk[20], followed by the estrangement and vacuum that arose around Liziukov, indirectly spoke to the fact that in the following days his superiors might draw the most unflattering conclusions about the actions of the army commander, with consequences that might cost the former army commander dearly.

Such conclusions had already been drawn at the level of Briansk Front. Political officers in Briansk Front's headquarters, who'd been sent to "bolster" the 5th Tank Army, reported numerous outrages in the course of organizing the offensive, while the Front's chief of staff disappointedly reported in telegraph discussions on the non-combative mood in Comrade Liziukov's units.[21] Finally, the Front's troop commander drove to the 5th Tank Army and during a personal meeting with its commander, in a loud voice accused him of cowardice …[22]

However, at that point the army was disbanded, and in Briansk Front's hastily-created operational group, the former army commander and now only a corps commander again had to face that same man, who had already humiliatingly flung the words "This is called cowardice, Comrade Liziukov!" at him, now in the role of his direct superior.

What conclusions can be drawn from all this? What feelings might have Liziukov been experiencing toward his direct commander, Lieutenant General Chibisov? Perhaps, he had already formed a deep personal antagonism toward Chibisov?

---

19 TsAMO, F. 331, op. 5041, d. 5, l. 49.
20 TsAMO, F. 331, op. 5041, d. 18, l. 15.
21 TsAMO, F. 202, op. 5, d. 489, l. 104.
22 Krivitsky, *Ne zabudu vovek*, (Moscow, 1963), p. 232.

Then there followed a new offensive under the command of that same belligerent superior and a new failure. In the process it turned out that Liziukov's tank corps had not only failed to carry out the task that it had been given, but of the two tank corps it had operated in the worst manner, while the corps command had allowed a number of crying shames to take place in its leadership over the subordinate units. For this, the guilty parties had to be held accountable, and first of all the corps commander had to answer for this.

In addition, there was one specific detail in Liziukov's biography that immediately gained particular significance after the general's disappearance: Liziukov had been arrested by the *organs* during the pre-war purges of "wreckers and traitors" in the Red Army. They later released him, but after all he had been arrested back then for *some reason*. Perhaps ever since he had harbored a grudge against Soviet authority, and had only been waiting for the right moment? If so, does this mean, judging from all the above, that it is possible to assume that the former army commander, who didn't have a completely clean past and had a sullied reputation at the present and who'd moreover been just demoted and was probably harboring a personal grievance, had grounds for going over to the enemy?

Based upon the documents and evidence known to us today, it is possible to assert with a great deal of likelihood that certain agents of the "special" organs didn't exclude such a turn in Liziukov's case. Affirmations regarding the death of a disgraced general "from the mouths of eyewitnesses" weren't taken by them as convincing proof of his death.

Meanwhile, the investigation conducted by Briansk Front's headquarters ended in a conclusion that Liziukov had perished. Colonel Sukhoruchkin, who prepared the staff report for Deputy People's Commissar of Defense Fedorenko and Briansk Front's Military Council, unambiguously stated in its opening: "Having researched the causes for the **death of the 2nd Tank Corps commander** [emphasis the author's] Hero of the Soviet Union Guards Major General Liziukov, I've established …."[23] An affirmation of Liziukov's death was made for the first time in an order from Briansk Front's Commander-in-Chief Rokossovsky on 28 July 1942.

However, seemingly not everyone agreed with their conclusions. The question regarding Liziukov's fate, seemingly being formally decided, actually remained unresolved for a long time. Moreover, the Supreme Commander-in-Chief, known for his suspicions and lack of trust even for individuals in his closest circle, probably to the end didn't believe in General Liziukov's integrity and honor.

Frontline journalist A. Krivitsky describes a scene in his book, which took place between Stalin and one "important military figure" who'd been summoned to the *Stavka* soon after Liziukov's death. Krivitsky, who wrote about this in the mid-1960s, for some reason doesn't disclose the name of this "important military figure", but according to the customary practice in the Caucasus to use the word "ty" [the intimate form of "you"] in conversations between fellow Caucasians which features in the cited dialogue, one can assume that this was Liziukov's former peer, the 5th Tank Army's commissar Tumanian, who in those circumstances was arguably a most important source for the suspicious Supreme Leader.[24] Let's take a look at what A. Krivitsky wrote in his book:

> Stalin was standing at a long table, hunched over and smoking a pipe. The military man announced his arrival. Stalin, as if not noticing him, began to pace back and forth at the table slowly and quietly. A strip of carpeting was muffling his footsteps. He made three steps in one direction, before turning and taking three steps in the other direction. Three steps in

23 TsAMO, F. 202, op. 50, d. 1, l. 306.

24 Initially I was inclined to believe that Stalin's conversational partner was Katukov, but I've since come to the conclusions that this was not the case.

> one direction, three in the other, six altogether, then just as slowly, without stopping, strode almost to the opposite wall, and from there, without turning, asked in a soft voice:
>
> "Do the Germans have Liziukov? Did he change sides?"
>
> This question carried from a distance, just like from a different, inscrutable world, and having flown across an enormous expanse, the cold words – each pronounced distinctly and separately, penetrated the realization of the military man. He felt a chill, and sensed something heavy gripping his heart, not allowing him to breathe.
>
> "Why aren't you answering?"
>
> So then, overcoming his anguish and feeling of suffocation, literally like escaping a narrow oubliette, the military man answered and was himself surprised and inwardly gasped at how firmly, just like iron, his words sounded: "Comrade People's Commissar, I knew Major General Liziukov well. He was a trustworthy son of the people, dedicated to the Party and to you personally."[25]

Well, not knowing all the circumstances of this complex, judging from Stalin's question, case, the "major military figure" left unnamed by Krivitsky nevertheless made no attempt to be cautious, and directly declared that he believed in the honor of the commander he knew well. Such an answer merits respect. As Krivitsky wrote, "Everyone, who knew Aleksandr Il'ich Liziukov, loved and trusted him. Only one man didn't trust him."[26]

But why all the same did Stalin so suspiciously ask one "major military figure" (which I believe was Tumanian) whether Liziukov had gone over to the Germans? Here, if you will, it is necessary to state that, which is in my view, the most important reason for the suspicions of the Supreme Leader, who didn't trust the conclusions of the official investigation completed by Briansk Front's headquarters about Liziukov's death. It had become known that the former commander of the 2nd Shock Army Lieutenant General Vlasov had been taken prisoner by the Germans. Leaflets bearing photographs of the captured general were being dropped over our trenches, but the most shocking were reports that Vlasov had begun to cooperate with the Germans.

On 12 September 1942, Vlasov made a public address with an appeal about the start of a joint struggle with the Germans for a new Russia. Stalin was quickly informed of this. For the Supreme Commander-in-Chief, this was a painful blow: one of his best generals had betrayed him and had openly joined cause with the Germans.

Thus, Liziukov's recent disappearance, especially given the still somewhat murky circumstances, immediately became suspicious. We'll recall that in the winter of 1941/42, at the time when Vlasov was commanding the 20th Army, Liziukov was none other than his deputy commander. Now, this recent joint service cast a long shadow over Liziukov, because *for Stalin* the fact of the strange disappearance of Vlasov's former deputy so soon after the announcement by the Germans that they had captured the commander of the 2nd Shock Army, acquired in the newly revealed circumstances a completely different, *special* significance…

Service under the command of an unexpectedly revealed "double agent and traitor of the Motherland"; the 5th Tank Army's failed operation, when there were all the prerequisites for success; and finally the reports and messages up the channel about the 2nd Tank Corps' poor leadership – all this, it seems, came together for the Supreme Leader into one suspicious, strange chain of events.

25 Krivitsky, *Ne zabudu vekov*, p. 236.
26 Ibid.

Indeed, what if the traitorous plans of both had ripened back during their joint service together and, taking advantage of a suitable moment that had come around, Liziukov had followed the example of his former superior, or surrendered to the Germans in order to escape responsibility?

Knowing Stalin's tendency to see betrayal and cunning even when there were none, it isn't difficult to imagine just how the "Great Leader" might have interpreted reports that the 2nd Tank Corps commander had disappeared, and "*no one had seen him again.*"

In the overturned system of values, where the presumption of innocence had become a bourgeois anachronism, given the fact that the circumstances surrounding the general's disappearance were contradictory and murky, no one could have convinced the Supreme Leader that Liziukov couldn't have gone over to the Germans.

Reports of Liziukov's death, especially from hearsay, were convincing proof only for a simpleton, who had succumbed to the lure of a cunning provocation set by German intelligence, but not for Stalin. Likely, even the fact of Liziukov's booklet found in the pocket of the corpse wasn't proof for the Supreme Leader: after all, it was impossible to identify the corpse by face ... which meant such a discovery might have been especially arranged, in order to feign Liziukov's death.

I repeat that such notions in my view might have been prompting Stalin, when he enquired of one "major military figure" whether Liziukov had gone over to the German side. I assume that the reader recognizes that I don't share these suspicions, and have cited them only as possible reasons for the Supreme Commander-in-Chief's lack of trust in his general.

Many years after the start of my research, when I had the opportunity to work with German documents, I was able to take a look at the events of the summer of 1942 in the Voronezh area from, as they say, the opposite side. Primarily I was interested in the subject of the 5th Tank Army's fighting and the following offensive operations by our forces on Briansk Front's left wing in July – August 1942. While examining a host of various materials, I was experiencing a certain agitation: what if in the German documents I unexpectedly came across any sort of mentions about Liziukov's fate?

The combat operations of July – August 1942 were covered in quite a bit of detail in the documents of the German divisions that were opposing our forces in this sector. In addition to operational reports, in the appendices to the divisional journals of combat operations I repeatedly encountered documents of a different nature. These were reports about captured equipment, maps, and other staff documents, as well as transcripts of prisoner interrogations, which contained their personal details and the unit in which they had served. These documents were of special interest, since they allowed one to establish not only the fact that one Red Army serviceman or another had not gone missing in action, but had been captured, but also they gave the possibility according to indirect indicators to determine the fate of individuals whose surnames weren't given.

The 2nd Tank Corps, the commander of which Liziukov became after the disbanding of the 5th Tank Army, was conducting combat operations against the German 387th Infantry Division in the offensive by Briansk Front's operational group. Having found this out, I decided that if there was some mention of a killed Russian general, then such a mention would be found in the files of the 387th Infantry Division. Knowing how valuable and informative the division's documents might be, in my search for any mentions about Liziukov, I planned to give its journal of combat operations, as well as all the division's reports, summaries, orders and radio messages for 23-25 July 1942 the most careful scrutiny.

Here, however, after so many valuable findings, complete disappointment was waiting for me. It turned out there are no files for the 387th Infantry Division in the archives, because the documents of this division hadn't been preserved. Alas, my hopes that I might probably be able to find some sort of mention of Liziukov, even an indirect one, in the documents of the 387th Infantry Division instantly and irreversibly collapsed.

In the absence of the 387th Infantry Division's documents, there remains only to ponder their significance and possible value for our search. I think that if these documents had been preserved, that in them there might have been at least a mention that on 23 July in the area northwest of Lebiazh'e, a Russian heavy tank had been knocked out, and that valuable documents and coded maps had been found on the bodies of two dead officers. However, this is only speculation.

At the end of July 1942, the 387th Infantry Division was part of the VII Army Corps. In the search for possible reports from the division to higher headquarters, I decided to look through the corps' documents. There turned out to be a lot of them, significantly more than in the files of the divisions, but unfortunately they were significantly less detailed. I looked through a multitude of corps documents that contained various accounts of combat actions and reports about combat episodes, but all the while I never came across any reference to General Liziukov.

If Major General Liziukov had been taken prisoner by the Germans, not only would the 387th Infantry Division have immediately reported about this important prisoner to the corps, but VII Army Corps also would have quickly reported this to the headquarters of the Second Army. I didn't discover any such communications. This fact once again indirectly confirms that General Liziukov was not taken prisoner.

The enemy command didn't know about the death of the commander and commissar of the 2nd Tank Corps (or didn't trust a soldier's story). Liziukov's name was known to the German command back from the preceding fighting of the 5th Tank Army, and there is no doubt that the enemy would have used the fact of Liziukov's death for propaganda purposes, if they had known about it. However, this wasn't the case. Accordingly, the German command didn't know about Liziukov's death.

Research in the US National Archive allowed me to use a completely unexpected source in my searches. The point is that in this archive's files of captured German documents, unique wartime German aerial photographs of our territory have been preserved. Having little hope that the Germans had photographed the Bol'shaia Vereika area at any time, or moreover that these photographs had been preserved, I nevertheless decided just in case to check whether there were any aerial reconnaissance photographs in the catalog that I might be able to use in my work on this book.

I was stunned. Practically the entire ground in the area of the front line between the Don River and the Kshen' River had been photographed by the enemy. I began to study the catalog of the needed map quadrangle attentively and to pick out specific sectors of the front, where the 1st and 2nd Tank Corps had fought. After a thorough screening, I ordered a roll of aerial photographs that had the most important characteristics for me: the photographed area, the date, the quality of the photographs and the scale. A day later they brought me this box of photographs from a special storage area, and I saw genuine German photographs of the series that I required. Approximately 60 photographs fixed in detail the work of the German reconnaissance airplane, as it methodically flew over the front lines and took aerial photographs of the broad area in the valleys of the Sukhaia and Bol'shaia Vereika Rivers, including the areas of the villages of Lebiazh'e, Bol'shaia Vereika and Kaver'ia. The aerial photographs were taken by the enemy early on the morning of 28 July, which is to say, five days after Liziukov's death.

Having arranged the photographs in the necessary sequence, I found a photograph of Hill 188.5 together with the woods west of it. The quality of the photograph was very high; the picture was snapped in cloudless weather, and the large, square aerial photograph had been obviously produced from a broad negative, which allowed much to be seen. With the help of a large magnifying glass, I began to study the terrain attentively, focusing on each tiny detail. This was exciting … I could easily make out the large craters left by bombs, the thin zigzag lines of trenches, and anti-tank ditches … It was hard to believe that more than 60 years after the end of the war, I was virtually sitting in the German reconnaissance airplane, flying over the front lines, and from an altitude of 5,000 to 6,000 meters, I was seeing the battlefield just as it was on that day of 28 July 1942.

The road running from Bol'shaia Vereika to Somovo was completely worn and well-traveled, with numerous paths leading from it. Both on the road and near it I sometimes made out the dark rectangles of tanks or vehicles. Meticulously, centimeter by centimeter, I looked over the ground in the photograph, moving in the general direction of the 2nd Tank Corps' offensive to the south.

Then suddenly, to the right of the road, not far from the southern fringe of the woods lying west of Hill 188.5, I discerned a solitary, dark rectangle in a field. Its contours clearly stood out against the whitish background of the field, and its large dimensions spoke to the fact that this was a large object, like a tank or truck. However, a truck could hardly have wound up so far from the road in the middle of field of tall rye. … Probably it was a tank, and judging from the dimensions of the black rectangle, a medium or heavy tank.

I took a shot in the dark. I once again pored over the ground around, but there were no other dark rectangles in the field close to the patch of woods. Was I really looking at Liziukov's knocked-out KV tank?! Could this possibly be? I considered the facts.

Liziukov was killed on 23 July. The aerial photograph was taken on 28 July. Five days had passed. Judging from the materials of Colonel Sukhoruchkin's investigation, Liziukov's tank had still not been found by the beginning of August, which means it hadn't been evacuated from the battlefield (having analyzed an excerpt from Katukov's book and having found in it a large number of discrepancies with the facts, I think it is possible to say that Katukov's assertion that Liziukov's tank had been evacuated from the front immediately doesn't correspond with reality). By the morning of 26 July, our forces had retreated from this area, leaving the battlefield to the enemy, and it had become impossible to evacuate knocked-out equipment. On the day the aerial photographs were taken, most likely Liziukov's KV was still in that very location where it had been knocked out on 23 July. *If this is so, then it was in the photograph that I was holding in my hands.* Even if not in that same location, where I saw the solitary dark rectangle, even if it was in a different location, but at least somewhere on the field at which I was looking from an altitude of several thousand meters, Liziukov's tank was there.

Alas, our command didn't have similar aerial photographs; requests for aerial reconnaissance remained for the most part unanswered. Over all my time of work in the Russian Ministry of Defense's central archives in Podol'sk, not once did I come across aerial photographs of an area of interest to me, neither in the documents of the Briansk Front's ground forces, nor in the documents of the Front's air units.

Again and again, I carefully examined the dark rectangle in the field. If this was the very tank in which the commander of the 2nd Tank Corps had set out from Bol'shaia Vereika on the morning of 23 July, then the place where the KV was standing is also the location where General Liziukov died. Sometimes it seemed to me that I could make out the tank's characteristic silhouette: the forward hull, the rear deck, the turret and even the main gun's barrel, but again and again I would direct the magnifying glass off to one side and realize that in fact I wasn't seeing any of this; I only wanted to see all of these features. Unfortunately, in distinction from the pilots who conducted the filming, I couldn't lower my altitude and examine this dark rectangle more closely.

Did I see Liziukov's knocked-out tank in the photograph? I can't be certain. It might have been a completely different tank. Moveover, it is also impossible to assert unambiguously that the dark rectangle in the field is a tank. I can only suppose that I am likely seeing the spot where the commander and commissar of the 2nd Tank Corps were killed.

Examining this large German aerial photograph back then, I experienced a strange feeling: here, in Washington, D.C., far away from my home and decades after the war, I was suddenly and actually in the summer of 1942, and from the cockpit of a German reconnaissance aircraft I was seeing the field where General Liziukov's last battle took place.

But let's return to August 1942. Soon after Liziukov's death, a letter arrived at the People's Commissariat of Defense (as A. Krivitsky writes) from Engineer-Captain Tsvetanovich, who served in the 5th Tank Army's Department of Armored Forces (plainly here Krivitsky is mistaken, as the 5th Tank Army's headquarters didn't have such a department; most likely he means Briansk Front's Department of Armored Forces).

Judging from the fact that the documents of Briansk Front's official investigation don't make any mention of Tsvetanovich's testimony, his letter appeared only after Colonel Sukhoruchkin concluded his work. In the letter, Tsvetanovich provides several details, which might partially explain the motives that drove General Liziukov to head out personally in his tank. The orders, issued to the 2nd Tank Corps commander (by the commander of Briansk Front's operational group, Lieutenant General Chibisov), writes Tsvetanovich, were insulting to Liziukov's honor in both style and contents.

However, that section of the letter in which he writes about the circumstances of the general's death is of particular interest to us. Tsvetanovich provides the following description in the letter of the final minutes of General Liziukov's life (during my long research in the Podol'sk archive, I wasn't able to find the indicated letter, thus I will cite in full its further text from A. Krivitsky's book):

> Of the tank's entire crew, only the wounded driver-mechanic of this tank returned and said that the tank had been knocked out by a direct hit of an armor-piercing slug. The crew received an order from Major General Liziukov to abandon the tank. The radio operator was killed as he exited the tank. Comrade Liziukov was killed by submachine gunners [sic] as he emerged from the tank.[27]

Let's analyze the description given by Tsvetanovich. Judging from everything, it is based again on the wounded junior driver-mechanic Mozhaev's story, as retold by Mussorov, and subsequently retold again and again by others. As we can see, the details of what happened already diverge from the description given in Colonel Sukhoruchkin's report. According to Tsvetanovich, after the German armor-piercing, discarding sabot round hit the tank, General Liziukov was still alive and conscious, and issued an order for the crew to abandon the tank; he was killed already after this. However, isn't this version of the events just a consequence of the distortions that unavoidably arise when a story is repeatedly passed on in someone else's words? Alas, all sorts of rumors came to be accepted as the truth and the "retelling of tales" plainly became back then the reason for much innuendo and speculation.

In Konstantin Simonov's book *Razynye dni voiny* [*Various days of the war*] we find a clear substantiation for this. He cites a letter from a war veteran about one encounter that he recalled, which occurred at the end of July 1942:

> Back then, in the beginning of July 1942, I commanded a platoon of 76-mm guns of the 237th Rifle Division's 835th Rifle Regiment. On one of these days (I can't recall which), I had an encounter that in a strange manner was connected with the fate of army commander Liziukov. The platoon was occupying a firing position somewhere in the area of Lomov [sic – Lomovo]. Fierce tank clashes had already been going on for several days, and with each passing day the hope for success dwindled. This was sensed even by soldiers distant from the headquarters.
>
> Incidentally, it can be that it is exactly the soldier at the front who is the first to sense the threatening symptoms of failure. Our tanks were burning out in front of us. I remember these tall funeral pyres, columns of smoke that were black like soot. That evening, a tanker

27 A. Krivitsky, *Ne zabudu vovek*, p. 235.

> with a head wound stumbled into our firing position. Having taken a seat on the parapet of a trench, he, as is typical, had a smoke and said that the commander of the 5th Tank Army had been killed in front of his eyes; that he had watched (or even taken part in this) how his burned corpse was recovered from the blackened tank. … The army commander's surname was given – General Liziukov.[28]

From the tale of the wounded tanker, it turns out that the tank burned, and the burned corpse of the general was inside the combat machine.

Further on in Simonov's book, he himself cites a version of junior driver-mechanic Mozhaev's story, which he heard back in 1942:

> After 2 or 3 kilometers, when he [General Liziukov] was approaching the edge of some woods, his tank was fired upon at point-blank range from German guns that were concealed in ambush. Only the turret machine gunner was able to save himself – he managed to leap out, hid in the rye, and from there watched what happened next.
>
> In his words, the fascists encircled the tank, dragged out the bodies of the dead from it, including Liziukov's corpse, and from documents realized that this was a general. As proof of the fact that he'd been killed, they took his documents, cut off the corpse's head, and brought it along with them.[29]

Many years later Simonov, recalling the several days he spent at the Briansk Front in July 1942, at a time when our forces were engaged in heavy and unsuccessful fighting, wrote: "In this episode, told very simply, there was something unique and desperate, characteristic for those desperate days …"

After concluding that Major General Liziukov had been killed, the Briansk Front headquarters' official investigation came to an end. The new corps commander and commissar hastily assumed command. The war continued, and more fighting lay ahead …

However, the commission's conclusions did not in fact give an answer to one of the most important, human questions: Where was General Liziukov buried, or was he even buried at all? Back then, in the heat of the fighting, after the conclusion that the 2nd Tank Corps commander was dead, the individuals who conducted the investigation were much more interested about what documents fell into enemy hands as a result of Liziukov's and Assorov's deaths, than they were about whether or not the deceased men had been buried.

Nothing definite was reported to Liziukov's wife either; according to A. Krivitsky, "No matter how she tried to find out, she didn't receive any notifications of her husband's death." Already after the war's end, she wrote three letters to Stalin with a request to clarify Liziukov's fate for her, but she didn't receive an answer to any of these letters. In one of these letters she wrote, "I'm appealing to you with a request. I want to know: where and how was my husband killed, and where was his corpse left?"

Stalin remained silent; a wall of silence formed around Liziukov's name, and many military leaders preferred not to say anything at all on this touchy subject. Only in the summer of 1943, after a sufficiently large amount of time had passed and having obviously come to the conclusion that Liziukov hadn't been captured and wasn't cooperating with the Germans, Stalin's anger changed to a pardon, and he granted his approval to give Liziukov's name to the Saratov Tank School, thereby posthumously removing any suspicion of betrayal from him.

28 Simonov, *Raznye dni voiny*, p. 156.
29 Ibid., p. 155.

In 1947, five years after Liziukov's death, his wife unexpectedly received a letter from the former deputy commander of the 1st Tank Corps' 89th Tank Brigade N.V. Davidenko, in which he said the general's body had been found. He wrote, "My scouts brought a document to me – a booklet bearing the name of Major General Liziukov that had been found on a body."[30]

So, was General Liziukov buried or not? This tormenting question remained as an unhealed wound for his widow, because she never received an unambiguous answer to it up until her very death. Meanwhile, already back then there was a document in the Ministry of Defense, which could bring clarity to this question, but Liziukov's widow likely never had the chance to read it.

Already after the war, a staff report on the circumstances surrounding Major General Liziukov's death was sent to the Red Army's Main Armored Directorate, but for almost 30 years nothing was known about its contents to a broad circle of scholars. Indeed, only in the middle of the 1970s, thanks to Konstantin Simonov's book, did a portion of this staff report become disclosed. I will cite its text, emphasizing what in my view is the most important for the subject of interest to us:

> On that day, having no information about the 148th Tank Brigade's 89th Tank Battalion that had gone missing in the area of the Gvozdevsky hills, General Liziukov and Regimental Commissar Assorov drove off in a KV tank in the direction of the woods west of Hill 188.5, and never returned to the unit. From the testimony of the former deputy commander of a tank brigade Guards Colonel Nikita Vasil'evich Davidenko it is known, that during his brigade's operations in this area, a knocked-out KV tank was discovered, on the turret of which was the body of Regimental Commissar Assorov; approximately 100 meters away from the tank, there was an unknown body dressed in overalls, with a crushed head. General Liziukov's property booklet was in pocket of the overalls. **At the order of Guards Colonel Davidenko, the indicated corpse was brought back to his observation post and buried near the woods lying west of Hill 188.5.** Soon the brigade was forced to retreat from this area. Other information on the death and interment of General Liziukov is not available.[31]

Thus, we've reach a point very close to an answer to the question of what happened with Liziukov's body and where someone should search for his grave. Here we must return again to that ill-fated day of 23 July 1942 and resume the discussion of the possible course of events after the wounded Mozhaev crawled back to friendly lines and stopped observing the knocked-out tank of the 2nd Tank Corps' commander.

Straight away we must say that here, reliable information comes to an end and speculation begins. However, the documentary sources in our possession give us a substantial basis for a logical version about what happened next.

Consider the following facts. In the words of the 1st Tank Corps' scouts, who approached Liziukov's knocked-out KV tank, Regimental Commissar Assorov's body was *hanging out of the turret hatch.*[32] Meanwhile, from the story of the sole surviving eyewitness of Liziukov's death, junior driver-mechanic Mozhaev, it follows that after the German projectiles struck the KV, Assorov *didn't even make an attempt to climb out of the tank.* This can be explained only by the fact that he was killed instantly or badly wounded. He wasn't killed *while exiting the tank and wasn't left "hanging" dead from the turret hatch.* Mozhaev was observing the tank from a rather close distance and watched as the Germans climbed onto the tank, climbed inside it, dragged out a map

30 Ibid., p. 237.
31 K. Simonov, *Raznye dni voiny*, p. 155.
32 TsAMO, F. 202, op. 50, d. 1, l. 305.

case, and then began examining the captured documents, and thus there is no basis to say that he simply couldn't see Assorov's corpse.

What follows from this comparison of the facts? It follows that Assorov's corpse was hanging from the turret because *he was partially dragged out of it.* Now we'll recall that an unidentified body with Liziukov's booklet was found approximately 100 meters from the tank. How did he wind up there? The supposition that Liziukov hadn't been killed, but only badly wounded (and the Germans didn't notice this!), then regained consciousness, independently climbed out of the tank and crawled away from it with a crushed head is, from my point of view, baseless.

Accordingly, he didn't wind up 100 meters away from the tank on his own, but because *his body had been dragged there.* At the same time it is completely obvious that this was impossible to do as long as Assorov's corpse blocked the exit through the turret's hatch, *because the KV tank had only one turret hatch.* (It seems completely improbable that the Germans abandoned Assorov's body in the turret hatch and then turned to the task of dragging Liziukov's body out through the driver-mechanic's hatch in the front of the tank, or the emergency hatch in the bottom of the tank.)

From these facts it is possible to make the following assumption: After the bleeding Mozhaev stopped observing the Germans' actions, left the place where the tank crew perished, and started his long and dangerous journey back to friendly lines, *the enemy soldiers dragged Liziukov's body out of the tank,* and then decided to remove Assorov's body from it as well, but for some reason abandoned the effort before it was completed.

The German soldiers undoubtedly guessed that of the four dead tankers, at least two of them were important Russian officers. I suggest that the map cases containing the documents (the dead Assorov also had a map case on his body[33]) prompted the Germans to the thought that they should also check the pockets of the dead men. One of the German soldiers got in to unfasten Liziukov's tanker overalls, in order to take his documents and immediately discovered the decorations. Beneath the overalls, the dead man was wearing Orders and medals. Of course, that said a lot to the enemy.

Obviously having flipped through the documents in the pockets of the dead men and having uncovered the Orders and medals, the Germans realized that a Russian general and important commissar had fallen into their ambush, and decided to drag their corpses out of the tank. Probably, Liziukov's head was disfigured by striking fragments or totally crushed as a result of a shell hit (this subsequently could have started the talk about the general's head, which had been torn off or fully cut off by the Germans). It wasn't an easy task to remove a dead body from the tank through the single turret hatch, but the enemy soldiers were plainly in no hurry and not fearing an attack. Liziukov's corpse was hauled out of the turret and dropped (the tongue doesn't work to say the word "tossed", although most likely, that's just what they did) onto the ground …

Then some of the Germans began to drag Liziukov toward the woods, while others clambered into the tank for Assorov's body. Ultimately, they also hoisted it up to the hatch. Then something happened – but what?

Most likely, it seems to me, this is what happened: From the documents of Colonel Sukhoruchkin's investigation, which are confirmed by operational documents of the 2nd Tank Corps' units, in the morning the Luftwaffe conducted several massed and lengthy raids against the tanks of the 26th and 27th Tank Brigades, which at this time were located not more than 1.5 kilometers from Liziukov's tank that was standing on the road. On 23 July, the 2nd Tank Corps undertook a final attempt at an offensive, which was disrupted primarily by the furious attacks of German dive

33 TsAMO, F. 202, op. 50, d. 1, l. 303. This follows from the testimony of Regimental Commissar Assorov's assistant, Junior Political Instructor Savel'ev.

bombers. For the sake of justice, it should be said that in the captured German documents one comes across a mention of the actions of Soviet aircraft in the same area.

It is possible that it was just in these minutes, when the German soldiers, sweating profusely from their exertions, had hoisted Assorov's body to the hatch and begun to drag it out that they heard the howl of approaching aircraft. They were quickly closing upon the area of the woods and the road to Bol'shaia Vereika that lay east of them. There is no need to say that the enemy feared an attack by our ground attack aircraft but even the approach of their own aircraft in that situation didn't bode well for the Germans. They were on a Russian heavy tank, openly standing without any camouflage on the road that served as the axis of a large Russian offensive. The German soldiers didn't have the slightest inkling of the intention of the Luftwaffe pilots. The pilots might have gone into a dive on the attacking Russian tanks to the north, but they might have simply pounced on the solitary KV tank, serving as the enemy's "vanguard", with no idea that there was no longer any living Russians there and that only German soldiers were around the tank. In any case, it was safer first to take shelter in the trenches, and only later determine whose aircraft were approaching the battlefield.

Having quickly assessed that an airstrike was threatening them, and the sort of mess that the "Il-2s" or "Junkers" might make of the entire area around the immobile tank, the Germans weren't about to test their luck and sought to clear the road and make it back to their foxholes and slit trenches in the fringe of the woods as quickly as possible. (It is possible that here they had special flags or sheets to mark their positions for the German pilots.) Thus, they in fact left Assorov's body hanging partway out of the turret hatch, while Liziukov's body had only been dragged 100 meters from the tank.

One can also assume the following: Exhausted by the effort to drag first one, and then a second corpse from the tank, and with heavy exertion having hoisted Assorov's body part way out of the turret hatch, the German soldiers decided that it made no sense to drag the "Red commissar" together with the general and left him on the turret, having first removed his documents. Thus, Assorov's limp body was hanging headfirst from the turret, which in fact the 1st Tank Corps' scouts saw several hours later.

It is impossible to discount the possibility of the enemy's swaggering courage over the dead Assorov, which they dragged out of the turret and left hanging in order to stage a dramatic photograph: the colossus of a destroyed Russian heavy tank with a dead Bol'shevik commissar hanging from its turret! As they say, in order to illustrate the all-devastating power of the German weapon!

German troops undertook the effort to drag the dead Liziukov across the field of rye, but having dragged him 100 meters, also left him there. Most likely, the same notions were governing their actions here: there was no need to drag the corpse into the woods; they could demonstrate their success even without this and moreover, it wasn't far to make it back to the general's body from the woods in case the dead general had to be displayed.

Then finally, one can fully suppose that a combination of numerous factors was the real reason why Assorov's body was abandoned on the turret, while Liziukov's body was laying 100 meters from the tank. In any case, documents and decorations of the dead men were in the hands of the German soldiers, so they believed it wasn't necessary to drag the corpses into their positions in the woods as well.

It is possible that in the process, the Germans decided to remove Liziukov's field tunic as convicing evidence of their triumph. This tunic with all of its decorations spoke eloquently about its owner's high rank and plainly couldn't leave their superiors doubtful. The Gold Star of Hero of the Soviet Union, two Orders of Lenin, a medal for 20 years of service in the Workers' and Peasant's Red Army were hanging on it, and below them, the pin for "Excellent handling of a tank" was attached. The shoulder belt and officer's belt with a buckle in the form of a star could also be of definite interest to the Germans. In addition to the honors on the tunic were the collar insignia of a major general, with two stars on each, and chevrons on the sleeves. There cannot be any doubts that in the eyes of a German soldier, a general's uniform was a trophy in and of itself...

Thus, the enemy soldiers most likely fully removed Liziukov's tunic from his corpse, having stripped off or ripped apart his tanker's overalls in the process. Arguably, it is this factor that can explain the odd phrase in Colonel Sukhoruchkin's account, when he wrote that the 1st Tank Corps' scouts found the unidentified corpse "of a Red Army man" 100 meters away from the knocked-out tank. This could only be said about a corpse, on which the scouts didn't find any signs speaking to the possibility that the dead man was a member of the command staff.

This means that Liziukov's body was wearing no tunic, no peaked cap (possibly, in place of it on his head was an ordinary tanker's helmet) and no general's boots (obviously, knowing that he was heading into combat in a tank, he put on simple "work boots" in their place; we can find an assertion for this in A. Krivitsky's memoirs.[34] Another reason for choosing not to wear his general's boots might have been the sticky mud after the downpour on the evening before). There is no way Liziukov could have been wearing his general's riding breeches with the broad red piping.

Among the documents taken from the bodies, the Germans seized Liziukov's working map with his notes; a map on the scale of 1:100,000 with the coding of the Front headquarters and corps' headquarters; Regimental Commissar Assorov's working map; various papers found in Liziukov's and Assorov's map cases; and most likely, their personal documents.[35] These included the Party membership card, personal identification card, Order booklet, and possibly pay books.

So only Liziukov's thin property booklet, showing his assigned uniform articles and military equipment remained on the corpse. This is an indisputable fact, confirmed by documents. Why was it left with the dead man? We can't know this for sure. Possibly, in distinction from the other documents, this booklet was for some reason not in a pocket of his general's tunic, but in the overalls separate from the other documents. There, it didn't quite stand out through the fabric of the overalls, so the Germans believed that there was nothing special lying in its pocket and made no effort to check it. In any event, one can only say definitively that they never removed it from the pocket. There are no doubts that if they had found it and for some reason decided not to bring it along with them, they would have simply tossed it aside, *and wouldn't have stuck it back in the dead man's pocket.*

The subsequent events in the area of the death of Liziukov and his crew can be approximately resurrected on the basis of Soviet and German documents. On the morning of 23 July, the patch of woods south of Lebiazh'e remained in essence the last German defensive strongpoint, which was checking the advance of our forces to the south on a 3-4 kilometer sector of the front. After the tanks of the 1st Tank Corps broke through to the approaches to Somovo and Bol'shaia Treshchevka east and west of the patch of woods, the elements of the German 542nd Infantry Regiment of the 387th Infantry Division that were defending the woods wound up encircled. Although our rifle units made almost no advance to the south here, and only Soviet tanks were cruising around the woods, the enemy without any doubts was feeling quite uncomfortable here. The ambush, in which Liziukov's tank fell next to the woods, was one of the final combat episodes for the German anti-tank artillery element that was operating here.

History is silent about where the enemy soldiers, who took Liziukov's documents and decorations, went with their prizes. It is possible to assume that they later talked about their success and even carried the captured papers, maps and Russian general's tunic to their superiors, but no mentions whatsoever about Liziukov's death were left behind in the preserved captured German

34 Krivitsky, *Ne zabudu vovek*, p. 237.
35 Ibid.

documents. Just as there is no mention in Soviet documents about the fact that Liziukov's and Assorov's documents and awards were ever found on any dead German soldiers.

Perhaps, in the documents of the 387th Infantry Division's 542nd Infantry Regiment there was some reference to Liziukov's death, but the documentary files of these units weren't preserved. Only in the archival files of the VII Army Corps did I come across one brief line, which arguably was the only mention in the preserved German documents about what took place at the woods south of Lebiazh'e. In a daily report from the 387th Infantry Division to the corps headquarters for 23 July, it was reported: "German dive bombers put 8 enemy tanks out of commission; 1 tank was knocked out by the division's forces."[36]

The comparison of Soviet and German documents and the chronology of the fighting in this area allows one to assume with a great deal of probability that this solitary tank (regarding the actions of our units, the division headquarters provided only verified data in the summary, without far-fetched conclusions or unfounded assertions), was most likely Liziukov's KV tank, which was knocked out near the patch of wood's southern tip …

On the afternoon of 23 July, a tank patrol from the 1st Tank Corps' 89th Tank Brigade reached Hill 188.5 south of Lebiazh'e, and from the march rolled beyond the wood's southern spur[37], passing Liziukov's knocked-out KV tank in the process. No one fired at them from the woods. The Germans, judging from everything, had taken up an all-round defense in the broad central area of the woods, fearing to remain in the narrow southern spur that could easily be swept by enemy fire. As was indicated in the documents of Colonel Sukhoruchkin's investigation, the scouts were at the knocked-out tank, saw a body with four bars on the tunic hanging from the turret hatch, but didn't take a look inside the tank …[38]

Today, from the vantage point of modernity, knowing how much remains unexplained in the fate of the deceased Liziukov, it is hard for us to understand why those scouts passed the knocked-out tank with such indifference, with barely a glance at the dead regimental commissar (!) and not even making any attempt to remove his body from the turret. It is hard for us to understand why they didn't take a glance inside the tank in order to check whether there were still wounded tankers inside it.

However, in order to better understand this "Why?", it is necessary to picture the terrible situation of those days, when blood and death, fragments of human bodies and corpses rotting in the heat, burned out tanks and the odor of burned flesh near their blackened wreckage already had little effect on the men left insensate by what was happening around them. A certain psychological shield was operating – don't think about what you've seen, or else you might go out of your mind. Not a single normal psyche would have been left, if the men had deeply and emotionally reacted to each body that they came across on those bloody fields. One can add to this their extreme fatigue, the constant stress of combat actions, and the exhausting nervous tension. In addition, by then they had seen so many knocked-out and burned-out tanks, that it made no sense to climb inside and glance around another one, especially because for them, this was "someone else's tank", not of their own unit.

Toward the evening the 89th Tank Brigade went on the attack toward Bol'shaia Treshchevka, and until nightfall was engaged in difficult fighting with a stubbornly defending enemy. That night, the brigade's deputy commander Lieutenant Colonel Davydenko's subordinates reported to him that troopers had discovered a disfigured corpse in the field that had General Liziukov's booklet on it. The corpse had been found in a rye field, about 100 meters from a knocked-out KV

36 NARA, T-314, roll 353, fr. 001339.
37 TsAMO, F. 89 tbr, op. 1, d. 1, ll. 28-29.
38 TsAMO, F. 202, op. 50, d. 1, ll. 304-305.

tank. At Davidenko's direction, the corpse was carried to the observation post. There was no way to recognize the dead man, because his head had been smashed or crushed. So Davidenko wound up facing a difficult choice.

Had this happened at the command post at any of the 2nd Tank Corps' brigades, which were standing less than 3-4 kilometers from here, everything would have gone differently from the beginning. But this didn't happen, and the dead Liziukov was brought to a command post of one of the tank brigades of the neighboring tank corps. General Liziukov's faceless corps was lying in front of Davidenko, who most likely simply couldn't believe this. Even in the 2nd Tank Corps itself, they still didn't even know about the disappearance, much less the death of their commander. At the 2nd Tank Corps headquarters, everything was quiet, because everyone there still thought that the general was located somewhere among the tank brigades that were striving to break through to Medvezh'e.

For Davidenko, the unidentified corpse he'd been brought was a hard to explain puzzle. The booklet was in the general's name, but the appearance of the dead man was plainly telling him that this was the body of a simple tanker. So suddenly, an unexpected question rose in front of Davidenko, whose head even without this riddle was busy with a multitude of urgent matters to organize the next day's combat: What to do with the body?

It was impossible to identify the body, and judging from everything, he had no radio or telephone contact with brigade or corps headquarters, and there was no way Davidenko could drive to the rear and find out what had happened from the neighboring corps headquarters (and unavoidably abandon his command over his own units in the process)! Of course, he should have reported about the strange corpse and asked for orders from higher command, but Davidenko didn't send one of his tankers that night to the rear to seek out a higher headquarters. They faced new, hard fighting with the sunrise, and the crews had to be given at least some rest.

Moreover, it mustn't be forgotten that Davidenko didn't have any information about the location of the neighboring corps commander, and couldn't even assume what had happened there. No one briefed him on searches for the missing Liziukov. He didn't know anything about the fact that the 2nd Tank Corps commander that morning had set out in a tank to the south, and hadn't yet returned. Most likely, he would have acted differently, had he known that Liziukov was missing and that everyone was looking for him! But in the 2nd Tank Corps, no one was even thinking about searching for Liziukov yet! Moreover, no one was searching for Liziukov in the neighboring 1st Tank Corps, where they knew little at all about the actions of a neighbor.

It is no secret that accurate and timely information in war at times is decisive. Alas, Davidenko didn't have any reliable information at all about Liziukov. *On that night he had to make a decision not about whom to inform and where to take a dead general, corps commander and Hero of the Soviet Union, but what to do with an unidentified corpse in a tanker's overalls and ordinary boots.*

Lacking any information from higher command about searches for a missing Liziukov and not even aware of the tragedy that had happened, Davidenko plainly decided that the unidentified corpse had to be buried in any case, while the origin of the booklet found on the body could be ascertained later. That's likely how this decision was taken.

At Davidenko's order, the unidentified corpse, which most likely were the remains of General Liziukov, was carried off to the edge of the woods and buried there at night without any sort of honors or monuments. There seemed no need for this. Only a few hours remained until dawn, and with the sunrise the men had to go into battle again. Possibly, not even a wooden star was found to mark Liziukov's grave, and nothing was left at the site in the fringe of the woods but the burial mound.

Most likely, the bodies of Assorov, the driver-mechanic and the radioman from Liziukov's crew didn't even get this treatment …

At sunrise on 24 July, after the initial alarming thoughts about the fate of the corps commander who had failed to return, at an order from the 2nd Tank Corps headquarters the commander of the 27th Tank Brigade sent two light T-60 tanks on reconnaissance with the task to follow Liziukov's route toward Medvezh'e. Having come under fire, the tankers didn't get far before coming back.[39] The lack of word about the corps commander's fate was only beginning to grow into a suspicion that something had happened to him, but *no one in the corps even knew yet that Liziukov would never be found alive or dead.*

The headquarters of the 2nd Tank Corps and Briansk Front headquarters learned about the information from the 1st Tank Corps' scouts far from right away. At least several days passed before the scouts' important information passed through brigade headquarters and corps headquarters and finally reached the headquarters of Briansk Front. By this time, it had already become impossible to pinpoint the possible location of Liziukov's grave, because the area of combat operations had been left to the enemy.

The uncoordinated actions, lack of communications and absence of cooperation between the two tank corps, as well as the fact that the 2nd Tank Corps' headquarters itself, remaining in complete ignorance, didn't report to the neighbors about Liziukov's disappearance on time, led to the fact that in the headquarters of the 1st Tank Corps, and moreover in that of the 89th Tank Brigade, no one knew that the commander of the adjacent tank corps had gone missing. At the same time, the 1st Tank Corps' scouts (obviously from the 89th Tank Brigade) themselves didn't know that they had found his knocked-out tank and had quickly buried an unidentified corpse of a man who was most likely General Liziukov.

Is it really possible to consider that the dead tanker who'd been buried at Davidenko's order wasn't in fact Liziukov? Of course, we don't know everything, and obviously there is no 100% certainty in this conjecture. However, it is even more obvious that all the other versions and hypotheses have much less merit. One very important argument speaks in favor of the belief that Liziukov's body was buried by Davidenko's tankers – the fact that Liziukov's booklet was found on the disfigured body. There is only one most logical and natural explanation for this: the booklet was found in the unidentified tanker's pocket precisely because **the tanker was Liziukov**.

The most widely-circulated argument against this interpretation is the conclusion that somehow Liziukov's booklet wound up with one of the other members of his crew. However, given an attentive examination of the events it becomes obvious that this suggestion is highly improbable, while the alternative that Liziukov's orderly might have taken the general's booklet (according to Soviet army practice, an orderly could "stand in" for his commander to obtain the general's army-issue items (new boots, belts, etc.) due to him, and thus he had it with himself on 23 July) is completely untenable.

Liziukov's personal adjutant (and not an orderly), who hypothetically might have received the booklet from the general, was Captain Vladimir Pendak. However, on the morning of 23 July, Pendak had already been burned alive in a tank the day before, together with whatever documents he had in his possession at that time, and remained somewhere on the approaches to the village of Medvezh'e, many kilometers from the location of Liziukov's death.[40] Thus, there is no way he could have taken the general's booklet on 23 July! Yet if we assume he had obtained it from the general previously, didn't return it, and somehow took it along on the deep raid into the enemy rear, then in that case there is no way that the intact booklet could have been found on the adjutant's unburned body in the vicinity of the woods near Lebiazh'e.

Did Liziukov have an aide de camp? Yes, he did; Senior Lieutenant Vafin was serving as the general's assistant or speaking more accurately, personal runner. Could Liziukov have given him the booklet, so he wouldn't have to deal with it? Let's assume he did. But where was Senior

39 Ibid.

40 TsAMO, F. 148 tbr, op. 1, d. 3, ll. 37-38. See also the records in the "Memorial" database.

Lieutenant Vafin on 23 July? It is known with certainty that on the morning of 23 July, he was alive and well and located at the bridge in Bol'shaia Vereika, where he fruitlessly remained for a long time, waiting for the general to return, as he later stated in his own testimony![41] So there is no way the recovered booklet could have been with the general's adjutant or aide de camp!

Who else could Liziukov have given this document, and more importantly, why? Who else was with him on that fateful morning? We don't even have to guess at this, since the circle of individuals is known. No one other than the tank crew members was with Liziukov. Hypothetically, the general might have given his booklet to Commissar Assorov for some reason (but again, why?). However, it is reliably known that this document wasn't found on Assorov's body! Assorov's body was hanging from the tank's turret hatch, and not found 100 meters from it.

Sergeant Mozhaev, who survived, was together with Liziukov in the KV's turret, but he also didn't have the general's booklet. Who else remains? Only three men are left: Liziukov himself, and the senior driver-mechanic and radioman, who were sitting in the front of the tank's fighting compartment.

We mustn't forget that Liziukov didn't have his own command tank with his own crew. The KV tank, in which he and Assorov set out on the morning of 23 July, had been offered to him by the commander of the 27th Tank Brigade Captain Luchnikov together with its assigned crew, the members of which were unfamiliar to Liziukov. Why in the world would Liziukov give his general's property booklet to someone among the ordinary tankers who were unknown to him? So they could take it and protect it (!), or go off to vouch for the general right before a battle!? The absurdity of this hypothesis is obvious! It is completely apparent that Liziukov had not the slightest reason to give his general's property booklet to an unfamiliar driver-mechanic or radioman from the crew assigned to his tank!

However, perhaps they had taken the general's documents after his death, and later the general's booklet was found on one of their corpses? This hypothesis is also unsubstantiated, since the driver-mechanic and radio operator were killed practically right away; thus it can be asserted with almost a guarantee that after Liziukov's death, his general's property booklet was located precisely with him, and not with anyone else!

Neither our tankers nor the German soldiers had any reason to take the booklet from the dead general and then stick it into the pocket of a dead soldier. There is simply no rational explanation for such a "cloak and dagger" stunt. Our scouts, having found the general's booklet on the dead man's body, would have reported about this to their superiors, *which in fact is just what happened.* If the Germans had found it, they would have taken it as a prize, together with the Russian general's other documents, or would have simply tossed it aside as a useless item.

However, it is impossible to imagine that having taken all of the general's documents, the "tender-hearted" German soldiers would have been ashamed of their act, and would have conscientiously stuck his booklet back into the pocket of the bloody overalls – or would have placed it in the pocket of an ordinary dead, disfigured soldier. For what reason? For what purpose? Who would they be fooling? Even if we assume that they had some unknown motives for doing this, the enemy soldiers had no assurance that someone in the nearest future would take notice of a soldier's mutilated corpse and check it in the search for any documents! Yet even if this did take place, no definite conclusions could be drawn from this fact.

Completely obvious is the fact that the actions of the German soldiers after Liziukov's death were not distinguished by a great deal of forethought. *They were surprised themselves by what had happened.* Their decisions were spontaneous, and no sort of "cunning plan" or premeditation is apparent behind their actions. Of course, if professionals from the *Abwehr* or officers of a propaganda company had

41 TsAMO, F. 202, op. 50, d. 1, ll. 301-302.

been in their place, they would have quickly decided how to extract the maximal advantage out of what had happened. However, there plainly weren't any of them among the German soldiers at the front, who were worn-out, weary, filthy, and calloused by the on-going fighting.

For them, what had happened was no less a surprise than it had been for the crew of the knocked-out KV. After all, none of them could have imagined that a Russian general and his commissar would fall into their hands that morning! Thus they were acting not according to the "crafty setups of the *Abwehr*", but according to their own simple soldier's thinking, which wasn't burdened with the cunning ideas of military intelligence or propaganda.

If the Germans did have the need to create the appearance that the dead "Red Army man" was in fact Liziukov, they probably would have left something more than a thin property booklet (which lacked a photograph) on the disfigured corpse. This could have been the general's tunic with its decorations and documents. In addition, there would have been no need to drag the corpse so far from the tank.

If, on the other hand, they needed to make sure no one knew where Liziukov was located and what had really happened to him, they would have dragged away his corpse together with all of his documents, and wouldn't have left *any incriminating pieces of evidence* at the location of the general's death. In that situation, it wouldn't have been any trouble for them to destroy any and all evidence of the tragedy, including the tank itself, which they might have set ablaze together with the crew members *and not leave Assorov's corpse hanging so ostentatiously from the turret hatch.*

The fact of the discovery of the general's property booklet on the dead man most likely can be explained by the fact that after the discovery of Liziukov's personal documents in his tunic, the Germans didn't bother to explore the pocket of his bloody overalls, and the general's unnoticed booklet was left there.

Here it is necessary to say why they preferred not to come to any categorical conclusions about Liziukov's fate in the summer and autumn of 1942 within the Red Army's leadership. I assume that the reason for this is obvious: **there was no guarantee that the general hadn't wound up as a prisoner!** Thus, considering the obvious absence of available, reliable information, the attitude toward the available evidence was very cautious. Moreover, the location of Liziukov's death remained in enemy hands and was inaccessible for any searches or the discovery of his possible gravesite.

It isn't surprising that the discovery of Liziukov's booklet on a disfigured corpse wasn't considered in those circumstances as proof of his death. There was only one inarguable and concise truth at that time – Liziukov was missing. There was no assurance that the discovery of Liziukov's property booklet wasn't an enemy provocation, and that Liziukov wouldn't suddenly and completey unexpectedly appear as a German prisoner, and Goebbel's propaganda wouldn't start trumpeting the news of a second Vlasov!

Therefore, it is hardly strange that the Briansk Front command didn't draw any conclusions about Liziukov's death, based on the evidentiary materials that were available. In Colonel Sukhoruchkin's investigation (regarding Liziukov's fate), there was primarily only a recitation of the available facts without any commentary about their reliability or significance. He was plainly being cautious and didn't want to say anything beyond that.

In the higher levels of the Red Army command and in the NKVD, they didn't come to any final conclusions about Liziukov's death for at least another entire year! This year was a period of uncertainty and tense waiting, and anything back then could have been expected – there was too much unclear and unambiguous in the circumstances surrounding the disappearance of the disgraced general. This matter, it seems, was finally closed only in July 1943, when the Saratov Tank School formally acquired the name of Hero of the Soviet Union General Liziukov. Such a decision was in essence an official recognition that he wasn't missing in action and had not wound up as a German prisoner, but had been killed in action and remained a hero.

In connection with this, the suspicions inevitably fell away, and the significance of all the available facts about Liziukov's death grew. With time it became clear that **the discovery of the general's property booklet on the disfigured corpse was not a German-staged scene in order to conceal the general's capture**. The final doubts finally evaporated already after the war, when no information was discovered to show that Liziukov had spent time as a German prisoner. Moreover, there couldn't be any now, after so many decades have passed since the victory.

Now, when this had become totally clear, the fact of the discovery of Liziukov's property booklet acquires much more significance for us, than it did for those who were questioned about the missing general's fate in 1942. It is difficult to over-evaluate the significance of this evidence! From its interpretation, one can now fully exclude the main element of the suspicions that existed back then – the possibility of a German provocation.

Thus, one can now declare with full responsibility that the discovery of Liziukov's property booklet is at the very least a serious basis for considering that the **tanker found in the overalls was none other than Liziukov, if not proof**.

An indirect acknowledgement of this is also Davidenko's postwar letter to Liziukov's widow, in which he essentially confirmed his official staff report. Without having any formal proof, with this letter Davidenko plainly expressed his own personal opinion that his soldiers back in July 1942 had most likely buried her husband in the fringe of the woods. Excerpts from this letter are given in the recollections of the writer Krivitsky, who repeatedly met with Liziukov's son, and knew first hand all of the complex twists and turns of the unsuccessful searches for his father.

Is it possible to assume that the Germans actually carried the general off in an unknown direction, as the authors of a book about Liziukov's brothers wrote? Of course, it is impossible to reject this alternative completely. Yet nevertheless, it is very doubtful.

In the first place, in order to confirm this hypothesis, one has to explain *why the Germans, who "were carrying away Liziukov's body in an unknown direction" for some reason stuck his property booklet in the pocket of a dead "Red Army man", who was lying 100 meters from the knocked-out tank.* We've already talked about the plain dubiousness of such explanations above.

Secondly, on that day it would have been a quite difficult and risky matter to carry away the dead Liziukov from the patch of woods to the German rear. Given the penetration by our tanks east and west of the patch of woods, when fighting had already developed 3-4 kilometers to the south, and the woods wound up in a pocket, the line of communications of the enemy elements in the woods had been severed.

Any German vehicles heading toward the woods on that day might simply have been destroyed by our tanks or have become easy prey even for the forward reconnaissance groups of the rifle units. Only in the evening in the course of a counterattack by the enemy's 9th Panzer Division did German tanks reach the woods and give the German infantry ensconced within them a chance to rest.[42] Thus, to "arrange for" a vehicle in order to transport the dead body of a Russian general out of the woods, much less to carry it out, was not at all simple for the enemy on that day, if not impossible.

Finally, there is the third and most important counterargument to the idea that the Germans carried off Liziukov's body "in an unknown direction". It is completely obvious that if such transportation had been arranged and carried out by the enemy, in the German documents there would have to be some mention of the fact that the body of General "Lisukow" had been delivered to the command post of some unit together with all of his papers. This event would have been so important, that it would have been immediately reported up the chain to the VII Army Corps' headquarters, to which the 387th Infantry Division was subordinate. In this case, even in the

42 NARA, T-314, roll 353, fr. 000404.

absence of any archival files of this division, there would have been some mention of Liziukov in the documents of the VII Army Corps. However, there is nothing like this in them.

Of course, it is fully possible that Liziukov's documents and tunic eventually reached a regimental headquarters – if, of course, the German soldiers in the woods didn't "requisition" the tunic because of the general's valuable decorations. (In connection with this, it is fully possible to assume that Liziukov's Orders and medals even today are being kept somewhere in a private collection in the West, the owner of which either has no inkling of the tragedy standing behind them, or does know, but for understandable reasons keeps silent and doesn't flaunt their origin.)

However, it is one matter if a higher command is presented with the corpse of a Russian general, together with his documents, as direct material proof, but a completely different matter, if a bloody and tattered tunic and the acquisition of documents *under quite strange circumstances* are reported back to headquarters from the front. Obviously, it would have been extremely difficult for a pragmatic German staff officer to believe that a Russian general and a highly-posted commissar had gone to the front without any cover and fallen into an ambush, as the soldiers were saying from the front.

Thus, in regiment headquarters, most likely they believed that the tunic and documents they'd been brought weren't a sufficient basis for any confident announcements or conclusions, so they didn't bother to report about this to division headquarters. Thus, the fine thread of information about the incident flowing up the chain of command was broken, and no traces of Liziukov's death were left in German documents. (It is possible as well that having acquired the general's decorations, the German soldiers tossed aside his tunic as something unneeded and simply didn't bother to report about what happened to their officers. The same fate might have befallen the captured documents. It is also impossible to exclude the possibility that these soldiers were quickly killed in the course of the fighting, and thus for understandable reasons simply were unable to report about the incident to the command staff.)

Thus, it is unlikely that the Germans could drag off Liziukov's body anywhere away from the woods. Thus, no matter how paradoxical it seems, from the point of view of searches for Liziukov's grave, it is now no longer important whether the "Red Army man" buried next to the woods on 23 July 1942 was Liziukov or not, *because one way or another Liziukov's grave must be somewhere around there.*

The question consists only in who performed the burial, and when. It is possible to assume anything here: This might have been done by the Germans or our guys, and the burial might have been done either during the fighting, or after it ended by local residents in the spring and summer of 1943.

Let's summarize the evidence: Two reliable sources speak in favor of the version that Liziukov was buried in the fringe of the woods south of Lebiazh'e: the materials of the 1942 investigation and Davidenko's staff report from 1947. In addition, this staff report is confirmed by a third source: Davidenko's postwar letter to Liziukov's widow.

On a 1941 military map, Point 188.5 is marked in a field southeast of the village of Lebiazh'e approximately 2,200 meters from the church. The patch of woods west of Hill 188.5 still exists, and its boundaries have changed little over the postwar years. Guards Colonel Davidenko in 1942 was the deputy commander of the 1st Tank Corps' 89th Tank Brigade. On 23 and 24 July, from its jumping off positions in the woods south of Lebiazh'e, the 89th Tank Brigade became engaged in offensive fighting northeast of the villages of Somovo and Bol'shaia Treshchevka.

In order to observe the course of combat operations, the brigade commander's observation post was supposed to be positioned within eyesight of these villages, and with consideration for the gradually rising terrain to the south, no further than 2-3 kilometers from them. At the same time, the observation post could not have been situated north of the southern edge of the woods, because observation of the battlefield would have been impossible from this location. Accordingly, the probable location for the 89th Tank Brigade's observation post might have been a point on a hilltop somewhere south of the woods. If this is the case, then it is possible to conjecture that the body of Major General Liziukov that had been brought to the observation post was possibly buried later *in the nearby fringe of the southern spur of the woods, which are located south of the village of Lebiazh'e.*

Back then, in the heat of heavy combat, the worn-out soldiers could hardly have left behind any sign on the grave of the fallen general, other than a little mound with a wooden star and, in the best case, an entry on a name plate: "An unknown soldier". But soon the brigade had to retreat from this area, and Liziukov's grave would have remained in German-occupied territory. What became of the gravesite back then is hard to say. In any case, there was no one to tend to it, and the traces of Liziukov's burial site began to fade away. The earth settled, the autumn rains washed away the little mound, and probably the marker also disappeared, if it still existed by that time. Later winter arrived, and the grave site was likely covered by deep snow …

In January 1943, fearing encirclement, the German units abandoned their occupied positions and quickly retreated to the west. Our forces went on the pursuit, and without combat advanced across the fields of the bloody fighting from the summer of 1942, which by that time lay under a thick blanket of snow. Liziukov's grave remained under that snow, and it was hardly possible that anyone noticed it back then. So only in the spring of 1943, once the snow had melted, would it have been still possible to find the place where the general was buried. However, there were no troops around: the front was already far to the west. Later, local residents began to return to their devastated villages, but they could hardly have noticed a solitary burial mound in the fringe of the woods. Hundreds of still unburied corpses were lying everywhere in the fields. It isn't surprising that Liziukov's grave gradually disappeared from sight and settled into the ground. At a time when people still had to think about how to survive, they had little concern for the dead.

What is surprising is something else. After liberating the ground, where the fighting went on, no diligent searches in order to find the grave of a prominent general, a Hero of the Soviet Union, and at least memorialize his memory, were undertaken by the Soviet command. According to some information, in the spring and summer of 1943 Liziukov's widow traveled to the place of fighting with a group of military servicemen who'd been specially-assigned for this search, but their attempts to find Liziukov's gravesite were unsuccessful.

Nevertheless, it still might have been possible to find eyewitnesses, who could have shown where Liziukov had been buried (as we've seen, Colonel Davidenko was still alive, because he wrote a letter to Liziukov's widow in 1947), but no decisive steps to establish the spot where the general was buried were undertaken. So his grave finally became lost.

Here it is worth talking about the surprising continuation of General Liziukov's posthumous drama. In May 2008, the leaders of "Don", a Voronezh search group, announced that they had supposedly been able to locate the general's gravesite at the church in the village of Lebiazh'e, and news media, seducible to sensations, were broadcasting this news to the entire nation. However, upon scrutinizing the historical validations of the findings that were offered by the group, it became clear that they couldn't stand up to any critique and the loud declarations by the "discoverers of Liziukov's gravesite" simply had no correspondence with the truth. One can read in detail about the discussions that went on over these questions in the book *Taina gibeli generala Liziukova* [*Mystery of General Liziukov's death*].

Do Liziukov's remains still remain somewhere in a fringe of woods in a gravesite that became lost after the war? It is fully possible, but also not a fact. Over the postwar years, much has happened on the edge of the field next to the southern patch of woods. An asphalt highway was laid down here, with the deposition of soil beneath the bed of the road, which ran practically right next to the southern spur of the woods. Later, an electrical cable was conducted through here, and deep holes were dug here for 30-meter-tall concrete supports. Finally, numerous diggings have been done in the forest fringe: official ones, and often also independent ones.

Many did diggings here: local children, search teams and even speculators interested in making money off of any uncovered artifacts. There are also mentions that among the remains found in the area are those of tankers, who were recognized by fragments of tankers' headgear and overalls stained with residual fuel oil. Who were these tankers? We don't know. Illegal diggers haven't written accounts of the "work" they've done, and it is unknown where the remains of the dead later went.

Archival records allow us to presume that dozens of tankers were killed in the fields of fighting around the woods and have been left behind. The number of infantrymen killed here can plainly be counted in hundreds, if not thousands. Only a small fraction of them were buried in fraternal graves; the majority of them lie in lost and forgotten sanitary landfills from the years 1943 and 1944, for which purpose primarily enormous bomb craters in the fields and countless trenches were used. Many of them never received a proper burial at all, and remain forever lying in fields, gullies and patches of woods. Such are the facts.

The area of Liziukov's possible gravesite is undoubtedly close to the area where his tank was knocked out. Judging from investigations of the terrain, it is possible to suggest with a great deal of probability that Liziukov's KV tank was knocked out in a very narrow portion of the field between the eastern spur of the woods that approach the highway from the west, and the contemporary road that branches off in the direction of Skliaevo. Here, too, a body clad in overalls was later found. The extent of the wooded fringe in this area amounts to around 1 kilometer. Perhaps, it is precisely here that one should seek General Liziukov's grave?

It is even possible now to do this? That is a difficult question. Even if someone began to excavate a trench in the fringe of the woods, it is fully possible human remains would be encountered; after all, so many people were killed here during the war! However, where is the guarantee that these would be Liziukov's remains?

As it seems to me, the question lies in something else. Because of the circumstances, we can hardly ever establish precisely the exact location of Liziukov's grave. In any case, in my view there should be a monument to him next to the southern fringe of the patch of woods west of Hill 188.5. This place is not only the area of his probable burial, but without a doubt, it also marks the field of his final battle. In the summer of 2009, a stone monument was set up on the eastern fringe of the woods, supposedly marking the location of the general's death, but it is completely obvious that the responsible parties who decided upon the location for the marker had only a totally vague notion of the circumstances surrounding Liziukov's last battle. Even so, the fact of the appearance of a stone memorial can only be welcomed, but the fact that it was set up in the wrong location is a cause for regret.

Of course, it would be more correct to establish a monument to General Liziukov at the fork in the Zemliansk highway that leads to Bol'shaia Vereika. This would be not only a monument to General Liziukov, who was buried somewhere nearby in a nameless grave, but also to our numerous soldiers and commanders, who didn't even share this fate back then.

Let's recall Regimental Commissar Assorov, whose last mention was only that his dead body was left hanging from the turret hatch of the knocked-out tank. Where should we look for his remains?

Let's recall the driver-mechanic who was killed in the tank, and the radio operator who was killed in the rye field after he emerged from the tank. Most likely, no one buried them after our forces withdrew. Let's recall the hundreds of other warriors, who were left back then to lie unburied on the hills soaked with blood. Their bodies were later dragged into large bomb craters or hastily dumped into crumbling trenches, and they never received after their death either a grave or a monument. Their bones, most likely, continue to reside in the ground or on the expansive field that contains Point 188.5.

An obelisk here to Liziukov would also be a general monument for many thousands of our soldiers, who were killed or went missing in action in the bloody battles of the summer of 1942 at Bol'shaia Vereika. We have no right to forget them. May they be remembered forever!

Conclusion

On 23 July 1942, the chief of staff of Briansk Front's operational group (the future 4th Army and subsequently the 38th Army) Colonel Pilipenko had sent General Liziukov the following order:

> The army commander has ordered to make fuel, ammunition and food ready for the 148th Tank Brigade, so that with the onset of darkness on 23 July, they can be sent aboard tanks to its area of operations. Prepare the 26th and 27th Tank Brigades for operations to the southeast on the night of 23/24 July. An order about the time set for the 26th and 27th Tank Brigades' offensive will follow.[1]

Judging by this order, neither army commander Chibisov, nor his chief of staff even knew yet that there was for the most part no one to whom to deliver the fuel, ammunition and food requested by the 148th Tank Brigade, that the battalions that had set out on the nighttime raid had been wiped out, and that just a little more than 10 of their men remained alive. Of course, they were in great need of food and water, but it was hardly possible to find them, hiding in the German rear amid the broad expanses of the Don River area, and give them genuine aid. Moreover, the corps commander wasn't at the 2nd Tank Corps' headquarters, and the staff officers didn't know exactly where he was located. In his absence, no one at the headquarters was willing to make important operational decisions in his place …

On that same day, in the evening, Colonel Pilipenko sent Liziukov one more order:

> After my report to the Front's chief of staff I received an order from the Front Commander-in-Chief for the entire 2nd Tank Corps to reach the Medvezh'e, Sviridov area in the remaining daylight hours, and to report on this to army and Front headquarters at 2400. I'm informing you that on the morning of 24 July, neighboring units will be attacking to the west from beyond the Don River in order to link up with you. The Front Commander-in-Chief has ordered you personally to implement command and control over the tank corps from a tank among its combat formations. Confirm receipt. Report on your departure.[2]

Liziukov, whom Rokossovsky was ordering to command the corps "personally from a tank among its combat formations", was already dead and could neither command the corps, nor report on anything, but neither the Briansk Front Commander-in-Chief nor the 38th Army's chief of staff, nor anyone else other than Sergeant Mozhaev, who had survived by a miracle, knew this yet.

Germans had searched Liziukov's lifeless body, the commander's and commissar's papers had already fallen into enemy hands, but the meticulous Pilipenko was sending him a new message with an insistent demand: "Report whether or not you have received the order and what you have done to carry it out."[3]

1 TsAMO, F. 202, op. 5, d. 258, l. 42.
2 Ibid., l. 43.
3 Ibid., l. 44.

An astonishing series of command orders followed that were addressed to the already dead commander of the 2nd Tank Corps! However, considering the overall situation of those desperate days, the absence of reliable information and the woeful situation with communications, only at first glance can this be called astonishing. Most likely, this was one more manifestation of the plain disarray in command of the troops and lack of coordination in the work of the command and headquarters, which alas was characteristic for the entire operation of Briansk Front's operational group.

The crews of the 148th Tank Brigade that had broken through earlier that day to Medvezh'e for the most part had already laid down their lives there. All of their tanks had been destroyed. Just 2 KV and 10 T-60 tanks were all that was left of the brigade's combat-ready machines.[4] The 26th and 27th Tank Brigades spent the entire day standing in a wooded ravine, enduring airstrikes and making no advance.[5] The 2nd Motorized Rifle Brigade didn't set out anywhere without the tanks and moreover didn't dare to do so. Who was to direct the offensive? The corps commander, but where was he? The staff officers still didn't know. In his absence, they couldn't offer any concrete answer to Pilipenko's direct question.

Having failed to receive anything intelligible from the 2nd Tank Corps in response to his preceding orders, and because of this being unable to supply the information being demanded by the Front headquarters, Pilipenko dryly informed Liziukov, who for some reason had been silent since the morning of 23 July, about the command's growing impatience and dissatisfaction: "The Front's chief of staff has ordered to warn you that if the corps isn't in the Sviridov, Medvezh'e area by 2400, then the matter will be viewed as the failure to carry out a combat order."[6]

The day passed. Pilipenko's order (and correspondingly Chibisov's order) remained unfulfilled. In the headquarters of the 2nd Tank Corps, they had initiated searches for Liziukov, but obviously hoping the worst hadn't befallen him, were thus far not hurrying to inform higher headquarters of the "ChP" that had taken place, and thus the higher command knew nothing and for the second day after Liziukov's death they were still prodding him forward and even threatening to court martial him!

On 25 July, Chibisov's patience came to an end, and now bypassing his chief of staff, he personally sent the 2nd Tank Corps commander a curt and strict order in the spirit of his previous scathing declarations:

> According to a report from the 193rd Rifle Division, up to 40 enemy tanks at 1500 on 25 July were in movement from Lomovo and Lebiazh'e. The 2nd Tank Corps is to hasten the destruction of the enemy in the Lomovo area and with a decisive attack toward Hill 181.8 to smash completely the enemy that is attacking toward Bol'shaia Vereika. Your actions are criminally slow. I demand energetic actions and the fulfillment of the order. Army commander CHIBISOV.[7]

It is astonishing, but it turns out that even on 25 July, the commander of Briansk Front's operational group still had no knowledge even that the commander of the 2nd Tank Corps was missing, much less dead, and was still demanding the dead general "to smash the enemy completely" and according to his already formed, mean-spirited "habit", was accusing him of criminal delay!

4 TsAMO, F. 148 tbr, op. 1, d. 3, l. 39.
5 TsAMO, F. 202, op. 50, d. 1, l. 308.
6 TsAMO, F. 202, op. 5, d. 258, l. 50.
7 Ibid., l. 64.

Finally, toward the end of 25 July, having plainly become angered by Liziukov's "irritating silence" in response to all of his orders and warnings, Chibisov through his chief of staff sent a demand to the 2nd Tank Corps commander to make an immediate appearance, "upon receipt of this message" in front of the Front's Military Council in Bol'shaia Poliana![8] Considering the threatening atmosphere of those days, which was even deteriorating in connection with the operation's clear failure, as well as the woeful experience of the unpleasant personal relationship between Liziukov and Chibisov, I think that this was most likely meant to be a genuine "call to the carpet" ....

However, Chibisov, who was ready to give Liziukov another harsh rebuke, was still unaware that Liziukov could now never come to the Military Council nor appear in front of anyone else, no matter how threatening the orders he sent; or that it was now too late to demand energetic actions and fulfillment of orders from him, while bossy threats at his address were pointless ...

For several days, higher command had no accurate information about the fate of the 2nd Tank Corps commander. Telegraph discussions between Colonel Potapov, who'd been assigned to the headquarters of Operational Group Chibisov, and Briansk Front headquarters show that by early in the morning on 28 July, the operational group's command had only unverified information that Liziukov had been wounded.[9] Only later that day, five days after the general's disappearance, after checking and comparing all the available information, was the determination finally made that he'd been killed. In his directive, Briansk Front's Deputy Commander for Armored Forces, addressing the shortcomings in their actions, wrote: "When directing a battle, the commanders of units and even formations become distracted by specific episodes of the battle, enter the dynamics of the combat themselves, and in the best case do not direct the fighting for a time, and in the worst case, which is what happened to the commander of the 2nd Tank Corps, get themselves killed."[10]

Here, however, it is impossible not to recall the order from Rokossovsky, the Commander-in-Chief of Briansk Front, who five days before had demanded that same commander of the 2nd Tank Corps to direct the fighting "with your personal leadership from a tank in the combat formations ...."[11] Incidentally, this demand did not refer to Liziukov alone. Katukov, the commander of the 1st Tank Corps, received a similar order on 23 July:

> Following a report from the Front's chief of staff, the Front Commander-in-Chief expressed dissatisfaction with your slow actions and ordered by your personal leadership from a tank within the combat formations to complete the enemy's destruction in the Bol'shaia Treshchevka, Malaia Treshchevka, Somovo, Gremiach'e area. Report on the execution by the morning of 24 July to the army headquarters and Front headquarters. Confirm receipt. Report on the steps taken.
>
> [Signed] Army chief of staff Colonel Pilipenko[12]

In the process, as opposed to Chibisov, Rokossovsky expressed his dissatisfaction precisely with Katukov's slow actions, not Liziukov's (we'll recall his radio message to the commander of the 1st Tank Corps on 22.7.42 about the fact that "the corps is criminally idling in place" and that his actions "were not worthy of the title of tankers").

8 Ibid., l. 63.
9 TsAMO, F. 202, op. 5, d. 489, ll. 241-242.
10 TsAMO, F. 202, op. 50, d. 1, l. 286.
11 TsAMO, F. 202, op. 5, d. 258, l. 43.
12 TsAMO, F. 202, op. 5, d. 258, l. 41.

It would seem that it was precisely the commander of the 1st Tank Corps who was primarily supposed to concern himself with the execution of the received order about commanding the tank corps from within its combat formations. Nevertheless, the two similar orders were interpreted by the commanders of the neighboring tank corps differently. Liziukov carried out the order and took a seat in a tank. No one later saw him alive. Katukov had no intention of following this point in the order and didn't lead his corps' attack from within a tank. He remained alive and wrote his memoirs.

Incidentally, Katukov's disagreement with his received orders and directives regarding the actions of the tank forces in those battles was personally expressed by him in a message he wrote three days later, in which he openly revealed his thoughts to higher command:

> I consider it a duty to report to you that it is better, when giving me an attack order, to subordinate some infantry division and artillery to me, as well as additional artillery regiments, and not [for them] to cooperate with us, since it is impossible to put together a firm plan of attack or the artillery's plan of work to suppress enemy strongpoints in cooperation with the tanks, and you can't implement one. The reliance upon frontal assault by tanks against enemy artillery is incorrect, no matter how much you berate us.[13]

The story, as is said, is full of coincidences. How might the literal execution of Rokossovsky's order have turned out for Katukov, especially if it is recalled that on that same evening of 23 July, the tanks of the 9th Panzer Division launched a counterattack and advanced through the same area of operations of the 1st Tank Corps at Somovo? In such case, he would have then, at a minimum, had to conduct the battle personally as part of a tank crew. There is a good chance that Katukov himself might get killed in such a situation. However, Katukov didn't carry out the order – perhaps because he was sick on those days. Possibly as well because he could easily imagine the consequences that such a command style might have for himself and for his subordinate troops. In any case, he had not only a solid reason to refuse to carry out such an order, but also an *appropriate excuse* ... Katukov was ill at his command post in Lebiazh'e, spent the entire time of the operation there (according to an account from the 1st Tank Corps headquarters), and plainly wasn't directing his brigades "with personal leadership among the combat formations". Perhaps that is why he remained alive. Had he gone into battle that day in a tank and wound up in the path of the German counterattack that evening, who knows what that might have cost Briansk Front's Operational Group Chibisov to lose two tank corps commanders simultaneously on one day? However, the ill Katukov sensibly remained at his command post.

Was Liziukov's death a coincidence? I think that here the best answer would be to say both yes and no. A chain of events led to the death of the 2nd Tank Corps commander, but nevertheless it was initially prompted by his own decision to conduct a nighttime attack with the tank corps on the night of 21/22 July 1942. It was this decision that ultimately led his solitary KV tank toward the positions of German anti-tank guns on the morning of 23 July.

How is it now possible to assess Liziukov's decision to launch an attack with his 2nd Tank Corps on the night of 21/22 July? Based on the documents and the analysis of the events that took place, it is possible to conclude that this decision was ultimately mistaken. In the situation where the brigade commanders lacked the time to work out the task properly, to make it known to subordinates, and most importantly, to plan the attack and to organize communications, cooperation and clear command and control over their units on totally unfamiliar ground in nighttime conditions, the corps' nighttime foray turned into a series of spontaneous, poorly organized and

13 TsAMO, F. 202, op. 5, d. 238, l. 464.

disjointed actions instead of a powerful attack against the foe, and became a tragedy for the 148th Tank Brigade.

Even in daylight hours, the introduction into a breakthrough and a tank corps' offensive in the depth of the enemy's defenses were on their own complex elements of an independent combat operation. But at night, when the commanders had no opportunity to orient themselves as they should in enormous fields that were indistinguishable from each other, these problems worsened the already difficult position in which the attacking elements found themselves, and placed the implementation of the order they had received on the verge of collapse.

It is completely obvious that the decision Liziukov made to launch a nighttime attack was neither properly thought out nor worked out, but became an improvisation, prompted by the desire to carry out an order at whatever the cost and by any means. However, it has long been observed that even a good improvisation is always based upon good preparation. In the case of the 2nd Tank Corps' improvisation, there can be no talk about any thorough preparation on the evening of 21 July. Not only the ordinary tankers, but also the unit commanders were unable to orient themselves properly in the unfamiliar terrain, and instead of a concentrated and daring raid that would thrown the adversary into panic, they blindly wandered around the fields in search of the needed directions.

(Here it is impossible not to recall that two weeks before this Liziukov, who was then the commander of the 5th Tank Army, in a fit of anger ordered the 11th Tank Corps' operations chief Lieutenant Colonel Khlebalov to be shot without any trial or investigation. His guilt consisted in the fact that instead of continuing the offensive at night, he had decided to dig in on the occupied line until morning. The enraged Liziukov accused Khlebalov back then of disrupting the offensive, as a result of which the corps supposedly failed to carry out the task it had been given.[14])

Two weeks after this summary execution, like an admonition for this arbitrary act he had committed, fate presented Liziukov with the opportunity to see for himself how fruitless and disastrous it was to conduct a spontaneous nighttime attack by brigades that hadn't been prepared for this.

By a strange confluence of events, the death of Liziukov itself was to a great extent connected with his own decision for the 2nd Tank Corps to launch a nighttime attack – a decision for which he had quite recently taken the life of a subordinate for the latter's failure to do so. It is impossible not to note as well a different coincidence in the fates of the former commander and subordinate. The grave of Liziukov, who had given the order to execute Khlebalov, became lost in obscurity, just like the grave of his victim Lieutenant Colonel Khlebalov, who was shot on 9 July 1942 in front of the assembled staff officers.

To conclude this short digression, it must be said that Lieutenant Colonel Vasilii Safronovich Khlebalov was posthumously rehabilitated a quarter of a century after his death – in 1967, while the order from the commander of the 5th Tank Army Liziukov to shoot him was summarily reversed as an order contradictory to the law.[15] Such is a little-known stain of bitter truth on the well-known image of the legendary army commander.

Most likely, Liziukov's calculations on the raid's success were based on the belief that after a noisy breakthrough by the tanks into the German rear, accompanied with indiscriminate fire, the foe would flinch, go into a panic, and terrified of encirclement, abandon their occupied positions, as a result of which his entire front of defense would collapse. However, this belief proved to be mistaken. The units of the German 387th Infantry Division, which had just taken up their defensive line shortly before nightfall, didn't quail, and having allowed the Soviet tanks to pass into their rear, remained in their occupied positions and held them against the following infantry's attack.

14 TsAMO, F. 11 tk, d. 14, l. 25.
15 USSR Ministry of Defense Order No. 196, 21 August 1967.

All of the following attempts to break through and go to the relief of the 148th Tank Brigade suffered failure, which to a significant degree was the fault of the 26th and 27th Tank Brigades' leadership, as well as that of the 2nd Tank Corps commander himself. The 167th Rifle Division was also unable to penetrate the enemy's defense, but the misleading report from the division commander about the division's headway by the morning of 23 July, and the supposed lines reached by its forward units, plainly misinformed the commander of the 2nd Tank Corps about the existing situation.

In reality, German units and anti-tank guns were still defending both the southern slopes of Hill 188.5 and the patch of woods west of it, as well as the area of the southern spur of the patch of woods, which according to the report from the headquarters of the 167th Rifle Division had already been cleared by the division; this proved to be fatal for the 2nd Tank Corps commander and commissar. The unexpected, close-range flanking fire from the Germans at Liziukov's tank as it incautiously rolled "along the route" didn't give him or his crew any chances, except for Mozhaev, who survived by some miracle. Neither Liziukov nor Assorov were now able to size up the situation or report the ambush. Moveover, they could no longer narrate about what happened later in their memoirs, which were never written, in which they could also have talked about a lot else.

The surviving Katukov and Ivanovsky wrote memoirs, in which with decades of hindsight after the war for one reason or another they strongly distorted what really happened and substituted a fictitious narrative for the historical truth. Ivanovsky, as I assume, wanted to put his actions as the 2nd Tank Corps' intelligence chief in the best possible light. Yet why did Katukov do this? Here, the question, as it seems to me, is more complex. Katukov wasn't Liziukov's subordinate, and in distinction from Ivanovsky, he didn't have to justify his actions or inactivity. He could have opted not to write anything about what he HAD NOT SEEN, what he HAD NOT EXPERIENCED, and what he DID NOT KNOW. However, in his memoirs he gave an eloquent picture of Liziukov's death, which doesn't have ANY CONNECTION with the truth. Why?

The answer, it seems to me, is obvious. This was a white lie, an attempt to present the matter as if there were no questions in the fate of the missing Liziukov, as if the glorious general had died the death of a hero in battle, and didn't go missing in action, or moveover, fall into enemy hands.

From the question about Liziukov, we'll now turn to an analysis of the operation and overall conclusions. The operation ended in failure, if not to say, a defeat. It failed to achieve a single one of its objectives, the enemy opposing Operational Group Chibisov was not routed, and the operational group's forces were unable to reach Semiluki and Gubarevo, in order to pose a threat to the German-held Don River bridges and contribute to Voronezh Front's offensive. At the same time, the troops of Operational Group Chibisov suffered heavy losses.

What were the reasons for the operation's failure? The operational group's command and that of several of its units attempted to answer this question soon after the fighting ended. Summing up the operation's results, the army's chief of staff wrote:

> This operation demonstrated:
>
> 1. The weak preparation of the regimental and divisional headquarters in organizing cooperation.
> 2. The enemy's aerial superiority, which acted on the morale of our infantry.
> 3. The ignorance of the combat and numerical strength of the units and formations.
> 4. The lack of discipline of the unit and formation commanders, which led to encirclement and large losses.[16]

16 TsAMO, F. 38 A, op. 9005, d. 39, l. 14.

We've already spoken above about the reasons for the failure of the 2nd Tank Corps' nighttime attack. In distinction from the 2nd Tank Corps' dead commander and commissar, who could no longer say anything about their view of the conducted operation, the 1st Tank Corps command wrote a comprehensive report about it, where they laid out the reasons for the failure in detail. This section of the report is worth citing here in full, with a few small corrections:

1. The organization of the offensive operation was conducted in a short period of time, in the course of the single day of 20 July, as a result of which even the battalion commanders were unable to familiarize themselves on the spot with the layout of the enemy's defense, study the nature of the terrain, and consult with the infantry and artillery commanders.
2. The written order for the offensive arrived at corps headquarters only by the evening of 20 July, as a result of which only a single night was left to the corps headquarters, the brigade headquarters, the battalion headquarters and the company commanders to organize the work according to the order and to clarify questions of cooperation.
3. The enemy's forward edge of defense wasn't ascertained by the rifle units, as a result of which it was assumed that the enemy's line of combat outposts ran along the line of Hills 218.7, 214.6, 213.8 and the northern outskirts of Bol'shaia Vereika, thus the aerial and artillery preparation was conducted against the depth of the enemy's defenses in the areas of Gremiach'e, Bol'shaia Treshchevka, Lebiazh'e and Kaver'ia, while the main firing positions, which proved to be on the forward edge of defense along Hills 214.6, 213.8 and 191.3 remained unsuppressed, and came alive with the start of the attack by the infantry and tanks.
4. The rifle divisions were poorly prepared for the offensive and the infantry wasn't organized; given the slightest fire resistance, it failed to advance behind the tanks and ran away ... expecting that the tanks would carry out the main combat role; as a result, the majority of the 284th, 340th and 193rd Rifle Divisions failed to carry out their task, and lay prostrate in the rye.
5. The tanks, which lacked organized infantry and artillery support, while at the same time the tank corps have no artillery means and little infantry, ran into anti-tank areas and minefields, and suffering losses, were not able to resolve tasks on the achieved lines. Lacking infantry, artillery and firing means, the tanks cannot fortify [the ground], and to avoid losses from enemy infantry's grenades and Molotov cocktails were compelled to fall back from the occupied position.
6. The enemy air force throughout the entire operation reigned supreme above the battlefield and bombed the combat formations and command posts with impunity, knocking out materiel and men ... and slowing the units' advance, and sometimes even disrupting command and control over the units and elements.
7. The rifle divisions didn't carry out the tasks to break through the defense; the tank corps, instead of entering a breach in the secured and prepared line of the Sukhaia Vereika River, was compelled to break though the enemy's defense itself in the Lebiazh'e area, destroy his anti-tank means, build bridges and clear passages through minefields, while suffering losses in tanks and personnel from the enemy's anti-tank means. The rifle divisions' powerful artillery, not unified into single hands for a powerful blow on the main direction, remained inactive and didn't render any support to the tank corps.
8. Timely assistance to the attacking units of the 1st and 2nd Tank Corps with an attack by other formations from the north didn't follow, and the moment was missed, when the enemy, having seized the initiative, launched a counterattack, and having shoved back units of the 284th, 237th and 340th Rifle Divisions, seized a portion of the ground and created a threat [of encirclement], partially even encircled units of the 1st and 2nd Tank

Corps and the 193rd Rifle Division [in fact the 2nd Tank Corps didn't fall into encirclement; rather, two regiments of the 340th Rifle Divisions were encircled together with the 193rd Rifle Division – I.S.] and eliminated the breakthrough by our units.

9. Units of the 7th and 11th Tank Corps, which were positioned in reserve, weren't timely used for active tasks and their entire role during the enemy breakthrough amounted to holding back his further advance to the north, but no assistance was given by their actions to the encircled units of the 1st Tank Corps and 193rd Rifle Division.
10. As a result of the rifle divisions' failure to carry out the tasks of breaking through the defense, the independent breakthrough of the forward edge and the securing of bridges by the tank brigades caused the offensive's pace to slow; the enemy, fortifying on new lines, and having brought up reserves, found a weak sector in the defense of the 340th and 284th Rifle Divisions [in reality – the defense of the 237th Rifle Division – I.S.] and launched a decisive blow into the shock grouping's flank, creating a threat of encirclement with penetrating units. The parrying of the counterattack was organized too late, and the shock group's reserves were drawn into the fighting.[17]

As we see, the 1st Tank Corps' command, and primarily the corps commander Katukov himself, expressed critical comments not only on the subject of the neighbors' actions, but also of his own superiors, which is completely apparent despite the vague, impersonal wording (for example, the authors of the account wrote that the 7th and 11th Tank Corps "weren't used", instead of directly saying that "the command of the operational group didn't use" them). After the passage of many decades, we have the opportunity to supplement these *conclusions written soon after the fact* and talk about those various reasons that weren't expressed back then.

In their accounts and conclusions, the Soviet command staff at various levels was very cautious regarding the criticism of higher command, as well as in the acknowledgement of their own sins and blunders (with the exception, arguably, of the unusually honest and self-critical entries in the 237th Rifle Division's combat diary); as a rule, in the headquarters they preferred to avoid such commentary or to present what happened as a result of circumstances that were totally beyond the control of the leadership. The 38th Army's account was also no exception, where almost all the blame was laid upon "unruly" subordinates.

Meanwhile, a significant share of the responsibility lay upon both Operational Group Chibisov's leadership, as well as that of the Briansk Front. Analyzing the operation, one can't help but notice the unsynchronized actions of the tank corps. At the time when one tank corps was attacking, the other was often late in starting or totally failed to go over to active operations, or began them at a time when the first tank corps was already running out of steam, which gave the Germans the opportunity to repel their attacks in turn, making efficient use of their quite limited available forces. Arguably, only on the first day of the operation was the attack launched by the forces of Operational Group Chibisov on the main axis conducted more or less simultaneously and in coordination, which doubtlessly reflected upon the results of the fighting: the German positions were breached and the troops were able to make an advance. Unfortunately, subsequently the coordination in the actions of the operational group's units increasingly broke down, which also reflected upon the results of the combat actions.

It is also worth noting the extremely cautious and timid use of the tank corps during the period of the German counterattack, when almost half of the available forces in them stood still and took no part in the fighting at all. Both the tank corps' headquarters and the command staff of the operational group constantly acted hesitatingly, as if fearing some new German "nasty tricks", at a

17 TsAMO, F. 1 TK, op. 1, d. 4, ll. 14-15.

time when the German command was anticipating "with sinking hearts" that the Russian forces that had approached from the north would at any moment scatter the 9th Panzer Division's thin covering screen and strike the division in the flank and rear.

Of course, it is easy to see all of this today, from the vantage point of hindsight, when the strength of the opposing sides, their plans and their real actions are known exactly, so the author from today's vantage point isn't pretending to "instruct" those who actually fought back in 1942. There were often quite weighty reasons for the Soviet command's extreme, hesitating caution, the main one of which was the completely inadequate information about the enemy forces that were opposing them, as well as their regroupings and movements. In distinction from the German commanders, who were accustomed to the effective work of aerial reconnaissance and regularly relied on its information when making operational decisions, the Soviet commanders in this respect were sitting on a starvation diet, or else received no information at all from reconnaissance aircraft. In comparison with the enemy, the Soviet units took much fewer prisoners, who were also an important source of information in order to assess the enemy's strength and intentions.

Here it is appropriate to point to the German General von Mellenthin, who wrote that in the period of the summer battles of 1942, the German command was able to "look in good time" at "the other side of the hill", was aware of the Russian movements, and accordingly outpaced the Russian command in reacting to changes in the operational situation.[18] Although Mellenthin himself fought in a different sector, the characteristics of the fighting noted by him can be fully applied to the operation of Operational Group Chibisov as well. The German command as a rule knew in advance of the approach of Soviet tank columns to the front, which cannot be said about the Soviet command, which for the most part was forced to guess about the assembly of major German panzer groupings, and at times "found" them in places where they were not at all expected.

Such an unsatisfactory situation can already serve as a rebuke to the Briansk Front command, which in reality solely controlled the work of aerial reconnaissance and made all the decisions about where and when to send reconnaissance aircraft. In the documents of Operational Group Chibisov's units, one often comes across requests for aerial reconnaissance in one or another area, but in them one rarely finds any trace of whether these requests were ever carried out.

As a result, at the most intense moment of combat operations, the Soviet headquarters significantly exaggerated the enemy strength in tanks, "having discovered" (Katukov) opposite him a mythical "Hungarian panzer division" with up to "230 armored vehicles" in addition to the 9th Panzer Division. However, even when the composition of the opposing operational group of German units was sufficiently known through the result of the fighting and the testimony of prisoners, the Soviet commanders were still slow to overcome a certain timidity in front of a hostile panzer grouping, anticipating to the final moment that the Germans would, to put it figuratively, "devise some new sleight of hand" and catch them by surprise (and therefore they were keeping up to half their forces in reserve "just in case" and fighting with just the other half), while in fact the German command after 24 July no longer had the time or strength for this.

Right on cue, it is impossible not to recall the quite eloquent comment of Briansk Front's former chief of staff General Kazakov, who wrote self-critically in his recollections:

18 Von Mellenthin, *Tankovye srazheniya 1939-1945: Boevoe primenenie tankov vo vtoroi mirovoi voine* [*Panzer battles 1939-1945: Combat employment of armor in the Second World War*] (Moscow: IL, 1957), p. 143. This book has been translated into English as *Panzer Battles: A Study of the Employment of Armor in the Second World War* and published initially in 1956 by the University Press of Oklahoma.

> The events on the Voronezh axis in the summer of 1942 came right at a time when both the Front headquarters and the army headquarters were still only gaining experience in handling troops in the conditions of a complex operation, when, to say it openly, we hadn't yet succeeded in eradicating that timidity when facing enemy tank formations. This basically explains almost all of our shortcomings back then in command of the troops.[19]

The totally unsatisfactory support of the attacking units from the air affected the outcome of the operation to an even greater degree than did the insufficient conducting of aerial reconnaissance flights. Some commanders never saw any such support at all, although the units of the 2nd Air Army unquestionably exerted a lot of effort to assist our forces; in the documents of the German divisions, one regularly encounters mentions about attacks by Soviet aircraft. What is the reason behind this paradox?

Here, it seems to me, two important factors must be mentioned. When conducting the operation, the aviation of the Briansk Front as a whole, as well as that part that was supposed to support Operational Group Chibisov in particular, weren't reinforced in a fundamental manner in order to address the Front's undoubted main task at that moment on its left wing. A significant portion of the aircraft of the Briansk and Western Front's aviation grouping continued to remain on those sectors of the front where there were no active operations underway. The Soviet command didn't conduct a decisive shift of air strength from passive sectors of the front to active sectors, and instead of a rapid build-up of air strength on the left wing of Briansk Front, the air force continued to carry out a multitude of missions in its other sectors, which in essence led to a dispersal of its efforts.

The desire to have air support everywhere unavoidably led to the fact that on the decisive axis, there plainly wasn't enough combat aircraft. In this respect, the quite modest possibilities of the Luftwaffe, as it seems to me, were used much more effectively, since with a timely maneuver of air units from passive sectors of the front, the German command succeeded in timely strengthening the decisive Voronezh axis as a whole, and the VII Army Corps' sector in particular, and managed to support them with a highly intense number of combat sorties throughout the entire operation, although now on a lesser scale than was the case during the time of fighting with the 5th Tank Army two or three weeks previously.

The second negative factor consisted in the fact that there was also a lot to be desired in the effectiveness of the use of the available air units. In the first place this relates to the exceptionally important work of aviation tactically on the battlefield during the course of combat operations. The attacks by Soviet aircraft as a rule took place in the rear zone of the German forces, and although they inflicted some damage, they didn't have the needed operational effect for the Soviet ground units, which had much more significance for the success of the operation than the simple weakening of the enemy as a whole.

In contrast to the German aircraft, which were literally "hanging" above the battlefield through all those days and time after time disrupted the attack of our infantry and tied down the actions of our tanks, Soviet air units only periodically showed up above the battlefield, and because of the failure to work out cooperation, the fear of striking friendly forces, inadequate experience or erratic vectoring, they as a rule strove to attack "guaranteed" enemy targets, which were naturally easier to find in the German rear.

In sum, it is possible to note the rather characteristic way that ground units perceived the actions of enemy aircraft. In the headquarters of the German divisions, raids by Soviet aircraft seemed quite frequent, while the commander of the VII Army Corps, as we recall, even expressed the

19 *Voenno-istoricheskii zhurnal,* No. 10 (1964), p. 43.

opinion that the Soviet air force at times had aerial superiority (if only he could have heard the commanders of the Soviet units ...), but to our forces that were conducting the offensive, such Soviet air raids seemed to be of little benefit. At the decisive moment of battle, Soviet aircraft weren't suppressing the enemy resistance on the battlefield and not protecting them against attacks by enemy bombers.

The strikes by German aircraft against our forces (primarily, the infantry) had an enormous effect on their morale, which almost all of the Soviet commanders noted. The regular attacks by enemy bombers and dive bombers often had most detrimental consequences for the rifle units, and at times led to catastrophic results: a stampede from their positions, panic, and the loss of combat effectiveness. The appearance of Soviet aircraft above the battlefield also had the same enormous morale-boosting significance for our soldiers, which the commissar of the 27th Tank Brigade clearly expressed in his report:

> [Our] air force appears above the battlefield, but quickly flies away, and it rarely happens that it drives away the German bombers. The mood of the soldiers and commanders is very good whenever German aircraft are shot down. The fall of a German aircraft was seen repeatedly between 23 and 25 July. With the appearance of our fighter aircraft, the soldiers rise and joyfully charge ahead, even though the fire isn't slackening.[20]

Joyfully charge ahead ... That's the effect that air support for our ground troops had on morale. It is only a shame that it happened so rarely.

One more characteristic of the completed operation was the constant complaints of our tank commanders about the "bad" infantry, which ruined everything for them. In reality, the devastating raids by the Luftwaffe and the fierce mortar and artillery fire had a much greater effect on the infantry than on anything else. This effect was even more calamitous because of the fact that more than half of the rifle units that took part in the operation weren't veteran units, seasoned in battle, but totally green units. For example, the 167th and 237th Rifle Divisions, and in essence the 104th Rifle Brigade, were "seeing the elephant" for the first time ever in the fighting, while it was just the second time in combat for the 193rd and 284th Rifle Divisions (prior to this, the 193rd Rifle Division had fought for exactly two days, in the course of which it was virtually destroyed). Only the 340th Rifle Division had served at the front since December 1941 (with one withdrawal into the rear for replenishments in April 1942), and its command staff had significant frontline experience, which undoubtedly allowed this division to retain its combat effectiveness and come out of the battle with less heavy losses.

Nevertheless, as it seems to me, both the excessive expectations and the carping of the commanders of the other types of forces toward the infantry, which in their thinking was supposed to "accomplish marvels", and to advance fearlessly in the face of savage air attacks and fierce barrages, were unjustified. No specially-chosen bravehearts and "wonder warriors" from around the country were fighting in the rifle divisions, but simple, mortal men, the majority of which had wound up at the front for the first time in their lives and immediately became engaged in very hard combat conditions. Among the command staff, there was a significant layer of those who had just finished an accelerated course of combat schooling, as well as those civilians with a higher level of education who'd been made chiefs of the political command staffs, which didn't at all necessarily mean that they had an adequate military competency.

Thus, it isn't surprising that the personnel of those rifle units in those specific combat conditions didn't justify the hopes of the tank commanders, who were so angered by them, and on the

20 TsAMO, F. 2 TK, op. 1, d. 224 (b), l. 97.

whole didn't prove to be models of fearlessness on the battlefield. However, Chibisov didn't have any other infantry ... time and the bloody experience of war was necessary, so that the surviving number of yesterday's collective farmers, workers and intellectuals that had been called up into the Red Army could develop into tenacious, experienced and capable soldiers and commanders, and become the backbone of the Red Army's units and formations that eventually drove back the enemy. Meanwhile, they would have much to learn, and have to pay for this invaluable frontline experience with their blood and lives.

In the same way, the command staff of both the operational group and of Briansk Front should have done everything possible so that this education came with fewer casualties, and so that the combat baptism of units that were arriving at the front didn't turn into a debacle for them in almost the very first battle. For example, the solution to the calamitous effect that the Luftwaffe had on the morale of unseasoned infantry almost fully depended not on the leadership of the rifle divisions, but on the higher-standing command, which was supposed to mitigate the effect of this negative factor on the inexperienced troops with all available measures and ensure their introduction into combat following a less pell-mell timeline. Even if there had been no way to give support to the attacking troops on the battlefield with strikes by bombers and ground attack aircraft against the enemy's firing positions, had they at least been covered against continuous, unpunished bombing attacks, the actions of the operational group's rifle units would have undoubtedly been more effective. This, in turn, would have to a great extent determined the success or failure of the operation.

By the way, the German infantry divisions that took part in the operation were also not seasoned veterans of the Eastern Front. They had all been formed in the spring of 1942 shortly before the start of the summer campaign; lacked any preceding combat history; were staffed largely with conscripts and volunteers, not regulars; and had entered combat already in the summer of 1942. However, judging from everything, their personnel had nevertheless gone through a more effective course of combat training, and moreover, had participated in the fighting at least since 28 June and thus before the operation had already managed to obtain some irreplaceable frontline experience. The situation with these divisions' air support was incomparable to that which our rifle units had to experience for themselves.

Pondering the reasons for the operation's failure, it is also not possible to fail to note the problem of communications. The situation here, just as in the 5th Tank Army's preceding operation, remained unsatisfactory, and if you will, all that was noted in the *Stavka*'s 24 July order regarding communications was the clearest illustration of all this. From the analysis of the documents of the operational group's headquarters and units it follows that the primary form of communications during the operation was still by means of wire communications or liaison officers, who were supposed to deliver the paper to the necessary headquarters. As a result of this, often hours passed between the time when the order was compiled and when it was received. It isn't surprising that given such a form of communications, with a break or cutting of the wires, the Soviet command was constantly late with an operational reaction to the changes in the situation, and at times had no knowledge of the real situation on the battlefield. The subordinates, in their turn, didn't receive the necessary directives and orders on time and lost control over the course of the combat operations.

Let's turn now to the question of losses. Unfortunately, the available documentary information permits a more or less accurate assessment only on the losses of the two sides in men and tanks. At the start of the counterattack (on the evening of 22 July), the total number of serviceable tanks in the 9th Panzer Division amounted to 94. In the course of the fighting, this number fell by 24 tanks and by the end of 28 July, amounted to 70 – the smallest number over all the days of the operation. Primarily the number of operational Pz III tanks decreased (from 64 on the evening of 22 July to 52 by the end of 28 July), which isn't surprising: as the most numerous tanks in the

9th Panzer Division, they bore the main burden of the fighting. Nevertheless, not a single one of the Pz III tanks were lost irrecoverably. The only irrecoverable losses of the 9th Panzer Division in tanks between 23 and 28 July were two Pz IV tanks.[21] One assault gun of the 201st Sturmgeschütz Battalion was also left burned-out and completely destroyed.[22]

In the course of fighting between 21 and 29 July inclusively, the Soviet tank units irrecoverably lost the following number of tanks:

1st Tank Corps – 2 KV, 31 T-34, 7 T-70 and 5 T-60.[23]
2nd Tank Corps – 14 KV, 22 T-34 and 3 T-60.[24]
7th Tank Corps – 7 KV, 8 T-34 and 2 T-60.[25]
11th Tank Corps – 1 Mk II Matilda.[26]
118th Tank Brigade – 3 KV, 5 T-34 and 5 T-70.[27]

The losses of the 201st Tank Brigade in tanks are unknown. On 21 July the brigade had 18 British Mk II Matilda tanks and 16 T-60.[28] On 29 July the brigade had 12 Mk II (two of which were under repair) and 11 T-60 (two of which were under repair) still remaining.[29]

Thus, 24 KV, 66 T-34, 1 Mk II, 10 T-60 and 12 T-70 tanks were irrecoverably lost. This yields a total (excluding the 201st Tank Brigade) of 123 tanks irrecoverably lost, of which 90 were T-34 or KV tanks.

The main burden of struggle with the Soviet tanks fell to the German anti-tank artillery, the losses of which can only be presumed on the basis of information on the availability of heavy, combat-ready anti-tank guns (75-mm German anti-tank guns and 76-mm updated French and Soviet guns) in the elements that took part in the fighting. If one considers that the decrease in the number of anti-tank guns occurred as a result of combat losses and not as a result of guns knocked out of commission due to breakdowns (a gun is not a tank, and malfunctions here are much less likely, although still possible, and thus we believe that in the majority of cases, an anti-tank gun was rendered inoperable as a result of enemy actions); if so, then taking into account possible replacements[30], it is possible to assume that the German anti-tank gun elements lost approximately 32-37 heavy anti-tank guns.[31] Undoubtedly, there were comparable losses in anti-tank guns of a smaller caliber.

It is worth observing that many Soviet commanders noted the key, decisive role played by the German anti-tank artillery in the struggle with Soviet tanks. The sharpest and most emotional, if you will, is the statement by the commander of the 11th Tank Corps General Lazarev, who in his account of the recent fighting wrote about something painful, without restraining himself in his words:

21 NARA, T-315, roll 2199, fr. 000839.
22 Ibid.
23 TsAMO, F. 1 TK, op. 1, d. 4, l. 28.
24 TsAMO, F. 202, op. 5, d. 238, l. 496; and F. 27 tbr, op. 2, d. 3, l. 27.
25 TsAMO, F. 38 A, op. 9005, d. 42, l. 20; F. 62 tbr, op. 1, d. 4, l. 30; F. 87 tbr, op. 1, d. 5, l. 162; and F. 87 tbr, op. 1, d. 5, l. 158.
26 TsAMO, F. 11 TK, op. 1, d. 19, l. 163.
27 TsAMO, F. 202, op. 50, d. 14, l. 291.
28 TsAMO, F. 201 tbr, op. 1, d. 5, l. 5.
29 TsAMO, F. 202, op. 5, d. 238, l. 504.
30 I couldn't find information in the captured German documents regarding the replacements for the enemy's anti-tank battalions during the fighting. It is fully possible that some of the battalions received replacements, as indicated by a slight increase in the number of combat-ready guns over the period from 26 to 28 July.
31 NARA, T-314, roll 354, fr. 000201-219; roll 354, fr. 001266-001268.

> On our front, there is some particularly cowardly artillery in the 193rd, 237th and 340th Rifle Divisions. As soon as enemy tanks appear, they flee beyond the Don. An end must be put to such a situation, and we will do this. The artilleryman's honor is to conduct the struggle against enemy tanks. Our superb 76-mm Model 1939 divisional cannons easily penetrate any enemy tank. The gun is cheaper than a tank, so even if it is lost, then it is to our advantage.
>
> The enemy artillery confronts our tanks; his tanks always cowardly hide behind it from our tanks. It is necessary for our artillery to do this too.[32] Given an enemy tank attack, the 76-mm battery should immediately occupy open positions on an anti-tank front. [...] The TP guns [tank support guns – I.S.] that are supporting the tanks must be in their place, and this must be checked. They should also appear timely on a new line, in order not to leave the tanks without cover. If necessary, they can be towed by the tanks.[33]

The total losses of the German units in personnel in the fighting with the forces of Briansk Front's operational group over the period from 21 to 29 July 1942 amounted to approximately 3,700 men killed, wounded or missing.[34] By German standards, these were very heavy losses.

Alas, our losses were much greater. The losses for the rifle[35] (including the 3rd Destroyer Anti-tank Artillery Brigade) and cavalry units (8th Cavalry Corps) over this same period amounted to approximately 26,000 men.[36] (The scale of the Soviet command's estimations of the size of the losses, judging from everything, is noticeably different from the German estimates. Moreover, in the headquarters of Operational Group Chibisov, they optimistically believed that the enemy had suffered greater losses than the units of the operational group ...[37]). Approximately 6,000 of our military servicemen went missing in action. A significant share of them became prisoners, the rest were killed in battle, but weren't considered KIAs in the documents. According to German data, in the fighting between 21 and 26 July, 2,643 Soviet soldiers, commanders and political staff members were taken prisoner (according to other data, 2,718[38]), and on the battlefield "the bodies of approximately 5,500 dead enemy soldiers were counted" (having in mind only the area of operations of the 9th Panzer Division and the 340th, 385th and 387th Infantry Divisions, and excluding the 82nd and 377th Infantry Division's sectors of defense).[39]

After the fighting between 21 and 28 July, the 193rd and 284th Rifle Divisions had taken so many casualties that Briansk Front's command was compelled to pull them from the front and

---

32 Lazarev's desire to disparage the hated foe by calling him cowardly is understandable. However, arguably it was more correct and accurate to say that the withdrawal of the German tanks behind the anti-tank artillery was not at all a manifestation of the German tankers' cowardice, but a tried and tested tactical practice, which allowed the German command to conserve their costly tanks in order to carry out decisive tasks on the main axis. In the conditions as they existed at that moment, such a tactic for the Germans made even more sense because of the fact that in an open battle with Soviet T-34 and KV tanks, the overwhelming majority of the German tanks were in a disadvantageous situation because of their lesser firepower and thinner armor. Thus the enemy conserved them, avoiding any tank duels, and as far as possible sought to avoid any tank clashes with our tanks. In essence, this was just what Lazarev was proposing when he acknowledged with annoyance the correctness of such "cowardly" enemy actions.

33 TsAMO, F. 2 TK, op. 1, d. 55, l. 52.

34 This follows from the summation of the available data for the divisions and a statistical assumption for the 82nd Infantry Division. NARA, T-314, roll 355, fr. 000505-507.

35 I could not find information on the losses of the 119th and 106th Rifle Brigades in the archive, but since their participation in the fighting was quite limited, it is possible to assume that they didn't suffer many casualties.

36 TsAMO, F. 202, op. 7, d. 72, ll. 433-455, with the inclusion of data for the 284th Rifle Division taken from the lists of irrecoverable losses in Memorial's consolidated database.

37 TsAMO, F. 38 A, op. 9005, d. 39, l. 15.

38 NARA, T-314, roll 353, fr. 000420.

39 NARA, T-314, roll 353, fr. 000912-915.

send them to the deep rear for replenishments and regeneration. For the sake of justice it must be said that by the start of the Soviet offensive, both of these divisions had been already engaged in combat operations (the 284th Rifle Division had defended Kastornoe for three days, then came out of encirclement and conducted combat operations for several more days before the start of the operation, while the 193rd Rifle Division had fought for two days as part of the 5th Tank Army), but it was precisely Operational Group Chibisov's operation that ultimately rendered them combat-ineffective.

Of the eight tank and two motorized rifle brigades that took part in the fighting (excluding the tank brigades of the 7th Tank Corps, which took part only in the counterattack on 25 July), there are data on the irrecoverable losses [killed or missing in action] for only eight of them (there are no data for the 27th Tank Brigade and 2nd Motorized Rifle Brigade). The total number of just the irrecoverable losses of personnel for these brigades (minus the 1st Motorized Rifle Brigade) amounts to 725 men.[40] The headquarters of the 1st Motorized Rifle Brigade reported on 28.7.42 that the brigade had lost 549 men, of which 404 failed to come out of the Lebiazh'e pocket.[41] One can assume that with the inclusion of the two other brigades, of which one was a motorized rifle brigade, the irrecoverable losses of the operational group's tank and motorized rifle units exceeded 1,400 men. (According to the incomplete data of the 1st Tank Corps' headquarters alone, the total losses of the corps in that operation amounted to 820 men.)[42] If you take as an average statistical correlation of wounded to killed and mortally wounded as 3 to 1 (it was often even greater), then the total manpower losses of the 1st and 2nd Tank Corps and the 118th and 201st Tank Brigades in killed, wounded and missing in action most likely substantially exceeded 3,500 men.

With the inclusion of the losses of the 59th Tank Brigade, the tank and motorized rifle brigades of the 7th Tank Corps, the artillery regiments as well as other specialized units of Briansk Front's operational group, its total losses in the operation amounted to approximately 30,000 men, which is approximately 8 times greater than the enemy's losses. Such was the cost to "grind down" the enemy forces – an expression to which some historians frequently resorted (and continue to do so!), trying to find something positive even in failed operations. In reality, from my point of view, it is totally impossible to speak of anything positive coming out of this operation, since to put one hostile soldier out of commission, our troops had to lose eight of their own. It must be said directly that in such operations, the Soviet command was grinding down not so much the enemy as their own men.

At the same time, this author is far from the viewpoint of considering the completed operation a glittering German victory and some model to imitate, despite, it would seem, the success achieved. On the one hand, the German command had every right to consider (and did consider) the outcome of the fighting successful: the German counterattack's main objective was achieved, the crisis on the front of the VII Army Corps had been eliminated, and the tottering defensive front restored. However, on the other hand the enemy didn't succeed in implementing what had been planned in full measure and plain hitches and uncoordination in the actions of the German units' fighting were also observed, although not on the same scale as in the case of Operational Group Chibisov's forces.

In addition, this operation plainly demonstrated once again, if you will, the main defect in German strategy, which became increasingly obvious as the war continued: the available forces were incommensurate to the assigned tasks. In the fighting of local significance against Operational

40 According to the available data in Memorial's consolidated database and the information in the operational documents.

41 TsAMO, F. 19 mbr, op. 1, d. 6, l. 158.

42 TsAMO, F. 1 TK, op. 1, d. 4, l. 28.

Group Chibisov that had just passed, this problem was reflected as if in a drop of water. Even at the start of the German counterattack, the strength of the German grouping was inferior to the opposing Soviet units in numbers, and with the approach of the reserve 7th and 11th Tank Corps to the front (even if they hadn't yet been brought back up to full strength after the preceding battles), the numerical superiority of the operational group's forces over the enemy, particularly in tanks, became obvious.

Against the 96 tanks of the 9th Panzer Division that were available on the evening of 24 July, of which only four were Pz IV armed with the long-barrel 75-mm gun;[43] in the Soviet 1st, 2nd, 7th and 11th Tank Corps and the 118th and 201st Tank Brigades there were approximately 330 operational tanks, of which 135-140 were medium and heavy tanks with the 76.2-mm gun, the armor-piercing shells of which could penetrate any German armored vehicle. By 26 July, the number of combat-ready German tanks was likely even lower as a result of the fighting on 25 July. It isn't surprising that the German tanks constantly declined battle with our tanks, and the Germans sought to confront our tanks with anti-tank artillery while conserving their own tanks (which was frequently taken by our tank crews as a sign of the German tankers' cowardice and their fear of Soviet tanks).

It is worth noting that the chronic lack of strength forced the German command to improvise continually, to shift forces from passive sectors of the front to active sectors, to create various sorts of improvised combat groups in order to resolve short-term tasks, and in general and on the whole to take great risks in operations, placing them on "a knife's edge", relying upon not the objective correlation of forces, but on the blindly accepted conviction that the German command and German soldier were superior to their Soviet counterparts. Moreover, as the fighting became increasingly bitter, the length of the frontline extended, and the Wehrmacht's strength increasingly dwindled, the German commanders at various levels of command were compelled to resort to risky decisions increasingly more often. In the long-term perspective, this inevitably led to the situation when one more risky decision would ultimately turn into a catastrophe, since in the command of the troops one mustn't rely on the fickle factor of "qualitative superiority" to the extreme and overindulge in risky decisions.

In the just completed operation, the Germans got away with such an approach. Because of mistakes by the Soviet command and the effective countermeasures by the German command, (let's acknowledge this directly), the enemy wasn't crushed or even shoved back to the south, although the forces of the operational group had sufficient capabilities to accomplish this. However, the war didn't end with this. Its Moloch continued to roll to the south, toward Stalingrad and the Caucasus, where its decisive battles were soon to take place. The bitter lessons of the summer campaign, the continuous quantitative and qualitative improvement of the Red Army and the accompanying weakening of the Wehrmacht, which was already straining its human and material resources, meant that a fundamental turning point in the Great Patriotic War was inexorably approaching.

However, the path to it was long and bloody …

43 NARA, T-315, roll 541, fr. 000725.

Afterword

More than 70 years have passed since the events described in this book; the overwhelming majority of our country's citizens has been born and grown up already since the war, and several generations have come and gone in the world. New trees have sprung up in the woods and groves once torn apart by shell fragments, the battlefields have been plowed, seeded and harvested many times, and more than 70 times the spring floods have filled and washed away the craters, trenches and bunkers left behind by the war.

Almost no visible traces of the war at the places of past battles from 1942 remain, which isn't surprising. Time and nature gradually "healed" the wartime scars left behind on the earth, but of course the main reason for their disappearance was human labor. Work grandiose in scale to convert the former battlefields into peacetime fields began soon after the local residents returned in the spring of 1943 to the villages and hamlets left devastated by the war. The first labor brigades (consisting in their overwhelming majority of women and adolescents) of the revived collective farms on liberated territory took up work that was completely foreign to them – erasing traces of the war from the farmland. Yet they immediately ran into a problem, which they couldn't resolve through their own efforts – the fields that were once part of the front were strewn with unexploded munitions and minefields.

Of course, military men were supposed to have gathered all of the explosive devices and cleared the former minefields, but in connection with the rapidly receding frontline, there were almost no military units left in the liberated areas by the spring of 1943, which might have taken up this important task. The attacking Red Army had pushed far to the west, and the clearing of mines in the rear areas given the acute lack of specialized sapper elements became a question for an indeterminate future.

The problem with the "legacy" left behind by the war arose immediately. Already soon after the return of people to the liberated areas, the number of mine detonations and explosions of live ammunition became frightening. Having returned to their native lands, the local residents saw that there was simply nowhere for them to live, since almost all of the structures in their villages had been burned down or blown apart. At first many were simply forced to find shelter in abandoned dugouts, including those that had once been along the front, with all the mine fields remaining there. In the search for building materials, they took apart the empty bunkers and carried away lumber from their overhead cover back to their devastated villages, and then headed back again, searching time after time for whatever they could scrounge in the positions left behind by the troops and take back to use for their households and farmsteads. Thus, the appearance of both adults and children on the fatally dangerous battlefields was not at all a coincidence, but a necessary measure.

The local residents first had to follow well-trodden footpaths along the former front – so serious was the risk of a mine explosion. But whereas adults observed all the necessary precautions and were fully cognizant of the danger lurking in the fields, one can't say the same about adolescents and children, unfortunately. For the most part left on their own, they naively believed (in accordance with their ages) that nothing would happen to them personally. They often ignored the danger, and in violation of stern warnings, they nevertheless went out to the places of past fighting not only to search for needed items, but also to "investigate" them out of childish curiosity. There, they would trigger explosions and pay for their lack of caution with crippling injuries or death.

In addition, it was impossible to do any work in the fields at the former battlefields before eliminating the threat of triggering mines or live ammunition. According to the recollections of elderly people, in the spring of 1943 small teams of sappers arrived in the district and had just started work to remove the mines, but soon, obviously in connection with the fighting that had started around the Kursk bulge, they were called back by command, without having completed what they had started. In the existing situation, before departing they could only mark dangerous sectors on the former frontline with warning signs and hang warning markers in the patches of wood that were crisscrossed with barbed wire and "blanketed" with unexploded ammunition in the hope of one day returning to resume work on completely clearing the mines and cleaning up those places, thereby at least protecting the local residents before that time arrived. The engineers departed, and the patches of woods, meadows and fields not fully free of mines remained behind …

A resident of the village of Spasskoe A.I. Bukovshin recalled that he often roamed across the former frontline positions accompanied by other adolescents, where "there was still a lot of stuff". In the fields it was still possible to find a rifle and even mortars; they often found our Moisin-Nagant rifles, but it was hard to come by the 7.62-mm ammunition for them on the battlefields. On the German side of the lines, everything was the opposite: there were more than enough mortar rounds, shells and bullets in abandoned cases, belts, magazines or simply scattered on the ground, but they rarely came across a weapon, which created certain difficulties for the lads in amusing themselves with target practice. Nevertheless, these difficulties were overcome with "excellent" searches, and the adolescents quickly learned through the process of trial and error how to handle any gun they found. A.I. Bukovshin told me, "When already after the war I arrived in the army, my commander was surprised that I easily knew how to handle a firearm or a grenade, and could shoot like a real marksman."

The problem of clearing the mines was very serious, and it had to be resolved as soon as possible, but the Red Army had no means for this in the existing circumstances, and, it seems, this couldn't be anticipated any time soon. So the leadership of the liberated areas together with the military enlistment offices took the only reliable decision in the situation that had arisen: to organize special teams from local adolescents, to teach them about mines and blasting work, and under the direction of assigned soldiers set to work to completely clear the ground of mines. A lot of such teams were formed in a short time in the areas of Voronezh, Orel and Kursk Oblasts that had been liberated in the winter of 1943.

For the extent of at least two years, they were busy with this dangerous work, going out into the fields, ravines and patches of wood almost daily, and methodically, step by step, clearing them of the enormous quantity of mines and munitions left behind by the war. For the 14- to 17-year-old adolescents and youth, this became, in essence, an everyday job, in the course of which they quickly grew up, demonstrating self-sacrifice and courage on their trips to clear the mines. In silent, tiring, constantly stressful and extremely dangerous encounters with lurking death, many of them became genuine professionals at what they were doing. Alas, the work didn't go by without casualties. In the mine clearing groups, there were killed and maimed among the adolescents, who met their soldier's fate even before they could become soldiers, having barely left childhood. I bow my head before their memory and courage.

Unfortunately, their accomplishment remained, for the most part, unrecorded, and the history of their military service to the Motherland even before being called up into the army has in essence not been researched. That makes the testimony of eyewitnesses to those long ago events that come to us even more valuable, especially if they were direct participants. In 2010 I was able to have a conversation with one of them. Here are his recollections (my interviewee's style of speech has been preserved):

Petr Grigor'evich Samodurov, born in 1927, village of Bol'shaia Vereika
The Germans came, surrounded our guys, and took a lot of prisoners here. The Germans made a clean sweep of the residents and evacuated them. We went every which way. They drove us away to the Zemliansk area, and [from] there – some to Kursk, some to wherever else. We came back to our home, it had a ruined stove; we had made it ourselves. We made a cooker outside; that's when neighbors came running up to us: "There she goes, let's boil something up; who -- whatever". We dug up old potatoes.

The Germans never explained anything – anything, nothing! "Rus'! Get moving!" and showed us which way to go. We went, some wearing nothing but a shirt! Whatever anyone could grab, some just the underclothing at hand …

The collective farm was called "Lenin's path". There were 13 collective farms in our village. The center of it had been heavily mined, where our shop is now and on that side. On our side it wasn't dangerous. The Germans had laid a lot of mines; I myself went to clear them. They gathered us through the military enlistment center and they sent a specialist. They registered us. They trained us about a month. We arrived in the month of March, and in April we already went to clear mines. They led us into a field where the Germans had been. We cleared the front-line and bunkers of mines, and I was wounded by a mine explosion. There were anti-personnel mines, and they had three prongs; they sent us to clear them and told us to walk cautiously. There was a senior lieutenant with us. He warned us, "Careful, when you see a spike, remove it!" Well, we would insert a linch pin and fish out this mine. But some guy was next to me, how should I call him? A damned fool, he stepped on a mine (after all, when a guy stepped on a mine, he had to say "Get down!"); some guys dropped, but I was on my hands and knees, handling a mine, and caught a splash of pellets in both legs! These mines had 360 pellets, and one pellet would break apart into four pieces. The mine springs up a half-meter and explodes.

Somehow they dragged me away from there. The other guy got hit in the back by the pellets, but he survived as well. Well, they carried me further, we had some medical unit nearby, there was a doctor; they bandaged me and I made it home somehow with a crutch. In sum, it hurt for another month, though true the pellets didn't hit a bone, but simply soft tissue …

The mine's prongs were already visible. But they were in tall weeds. In some places there were trip wires, but not many. They weren't metal wires, but from a material that had already rotted. We all survived, we had an experienced senior lieutenant, a Siberian. He was also a war invalid; they sent him from the military enlistment center. He was alerting us all the time and giving us instructions.

We would get there about 8:00 or 9:00 in the morning. What did you bring along? A boiled potato and that's all, nothing more! Later we protested in the enlistment center – we won't go! Give us military rations! They began to give us military rations. Flour, butter, a little sugar … We went to Lebiazh'e, to Pavlovka, to Lomovo, we were everywhere. There was a machine-tractor station (now a gas station); there we had a round shed, and there we would gather from all the surrounding villages, since we had one team. There were about 30 of us. We went all summer and all fall to clear mines, and we didn't get any days off.

The anti-tank mines, they weighed about 8 kilograms; they didn't corrode a bit. Our mines made from wooden boxes were all falling apart; everything had deteriorated from the sun … We gathered the mines into a pile and blew them up in a field. We'd dig out a small hole, lay them in it, attach a blasting fuse and run away; this fuse was short, we'd light a piece of cotton wadding, then get under cover or run away. Next we'd wait for the signal. Then it would blow up.

We cleared mines until the month of September 1944. Later on 29 November we were called up into the army.

The first collective farmer brigades would move into the cleared fields in the wake of the adolescent-sappers. Their primary task was to gather and bury the corpses that hadn't been collected since the summer battles of 1942, which showed up in large numbers after the springtime thaw of 1943. With the warmer weather, the bodies of the dead that had frozen in the winter began to thaw under the warming rays of the springtime sun, filling the silent fields of the former front with a rotting stench.

The burials in the spring and summer of 1943 were carried out in various ways. Wherever there was the possibility, the located bodies were taken to nearby villages and buried there in fraternal graves. For example, P.G. Samodurov recalled, "In the fields there was a lot of dead bodies … there was a lot of our dead. … But when did we have time to bury them? We had no time for this. Our job was to clear mines. The dead were especially gathered in the collective farm; they assigned horses and carried the bodies to the place where we now have this monument. For each corpse we found, they'd pay us 5 "labor days".[1]

If there was no way to transport the bodies to a village (or there was not any time or strength for this), they were buried wherever they were found – in fields, patches of woods and ravines. As a rule, such sanitary burials were done in a nearby shell crater or trench, without searching the rotting corpse for documents or the death medallion.[2] At the same time, according to numerous statements by the elderly, in the overwhelming majority of cases, the bodies that were found were those of our soldiers, while unburied German dead were many times fewer. The Germans timely buried their own dead in cemeteries that had been created for that purpose in the near rear. After the Germans retreated, these cemeteries everywhere were leveled to the ground, leaving no trace of them behind, while if the Germans burial sites were established in well-known public places, then all the graves were exhumed and the despised corpses were hauled away.

After the collection and burial of the dead, the local residents set to work to prepare the fields for planting. There were so many craters, trenches and bunkers in them that it required a lot of time to fill them in, gradually and step by step, and to collect the barbed wire (which was often subsequently used to protect gardens, where it continues to "carry out its service" even to this day), and finally, to put the field in suitable condition for agricultural work. Only knocked-out vehicles and tanks continued to remain for many years on commemorative hilltops marking the fighting of 1942. At the end of the 1940s and beginning of the 1950s, they began to haul them away as well. Brigades of workers arrived in the fields and used blow torches to cut up the military equipment that had stood there since 1942 and carried it away for scrap metal. Thus, the last sad "monuments" gradually disappeared from their combat positions. Plowing of the fields gradually concealed even the war's smaller bits of metal – the countless shell fragments and cartridges.

In the early 1950s in the course of a large-scale Stalinist campaign to recreate nature, the hills that had been profusely soaked with blood were planted with forest belts, which strongly altered the appearance of the battlefield and restricted the line of sight from the hilltops. By that time, there were already no clear traces of the war left on the cultivated areas of land; old craters, trenches and bunkers could be found only in those places where they didn't get in the way of people – in the remaining uncultivated meadows, and in ravines and patches of woods. In one such wooded ravine, I had my first encounter with the war that had thundered so many years ago.

1 Ed. note: Under Stalin, collective farmers weren't paid any money. Instead, at the end of the agricultural season, they would receive products like kilograms of flour, butter, millet, etc. for each day of labor. They would then try to get to a market to sell what they could to obtain money.

2 Ed. Note: These medallions were given to Red Army soldiers early in the war. They were small wooden boxes or plastic capsules that contained each soldier's ID written on a rolled-up slip of paper. Soon, most soldiers stopped wearing the medallions, because they superstitiously thought that they were sure omens of their own impending deaths in battle.

In the autumn of 1981 as part of an expedition to the battle locations that had been organized by the history department of a local university, for the first time I saw visible traces of the distant fighting from 1942. On the slope of a ravine, you could clearly see a very lengthy communications trench leading up to a rifle pit. We climbed the trench, scrambling through the branches of trees that had grown up around it, before stopping in the pit and quietly taking in the view of the empty field that stretched far into the distance and looking around. Within the rifle pit itself, just out of curiosity I briefly scraped the dried autumn leaves beneath our feet with my shoe. Imagine my surprise when from beneath my shoe, a dark Soviet rifle cartridge rolled out on the bottom of the pit that had been partially filled in with the passage of time. Next to it I immediately found several more of its silent sisters.

For me, born almost 20 years after the war's end, this unexpected finding was a genuine discovery. It turned out that visible evidence of the war hadn't totally disappeared; they were simply hidden from your eyes, but were quite nearby, literally under your feet. Someone had been firing from this rifle pit back in 1942, had climbed and descended along this communications trench, and lived and fought in his combat post in this now silent ravine. Who was this fighter? In what unit did he serve? How did he fight?

I recall that at the time I was suddenly seized by the desire to find out what had happened here, and what events had unfolded on these now peaceful fields and hills. At the same time, my first scholarly interest in that which was connected with the military history of those places woke up inside me.

Subsequently on numerous trips to the places of fighting, my friends and I visited all the memorable fields, patches of woods and hills described in this book, and went over the length and breadth of the former front and preserved combat positions. On these trips, I came across metallic relics of the war that were lying here and there on the ground.[3] However, I never conducted a search and at first wasn't even familiar with searchers, although I repeatedly came across the traces of their diggings. In May 1992 I even unexpectedly stumbled upon an entire group of Voronezh searchers who were at work in a patch of woods, and with my own eyes I saw how much the earth is still concealing.

With the appearance of readily-available metal detectors, the number of recovered historical artifacts has grown several-fold. There, where previously I had come across only rusty pieces of metal lying under my feet, now one comes upon deposits of military hardware that have been dug up and abandoned by diggers, and one can only guess what they carried away with themselves back then. Gradually, the owners of metal detectors "checked out" and "hollowed out" all of the still-preserved trenches, bunkers and shell craters in the area and switched to searching the still unexplored fields, where for years no traces of the war have remained on the surface. Here, success of a search now greatly depended upon simple luck in "snagging" a long ago filled-in trench, in order to then have a stroll along its approximate configuration.

3 In September 1991 on one of my trips with friends, when passing through Lebiazh'e we stopped at one of the residences and asked for water. We spoke with the homeowners. Having learned about what was compelling us to "walk around the surrounding fields and patches of woods with heavy backpacks", the elderly head of the family unexpectedly announced that they also had a trace of the war in their yard – the barrel of a genuine cannon! To my astonishment this proved to be the truth, which he eagerly demonstrated to us. Along a wall of the residence, there was the barrel of a 76-mm divisional gun, raised at a height that was comfortable for sitting. For long decades, it has been resting here, used by the homeowners as a unique bench for get-togethers. I couldn't restrain myself, and not fully trusting my eyes, laid my palm on the cannon's cold metal, which had been silent since 1942. It was remarkable: Almost 50 years since the fighting had died away I was unexpectedly touching a mute eyewitness to it and participant in it.

Searches on the ground have also permitted the confirmation of archival documents with factual evidence. For example, in the former sector of the German 340th Infantry Division's combat, a multitude of items of French manufacture has been found, which is readily explainable, since this division had formed up in France in the spring of 1942. It is completely obvious that prior to its departure to the Eastern Front at the threshold to the summer campaign, the soldiers and officers of the 340th Infantry Division stocked up on a large quantity of fashionable everyday French trinkets, which were later left on Russian soil. Just like, incidentally, many of their dead owners, who didn't survive until the winter of 1943 when the 340th Infantry Division, fearing encirclement, hastily abandoned these places forever and retreated.

I personally held one of these French items in my hands at the end of the 1990s, when we found it lying unnoticed in slightly withered foliage in German positions in the woods on Hill 218.7. It was a delicate, round container with a rather well-preserved inscription on a coarse-grained surface that had darkened with time. At first we couldn't even figure out what it was. Indeed, later, when its double lid was pried apart with a knife and the top cover had popped off, having removing the lower lid, we found the container lightly packed with a substance of a delicate pink color. Only then did it become clear that this had been part of some sort of traveling kit of small lidded jars, one of which contained toothpaste. Most surprising was the fact that it still had a clearly discernible, characteristic pleasant aroma! I repeat that we found this little jar lying directly on the ground.

However, I never suspected back then how many similar types of relics were under the ground! Reports from searchers allow us to make this judgement. In the area of the German division's positions, a large number of items have been found, which even after the passage of more than 70 years since the fighting of 1942, eloquently testify who their owners were, and from where all these "goods" wound up in Russia's interior. These include tin cans of Portugese sprats supplied to the Wehrmacht (which still have well-preserved lettering and color, some already semi-opened by a key that spins around the metal lid); numerous collapsible tubes of various types with easily read brand names on their colorful sides; little tin boxes of various types and sizes; tent pegs, buckles, buttons and similar metal "gimmicks"; and even well-preserved sheaves of paper. In one of the bunkers, an overseas cockleshell was found, which served as an ash tray for its inhabitants.

It is characteristic that on our side of the frontline, one practically never encounters a similar type of foreign "sheen"; the everyday items that have been found are simple and plain, and the "company" labels on them are not brand names, but the names of the possessor scratched into the surface with something sharp. Instead of aluminum canteens, which the Germans had, in the findings on the Soviet side of the line one frequently encounters heavy glass flasks – a typical sign of a Red Army soldier's equipment in 1942. Together with the ammunition, these flasks, found together with a set of human remains, eloquently speak to the fact that a soldier of the Red Army was their owner.

Here, it is time to talk about one more, alas, typical characteristic, which distinguished and still distinguishes searches on the Soviet side of the frontline (here, of course, the discussion is about the areas that were the focus of this study): together with the personal ammunition and equipment on the former battlefields, one still finds the remains of our soldiers as well. Frequently they are found thanks to the sound of metal objects that remained with them in the earphones of the metal detectors. The discovery of German remains on the battlefield happens much more rarely. How can this be explained?

In my view, it is possible to explain this with the fact that right up until the enemy's hasty retreat in the winter of 1942/1943, the German units as a rule managed to keep possession of the battlefield, restore the lines they had lost, and thus had the possibility to bury their own dead in the cemeteries dedicated for that purpose in the near rear. The German traits of organization and order in this matter important for maintaining the troops' morale are evident. The soldier at the front shouldn't have to see the rotting, unburied corpses of their combat comrades.

Unfortunately, no matter how bitter it is to write this, it must be acknowledged that the matter with the search and honorable burial of the fallen stood much worse in our units. Even in those areas where the outcome of the fighting left the battlefield in Soviet possession, the dead often continued to lie wherever they fell, or they were buried on the spot, in the nearest shell crater, covered only with a shallow layer of dirt, often without even removing their documents and death medallion. Because of such an attitude, many of the dead soldiers were left as missing-in-action in the documents, even though they were in fact killed.[4]

Unfortunately, their ultimate oblivion was pre-determined by the fact that the subsequently conducted sanitary burials were not satisfactorily marked, and in the fields not marked at all. The little stars (or else simply markers) on the graves scattered everywhere, which were crafted from whatever material that was at hand, quickly fell into a state of decay, disintegrated, and as a result the hastily conducted burials for the most part became lost to time.

Such a historical-cultural "inheritance" greatly hinders today the discovery of the fates of those soldiers who went missing in action and the proper military burials, but will ensure the work of searchers for more long years. Their primary aim, of course, is not the discovery of all types of "things", but to find and give a proper burial to the soldiers' remains that have yet to be found on the battlefields or continue to lie in graves that became lost after the war.

It must be noted that the accuracy and effectivenesss of the searches in recent years has grown substantially due to the fact that high-quality aerial photographs from the war years have become accessible to scholars. With the assistance of special computer programs and contemporary satellite images, it is now possible not only to compare the terrain, but also to "fix" accurately on them those trenches, shell craters, gun pits and bunkers from 1942 that are today not visible on the surface of the ground.

Thanks to this, successful targeted searches have been done in recent years on the formerly enormous, featureless fields, where it would seem even the slightest trace of the former positions had already been lost forever. The discovery of the remains of a T-34 tank of the 62nd Tank Brigade's forward detachment, which was destroyed in the brigade's first combat action on 6 July 1942 in the area north of the village of Malopokrovka, can be given as an example of one such exploration. Specific pieces of this tank were found exactly on the spot where it had been fixed on a large-scale aerial photograph, and the fact that according to historical documents, there were no T-34 tanks from other brigades in that area throughout the extent of all the fighting, allows the virtually unambiguous assertion that the recovered pieces belong specifically to a tank from the 62nd Tank Brigade's forward detachment (one can read about this episode in my previous book, *General Liziukov i ego armiia* [*General Liziukov and his army*], which will be translated and published by Helion Press at some point in the future).

One more example of such a targeted search is the recent discovery on Hill 188.5 of the remains of tanks identified on a 1942 German aerial reconnaissance photograph. In the associated spot in the field, searchers discovered pieces of armor and a large quantity of 20-mm shell casings from a ShVAK cannon – the sign of a Soviet T-60 tank. Another tank proved to be a destroyed T-34 or KV, judging from the large amount of metal in the large pits, as well as the remnants of a DT machine gun, the ammunition load and other details. A set of human remains was discovered next

4 It is worth citing here an excerpt from a political report written by the 118th Tank Brigade's political chief Battalion Commissar Kudriagin on 30.7.42: "So far I've been unable to establish the individual names of the dead and missing-in-action. The soldiers and commanders who were buried on the battlefield on 28 July were in their majority unidentified, since they had decayed; some had been run over by tanks, and another portion burned beyond recognition." In this same report he reported that the brigade's casualty count he had provided didn't include the losses in the motorized rifle battalion, which at that moment still hadn't been determined. (TsAMO, F. 118 tbr, op. 1, d. 47, l. 33.

to it. The remains had no identifying signs, but the absence of infantry equipment (helmet, gas mask, cartridge pouch, etc.) speaks to the fact that most likely he was a tanker.

As discussed previously, a recently discovered German aerial reconnaissance photograph also allows an assumption regarding the exact location of Liziukov's knocked-out KV tank with a great degree of probability. The point is that the only photograph of the area of the 2nd Tank Corps commander's death previously available to me was an aerial photograph taken on 28 July 1942, which because of its scale, photography conditions and time of year made it extremely difficult to determine where knocked-out tanks might be located. A majority of the tiny objects merged so completely into the generally dark gray background of the July field that it wasn't possible to speak confidently about any unambiguous identification of machines.

A winter-time photograph of this same area yielded totally different possibilities. In the first place, the snow-covered fields ensured a flat, white backdrop, against which anything dark clearly stood out. In the second place, the identification of the objects rising above the snow was substantially eased by the lengthy shadows they cast due to the low winter sun. Thus, in the area of the southern fringe of the woods south of Lebiazh'e, several dark objects are clearly distinguishable on the photograph, which are located on the road and off to the side of it. Judging from the fact that Liziukov's tank wasn't evacuated and remained on the battlefield (which follows from Soviet documents), one can assert with a great deal of confidence that one of these dark objects is in fact Liziukov's knocked-out KV tank. Incidentally, in message threads on historical Internet forums, there are already mentions that several fragments presumably from a KV tank have been found in this area. By "linking" the found aerial photograph to the actual ground, someone can conduct an accurately targeted search on it and try to uncover the remnants of tank parts in the designated places.

During my work on this book, I received several letters from the ancestors or relatives of Soviet soldiers that fell in those battles. These letters that contain a story of the fate of the KIAs, the search for their gravesite, and a desire to learn the truth about their last battle and deaths allowed me, so to speak, to "see the faces" of the ordinary participants in the events described here (which are usually hopelessly lost somewhere in the background, when talking about the actions of armies and generals) and to learn about carefully preserved family relics and both the memory and the pain, which to the present day don't give any peace to our contemporaries. For them, the deceased fathers and grandfathers were not faceless numbers in the tally of irrecoverable losses, but those singular and beloved men, the death of which remains for their ancestors as an irreparable loss even today.

Hills 217.8 and 212.9 comprised the area of the fiercest fighting described in this book. Today they are both cross-sectioned by tall forest belts, and the low ground between them has become heavily overgrown with woods; the patch of woods that existed back in the war has almost merged with the woods in the ravine. Now, the view of both the hills and the view from them are greatly restricted.

Searchers are still finding the remains of our soldiers here. For example, on Hill 217.8 in the autumn of 2012, the remains of several Soviet soldiers were discovered, as confirmed by the ammunition, helmets, gas masks, glass flasks, cooking pots and other equipment articles found with them. All of the fallen were not found in one place, but were lying apart from each other, so one can say that most likely they were killed in action and left where they fell (and were not, for example, killed during an enemy artillery barrage before or after the fighting directly on the hill, since in that case the soldiers wouldn't have been buried separately, but would have been gathered together on the field for burial in one fraternal grave, or would have been evacuated to the rear).

Moreover, the completely shallow depth of the remains' discovery speaks to the fact that the dead men were only hastily covered with a shallow layer of dirt, and not buried in graves especially dug for them. It is possible that the discovered soldiers joined combat each in their own shallow foxhole, which seems likely given the relatively equal spacing between them on the field, and remained in them after being killed.

How and when did they die? To which unit did they belong? Alas, they didn't have any death medallions with them; only one set of remains had a spoon with the initials "M.A." scratched into it, while another had a soap box with the letters "E.V.A.". Unfortunately, this is completely insufficient for any sort of identification of the remains, but the available information allows us to give at least the designations of those Soviet units, in which these military personnel most likely served.

From the documents it follows that there three separate combat actions took place on Hill 217.8, in which the discovered infantrymen could have been killed: On 6 July 1942, the 2nd Motorized Rifle Brigade's 449th Motorized Rifle Battalion fought here; on 13 July, elements of the 7th Motorized Rifle Brigade and possibly the 193rd Rifle Division fought here; on 24 July, it was the 237th Rifle Division's 835th and 841st Rifle Regiments that were defending here. On all three occasions, our units came under an attack by the German 9th Panzer Division, and each time the battlefield was left in the enemy's possession, which didn't allow the possibility to gather up the dead and give them a proper burial.

By the way, on this same hill the presumable remains of a German soldier were found, which could be determined only from a button on the uniform that had rotted away, and the remnants of one boot. There were no other distinguishing signs with the remains (a mug, a cartridge, a helmet, etc.); the German body was, in the words of those who found him, "totally pilfered". If for our three sets of remains, it is possible to give at least three most likely dates of their deaths, it is possible to give a much more concrete date for when and how the dead German soldier wound up on Hill 217.8, since on only one occasion – on 25 July 1942 – did it happen that our units seized this hill and didn't give the Germans the opportunity to recover their own dead.

On that day, tankers of the 3rd Guards Tank Brigade overran and destroyed the 5th Company of the German 10th Panzer Grenadier Regiment, which had been detached to screen the tanks of the 9th Panzer Division that were attacking northeast of Lomovo. Thus, it can be said with considerable certainty that the remains of one of the 15-20 KIAs of that same shattered company, of which only 8 men were able to return to the battalion and 55-60 were taken prisoner, were found on the hill.

As in the case with our soldiers, the German's remains were found approximately 1-meter beneath the ground, which again speaks to the fact that he wasn't buried, but only covered over with dirt. Why this took place with the German is understandable: no one wanted to bother with the body of a hated foe. However, the same sorry fate befell our dead Red Army men as well – they also remained lying on the hill, despite the fact that the enemy had not only been driven from it on 25 July, but the front had already moved on another 4-5 kilometers.

After the end of active combat operations and the final stabilization of the front lines, Hill 212.9 also wound up close behind the Soviet lines, but even then, judging from the sad discoveries of the present day, many of our fallen soldiers weren't given honorable burials. Late in the autumn of 2014, the remains of at least 10 Red Army soldiers were found on the southeastern slopes of this hill. As on Hill 217.8, they were discovered by the audible tone of metallic items of equipment and ammunition (helmets, bayonets, ammunition) produced in the headsets of metal detectors. Just as in that case, the remains weren't found deep in the ground; here too, judging from everything the dead were lying directly in their fighting positions. However, there was one very important difference. Upon a careful inspection of the remains, it turned out that this time the searchers were unbelievably lucky: the death medallions were found for six of the fallen men (a rare success for any search team!).

From the available evidence, for the most part ordinary riflemen were lying in their foxholes, but in one digging, two rusty detachable wheels from the mounting for an 82-mm mortar and supplementary charges for the shells were found together with the remains of two men, from which it is possible to assume that these were mortarmen. In addition, one was an officer, about which the remnants of his leather sword belt eloquently spoke. However, these suppositions remained no more than guesses, until a rare search success again smiled at the author of the discoveries (for the second time on that memorable day!): a death medallion that was found could be read. On a narrow, unfolded strip of paper, which had been lying in a tightened plastic capsule for more than 72 years, the words "Lieutenant Petr Fillipovich Blinov, born 1923" were barely distinguishable in pencil.

It turns out that he was just 19 years old in 1942 ...

A search through Memorial's consolidated database confirmed and expanded the initial information. It turned out that Petr Blinov had been serving in the Red Army since 1941, was the commander of a mortar platoon in the 237th Rifle Division's 841st Rifle Regiment, and in August 1942 he was listed as missing in action. The discovery of the remains together with the discernible contents of the death medallion and the compilation of all the available information became a genuine breakthrough in the matter of determining the truth, and finally removed any uncertainty about the fate of the killed lieutenant, which had been shrouded for more than seven decades.

Now it was completely clear that Lieutenant Blinov hadn't gone missing in action at all, as was mistakenly recorded in a military enlistment center in Kemerov Oblast after the war, but was tragically killed in the unequal fighting on 24 July 1942, when German tanks smashed the 841st Rifle Regiment that had been standing in reserve, having encircled it on Hill 212.9. Most likely, that was when the other bodies found not far from the young lieutenant were killed. The location of their deaths not far from branches of the ravine on the southeastern slopes of Hill 212.9 gives the basis to assume that they all came under an attack by enemy tanks and tank riders, when they began to encircle the hill after reaching it through the narrow neck of ground between the two ravines, and struck the battalions of the 841st Rifle Regiment that lay in their path of advance in the flanks.

Not far from the lieutenant's remains, the remains of another soldier were discovered in the ground, and the note in his death medallion was also legible. They proved to be the remains of Private Vasilii Trofimovich Danilov of the 841st Rifle Regiment, who was listed in a report from the 237th Rifle Division as "missing-in-action" on 24.7.42 in the area of "the northern outskirts of the village of Lomovo", which actually lies 3-4 kilometers from his place of death.

A third set of remains found with a legible death medallion proved to be artilleryman Arkadii Mikhailovich Mogilev of the same 841st Rifle Regiment. In a casualty report put together by the headquarters of the 237th Rifle Division on 29 September 1942, he was listed as "killed and buried on 24 July 1942 on the northern outskirts of Lomovo". He was born in the Krasnogorsk District of Kirov Oblast and was called up in October 1941. From the information of the military enlistment center, the 19-year-old's mother learned of her son's death only on 17 February 1943.

Not far from Mogilev's remains, the remains of two more soldiers were found. They didn't have death medallions, but the very same report from the 237th Rifle Division gives us the basis to suggest who they were. Possibly, the searchers "raised" Mogilev's combat comrades from his artillery battery or even his own crew, who were killed, according to the 237th Rifle Division's casualty list, in the same place and on the same day: the gunlayer Andrei Atamanovsky and the breech operator Boris Porfir'evich Vovchenko.

There is no doubt that the tragic death of these artillerymen of the 841st Rifle Regiment on 24 July 1942 was connected with the regiment's combat on Hill 212.9, when their gun crew wound up in the path of the German tanks that had broken through. One can assume one of the survivors of this terrible slaughter saw that the artillerymen had been killed, and later reported about this to his superiors, thanks to which they were listed as KIAs in the report from the 237th Rifle Division's headquarters, not as missing in action. However, as we see, the entry that they were supposedly buried somewhere on the northern outskirts of Lomovo is incorrect, both with respect to the accurate location of the place and, alas, the meaning of the term "buried" itself. In reality, they remained lying at the place where they were killed.

These facts give us considerable justification to doubt in the accuracy of the entries about the other fallen personnel of the 237th Rifle Division and the location of the area of their burials as indicated in the documents.[5] The comparison of all the available documents allows one to assert with a great deal of likelihood that the absence of mentions in the casualty lists about the burial of the dead in specifically designated fraternal graves tied to a location most often means that the dead weren't at all buried in the proper fashion, and the entries (in the column "where buried") specifying hills, fields and villages are no more than a general orientation about their place of death.

One more detail: in the area of the southern slopes of Hill 212.9, in one of the pits that contained the remains of two men, an entire pile of 14.5-mm cartridges for an anti-tank rifle was found. There were also matches and some sort of rolled up instruction sheet, plainly prepared for self-rolled cigarettes. Likely, the dead men were members of an anti-tank rifle team and were in their fighting positions, but it is noteworthy that given the bountiful supply of 14.5-mm cartridges found around them, there was not a single empty casing. Possibly, they were killed right away, before being able to fire a single shot at the enemy, and this happened most likely at the very start of the charge by the German tanks toward the hill, when a storm of fire from hundreds of German

5 According to information provided by the Voronezh search team "Patriot", on 11 September 2014 the remains of 64 soldiers were buried at the area of the military memorial in the Ozerki area. Another 18 sets of remains were buried there in May 2015. At the present moment, the names of 21 of these men, whose remains were buried in September 2014, have been established. They are:

1. Junior Sergeant Aleksei Grigor'evich Dvoriankin
2. Private Ivan Grigor'evich Sysoev, a rifleman of the 841st Rifle Regiment
3. Private Nikolai Ivanovich Stupnikov, a rifleman of the 841st Rifle Regiment
4. Private Fedor Ivanovich Rybinsky, a rifleman of the 841st Rifle Regiment
5. Private Il'ia Egorovich Mamontov, a gunlayer of the 841st Rifle Regiment
6. Private Timofei Vasil'evich Akimkin, a rifleman of the 841st Rifle Regiment
7. Private Nazar Alekseevich Alekseev, a gunlayer of the 841st Rifle Regiment
8. Private Ivan Andreevich Oleinikov, a gunlayer of the 841st Rifle Regiment
9. Sergeant Il'ia Ivanovich Andrechuk, squad commander of the 841st Rifle Regiment's machine-gun battalion
10. Private Anatolii Gerasimovich Demarchuk, a rifleman of the 841st Rifle Regiment
11. Sergeant Ivan Andreevich Nazarov, squad commander of the 841st Rifle Regiment
12. Private Ivan Nikolaevich Konovalov, rifleman of a separate company of the 841st Rifle Regiment
13. Private Nikolai Georgievich Kutilin
14. Sergeant Anton Ivanovich Andrianov, deputy squad commander of the 841st Rifle Regiment
15. Private Petr Fedorovich Buaganov (medallion)/Burganov (Memorial database), rifleman of a separate company of the 841st Rifle Regiment
16. Private Khabibrakhman Gabrakhmanov, a rifleman of the 841st Rifle Regiment
17. Private Dzhambai Kul'boev, a rifleman of the 841st Rifle Regiment
18. Private Kakui/Kokui Samoev (Samaev), a rifleman of the 841st Rifle Regiment
19. Private Vladimir Ivanovich Burdiuk (in the Memorial database), Grigorii Ivanovich (medallion), a rifleman of the 841st Rifle Regiment
20. Private Anton Stepanovich Ignatovich
21. Private Ivan Fedotovich Artishchev, gunlayer of the 841st Rifle Regiment

There were no weapons at all found with the remains, but there were ammunition and various items of equipment and personal usage: spoons, mugs, flasks, cigarette holders, razors, knives, money (one even had Mongolian money), gas masks, helmets (almost on each), and insignia. Many of the helmets had been shot through by bullets from behind. There was no continuous line of defense, only foxholes, with 2-3 men in each. Most often they were lying face down. There were three officers, judging by the bars, but not a single belt, map case or holster on them; they'd all been removed …

barrels fell like a thunderclap on the unseasoned, stunned Red Army elements. Let's not forget that for the overwhelming majority of the regiment's men, this was their very first combat. For very many of them, alas, it proved to be their last.

In that terrible meatgrinder, into which the regiment fell on Hill 212.9 on 24 July 1942, the living plainly had no interest in the dead, and there was simply no one to bury them. We'll recall that of the two full-strength battalions, which is to say approximately 1,200 men, only around 200 made it back to friendly lines after the battle. For a long time, at the headquarters of the 237th Rifle Division, they simply had no information about the fate of the rest. Only on 15 August, already at a time when a new offensive operation was in full swing and three weeks after that unforgettable introduction to combat did the division headquarters submit to higher command its first (!) list by name of the irrecoverable personnel losses on six pages, which was far from complete.

The confusion and chaos of the division's first battles, which affected the tracking of casualties in such a woeful manner, were deepened by the fact that during one of the airstrikes, a bomb destroyed the wagon that had all of the corresponding documents on it. The 237th Rifle Division's chief of staff Major Marol' explained to higher command: "For some of the men, the lists were compiled without indicating relatives, in view of the fact that documents for the personnel were destroyed together with the wagon by a bomb, as a result of which information in the presented lists was drawn from rough drafts kept by the squad and platoon commanders and from other sources."

The study and analysis of the 237th Rifle Division's lists of irreplaceable casualties allow one to conclude that the division headquarters was able to obtain more or less accurate information on the dead and missing only by October 1942, almost two months after the bloody drama of the first battle, yet even then the information wasn't complete, as eloquently demonstrated by the case of Lieutenant Blinov, who was killed in action, but whose name didn't appear on a single one (!) of the 11 casualty lists generated by the 237th Rifle Division in the summer and autumn of 1942. During an attempt to find him in Memorial's consolidated database, the researcher receives only a reference to a 1948 postwar order about excluding the 19-year-old lieutenant from the roster of the armed forces as … missing-in-action in August 1942.

Were there any other military servicemen killed or missing in action that didn't show up in the division's casualty lists? It is hardly possible to answer that question accurately, but it is fully possible to assume that there were. After all, if an officer killed in action went uncounted, then what can one say about ordinary Red Army men? At the same time it should also be noted that in the casualty lists generated by the headquarters of the 237th Rifle Division, numerous cases of double entries for one and the same man are encountered.[6]

Let's sum up the results. Of the available reports for the corresponding period it follows that over the entire time of the operation, the units of the 237th Rifle Division lost approximately 2,000 men irrecoverably (killed or missing in action), of which approximately 1,600, or more than 75% were lost in the first two days of fighting. Around 1,300 of the total number of irrecoverable losses were men missing in action.[7]

It is worth noting that these summary figures differ from the information in the journal of Briansk Front's headquarters that tracks losses, which was compiled no earlier than September 1942. At the same time, it is impossible not to observe that the information for the 237th Rifle Division in this journal suffers from plain inconsistencies and contradictions. For example, if you

6 These cases were taken into account when making final summations.

7 On one of the casualty lists, the first three pages have no information for 112 personnel, but the document's overall framework of time and information on the following pages made it possible to conclude that these pages primarily relate directly to the losses on 23-24 July, a significant share of which were missing-in-action.

sum the numbers given for the killed, wounded and missing in action in the corresponding tables (categorized by rank), it turns out that the division lost 198 command staff, 662 junior command staff, and 2,050 rank and file in the fighting (or 336 killed, 1,343 wounded and 1,231 missing, for a total of 2,910). However, in the summary table of losses, the numbers for these same categories of rank grow respectively to 340 killed, 1,085 wounded and 3,523 men, for a total of 4,948 men (of which 1,567 were either killed or missing in action); the journal kept by Briansk Front's headquarters doesn't offer any explanations for this discrepancy.

In my view it is possible to explain such a contradiction in the documents by the fact that at the time the headquarters of the 237th Rifle Division put together the final summary, it still didn't have complete information on either the total number of casualties, nor on the structure of the losses suffered by the division, and in the absence of this in the document of tables, the "uncounted excess" increased the total number of losses, based upon the missing men revealed by roll calls after the fighting. On the basis of amended lists (although still incomplete) on the irrecoverable losses that were put together much later, one can assume that the total losses of the 237th Rifle Division were still fewer than the 4,848 men indicated in Briansk Front's journal, primarily because many of the servicemen who at first disappeared from their shattered units were subsequently found and returned to duty. But at the same time, the number of irrecoverable losses proved to be substantially higher than in the 237th Rifle Division's summary report to Briansk Front headquarters.

Generally speaking, it is necessary to note that the reports from the 237th Rifle Division's headquarters regarding the missing-in-action stand out for being more complete and, if you will, honest than the same reports from other units of the operational group. The general tendency of the latter was to reduce substantially the number of missing-in-action, or to avoid reporting them at all to higher command, which is most likely explained by the desire to avoid unnecessary questions from above and the subsequent awkward explanations …

The headquarters of the majority of the units, in order to paper over unpleasant information preferred to transfer the numbers of those missing in action to the category of "killed-in-action", although even in this case the total number of irrecoverable losses in the submitted summaries to the command proved to be reduced. For example, the headquarters of the 167th Rifle Division in its final report on the conducted operation didn't report anything at all about the missing-in-action cases (even though by the time the report was put together, it was completely clear that there were such cases, and in a significant number), but wrote instead "around 800 killed and approximately 2000 wounded".

Later, in a report on losses that was submitted to Briansk Front headquarters, the division command reported 471 killed and 1,715 wounded, but placed dashes in the category for missing-in-action. In this fashion, the total number of losses was reduced to 2,186 men in comparison with the report. In fact, the losses of the 167th Rifle Division according to the casualty lists that were compiled in the period between July and November 1942 were substantially greater, and in the irrecoverable losses of 1,262 men, there were 674 men who went missing in action. It is completely obvious that the losses of the 167th Rifle Division given in its journal were incomplete both regarding their total number (which was lower by 791 men) and regarding its individual categories.

A similar picture can be seen in the data for the 340th Rifle Division. According to its combat journal, the irrecoverable losses of the 340th Rifle Division amounted to "only" 382 killed and 160 missing-in-action, although according to adjustments bassed on the materials of the Memorial consolidated database, it follows that in fact the division lost 517 killed and 653 missing in the operation, or 628 more than in the journal. Together with the 1,550 wounded indicated in the report, this yield a total number of 2,720 casualties (whereas in the journal – 2,125 casualties including 33 sick).

Unfortunately, the reports on the irrecoverable losses of many of the operational group's units could not be found, but a statistical analysis of the data for some of them that offer lists by names (the 167th, 237th, 340th Rifle Divisions, the 104th Separate Rifle Brigade, the 26th, 49th and 118th Tank Brigades and the 1st Guards Tank Brigade) show that the number of irrecoverable losses in them were much greater than indicated in the operational documents. This gives a serious basis to believe that for the other formations, the official data on the irrecoverable losses suffered by the forces in the operation were incomplete even by the autumn of 1942.[8] Thus it is possible to assume that the total losses among the operational group's forces were even higher than the 30,000 casualties mentioned previously.

Let's return again to the 237th Rifle Division and its soldiers' remains that were found in the fields. How many of them might remain forever in the area of the division's first combat action, on those tragic hills of that unsuccessful operation? In order to give an answer to this question, I decided to study carefully the lists by name of the 237th Rifle Division's irrecoverable losses available in Memorial's consolidated database.[9]

Several weeks of daily work were necessary to do this, but the analysis of the studied lists help reaching certain statistical conclusions. For example, it turned out that several men of those listed as "missing-in-action" of the 237th Rifle Division actually made their way to other units on the days of the division's destruction, and were killed or died later in hospitals. At least six men were found who continued to serve and successfully survived the war. Many were double-counted, at times as both killed and missing in action.

The most surprising case, if you will, involved the tribulations of Junior Lieutenant V.V. Leonov. On 5 October 1942, in a report from the headquarters of the 237th Rifle Division, it was written that he was killed in action when fighting for the Motherland on 24.7.42 and was buried on the northern outskirts of Lomovo. The 20-year-old lieutenant's family received a death notification, and at an order from the Main Directorate for Personnel, he was dropped from the roster of the Red Army. In fact he was taken prisoner, spent almost three years as a German prisoner, and was freed only in May 1945 (and repatriated on 23.6.45). Only in October 1954 was his name re-added to the rosters of the Soviet Army as "counted as a combat loss, but in fact wound up as a prisoner". However, on paper he'd already been buried.

From the lists of burial by name it follows that Junior Lieutenant V.V. Leonov, who was killed on 24.7.42, was buried in a fraternal grave in Lomovo and appears as No. 312 on a corresponding list. A momument (with the names engraved in the stone) was erected in Lomovo in 1962, almost 20 years after the fighting of the summer of 1942. It isn't known whether the 40-year-old former Junior Lieutenant Leonov was still alive in 1962, and if he was, whether he knew about his "burial". It must be thought that he would have experienced a strange feeling, had he in subsequent years visited the place of his first and last battle, capture, "death" and "burial". What thoughts might he have had when gazing at his own name on the monument stone? He, undoubtedly, was lucky to

8 In the Briansk Front's journal of losses, the accounting period for Operational Group Chibisov was 21-28 July 1942, but the absence in the document of any mention whatsoever of the losses suffered by its units between 29 and 31 July (which there were, in fact) leads one to think that the cited data weren't limited by these dates, but were summed up for the entire period of the operation. However, even if this isn't so, the attrition in the operational group's troop strength over these three days (29, 30 and 31 July) were incomparably fewer than the losses suffered in the preceding days, and thus could not yield a sharp increase in the presented figures. Thus, this vagueness regarding the dates doesn't alter the overall conclusion.

9 I want to express my enormous gratitude for assistance in this troublesome and painstaking search to my fine comrade and associate from the city of Samara, Aleksandr Barkov, who personally dug, one by one, through the hundreds of family names of the soldiers and officers of the 237th Rifle Division available in the search engine.

survive that war and fortunate, having refuted his death notification, to return alive to his family and friends, who for three years had believed he was killed. Alas, the case proved to be a rare exception. Only one other man listed in the report as killed on 24.7.42 wound up as a prisoner and survived the war (I.S. Solomin).

If you assume that the dates presented in the divisional lists are accurate (which isn't actually the case), it turns out that on 24 July alone on the battlefield of the 237th Rifle Division, primarily in the area of Hills 212.9 and 217.8 and the western outskirts of Lomovo, approximately 1,060 men were killed or went missing in action (of which 178 were counted in the reports as killed).[10] Only in rare cases as a result of a search through Memorial's consolidated database were men of the 237th Rifle Division who'd been listed as killed or missing in action later found as prisoners in captured German documents. Only 20 prisoners were found among the more than 1,000 men entered in the lists. Of these 20 men, nine died in imprisonment. Even if we assume that not all of the captured German documents were preserved and that not all of the men taken prisoner were registered by the enemy, and their number was in fact even greater[11] (let's assume that in fact the figure exceeded those found in the captured documents twice over), then all the same the summary data makes the following conclusion obvious: the overwhelming majority of those soldiers, officers and political staff members of the 237th Rifle Division listed as missing-in-action were in fact killed and never became German prisoners.

In the division's very first battle, they continued to resist desperately, despite all the tragedy and hopelessness of the existing situation, when the totally unseasoned battalions (primarily of the 841st Rifle Regiment) that had never previously served at the front, simultaneously came under an attack from dozens of German medium tanks and accompanying infantry. Left without support or assistance, they nevertheless fought to the end and died without surrendering, and many of the wounded, probably, were finished off where they lay by the enraged foe. We bow our heads before their memoiries and courage! Statistics speak eloquently to the fact that there was no massed, organized capitulation by the men of the 237th Rifle Division in this battle ... Encircled by the enemy on the exposed heights, the warriors stood to their deaths and were killed in their positions that were repeatedly overrun by tanks, crushing the living and the dead beneath their tracks.

The hopes to find the division's nurses and female combat medics among the survivors and missing-in-action weren't justified; it would seem that they had better chances to survive in the defeat and encirclement that took place. Not a single one of them is listed in the German card files as a prisoner, and not a single one was added later in a happy addendum to the division's list as "turned up alive", and not a single one returned home after the war. The majority of them were just 18 to 20 years old; they still had much life to live, to get married and to have children. However, having been caught together with the men in the enemy's path, they remained in those terrible fields forever, killed young and having no chance to give life to others.

The majority of the division's fallen soldiers, many of whom were still youthful, had no chance to grow into full adulthood, having just barely donned their soldiers' boots. At a time of heavy trials, they courageously rose in defense of the Motherland, but were alas killed in their very first battle. Together with them, older reservists, who had become fathers, and all those who were between these two extreme call-up categories, someone's husbands, sons, daughters, brothers and

10 To the number of those killed and left behind on the battlefield on 23 and 24 July, one should add approximately 150 killed and missing in action in the course of fighting on 28 and 29 July in the same area.

11 It is known that in distinction from the period of the autumn and winter of 1941, when no proper account in the Wehrmacht of the millions of Soviet military servicemen taken prisoner was ever organized, and the mortality among them was very high, the soldiers, commanders and political staff members of the Red Army, who became prisoners later, had a much greater chance to survive the war and return home.

sisters, also perished. The war wasn't selective and wasn't sparing, and that's how it was in all of the operational front's units, and throughout the Red Army that was fighing on an enormous front.

The soldiers of many Soviet units fell in the fierce fighting of the summer of 1942 on the tragic hills in the triangular area between Bol'shaia Vereika, Kamenka and Ivanovka. The total number of dead Red Army men who were killed and left abandoned back then on those battlefields in this area likely numbers in the thousands.

On 5 May 2015, almost 73 years after their deaths, the remains of soldiers of the 237th Rifle Division found by searchers were buried with all military honors in a fraternal grave in the memorial complex in the village of Ozerki. Here, at a proud and touching monument to the defenders of the Motherland, they finally acquired their posthumous honor and eternal peace after so many decades of bitter obscurity and oblivion.

Relatives of the fallen soldier Mogilev – Sergei and Nikolai Mogilev – arrived from Siberia for the reburial.[12] Together with the rest of the people who had gathered that day for the ceremony, they placed a bright and sorrowful period on the fate of the found soldiers, having tossed a handful of Russian earth into the fraternal grave in worth memory of the fallen.

I spoke with Sergei and Nikolai. The brothers told me about the Mogilev family. The head of the family fought in the war, was wounded, but survived. Of his four sons, three went to the front (the youngest son was born in 1929 and didn't reach draft age by the time the war ended), and two of them were killed. That's a family history that is so familiar in our country. For a long time, the family clung to the hope that Arkadii hadn't been killed, but had been taken prisoner, and hadn't returned after the war to the USSR for some unknown reasons. These hopes, literally giving rise to a legend, strengthened after 1991, when never-before-seen changes in the life of our country made possible that which had been even impossible to imagine before: Might Arkadii still be living somewhere abroad, and now make himself known, when nothing would happen to him for this? Would he come forward after the decades? However, the years passed, the world changed unrecognizably, that former country was now no longer, and news from Arkadii didn't come …

Then unexpectedly a message arrived from the military enlistment center. Arkadii's remains had been found on the battlefield, recognized by a legible name in his death medallion, and he had been lying unknown all this time in native soil …

Later, when the official speeches accompanied by an orchestral performance had ended, when the salute had been fired and the fresh graves strewn with flowers, the time arrived for a more personal meeting, outside the purview and commotion of others. Ruslan Ermolov, through whose efforts and stubbornness Arkadii Mogilev's remains and the remains of many other soldiers had been found, was ready to show us the location of Arkadii's final battle. So we headed together with Nikolai and Sergei Mogilev to the place of their uncle's death – an eternal 18-year-old, who was now decades younger than his nephews that he had never known and never seen. Our path was short – Hill 212.9 is separated from Ozerki by just a few kilometers.

The cars raised clouds of dust along the dirt road, then turned off into a field and headed along a barely-noticeable track through the cultivated field. We stopped short of a wooded ravine. A cold wind was blowing along the slopes of a large hill, pressing the crops that had just sprouted to the earth, rustling the trees in the ravine with their newly opened leaves – it was spring, in which once again nature was engendering new life under the sun's warmth. Yet we were standing in a field, where so many young lives had once been cruelly harvested by the war …

12 Unfortunately, there were no relatives of other of the fallen soldiers found by the searches at the reburial ceremony: many close ones of the fallen couldn't be found, and some of those who could be found couldn't attend. The remains of one or two of the soldiers had been previously transported away to the Urals for reburial in their native soil.

Our guide led us to a raised circle of recently excavated earth, which was hardly noticeable at first glance, and briefly said, "Here's where they were lying." Taking a look, we saw not far away other similar markings of diggings, which sorrowfully crowned the places of death and lengthy oblivion of many more of our soldiers. They were men who'd been tragically killed in their very first and last battle, and who hadn't received proper burial. Now we were standing on that same spot, where everything had happened back then, in 1942; standing, looking around, and pondering the sad significance of the minutes we were experiencing.

The nephews who had arrived at the place of death of their uncle, laid scarlet tulips on the black earth that had been overturned by the diggers, and so that the wind didn't blow them away, placed the hefty nosecone of a shell and a rusty, heavy shell fragment that they'd found nearby on the stems. It seemed to me back then that these dark traces of the war hadn't almost immediately turned up nearly right under our feet by accident at this moment, and that there was something special and deeply symbolic in this. We were silent, gazing at the tulips and at the empty field surrounding us. It seemed that words simply weren't necessary at this, our unexpected encounter with the past and with remembrance.

I was turning over a lot in my mind back then. The terrain has largely remained unchanged since the war; not far to the west, the last branch of the ravine that runs to the east was clearly visible, as was the patch of woods, behind which (in front of the upper reaches of another deep ravine, which leads toward Ozerki) there opened the only passage to Hill 212.9 from the southwest. The corridor is only several hundred meters wide, which gave the enemy command a better (if not the only) possibility for a rapid breakthrough to the hills, and to develop an attack along it into the flank of our attacking grouping back then.

Knowing well that we were standing on a line of rifle pits of the 841st Rifle Regiment, I was trying to imagine what had happened here back then on that tragic day of 24 July 1942, when the totally green regiment came under the massed attack of German tanks in its very first battle. As the rumble of combat began alarmingly to approach from the hills that were unseen from behind the copse of trees following the fierce air raids and savage artillery bombardments, dozens of German tanks suddenly emerged on the hill from behind the branch of the ravine with a clattering of tracks and roaring of engines; pursuing the men from the elements positioned out in front that were fleeing across the planted fields, they were raking the fields out in front of them with cannon and machine-gun fire, advancing along its slopes toward the firing positions of the regimental artillery and the foxholes of the stunned infantrymen …

We don't know what happened next and how our soldiers were killed here (most likely, we'll never know), but the scene of what was happening was likely horrific …

The details of that tragic battle remain unknown, as does, incidentally, much else, since the documents don't discuss them and no eyewitnesses remain. However, even more than seven decades since the fighting, the war reminds us about its hidden secrets, which remain uncounted to the present day. The remains of our fallen troops, found in the positions of the 841st Rifle Regiment on the slopes of Hill 212.9 among the remnants of ammunition, equipment and combat supplies, are one of the examples of this partially-revealed mystery. The mute eyewitnesses of that terrible combat might have a lot to say to us, but the dead soldiers are silent, and only their restless spirits, as it seems to me, still call to our hearts and minds. Because the ground of those fields still contains a lot of bitter reminders and secrets.

The reburial concluded, and new names were added to the memorial stones. Through the efforts of the searchers, approximately 100 of our Red Army men and women, commanders and political workers who'd been lying in obscurity had been pulled out from the bondage of tragic abandonment, their bones from the repeatedly tilled soil, and many of them have been identified by name.

Yet how many have yet to be found around the entire area, who arrived here in 1942 from various corners of our one-time country, and now lie silently in unknown graves and lost burial sites, or who were simply hastily covered with dirt in the trenches and shell craters back then? We don't know, but obviously a lot. They, who have yet to be found, are waiting. They've been waiting now more than 70 years since the war. We must continue our searches and remember that the war isn't over, until the last dead soldier from it has been buried.

Appendix I

Documents relating to 23-24 July 1942

A. The commissar of a rifle battalion of the 284th Rifle Division's 1047th Rifle Regiment Junior Political Instructor Il'ia Maksimov recalled:

> On 23 July 1942 at 0430 our battalion received a combat order – to capture a patch of woods and take up a defense on the slope in front of the river. It was a marvelously clear and sunny morning. The day was going to be a hot one. The order was passed down to each commander and soldier; command and control signals were established, as well as communications with neighboring battalions. However, as soon as we had advanced about 500 meters, we lost contact with the neighbors, who weren't using the signals. The commanders were not at their posts; instead, they were running at full height from platoon to platoon and to each soldier, not directing the battle with signals, but with their own voices; in other words, they were taking over the functions of lower-ranking commanders. They were unable to exert good control over the elements and were more frequently themselves winding up killed or wounded.
>
> Heroism and fearlessness are good things, but competence is also necessary, otherwise there will be needless casualties. I was a battalion commissar, and the order was to drive the enemy out of the woods; Junior Lieutenant Nechaev's rifle company went on the attack on the left flank with a team of the battalion's command staff. Comrade Nechaev made a number of mistakes: he didn't direct the platoon commanders, but instead ran from platoon to platoon and issued directions to each individual soldier, failed to keep solid contact with the neighbors on the right and left, and wound up isolated in front of the neighbors, which weren't supporting him. The enemy concentrated all of his fire at Nechaev's rifle company, inflicting needless casualties, and Nechaev himself was wounded.
>
> Our forces were fewer than the enemy's. In order to beat him, resourcefulness, wit and nimbleness are necessary. We didn't use these, but instead launched a head-on attack and had no success. We might have been able to take this patch of woods from the flank, where the enemy wasn't expecting us, while small groups of riflemen supported the attack with suppressing fire from the front. We didn't do this, and thus we failed. We also suffered many casualties because we made no use of the terrain or employ any tactical techniques on the attack. We made lengthy runs in places where it was necessary to move at a crawl. Those soldiers who were nearer to me kept low when moving, snaking along on their bellies with their forearms, and thus saved their lives. [...]
>
> In nighttime conditions one shouldn't always pay attention to various soldiers you come across. Around 01:00 on 23 July, we had just taken a small grove of trees; to the right of us the training battalion's machine-gun company was attacking. At this time a man wearing a Red Army uniform stepped out of a large patch of woods about 50 meters out in front of us and loudly called out in Russian: "Why are you being slow? Come on into the woods, your

submachine gunners have already cleared it and the Germans have retreated." I knew that no submachine gunners were operating with us and that they couldn't have cleared those woods, and moreover that the enemy had just fired at us from the machine gun of a tank that was emplaced in front of the woods, so we stayed put. The training battalion's machine-gun company stood up and headed toward the woods in a bunch. This decoy simply darted into the woods, fired a burst from a submachine gun, and the fascists began to shower the machine gunners with grenades, forcing them to retreat ....[1]

B. *STAVKA* DIRECTIVE No. 170526 TO THE FRONT COMMANDERS AND THE COMMANDER OF THE 7th SEPARATE ARMY REGARDING THE USE OF RADIO COMMUNICATIONS FOR TROOP CONTROL

24 July 1942

Combat experience demonstrates that our command over the troops remains at an impermissibly low level. Unfortunately, it is necessary to note once again that the majority of our commanders continue to consider wire communications as the primary form of communications.

Command and control over the forces lasts for as long as wire communications continue to exist, but one only has to break wire communications, and immediately command and control are lost.

As before, radio means of communications are being used reluctantly, under protest; there is no thought given to radio sets, keeping them distant from command posts and sometimes with the rear echelons of headquarters. Insufficient attention is being given to the training of radio operators; our radio operators in the majority work slowly and have little knowledge of the technical aspects of radio communications.

The loss of contact is the loss of command, and loss of command over the troops in battle leads inevitably to defeat.

In the future such a situation cannot be tolerated.

The *Stavka* of the Supreme High Command orders:

1. Under the personal responsibility of commanders and commissars of all levels, the under appreciation of radio means of communication in headquarters, units and by the political command staff of the units and elements is to be eliminated in the shortest amount of time. When organizing communications with the troops, it is necessary to consider communications reliable only in the event that radio communications have been set up well, and this question must be given primary attention when organizing any type of combat or force maneuver. Permit the free use of radio communications in all instances of troops' combat activity, as long as it is not banned by a higher-standing chief or headquarters. Place a limitation on the use of radio transmissions only in periods of regroupings and the assembly of forces ...[2]

1 Arkhiv IRI RAN, F. 2, razdel 1, op. 31, d. 22, ll. 96-98.

2 *Russkii arkhiv. Velikaia Otechestvennaia. Stavka VGK: Dokumenty i materialy, 1942; Tom 16* [*Russian archive. Great Patriotic War. Stavka of the Supreme High Command: Documents and materials, 1942; Volume 16*] (Moscow: Terra, 1996), pp. 324-325.

C. From a political report of the 12th Separate Reconnaissance Battalion:
On 24 July at an order from the corps commander we set out from the area south of Murav'evka to the area of Bol'shaia Vereika, where the enemy was strafing from the air. We camouflaged the machines in the village and dug in. Two soldiers went out on a patrol and returned safely. At 1100 an order was given to fall back toward the Vereisky hills to an area south of Murav'evka. The enemy was conducting heavy fire from the air and during the movement 3 men were killed (and buried), and 2 were wounded and sent to Hospital No. 2118. We assembled in the area south of Murav'evka at 2300 on 24 July. The enemy bombed us at 0400 on 25 July. There were no losses. Two armored cars were sent out on a combat mission, which were subjected to an aerial attack by bombers, as a result of which 1 armored car was left burning, while the second [indistinguishable – I.S.] and the crew was unharmed.[3]

D. From a political report of the 340th Rifle Division for 24 July:
Gathered [on the battlefield – I.S.]: 49 rifles; 6 light machine guns; 7,000 cartridges; 162 ammo drums from PPSh submachine guns, 16 from RPD light machine guns; 2 machine-gun belts; and 46 gas masks. Seized booty [obviously at the start of the operation – I.S.]: 82 rifles; 5 cannons; 2 heavy machine guns; 7 light machine guns; 1 mortar; 17,000 cartridges; a radio; 27 bicycles; 3 motorcycles; 1 light vehicle; 31 prisoners have been taken. Domestically-manufactured weapons: 200 rifles, 16 light machine guns and 3 82-mm mortars.[4]

E. From an account of the 1st Guards Tank Brigade's command:
Enemy actions were of a restraining nature, primarily artillery blocking fire and rather strongly fortified terrain … all of the artillery was positioned in bunkers or in the foundations of stone buildings. […] There was a strong nest of resistance on the axis of the brigade's actions. Among the characteristic features of the enemy's actions were:
a) Skillful maneuvering of artillery means across the front and in the depth
b) Organized adjustment of artillery and mortar fire by means of:
    1. Spotting aircraft
    2. Infiltration through the combat formations of the infantry into our rear by submachine gunners [sic] and a forward observer equipped with a small radio set
    3. Adjustment of artillery fire by flares and at night with light signals in the sky
c) Fascist tankers fear our tanks. It is sufficient for 2-3 of our tanks to open fire at a numerically superior group of German tanks, and they will refuse combat and retreat …
d) The placement of mines in the rear of our advancing tanks. For example, from the western outskirts of Somovo separate tanks began to move to the southern outskirts, when on their way back, their route had been mined.

One of the characteristic details of the German aviation in the Khruschevo – Bol'shaia Vereika sector of the front was the high density of aircraft, which made 500 individual sorties a day; the German air force was bombing the combat formations and approaching reserves at intervals of 10-15 minutes.

3 TsAMO, F. 8 gv TK, op. 1, d. 224 (b), l. 158.
4 TsAMO, F. 340 sd, op. 1, d. 91, l. 437.

a) Bombers: He-111, Ju-87 and Ju-88
b) Fighters: Me-109F
c) Reconnaissance: Fw-189 and He-126

In the process the actions of the German aircraft featured:
a) Large and incessant echelons of twin-engine He-111 bombers, occasionally alternating with Ju-87 dive bombers;
b) The escorting of the Ju-87 dive bombers toward their target by Me-109 fighters;
c) The summoning of other echelons of aircraft to a clearly identified target by means of homing pigeons. [How this became known to the command of the 1st Guards Tank Brigade, or whether this was in fact a genuine practice remains an open question – I.S.][5]

F. From the recollections of a military surgeon of the 340th Rifle Division, Konstantin Boldin:

On 19 or 20 July we were setting up in Bol'shaia Poliana. My platoon was given a somewhat cramped, but very suitable building of a former outpatient clinic. Local women were cleaning it and we barely had time to move in our equipment when wounded men started to arrive. The nurses were catching some sleep for three or four hours, but I barely had time to lie down. I've already lost track of the sleepless nights!

Fierce combat was continuing. General Liziukov's tank army, to which our division was attached, was suffering heavy losses in tanks and men [by this time the 5th Tank Army had already been disbanded and the forces of Operational Group Chibisov was conducting the fighting, but as we see, Military Doctor Boldin wasn't aware of this – I.S.] According to the wounded, the last tanks were being knocked out. There was no success. The wounded tankers explained this with the fact that our tanks were being thrown into the fighting in small groups; instead of a strike with a clenched fist, there was prodding with extended fingers.

With the passage of time historians explain everything in an epic tone – for whatever reason and why, but today the pain is the same for such lack of skill or thoughtlessness!

… During breaks between operations I would step out just as I was dressed, in a surgeon's gown over which I wore a red oilcloth apron, and wearing black rubber surgical gloves I would take a rest on the steps from the smell of ether and iodine, and smoke a self-rolled cigarette of cheap tobacco. Shrapnel shells were exploding over the outskirts of the village; our cannon standing somewhere not far away was replying. You could hear the shell explosions, the chattering of machine guns, and the snapping of rifle fire. For some reason we were right next to the front! I guess we'd been a bit further away from it the day before.

…. We managed to regulate rest (we were now able to sleep for 5-6 hours a day). They improved our food – they were giving us meat, herring and butter. Shakhbazian arrived and informed us that our division was being transferred to a different army, because Liziukov's formation (or that which remained of it) was heading for reforming.

One morning, when the faces of the patients in the corridor became visible, among them I spied the face of Lieutenant Roginsky. The right forearm of the former pianist and singer was smashed and the radial nerve was damaged. I recognized him with difficulty. His face was covered with blood and dust, and he was pale. Having spent the entire night

5 Arkhiv IRI RAN, razdel 1, op. 36, d. 13, ll. 39-40.

on a stretcher, he was completely done in. His uniform was greasy, torn, bloody and filthy. He didn't stand out in any way from the dozens of soldiers that were lying next to him. I quickly checked him, gave him a smoke and a bit of vodka, and arranged for him to be on the first vehicle that was going to a hospital.

In the morning, we carried out the dead, who'd been unable to wait for medical attention, out of the corridor. After all we didn't even have any flashlights to illuminate the wounded man, prostrate on the floor, in order to find out where he'd been wounded and what sort of help he might be given! What could be done? We didn't have enough people. The operating table and six bandaging tables were constantly busy, and we couldn't deal with the overflow of patients. Several more men from an orchestra had been assigned to our five medics, and still … the medic would take a seat to have a smoke, his head would start nodding and he would doze off, forgetting about the cigarette. At night you'd go out into the darkness – there's someone standing in the corner. You'd switch on your flashlight (I still had a captured German flashlight) – and see a medic, standing, sleeping, but somehow not falling!

When I went out to see off Roginsky, I ran into the investigator Saninsky. He asked in a low voice, "Have you seen German tanks?"

I replied that a year ago I had even run away from them.

"But this year, have you seen any? On the loose?"

I answered, "No!"

"Then let's go and I'll show you!"

It turned out that from the outskirts of the village, German tanks were visible (more than a dozen of them), which had broken through our defense.

The picture, it turns out, was a "merry" one! At the time I still didn't know that our neighboring division had been crushed, that we were running out of ammunition, that the losses in the division were very heavy, or that the Uzbeks and Kazakhs that had arrived as replacements proved to be totally green. I didn't know that the situation was extremely critical.

I didn't go to get a look at the German tanks "on the loose" – work didn't allow it, and indeed somehow it was indifferent to me, where the German tanks were rumbling – outside the village or in the village itself. Extreme fatigue had numbed my instinct of self-preservation.

One night, at the peak of heavy work, when the head swells, the feet scream, and your eyes close just as soon as you lean against a wall, and you can't walk along the corridor without stepping on a wounded man, I heard the swearing of a man's voice, which a woman's voice was echoing in the same strong language. Her swearing was using the choicest words, but coming from a woman's mouth, it sounded somehow unconvincing. I stepped out, and an argument was going on between a *feldsher* [a medical assistant] of some unit and my nurse on the matter of the wounded, which the young lady didn't want to transport to triage, intending instead to offload them then and there onto the floor. I caught her saying, "You've found a comfortable hideout here … Fuck your mother, you don't want to do anything!"

Her driver was giving support to the spirited young lady, toying with a pistol to back her up. I understood the nurse's desire to ram the wounded through to the operating table as quickly as possible; other casualties were waiting for her; she was frazzled, exhausted and feeling great sympathy for the guys who'd been mutilated in this slaughterhouse. However, no sort of remonstrations had any effect on the two, so I switched to swearing and sent the nurse and driver both packing into the street. The driver once again had the notion to "shoot everyone", including me, but thought better of it and drove off to triage.

The next morning they brought in this same young nurse with a penetrating wound of the stomach. The woman's voice was quite feminine, and I felt great pain for her, even more than she had shown her fellows ….

Appendix II

Summary protocol of the interrogation of 11 prisoners of the 5th Company of the 9th Panzer Division's 10th Panzer Grenadier Regiment, captured on 25.7.42

On 25.7.42 in the area south of Perekopovka (Spasskoe area), the remnants of the 5th Company of the 10th Motorized Regiment (9th Pz. D.) numbering 60 men were taken prisoner. The company, positioned in a forward outpost, was attacked and encircled from the front and the flanks by our tanks. Company commander Lieutenant Füller was located in the company's rear and fled during the tanks' attack (according to the testimony of other prisoners, he was killed). [According to the data on the losses of the 9th Panzer Division, there were no officers killed or missing in the 10th Panzer Grenadier Regiment on that day – I.S.]

Left without leadership and having no path of retreat, individual soldiers began to surrender. Having been convinced that our tankers weren't shooting prisoners, the other soldiers ceased resistance as well.

There are no officers among the prisoners. Among the interrogated soldiers, many had returned in the month of July from Germany after convalescing from wounds or after leaves of absence. For example, *Oberfeldwebel* Egol Alsis on 23.7.42 returned to the company after a month-long leave of absence to Germany, and on that same day he was appointed commander of the 2nd Platoon and sent into combat.

The soldier Kogan Heiden returned from Germany on 11.7.42., where he was under treatment after being wounded. *Unter-offizier* Josef Sattlecker, who worked for five years as a mechanic in military motor repair shops, returned from leave to Austria on 20.7.42 and was made squad leader without any training.

In the 5th Company, most of the soldiers are between 25 and 33 years of age, but some are young men 18-20 years of age who arrived as replacements in July 1942. The majority of the soldiers of the 5th Company, as in the entire 9th Panzer Division, are Austrian. Among the military prisoners are soldiers who've been with the 9th Panzer Division since November 1938. Prior to then, the 9th Panzer Division was called the 4th Light Panzer Division (obviously, the 9th Panzer Division was formed on the basis of the 4th Light Panzer Division). For example, *Obergefreitor* Oskar Tylo was transferred to the 9th Panzer Division in November 1938 from the 1st Panzer Division (Weimar). *Obergefreitor* Hans Frieder was transferred to the 9th Panzer Division in November 1938 from the 23rd Panzer Division (Stuttgart).

This allows one to assume that the 9th Panzer Division was formed up in the autumn of 1939 through cadre soldiers of other units ... Among the replacements that arrived in November 1941 as well as at the beginning of 1942 there are soldiers who were previously serving in security battalions and militia battalions. Wounded soldiers after spending time in hospitals were directed to the 10th Reserve Battalion, where they served in a convalescent company, before being sent to the panzer division together with a batch of replacements from other companies. [...]

Some of the prisoners of war tried to maintain that they surrendered voluntarily, but were compelled to acknowledge that they had no other way out and were in fact taken prisoner by our tankers. The majority of them are confident in Germany's victory. They all want the war to be over as soon as possible and to return home, but only after a successful outcome of the war for Germany. The heavy losses suffered by the regiment in recent days, as well as the hard recent combats have begun to force the prisoners to start to ponder questions of ceasing the war, but haven't yet shaken their faith in the strength of German arms.[1]

1 TsAMO, F. 202, op. 12, d. 499, l. 1107-1110.

Appendix III

Lieutenant Shuklin's exploit: fact and fiction

An article written by the well-known military correspondent Konstantin Simonov appeared in the *Krasnaia zvezda* [*Red Star*] newspaper on 9 August 1942. Entitled "Edinoborstvo" ["Single combat'], the article focused upon the combat of a 76-mm anti-tank gun crew directed by battery commander Lieutenant Shuklin of the 284th Rifle Division against German tanks. Thanks to this correspondent, this article became widely circulated and was mentioned in documents and recollections, and later became known in local history circles as "Lieutenant Shuklin's exploit". The fact that this incident took place during the events that we are examining presents a good opportunity to take a closer look at it in the pages of this book.

For a start, let's look at Konstantin Simonov's article. On its own it is of doubtless historical value to scholars, since Simonov was assigned to Briansk Front in July 1942 and personally met with Shuklin and had a talk with him (and didn't pass on a later version written by staff officers who hadn't witnessed the action). Simonov wrote the correspondence immediately after the events and preserved names and details in it, which weren't left behind in the "dry" TsAMO archival documents. This article is also valuable because very few eyewitness accounts of direct participants in those July battles remain, and each of them is of great interest for our research.

With a great deal of confidence it can be stated that Simonov's article is a literary re-working of Lieutenant Shuklin's own story, and allows us today to see this combat episode through Shuklin's own eyes. It was for this reason that it became for the majority of scholars the firsthand source from which they learned about the hero. Because of its doubtless value – the reliability of the contents, the accurate description of events and Simonov's lively writing style – it is worth starting the conversation regarding Shuklin's exploit with excerpts from the *Krasnaia zvezda* article. In addition, this will allow the reader to better and more quickly grasp the essence of the questions examined subsequently. So, a passage from Konstantin Simonov's article "Edinoborstvo", published in *Krasnaia zvezda* on 9 August 1942:

> It is possible to call this story "Chetyrnadtsat' i odna" ["Fourteen and one"]. The fourteen are tanks. German medium Mark III tanks, the 1939 model. A 50-mm cannon, 2 machine guns, and a crew of four. The one is an anti-tank gun – a Russian, semi-automatic 76-mm cannon. When we speak about the cannon, this means we're implying the gun crew – seven priceless warriors and their commander Lieutenant Shuklin.
>
> [...] In the latter half of July the division was firmly entrenched in positions and then launched an offensive. Immediately, life somehow became merrier. If before, during the retreat, commanding his battery, Shuklin felt only hatred and malice, then now for the first time he was flushed with the intoxication of combat. Passing by the place at which he'd been firing, he could finally see the results of his work. If previously, after a battle, in the brief minutes when he could snatch some sleep, he could quietly close his eyes and instantly fall asleep as if falling into a bottomless black abyss, then now, as if he wasn't fatigued, before

going to sleep he didn't mind talking about what had happened that day, suddenly recalling all the details of the fighting. Indeed, he observed that his soldiers were sharing the same feeling. For the first time ever, in the evening they would gather into a circle, take a seat, and croon, while the life of the party and enthusiastic dancer Akinshin would imitate musical instruments with his voice.

The guns were doing a lot of work, like never before; one day just before evening specialists from the repair shop arrived at the battery and announced that without urgent repairs, it was dangerous to fire the guns; putting it more briefly – it shouldn't be done. The artillery battalion commander ordered for the guns to be withdrawn into a small patch of woods behind the nearest village. All night and the next morning, they worked to repair the guns. But around 1200 in the daytime, while the work was proceeding feverishly, an increasingly fierce cannonade could be heard from the forward positions. The assistant regiment commander came galloping up on a foaming horse and without even dismounting asked about the condition of the guns and whether it was possible to fire them. The repairmen told him that at the moment, it was only possible to fire one gun, but that – now they shook their heads – they couldn't rule out that the gun barrel might burst.

"It will do!" – Gun commander Sergeant Akinshin suddenly blurted out; "That won't happen, my gun won't explode, I know it. Let's go, Comrade Lieutenant!"

But it wasn't necessary to give this prompting to Shuklin. He was already issuing an order to move out. The assistant regiment commander said that German tanks, striving to check our offensive, had launched a counterattack and now there was not a single other gun at hand, except this one. The gun was hitched to a tractor and the tractor started rolling. Shuklin was already nowhere around; he had leaped upon a horse and galloped away in order to select a position in advance. Platoon commander Lieutenant Mal'tsev left together with him. Shuklin selected a position in a dense field of rye on the crest of a hill, which offered a splendid field of vision; the crest of the adjacent hill, where the German tanks should be appearing, was clearly visible. Shuklin impatiently waited for the gun. Finally, it arrived with the tractor, with a full load of ammunition. The lieutenant unlimbered the gun and deployed it in the position, before again galloping up to the crest of the hill. Just at that moment he caught sight of tank silhouettes on the horizon, which were moving toward a village lying to the left of his hill.

First he counted 10 tanks, but then more and more. Altogether, he counted 30 of them. One after another they appeared on the crest of the adjacent hill. This was a very obvious place, for there was an intersection of roads there marked on the map. Shuklin checked this spot on the map, calculated the range, took aim, and with the very first shot set fire to a German tank. The tanks were moving toward him, skirting the hill. An entire series of shots followed the first one. Sitting on a horse 20 meters away from the gun, he was correcting the fire and constantly giving the command "Fire!"

When the third tank was knocked out, the remaining crews obviously spotted the gun's position and opened fire at it while on the move. Shells were exploding all around. At Shuklin's order the gun instantly shifted position and resumed fire. Having lost several more tanks, the Germans once again detected the firing position. Now the shells were landing quite nearby. Shuklin was continuing to correct the fire without dismounting from his horse. The rye was tall, and it was possible to see the battlefield as he should only from atop the horse. With the tenth knocked out tank, the gun began to run low on shells. Shuklin ordered the tractor driver Osadchy to drive a kilometer to the rear and bring up more shells. The tractor headed out directly across an open field. Shell fragments whistled around it, but the tractor was chugging and kept moving. That meant the driver was still alive.

Meanwhile Shuklin was continuing to direct the fire. A shell fragment wounded the thigh of platoon commander Mal'tsev, and immediately thereafter the gun layer Romashev was hit.

Private Kaiumov took over his position at the panoramic sight. The shells had just about all been expended when the tractor returned with a new supply. Osadchy together with signalman Private Lonchakov began to deliver the shells, but at this minute Osadchy was also wounded in the side.

Now 12 German tanks were smoking out in front of them. The remaining, turning around, began to retreat behind the hill, but two of them, which had stopped on the hill, were now firing not while on the move, but from fixed positions. It was necessary to change position again, but the wounded tractor driver was now lying motionless in the rye. For the first time during the combat action, Shuklin climbed down from his horse. Having hitched the gun to the tractor, he took a seat behind the wheel and hauled the gun another 50 meters to a new position. At this moment, a runner from the division headquarters galloped up.

He briskly asked, "Who here is directing the fire?"

"I am", Shuklin said with fatigue, clambering down from the tractor.

"The division commander ordered me to relay his gratitude!" the runner shouted. Shuklin again climbed up on his horse, and the anti-tank gun started barking again. After several hits, two more tanks were knocked out. The last hit, the fourteenth, was particularly successful; the target immediately exploded.

A minute of calm arrived. Then from around one side of the hill, five German trucks with infantry emerged directly out of the rye. They skirted a ravine and headed directly toward the gun. Shuklin fired several rounds, which exploded short, and then ordered Akinshin immediately to elevate the fire and shift it to the edge of the ravine. Frightened by the first shots, the Germans turned around and were delayed at the edge of the ravine. There they were caught by an entire series of shells. Only two of the trucks managed to descend into the ravine. Three, set ablaze by direct hits, were left burning in place. The shot that brewed up the last German truck was the gun's final round. The predictions of the repairmen became true in part: the semi-automatic mechanism stopped working and breech refused to close.

But from out of a woodlot behind them, new guns that were coming up from the rear in order to help finally showed up. Fourteen knocked-out and burned-out tanks were now clearly visible on the adjacent hill. Some were still smoking, while others were simply immobile, blackened hulks in the rye ..."

Unfortunately, for understandable reasons Simonov didn't inform his readers in 1942, where and when this battle he described occurred, but at the time this wasn't important: obviously, the author was trying to raise the soldiers' morale and strengthen the combat spirit of the fighting army and wasn't thinking at all about accommodating the postwar historians. But now, many decades later, the question about exactly where, when and how this combat took place is of undoubtable interest for our research, and available sources allow us to answer these questions with reasonable accuracy.

The comparison and analysis of archival records unequivocally speak to the fact that the described battle took place on 24 July 1942 at the time when the counterattack by the 9th Panzer Division began. This is also confirmed by the initial recommendation for a combat decoration written up for Lieutenant Shuklin (in later award lists, the date is mistakenly given as 26 July; in the August 1942 report of the commander of the 284th Rifle Division on the results of the fighting and the combat lessons gained from it, the action described by Simonov isn't mentioned at all).

To the question as to where exactly this combat action took place and where the valiant artillerymen's firing positions were, for a long time I was unable to give a concise answer, since the studied documents in TsAMO were in this respect insufficiently informative, reporting only that the battle took place "near Perekopovka". Such a "reference" to the location didn't allow the possibility to determine where the anti-tank gun crew's firing positions were located, and only a comparison with captured German documents, from which the axis of the German panzer grouping's actions, its objectives and tasks became clear, permitted an approximate assumption that these firing positions were somewhere northwest, north or northeast of Hill 214.6.

Only relatively recently among archival documents of the IRI RAN [Institute of Russian History of the Russian Academy of Sciences] were materials discovered that allow us to cast conclusive light on this matter.[1] It turned out that back in the war years, in the course of assembling the stories of the frontline men about the fighting that took place, the recollections of veterans of the 284th Rifle Division were recorded, including those of Shuklin himself! In the collection of materials on the 79th Guards Rifle Division (the former 284th Rifle Division), not only his story and a pencil-sketched portrait of him are preserved, but also a scheme of the action drawn by him, which when compared with a map and the text permitted a relatively accurate pinpointing of the area of his guns' firing positions on 24 July 1942. This unexpected discovery in turn allowed a better understanding of how the battle itself went, as well as an assessment of its results.

Supplementing the essay "Edinoborstvo" that he had read in 1942, Lieutenant Shuklin wrote:

> We happened to take direct part in the battle described in the article "Edinoborstvo". Our battery was defending a sector of two villages: O. and P. [Ozerki and Perekopovka – I.S.]. [...] Carrying out the command's order, we manhandled a 76-mm gun onto the crest of a hill, where it, maneuvering and conducting targeted fire, repulsed the attack of a fascist tank column. [...] Having received the order from the chief of artillery to stop the movement of the German tanks, I ordered Akinshin to follow me with the gun, while I hurried ahead on my horse in order to choose a firing position. A low hill, located between the two villages of O. and P. turned out to be a satisfactory place for it.
>
> On a map I determined the firing coordinates out to the nearest line – a ravine. It was possible to do this by ocular means as well. But I didn't want to make a mistake in determining the coordinates or expend excessive shells for registration fire, and I didn't want to waste time. The elevation setting to the ravine was + 50. I noted alternate positions and selected reference points.
>
> In the distance, at a range of 4 kilometers from us, hostile tanks appeared. I counted 30 of them. They were medium tanks, moving rather quickly. Although they were already within reach of our fire, I waited: I considered it advantageous to allow the tanks to close and to fire more surely. When the lead machine drew even with the ravine, which lay at a range of 2.5 kilometers from us, I selected the most tempting group and opened fire. The very first shell struck a tank. The shell's tracer streak signaled a direct hit. I issued a command to open rapid fire. Another tank began to smoke. A third tank quickly moved off to one side. I didn't begin to track it. From the start, I decided to fire at large clusters, consisting of 3-4 tanks each. My calculations were justified: we were firing at such groups almost without a miss. For sure, we kept hitting some target. We destroyed another 2 tanks in the next group. Then the enemy spotted us and opened return fire. The shells were striking the forward slope of the hill. Having spotted a firing tank, I issued the command: "At the tank conducting fire, elevation + 42, one shell, fire!"
>
> The shell overflew the target and exploded to the right of it. I corrected the fire and at elevation + 40 destroyed this machine as well. Other tanks began to fire. The shells were exploding 5-10 meters away from the gun. It was impossible to stay in one place. I gave an order to roll the gun over to a different, previously designated position, which stood 20 meters from the crest. The foe lost sight of their target, and having noticed our silence, headed in our direction,

1 The author wishes to express his gratitude to Konstantin Sergeevich Drozdov, an employee of the Institute, for his assistance in the searches.

apparently believing that they had knocked out our gun. When the machines closed to within short range, we suddenly opened fire and again began to fire at clusters of tanks. Immediately we knocked out 2 tanks. The remaining tanks began to answer while continuing to advance slowly toward us. An artillery duel began.

Under enemy fire we rolled the gun 150 meters off to one side. Here we stopped and continued our gunnery. This maneuver disoriented the foe. He again lost sight of us. Taking advantage of his confusion, we knocked out 2 more tanks. We were running out of shells. We had just five left.

I ordered the tractor driver Osadchy to go for more shells, which were stockpiled next to a church in O[zerki]. Leaving behind platoon commander Lieutenant Mal'tsev to direct the fire, I set off to follow the tractor. I wanted to hurry the loading and delivery of the shells. Along the road I encountered a truck that was carrying 76-mm shells for a neighboring unit. I rejoiced at the pleasant surprise and ordered the truck driver to immediately take the shells to our gun. The driver carried out my order, delivered the shells, and Mal'tsev destroyed two more tanks.

Again we changed positions. Heavier fire was coming from the tanks. The gun layer Sergeant Romashov, two range setters Privates Shmonov and Panin, and then Lieutenant Mal'tsev himself were wounded. However, none of them agreed to leave the battle. Only after a second wound was it necessary to replace the gun layer. The breechblock operator Kaiumov took his place and no less skillfully directed the fire over open sights. He aimed the gun at a target in 5-7 seconds. The training to be able to take over other duties proved very beneficial.

By the end of the first hour of the battle, our gun had destroyed 12 enemy tanks. The remaining tanks couldn't withstand the destructive fire and retreated. Their withdrawal was covered by 2 tanks. We concentrated our fire at them and quickly knocked them out. Unexpectedly on the road leading to the ravine, trucks appeared carrying German infantry. Allowing them to approach to the registered landmark, we began to fire at them at elevation + 20-21. One enemy truck blew up into the air. The others quickly turned back. Our shells flew after them. Another three trucks were destroyed. Our gun crew's combat with 30 medium German tanks lasted approximately 2 hours. The outcome of the action: the enemy's tank attack was repulsed, 14 German tanks were destroyed or knocked out, 4 fascist trucks were destroyed, and approximately 100 Nazis were annihilated.[2]

When comparing Shuklin's own account with Simonov's article, we can see that for the most part they are similar and lay out the course of the battle and its results in primarily the same way. At the same time, though, it is worth noting Shuklin's modesty when he made no mention of the division commander's personal gratitude or his personal bravery, when he kept directing the fire while mounted on his horse, refusing to acknowledge the enemy's fire by taking cover. He also didn't mention taking a seat in the tractor in place of the wounded driver while under fire, or the "fright" of the Germans in the trucks, which was plainly contrived by Simonov, but which neither he nor Shuklin could know about with any certainty. The absence in Simonov's article of the episode regarding Shuklin's requisitioning of the truck that was carrying shells to a different unit is also fully explainable – it was plainly undesirable to write about such an emergency means of self-supply with ammunition in the Red Army's central newspaper. It is unsurprising that instead of the requisitioned truck, according to Simonov a "tractor with a fresh supply" delivered the shells to the artillerymen and at the end of the battle, "new guns from the rear" were arriving to help the valiant crew, which in fact never happened.

2 Arkhiv IRI RAN, fond 2, razdel 1, op. 21, d. 15, ll. 25-27.

At a conference of the command staff in Krasnoufimka, to where the 284th Rifle Division had been withdrawn after the fighting for rest and replenishment in August 1942, the 284th Rifle Division's commander Colonel Batiuk paid particular attention to the combat at Perekopovka, but in the process didn't mention at all the name of Lieutenant Shuklin, shifting the honors to the gun commander subordinate to him and the commander of a neighboring battery:

> During the battle, all of our guns began to reach a technically dangerous condition. They were under extreme stress, because we had decided to fire to the utmost and fired according to the demands of the situation. Only one gun remained that was capable of fighting. The task was carried out. In this action there were models of exceptional courage, and never-before-seen achievements were accomplished here. Commander Akinshin with one 76-mm gun destroyed 14 tanks. Battery commander Iurchenko, who destroyed 5 tanks, 3 vehicles and killed up to 500 fascists performed brilliantly on this day.[3]

Why Batiuk failed to write about Lieutenant Shuklin remains unclear, and there is now no one to ask about this …

Now, after reading all three sources and on the basis of all the information contained therein, we'll try to analyze the course of the battle and its results. In reality, on the morning of 24 July, several dozen German tanks did appear within Lieutenant Shuklin's field of vision, when they first arrived on a hill at the southern end of the long, broad Ozerki ravine, and then began to advance toward Hill 212.9. These were the tanks of the 9th Panzer Division's shock grouping, and I have no doubts that their approach took place just as Shuklin described it. However, his interpretation of the enemy's intentions and actions was inaccurate. He believed that the hostile tanks were attacking toward Ozerki and striving to break through the line occupied by his artillerymen, when in fact the 9th Panzer Division had no such task. Its objective was to overrun the positions of the 237th Rifle Division on the hills south and east of the lengthy Ozerki ravine, crush the resistance on Hills 212.9 and 217.8, and create the basis for a deep envelopment and subsequent encirclement of Operational Group Chibisov's shock grouping.[4]

For this the panzer regiment of the 9th Panzer Division was to operate not to the north toward Ozerki, but to the northeast, in order to reach Surikovye Vyselki from the west while bypassing Lomovo. Thus, pursuant to their order, the German panzer elements were increasingly diverging away from Ozerki, gradually exiting Shuklin's field of vision, and disappearing from sight in the hilly terrain. Unobserved from Shuklin's position, after destroying the regiments of the 237th Rifle Division, they totally vacated Hill 212.9 with their main forces, leaving behind their infantry to mop up the hill, and continued to attack to the northeast. However, ignorant of the foe's real intentions, Shuklin and his artillerymen believed, they had repulsed an offensive by 30 German tanks with the fire of their single anti-tank gun, having destroyed or knocked out 14 of them and forcing the rest to retreat!

As we see, the incorrect interpretation of the enemy's actions led Shuklin and his artillerymen to draw mistaken conclusions regarding the course and outcome of the fighting. It must be stated directly that a purposeful attack of German tanks directly toward their position never really happened, and thus the assertion that Shuklin's gun repelled a simultaneous attack by 30 German tanks is incorrect. Indeed, the crew of a single gun could hardly have done this even had such an attack really happened as many other episodes of those battles eloquently testify, when anti-tank

3 TsAMO, F. 1227, op. 1, d. 6, l. 28.
4 NARA, T-315, roll 541, fr. 001112-114.

guns even in a much larger number proved unable to withstand the massed attacks of armor and perished under the fire and tracks of the attacking tanks.

I'm confident that in such a situation, Lieutenant Shuklin and his men would have fought to the finish, but considering the enormous superiority in firepower of the approaching German tanks – 30 cannons and approximately 60 machine guns – one can hardly doubt that in the end, the tanks would have overwhelmed the firing anti-tank gun (possibly in a literal sense as well), and the fate of its crew under the storm of machine-gun and cannon fire would not have been enviable. The clearly lopsided (I would even say, incommensurable) force in such a situation and the numerous examples of the war's combat experience speak to the fact that the crew of one single anti-tank gun was unable to oppose the attack of an enemy armored armada for very long.

Let's turn now to the question regarding the German losses. Lieutenant Shuklin believed that in addition to the 4 trucks and "approximately 100 wiped-out Nazis" his artillerymen destroyed or knocked out 14 tanks in this battle. How objective is this belief? It is clear that in distinction from the infantry and trucks, which were unprotected by armor, the tank presents a much more difficult target for an anti-tank gun, since even fragments from a nearby exploding shell are not a threat to it. In order to knock out an armored vehicle, it is necessary first of all to achieve a direct hit against it, and secondly this hit must be sufficiently destructive, in order to inflict enough damage to the tank (or its crew) to deprive it of combat capability or fully make it an irrecoverable loss.

Let's examine the first of these necessary conditions. How difficult was it to hit a target at a range of several kilometers? For contemporary military equipment with laser range-finding, computer calculations of the ballistic information, and the rapid, automatic achievement of a firing solution (even considering a multitude of most diverse factors), it is most likely impossible to call this task very difficult. However, as we understand, in 1942 Lieutenant Shuklin didn't have any of these benefits of modern technology, but was forced in the battle on 24 July to use a map, an optical sight, and his own visual estimations.

Would they be sufficient to strike a tank accurately at a range of 2.5 kilometers with the very first shot? In my opinion, no, though of course the element of chance and a great deal of luck can't rule this out. But what if this tank is not immobile, but moving, especially at a lateral angle of deflection with varying speed, an unpredictable heading, and with stops? These factors greatly complicate a task that isn't even simple without them, and the absence of special targeting systems makes this most difficult to do. As we understand, Shuklin didn't have any such targeting systems; in the best case he could use binoculars for observation and in order to adjust the fire (although the lack of any mention of them in his account, just as in the case of Simonov's article, suggests that he possibly didn't have any binoculars).

Let's give a thought to this. The muzzle velocity of the authorized 76-mm armor-piercing shells, which the Red Army had in 1942 varied between 655 and 662 meters per second (but to simplify calculations, let's round this off to 660 meters/sec). Understandably, in the ensuing moments the shell's velocity dropped, and in order to overcome the 2.5 to 3 kilometers to the enemy tanks, at which range this exchange of fire primarily took place back then, required not 4-5 seconds, but even more. Over this interval of time, a tank moving at an average speed (let's assume 20 to 25 kilometers an hour) would cover several dozen meters.

At the same time, the anti-tank gun crew, as one can understand from the description of the battle, didn't have a good field of vision. The gunners were firing at Shuklin's command, who was mounted on a horse in order to see over a field of rye that was taller than a man's height and get a better look at what was happening. The gun layer, in essence, was forced to "search" through the tall grain that was hindering observation, which of course complicated aiming. The crew didn't have enough time or men to clear the grain in order to create an adequate field of view in the situation, and moreover, such an activity carried the risk of worsening the camouflage and might have made the anti-tank gun more noticeable for the German gunners that were searching for it. Thus, we'll once again note that obtaining a direct hit against a mobile target (Shuklin himself commented that the German tanks were moving "rather quickly") at such a range and in such unsatisfactory conditions was, putting it gently, an extremely complex and difficult task. The factor of the wear on the anti-tank gun's barrel, which unavoidably reduces the accuracy of its fire, makes this even more difficult.

Nevertheless, Lieutenant Shuklin believed that without any preliminary registration fire, the very first shell discharged by his gun accurately struck the German tank at a range of 2.5 kilometers and immediately brewed it up. Such an amazing result can be explained by the impressive gunnery of a military professional, a rare stroke of luck … or by Shuklin's self-deception, who was <u>feverishly</u> replacing reality with the desirable in his assessment of the accuracy of his shot.

Attention should also be given to Shuklin's entirely unique method of targeting – at clusters of German tanks. It is completely obvious that these groups of German tanks seemed tightly clustered only from long range, whereas from close up the distance between their tanks (which were moreover moving) was more likely dozens, or perhaps even hundreds of meters. What then was the targeting aim point? Some perceived center of the group? However, in such a case such gunnery was akin to area fire with all the deleterious consequences this would have on the accuracy of hitting individual armored targets. The effectiveness of such fire at tanks several kilometers away could hardly be high …

Now let's look at the problem of the accuracy of fire from the opposite side. Understandably, a 76-mm anti-tank gun was substantially lower and smaller than a tank, and it was much more difficult to catch sight of it in the tall rye. Nevertheless, according to Shukin's own story, in the course of the action the German tanks each time spotted the gun and blanketed it with dense fire, forcing him to alter firing positions three times. Aside from the gun that was concealed in the field, however, there was the battery commander on horseback not far from the gun, and also the much taller tractor and truck which were more easily distinguishable from a distance that moved across this very same field during the battle, approached the gun and disclosed its position.

Undoubtedly, they were within direct eyesight of the German crews. Nevertheless, even the fire of many tanks, the gunners of which were using the high-quality Zeiss optics and the most up-to-date sights at the time, failed to produce a single direct hit against the gun, much less either the truck or the tractor. The best these gunners were able to achieve was the placement of their shells within 5-10 meters of the gun, according to Shuklin's story.

Of course, the fragments of the shells that were exploding close to their firing position wounded an increasing number of its crew, but the anti-tank gun itself remained serviceable and continued to fire, until it was knocked out of action due to mechanical problems. Only a direct hit might have destroyed the gun itself, but the adversary didn't manage to achieve this. On the basis of these facts, one can assume with complete justification that if the dense fire of many German tanks at a range of several kilometers failed to generate a direct hit, then the probability of 16-18 direct hits in a row (including the trucks) against moving targets from just the same range, given the fire of just a single gun, seems to me to be dubious, putting it gently.

It is worth noting as well that K. Simonov didn't give the range to the German tanks from the position of Shuklin's anti-tank gun in his article. Possibly, this was not a coincidence, since he clearly understood that material published in the *Red Star* newspaper relating that a single 76-mm anti-tank gun by itself destroyed 14 enemy tanks with direct hits <u>*from a range of 2-3 kilometers*</u> might have prompted extreme doubts among professional artillerymen in the reality of such super-accurate gunnery, the improbable armor penetration, and the described victory itself ….

Now we'll switch from discussing the problems related to the accuracy of the fire to a discussion of the degree of its effects on the tanks. We don't know which particular 76-mm gun that Shuklin's artillery crew was using at the time. Let's assume that they were using the most contemporary model at that time – the famous divisional ZIS-3 cannon, which entered widespread use among the troops in 1942. A contemporary review of it states: "In its armor-penetrating effects before the beginning of 1943, the ZIS-3 was capable of penetrating the frontal armor of virtually any model of German tank from a range of 500-700 meters." Let's note an important consideration for our question: the review specifies a range of 500-700 meters, not at all 2.5-3 kilometers! According to the statistical table, even with the most beneficial angle of incidence of 90 degrees, the 76-mm armor-piercing shell could only penetrate up to 50 mm of armor from a range of 1,500 meters. But what about a range of 2.5 to 3 kilometers? There is simply no information for the effects of fire from that range in the table, but obviously, armor-penetrating capabilities don't improve at all with an increase in range, but decline. At the same time it is necessary to note that the 9th Panzer Division, as one of the panzer divisions of Army Group South that was designated for conducting Operation Blau, was primarily equipped by the start of the offensive with the latest models of medium tanks with a frontal armor of 50-70 mm, and 30-50 mm for the side armor of the hull and turret.

It is completely obvious that when taking into consideration these factors, the likelihood that a 76-mm shell would penetrate the armor of enemy tanks at a range of several kilometers cannot be called "high". If you take into consideration the fact that with the increase in range to the target from 500 meters to 1,000 meters, and then to 1,500 meters, the armor penetrating capability decreased from 70 mm to 60 mm and 50 mm respectively (again given the most beneficial angle of incidence of 90 degrees), then it can be assumed that at a range of 2.5 to 3 kilometers, the shell might be theoretically capable of penetrating only armor thinner than 50 mm.

If at the same time the angle of incidence is less than optimal, the probability of which was very high given the tank's movement, its angle relative to the firing gun and the descending trajectory of the shell's flight at great ranges, then the shell's penetrating capability dropped even further. The strike and explosion of a 6.5 kilogram shell with 119 to 155 grams of explosive material would of course be sufficient to damage the tank; however, to knock it out irrecoverably (to set it ablaze) would become a quite problematic matter.

However, perhaps all of these hypothetical considerations are worth little in the attempts to explain the practical realities of that specific combat action and cannot provide a serious basis to doubt in the objectivity of its direct participants? Let's assume so. It must be acknowledged that resting on only hypothetical considerations in historical research can hardly be sufficient to draw any categorical conclusions.

In that case let's return to the documents that might confirm or refute our considerations and assumptions. It is completely apparent that the loss of 14 tanks (of which 12 were destroyed!) in a combat with one Soviet anti-tank gun alone, together with the losses of combat machines sustained in the numerous other combat episodes that day, would have substantially reduced the number of operational tanks in the 9th Panzer Division by the evening of 24 July 1942. However, the German documents unequivocally inform us that this didn't happen.[5]

If on the evening of 22 July there were 94 combat-ready tanks in the 33rd Panzer Regiment (not including the 5 Pz-I tanks, which were no longer being used in combat and were employed primarily as tow vehicles), then on the evening of 24 July, which is to say after one and a half days of combat, the panzer regiment now had 96 operational tanks, albeit the composition had changed (there were 3 fewer Pz-II tanks, although not one of them had been lost irrecoverably; in addition, the number of Pz-IV tanks had decreased by 4, but considering the intensity of the combat actions on other days and in other areas, it is very doubtful that they were all lost irrecoverably on 24 July, whereas the number of serviceable Pz-III tanks increased by 8, which had obviously returned from repair by that time).

5 NARA, T-315, roll 541, fr. 000708-725.

The information on unrecoverable loss in equipment of the 9th Panzer Division also leave no doubt that the assertion regarding 12 destroyed German tanks in that battle is fiction. Even over all the days of combat with the Soviet units that were opposing it, the 9th Panzer Division's irrecoverable losses in tanks were much lower than the number given by Lieutenant Shuklin.[6] If we examine 24 July specifically, then on that day the 9th Panzer Division was engaged in bitter fighting primarily with the 237th Rifle Division, and only partially with the 284th and 340th Rifle Divisions and the 201st Tank Brigade, and subsequently entered into an exchange of fire with the 2nd Tank Corps' 148th Tank Brigade with its forward units. All of these formations reported knocking out and destroying enemy tanks, the total number of which on paper reached many dozens. Shuklin's share in these declared (but not real!) enemy losses came to approximately one-fifth.

Analyzed captured German documents don't give us the possibility to confirm or refute Shuklin's assertion about the destruction of four trucks by his artillerymen. I am inclined to believe that at the very least, the likelihood of such a result is much higher than in the case with the tanks, considering that even fragments of nearby exploding shells were able to destroy and set ablaze unarmored vehicles. It is fully possible that several enemy trucks were in fact destroyed as a result of the fire of Shuklin's anti-tank crew. The losses in personnel of the German divisions are known: the 9th Panzer Division lost 34 men killed and 226 wounded on 24 July.[7] The 340th Infantry Division correspondingly lost 20 killed, 224 wounded and 31 missing in action.[8] Altogether, 54 men were killed and 31 went missing in action, which yields a total of 85 men (a certain portion of the missing in action wound up as prisoners of war, and correspondingly weren't "wiped out"). Yet this was *over the entire day* of 24 July in combat *with all of our units* and not just *with the crew of a single 76-mm anti-tank gun* of the 284th Rifle Division. How many of these "wiped out Nazis" went to the share of Shuklin's artillerymen? That isn't known precisely, but it is totally clear that it was *much* less than Shuklin reported.

As we see, from the available materials it follows that the real losses inflicted on the enemy was not at all like the young battery commander believed, which once again confirms the general, persistent tendency of those times: enemy losses in the reports were greatly exaggerated. In the case with Shuklin, this obviously was connected with the fact that in the heat of the battle, given the poor field of vision and the long, even extreme range of fire, it was extremely difficult for his comrades and him to assess objectively the real results of their combat activity. The ashes, dust and smoke from the explosions in the area of the enemy's penetration of the 237th Rifle Division's defenses, where fierce fighting was seething with the participation of other artillery units and rocket launchers, made this even more difficult. In addition, the battlefield in the end remained in the Germans' possession, so it was impossible to investigate it to ascertain the enemy's losses. Thus Shuklin's bold conclusions could not be confirmed and were based exclusively on observation from a range of several kilometers, which was plainly inadequate for accurate assessments.

Then what might have been the tactical significance of this combat action? Undoubtedly, the fire of a Soviet 76-mm anti-tank gun even from a range of several kilometers delayed the advance of hostile tanks and diverted a portion of them from fulfilling the main task. Instead of focusing on actions in the area of the hills along the eastern side of the Ozerki ravine, the crews of the left-hand shock group of the 33rd Panzer Regiment were forced to pivot from the northeast direction due to Shuklin's fire, time and again had to search for the anti-tank gun's new firing position, and

6 Ibid. fr. 000751.

7 NARA, T-315, roll 541, fr. 001431.

8 NARA, T-314, roll 354, fr. 000726-727.

again and again open fire at it in the attempt to destroy this "fiendish Russian thorn" that was hindering them. As we see, their fire had no great success.

In the account of the 9th Panzer Division, there is a quite eloquent mention of its tank wedge's "loss of traction" in the launched counterattack: "As was presumed, the 33rd Panzer Regiment ran into fierce resistance south of Hill 212.9. A large quantity of anti-tank weapons [of the Russians] initially blocked the path of the offensive, and now and then numerous enemy tanks, launching flank attacks, tried to disrupt the attack."[9] There are no doubts that in this fierce Russian resistance noted by the enemy, Lieutenant Shuklin's artillerymen played no small role, the fire of which the annoyed German tank crews might have fully taken as the flank attacks of numerous, unknown Russian tanks, which judging from all available evidence were simply not present at all in those hours. If you will, the tactical effect and undoubted success of Lieutenant Shuklin's artillerymen indeed consists in this diversion of part of the hostile shock grouping and the fixing of the actions of the German tanks; through their self-sacrificial resistance, the anti-tank crew helped the adjacent 237th Rifle Division, which had come under an overwhelming armored assault, as best they could and in this sense, they did their duty. They could do no more in the situation that had arisen.

Now we will turn to the main question, which most likely comes to the meticulous and sharp-eyed reader after reading all of the above: If Lieutenant Shuklin and the anti-tank gun crew were in fact unable to stop the German offensive and didn't inflict heavy losses to the foe, then what was their exploit, and was there one at all?

I will give an unambiguous answer to this question: their exploit, of course, was real, and it can be called such without any quotation marks. However, it consisted not in the figures of the losses inflicted upon the Germans nor in the disruption of their offensive, but in the moral victory of Shuklin and his combat comrades, who didn't give way in a mortal combat with a vastly superior enemy force.

It shouldn't be forgotten that we are judging those long ago events with the benefit of hindsight. We know now that the 9th Panzer Division's massed armored attack was directed not at Shuklin's position, but to the northeast of it, and that the 33rd Panzer Regiment didn't have the direct task to break through the position that he occupied. However, Shuklin and his comrades didn't know this, and couldn't know it (indeed, the higher command also had no knowledge of the German plans …). Thus, having seen the German tanks out in front of him, Shuklin had every right to believe that they were going to attack his position – with 30 tanks, against his anti-tank gun alone. At the same time he couldn't expect any help, and his worn-out gun itself might refuse to work at any moment (as eventually happened).

Yet despite all this, Lieutenant Shuklin accepted battle, striving at whatever the cost to stop the attack of 30 hostile tanks, knowing full well how this battle might end for him. Just by itself, this very decision and the self-sacrificial resolve to stand to the end in those particular circumstances can already be called an exploit. But what of the clash itself? One gun traded fire with a horde of enemy armored vehicles. Their gunners were time and again searching for it, furiously firing fragmentation shells at the firing position, which caused growing casualties among the crew. At any moment the next shell might envelop the gun and its entire crew with a final, deadly explosion. What nerves and will must the battery commander have had, in order to stand up to this punishment and not "break"? To refuse to seek shelter on his horse in a nearby defilade, and having spat at it all, to withdraw from combat as quickly as possible, pointing to the "threat that the barrel might burst", the lack of help, and the impossibility of repulsing all alone a simultaneous attack by 30 fascist tanks? However, neither Shuklin nor any of his combat comrades flinched. Even the

9 NARA, T-315, roll 541, fr. 001111.

wounded artillerymen refused to leave the battlefield and stood to the death in the position they occupied. This was their exploit.

It is even more significant because in those desperately hard days of the new German successes and our defeats, there were, alas, a multitude of examples of a completely different nature, when even in a much less dangerous situation and given a more satisfactory correlation of forces, the Soviet elements couldn't withstand an audacious enemy onslaught and fled in disarray, or else abandoned their positions in panic without combat, tossing aside their weapons and equipment. In that depressing situation of heavy losses and bitter defeats, Shuklin's combat was a splendid example of how one must fight and do his military duty.

It isn't surprising that having learned about this combat episode, Konstantin Simonov, who had seen a lot on the Briansk front (it was here, devastated by what he had seen and heard, that he grasped the intent of the famous Order No. 277 [the "Not one step back" Order] that had arrived in the troops and had been read to him), decided to write a special article about Shuklin. In it he showed a simple, provincial Russian fellow, who was heroically fighting for the Motherland. So Shuklin became an example and model for inspiring very many soldiers, commanders and political workers of the Red Army, who saw in him not the artist's depiction of a poster board hero, but a flesh-and-blood man with feelings, hopes and aspirations that they all understood. They saw that the combat hero was similar to them, like them, and one of them. Just like a combat comrade in a neighboring foxhole.

The ending of Simonov's article is touching with its inspiration, faith and optimism, as if he was conversing with the reader: With such people like Shuklin and his combat comrades, we absolutely will endure and emerge victorious no matter how hard things are now:

> The artillerymen are preparing a soup from young potatoes in their pots. An enticing steam rises from the pots. German long-range artillery is bombarding the woods, and an as of yet undispersed bluish-gray smoke is also rising above the fresh shell craters. We are sitting together with Shuklin. He has piercing black eyes and a merry, very young face. But he suddenly takes on a serious, manly expression when he talks about the battle. The word "exploit" is not in his lexicon. Perhaps, even if he had performed one, he doesn't consider it an exploit, but from the happy expression on his face one can sense that this combat action was the fulfilment of his most cherished and strongest desires. He recalls why he had come to the front, and his childlike face immediately becomes the inspired face of a warrior and man.
>
> Then, giving some thought, he suddenly begins to recall recent events and people, which have no connection with the war – his mother and father who reside in the distant city of Oyrot Tura [present-day Gorno-Altaisk, the administrative center of the Altai republic]; his Komsomol comrades from Oyrot Tura, where he was a bureau member of the Komsomol district committee; and a young woman, Valia Nekrasova, who had left to join the fleet in the Far East and had recently sent him a letter while en route, from Novosibirsk.
>
> I hope that having read this newspaper edition, Shuklin's mother and father were proud of their son, that the Komsomol members of Oyrot Tura recalled their comrade, whose example they need to follow and that the young woman Valia Nekrasova knows that a genuinely fine man with the direct gaze and strong hand of the soldier loves her.

What was the further fate of Lieutenant Shuklin? For the action at Perekopovka, the division command put him up for the Order of the Red Star. The article about the famous artilleryman of the 284th Rifle Division was later published in the *Pravda* newspaper as well. After rest and replenishment, the 284th Rifle Division was sent to Stalingrad, and there Shuklin again fought with his battery in a most intense stage of the fighting, and was decorated with another combat Order. There, on the banks of the Volga, he, like thousands of other experienced, valiant frontline men who'd been forged in battle, became the foundation of that invincible army, who (like Shuklin had once done in the battle near Perekopovka) refused to break under the enraged onslaught of the Germans, but only became compressed like a steel spring, before releasing, answering the foe with the crushing Stalingrad offensive.

At the beginning of May 1943, for the courage and heroism he had displayed, the division command wrote Il'ia Shuklin up for the highest honor, the title "Hero of the Soviet Union". On 5 June, after passing up the chain of command, the Commander-in-Chief of the Southwestern Front General of the Army Malinovsky wrote his final resolution on the recommendation: "Worthy". But it wasn't until 26 October 1943 by a decree of the USSR Presidium of the Supreme Soviet that Guards Senior Lieutenant Il'ia Zakharovich Shuklin was awarded the title "Hero of the Soviet Union" "with the bestowing of the Order of Lenin and the Gold Star medal".

Alas, he was no longer able to receive them, nor could he know about his heroic title. By this date of awarding, he was no longer among the living. On 21 July 1943, just 12 days before his 21st birthday, he was killed in action on the Severskii Donets River during the Soviet counteroffensive after the victory at Kursk. In the recommendation written to bestow him with the Order of the Patriotic War posthumously, it was written:

> In the area of Belaia Dolina in the offensive fighting of our units to liberate the Donbas region, on 21-22 July 1943 Comrade Shuklin took up open fighting positions in order to escort our infantry and was moving in the infantry's combat formations. In this battle Comrade Shuklin's battery repelled two enemy tank attacks in its sector, destroyed 7 tanks and 2 anti-tank guns, and killed more than a platoon of enemy soldiers and officers. Comrade Shuklin behaved heroically in this battle, personally correcting the fire over open sights at the fascist tanks and firing positions. In this battle, Comrade Shuklin was killed in a blaze of glory.

Reading this recommendation, the thought involuntarily comes to mind that the details of this battle and the death of the heroic artilleryman are very reminding of the circumstances of the combat action at Perekopovka. The situation was similar – a stalwart, fearless commander, who was personally directing his battery under enemy fire and laying direct fire from an exposed firing position. Just as it had been in July 1942 …

Unfortunately, this time the frontline Fates didn't spare the hero, like they had done a year before, when not a single bullet or shell fragment touched him as he was mounted on his horse in close proximity to the German shells that were exploding around him. Alas, life at the front was often short. Lieutenant Shuklin fought heroically at the front for just more than a year, but still managed to accomplish the main thing: Looking up to him and inspired by his example, other lieutenants arrived to replace him, who unstoppably led their soldiers to the west.

Guards Senior Lieutenant Shuklin was buried in the liberated soil of the Ukraine, close to the village of Golaia Dolina in a "Pioneer's Camp on the left bank of the Severskii Donets River". Our eternal gratitude to him, and may we forever cherish the memory of him!

Appendix IV

A veteran tanker's recollections of the fighting on 25 July 1942

I began collecting the materials for this book more than 30 years ago. A lot of veterans of the war were still in good health back then and were able to share their recollections with me. I understood that time was fleeting and there was much to be saved, so I initiated a search for more veterans.

In 1989-1990, I was fortunate to attend gatherings of veterans of the 1st Guards Tank Brigade and personally became acquainted with many of them. Their stories about their service, the war years, and their experiences at the front were a genuine discovery for me. They helped me better picture and understand what it was like back then to fight, and what our soldiers at the front were thinking about and feeling; how they lived and, alas, died in those fierce battles. Subsequently I corresponded with and met with these 1st Guards Tank Brigade veterans and I'm proud of these meetings and letters. One of them, Vasilii Vladimirovich Iaroshenko, sent me a notebook with many pages of entries back in 1990, which I preserve as precious relic.

I will cite a lengthy excerpt from his recollections; in distinction from the staff documents that reflected the view of the command, as they say, "from atop a high hill", they offer us the rare opportunity to see those battles through the eyes of an ordinary tanker in his combat machine.[1] Thus, a participant in those heated battles in the summer of 1942 Vasilii Vladimirovich Iaroshenko, a former driver-mechanic of the 1st Guards Tank Brigade, recalls:

> It was an unbearably hot summer, not a single cloud and inside the tank it was literally like a hot oven – it was impossible to breathe. In the daytime the armor was so hot that it was impossible to touch it. During a battle, when the main gun and machine guns were firing, a lot of the propellant fumes remained in the tank's fighting compartment, because the tank had no special exhaust ventilators, and the sole exhaust fan was the turbine of the master clutch through the wall that separated the engine compartment from the fighting compartment.
>
> In such cases the crew simply had no way to breathe, sweat was streaming down your face, trickling into your eyes, worsening the already restricted view through the observation lenses. Your mouth became dry due to the propellant fumes and your throat burned. In intervals of calm during a battle, each crewman would thirstily fill a cup or two of water from a canister that we always kept in reserve. There was also always a self-rolled cigarette with shag tobacco dangling from your mouth, a distinctive "narcotic" for calming the nerves.
>
> The day stretched on unbelievably slowly, and with the onset of darkness, they set out on a march to the assembly area that didn't allow even the slightest rest. As was the established routine back then, the commanders were busy with tactical discussions, while the crews readied the equipment on those short summer nights, showing no regard for themselves. At the same time I'll allow myself to repeat that the main burden was placed on the

1 1990 papers, author's personal collection.

driver-mechanics, on whose skill and bravery rested not only the success in battle, but also the lives of the rest of the crew. However, in every respect, these were humans and their capabilities weren't limitless. Therefore on the second and especially the third day of battle, despite the responsibility placed on them, the sense of reaction to the surrounding situation became sharply dulled, and the real danger of battle faded into the background, and all movements to handle the machine, in response to the situation, were seemingly carried out automatically.

Not everyone can image it what it means to go 2-3 days without rest, and even more so, not everyone believes that you can fall asleep during a battle. Yes, this even happened with me while maneuvering in combat; having identified a target and coming to a stop, you squeeze both clutch levers and instantly your eyes close automatically and you drift off to sleep. The gun fires, the tank's body rocks, your eyes open and your hands release the clutches, your foot gives gas to the engine, and again you advance, altering your direction and searching for a target. This keeps repeating until the crisis passes. After such battles, among those who survived, it is hard to recognize a man. It seemed that not real men emerged from the machines, but bogeymen, with grimy faces and scruffy beards, reddened eyes in deeply sunk sockets and hollow cheeks. What willpower did one have to have to endure all this?

The situation grew tense and was changing by the hour. On 25.7 the Germans broke through in one of the neighboring sectors and with their subsequent advance created the threat of reaching the Don River. That night, our four crews marched 12-15 kilometers to this sector and took up a defense within 1 kilometer of the river itself. [Judging from the documents, the esteemed veteran is mistaken, because the 1st Guards Tank Brigade's command didn't send any separate tank groups to the Don River. Over all these days, the 1st Guards Tank Brigade, like the other brigades of the 1st Tank Corps, was operating around Lebiazh'e and to the southwest of there. Most likely, the night march that Iaroshenko writes about was conducted not toward the Don River, but to somewhere in the Lomovo area, in order to screen the tank brigade's actions from the north, which is partially confirmed by the documents in the "Memorial" Consolidated Database regarding the losses of personnel of the 1st Guards Tank Brigade – I.S.] In the sector of defense of a rifle unit that numbered no more than a battalion, we dispersed our machines in the anticipated direction of the enemy.

The sun began to rise. Climbing out of the machine, I began, as was my job, to inspect the machine and the surrounding terrain, in order to camouflage it. Suddenly a cannon shot rang out from the right and struck below the turret of Lieutenant Koshkarev's tank, which was positioned 150 meters to the right. From the hit, the turret hatches flew open and a small stream of smoke poured out of the turret. Immediately driver-mechanic Liubushkin and radio operator N. Etnenko exited the tank and came running toward our tank, which was standing closer to a deep, wooded draw that extended from the river.

I realized that the Germans, undetected by the infantry, at dawn had rolled up anti-tank guns to somewhere close by, and over open sights from extremely close range, invisible in the tall vegetation, began to fire at our tanks. Instantly leaping into the tank, I began to back the machine up. Simultaneously, in order to decrease the likelihood of a shell hit in the flank, I began to pivot the tank to face the enemy's direction, thereby creating a more acute angle.

All of my attention was so focused on this task that having put the machine in rear gear and stepped on the gas, with both hands I was clutching the left lever, before I'd even had time to close the forward hatch. The shot from the German gun, and then my subsequent actions, were a puzzle to the rest of the slumbering crew, who had opened their eyes in bewilderment after their sleepless night and were looking at me.

At that instant, the first round struck the right side in the lower portion of the fighting compartment, and through the roar of the engine I heard as the diesel fuel began to bubble from the penetrated side tank. I hauled back on the lever with all my might, pivoting the tank, while my brain was working feverishly: faster, faster, so that the second shell, which might be an incendiary shell, doesn't brew up the tank …

Just at that moment, the second armor-piercing slug struck the second road wheel, after which the track began to scrape against the deformed, broken wheel. Immediately a third armor-piercing slug struck the forward idler wheel just when the tank had almost completed pivoting to face the German gun; the hit happened in front of my eyes through the open hatch, and I saw the sparks of the shell hit flying off in every direction together with pieces of the smashed track cover. At that moment, the tank took cover in the draw behind a finger of the woods. Liubushin and Etnenko, who had come running up to our machine said that Lieutenant Koshkarev and gun commander K. Beliaev were instantly killed by the direct hit of the shell. There was no need to doubt their words, because both of their uniforms and caps were bloody and flecked with pieces of human flesh.

After my advice to evacuate the knocked-out tank that had been abandoned by the crew, driver-mechanic Liubushkin ran over to the tank. Obviously, the Germans realized his intention, and even before he had reached the tank, one shot rang out, followed by a second. Koshkarev's tank erupted and blew apart, since it still had a full load of shells and full tank of fuel and the Germans' incendiary shells did their work.

The running gear of our tank was so damaged that it could no longer move under its own power. The tank company commander Lieutenant Kolganov (later, in August, he was badly wounded and lost both legs, and now [in 1990 – I.S.] resides in Moscow], gave an order to platoon commander Lieutenant Kazakov to destroy the German anti-tank gun. The tanks of the company commander and Lieutenant Kazakov were located in a hollow behind a projection of woods, and thus were sheltered from the German fire.

Unfortunately, Lieutenant Kazakov had arrived in the brigade together with a batch of replacements during the Voronezh fighting, and judging from his actions, he didn't have enough experience; from the start he failed to establish the direction of the enemy's position through observation, and he hurried to fulfill the order. Straight away, not having even advanced 200 meters, his tank was struck by the first shot after it had climbed a low rise. The tank burst into flames and none of his crew was able to escape the tank; they all died in the fire. Only Lieutenant Kazakov climbed out of the tank, but his overalls were burning (even though it was thought that they were fireproof, having been impregnated with a special mixture); the lieutenant rolled around on the ground, trying to smother the flames, and the nearby infantry only passively looked on, making no attempt even to rescue him.

That's how driver-mechanic A.I. Lymar', Lieutenant Kazakov, and Senior Sergeant V.M Zlobin perished. There is a Russian saying: "Each individual is strong with hindsight" [or "Hindsight is 20/20"]. Thus, without judging the living or the fallen, I want to say that because of our lack of caution, and at times even stupidity and laziness and God knows what other obvious characteristics we have, we suffered unjustified losses in the war.

Plainly, by paying heed to the Golden Rule – reconnoiter before all else – these losses might not even have happened, if the company commander had first arrayed the tanks in the combat formations of the infantry, which were dug into a potato field, had initially camouflaged them in a stand of woods, and only then initiated the action.

There's even more as far as the death of Lieutenant Kazakov is concerned. We, who had learned on the basis of bitter experience, didn't have the chance to advise the lieutenant that when going into battle, especially in overalls, one mustn't tighten up the belts. Unfortunately, young lieutenants would tighten a belt over the overalls and criss-cross the shoulder straps. Thus in such cases it was simply impossible to wriggle out of the burning clothing by yourself. The company commander might have told him this in the mandatory council, especially because in the summer battles we not only didn't wear the overalls, we didn't wear waist belts either; our pistol was always behind one bootleg, and a knife behind the other.

Thus, of the 4 tanks we now had only 2, of which only one – the company commander's tank – was serviceable; our tank couldn't move on its own and needed to be towed. The Germans, seeing the damage they'd done to us, became bold and began to harry our infantry with automatic weapons fire, while moving up a gun under its cover in order to deal with our remaining tanks. Infantry observers reported this. Therefore the company commander Kalganov decided to destroy the enemy gun. Having given our crew an order to imitate the movement of a tank by working the engine while simultaneously firing periodically in the direction of the position of the enemy's anti-tank gun, Kalganov emerged on its flank and destroyed it. However, just as our tank company commander attached a tow to our machine in order to evacuate it to a collection station for repair, the Germans launched an attack.

By midday the situation became complicated. Our rifle elements, having no means of reinforcement and support, began to retreat, and then began running away, tossing aside their weapons. A panic developed. Here for the first time I saw what a terrible foe this was – panic, especially in the case when there are no clear justifications for it. No shouts or threats of the commanders with a pistol had any effect; the soldiers were running like a herd of animals prompted by some unseen fear, throwing away their weapons. To the Don River there remained only 400-500 meters. Our 2 tanks remained face to face with the adversary – my immobile, damaged tank, and the company commander's tank. Their firepower put a stop to the German infantry's attack, and an hour or two later our infantry began to return, timidly looking about themselves. At 1800 reinforcements began to arrive – a rifle unit and the 49th Tank Brigade, which had been moved up into the first echelon from the second echelon. They pulled us out of combat; my tank was towed away to a collection point for damaged machines about 4 kilometers to the rear.[2]

2 A comparison between these recollections and both German documents and the "Memorial" Consolidated Database records gives strong justifications to presume that the described events took place in the vicinity of the extended patch of woods east of Hill 213.8 (which the Germans called "the Crocodile Woods", where a group of tanks of the 1st Guards Tank Brigade fought against 4 assault guns of the 201st Battalion of StuG assault guns during an attack by the 385th Infantry Division's 537th Infantry Regiment that they were supporting. In his report, the commander of the German assault gun battery wrote: "On 25.7.42 at 0500, 4 guns began an attack toward Bol'shaia Vereika from out of a swale that stretched from Lomovo to the southwest … In the process, the battery engaged hostile tanks that showed up out of the Crocodile Woods. Five T-34 and one 20-ton [sic] were knocked out, and the crews of two of the tanks were forced to abandon their machines. During the further attack and the shelling of a column of trucks, one assault gun was knocked out by a Russian tank or anti-tank gun from the exposed right flank and became fully consumed in flames; the leader received severe burns and the loader – light burns" (NARA, T-315, roll 2199, fr. 000839).

Appendix V

Excerpts from documents

From a 1st Tank Corps intelligence summary:

...the interrogation of Feldwebel Friedrich Schöner, who voluntarily came over to the Red Army's side in the vicinty of Bol'shaia Vereika, confirms the actions of the 385th Infantry Division's 537th Infantry Regiment, which arrived in the sector on 22.7.42 from the Kshen' River. Soldier Rudolf Czervinger, a Czech, who came over to the Red Army in the Lebiazh'e area, belonged to the 385th Infantry Division's 579th Infantry Regiment, which arrived in the new sector on 22.7.42 from the Kshen' River. Soldier Robert Petler, a Czech, [belonged] to the 340th Infantry Division's 695th Infantry Regiment. Soldiers Petler and Czervinger indicated that Hungarian motorized infantry and more than 100 Hungarian tanks are backing up their divisions. Conclusion: the enemy continues the offensive and presumably has the aim of advancing beyond Kon' Kolodez' and encircling the right-flank grouping in the area of the Don River.[1]

From the operational summary of the 1st Motorized Rifle Brigade:

From the interrogations of Robert Pelsher [sic], a Czech by nationality, it has been revealed that the 340th Infantry Division, which had been shifted from Zemliansk on 23.7.42, is operating opposite our front. The division formed up in France. The division's personnel is multi-national and their morale is shaky ...[2]

From an 87th Tank Brigade political report:

The enemy by all appearances is quite nervous because of the fact that all of its aerial bombings are not yielding the needed results. Our combat formations over the evening didn't suffer a single casualty, while communications continued to support the combat readiness of men and equipment. The rabid foe already for the third day in a row is dropping bombloads on peaceful citizens. Over three days the villages of Perekopovka, Ozerki, Kamenka and Pokrovskoe have been subjected to multiple airstrikes, as a result of which up to 100 buildings and other collective farm structures have been completely demolished; up to 40 head of horse and cattle and a lot of chickens have been killed. The population is burning with hatred for the fiends and giving all-possible assistance to our units. After the Germans took half the village of Perekopovka on 12 July, they drove approximately 150 residents to a point somewhere behind their lines; the remaining residents of the village and of other villages, where the frontline passes at the current moment, are leaving their villages and heading to the rear.

1 TsAMO, F. 1 TK, op. 1, d. 235, l. 70.
2 TsAMO, F. 19 mbr, op. 1, d. 6 , l. 148.

With the exception of 82-mm mortar shells, the units and formations are fully supplied with fuel, lubricants and ammunition. The army stockpiles for some unknown reasons are not delivering supplies. Because of this the mortar crews are firing while keeping an eye on their remaining ammunition, and are silent at times. I believe it necessary to make the following known to the corps' military commissar:

1. In the sector occupied by the corps' formations, there are a lot of dead horses, both the army's and the peasants'. They are lying about the villages, rotting and threatening outbreaks of epidemics. No one is undertaking any measures to dispose of them, plainly waiting for someone else, but so far no such bravehearts can be found. I ask your instructions on this matter.
2. Combat security and rear security are absent everywhere; it is possible to infiltrate any brigade's position without hindrance. Now the nights are quite foggy, and given the absence of any sentries the enemy can easily cross our lines and organize an act of sabotage. I request your orders.[3]

3 TsAMO, F. 87 tbr, op. 1, d. 5, ll. 159-160.

Appendix VI

The recollections of local residents

Ivan Petrovich Russkikh, a resident of the village of Churikovo born in 1930

When the Germans arrived, there was no fighting whatsoever. There were no battles, it was quiet. At night the Russians kept marching past. They were marching right here along the well-traveled village road, there was no asphalt, toward the Don over there, toward Zhivotinnoe, toward the bridge. The Germans arrived; three motorcyclists drove up, talked about something among themselves that the locals didn't understand, turned around and left. They drove off and later there came a column of vehicles, again rolling along the high road and into the woods.

Then infantrymen – the Germans arrived; there were a lot of households back then, but no one lives there now. "Momma, eggs!" Straight away, they caught cows and milked them. The Germans started to take photographs ... they were well-equipped and orderly, with submachine guns.

At the time there was not a single shot fired. But when there was fighting, by then they had already kicked us out [of the village]. There were a lot of dead in the meadows and around the vegetable patches ... The Germans drove us out on the following day. They had dug some trenches right here, in this very village.

We returned from Kaver'ia in the morning, and there was already a field kitchen standing in our yard, screened by willow bushes. ... They were digging trenches directly along the river. Somewhere around 200-300 meters from the river. The Germans came from Bol'shaia Vereika.

We were spending the nights in cellars; some moved into a brick hut for safety reasons, others into trenches. The Germans rounded us up into a ravine. Those of our elderly villagers who'd been prisoners in World War I understood [the Germans] a little. The Germans were saying, "Get moving! Or else 'Bang', we'll shoot!"

We were coming back from the village, my mother and my aunt; they had wanted to get some stuff. Well, seemingly here the fighting had quieted down; there wasn't any. But they intercepted us in the woods and forced us to dig bunkers, and the four of us were still young children. They put us to work – "Don't you dare leave, or else 'Bang'! We'll shoot you instantly!"

There were berries ... We wanted to pick the berries, we were hungry, and our women were digging trenches in the woods the entire day and the Germans didn't give us anything to eat, not even a piece of bread. So we [the little children] spent the day sitting. ... However, by evening they released us. But we didn't reach here, they turned us around – and showed us where to go, or else "Bang!", they'd shoot. "Move away from here, or else ...". They chased us away.

Yet as I said in the morning some Germans came, but they didn't force us all to keep moving; some villagers managed to stay behind. But they forced us into a ravine; we took along our cows. All night long, planes were diving and launching signal flares, along the village road there was a ruckus – tanks. ... We were lying on bare ground; there was some sort of haystack there, but among us was an old man who had been in war – "Don't go near the haystack! Keep lying right here among the sunflowers on the bare ground!" Well, somehow we made it through the night, fearing that a bomb would drop on us … The cow, terrified, came along with us. After all, they [the Germans] might spot a target and open fire. … Well, in the morning we rose and were now heading home. An upright horseman rode up. Our cow was in good health … "Momma! Catch the cow!" Momma caught it. I took the cow and led her into some woods. The woods on the hill are called the Kaver'ia Woods.

Joint interview with Lidiia Arkhipovna Russkikh, born in 1932; Mar'ia Vasilev'na Sukovatykh, born in 1935; and Ivan Petrovich Russkikh, born in 1939

I had a sister in my care, who was born in 1941 … She was trailing behind me, with a loaf of bread, and I was dragging her along by the hand. So we left Kaver'ia and went on foot as far as Zemliansk. We were walking barefoot. I had only a frock; nothing on my feet, no cover. Prior to this, our soldiers had told us, "Seal up the windows!" and advised us to find some place to hide, some way out. Our military construction brigades were there and began to build mortar emplacements right there. … But when the Germans came, there was no one to be found! Not a single Russian, they were already beyond the Don. The Germans arrived – they were masters, well-equipped, with tidy uniforms, cameras, everything!

In a meadow by the river our dead were lying in piles; it was a horror! In the spring of '43 they were collected for burial. A lot of them were buried in the fields there. … You'd walk up – it [the corpse] was fully-uniformed and wearing boots. You'd dig a hole, but it [the body] would all fall apart, like there was no body any longer, just bones … It is all overgrown there now, you won't find anything. Two or three years after the war, it was still possible to find a lot.

Did any of the arriving Germans speak Russian? I'll tell you now … We were in Khokhol. I was having a smoke with an elder, Vania. A German officer drives up, polished leather boots, a dagger hanging right here, and carrying a machine pistol. … "Uncle" Vania said, "Sir! Give me some paper for a cigarette" – he wanted to smoke a cigarette. But the other says, in Russian no less: "And you, old man, are from what area?" Vania replied, "Heigh ho, I'm from the Zemliansk area."

– Do you know the village of Skliaevo?
– Of course, how could I not?
– When you make it back to Skliaevo, give my greetings to the Skliaevskys!
– Huh, and you are? Give your greetings to whom?
– That doesn't matter!

Thinking about it, now that I'm grown and have become old, this guy was a traitor, the swine! Look here, he spoke pure Russian, just like we all speak, but he was wearing a German uniform, of course. … I heard this personally.

The residents were forced to go to Kaver'ia. We spent about three days there. The Germans blew up the church there; a windmill was still standing there, and they blew it up too.

Ekaterina Ivanovna Parina, born in 1924 (as told by her granddaughter)

The Germans began to force her and another girl, they were already 16 years old, to dance. Gesturing with their machine pistols – dance! At this time, an old man named Evrodich began playfully to dance around, and while the Germans were laughing, the girls quickly darted away. They took on disguises, the old women covered them with some kerchiefs, so they …. Well, the Germans wanted to shoot Evrodich, because he had distracted them from the girls.

There was one German who showed [a photograph of] his family. He summoned my Momma (Dar'ia Ivanovna Dolgikh, who was 12 years old back then). She said that they were afraid, when at first she began following them – they took her bucket from her, and it was the only one they had. The Germans undressed, lowered the bucket in the well, and poured the water all over themselves. She said, "Give it back, sir, give me back the bucket!" But he said, waving his machine pistol, "I'll shoot you right now!" But a second German spoke up, called her over, and gave her a piece of chocolate: "Don't cry, you'll get it back soon; they'll leave the bucket here."

He added, "Don't be afraid" and showed her a photograph; his wife, he said, a beauty, and two children in the photo – I wasn't willing to go to war, they've forced me to come here. He was using gestures to make this known to them, and they understood him. They took the chocolate and ran.

The Germans weren't in Lomovo long. Grandma told us: "You step out on the porch – Germans! They're marching past: "Mama, milk, eggs!" Three or four hours pass, you step out – now they're Russians: "Mother (in a whisper), where are the Germans?" They were just here ....

There were 4 or 5 roads through the vegetable patches, and there were trenches and positions down around the river. So, she said, once we took a look, and there was grass over there – Russians had lost a rifle and wanted to shoot the kids, because they thought they had taken it and hidden it in the grass. But then, she told me, some grown-ups intervened, some old women and women, and made things clear to the commander.

Everyone was concealed over there in our Marinikhin Woods near Pavlovka, while our Katiusha rocket launchers were standing over there where the cemetery in Lomovo is. Quickly, she said, they dispersed and concealed the trucks and brought up shells, but someone warned the Germans and they had abandoned their positions. Yet by this time Russians had occupied the former German positions and the Katiusha fire struck them. There were a lot of wounded; everyone there, of course, were swearing Stalin was responsible. They killed friendlies, and already within a half hour the Germans were again occupying their entrenchments, there in the Marinikhin Woods. But the Germans didn't kick the locals out and force them to the German rear; she said the locals were being evacuated to Ksizovo [in the Russian rear] ....

Nina Danilovna Vorontsova, born in 1926 and a resident of Bol'shaia Vereika

How did the Germans arrive? There'd already been a cannonade; the fighting was approaching us. The Germans were rounding up the residents; our guys didn't evacuate us. We were already going to a kolkhoz. Back then they were planting tobacco; they would gather the girls, and we would water it. Then one day a brigade leader showed up; they wanted to take us somewhere and were gathering us together, collecting the young adults who'd been born in 1926 or 1927, and they took us to Gremiach'e, which is now known as Pavlovsk. An aircraft appeared overhead and began to bomb us, and we scattered in every direction. But the Russians had brought us to Gremiach'e; I don't know where they were going to take us before the Germans arrived. So we returned home. Soon, in fact, the Germans came.

They bombed us. We ran to Grandma's place – she had a brick home, and Mama swooped us up, we were 4 young kids, and we went to Grandma's. We arrived there to find that there were people already there who'd been evacuated from the Kshen River [a river about 60 kilometers to the west]! So we're sitting there, and this gray-haired man, he was elderly, kept telling us, "Oh, kids, don't worry, the shell has already passed!" He understood that if you could hear the shell's whistle, it meant it was already passing you. So we're sitting there, huddled together. ... We lived a long time here in the trenches. But the front was right there – we'd get up in the morning – Germans! A day would go by, and in the morning we'd get up – now our Russians were coming. When the fighting was going on, we were still here, until a German ousted us. The German kicked us out on 12 July. It was a religious holiday, Petrov's Day.

I remember clearly, because our Momma was telling us, "Oh, children, soon the potato will be young (we'd already put in some potatoes); soon the potatoes will be ready, and everything will be fine for us." First they forced us to go to Churikovo, we spent a night there, and then spent a night in Kaver'ia. Grandma, she had a little girl from a daughter, an orphan, and a little boy from a son; two orphans and the four of us from Momma, so there were six of us, plus Momma and Grandma – 8 people. From Kaver'ia we were removed to Erofeevka, then to Treshchevskie Vyselki. We spent the winter in Perlevka.

The Germans there went around, and if you were walking near a building, it was "*Ap, ap*!" [Scram! Get out of here!] with a gun-butt and a kick to your backside, and they wouldn't allow you to approach the building! They drove us out without any of our things! Whatever you managed to grab! Momma even brought along a cow; we smeared the cow with dung, so they wouldn't take it away. They were taking the cows from everyone, but when they came for ours: "O, Momma, *schiesse*! *Scheisse*!" [shit]. Momma had deliberately smeared the cow all over with dung, so they wouldn't take it!

Maria Antonovna Dolmatova, 1925 year of birth, a resident of Kaver'ia

The Germans that came were frontline men, they left us alone. Then they gathered to retreat and began to pull out, but in the daytime the Germans arrived overhead to bomb us, thinking our guys had already moved into the village. But then the German troops unfurled a fascist flag, and they stopped the bombing. Later the Germans began to force us out, no one understood anything! It was "*Veck*! *Veck*! [Get lost! Scram!]" But what this "Veck! Veck!" meant, nobody knew. They marched us first to Treshchevka. Then to Bol'shaia Perlevka. And then to Kursk Oblast. First we walked on foot from Perlevka to Kurbatovo. There they loaded us on a train, which took us to Kursk Oblast. In Kaver'ia the Germans were telling us, "Take something with you!" Well, whatever someone managed to grab, that's what they took. My father even brought along a goat.

We were put to work repairing roads. Then a shenanigan happened. Such bullshit! This village elder proved to be such a swine; they weren't going to evacuate us to Germany, but he insisted on the contrary – and they evacuated us! He told us to add our names to some list. But who knew? … They forced us into some commandant's office, where they began to register us. Lo and behold, 10 of us from Kaver'ia were selected and everyone to Germany! They told us to run home and say good-bye to our families …

The Volga Germans [the descendants of Germans who had settled in Russia under the reign of Catherine the Great back in the 18th Century; when the war broke out, they were forcibly removed to Kazakhstan, but as we can see from the story, some of the Volga Germans still remained in occupied territory], there were around 40 of them, they were kept separate. Our 10 from Kaver'ia were also kept separate, and we had a police goon now with a submachine gun. In October they were already shipping us to Germany. They crowded us into a large railcar. There were two German police chiefs and 6 police goons to keep an eye on us. Now things were bad, very bad.

In 1945 we were living in a German village, and at first Vlasov's men [members of the Russian Liberation Army formed by the Germans, who were commanded by General Vlasov, who'd been captured by the Germans in 1942] arrived there. They were uniformed and equipped just like a German, down to a "T", only they spoke Russian. But in February 1945, our guys liberated us. They called us "trophies" back then. I had to work in a hospital as a civilian employee. A senior counterintelligence official showed up there one day and was asking us, "How and why did you wind up in Germany?" But our group leader was standing there, he was our chief of food supplies, "Uncle" Fedia. So he is standing there and says, "And why did you allow it to happen that they wound up in Germany?! You're the guilty party!" They gave us verification letters for our work in the hospital. Well, later one certain muttonhead refused to work -- Why did I need these papers?

Bit by bit I lost everything and came back to the communal home – poor as a church mouse, with absolutely nothing! I brought back for myself a few things, so I would at least have something to wear.

Our guys blew up the church in Kaver'ia, not the Germans. It was very visible. This was before the Germans arrived.

Maria Antonovna Gladunets (Alekhina), 1931 year of birth, resident of Kreshchenka

When the war started, I was 10 years old. It was the summer of 1942. An aircraft flew in, a large illumination bomb was dropped, so big it became light as day in the village when it ignited. People filled the streets and were saying "The German has come." But there were no Germans in the village; it was our guys, Russians, the Red Army.

A German patrol arrived in the village. Scouts were walking around the village; they were riding in a tank …

We had these settlements, "Krasnaia Step'" they were called. In this Krasnaia Step' the Germans rode in this tank and were firing at everyone they came across. They found one of their scouts dead, laid him on the tank and carried him through the village. They carried him around for a long time.

Then they came to our village and once we caught a German. Our village street was a well-worn dirt road, and we all went running along it until we came to this little cottage. An old man had been living there once, but now no one was living there. We found a German scout sitting on its little porch; he was young, very handsome, and he kept pointing to this brooch. Our guys opened this brooch, took a look, and saw that he had 3 children, while he kept insisting through the interpreter that we had no quarrel, we didn't need this war, and that it was our government officials that were fighting. It was Hitler that wanted to seize all of Russia and conquer it. But wherever they were going to take him, this scout, he was begging not to be shot.

Three days later these Germans arrived, occupied our village, and were going around plundering everything, especially eggs. We had some sort of chests, they were called trunk boxes; they contained all we had, and the Germans took everything. Then our side drove them out, and up until 1943, the month of January, we had no Germans. We were evacuated in the fall to the village of Sindiakino. Then, they took all our animals, drove them away in herds, but we were able to keep our cows; no one touched them.

We twice had Germans in the village. We had them there for a total of 2 days, but in Fomina-Negachevka, the Germans were there three days. I personally saw them; they were marching upright, carrying submachine guns. It was at a time when there was no underbrush and the village was totally barren. They were marching just like you see in the movies, their hands on their submachine guns. They were going along and killing chickens, dragging away piglets and stealing grain. Where they managed to put it all, I can't even imagine, but they plundered all food and milk.

They were marching right along this street. They also flew over to bomb us. They bombed us very often. A "Rama" [an FW 189 Uhu – the Russians called it the "Frame" because of its twin boom construction] would appear overhead, reconnoitering and watching everything happening down below, and then the bombing would begin.

They would approach the church, ours had icons on the right and left side, and they would fire at them. Both the Germans and our guys would fire at them.

We had a [Russian] scout sitting in the church. His name was Nikolai, but I forget his family name … back then, you know, we were all illiterate. He was sitting there, and soldiers would bring him something to eat in a kettle. He had a rope and would lower it, they would attach the kettle to it, and he would raise it. Well, once he had to go on patrol, and he came by to say to my Momma: "I'm leaving, my dear little old lady, and I dropped by to say goodbye. I'll return to you. I'll come back and resume my duties." But in fact he never returned from the patrol. He was killed.

We asked about him; some chief was staying here in our cottage, in this very home. It is an old home, my parents'. My father was born in 1907 and he lived in this home. All the cottages had thatched roofs, but after the war we covered them. The chief was in our cottage, a field kitchen stood in the yard, and a medical aid station was over here [gesturing], above the cemetery; the aid station was next to the cemetery. The field kitchen was only for the military commanders.

We had bunkers there in the woods, and that's where the command staff was. Vehicles would drive up to the cottage and stop right in front of it, like in the movies. They were not camouflaged; they were never camouflaged. There was no security, no sentry, nothing. The headquarters was in the school. A Katiusha rocket launcher was standing over there, near the medical aid station, and it was firing at Bol'shaia Vereika, while the Germans were firing back from behind a hill. On this field they were reaping a very large harvest of grain, and we were being sent to drag away the sheaves. There were so many dead! When the Germans were driven back in 1943, there were a very large number of bodies in the fields. We collected them and were burying them directly in the trenches.

They had wrapped one killed tanker's body in a thick cloth, and that's how they buried him without a coffin. They brought him on a tank and some people said it was actually his own brother who buried him. Later I told a former tanker, who came back to the village after the war: "You were going along the road, we three girls were standing here, and you gave each of us a red 10-ruble banknote."

The dead tanker was a major, and he was there in the school when a bullet flew in and struck him. We ran to check on him, but he was mortally wounded and passed away. This was before the Germans arrived. His wife came to the village after the war; she took a clump of soil from here and never returned.

The Germans were heavily bombing the Don River. There was no bridge back then, and everything was crossing on boats in Dmitriashevka.

The soldiers were very hungry. We fed them. They were always coming to us in the evening with kettles, and we filled them. But then an order came down not to feed them – a strict order! But why? Because the command didn't want them going around, or locals might say that the Red Army was hungry … or else the Germans would scatter leaflets saying that the people were feeding the Red Army soldiers, because the army couldn't! The kitchen was standing right there in the yard. At last they started to bring enough victuals here and even began to treat us, the children, with food.

The Germans were the first to arrive in the village, our guys weren't even here. A "Frame" arrived in the sky above us, flares were suspended in the sky, and it became as bright as daytime! Right above our village. We had one old man Ivan Ivanovich, he had fought back in the German war (the First World War), and he told us, "Well, women, the German has come to us!" But my Momma was in Vereika, digging anti-tank ditches so the tanks couldn't pass. They came back in the morning, our parents, but the Germans were already occupying this spot by lunchtime. I clearly remember this; I was 10 years old.

The Germans came by our cottage; one of them spoke Russian with an accent: "Mother, mother, milk, eggs!" They took everything we had. But they didn't burn our cottage. They spent some time with us and headed back to Vereika. Altogether they might have been with us for 5-6 hours. They spent more time in Fomina-Negachevka. They came for a second time several days later. Vereika changed hands many times. The headquarters was in the old log school building. But the main headquarters was in the woods. The "Manor House" woods, it was called.

The Germans came and found a Russian scout. It happened that there was a local man in the village who had come back from the war after being discharged because of his wounds. He was in the vegetable garden, and the Germans happened to come across him and shot him. Next they rounded up the entire population and drove us to Sredniaia Dolina, Blagodatnoe and Step', to a school where they imprisoned us. Our people who had run to hide somewhere also wound up there. People were running to hide in every direction: into a ravine, but the Germans were firing into the ravines, and we were hiding in them! Nobody knew what to do! They piled bundles of hay up against the school and poured gasoline over them, but then a reconnaissance aircraft arrived overhead; they had a chat with it over the radio and immediately left, but without freeing our people. Well, there our people knocked out the doors and windows and left. They [the Germans] never returned.

There is nothing left of that school in Sredniaia Dolina; only memories of it remain. During the war, there were none of these planted forests we have now [such forests were planted in the steppe region in the 1950s]. We had very large gardens. We had a school – a former manor house in Sredniaia Dolina. I was baptized in Vereika; our church was no longer active. During the war it was fully intact: it had both floors and hanging chandeliers. A circus troupe came and performed there during the war; the altar was very beautiful and all the glass was intact. We even have a bell hanging in the church now. The church was destroyed already after the war. A school director has begun to build here. They're taking bricks from the old church. Later they used the church as a granary. They stopped storing grain here back in 1975. Both our side and the Germans fired at the icons in the church.

Appendix VII

Order of the USSR People's Commissar of Defense On measures to strengthen discipline and order in the Red Army and to forbid the voluntary retreat from combat positions

No. 227

28 July 1942

Moscow

The foe is hurling more and more fresh forces to the front, paying no regard to his heavy losses, and is creeping forward, penetrating into the depth of the Soviet Union, capturing new areas, pillaging and plundering our cities and villages, and raping, robbing and killing the Soviet people. Fighting is underway in the Voronezh area, at the Don, and to the south at the gates of the Northern Caucasus. German occupiers are lunging toward Stalingrad, to the Volga, and want at any cost to seize the Kuban', the Northern Caucasus with their oil and grain riches. The foe has already taken Voroshilovgrad, Starobel'sk, Rossosh', Kupiansk, Valuiki, Novocherkassk, Rostov on the Don, and half of Voronezh. A section of the troops on the southern front, yielding to panic mongers, abandoned Rostov and Novocherkassk without serious resistance and without an order from Moscow, coving their banners with shame ...

The population of our country, who relate to the Red Army with love and respect, is beginning to be discouraged in it, losing faith in the Red Army, and many of them are cursing the Red Army for leaving the people under the yoke of the German oppressors and itself flees to the east.

Certain stupid people at the front comfort themselves with talks that we can in fact retreat further to the east, since we have a lot of territory, a lot of land, a lot of people, and that we will always have bread in surplus.

By doing so, they want to justify their shameful behavior at the front. But such talks are false and deceptive through and through, and beneficial only to our foes.

Each commander, Red Army soldier and political worker should understand that our means are not limitless. The territory of the Soviet state is not a desert, and the people – workers, peasants, intellectuals – are our fathers, mothers, wives, brothers and children. The territory of the USSR that the foe has seized and is attempting to seize – is bread and other products for the army and rear, metals and fuel for industry, factories and plants that supply the army with weapons and ammunition, railroads. After the loss of the Ukraine, Belorussia, the Baltic republics, the Don basin and other regions, we have much less territory, and thus much less grain, metals, factories and plants. We have lost more than 70 million people, more than 800 million tons of grain per year and more than 10 million tons of metals each year. We no longer have superiority over the Germans in human resources or grain reserves. To retreat further means to bring ourselves to ruin, and bring our Motherland to ruin. Each new piece of territory abandoned by us will strengthen the foe and weaken our defense, our Motherland, in every possible way.

Thus it is necessary to eliminate root and branch the talk that we have the possibility to retreat endlessly, that we have a lot of territory, our country is great and rich, the people many, and that we'll always have bread in surplus. Such talks are false and harmful, they weaken us and strengthen the foe, since if we don't stop the retreat, we'll remain without bread, without fuel, without metals, without grain, without factories and plants, without railroads.

From this it follows that it is time to end the retreat

Not one step back! Such should now become our main slogan.

It is necessary to defend each position, each meter stubbornly, down to the last drop of blood, to cling to each clump of Soviet land and defend it to the last possibility.

Our Motherland is experiencing hard days. We must stop, and then throw back and smash the enemy, regardless of the cost. The Germans are not so strong, as it seems to the panic mongers. They are straining their last forces. To withstand their blow now means to secure our victory in the next few months.

Are we able to withstand the blow and then throwback the foe to the west? Yes, we can, because our factories and plants in the rear are operating splendidly now, and our front is receiving more and more airplanes, tanks, artillery and mortars.

Then what do we lack?

We lack order and discipline in the companies, battalions, regiments and divisions, in the tank units and in the air squadrons. This is now our main shortcoming. We must establish the strictest order and iron discipline in our army, if we want to save the situation and defend our Motherland.

We can no longer tolerate commanders, commissars, political workers and units and formations that voluntarily abandon their combat positions. It is impossible to tolerate it any longer, when commanders, commissars and political workers allow just a few panic mongers to determine the situation on the battlefield, to carry away other soldiers in retreat and expose a front to the enemy.

Panic mongers and cowards must be executed on the spot.

From this point on, discipline for each commander, commissar, Red Army soldier and political worker must be an iron law – not one step back without an order from higher command.

Company, battalion, regiment and division commanders, and the corresponding commissars and political workers, who retreat from a combat position without an order from above, are traitors to the Motherland. It is necessary to treat such commanders and political workers as traitors to the Motherland.

Such is the slogan of our Motherland.

To carry out this call means to defend our soil, to save the Motherland, to eradicate and beat the hated foe.

After our winter offensive under the onslaught of the Red Army, when discipline was shattered in the German forces, in order to restore discipline the Germans took several harsh measures, which yielded pretty good results. They formed more than 100 penal companies out of the soldiers who were guilty of violations of discipline due to cowardice or a lack of steadiness, positioned them on more dangerous sectors of the front and ordered them to atone for their guilt with blood. Further, they formed approximately a dozen penal battalions out of officers who were guilty of breaches of discipline due to cowardice or a lack of steadiness, stripped them of their Orders, positioned them on more dangerous sectors of the front, and ordered them to atone for their guilt with blood. Finally, they formed special blocking detachments, positioned them behind unsteady divisions, and authorized them to shoot panic mongers on the spot in the event of voluntary attempts to abandon positions and in the event of attempts to surrender. As is known, these measures had an effect, and now the German troops are fighting better than they did in the winter. Now it happens that the Germans troops have good discipline, even though they have no higher aim of defending their own motherland, but only one rapacious aim to enslave a foreign land, while our troops, having the higher purpose of defending their desecrated Motherland, do not have such discipline and in view of this suffer defeat.

Shouldn't we now learn from our foes, just as in the past our forefathers learned from their adversaries, and thereby achieved victory?

I think we should.

The Supreme High Command of the Red Army orders:

1. Front Military Councils and first of all Front commanders:
   a) Eliminate defeatist moods in the troops unconditionally, and with an iron hand ban propaganda that says we can and should supposedly retreat further to the east, and that such a retreat will cause no harm.
   b) Unconditionally remove army commanders from their posts who have allowed a voluntary retreat from occupied positions, without an order from the Front command, and send them to the *Stavka* for court martial.
   c) Form one to three (depending on the situation) penal battalions (of 800 men each) within the boundaries of each army, to where you will send mid-level and senior commanders and corresponding political workers of all types of troops who are guilty of breaches of discipline due to cowardice or unsteadiness, and position them [the penal battalions] on the harder sectors of the front, in order to give them the possibility to atone for their crimes against the Motherland with their blood.

2. Army Military Councils and first of all army commanders:
   a) Unconditionally remove commanders and commissars of corps and divisions from their posts, who have allowed a voluntary troop withdrawal from occupied positions without and order from the army command, and send them to the Front's Military Council for court martial.
   b) Form within the army's boundaries 3-5 well-armed blocking detachments (up to 200 men in each), position them in the immediate rear of unsteady divisions and compel them in the event of panic and a disorderly retreat of a division's units to shoot panic mongers and cowards on the spot, and thereby help the division's honorable soldiers fulfill their duty to the Motherland.
   c) Form within the army's boundaries five to ten (depending on the situation) penal companies (from 150 to 200 men in each), to where you will send ordinary soldiers and junior commanders guilty of breaches of discipline due to cowardice or unsteadiness, and position them [the penal companies] on the hardest sectors of the army, in order to give them the possibility to atone for their crimes against the Motherland with their blood.

3. Corps and division commanders and commissars:
    a) Unconditionally remove from their posts the regiment and battalion commanders and commissars who have allowed a voluntary retreat of the units without an order from the corps or division commander, strip them of their Orders and medals, and send them to the Front Military Councils for court martial.
    b) Render any and all help and support to the army's blocking detachments in the matter of strengthening order and discipline in the units.

Read this order in all companies, cavalry squadrons, batteries, air squadrons, commands and headquarters.

People's Commissar of Defense
I. Stalin

Appendix VIII

The formations and units of Briansk Front's operational group under the command of Lieutenant General Chibisov that took part in the operation

Tank:

1st Tank Corps – Major General Katukov
    1st Guards Tank Brigade – Colonel Chukhin
        1st Tank Battalion
        2nd Tank Battalion
    49th Tank Brigade – Colonel Chernienko
        49th Tank Battalion
        253rd Tank Battalion
    89th Tank Brigade – Lieutenant Colonel Zhukov
        202nd Tank Battalion
        203rd Tank Battalion
    1st Motorized Rifle Brigade – Colonel Mel'nikov

2nd Tank Corps – Major General Liziukov
    26th Tank Brigade – Colonel Burdov
        270th Tank Battalion
        282nd Tank Battalion
    27th Tank Brigade – Captain Luchnikov
        436th Tank Battalion
        239th Tank Battalion
    148th Tank Brigade – Lieutenant Colonel Mikhailin
        89th Tank Battalion – Senior Lieutenant Zaporozhets
        260th Tank Battalion – Senior Lieutenant Tiunin
    2nd Motorized Rifle Brigade – Lieutenant Colonel Borodavkin

7th Tank Corps (from 25.7.42) – Colonel Rotmistrov
 3rd Guards Tank Brigade – Colonel Vovchenko
 87th Tank Brigade – Colonel Shabarov
 62nd Tank Brigade – Lieutenant Colonel Gumeniuk

11th Tank Corps (from 25.7.42)
 59th Tank Brigade – Colonel Krupsky (of the entire corps, only the 59th Tank Brigade took any part in the fighting)

Separate Tank Brigades:

118th Separate Tank Brigade – Lieutenant Colonel Bregvadze
201st Separate Tank Brigade – Colonel Taranov

Rifle Units:

167th Rifle Division – Colonel Mel'nikov
 465th Rifle Regiment
 520th Rifle Regiment
 615th Rifle Regiment
  576th Artillery Regiment

193rd Rifle Division – Major General Smekhotvorov
 685th Rifle Regiment – Colonel Moiseev
 883rd Rifle Regiment
 895th Rifle Regiment
  384th Artillery Regiment

237th Rifle Division (from 23.7.42) – Colonel Tertyshnyi
 835th Rifle Regiment
 838th Rifle Regiment
 841st Rifle Regiment
  691st Artillery Regiment

284th Rifle Division – Lieutenant Colonel Batiuk
 1043rd Rifle Regiment
 1045th Rifle Regiment
 1047th Rifle Regiment
  820th Artillery Regiment

340th Rifle Division – Colonel Martirosian
 1140th Rifle Regiment
 1142nd Rifle Regiment
 1144th Rifle Regiment
  911th Artillery Regiment

104th Separate Rifle Brigade – Lieutenant Colonel Stodukh

Separate Artillery Units:

124th Howitzer Artillery Regiment, 396th Howitzer Artillery Regiment, 611th Destroyer Anti-tank Artillery Regiment, 1244th Destroyer Anti-tank Artillery Regiment (all of the Supreme Command Reserve); 3rd and 4th Destroyer Brigades of the 2nd Destroyer Division

Guards Mortar Units [of Katiusha rocket launchers]:

65th Guards Mortar Regiment, 66th Guards Mortar Regiment, 72nd Guards Mortar Regiment

Appendix IX

German formations and units of the VII Army Corps that took part in the battles with units of Operation Group Chibisov

Infantry Units:

340th Infantry Division – General Butze
694th Infantry Regiment
695th Infantry Regiment
696th Infantry Regiment
340th Artillery Regiment

387th Infantry Division – General Jahr
541st Infantry Regiment
542nd Infantry Regiment
543rd Infantry Regiment
387th Artillery Regiment

385th Infantry Division (from 24.7.42) – General Eibl
537th Infantry Regiment
539th Infantry Regiment
385th Artillery Regiment

Attached Units:

A reinforced battalion from the 168th Infantry Division's 417th Infantry Regiment and 442nd Infantry Regiment (between 23 and 25.7.42)

One company (4 self-propelled guns) of the 201st Stürmgeschutz Battalion (between 25 and 27.7.42)

The 654th, 559th (from 22.7.42) and 560th (from 24.7.42) Panzerjäger Battalions, and a portion of the 323rd Infantry Division's Panzerjäger battalion (from 23.7.42)

A battalion of the 62nd Artillery Regiment, a battalion of the 71st Artillery Regiment, a battalion of the 108th Artillery Regiment, and two battalions of the 109th Artillery Regiment (from 23.7.42)

221st Pionier [Engineer] Battalion (from 22 to 26.7.42)

Panzer Units:

9th Panzer Division (from 23 to 27.7.42) – General Baesler
- 33rd Panzer Regiment
- 10th Panzer Grenadier Regiment
- 11th Panzer Grenadier Regiment
  - 102nd Artillery Regiment

Bibliography

Unpublished materials

TsAMO:
Large number of documents, including F 148, 202, 331, 1657. All specific references are listed in the footnotes.

National Archives, Washington DC:
Captured German records, especially microfilm rolls T-314 and T-315. All specific references are listed in the footnotes.

Other unpublished materials:
Materials at the Institut rossiiskoi istorii RAN (IRI) . All specific references are listed in the footnotes.
Materials of the Kon'-Kolodez' Museum, Khlevenskii District, Lipetsk Oblast.
School museum in the village of Sklaievo, Ramonskii District, Voronezh Oblast.

Printed materials

Devidov, P.M., *Na sluzhbe y boga voiny [In service of the 'God of War']* (Moscow: Iauza-Eksmo, 2007).

General'nyi shtab v gody VOV, Tom 23: Materialy i dokumenty [The General Staff in the years of the Great Patriotic War, Volume 23: Materials and documents] (Moscow: Terra, 1999).

Halder, F. *Voennyi dnevnik: Ezhednevnye zapisi nachal'nika General'nogo Shtaba Sukhoputnykh voisk, 1939-1942* (Sankt Peterburg: AST, 2003), p. 822. This is the Russian language edition of Halder's war diary. The English translation comes from Charles Burdick and Hans-Adolf Jacobsen (ed.), *The Halder War Diary, 1939-1942* (Novato: Presidio Press, 1988).

Ivanovsky, E.F., *Ataku nachinali tankisty [Tankers launched the attack]* (Moscow: Voenizdat, 1984)

Krivitsky, A., *Ne zabudu vovek [I will never forget]* (Moscow, 1963).

von Mellenthin, F.W., *Tankovye srazheniya 1939-1945: Boevoe primenenie tankov vo vtoroi mirovoi voine [Panzer battles 1939-1945: Combat employment of armor in the Second World War]* (Moscow: IL, 1957). This book has been translated into English as *Panzer Battles: A Study of the Employment of Armor in the Second World War* and published initially in 1956 by the University Press of Oklahoma.

Poklonimsia velikim tem godam: Vospominaniia veteranov 167 sd [We *bow down before those great years: Recollections of veterans of the 167th Rifle Division*] (Lipetsk, 1995).

Postnikov, M., *Bronezaschita tiazhelykh tankov KV i IS, 1941-1945 [The protective armor of the heavy KV and IS tanks, 1941-1945]* (Moscow: Eksprint, 2006).

Rodinsky, D., and Tsar'kov, N., *Povest' o brat'iakh [Tale of brothers]* (Moscow: Politizdat, 1976).

Rokossovsky, K.K., *Soldatskii dolg [Soldier's duty]* (Moscow: Voenizdat, 1988).

Russkii arkhiv. Velikaia Otechestvennaia. Stavka VGK: Dokumenty i materialy, 1942; Tom 16 [Russian archive. Great Patriotic War. Stavka of the Supreme High Command: Documents and materials, 1942; Volume 16] (Moscow: Terra, 1996).

Stalingrad 1942-1943: Stalingradskaia bitva v dokumentakh [Stalingrad 1942-1943: The Battle of Stalingrad in documents] (Moscow: Biblioteka, 1995).

Index

INDEX OF PEOPLE

INDEX OF PLACES

INDEX OF GERMAN MILITARY FORMATIONS & UNITS

INDEX OF SOVIET MILITARY FORMATIONS & UNITS